1999

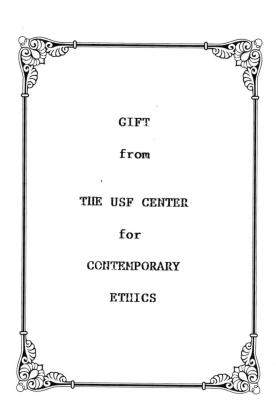

GIFT

from

THE USF CENTER

for

CONTEMPORARY

ETHICS

A Companion to Business Ethics

Blackwell Companions to Philosophy

This outstanding student reference series offers a comprehensive and authoritative survey of philosophy as a whole. Written by today's leading philosophers, each volume provides lucid and engaging coverage of the key figures, terms, topics, and problems of the field. Taken together, the volumes provide the ideal basis for course use, representing an unparalleled work of reference for students and specialists alike.

Blackwell Companions
to Philosophy

A Companion to Business Ethics

Edited by
ROBERT E. FREDERICK
Bentley College

 BLACKWELL
Publishers

Copyright © Blackwell Publishers Ltd, 1999

First published 1999

2 4 6 8 10 9 7 5 3 1

Blackwell Publishers Inc.
350 Main Street
Malden, Massachusetts 02148
USA

Blackwell Publishers Ltd
108 Cowley Road
Oxford OX4 1JF
UK

Library of Congress Cataloging-in-Publication Data
A companion to business ethics / edited by Robert E. Frederick.
        p.   cm. — (Blackwell companions to philosophy ; 17)
    Includes bibliographical references and index.
    ISBN 0–631–20130–0 (hc. : alk. paper)
    1. Business ethics.   I. Frederick, Robert.   II. Series.
  HF5387.C655   1999
  174'.4—dc21   99–19775
                                                          CIP

British Library Cataloguing in Publication Data

A CIP catalogue record for this book is available from the British Library.

Typeset in 10 on $12\frac{1}{2}$ pt Photina
by Graphicraft Limited, Hong Kong
Printed in Great Britain by T.J. International, Padstow, Cornwall

This book is printed on acid-free paper.

Contents

Contributors

M. J. Abdolmohammadi,
John E. Rhodes Professor of
   Accountancy,
Bentley College,
Waltham, MA 02452,
   USA
mabdolmo@bentley.edu

Douglas R. Anderson,
Pennsylvania State University,
Department of Philosophy,
240 Sparks Building,
University Park, PA 16802,
   USA
dra3@psu.edu

John R. Boatright,
Raymond C. Baumhart, S.J. Professor
   of Business Ethics,
School of Business Administration,
Loyola University of Chicago,
820 N. Michigan Avenue,
Chicago, IL 60611,
   USA
jboatri@luc.edu

Norman E. Bowie,
Executive Vice-President, Seminars,
The Aspen Institute,
PO Box 222,
Queenstown,
   MD 21658 USA
norman.bowie@aspeninst.org

George G. Brenkert,
Georgetown University,
Director, Connelly Program in
   Business Ethics,
290b Maguire,
37th and "O" St. NW,
Washington, DC 20057, USA
brenkg@gunet.georgetown.edu

Rogene A. Buchholz,
Legendre-Soule Professor of Business
   Ethics,
School of Business Administration,
Loyola University of New Orleans,
6363 St. Charles Avenue,
Box 15,
New Orleans, LA 70118, USA
buchholz@loyno.edu

Archie B. Carroll,
Scherer Professor of Management,
Department of Management,
Terry College of Business,
University of Georgia,
Athens, Georgia 30602, USA
acarroll@arches.uga.edu

Joanne B. Ciulla,
Coston Family Chair of Leadership and
   Ethics,
Jepson School of Leadership Studies,
Jepson Hall – Room 244,
University of Richmond,
Richmond, VA 23173, USA
jciulla@richmond.edu

John R. Danley,
Department of Philosophy,
Box 1433,
Southern Illinois University,
Edwardsville, IL 62026–1433,
    USA
jdanley@siue.edu

Keith Darcy,
Executive Vice President,
IBJ Whitehall Bank and Trust,
One State Street Plaza,
New York, NY 10004,
    USA
kdarcy@ibjwhitehall.com

Richard T. De George,
University Distinguished Professor of
    Philosophy,
Department of Philosophy,
The University of Kansas,
3052 Wescoe Hall,
Lawrence, KS 66045–2145,
    USA
degeorge@ukans.edu

Robbin Derry,
James E. Holshouser Distinguished
    Professor of Ethics,
Department of Philosophy and
    Religion,
Greer Hall,
Appalachian State University,
Boone, NC 28608
derryr@appstate.edu

Joseph R. DesJardins,
Department Chairperson,
Department of Philosophy,
College of St. Benedict,
37 S. College Avenue,
Saint Joseph, MN 56374,
    USA
jdesjardins@csbsju.edu

Thomas Donaldson,
Mark O. Winkelman Professor,
The Wharton School,
University of Pennsylvania,
3620 Locust Walk,
2203 SH-DH Hall,
Philadelphia, PA 19104,
    USA
donaldst@wharton.upenn.edu

Joan E. Dubinsky,
President, Rosentreter Group,
3316 McComas Avenue,
Kensington, MD 20895–2225,
    USA
dubinsky@erols.com

Thomas W. Dunfee,
Kolodny Professor of Social
    Responsibility,
Director, Zicklin Center for business
    Ethics Research,
Department of Legal Studies,
The Wharton School,
University of Pennsylvania,
Philadelphia, PA 19104,
    USA
dunfeet@wharton.upenn.edu

Ronald Duska,
Executive Director,
Society for Business Ethics,
Charles Lamont Post Chair,
The American College,
270 S. Bryn Mawr Avenue,
Bryn Mawr, PA 19010–2196,
    USA
rduska@aol.com

Robert E. Frederick,
Department of Philosophy,
Bentley College,
175 Forest Street,
Waltham, MA 02452,
    USA
rfrederick@bentley.edu

William C. Frederick,
Professor Emeritus of Business
  Administration,
University of Pittsburgh,
1246 Murray Hill Avenue,
Pittsburgh, PA 15217, USA
billfred@vms.cis.pitt.edu

R. Edward Freeman,
Olsson Professor of Business
  Administration,
University of Virginia,
Darden School,
Olsson Center,
PO Box 6550,
Charlottesville, VA 22906, USA
freemane@darden.gbus.virginia.edu

Ronald M. Green,
Eunice and Julian Cohen Professor
  for the Study of Ethics and
  Human Values,
Dartmouth College,
6031 Parker House,
Hanover, NH 03755–3500, USA
ronald.m.green@dartmouth.edu

James Humber,
Philosophy Department,
Georgia State University,
University Plaza,
Atlanta, GA 30303, USA
phljrh@panther.gsu.edu

Jeffrey M. Kaplan,
Arkin Schaffer & Kaplan LLP,
1370 Avenue of the Americas,
New York, NY 10019–4602, USA
kaplan@arkin-law.com

Henk van Luijk,
Universiteit Nyenrode,
Straatweg 25,
3621 BG Breuklenen,
The Netherlands
vanluijk@nijenrode.nl

Tibor R. Machan,
School of Business & Economics
Chapman University
Orange, CA 92866
Machan@chapman.edu

Thomas F. McMahon,
Professor of Management,
Loyola University of Chicago,
Chicago, IL 60611, USA

Lisa H. Newton,
Director, Program in Applied Ethics,
Fairfield University,
Department of Philosophy,
Fairfield, CT 06430, USA
lhnewton@fair1.fairfield.edu

Mark R. Nixon,
Department of Accountancy,
Bentley College,
Waltham, MA 02452, USA
mnixon@bentley.edu

Lynn S. Paine,
John G. McLean Professor of Business
  Administration
Chair, General Management Unit
Harvard Business School
Morgan – 463,
Soldiers Field Road,
Boston, MA 02163, USA
lpaine@hbs.edu

Robert A. Phillips,
Georgetown University,
School of Business,
290b Maguire,
37th and "O" St. NW,
Washington, DC 20057, USA

Sandra B. Rosenthal,
Philosophy Department,
Loyola University of New Orleans,
New Orleans, LA 70118, USA
rosenth@loyno.edu

Milton Snoeyenbos,
Department of Philosophy,
Georgia State University,
University Plaza,
Atlanta, GA 30303, USA
phlmhs@langate.gsu.edu

Robert C. Solomon,
Quincy Lee Centennial Professor of
    Philosophy,
University of Texas–Austin,
Department of Philosophy,
Wagner 316,
Austin, Texas 78712–1180,
    USA
rsolomon@mail.utexas.edu

Diane L. Swanson,
Management Department,
College of Business Administration,
101 Calvin Hall,
Kansas State University,
Manhattan, KS 66506–0507,
    USA
swanson@business.cba.ksu.edu

Linda Klebe Treviño,
Professor of Organizational Behavior,
Department of Management,
416 Beam Business Administration
    Building,
Pennsylvania State University,
University Park, PA 16802, USA
ltrevino@psu.edu

Rebecca S. Walker,
Arkin Schaffer & Kaplan LLP,
1370 Avenue of the Americas,
New York, NY 10019–4602,
    USA
rwalker@arkin-law.com

Patricia H. Werhane,
Ruffin Professor of Business Ethics,
Darden Graduate School of Business
    Administration,
University of Virginia,
PO Box 6550,
Charlottesville, VA 22906–6550,
    USA
werhanep@darden.gbus.virginia.edu

Preface

Although the world of business is continually changing, some things in business seem to have stayed more or less the same for as far back as one might care to look. One is the desire to make a profit. Another is concern about ethics in business. From the code of Hammurabi to the latest issue of *The Wall Street Journal*, the record shows that worries about greedy, deceptive, and unjust business practices are common. Whether it be in Mesopotamia or Manhattan, there have always been people who tried to make a dishonest buck, and there have always been other people who complained loudly about it. This is vaguely comforting in an odd sort of way, maybe because it is reassuring to know that there are some constants in human nature.

It is worth noting, however, that even though the unethical business practices people worry about have remained very much the same over the years, the concerns they have had about those practices come in at least two distinct varieties. These two different kinds of concerns derive, in turn, from two different traditions regarding the essential nature or character of business. The first tradition, which is foreshadowed in the writings of Aristotle and reaches its ultimate expression in Marx and his contemporary heirs, takes business to be an inherently unethical activity. As Aristotle puts it, retail trade is "justly censured" and "unnatural." For Marx, the relation of capitalist to worker is necessarily one of "naked, shameless, direct, brutal exploitation." Thus, for these writers and the tradition they represent, it is inevitable that those who engage in business are ethically stained. Further, as long as one remains in business, nothing can be done to remove the stain, no matter how hard one may scrub.

In this tradition, then, the main concern is to avoid being ethically tainted by business activity. Aristotle's solution is straightforward – just don't engage in business beyond the absolute minimum necessary to keep one's household going. Since virtue can be attained only if activities destructive of virtue (e.g. business) are shunned, let the help take care of the details. For Marx, the situation is more complex, and more desperate. Capitalists and workers are bound in an exploitative relationship by the coils of history. Individuals can do nothing to escape; social revolution is the only way the bond can be broken. Without a complete overthrow of the existing means of production, society is condemned to exist forever in a capitalist purgatory, where ethics is just another device that the powerful selectively use to see to it that their interests prevail. Only the ingenuous – or the ignorant – hope for better.

The second tradition, represented by enlightenment thinkers such as Immanuel Kant and John Stuart Mill, takes a more sanguine view of business transactions. Business is not thought to be unethical or exploitative by its very nature. Rather, it is individual business people who sometimes choose to engage in practices that are deceptive, unjust or exploitative. They are not compelled to make these choices by the intrinsic character of business, or the forces of history, or some other factor over which they have no control; they could do otherwise. In business, as in other parts of their life, the decision to act ethically or unethically is, to a significant degree, theirs to make. Thus they are responsible for their business actions in a sense that neither Aristotle nor Marx could admit.

All of the contributors to this book – including those influenced by Aristotle or Marx and those who believe that enlightenment ethics is a failure and must be replaced – accept the second tradition's basic understanding of business. None of them believes that business is ignoble, or that it must be exploitative, or that individuals have no real control over the ethics of business practices. All of them agree that there is a genuine sense in which the ethics of business is up to the people in business. Moreover, all of them agree that ethics in business is important; and that it matters whether business is conducted ethically or unethically. Consequently, none of them believes – as some recent authors have claimed to believe – that business is an ethically free zone.

These agreements among the contributors give this book a certain perspective. For instance, those looking for a wholesale condemnation of all aspects of business will not find it here. On the other hand, those hoping for a paean to business will be equally disappointed. There is a big difference between the way business ought to be conducted and the way it is conducted, and none of the contributors lose sight of the distinction.

This should be not taken to imply, however, that agreement among the contributors extends much beyond the very broad understanding of the nature of business described above. Quite the contrary. Especially in the first and longest section of the book, which is devoted to placing business in the context of normative theories, there are deeply divergent views about what counts as an unethical business practice, about what should be done about unethical business practices, and even about the extent to which something can be done about them within the confines of the present socioeconomic system. Each chapter in this section explains, and to some extent defends, an alternative conception of ethics in business. There is some overlap, but no consensus, about what that conception should be.

The remaining articles in the book are equally diverse, but unlike those in the first section they are not primarily devoted to relating business to specific normative theories. The reason for this change in emphasis lies in the development of the academic field of business ethics. Over the past 25 years or so, there has been a sustained and intensive investigation of ethics in business, not only by philosophers, but also by social scientists and members of the business disciplines. This investigation has simultaneously proceeded along four different, but closely related, fronts. The first, represented in the first section of the book, relates ethics in business to normative theories. The second draws on work done in the first but is more "discipline focused," i.e., it reflects the interests and expertise of investigators in a specific business or social science discipline, and views ethics in business from the perspective of that discipline. So, for example, in the second section of the book, there are articles that place ethical issues in business in the context of disciplines such as management, finance, accounting, marketing, law, and economics.

The third line of investigation explores a series of complex issues that have arisen in business ethics as a consequence of attempts to apply the insights of normative and disciplinary research to specific issues. Thus there are articles on business ethics in an international setting, employee rights, ethics at work, and business ethics and the environment. This section of the book also includes an article on corporate moral agency, a problem which has its origins in philosophical concerns about the proper attribution of moral responsibility, and articles on the intricate relationships between business ethics and religion, and business ethics and the corporate responsibility movement.

The final section of the book begins with two articles that give some of the historical background of business ethics, and an article that describes the development of business ethics in Europe. The remaining articles derive from or are motivated by the experiences of people in corporations who have implemented corporate ethics programs. They deal with the very practical problems of starting and running ethics program, within a specific historical, economic, regulatory, and legal environment. Thus they are examples of the fourth line of investigation, i.e., the attempt to apply ethics in organizations.

Although work in business ethics has developed roughly along lines that correspond to the four sections of this book, it is worth emphasizing that neither the different lines of inquiry nor the articles that report some of their results are in any strong sense independent or separate from each other. Almost from the beginning, business ethics has self-consciously been an interdisciplinary effort. At its best, as it is in this volume, it draws from many different fields and uses many different kinds of expertise. For example, the more theoretical pieces in the book are invariably influenced by actual events and practices in the business world; and articles that take a disciplinary or problem-based approach rely on a theoretical background as well as the experience of people who work in corporations. In business ethics, there has been a real attempt to ensure that theory is informed by practice, and practice illuminated by theory. It is in this sense that business ethics is an applied discipline.

To conclude, I would like to offer a word of caution and a bit of explanation to the reader. The caution is that even though the articles in the book are as comprehensive and complete as the limitations of time and space would allow, they are not, nor are they intended to be, the final word on the particular topic addressed. Much more can be said, and has been said, about every one of them. The bibliography, suggested readings, and list of web pages, will, I hope, be of use to those who would like more discussion.

The explanation concerns those topics covered in the book. As in all books of this kind, not everything could be included. So, for good or ill, choices were made about what to put in and what to leave out. As a consequence, no doubt, some readers will not find what they are looking for. I regret that this must be so, but hope that there remains substance enough to alleviate the disappointment.

Finally, I would like to express my deep gratitude to the many authors who so kindly agreed to write for this volume. It is fair to say, I believe, that the work they produced is outstanding, and is some of the best that business ethics has to offer.

Robert E. Frederick

PART I

BUSINESS ETHICS AND NORMATIVE THEORIES

1

A Kantian approach to business ethics*

NORMAN E. BOWIE

Even the most cursory foray into business ethics will bring one face to face with Kantianism. Indeed Kant's influence on that branch of ethical theory known as deontology is so strong that some writers simply refer to deontology as Kantianism. Despite the fact that Kant's name is often invoked in business ethics, as of 1997 there was no published book that systematically applied Kantian theory to business. (However, Bowie (1999) fills this gap.) Kant is best known for defending a version of the "respect for persons" principle which implies that any business practice that puts money on a par with people is immoral, but there is much more to a Kantian approach to business ethics than this. In this essay, I focus on five key aspects of Kant's moral philosophy. I begin by showing some of the implications of Kant's three formulations of the fundamental principle of ethics. I then show why Kant's emphasis on the purity of our intentions in acting morally has created problems for a Kantian theory of business ethics. I conclude with a brief discussion of Kant's cosmopolitan and optimistic outlook, and show the relevance of those ideas to contemporary business practice.

Background

Kant was born in 1724 in Konigsberg in East Prussia, not far from the Baltic Sea. He spent his entire life within 26 kilometers of Konigsberg and died there in 1804. Today, Konigsberg is located in a small strip of Russian territory between Poland and Lithuania, and is called Kaliningrad. Kant's major writings on ethical theory occurred between 1785 and 1797. Kant argued that the highest good was the good will. To act from a good will is to act from duty. Thus, it is the intention behind an action rather than its consequences that make that action good. For example, for Kant if a merchant is honest so as to earn a good reputation, these acts of being honest are not genuinely moral. The merchant is only truly moral if he or she is honest because being honest is right (one's duty). Persons of good will do their duty because it is their duty and for no

* I am greatly indebted to Robert Frederick for his detailed and helpful comments on this manuscript. The ideas expressed here are more fully developed in my book *Business Ethics: A Kantian Perspective* (Bowie, 1999). Many others have commented on that work whom I will acknowledge upon publication of that work. Both this article and the book arose from a Ruffin lecture entitled "A Kantian Theory of Capitalism" delivered at Darden School, University of Virginia, and subsequently published in *Business Ethics Quarterly*, The Ruffin Series, Special Issue No 1, 37–60.

other reason. It is this emphasis on duty, and the lack of concern with consequences that makes Kant the quintessential deontologist.

But what does Kantian morality think our duties are? Kant distinguished between two kinds of duty (imperatives). Sometimes we do something so than we may get something else. We go to work to earn money or study to earn good grades. If you want good grades, you ought to study. Kant referred to this kind of duty as a hypothetical imperative because it is of the form if you want to do x, do y. The duty to study is dependent on your desire for good grades.

Other duties are required *per se*, with no ifs, ands or buts. Kant described these duties as categorical and referred to the fundamental principle of ethics as the categorical imperative. He believed that reason provided the basis for the categorical imperative, thus the categorical imperatives of morality were requirements of reason. Although Kant spoke of "the" categorical imperative, he formulated it in many ways. Most commentators focus on three formulations:

1   Act only on maxims which you can will to be universal laws of nature.
2   Always treat the humanity in a person as an end, and never as a means merely.
3   So act as if you were a member of an ideal kingdom of ends in which you were both subject and sovereign at the same time.

Kant believed that only human beings can follow laws of their own choosing (i.e. act rationally). Human beings are the only creatures that are free, and it is the fact that we are free that enables us to be rational and moral. Our free will is what gives us our dignity and unconditioned worth.

Kant's ethics then is an ethics of duty rather than an ethics of consequences. The ethical person is the person who acts from the right intentions. We are able to act in this way because we have free will. The fundamental principle of ethics, the categorical imperative, is a requirement of reason and is binding on all rational beings. These are the essentials of Kant's ethics. Let us see how they apply, specifically, to business ethics.

The self-defeating nature of immoral actions

Kant's first formulation of the categorical imperative is "Act only on that maxim by which you can at the same time will that it should become a universal law." Although the phrasing is awkward, Kant is providing a test to see if any proposed action, including actions in business, is moral. Since Kant believed that every action has a maxim, we are to ask what would happen if the principle (maxim) of your action were a universal law (one that everyone acted on). Would a world where everyone acted on that principle be possible? One example Kant used to illustrate his theory was a business one.

Suppose you desperately needed money. Should you ask someone to lend you money with a promise to pay the money back but with no intention of paying it back? Do your extreme financial circumstances justify a lying promise? To find out, Kant would require us to universalize the maxim of this action: "It is morally permissible for anyone in desperate financial circumstances to make a lying promise, that is, to promise to repay borrowed money with no intention of doing so." Would such a universalized maxim be logically coherent? Kant (1990, p. 19) answers with a resounding no.

And could I say to myself that everyone may make a false promise then he is in a difficulty from which he cannot escape? Immediately I see that I could will the lie but not a universal law to lie. For with such a law there would be no promises at all, inasmuch as it would be futile to make a pretense of my intention in regard to future actions to those who would not believe this pretense or- if they over hastily did so- would pay me back in my own coin. Thus my maxim would necessarily destroy itself as soon as it was made a universal law.

Notice what Kant is *not* saying here. He is not saying that if everyone made lying promises, the consequences would be bad – although they would. Rather, Kant is saying that the very concept of lying promises, when adopted as a principle by everyone, is incoherent.

Thus the categorical imperative functions as a test to see if the principles (maxims) upon which an action is based are morally permissible. The action can only be undertaken if the principle on which the action is based passes the test of the categorical imperative. A business manager who accepts Kantian morality would ask for any given decision, does the principle on which the decision is based pass the test of the categorical imperative, that is, can it be willed universally without contradiction? If it can, then the decision would be morally permissible. If it cannot, the action is morally forbidden.

Let us consider two other examples to illustrate Kant's point. First, theft by employees, managers, and customers is a major problem in business. Suppose that an employee, angry at the boss for some justified reason, considers stealing from the firm. Could a maxim which permitted stealing be universalized? It could not. Because goods and services are in limited supply and universal collective ownership is impossible, the institution of private property has developed. If a maxim that permitted stealing were universalized, there could be no private property. If everyone were free to take from everyone else, then nothing could be owned. Given the practical necessity of some form of private property, a universalized maxim that permitted stealing would be self-defeating. Thus, if the employee steals from the boss, the theft is morally wrong.

Another example found in the press concerns companies that try to renegotiate contracts. A favorite ploy of General Motors, especially with Jose Lopez in charge, was to demand price reductions from negotiated contracts with suppliers. In this way, General Motors cut costs and contributed to its bottom line. Would such a tactic pass the test of the categorical imperative? No, it could not. If a maxim that permitted contract breaking were universalized, there could be no contracts (and contracts would cease to exist). No one would enter into a contract if he or she believed the other party had no intention of honoring it. A universalized maxim that permitted contract breaking would be self-defeating.

Now consider an objection to Kant's no self-contradiction requirement raised by Hegel, Bradley, and several others. Simply put the argument runs like this: If there is a practice of private property, then a maxim that permitted stealing would be self-contradictory. However, there is nothing self-contradictory about a world without the practice of private property. So Kant's argument fails.

But as Christine Korsgaard (1996, p. 86) has argued, this criticism misses Kant's point. Kant is simply arguing that if there is a practice of private property then a maxim that permitted stealing would be logically self-contradictory. In all capitalist societies, and indeed in most societies, we do have private property and so a maxim that permitted stealing in societies with private property would be self-contradictory.

We can see this when we consider an example that does not have the ideological baggage that accompanies a term like private property. Take the practice of lining (queuing) up. There is nothing inconsistent about a society that does not have such a practice. However, in a society that does have the practice, cutting into line is morally wrong. The maxim on which the act of line-cutting is based cannot be made a universal law. An attempt to universalize line-cutting destroys the very notion of a line.

What is helpful about Korsgaard's response on behalf of Kant against Hegel and his other critics is that it allows the first formulation of the categorical imperative to work for the rules of any institution or practice. Indeed the test of the categorical imperative becomes a principle of fair play. One of the essential features of fair play is that one does not make an exception of oneself. For example, Kant (1990, p. 41) says:

> When we observe ourselves in any transgression of a duty, we find that we do not actually will that our maxim should become a universal law. That is impossible for us; rather the contrary of this maxim should remain as the law generally, and we only take the liberty of making an exception to it for ourselves or for the sake of inclination, and for this one occasion. Consequently, if we weighed everything from one and the same standpoint, namely reason, we would come upon a contradiction in our own will, viz., that a certain principle is objectively necessary as a universal law and yet subjectively does not hold universally but rather admits exceptions.

Thus the categorical imperative captures one of the key features of morality. Unless the principle of your action can be universalized, to make an exception for yourself is immoral.

I have frequently used these arguments with executives who may find them theoretically persuasive but who, nonetheless, think that their practical application is limited in the real world of business. They point out that, in the real world, contracts are often "renegotiated" and yet business people still engage in contract-making.

These executives raise an interesting point. However, an examination of what goes on in the business world does more to vindicate Kant than to refute him. Consider the following real-world situations.

- When on vacation in Ocean City, Maryland, my favorite seafood outlet had a large sign on the wall saying, "We do not cash checks and here is why." Below the sign and nearly covering the entire wall were photocopies of checks that had been returned with "Returned: Insufficient Funds" stamped in large letters. At least in this retail outlet, a threshold had been crossed. A sufficiently large number of customers wrote bad checks so that it was no longer possible to use checks in that retail store. Suppose a maxim permitting writing checks without sufficient funds in the bank to cover them was really universalized. There would be no institution of check writing.
- While lecturing in Poland in 1995, I was informed that, shortly after the fall of communism, there was a bank collapse because people did not pay on their loans. And experts generally agree that one of the impediments to the development of capitalism in Russia is the failure of various parties to pay their bills. A supplier is reluctant to provide a product if it is not known if and when payment will be received.

- Finally, there has been considerable speculation regarding the future of capitalism in Hong Kong now that the Chinese have regained sovereignty there. As business commentators have pointed out, Hong Kong had developed a legal system that enforced business contracts and limited the influence of politics. In China, political influence plays a much greater role. If the tradition of legal enforcement that has been developed is undermined, can Hong Kong survive as a thriving prosperous major center of business practice? A Kantian would agree with the economists here. Hong Kong would lose its premier standing as a commercial center and would suffer economically.

There are positive stories that illustrate Kant's point as well. By that I mean there are stories showing that when a certain threshold of morality is reached, certain institutions that, until then, were not feasible become feasible and develop. The development of a Russian stock market provides one such example. Russia had difficulties developing a stock market because company spokespersons would not provide accurate information about their companies. As a Kantian would expect, investors were not forthcoming. Gradually, a few companies including Irkutsk Enerego, Bratsky LPK, and Rostelecom were able to establish a reputation as truth tellers. These companies were then able to attract investors and have done well. The success of these honest firms has led other firms to be more honest to the point where the Russian stock market is thriving. The March 24, 1997 *Business Week* reported that the Russian stock market was up 127% in 1996 and had already gained 65% at that point in 1997. (Since 1997, the Russian stock market has plunged. However, the reasons for that plunge are completely consistent with the arguments made here.)

Thus the categorical imperative is not irrelevant in the world of business. If a maxim for an action when universalized is self-defeating, then the contemplated action is not ethical. That is Kant's conceptual point. And when enough people behave immorally in that sense, certain business practices like the use of checks or credit become impossible.

Treating stakeholders as persons

Since human beings have free will and thus are able to act from laws required by reason, Kant believed they have dignity or a value beyond price. Thus, one human being cannot use another simply to satisfy his or her own interests. This is the core insight behind Kant's second formulation of the categorical imperative: "Always treat the humanity in a person as an end and never as a means merely." What are the implications of this formulation of the categorical imperative for business?

First, it should be pointed out that the "respect for persons" principle, as I shall call it, does not prohibit commercial transactions. No one is used as merely a means in a voluntary economic exchange where both parties benefit. What this formulation of the categorical imperative does do is to put some constraints on the nature of economic transactions.

To understand Kant fully here, we need to draw a distinction between negative freedom and positive freedom. Negative freedom is freedom from coercion and deception. Kant scholar Christine Korsgaard (1996, pp. 140–1) has put it this way.

> According to the Formula of Humanity, coercion and deception are the most funda-
> mental forms of wrongdoing to others – the roots of all evil. Coercion and deception
> violate the conditions of possible assent, and all actions which depend for their nature and
> efficacy on their coercive or deceptive character are ones that others cannot assent to . . .
> Physical coercion treats someone's person as a tool, lying treats someone's reason as a
> tool. That is why Kant finds it so horrifying; it is a direct violation of autonomy.

However, simply refraining from coercive or deceptive acts is not sufficient for respecting the humanity in a person. Additional requirements can be derived from Kant's view of positive freedom. Positive freedom is the freedom to develop one's human capacities. For Kant, that means developing one's rational and moral capacities. In interacting with others, we must not do anything to diminish or inhibit these uniquely human capacities.

Thus, treating the humanity in a person as an end, and not as a means merely, in a business relationship requires two things. First, it requires that people in a business relationship not be used, i.e. they not be coerced or deceived. Second, it means that business organizations and business practices should be arranged so that they contribute to the development of human rational and moral capacities, rather than inhibit the development of these capacities. These requirements, if implemented, would change the nature of business practice. A few examples are in order.

American have been deeply concerned about the massive layoffs created by the downsizing of corporations in the early and mid-1990s. Are these layoffs immoral? A naive Kantian response would label them as immoral because, allegedly, the employees are being used as mere means to enhance shareholder wealth. However, that judgment would be premature. What would be required from a Kantian perspective is an examination of the employer/employee relationship, including any contractual agreements. So long as the relationship was neither coercive nor deceptive, there would be nothing immoral about layoffs.

What is highly contested is whether or not the standard employer/employee relationship is coercive and/or deceptive. Employers tend to argue that employees are well aware of the possibility of layoffs when they take a position and, furthermore, that employees have the right, which they frequently exercise, to take positions elsewhere. There is neither deception nor coercion in either standard labor contracts or in the implicit norms governing the employer/employee relationship. On the other hand, many employees argue that, in times of relatively high unemployment and job insecurity, employees really must accept job offers on management terms. You take what you can so as to eat, but you do not accept the threat of a layoff to enhance shareholder wealth freely. Moreover, in many companies, such as IBM, there had been a long tradition of job security in exchange for employee loyalty. The sudden unilateral changing of the rules amounted to both deception and coercion on the part of management, or so it is argued.

An examination of these opposing arguments would take us far beyond the scope of this chapter. However, by framing the issue in terms of whether or not coercion and/or deception has occurred, one has adopted a Kantian approach to business ethics.

Another concern about contemporary business practice is the extent to which employees have very limited knowledge about the affairs of the company. In economic terminology, there is high information asymmetry between management and the employees. Wherever one side has information that it keeps from other side, there is a severe temptation for abuse of power and deception. A Kantian would look for ways to reduce the information asymmetry between management and employees.

In practical terms, a Kantian would endorse the practice known as open book management. Open book management was developed by Jack Stack at the Springfield Manufacturing Company. Stack and his company won a prestigious business ethics award for the technique. Under open book management, all employees are given all the financial information about the company on a regular frequent basis. With complete information and the proper incentive, employees behave responsibly without the necessity of layers of supervision.

> How does open book management do what it does? The simplest answer is this. People get a chance to act, to take responsibility, rather than just doing their job. . . . No supervisor or department head can anticipate or handle all . . . situations. A company that hired enough managers to do so would go broke from the overhead. Open book management gets people on the job doing things right. And it teaches them to make smart decisions . . . because they can see the impact of their decisions on the relevant numbers (Case, 1995, pp. 45–6).

The adoption of practices like open book management would go far toward correcting the asymmetrical information that managers possess, a situation that promotes abuse of power and deception. Under open book management, if a firm faced a situation that might involve the layoff of employees, everyone in the firm would have access to the same information. Deception would be very difficult in such circumstances. Suspicion would be less and, as a result, cooperative efforts to address the problem would be more likely.

Open book management also enhances employee self-respect. Employees at Springfield Manufacturing Company use Kantian "respect for persons" language when describing the impact of open book management on working conditions. Thus, open book management lessens the opportunity for deception and supports negative freedom.

By enhancing employee self-respect, open book management supports positive freedom as well. What are the implications of Kant's theory of positive freedom for business practice? To treat the humanity in a person as an end in itself sometimes requires that we take some positive action to help a person. This is required by the "respect for persons" formulation of the categorical imperative, by some of Kant's own writing on the nature of work, and by the demands of Kant's imperfect duty of beneficence to help others.

The requirement that business practice be supportive of positive freedom has wide implications for business practice. I will focus on only one implication here. I believe Kant's moral philosophy enables business ethicists to develop a useful definition of meaningful work and that Kantian ethics would require companies to provide meaningful work so defined. Although I cannot cite all the Kantian texts in this brief chapter, I think the following conditions for meaningful work are consistent with Kant's views. For a Kantian, meaningful work:

- is freely chosen and provides opportunities for the worker to exercise autonomy on the job;
- supports the autonomy and rationality of human beings; work that lessens autonomy or that undermines rationality is immoral;
- provides a salary sufficient to exercise independence and provide for physical well-being and the satisfaction of some of the worker's desires;
- enables a worker to develop rational capacities; and
- does not interfere with a worker's moral development.

(Notice that these requirements are normative in the sense that they spell out what meaningful work ought to be. There is no requirement that workers who are provided meaningful work must themselves subjectively experience it as meaningful.)

A manager taking the Kantian approach to business ethics would regard providing meaningful work as a moral obligation. Some management attitudes and practices are more conducive toward meeting this obligation than others. Thus, Kantian managers need to create a certain kind of organization. A discussion of what a Kantian business firm would look like leads directly to a discussion of the third formulation of the categorical imperative.

The business firm as a moral community

Kant's third formulation of the categorical imperative roughly says that you should act as if you were a member of an ideal kingdom of ends in which you were both subject and sovereign at the same time. Organizations are composed of persons and, given the nature of persons, organizational structures must treat the humanity in persons with dignity and respect (as an end). Moreover, the rules that govern an organization must be rules that can be endorsed by everyone in the organization. This universal endorsement by rational persons is what enables Kant to say that everyone is both subject and sovereign with respect to the rules that govern them. I believe a Kantian approach to the organizational design of a business firm would endorse these principles:

1   The business firm should consider the interests of all the affected stakeholders in any decision it makes.
2   The firm should have those affected by the firm's rules and policies participate in the determination of those rules and policies before they are implemented.
3   It should not be the case that, for all decisions, the interests of one stakeholder automatically take priority.
4   When a situation arises where it appears that the interest of one set of stakeholders must be subordinated to the interests of another set of stakeholders, that decision should not be made solely on the grounds that there is a greater number of stakeholders in one group than in another.
5   No business rule or practice can be adopted which is inconsistent with the first two formulations of the categorical imperative.
6   Every profit-making firm has a limited, but genuine, duty of beneficence.
7   Every business firm must establish procedures designed to ensure that relations among stakeholders are governed by rules of justice.

I think the rationale for most of these principles can be derived from the explanation of Kant's ethics already provided. Principle 1 seems like a straightforward requirement for any moral theory that takes respect for persons seriously. Since autonomy is what makes humans worthy of respect, a commitment to principle 2 is required. Principle 3 provides a kind of organizational legitimacy; it ensures that those involved in the firm receive some minimum benefits from being a part of it. Principle 4 rules out utilitarianism as a criterion for decision-making in the moral firm. The justification for principle 6 is based on an extension of the individual's imperfect obligation of beneficence which Kant defended in the *Metaphysics of Morals*. There Kant (1994, p. 52) says:

> That beneficence is a duty results from the fact that since our self-love cannot be separated from our need to be loved by others (to obtain help from them in the case of need), we thereby make ourselves an end for others . . . hence the happiness of others is an end which is at the same time a duty.

The strategy here is to extend this argument to the corporate level. If corporations have benefited from society, they have a duty of beneficence to society in return. And corporations have benefited. Society protects corporations by providing the means for enforcing business contracts. It provides the infrastructure which allows the corporation to function – such as roads, sanitation facilities, police and fire protection – and, perhaps most importantly, an educated work force with both the skills and attitudes required to perform well in a corporate setting. Few would argue that corporate taxes pay the full cost of these benefits. Finally, principle 7 is a procedural principle designed to ensure that whatever rules the corporation adopts conform to the basic principles of justice.

A Kantian views an organization as a moral community. Each member of the organization stands in a moral relationship to all the others. On one hand, the managers of a business firm should respect the humanity in all the persons in the organization. On the other hand, each individual in a business firm, managed as a Kantian moral community, should view the organization other than purely instrumentally, that is, as merely a means for achieving individual goals. Organizations are created as ways of achieving common goals and shared ends. An individual who views the organization purely instrumentally is acting contrary to the "respect for persons" principle.

A manager who adopts the Kantian principles of a moral firm must also look at human nature in a certain way. In management terms, the theory Y view of human nature must be adopted rather than a theory X view. (The distinction between theory X and theory Y was made prominent by McGregor (1960). Theory X assumed that people had an inherent dislike of work and would avoid it if possible. It also assumed that the average person seeks to avoid responsibility. Theory Y assumes the opposite: that employees prefer to act imaginatively and creatively and are willing to assume responsibility. Although we can debate about which theory is descriptively more accurate, as a normative matter a Kantian manager should adopt theory Y. For it is theory Y that views human beings as having the dignity Kant thinks they deserve.

Moreover, both theory X and theory Y have the tendency to become self-fulfilling prophecies. By that I mean that people will tend to behave as they are treated. If a manager treats people in accordance with theory X, employees will tend to behave as theory X predicts. Conversely with theory Y. Thus the question becomes what kind of organization should the manager and the employees, working together, create. For the Kantian, the answer is clear. People should try to create an organization where the participants in the organization behave as theory Y would predict. People should seek to create an organization where members develop their rational and moral capacities, including the capacity to take responsibility.

One of the chief implications of Kant's ethics is that it acts as a moral critique of authoritarian hierarchical organizational structures. Principle 2 demands participation in some form by all the corporate stakeholders, especially stockholders and employees. A Kantian would morally object to a hierarchical structure that requires those lower down to carry out the orders of those above, more or less without question.

Kantian moral theory also requires worker participation; indeed, it requires a vast democratization of the work place. Certainly, a necessary condition of autonomy is consent given under non-coercive and non-deceptive conditions. Consent also requires that the individuals in an organization endorse the rules that govern them. As a minimum condition of democratization, Kantian moral philosophy requires that each person in an organization be represented by the stakeholder group to which he or she belongs, and that these various stakeholder groups must consent to the rules and policies which govern the organization.

This requirement for a more democratic work place is not purely utopian; it has some support in management theory and in management practice. Teamwork is almost universally praised, and several corporations have endorsed varieties of the concept of participative management. Levi Strauss and Singapore Airlines, to name just two examples, have democratic work places.

I hope I have convinced the reader the Kant's moral philosophy has rich implications for business practice. When the three formulations of the categorical imperative are considered together as a coherent whole, they provide guidance to the manager, both in terms of negative injunctions and positive ideals. The negative injunctions prohibit actions like contract breaking, theft, deception and coercion. The positive ideals include a more democratic work place and a commitment toward meaningful work.

However, Kantian ethics is not without its limitations and challenges. Kant had nothing to say about environmental ethics and had little understanding of the suffering of animals and thus held a truncated view of our obligations to animals. But the biggest challenge to the Kantian ethic is that the Kantian ethic is too demanding. Let us consider that objection at greater length.

The purity of motive

It is a central tenet of Kant's moral philosophy that an action is only truly moral if it is morally motivated. Truly moral actions cannot be contaminated by motives of self-interest. Since the good acts of even the most enlightened corporations are almost always justified in part on the grounds that such actions are profitable, it appears that even the best actions of the best corporations are not truly moral. Consider the following quotation from J. W. Marriott Jr (Milbank, 1996, p. A1) describing the decision of the Marriott Corporation to hire welfare recipients.

We're getting good employees for the long term but we're also helping these communities. If we don't step up in these inner cities and provide work, they'll never pull out of it.
But it makes bottom line sense. If it didn't we wouldn't do it.

A strict Kantian could not call Marriott's act of hiring welfare recipients a good act.
In Kantian language, the act would be done in conformity with duty but not out of
duty. But doesn't that make Kant's theory too austere to apply to business? Several
things can be said in response to this question.

We might say that Kant is mistaken about requiring such purity of motive. Yet even
if Kant is wrong about the necessity of pure motivation for an act's being moral, he
still has a lot to offer the business ethicist. Working out the implications of the three
formulations of the categorical imperative provides a rich agenda for the business
ethicist. However, a bit more should be said, especially in light of the fact that the
general public judges business from a strict Kantian position.

In discussing this issue, people seem to assume that actions that enhance the bottom
line are acts of self-interest on the part of the corporation. However, for publicly held
corporations and for partnerships, this is not the case. Publicly held corporations have
an obligation to make a profit based on their charters of incorporation, legal obligations
to shareholders, and an implied contract with the public. It would not be stretching a
point too far to say that the managers of a publicly held corporation have promised to
strive for profits. If that is so, the position of the Marriott Corporation is a moral one,
even for the strict Kantian. The Marriott Corporation is honoring its obligation to
realize profits and its obligation of beneficence. Thus, Kant's insistence that an action
must be done from a truly moral motive need not undercut acts of corporate beneficence
that also contribute to the bottom line.

So far all we have shown is that Kant's insistence on the purity of a moral motive
has not made his theory irrelevant to business ethics. But perhaps his insistence on the
purity of the moral motive has a positive contribution to make to business ethics and
is not simply a barrier to be overcome. Perhaps focusing on issues other than profits,
such as meaningful work for employees, a democratic work place, non-deceptive advertising, and a non-coercive relationship with suppliers will actually enhance the
bottom line. Many management theorists urge businesses to always focus on the
bottom line. However, perhaps paradoxically, profits can be enhanced if we do *not*
focus so exclusively on the bottom line. To put this in more Kantian terms, perhaps
profits will be enhanced if the manager focuses on respecting the humanity in the person
of all the corporate stakeholders. Perhaps we should view profits as a consequence
of good business practices rather than as the goal of business.

With this standard criticism of Kantian moral philosophy addressed, we can close
by considering briefly how Kant's cosmopolitan perspective provides a moral ideal for
international business.

Kant's cosmopolitanism and international business

One of the key features of the enlightenment was its cosmopolitan perspective, and
Kant was cosmopolitan in many ways. For Kant, national boundaries have, at most,
derivative significance. His greatest concern was with the human community and

with ways that the human community could live in peace. Contemporary capitalism is also cosmopolitan and is no respecter of national boundaries. Many have also argued that capitalism contributes to world peace. Kant would tend to agree. In addition, international economic cooperation provides the foundation for a universal morality that is consistent with Kant's philosophy.

To see how Kant's philosophy provides a foundation for a universal morality, we need to return to the first formulation of the categorical imperative. Interestingly, that formulation provides a convincing argument against a full blown ethical relativism (the doctrine that what a culture believes to be right or wrong really is right or wrong for that culture). At least within international capitalist economic relations, the maxims of certain actions if universalized, would be self-defeating. Thus, as capitalism spreads throughout the world, a certain minimum morality, what I have called the "morality of the marketplace", will be universally adopted. For example, I believe that international capitalism will necessarily promote increased honesty and trust among different cultures participating in capitalist economic relations, and I believe that international capitalism will undermine certain forms of discrimination, e.g. against women. However, I will illustrate my general argument by providing an argument against bribery – an argument which enables us to predict that we will see less bribery as capitalism spreads throughout the world.

I maintain that, if a maxim permitting bribery were universalized, it could not pass the test of the categorical imperative. (For purposes of this discussion, bribery is distinguished from extortion and facilitating payments.) Put most abstractly, the argument – for which I am indebted to Robert Frederick – goes like this:

If we understand the practice of bribery to be a secret attempt to gain a special advantage over others, an advantage these others would not agree to if they knew about it, then a principle permitting bribery could not be universalized. If everybody offered bribes, then the practice of trying to make secret attempts to gain special advantages would make no sense.

Bribery involves practical inconsistencies as well. Consider a company offering a bribe. Suppose the company could have received the contract on the merits of the product without offering a bribe. If so, paying adds to its costs and it will lose out to competitors that have equally good products but incur less costs since they do not bribe. Other things being equal, companies that do not bribe have a competitive advantage that will drive companies that bribe out of business. Since companies wish to stay in business, a maxim to offer a bribe cannot be universalized.

A similar argument can be made for a company taking a bribe. It receives a product of the same or even less quality for a greater expenditure. That puts it at a competitive disadvantage and, other things being equal, it will be driven out of business. The maxim of accepting a bribe cannot be universalized.

However, bribery is, allegedly, a fact of life in many countries. In those countries, an international firm doing business in that country would have to offer bribes to stay in business. There is some merit in that reply, but the nature of the reply shifts the argument to a higher level. If a country adopts the practice of bribery, it condemns itself to a much lower standard of living and to an ever-increasing gap between those countries where bribery is widespread and those countries where it is not widespread. It is widely maintained that one reason for the lack of economic development in many countries of Africa is the high level of corruption, especially the bribery that takes place there. As Hong Kong returns to China, business writers have commented on the economic danger to Hong Kong if political influence replaces arm's-length considerations of quality and price in business transactions. These theoretical considerations receive empirical support. Research has shown that corruption, including bribery, diminishes per capita income; a study by Johns Hopkins economist, Steve Hanke, is cited in Zachary (1997, p. A8). Specific figures have been given for Italy, where it is estimated that Italy's debt has been increased $200 billion by bribery (Penner, 1993, pp. 133–8). Given this data, and the fact that decreases in per capital income are nearly universally seen as undesirable, a country that practices bribery cannot universalize its practice.

Kantians would use arguments such as this to try to show that there is a minimum market morality that capitalist countries must adhere to, if they are to gain the economic advantages of capitalism. Such arguments would be useful in undercutting the relativism that is in intellectual fashion these days. But Kant's moral philosophy has even more to offer international business ethics. It shows how international business can contribute to world peace.

The thesis that commerce supports world peace was widely held in Kant's time. Exponents of the thesis included Adam Smith, David Hume, and John Stuart Mill. Kant (1963, p. 23) had this to say:

> In the end, war itself will be seen as not only so artificial, in outcome so uncertain for both sides, in after effects so painful in the form of an ever-growing war debt (a new invention) that cannot be met, that it will be regarded as a most dubious undertaking. The impact of any revolution on all states on our continent, so clearly knit together through commerce will be so obvious that other states, driven by their own danger, but without any legal basis, will offer themselves as arbiters, and thus will prepare the way for a distant international government for which there is not precedent in world history.

For all these thinkers, commerce is a way of bringing people together rather than keeping them apart. If commerce is successful in bringing people together, then the chances for peace among nations improves. Given the exponential growth of international business, it is not surprising that this view has many adherents today. During the 1970s and 1980s, trade agreements between the USA and the former Soviet Union were defended on the grounds that they would enhance the chances of peace. Similar arguments are heard today regarding the granting of Most Favored Nation Status to China. Such arguments are not limited to US spokespersons. A Mideast Common Market has been proposed as a cure of the continuing conflicts in the Middle East.

If these arguments are right, then business ethics from a Kantian perspective is not simply a matter of following the demands of the three formulations of the categorical imperative. International business has an opportunity to contribute to an ethical ideal. International business, if done from the Kantian perspective, can contribute to the long hoped for, but elusive, goal of world peace.

This concludes our brief analysis of the implications of Kantian moral philosophy for business ethics. I hope I have shown that Kant's moral philosophy is not a system of inflexible absolute rules. The categorical imperative does rule out certain practices such as the unilateral breaking of contracts, theft, and bribery. But Kant's moral philosophy is more than a series of negative constraints. If business is to be faithful to the second and third formulations of the categorical imperative, business managers should manage so as to provide meaningful work for employees, and business firms should be organized more democratically. Finally, firms engaged in international business can contribute to the goal of world peace. Kant's moral philosophy has rich implications for business ethics.

References

Bowie, N. E. 1999: *Business Ethics: A Kantian Perspective*. Oxford: Blackwell Publishers.

Case, J. 1995: *Open Book Management*. New York: Harper Collins Publishers.

Kant, I. 1963: What is enlightenment (1784). In L. White Beck (ed. and trans.) *On History*. Trans. Indianapolis: The Bobbs Merrill Company.

Kant, I. 1990: *Foundations of the Metaphysics of Morals* (1785). Trans. by Lewis White Beck. New York: Macmillan Publishing Company.

Kant, I. 1994: *The metaphysics of moral; The metaphysical principles of virtue* (1797). In I. Kant *Ethical Philosophy* 2nd edn, Trans. by James W. Ellington. Indianapolis/Cambridge, MA: Hackett Publishing Company.

Korsgaard, C. 1996: *Creating the Kingdom of Ends*. New York: Cambridge University Press.

McGregor D. 1960: *The Human Side of Enterprise*. New York: McGraw Hill Book Company.

Milbank, D. 1996: Hiring welfare people, hotel chain finds, is tough but rewarding. *The Wall Street Journal*. October 31.

Penner, K. 1993: The destructive costs of greasing palms. *Business Week*, December 6.

Zachary, G. P. 1997: Global growth attains a higher level that could be lasting. *The Wall Street Journal*, March 13.

2

Utilitarianism and business ethics

MILTON SNOEYENBOS AND JAMES HUMBER

This chapter states and clarifies act and rule utilitarian principles, enumerates several advantages of employing utilitarianism as an ethical theory in business contexts, and discusses the main difficulties with utilitarianism in such contexts.

Utilitarianism is a consequentialist ethical theory. It is an ethical theory because it is concerned with whether human actions are right or wrong; it is consequentialist because it tells us that an act's rightness or wrongness is determined solely by the act's consequences and not by any feature of the act itself. For example, if I make a promise to you and then act in such a way as to break it, my act has the feature of breaking a promise, and many people would claim my act was wrong because it has that feature. However, according to utilitarianism, that feature does not make the act wrong for that feature is irrelevant to whether the act is right or wrong. For the utilitarian, whether breaking a promise is right or wrong depends entirely on the act's consequences. The intuitive idea behind utilitarianism is that we should act to bring about the best consequences and, hence, whether an act is morally right or wrong depends on whether the act does or does not bring about the best consequences. Of course, we will have to say more about what we mean by "best consequences," but for now let us just use our ordinary concepts of benefit and harm to make sense of the notion. Of two acts, one of which causes you pleasure and the other pain, we would ordinarily say the former benefits you and the latter harms you, and that the former is better for you than the latter. Again, of two acts, one of which increases dividends and the other of which bankrupts a firm, we would commonly say the former benefits and the latter harms shareholders, and that the former is better than the latter for shareholders.

According to one version of utilitarianism, act utilitarianism, an act is morally right if and only if it maximizes utility, i.e., if and only if the balance of benefit to harm calculated by taking everyone affected by the act into consideration is greater than the balance of benefit to harm resulting from any alternative act. Although we will have to modify it slightly, this statement of act utilitarianism best enables us to see how the act utilitarian goes about determining which act is right in typical situations. In deciding to act, the act utilitarian will:

1 set out all the relevant alternative acts that are open to him or her;
2 list all the individuals who will be affected by the alternative courses of action, including oneself if affected;

3   assess how the individuals will be affected by the alternative acts, computing the balance of benefit to harm for each individual affected by each act; and
4   choose that act which maximizes utility, i.e., which results in the greatest total balance of benefit to harm.

Suppose, for example, that a person P_1 faces a situation in which there are four possible courses of action (A_1, A_2, A_3, A_4) and assume there are four people who will be affected by at least some of these acts (P_1, P_2, P_3, P_4). Assume, furthermore, that the balance of benefit to harm for each person affected by each act can be expressed quantitatively, with a positive value indicating an overall benefit and a negative value indicating an overall harmful effect. Finally, assume a calculation yields the following result:

Persons

		P_1	P_2	P_3	P_4	Totals
	A_1	+6	+2	−7	+4	+5
Acts	A_2	+5	−4	0	+6	+7
	A_3	−12	−1	−6	+15	−4
	A_4	−3	−1	−2	+7	+1

Here it may be that P_2 is both benefitted and harmed by A_1 (for example, P_2 benefits +7 but is harmed −5), but on balance he or she benefits to the extent of +2; similarly, P_3 may receive some benefits from A_3 (say, +1), but also some harm (say, −7), so that on balance he or she is harmed to the extent of −6. In the situation represented by the above chart, the act utilitarian will choose act A_2 because it provides the greatest total balance of benefit to harm (+7) when everyone affected by the acts is considered.

Using the chart, we can further clarify act utilitarianism and distinguish it from other consequentialist theories. First, act utilitarianism differs from ethical egoism in that, for the latter, an act is morally right if and only if, of all available acts, it provides the greatest balance of benefit to harm for the person performing the act. Accordingly, P_1, acting as an ethical egoist, will do A_1 because A_1 produces the greatest benefit to harm ratio for P_1 (+6), whereas P_1 acting as an act utilitarian would do A_2, since A_2 maximizes utility. Furthermore, act utilitarianism is not altruism. The altruists do not consider themselves in the benefit to harm calculation; they act to produce the greatest benefit to harm ratio when only others affected by the acts are considered. Accordingly, P_1, acting as an altruist, will select A_3 as the right act, since it produces a balance of +8 when considering the effects on P_2, P_3, and P_4, and this balance is greater than those for A_1 (−1), A_2 (+2) and A_4 (+4), whereas P_1 acting as an act utilitarian will do A_2. Of course, there will be many occasions on which the act required by ethical egoism will be the same as that required by act utilitarianism, and for that matter altruism. For example, CEOs may maximally benefit themselves by a singular focus on profit maximization, but at the same time maximally benefit customers, employees, shareholders, and society as well. Yet act utilitarianism, as a general ethical theory, is distinct from egoism and altruism; in calculating benefits and harms, the act utilitarians consider themselves equally with others, no less but no more.

Second, act utilitarianism is not the principle that we should maximize total benefits, rather, one should maximize utility. If we calculate just benefits, A_3 provides +15 and A_2 provides +11, hence A_3 would be the right act. However, in calculating utility, it is important to consider harms as well as benefits, which act utilitarianism does in judging A_2 to be the right act.

Third, the act utilitarian is not concerned solely with short-term benefit-to-harm ratios; long-term consequences also have to be calculated. However, this requirement is consonant with good business practices; research and capital expenditures are aimed at long-term benefits.

Fourth, act utilitarianism is not the theory that an act is morally right if its overall benefits outweigh its harms. A_4's benefits outweigh its harms (by +1), but A_2 is the right act according to act utilitarianism, and all the other alternative acts, including A_4, are morally wrong.

Fifth, act utilitarianism is not the principle that an act is right if and only if it provides the best consequences for the greatest number, where this means that to be right an act must maximize utility and, at the same time, maximize the number of individuals who realize a positive benefit to harm ratio. In our charted example, A_2 maximizes utility but A_1 maximizes the number of individuals who realize a positive balance of benefit to harm, since three individuals benefit (P_1, P_2, P_4) from A_1 but every other act benefits at most two individuals. Since none of the acts in our example satisfies the best consequences for the greatest number principle, none of the acts listed is morally right according to that principle, an odd result, since if we are consequentialists we would expect that one of these acts is right and, of course, A_2 is right according to act utilitarianism. This criticism of the best consequences for the greatest number principle also enables us to see a defect in our formulation of act utilitarianism. Suppose a person has three acts available, two of which produce the same overall utility, say +9, and a third which yields −4. In this case, since no one act maximizes utility, none of the acts is right. Accordingly, we have to revise our statement of act utilitarianism to read: an act A is morally right if and only if no other alternative act has greater overall utility than A. Thus, the result in the above example would be that both +9 acts would be morally right.

Since act utilitarians focus on maximizing benefits and minimizing harms, we now need to consider what they regard as benefits and harms. We shall discuss three major utilitarian value theories: hedonistic, pluralistic, and preference.

Hedonistic act utilitarians claim that pleasure (or happiness, construed as long-term pleasure) is the only intrinsically good thing, i.e., the only thing that is good in and of itself. Other things, when they are good, are good instrumentally, i.e., they are good as a means to other things. Money for example, is not always instrumentally good, but when it is good it is good as a means to other things; it is instrumentally, not intrinsically, good. The English act utilitarian Jeremy Bentham (1748–1832) attempted to establish a method for determining quantities of pleasure by listing seven criteria for pleasure and (what he took to be) its opposite, pain: other things being equal, of two pleasures P_1 and P_2, P_1 is greater than P_2 if P_1 is

1   more intense than P_2, or
2   of greater duration than P_2, or
3   more certain of realization than P_2, or
4   nearer in time than P_2, or
5   such that it will lead to other pleasures that P_2 does not lead to, or
6   purer, i.e., less mixed with pain than P_2, or
7   such that more people can realize it than P_2.

The idea is that we can assign numbers to each dimension of pleasure. To simplify matters, consider pleasurable experiences having only the dimensions of duration and intensity. We might say that a pleasurable experience of one hour duration is assigned +1, two hours +2, and so on. A pleasure of a certain intensity is assigned +1 and a pleasure twice as intense is +2. Accordingly, a three-hour pleasurable experience of intensity +4 is assigned +12 ($+3 \times +4$). In this way, pleasures can be measured and compared. Bentham's follower John Stuart Mill (1806–73) further developed the former's "hedonistic calculus." Among other things, Mill was concerned that Bentham's approach would allow beer guzzling to be better than doing philosophy, so he argued that the type of pleasure should be included as well as Bentham's factors, with "higher" pleasures being accorded higher values than "lower" pleasures. So, doing philosophy might be assigned +60, beer drinking +5. Accordingly, one hour of doing philosophy of intensity +2 ($1 \times 2 \times 60 = +120$) would be better than four hours of more intensely pleasurable (+3) beer drinking ($4 \times 3 \times 5 = +60$).

Although we might agree that Bentham's criteria are factors that should be considered in weighing alternative courses of action, it is questionable whether they allow us to make the precise, mathematical calculations utilitarians envisage. Duration can be calculated rather precisely, say, in seconds, but it is often difficult to say just when a pleasurable experience begins and /or ends. We can and do say that one pleasurable experience is more intense than another, one pain more intense than another, but we do not say that one experience is nine times more intensely pleasurable than another and it is doubtful we can attain such quantitative precision. If duration and intensity are not quantifiable, then the other five of Bentham's criteria, which depend on these two, are not quantifiable. Mill's proposal faces these difficulties, plus two more. His proposal requires us to rank pleasures (e.g., doing philosophy is "higher" than drinking beer) and then assign them numerical values. However, some people will rank drinking beer higher than doing philosophy; in fact, if we were to take a vote, more people might well rank beer drinking higher than doing philosophy. So how can Mill justify his belief that intellectual pleasures always must be ranked higher than physical pleasures? Even if we can rank doing philosophy as higher than beer drinking, what argument can be employed for assigning +60 to doing philosophy and +5 to beer drinking? Neither question has been answered satisfactorily.

Given these measurement and comparison problems with the concept of pleasure, act utilitarians have four main options. First, they can continue the pleasure quantification quest; after all, at one time we used "hot" and "cold" but we now have precise temperature concepts. Perhaps someone will devise a pleasureometer. Second, they can retain hedonism but abandon quantification, claiming that, even if we cannot measure pleasure with mathematical precision, we all know that some experiences are quite pleasurable and that some pleasures are greater than others, as we know that boiling water is hot, and hotter than ice. If, in some cases, rough judgments and comparisons are all that can be obtained, they are, nonetheless, useful and often adequate. Third, since utilitarianism can be construed as the claim that we should maximize that which is intrinsically good – and the theory itself leaves open what is intrinsically good – act utilitarians can claim that other things in addition to pleasure should be added to the list of things intrinsically good: knowledge, freedom, beauty, fairness, friendship, generosity, etc. In fact, some act utilitarians, known as pluralistic act utilitarians, have developed this approach. However, this strategy does not alleviate our measurement and comparison problems. How do we measure friendship and compare it with pleasure? Furthermore, if we allow different persons to weight (in some manner) these intrinsic goods differently, then overall utility calculations will differ. Which should we accept?

In this century, a fourth strategy, preference act utilitarianism, has been developed. If pleasure seems subjective and unmeasurable, our preferences, linked to our desires, choices and behavior, are more objective and may offer a firmer basis for a theory of value. If you prefer celery over pork, you behave in certain ways; you typically choose celery when presented with the two alternatives. So, we can say that celery has more value for you than pork, if you exhibit more preference for celery than pork. Economists have devised methods for assigning numbers to a person's preferences; hence, if we can determine how many people prefer celery over pork, we have a way of totaling preferences, i.e., a general method for determining which acts maximize total preference satisfaction.

Preference act utilitarianism has three major advantages over its hedonistic relative:

1   As noted, it handles the measurement and comparison problems better than hedonism.
2   It admits a greater range of values than hedonism: what is valuable to you is anything you prefer.
3   It is more tolerant than hedonism: other things being equal, the hedonistic act utilitarian will claim it is right to restrict what you prefer, if doing so will maximize happiness in the long run, whereas preference act utilitarianism is based on whatever you actually prefer.

The third advantage raises the main difficulty for preference act utilitarianism understood as a general moral theory. Some people prefer heroin to celery, and we commonly think this preference is wrong even if the choice of heroin affects no one else. Of course, some preferences do affect others, and we say that a manager acts wrongly in preferring to sexually harass an employee rather than treating him or her fairly. So the concept of preference, important as it seems to be in the development of an economic theory adequate to explain and predict actual market behavior, is initially problematic as a basis for value in an adequate moral theory. We seem to need the concept of an "acceptable" preference, i.e., a morally acceptable preference, but it is

21

not clear whether such a concept is even consistent with the notion of preference construed as a fact, and it seems to undercut the fact-based advantages preference act utilitarians claim their theory offers over hedonistic act utilitarianism. Moreover, although some preference act utilitarians argue that "unacceptable" preferences should not count in utility calculations because they interfere with others' "acceptable" preferences, it seems more plausible to say that such unacceptable preferences should count in the calculation; it is that they simply lead to unhappiness. The conclusion is that they should be factored into a hedonistic utility calculation. Some preference act utilitarians suggest the concept needed is that of "informed preference," roughly, the preferences a person would have, if fully informed about the relevant facts related to preference alternatives. However, critics argue that such preferences would simply be those that maximize happiness – we try to satisfy our preferences and those of others because doing so maximizes happiness. If so, the theory again seems to reduce to hedonistic act utilitarianism. Preference act utilitarianism also has difficulties with simple distributional issues. If you prefer X which costs 40 cents per unit, and I prefer Y which also costs 40 cents, and we have only 55 cents to distribute, pure preference act utilitarianism has no answer as to how the 55 cents should be distributed. Hedonistic act utilitarianism does: we figure out who would be made happier by getting what he or she wants. Finally, preference utilitarianism is not as simple as it seems. Our preferences change over time; some are added, some dropped. Should I maximize those I have now but will not have later? It would seem not, but how can I know now which preferences I will drop? Should I seek to maximize only the unchanging preferences? What are they? And how will this enable me to add new preferences? Surely, in some cases, it is rational to change preferences, but accounting for this will require a much more complex theory than one based simply on the preferences people do in fact now exhibit.

Although the measurement problems for act utilitarianism are severe, if they could be overcome the theory would have distinct advantages as an ethical theory in business contexts. First of all, as a thoroughgoing consequentialist theory, it has a commonsense plausibility. If your manager tells you to treat customers with respect, he or she probably adds that doing so will benefit the two of you: your firm, and your customers. In other words, we standardly base and explain our moral judgments on acts' overall consequences. In addition, unlike ethical egoism, act utilitarianism is impartial in that it takes into account each individual affected by the acts considered and requires that act which maximizes utility irrespective of who benefits. As an act utilitarian, businessmen will not seek to just maximize their utility or their firm's utility; they consider equally everyone affected by their acts. This squares with our commonsense idea that the "best" business transaction is one in which the "best result" is achieved when both buyer and seller are considered and benefitted. Moreover, act utilitarianism provides a definite method for determining which act is right. It cautions us not to act on our mere intuitions as to what is right and wrong, and requires us to enumerate alternatives, consider all their consequences, calculate utilities, and then act to maximize utility. Now businesses certainly engage frequently in this type of calculation. In considering whether to relocate a plant, alternative sites are listed and the consequences for the firm, stockholders, employees, customers, and the communities affected are analyzed in terms of benefits and harms. Act utilitarianism simply requires the businessperson to act to maximize utility.

Act utilitarianism also accounts for why certain business practices are held to be immoral. Breaking a contract is generally wrong because doing so, typically, does not maximize utility. If you promise your employees a wage increase, other things being equal, you should keep your promise, because doing so will generally lead to better consequences than breaking it. However, moral rules, such as "keep your contracts," are not inviolable. If you sign a contract to build a plant, but then discover that doing so will destroy an ecosystem and not maximize utility, you should break the contract. And if you have promised your employees a wage increase but your company suddenly loses money, maximizing utility may morally require you to break your promise. So, act utilitarianism can account for the moral rules we employ in business, while also permitting business the flexibility to break such rules when morality requires it.

Because it is universalistic, provides a definite method for determining which acts are right, and permits flexibility in adhering to moral rules we use in business, act utilitarianism has decided advantages in international business contexts. In some countries, bribery is prohibited; in others, it is permitted, while in yet others it may be required to do business. Which rules should a business follow? Well, all such rules are merely rules of thumb according to act utilitarianism. Following the rule "never bribe" may typically have utility in one society, while following the rule "always bribe" may typically have utility in another society. All such rules are breakable, and we are obligated to break them when utility maximization requires it.

Act utilitarianism also provides a basis for economics and social policy. Assuming that

1   value is based on preference and is measurable,
2   price is the exchange value of one good in terms of another, and
3   the "rational economic person" will act to maximize his or her own self-interest (i.e., his or her own utility),

economists are able to explain price behavior in a competitive market and show that the "free market" would enable consumers to maximize their own utility. A long line of economists, from Adam Smith to Milton Friedman, argue that the best way to organize the exchange of goods is to let people trade freely with whatever resources they possess, because doing so maximizes overall utility. These economists provide a utilitarian justification for the free market. In effect, Smith and Friedman make an efficiency claim for the free market: the market is said to be the most efficient means to maximize utility. However, the ordinary notion of business efficiency as applied to the individual firm also has a utilitarian basis. The efficient firm maximizes outputs in relation to inputs, which squares with the utilitarians' argument that one should act to maximize benefits and minimize costs. Profit, which in one sense is just a measure of efficiency, thereby has a utilitarian justification. Act utilitarians also argue that their theory provides the best basis for governmental and social policy. Given a set of policy alternatives, which should be chosen? Act utilitarians say we should choose the one that provides the greatest overall benefits at the least cost, the one that maximizes utility.

Act utilitarianism is also attractive to businesspersons because it provides the foundation for cost–benefit analysis, which in its purest form calculates benefits and costs in terms of money. Of course, the market itself places a monetary value on many goods, services, and activities; in addition, utilitarians have devised ingenious methods of placing a price on such seeming unmeasurables as aesthetic value, health, even human life. For instance, we can determine the value you place on your own life by examining the risks you do or would take and the insurance premiums you pay or would be willing to pay. We can also calculate the value of your life by discounting to the present your expected earnings in the future, or by calculating the losses others would experience from your death. Given that we can legitimately make such calculations, the basic strategy of cost–benefit analysis is straightforwardly utilitarian: enumerate alternative courses of action $A_1, \ldots, A_n$, calculate the benefits and costs of each alternative in monetary units, and if A_2's benefits outweigh its cost and A_2's balance of benefits to costs is greater than any other alternative, then A_2 should be done.

Finally, although some act utilitarians claim their theory supports the shareholder conception of corporate responsibility and others claim utilitarianism supports the stakeholder conception, all agree that utilitarian considerations are the sole basis for resolving the dispute. Briefly, utilitarians favoring the shareholder theory argue that maximizing shareholder interests (typically profit maximization) will, via Adam Smith's "invisible hand," tend to maximize overall utility. "Maximize profits" is thus a general rule of thumb, to be violated only if doing so is required by the utilitarian principle. Advocates of the stakeholder theory argue that all stakeholders (shareholders, employees, customers, suppliers, society, etc.) should be taken into consideration directly in the utilitarian calculation. In any case, act utilitarians agree the dispute is to be resolved by determining which approach actually maximizes utility.

In spite of its advantages in business contexts, act utilitarianism faces severe criticisms in addition to those involving the measurement of utility. Many critics focus on the utilitarians' claim that the only morally relevant feature of an act is its consequences, namely, its utility; according to act utilitarians, no feature other than utility even contributes to an act's rightness. So, if my alternatives involve keeping or breaking a promise and keeping it is morally right, then that act is right solely because it produces more utility than breaking the promise. If breaking the promise has more utility than keeping it, no other feature is morally relevant and breaking it is morally right. Critics point out that one intrinsic feature of an act of keeping a promise is that one is keeping a promise and one intrinsic feature of an act of breaking a promise is that one is breaking a promise. So consider two acts, A_1 and A_2, and features of these acts (where we assume the utility/disutility of keeping/breaking promises are factored into both utility calculations):

Features of acts

Acts		F_1	F_2
	A_1	+85 utility	keeping a promise
	A_2	+86 utility	breaking a promise

Utilitarians claim A_2 is morally right; A_2 maximizes utility, which is the only morally relevant feature. Some critics claim A_1 is morally right, believing that a small increase in utility should not override one's obligation to keep a promise. At the very least, critics claim, promise-keeping and promise-breaking are morally relevant features in determining which act is right and, since act utilitarianism does not regard them as relevant, the theory is defective. Now, clearly, promise-keeping is very important in just about every sort of business transaction, and if act utilitarianism does not provide a plausible account of the role and importance of promise-keeping in business, it is inadequate as an ethical theory for business.

Critics also allege that act utilitarianism does not adequately take into consideration individuals' rights when determining whether an act is morally right. For example, suppose executive X in company Q has worked for months to secure a contract between Q and another company D. Whether the contract is signed depends heavily on what X does, for negotiations are at a crucial stage. If the contract is signed, Q and D will increase profits and new jobs will be created. During final negotiations, Q's president by chance discovers that X has embezzled $\$50,000$ from Q. The president knows Q will be audited tomorrow and knows the auditors will discover X's theft. Q's president confronts X, who explains that the money was needed to pay for an emergency operation for a close relative, but notes that this relative has died and never again will X be pressed to steal money from Q. Also, X says that if the theft is made known to the negotiating team in D, they will no longer trust X and the deal will fall through. Since X's theft will be detected by the impending audit, the president says there is little that can be done. As luck would have it, however, there is a middle-manager, Y, in Q, who has had bad relations with his or her supervisors and is about to be fired. X suggests that Q's president make it appear as though Y embezzled the $\$50,000$. When Y is fired, the company will not press charges, and X will quietly repay the money stolen. The question then is this: should Q's president frame Y for the embezzlement actually committed by X? If, as it appears, doing so would maximize utility, then the act utilitarian would answer yes. However, framing Y seems morally wrong: it violates Y's right to be treated fairly and Y's right not to be falsely accused. Similar cases can be developed to show that managers, acting as utilitarians, would be required to trample on individuals' rights to privacy, due process, safe working conditions, and perhaps even the right to life. Such rights' violations pose powerful counterexamples to act utilitarianism.

In addition to difficulties with promising and rights, critics claim that act utilitarianism permits social injustice. For example, the following sort of utility calculation could be employed to "justify" what we would regard as an unjust act of enslavement:

Persons

		P_1	P_2	P_3	P_4	Totals
Acts	A_1	+33	+27	+30	−49	+41
	A_2	+10	+10	+10	+10	+40

It is conceivable that the enslavement of P_4 via act A_1 would produce slightly greater total utility than act A_2, which does not involve enslavement and also results in a more equitable distribution of happiness. Since the act utilitarian is committed to holding that A_1 is morally right, but A_1 seems morally wrong because it is unjust, act utilitarianism seems to be an inadequate moral theory.

In response to these three sorts of criticism, act utilitarians claim the counterexamples are contrived and not indicative of real-world situations. They claim that slavery would not maximize utility, so the value assignments in the enslavement counterexample do not reflect reality. Framing the innocent manager is contrived because, in the real world, there surely would be other alternative acts that could be selected. Finally, the promise-breaking case is either contrived because the full negative consequences of breaking a promise are not reflected in the utility calculation, or it is not contrived and the utility values are adequately represented, in which case the only morally relevant feature is utility and A_2 is morally right.

Other utilitarians, convinced these sorts of criticisms are decisive against act utilitarianism, have changed the theory to try to answer them. Although it has been formulated in a variety of ways, this type of theory, called rule utilitarianism, is based on two convictions:

1   Utility maximization plays a central role in an adequate moral theory.
2   Rules play an important role also, a more important role than is accorded them by act utilitarianism.

These two convictions are combined in the idea that we should employ the principle of utility maximization to determine which rules everyone should follow, and then, when faced with a decision as to which act is right in a particular circumstance, we simply determine which act is required by the rule everyone should follow. So, overlooking some terminological technicalities, according to one version of rule utilitarianism an act A in circumstance C is morally right, if and only if the utility of everyone acting according to the rule "If you are in C, then do A" is at least as great as the utility of everyone acting according to any alternative rule applicable to C.

To see how this principle works, suppose you are in a circumstance C in which you have made a promise and you have only two alternative acts available: A_1 (keep your promise) and A_2 (break your promise). Assume A_2 produces more utility than A_1. The act utilitarian will claim A_2 is morally right. The rule utilitarian will consider the rules applicable to this circumstance. Consider two rules: R_1 (If you made a promise, then keep it.), i.e., (If C, then A_1), and R_2 (If you made a promise, then break it.), i.e., (If C, then A_2). The rule utilitarian asks which rule, if followed by everyone, would maximize utility. Of these two rules, it seems clear that R_1 would maximize utility if it were followed by everyone, since if everyone broke his promises chaos would result. Accordingly, the rule utilitarian would claim A_1 is morally right. So, it seems that act and rule utilitarianism sometimes yield different results as to what is morally right, and that rule utilitarianism is sometimes more in accord with our ordinary notion of what is right. Consider another example, our earlier case in which corporation Q's president is to decide whether to frame the innocent Y for X's theft. Assume the president has a choice of two acts: A_1 (frame Y) and A_2 (do not frame Y), and assume that of these two acts A_1 produces more utility than A_2. According to act utilitarianism, A_1 is morally right, but this, as we noted, seems to violate Y's rights and seems intuitively wrong. According to rule utilitarianism, we should examine the rules applicable to this circumstance. Consider two such rules: R_1 (If you are in C, then frame the person.), and R_2 (If you are in C, then do not frame the person.). If, as seems plausible, everyone's following R_2 would maximize utility and everyone's following R_1 would not, then the act in accord with R_2, namely A_2, is morally right. In this manner, rule utilitarians claim their account establishes a central place for both the principle of utility maximization and for moral rules, and combines them into a theory that is able to meet the criticisms of act utilitarianism.

Critics of this version of rule utilitarianism claim that, in the case of the president framing the innocent employee, there is another rule which must be considered: R_3 (If you are in C, then do not frame the person unless doing so maximizes utility.). The critics point out that more utility would be produced by everyone's following R_3 than by everyone's following R_2; indeed, everyone's following R_3 will maximize utility whereas everyone's following a rule such as R_2 will not, since R_2 requires that one never frame a person in C, even when framing that person would maximize utility. So, by his or her own moral principle, the rule utilitarian is committed to R_3. However, applying R_3 to the president's circumstance will produce exactly the same result as applying the act utilitarian principle directly to the circumstance; on both, the morally right act is to frame the innocent employee. This argument is easily generalized. In any circumstance C, the rule that will maximize utility, if followed by everyone, essentially will be: "In C, act to maximize utility." However, when this rule is applied to a particular C, the act recommended as morally right will be exactly the same act recommended by the act utilitarian principle. Since there seem to be very good counterexamples to the act utilitarian principle that make it unacceptable to many people as a moral theory, and the same counterexamples apply to this version of rule utilitarianism, it also seems unacceptable.

Recently, several rule utilitarians have offered revised theories to meet the above criticism, one being Richard Brandt's optimal code utilitarianism. Instead of focusing on the utilities of individual rules, Brandt focuses on the utilities of entire moral codes. Roughly, a moral code (MC) for a society S is a set of shared desires and aversions, along with a complete set of moral rules governing what should be done in all circumstances that may arise in S. Brandt's basic idea is that although any one of a number of moral codes (MC_1 or MC_2 or . . .) could be employed in S, one such code would have more utility than the others if it were widely accepted in S. This is S's optimal moral code (MC_0). According to optimal code utilitarianism, then, an act A in society S is morally right if, and only if, A is not prohibited by the MC_0 for S. So, right acts in S are those permitted by the moral code optimal in S, and the optimal code in S is the code that, if it were widely accepted, would maximize utility. Since the optimal code for S will presumably prohibit framing an innocent employee, this theory seems to meet the counterexamples that undercut other versions of utilitarianism.

To the criticism that the optimal moral code for S would consist of one rule (MU) "Maximize utility," and hence the optimal code utilitarian principle yields the same results as the act utilitarian principle, Brandt replies that the critics would have to show that no code could have higher utility if widely accepted than the code which consists solely of MU, and he claims this is highly implausible. Some codes, if widely adopted, would undoubtedly produce high utility but, if MU were widely accepted, it probably would not. If your employees faced a moral problem and inquired about the rule governing such cases, you could only say "Maximize utility," and if they requested more specific advise you could only repeat "Maximize utility." MU is so abstract that if it were the only rule widely accepted in S, uncertainty and confusion would probably result; hence broad adoption of MU probably would not maximize utility. On the other hand, among all the codes consisting of relatively specific rules, there will be one which, if widely accepted, would maximize utility and allow you to provide specific advice to your employees. Hence, Brandt claims that optimal rule utilitarianism will not yield the same counterintuitive results as does act utilitarianism.

Still, optimal code utilitarianism is not defect free in business contexts. The theory rests on the notion of a "society," but any society will consist of subgroups, e.g., physicians, businesspersons. Do businesspersons constitute a society? Well, it is commonly said that they operate by their own set of rules, a set somewhat distinct from ordinary morality. If businesspersons do constitute a society, then the optimal code for the society of businesspersons may permit an act that is prohibited by the moral code optimal for the general society. When such a conflict occurs, what principle can be employed to resolve it? In addition, since the code optimal for S (the code that would maximize utility if it were widely accepted) is probably very different from the code that is actually widely accepted in S, a person following the optimal code may be at a serious disadvantage in a society in which only a few follow it. If the optimal code permits only strict truth in advertising, those who follow it will probably not prosper in a society in which puffery is widely accepted and practiced.

With a history of over two hundred years, utilitarianism has proven to be a durable and resilient ethical theory which is also an important foundation for economics and social policy. Although severe criticisms have been directed at the theory in recent years, the newer versions of rule utilitarianism may provide the basis for an adequate moral theory, and even those who believe that no version of utilitarianism will be able to handle the rights and justice criticisms will have to acknowledge that utilitarian considerations must be included as a part of any adequate moral theory.

Bibliography

Alston, W. P. 1967: Pleasure. In P. Edwards (ed.), *The Encyclopedia of Philosophy*, Vol. 6, New York: Macmillan, 341–7.

Bayles, M. D. (ed.) 1968: *Contemporary Utilitarianism*. Garden City, NY: Doubleday & Co.

Bentham, J. 1789: *The Principles of Morals and Legislation*. Oxford: Oxford.

Brandt, R. B. 1967: Happiness. In P. Edwards (ed.), *The Encyclopedia of Philosophy*, Vol. 3, New York: Macmillan, 413–4.

Brandt, R. B. 1979: *A Theory of the Good and the Right*. Oxford: Clarendon.

Brandt, R. B. 1992: *Morality, Utilitarianism, and Rights*. New York: Cambridge University Press.

Feldman, F. 1978: *Introductory Ethics*. Englewood Cliffs, NJ: Prentice-Hall.

Glover, J. (ed.) 1990: *Utilitarianism and its Critics*. New York: Macmillan.

Gorovitz, S. (ed.) 1971: *Mill: Utilitarianism – Text and Critical Essays*. Indianapolis: Bobbs-Merrill.

Hooker, B. (ed.) 1994: *Rationality, Rules and Utility: New Essays on the Moral Philosophy of Richard B. Brandt*. Boulder: Westview Press.

Jackson, J. 1993: *A Guided Tour of John Stuart Mill's Utilitarianism*. Mountain View, Ca.: Mayfield Publishing.

Lyons, D. 1965: *The Forms and Limits of Utilitarianism*. Oxford: Clarendon.

Lyons, D. 1994: *Rights, Welfare, and Mill's Moral Theory*. New York: Oxford University Press.

McInerney, P. K. and Rainbolt, G. W. 1994: *Ethics*. New York: Harper Collins.

Mill, J. S. 1957: *Utilitarianism*. Indianapolis: Bobbs-Merrill.

Miller, H. B. and Williams, W. H. (eds) 1982: *The Limits of Utilitarianism*. Minneapolis: University of Minnesota Press.

Mishan, E. J. 1982: *Cost-Benefit Analysis*. 3rd edn. London: Cambridge University Press.

Plamenatz, J. 1958: *The English Utilitarians*. Oxford: Blackwell Publishers.

Quinton, A. 1989: *Utilitarian Ethics*. London: Duckworth Press.

Ross, W. D. 1930: *The Right and the Good*. Oxford: Oxford University Press.

Ross, W. D. 1939: *Foundations of Ethics*. Oxford: Oxford University Press.

Sen, A. and Williams, B. (eds) 1982: *Utilitarianism and Beyond*. New York: Cambridge University Press.

Sidgwick, H. 1902: *Outlines of the History of Ethics*. 5th edn. London: Macmillan.

Sidgwick, H. 1922: *The Methods of Ethics*. London: Macmillan.

Smart, J. J. C. 1961: *An Outline of a System of Utilitarian Ethics*. Melbourne: Melbourne University Press.

Smart, J. J. C. 1967: Utilitarianism. In P. Edwards (ed.) *The Encyclopedia of Philosophy*, Vol. 8, New York: Macmillan, 206–12.

Smart, J. J. C. and Williams, B. 1973: *Utilitarianism: For and Against*. London: Cambridge University Press.

3

Business ethics and virtue

ROBERT C. SOLOMON

Business ethics, like most areas of ethics, often tends to focus on principles of action, on the action itself and its consequences. The most common contrast, typically presented as the focus of debate on most ethical issues, is between Kant and "deontology," on the one hand, and Bentham, Mill and "utilitarianism" on the other. The former focuses primarily on the principles of action, on their universality and justification; the latter focuses on the consequences of action, their goodness or badness (relative benefits and harms). Over the course of the last century or so, this debate has become quite subtle and sophisticated, and both deontology and utilitarianism have become quite subtle and sophisticated in turn. In business ethics, as in most areas of ethics, it is generally agreed that all three elements – the principles of action, the action itself and the action's consequences – must be taken into account. However, there is another option, not adequately covered by either deontology or utilitarianism, and that is what has recently come to be called "virtue ethics." Virtue ethics focuses not so much on principles or the consequences of action, nor even the action itself so much as on the agent, the person who performs the action, in the light of the circumstances and all of his or her other actions. One might say the focus is on the person's *character*, or alternatively, on those traits of character expressed in this and other actions, his or her *virtues*.

Virtue ethics has been suggested as a complement to traditional moral theory, and it has been defended as a radical alternative to traditional theory. The more moderate version insists only that traditional moral theory leaves something essential out of the account of our moral life, and virtue ethics will supply this. The more radical version insists that traditional moral theory has it all wrong. It is not just that questions of virtue and character are typically left out or pushed to the margins of deontological and utilitarian theories of ethics; questions of virtue and character undermine deontological and utilitarian theories, and show their accounts of moral life to be bankrupt, and their vocabulary of goodness and rightness to be misleading if not fraudulent. Here, we will consider only the moderate version of virtue ethics.

The most famous virtue ethicist, and in many ways still the starting point if not also the continuing focus of discussion for most virtue ethicists, is the great Greek philosopher Aristotle (384–322 BCE). In his *Nicomachean Ethics* (1954), Aristotle laid out a system of virtue ethics which still remains the starting point, if not the model, for most virtue ethicists. A virtue (*areté* which can also be translated as "excellence") for Aristotle was the "mean between the extremes," which was something more than the usual

Greek emphasis on moderation. Examples were courage (between cowardice and reck-lessness), temperance (neither gluttony nor prudishness) and justice (neither too much nor too little). Many of the virtues were traits that promoted congeniality, for instance, wittiness and friendship. Aristotle was, in essence, describing his own Athenian society – or at least his idealized version of what society could be. So, too, virtue ethics tends to begin within an established tradition or culture and pay attention to the specific attributes that are admired in that tradition or culture. This naturally raises the specter of "relativism" – the idea that there may be very different virtues in different societies – and, to be sure, we find very different virtues in, for example, the Homeric Greece of the Iliad, Aristotle's Athens, the medieval monastery, at IBM or at Microsoft, Inc. It does not follow, however, that there are not some non-relative virtues, virtues that can and must be found in every human society or institution, just because of the kind of creatures we are.

A very different and much more radical virtue ethicist is the nineteenth-century German philosopher Friedrich Nietzsche (1844–1900). In contrast to Aristotle, who insisted that the virtues are those traits that help us to get along and be congenial with one another, Nietzsche emphasized more solitary, artistic and (at least in his metaphors) warrior-like virtues, such as independence, creativity and risk-taking. In business ethics, we can recognize the difference in terms of the difference between the good corporate citizen and the entrepreneur. Of course, we would like to think that a person could have both sets of virtues, but this is a matter of some controversy. Aristotle defended a thesis often called "the unity of the virtues," in short, the idea that the various virtues support and reinforce one another, and do not come into conflict. The good person has them all. Nietzsche, on the other hand, argued that everyone has his or her own unique virtues, and that the virtues are often at war with one another. In Aristotle, the overriding image is one of living in harmony; in Nietzsche, the image is rather one of individual assertiveness. They provide us with two very different pictures of the virtues, reminding us that agreement on the importance of virtue ethics is by no means an agreement on what are to count as the virtues.

We might note that there is another ancient virtue ethicist who has been far more influential than Aristotle and Nietzsche put together, and that is Confucius (551–479 BCE). Chinese society, like many non-Western societies, might well be characterized as "virtue" societies, in which good-upbringing, good habits, good "instincts," are con-sidered at least as important as rules and considerations of the public good (to which, however, they are conducive). Confucius taught the way to universal harmony (*Tao*) through right action (*Jen*) in harmony with others (*Yi*). The virtues, particularly the virtue of "filial piety," were central to this vision.

Two important modern virtue theorists, one with special significance to business and the free enterprise system, are David Hume (1711–1776) and Adam Smith (1711–1776), both Edinburgh Scots who together (with several others) became known as the "moral sentiment theorists." They defended a portrait of human nature in which "fellow-feeling" and "sympathy" played a role as important (if not always as domin-ant) as self-interest, and in which the virtues were important as both pleasing and useful. It is of considerable importance for business ethics that Adam Smith (1880, 1948) preceded his writing of *Wealth of Nations*, the "bible of capitalism," by publishing his *Theory of the Moral Sentiments*, in which the two basic virtues of any decent society

– including, especially, modern market society, are justice and benevolence. Advocates of Adam Smith's economics too often ignore his ethics, but the former is unworkable without the latter.

One might argue that "our" ethical tradition is built around the importance of moral *principles* in ethics, formally stated rules. Examples range from the Ten Commandments in the Old Testament to the policy of "government by laws, not men" put into practice by the framers of the US Constitution. However, this emphasis on principles is not the whole of ethics, and there are many systems of ethics which do not place such stress on principles at all. Aristotle's Athens and Confucius' China, as opposed to the Jerusalem of the Judao–Christian tradition and Nietzsche's Germany, is like this. Virtue ethicists would argue that what is essential to ethics, even within the Judao–Christian tradition, is not universal rules and objective rational principles but rather an established way of doing things, a shared sense of value and significance, shared heroes and role models, a clear sense of *what sort of a person one should be.* Jesus, both as an example and as the exponent of an ethics of love, has often been considered such a figure.

With this in mind, the question of heroes and role-models, particularly in business, should concern us. What does it mean, for example, that recent management books extol the virtues of Attila the Hun and Machiavelli? What does it mean that our business heroes are often high-flying financial wheeler-dealers rather than good corporate citizens or creative entrepreneurs?

Essential to understanding most human activities is the idea of a *practice* – a shared cooperative activity with mutually understood goals and ways of doing things – and an idea of *excellence* in that activity, both in the sense of the specific skills and talents required for the activity, and in the sense of the more general traits and habits that make the activity possible. A game like football or soccer, for example, is first of all a practice. It also has rules, of course, but to think of the rules as *defining* the game is to get the account backward. The rules clarify the implicit understandings that make the game, the practice, possible. Everyone who plays the game understands that the objective is for the ball to go over the goal line while facing the opposition of the other team, within the "bounds" of the game, both the spatial boundaries circumscribing the field and the boundaries understood in terms of fair play. The rules clarify this; they delineate the various possibilities that enable one to pursue the objective (scoring, winning) without ruining the game. (Killing opposition players or destroying the ball mid-play, for example, would have this effect.) However, it is the practice that determines the excellences or virtues required for the game.

Each game has its characteristic activities – running, kicking, passing – and each of these is an invitation to excellence. It is not as if one is just able to run, kick or pass, but one does so well or badly, better or worse. Excellence is doing it best (although one should not leap to the conclusion that "best" necessarily means "best of all, one and only," nor should one retreat to the well-meaning but slightly defeatist attitude of "best that one can do"). Accordingly, every game has its exemplars or champions, whom both players and spectators admire. Those players excel in both the specific skills and activities and the more general traits and habits that make the game possible, such as a keen sense of competition and a sense of good sportsmanship. Without the specific skills and talents, the game becomes something of a joke, but without the more general traits, the game may become a battlefield.

Virtue ethicists, naturally, are interested in the most general traits, those that make all human activities, and harmonious human society, possible. One might think of society as a grand set of social practices, and the virtues, most generally, as those traits which, at their least, make the society civilized and workable and, at their best, make those who are virtuous and, perhaps, the society itself exemplary. One does not find the virtues outside of all social contexts and practices. Generosity, on a desert island, is no virtue at all. (On the other hand, generosity, in a society in which everyone already has more than enough of everything, is no virtue either.) "The virtues," as we usually use that term, refer to the most general, non-specific character traits that support the most general, non-specific social practices. Thus, trustworthiness and honesty are considered virtues, because they are crucial to almost any human interchange. Being able to kick a ball brilliantly or being able to scrutinize a corporate annual report are much more specific excellences and would usually not be counted as "virtues" at all.

The difference between "excellence" and "virtue," however, is by no means clear. The most general virtues are sometimes distinguished by being called "moral" virtues. There are also, on this account, "non-moral" virtues, for example, congeniality, or a good sense of humor. So, too, some business ethicists would insist on a distinction between business skills and business virtues, and this raises much the same question as whether there is a useful distinction to be made between moral and non-moral virtues. Are congeniality and charm, for example, merely "people skills," or are they moral virtues? Aristotle would probably not endorse any such distinction. (He often modeled his account of the virtues on comparisons with the craftsman's skill.) Nevertheless, he included in his list of virtues only those virtues that made a person a good citizen and a good neighbor ("a good person") and not those more specialized excellences that made one a good farmer, craftsman or soldier.

Business ethicists, understandably, are especially interested in what general traits allow the market, the free enterprise system, to work at full efficiency and which traits allow the market to work harmoniously in the midst of the larger society. These may, or may not, be identical (an empirical question). An efficient market, but at odds with the needs and interests of the rest of society, will be terminated. (Consider the forced closing of some markets in the midst of war or natural catastrophe.) On the other hand, it is one of the articles of hope, if not faith, that an efficient market that is harmonious with the rest of society will turn out to be the most prosperous and most happy of all societies. Whether this is so is an experiment still in the making. If the conclusion of that experiment is anything like what Adam Smith promised, the virtues of a successful business person and those of the exemplary citizen would be identical.

Needless to say, this is not a proposition, speculative as it is and contrary to some disturbing trends in the increasingly industrialized world, that is universally accepted. It has been argued by several recent authors that the virtues of business – competitiveness, individualism, economic self-interest – are destructive, and, in particular, destructive of a sense of community. On the other hand, arguments carried over from the eighteenth and nineteenth centuries, take business to be a highly civilizing activity and the prosperity provided by business to be the dominant factor in the economic well-being that supports and encourages social harmony. These issues are far too complex and controversial to be dealt with here, but it is important to mention them.

How one ultimately judges business ethics and virtue ethics in business will depend on how one thinks about these weighty issues. Insofar as business virtues are destructive of, or incompatible with, community, they will not be virtues; but insofar as business virtues are conducive to community, they will turn out to be very important social virtues.

Nevertheless, business is a distinctive practice and, as such, we would expect it to have some (more or less) distinctive virtues, something less than the most general virtues of the good citizen but more general than the specific skills – accounting, financial planning, marketing, managing – that make for success in business. Thus, among the business virtues, we would expect to find special versions of honesty, courage, temperance and justice. Honesty, for example, would be most important in the making and drafting of agreements, whether they had to do with the hiring and treatment of employees or dealing with customers or other companies. A special concern, of course, is advertising. Telling "the whole truth and nothing but the truth" ("our product isn't significantly different from its competitors, but we have our own attractive label on it") would be foolish. Lying, on the other hand, is unacceptable, and the ethical and practical challenge is finding the "mean" between imprudent truth-telling and prevarication. What is special to virtue ethics is not, however, the search for a general criterion for proper honesty. It has rather to do with the motives and habits of the person, whether he or she thinks in terms of "putting one over on others" or rather thinks in terms of the fairness of the situation, what information is appropriate to the relationship and the occasion, and "what an honest person would do."

So, too, courage, in business situations, takes on a number of forms, ranging from the willingness to assume risk (whether in investing or investing one's time or one's trust) to the special virtue of "moral courage," being willing to take a stand, even when there are serious threats to one's job, one's prospects, or one's career.

Temperance in business refers to one thing above all, and that is having a reasonable set of expectations and desires. The opposite, the virtue's corresponding vice, is greed (or avarice). Not being greedy (to put it negatively) is, perhaps, first and foremost among the business virtues. Typically, it is because of greed that people cheat, lie and act unfairly. With more reasonable demands and desires, the limits imposed by the other virtues come more clearly into focus. Finally, justice is an especially complex virtue in business, in part because of the complexities of the market. On the one hand, justice depends on merit: hard work, quality products and good ideas, taking care of customers. We think it unjust, for example, if the inventor of a product or the people that produce it do not enjoy a share in its rewards. On the other hand, we recognize that the market has a good deal to do with luck, and hard work is not always rewarded. Again, justice as a virtue is not to be conflated with that general philosophical search for abstract principles and policies. Aristotle saw quite clearly, for instance, that prior to adopting such principles and policies, a person must have a "sense" of justice and the desire to be just.

On rules: In business, one might say that the practice is defined by the activities of exchange and making contracts, while the rules (that is, legal regulations) clarify and codify that practice. However, not all need such codification, and the underlying insight of virtue ethics is that the richness of our pre-legal understanding overflows the possibility of clarification.

Some business virtues are easily misunderstood. The much celebrated virtue of "toughness," for example, is often conflated with ruthlessness, or with stubbornness, or with general hard-headedness. As a business virtue, however, toughness makes sense and is successful only within a context more broadly defined by cooperation and congeniality. A business is not a slave ship. Toughness, as a business virtue, presupposes other virtues as well.

Generosity is a virtue that is often denied to business, on the (false) theory that business people tend (more than most) to hold onto their money and ask, "what do I receive in return?" In fact, business people in general tend to be very generous, both as individuals and as members of corporations. Indeed, the overwhelming success of business is the modern world has meant that the ancient concept of noblesse oblige – the obligations of the nobility (here, the wealthy) – has passed onto the corporate world. Those who have are expected to give, in short, and give they do. Generosity, although not, perhaps, to the detriment of profits, has become a business virtue.

One of the more interesting complications of the introduction of the virtues into ethics is the complicated moral status of people who do not obey the rules but nevertheless emerge as heroes and exemplars. For example, there is that figure whom we might call the *rogue*. Some rogues – Robin Hood, for instance – might be morally defended as appealing to a "higher" morality than the laws of the land, but many of the heroes in American movies, for example, have no such thought in mind. They may simply be asserting their own freedom, or fighting for an idea. Yet they retain our admiration because of the characters they are. On the more respectable side of business, we find general admiration for the *entrepreneur*, the maverick businessman who takes high risks to launch a new idea or product on the market. The entrepreneur too is a rogue. Abraham Zeleznick (1989), a professor at the Harvard Business School, has written that "to understand the entrepreneur, you have to understand the mind of a juvenile delinquent." Nevertheless, we have no hesitation speaking "entrepreneurial virtues," so long, of course, as they do not seriously undermine even more basic virtues that are required for a decent society. (Entrepreneurs need to be ingenious; they are not supposed to lie or cheat.)

One feature of the virtues that is worth mentioning, and common to Aristotle, Nietzsche, Confucius and the Moral Sentiment Theorists, is the fact that they are cultivated responses and actions which may, at the time, require no deliberation whatsoever. Indeed, where deontology seems to require at least some deliberation in order for us to be acting on principle and utilitarianism encourages, even it does not require the calculation of utilities, the expression or manifestation of a virtue seems to require little or no thought. One acts "spontaneously" whenever the appropriate occasion arises. The truly honest person probably never even *thinks* of lying. The virtues, accordingly, do not as such *require* deliberation. Indeed, *too* much deliberation – "Should I be generous? Am I supposed to leave a 20 percent tip or can I get away with less?" – is evidence that one does *not* have the virtue (generosity) in question.

Many of the virtues become ridiculous if they are preceded by the sorts of deliberation encouraged by moral theorists. One does not display a sense of humor by coming to the realization that one *ought* to laugh. Of course, there are virtues that involve moral principles and a thoughtful person might well generalize about his or her virtues, or formulate various "rules of thumb," but the focus on the virtues is not primarily concerned with such thoughts and guidelines. Rather, it is the hallmark of a virtue that it be ingrained in one's character and – perhaps after years of cultivation and practice – seem perfectly "natural."

So, too, the virtues tend to undercut the distinction between altruism and egoism or selfishness that has been so much the preoccupation of moralists and moral philosophers. A generous person may take delight in the well-being of others, but he or she need not do so. He or she may simply *be* generous, one might say overflowing, or take great pride in being a generous person. One can try to raise the objection that such proud self-concern undermines or cancels out the generosity, but here the objection seems to lose its force. To be generous is to act and to be motivated by generosity, but no further claim need be made distinguishing self-interest, altruism and concern for others. To say that a person has a virtue is not to invite an investigation into his or her motives, or the consequences of virtuous action. If a person routinely acts courageously, one is justified in calling him or her courageous, and whether an act of courage has good or disastrous consequences for oneself or for others, it is, nevertheless, an act of courage. Of course, every such claim is defeasible if one discovers some unexpected ulterior motive, but we need not dig into the depths of the soul and demand some purely virtuous or public-spirited motive.

What counts as a virtue depends on the nature of the society in which it is embedded as well as on the overall character in whom it plays its role. Insofar as Hume is correct in saying that a virtue is a feature that is particularly pleasing and useful to others, it certainly depends on the nature of the context and the culture of the society in question. What was pleasing to Hume and his gentlemen friends in Edinburgh were, understandably, the virtues of a gentleman. What was pleasing to Agamemnon on the battlefield in front of the walls of Troy was a set of virtues that were certainly not gentlemanly. The fact that a virtue must be considered admirable within the context of one's particular society means that the virtues may well vary from context to context, whether they serve some specific practical function such as having good business sense in the corporate world, or knowing how to handle snakes on a snake farm, or because they appeal to the particular ideals of a culture. Being devout and faithful will be among the greatest virtues in a religious society. Being creative and even eccentric will be virtues in a society of artists or academics in which originality and individuality are conducive to creativity, while being honorable and acting honorably will be among the highest virtues in a society such as Japan, in which proper behavior is often precisely described and public shame is worse than (or equivalent to) death.

Virtues can become out-moded. Being able to fight well with a sword and being "the fastest gun in the West" are no longer virtues in late twentieth-century America. At most, they might be salable skills in Hollywood. Having the talent to be a crack computer programmer would not have been a virtue during the Trojan War and having a superb sense of humor would not have been a virtue in a medieval Carmelite monastery. The aging of virtues is almost always resisted and deplored as a loss of values, but the truth seems to be that as societies change – and not necessarily for the better – the virtues will change too. So, what once was a virtue may well become a vice, and what was a vice for one generation may well become a virtue for the next. Indeed, the most striking thing about the virtues is how they vary from culture to culture and through history.

This raises the difficult question of relativism, whether the virtues are indeed "relative" to the values and customs of a given society or whether there are at least some non-relative virtues that are essential in all societies. Those aspects of society which are necessarily shared – for example, the need to cooperate and live together, the need to supply the members of society with the necessities of life, the need to protect the society against foreign intruders and natural disasters, the need for dependable communication within society – all of this would suggest that, indeed, there must be such non-relative virtues, although, to be sure, with local variations and interpretations, such as courage, honesty, generosity, congeniality.

In a business society, in particular, trustworthiness and cooperation would seem to be non-relative virtues, that is, essential to any form of market (or non-market) society, and this would be so no matter how much the opposite virtues, of cleverness and competitiveness, are highlighted. Even the most devious business dealings presuppose an atmosphere of trust, and competition is possible (as in games) only within a context of general cooperation. One might say that the bottom line of the virtue approach to business ethics is that we have to move away from "bottom line" thinking and conceive of business as an essential part of a society in which living well together, rubbing along with others, and having a sense of self-respect are central, and making a profit merely a means.

References

Aristotle, 1954: *Nicomachean Ethics*. Translated by W. D. Ross. Oxford: Oxford University Press.

Smith, A. 1880: *Theory of the Moral Sentiments*. London: George Bell & Sons.

Smith, A. 1948: *Wealth of Nations*. New York, Hafener.

Zeleznick, A. 1989: *The Managerial Mystique: Restoring Leadership in Business*. New York: Harper & Row.

Further reading

French, P., Euhling, T. E. Jr and Wettstein, H. K. (eds) 1988: *Midwest Studies in Philosophy, Vol. XII, Character and Virtue*. Notre Dame: University of Notre Dame Press.

Hume, D. 1983: *An Enquiry Concerning the Principles of Morals*. Oxford: Oxford University Press.

Kaufman, W. (ed.) 1992: *Basic Writings of Nietzsche*. New York: Modern Library.

Kupperman, J. J. 1991: *Character*. Oxford: Oxford University Press.

Leys, S. (trans.) 1997: *The Analects of Confucius*. New York: W. W. Norton.

MacIntyre, A. 1984: *After Virtue*, 2nd edn. Notre Dame: University of Notre Dame Press.

Murdoch I. 1970: *The Sovereignty of the Good*. London: Routledge and Kegan Paul.

Nussbaum, M. 1985: *The Fragility of Goodness: Luck and Ethics in Greek Tragedy and Philosophy*. Cambridge, Cambridge University Press.

Sherman, N. 1989: *The Fabric of Character: Aristotle's Theory of Virtue*. Oxford: Oxford University Press.

Slote, M. 1992: *From Morality to Virtue*. Oxford: Oxford University Press.

Solomon, R. C. 1993: *Ethics and Excellence: Cooperation and Integrity in Business*. Oxford: Oxford University Press.

4

Social contract approaches to business ethics: bridging the "is–ought" gap*

THOMAS W. DUNFEE AND THOMAS DONALDSON

Social contract approaches to business ethics are now two decades old. Detailed, well-constructed versions of the social contract in application to business began to appear in the early 1980s, and have been gaining momentum ever since. An increasing number of scholars have joined the effort, with the result that social contract thinking is becoming one of the most significant tools used in analyzing ethical issues in business.

At the heart of the social contract effort is a simple assumption, namely, that we can understand better the obligations of key social institutions, such as business or government, by attempting to understand what a fair agreement or "contract" between those institutions and society, or among different communities within those institutions, entails. Prior to the mid-nineteenth century, most social contract attempts focused on the contract between government and the people. The seventeenth-century English philosopher, Thomas Hobbes (1651), asked what underlying agreement between people and sovereign was necessary to avoid chaos and war. The eighteenth-century French philosopher, Jean Jacques Rousseau (1997), asked what underlying agreement would be likely to enhance social welfare; and the eighteenth-century English philosopher, John Locke (1948) asked what agreement between state and citizenry was necessary to protect liberty and property.

With the advent of philosophy's applied turn in the middle of the twentieth century, a number of contract theorists began to focus on economics and business. John Rawls (1971) undertook his now celebrated attempt to articulate the principles of justice through the social contract, and he included an analysis of how to define "fair" economic distribution. Shortly after this, social contract theorists began to ask the fundamental questions, such as "What would a reasonable agreement between the members of society and modern corporations look like?" and "What obligations for business follow from the implicit ethical agreements existing in industries, trade associations, companies, and economic systems?" This turn for business ethics entailed great significance. For, if the social contract methodology could do for business what it had already done for government, i.e., clarify the ethical obligations of leaders and the institutions they govern, it would perform a critical service indeed.

---

* This paper contains portions of an earlier paper (Dunfee and Donaldson, 1995).

This chapter summarizes the development of the contractarian approach. It positions that development alongside other key theories and concepts in business ethics. It further describes the social contract theory entitled "ISCT" that we, the authors, have attempted to develop in some detail. Finally, in an attempt to set the tone for further research in this area, it identifies an important set of research issues related to social contracts in business.

Background: mapping the field of business ethics

As an academic field, business ethics should be considered a new entrant, although it has already succeeded in establishing its own research paradigms. Most of the important research has been conducted in the past three decades. The first serious efforts at business ethics applied either classical ethical theories to problems of business ethics or expanded concepts already familiar to business academics. A prime example of the former is the work of Norman Bowie (1982, 1988) in applying Kantian ethics in a sophisticated manner to a myriad of business contexts.

An elaborate application of the Bowie approach may be found in *Making The Right Decision* (Hall, 1993), a book based upon the Arthur Andersen program in business ethics. Similarly, in a classic article in the field of business ethics, Freeman and Evan worked out an elaborate Kantian-based model for stakeholder management (Evan and Freeman, 1988). (There is no shortage of attempts to apply Kantian concepts to issues in business ethics; see, for example, Green (1986).) Rights-based approaches informed by deontological ethical theories or theories of social justice have also been applied to issues of business ethics. As examples, see the work of DesJardins and McCall (1985) with regard to the question of the random drug testing of employees, and that of Werhane (1984, 1991) regarding a variety of issues within the domain of human resources management.

Social contract methodology is only one method that has been used to unravel ethical problems in business. So as to put the social contract approach in relief, it will be helpful to contrast it to a few others, in particular, "philosophical consequentialism," the "stakeholder theory," and the "empirical paradigm." Consequential approaches to ethics, i.e., ones that evaluate ethical behavior from the standpoint of its consequences, have been discussed by moral philosophers for centuries, and have recently been applied to problems in business ethics. An early example was the use of a consequential or "end-point" analysis by Pastin and Hooker (1980) in their controversial article attacking the ethical basis of the US Foreign Corrupt Practices Act. Later, Ronald Green (1991) used consequential moral reasoning in an attempt to demonstrate that the excuse "everyone's doing it" may actually serve as a valid excuse for business conduct – at least under specific, consequentially defined conditions. An extensive literature in business ethics involves researchers examining the claims that corporate ethics is justified consequentially through achievement of higher profit levels; see for example, Aupperle et al. (1985). In the domain of professional ethics, Dunfee and Maurer (1992) have employed an explicit consequential framework in analyzing the ethical dimensions of corporate attorney whistle-blowing.

Many articles in the business ethics literature employ multiple ethical viewpoints in evaluating particular business practices (Pastin and Hooker, 1980; Brummer, 1991), or incorporate both consequential and rights-based factors in lists of principles or questions to be applied by business decision makers (DeGeorge, 1993, chapter 3; Nash, 1981). In an early response to the tendency to apply multiple viewpoints, Cavanagh et al. (1981) proposed an elaborate decision model for sorting among three of the more common theoretical approaches.

Another theoretical approach that originates largely in the business ethics literature is the "stakeholder" concept. The original stakeholder concept appeared in traditional management literature through the work of scholars such as Dill (1958) and Aoki (1984), but most of the elaboration and extension of the concept has occurred in the business ethics literature (Freeman, 1984; Carroll, 1989; Goodpaster, 1991). (Dill himself, interestingly enough, did not use the term "stakeholder," yet is properly regarded as a key precursor of the stakeholder movement.) Donaldson and Preston (1995) have provided a framework for understanding this diffuse literature by classifying it into "normative," "descriptive," and "instrumental" branches. The normative stakeholder literature seeks to justify and identify recognizable ethical obligations on the part of firms to respond to the legitimate interests of corporate stakeholders (Kuhn and Shriver, 1991; Hosseini and Brenner, 1992). The instrumental approach establishes a framework for examining the connections, if any, between the practice of stakeholder management and the achievement of various corporate performance goals (Preston and Sapienza, 1990; Preston et al., 1991; McGuire et al., 1988). The descriptive stakeholder approach seeks to determine the extent to which firms can be described accurately in terms of stakeholder concepts, or to what extent extant law requires, or is at least supportive of, such approaches (Orts, 1992).

The greatest elaboration of the stakeholder approach has been in the work of Ed Freeman (Freeman and Reed, 1983; Freeman, 1984, 1991; Freeman and Gilbert, 1987; Evan and Freeman, 1988; Freeman and Evan, 1990). The concept has now reached a watershed in which certain critical normative questions must be resolved before it can achieve full status as a specialized "theory" of business ethics. For example, what serves to justify a particular claim by a stakeholder or, for that matter, the broader claim that someone is a stakeholder? An unqualified normative admonition that management has an obligation to respond to the self-defined needs of anyone affected by a corporate decision leads to the anomalous result that an armored car company must consider the interests of thieves as stakeholders in the context of a decision to improve the security of its cash delivery service. Another critical question involves the normative weighing of competing stakeholder interests in a context where the interests of one set of stakeholders is in direct conflict with important interests of other legitimate stakeholders. This issue arises, for example, when asking whether it is appropriate for a firm to give weight to non-shareowner stakeholder interests when the firm's core financial well-being is at stake. Should a firm allow itself to become unprofitable to avoid a plant shut-down that will affect hundreds of long-time employees? Or, in a less dramatic case, should a firm accept a 50 percent reduction in profits to achieve the same goal? Or 5 percent? This issue has received a rich and varied treatment in the business ethics literature, but it is fair to say that there is little consensus about how the plant-closing question should be resolved. Moreover, very little work has been done to date on the background theoretical issue of how to weigh stakeholder interests. (Note the complex methodology of Hosseini and Brenner (1992) which ultimately reduces to firm-perspective circularity.)

Another significant component of the business ethics literature may be called the "empirical" paradigm. This component contains the many empirical studies that attempt to give accurate descriptions and causal explanations of business ethics behavior. Thousands of such empirical studies have been undertaken in the preceding decades, and they have investigated questions such as "What do managers think the important issues are in business ethics?" (Deshpande, 1997); "Do environmental regulations spur innovations?" (Bhat, 1996); "Do employees prefer utilitarian or formalist forms of ethical reasoning?" (Brady and Wheeler, 1996); and "How do firms disclose their social responsibility?" (Robertson and Nicholson, 1996). This research has been crucial in providing an empirical foundation for modern business ethics. Unfortunately, by themselves, empirical studies are not capable of generating conclusions about what business managers should do. As is often pointed out, one cannot move simply from an "is" to an "ought." One cannot move from the fact that, say, most companies have failed to disclose certain aspects of their social responsibility posture, to the conclusion that companies ought to fail to disclose them. Empirical studies, by themselves, have no discernible foundation in ethical theory. We, and many others in the field, see this as problematic and, while we champion good empirical research, we regard it as only one part of a healthy approach to understanding business ethics.

Business ethics, in short, requires not only empirical facts, but also a normative compass. Without a normative compass, business ethics too often reflects either a particular author's intuitive response or political bias. Without a normative compass, the analysis of individual case studies often is used as a substitute for general theory, and false inferences to unrelated cases are drawn. More than once, business ethics has deserved the criticism sometimes made in common law contexts that "hard cases make bad law." Also, a-theoretical, case-by-case approach lacks the consistency and legitimacy essential for offering anything other than unreliable, politically contaminated guidance.

The evolution of social contract approaches to business ethics

The evolution of theoretical approaches in business ethics has been influenced by certain seemingly intractable constraints and problems. With the notable exceptions of the still unfolding stakeholder theory and the market-based morality championed by economists such as Milton Friedman (1970), only contractarianism has been able to establish a beachhead as a practicable, generally accepted core paradigm in business ethics. The attempts to apply classical traditional philosophical ethical theories, such as consequentialism, to business problems have been handicapped by the generality of the theories and the difficulty in applying them to the "artifactual" environment of business, i.e., an environment that is largely created by economic participants in contrast to being a product of nature. As we have explained elsewhere (Donaldson and Dunfee, 1994, 1995), business is different from other key social institutions, such as the family, in being almost entirely the product of human artifice. This "artifactual" character of business means that the rules and structure of business can vary dramatically from culture to culture, from industry to industry, and from company to company. Furthermore, it raises Herculean problems for ethical analysis. Those who seek to apply the same broad, traditional ethical theories that philosophers have applied to social issues to hard-core business problems, such as nepotism, bribery in Third World cultures, drug-testing and insider trading, usually reach vague, unsatisfying conclusions. Frequently, indeed, these conclusions are inapposite ones; a phenomenon lending weight to skeptical claims that the field lacks substance.

Perhaps the most intractable aspect of the "artifactual" problem in business ethics is that of cultural variety. Economic institutions, even more than most human ones, exhibit cultural diversity. Some cultures emphasize property right dimensions of intellectual property; others emphasize cooperative behavior and societal sharing of innovations (Swinyard et al., 1990). Some tightly constrain the use of firm-derived (inside) information in securities markets, while others show considerable indifference to the phenomenon. How are these differing responses to be reconciled? Is a society which de-emphasizes property rights, in favor of cooperative sharing, immoral? Or vice versa? Is there only a single approach to the use of inside information in securities transactions that satisfies the normative standards of business ethics? That is, does (or should) business ethics theory mandate a particular form of restriction on insider trading? Application of broad theories of ethics such as Kantianism or utilitarianism are unlikely to provide clear answers to such questions. What, then, constitutes the source and justification of many of the detailed, day-to-day ethical standards for business activities around the world?

A contractarian approach derived from classical political theory has evolved as a significant alternative for trying to answer such fundamental questions. In general, contractarian theories utilize the device of hypothetical consent to justify principles, policies, and structures. The normative authority of any social contract derives from the assumption that humans, acting rationally, would consent to the terms of some particular societal agreement. However, even in the context of such hypothetical consent, contractarian approaches can be designed to take existing artifactual institutions and business practices into consideration, thus providing the essential context for rendering normative judgments concerning economic behaviors.

The first application of a contractarian approach to business ethics was by Donaldson (1982) who sought to construct the outlines of a social contract for business capable of providing concrete insights into the nature of corporate obligations. Following the classical tradition of using a hypothetical agreement as a device for parsing specific rights and responsibilities, he imagined the terms of an agreement between business firms (all productive cooperative enterprises) and society (individual members of a given society in the aggregate). Using this device, he identified the reciprocal expectations of the parties to the contract who were both assumed to be interested in maximizing the benefits (e.g., specialization, stabilization of output and distribution, liability resources, increased wages) and minimizing the drawbacks (pollution, depletion of natural resources, destruction of personal accountability, worker alienation) of productive organizations. The terms of the contract incorporate, for example, a process by which tradeoffs between these various factors can be realized. Donaldson's initial effort produced a variety of responses, including one from Hodapp (1990) questioning whether the approach was founded upon an adequate normative basis, or was instead circular, presupposing the very terms it claimed to generate. Another, from Kultgen (1986) questioned whether, by disallowing status as a real agreement or set of actual contracts, the effort represented a "minor heuristic exercise." Others urged Donaldson to commit personally to the existence of a real social contract (Levitt, 1986). Attempts were also made to apply Donaldson's model to specific contexts, such as agribusiness ethics. Donaldson responded vigorously to criticisms generated by his 1982 exposition and in the process clarified and expanded upon his original concept (1988, 1989, 1990).

Other attempts to connect the social contract concept to business and economic events emerged during the 1980s. Norman Bowie (1982) offered a brief description of the "social contract" between business and society in his book, *Business Ethics*. David Gauthier (1986), in his book, *Morals by Agreement*, utilized concepts of economic rationality to advance a hypothetical "agreement" among rational, self-interested agents that formed the basis for a collective morality. Gauthier noted that, ironically, it was self-interestedly rational for agents to bind themselves to moral commitments that flouted self-interest in the short term to gain greater offsetting interest satisfaction in the long term. Michael Keeley (1988) developed a progressive theory of organizations using social contract concepts in his book, *A Social Contract Theory of Organizations*. Keeley uses the contract metaphor in a non-traditional way, viewing the firm as a series of contract-like agreements about social rules. Keeley's recurring emphasis is on voluntariness. In the process, he identifies a series of rights whose existence he argues are essential to preserve voluntariness. Keeley's social contract view contrasts sharply to the "organismic" model of the firm, a view he criticizes for subordinating the welfare of individuals to the welfare of the organization.

In 1989, Donaldson extended a modified version of his social contract model to the global level. Using again the imaginary social contract as a heuristic device, he relied upon reason and intuition to identify terms in the contract that establish a minimal floor of responsibility for global corporations (Donaldson, 1989). From this, he recognized sets of explicit and implicit derivative obligations for global corporations which require them to:

- enhance the long-term welfare of employees and consumers wherever they operate
- minimize drawbacks associated with developing productive societies, and
- refrain from violating minimum standards of justice and human rights.

These obligations translate into an obligation to avoid depriving and, under some circumstances, a duty to protect from deprivation a set of ten fundamental human rights.

Dunfee (1991) emphasized real or "extant" social contracts as constituting a significant source of ethical norms in business. When these real, but usually informal, social contracts are based upon uncoerced and informed consent, and the norms they produce are consistent with the principles of broader ethical theories, they become prima facie obligatory. The completion of Dunfee's work raised the intriguing possibility that a contractarian theory might be developed that would combine the concept of a hypothetical social contract (not unlike that discussed earlier by Donaldson) and real social contracts (not unlike that discussed earlier by Dunfee). The aim of integrating the two approaches would be to put the "is" and the "ought" in symbiotic harmony in a way requiring the cooperation of both empirical and normative research in rendering ultimate value judgments.

Integrative social contracts theory (ISCT)

In recent work, we (the authors) have formally attempted to bridge this "is" "ought" gap by developing "Integrative Social Contracts Theory" (ISCT). ISCT (Donaldson and Dunfee, 1994, 1995, 1999) attempts to unify normative and empirical streams of research by utilizing extant, generally understood, social contract norms, even as it relies upon a classical, hypothetical contract the kind used earlier by Rawls (1971), Hobbes (1651) and Locke (1948). The term "integrative" in the theory captures the fact that the theory encompasses two very different types of social contracts: a hypothetical social contract used as a heuristic device and extant social contracts based within living communities. The use of the plural word, "contracts," has two intentional meanings: first, the word reflects the fact that two kinds of contracts are relevant in business ethics, namely, contracts that are both hypothetical and actual; second, it acknowledges the fact that more than one real contract is relevant – indeed, there may be literally thousands of community-based social contracts whose norms are important in rendering normative judgments in business ethics.

ISCT is grounded in the familiar idea that social norms serve as the foundation for rules of behavior within communities. In this respect, ISCT's derivation is similar to both the political principles employed by many of the framers of the US Constitution and Declaration of Independence, as well as Rawls's theory of justice as fairness. Following classical contractarians, we envision global humanity seeking to design a binding, though unwritten agreement establishing the parameters for ethics in economic relationships. To justify consent on the part of the contractors, we limit ourselves to parsimonious assumptions and a minimalistic global social contract.

The terms of the contract are based upon two assumptions. First, it is assumed that the contractors are aware of, and concerned about, bounded moral rationality. Bounded moral rationality represents an extension of the well-known idea of bounded economic rationality to the moral sphere. As in the analogous case of bounded economic rationality, it is assumed that individual moral agents lack sufficient information, time and emotional strength to make perfect judgments consistent with their moral preferences. Thus, an engineer concerned about the effect of temperature on the "O" ring of the Challenger NASA rocket may not be sure where to begin in situating the ethical duty to terminate the launch or to blow the whistle. Similarly, a Challenger engineer who is a committed utilitarian may not be able to apply his or her preferred theory due to a lack of time and information to determine the net consequences of potential courses of action.

The other dimension of bounded moral rationality concerns its acknowledgment of the difficulties that even rational global contractors have in agreeing to a single comprehensive moral theory or set of ethical principles. We assume, pace Williams (1985) and others, that moral theory is fraught with opaqueness in application to concrete events. Accordingly, ISCT presumes that the individual contractors would wish to retain the right to select their own values to the maximum extent possible, and that they would "desire to participate in economic communities that reflect their personal and cultural values" (Donaldson and Dunfee, 1995, p. 93). In so doing, contractors recognize the limits that bounded moral rationality imposes upon all decision contexts for a diverse humanity.

The second of the assumptions, on which ISCT is based, is that global contractors would, in response to bounded moral rationality, recognize the need for a community-based moral fabric as a necessary condition for both the generation of wealth and the maintenance of an environment conducive to a good and productive life. Without such a moral fabric, there is the threat of social denigration into Hobbes's (1651) notorious state of war, pitting "man against man" and yielding lives that are "nasty, brutish and short." Even short of such a disastrous state, a successful society requires agreed-upon norms. Individuals must work in organizations, and interact with others, to facilitate economic life efficiently. In turn, those organizations and relationships are based upon implicit understandings concerning proper bounds of behavior. Rational contractors would want to set up an arrangement that recognizes the key role of relationships and groups as well as the need to tailor norms to fit a particular organizational or relational context. This process of tailoring norms to fit particular contexts is critical. Rational contractors would want for the process only to be undertaken by the members of particular economic communities, and for the resulting agreements or "contracts" to be binding upon all members.

Consider marketing ethics and the issue of setting ethical standards for advertising among different industries and cultures. Any such standards should deal with questions such as the ethics of comparison advertising or of appropriate disclosures in marketing research. Yet the parameters of ethical behavior in advertising may vary legitimately between Japan, France and the USA. In turn, ISCT acknowledges that communities should be allowed, acting within their moral free space, to generate "authentic" ethical norms. A norm is defined as "authentic" when it is supported by the attitudes and behavior of a substantial majority of the members of a community. Although ethics codes and statements are often proxies for authentic norms, they may also diverge from the true or underlying morality of a given economic community. For example, the ethics code of the American Marketing Association specifies that there should be "identification of extra-cost added features" in product development and management. If a substantial majority of marketing practitioners hold the opposite view, then the AMA provision does not constitute an authentic norm for the community of marketing professionals. The ultimate, definitive source of norms must be the attitudes and behaviors of the members of the relevant communities.

ISCT imposes two additional requirements on the operation of the community. First, the community must respect the right of members to withdraw or exit from membership within the group. Thus, a dissenting member of a community who is quite distressed about a particular authentic norm may elect to leave the community. An employee may, and generally should, leave a corporation whose values are significantly at odds with the employee's important personal values. Second, an individual should have the opportunity to exercise voice within his or her economic community. This axiom is consistent with much of the organizational justice literature, which identifies the crucial role of procedural justice in organizations. Individuals have a right to influence – in some manner or other – the development and evolution of norms, and, still more important, they have a right to participate in removing norms they find objectionable.

So long as these requirements of community recognition of voice and exit are met, and so long as a given norm is supported by the attitudes and behavior of a substantial majority of the membership of a community, the norm qualifies under ISCT as an authentic norm.

Were ISCT to stop at this point, it would be morally inadequate. Given the description of ISCT to this point, the only thing that could protect a dissenting individual from having an ethical obligation to comply with a distasteful norm is the right to leave the community or to try to change the norm. Beyond that it appears as though the "naturalistic fallacy" has been committed, and that the "is" of community consent has been transformed into an "ought." The simple affirmation by a community of a norm (the "is"), appears to have been counterfeited into the right thing for a member to do (the "ought"). But what happens when a community adopts a morally untenable norm? What happens when a corporation practices intentional racism or sexism? Because extreme ethical relativism is untenable, and because communities do sometimes develop authentic norms supporting fundamentally immoral practices, ISCT assumes that the original contractors would want to adopt a thin set of universal principles capable of constraining the relativism of community moral free space. Hence, an additional axiom of the microsocial contract is the following: To be obligatory, a microsocial contract norm must be compatible with hypernorms.

Under ISCT a "hypernorm" constitutes, by definition, a norm sufficiently fundamental that it can serve as a guide for evaluating authentic but less fundamental norms. In this sense, a hypernorm is a "first-order" norm, capable of evaluating "second-order" norms. Hypernorms are "principles so fundamental to human existence that . . . we would expect them to be reflected in a convergence of religious, philosophical, and cultural beliefs . . ." (Donaldson and Dunfee, 1994, p. 265). As interpreted by Walzer, they constitute a thin "set of standards to which all societies can be held – negative injunctions, most likely, rules against murder, deceit, torture, oppression, and tyranny" (Walzer, 1992, p. 9). ISCT employs the term "legitimate" to describe a second-order, authentic norm that has passed the hypernorm test.

An obvious question is how one should handle norm conflicts among economic communities. If one of two conflicting norms is illegitimate, i.e., is inconsistent with hypernorms, the answer is straightforward; namely, the illegitimate norm lacks moral authority. But what happens when norms from two communities conflict, and both happen to be legitimate? Drawing on well-accepted principles of conflict resolution in international law, ISCT prescribes the following set of priority rules to handle such conflicts:

1 Transactions solely within a single community, which do not have significant adverse effects on other humans or communities, should be governed by the host community's norms.
2 Community norms for resolving priority should be applied, so long as they do not have significant adverse effects on other humans or communities.
3 The more extensive the community which is the source of the norm, the greater the priority which should be given to the norm.
4 Norms essential to the maintenance of the economic environment in which the transaction occurs should have priority over norms potentially damaging to that environment.

5   Where multiple conflicting norms are involved, patterns of consistency among the
    alternative norms provide a basis for prioritization.   .
6   Well-defined norms should ordinarily have priority over more general, less precise
    norms.

These rules are not given priority themselves; rather they are to be loosely weighed
and applied without a strict calculus of relative value.

Consider, again, marketing ethics as an illustration. Many of the more challenging issues of marketing ethics involve conflicting legitimate norms. The marketing
research community, for example, may believe that some "soft" deception is acceptable to obtain results that further the goals of marketing research and contribute
to general economic welfare. Yet other communities may have an opposite norm,
thinking that full disclosure is necessary to justify the respondent's participation in
the research. Both norms may pass the hypernorm and exit/voice tests, and hence
both may be legitimate. What should be done? Under ISCT, the priority rules
would be applied to the practice of soft deception in marketing research as a set.
ISCT invites anyone attempting to resolve this conflict to ask a series of questions,
including: "Is soft deception in marketing research essential to the maintenance of
the economic environment in which the advertising occurs?" (Rule 4); "Are there
significant adverse effects on other humans or communities from soft deception in
marketing research?" (Rule 1); and "Is there a pattern of consistency among the
alternative norms in various communities regarding soft deception?" (Rule 5). Depending on the answers one gives to these questions, soft deception is determined to be
permissible or not.

Contractarian approaches are now being used to evaluate a host of issues. Kim
Scheppele (1993, p. 151) has supported restrictions on insider trading through a
contractarian analysis that she stresses is capable of providing "concrete guidance in
working out how to think about the ethics of insider trading." She argues that consent
must be "based on more detailed and context-dependent knowledge of specific features
of American life and of particular individuals." After extensive analysis along these
lines, she justifies restrictions on insider trading based upon a contractually derived
desire to provide equal access to financial markets. Similarly, Robert Frank (1993) has
advanced a contractarian view of regulatory policy in emerging market economies,
noting that "recent decades have seen a resurgence of contractarian thinking about
the nature and origins of the state (p. 258)."

Remaining issues and promising research directions for contractarian business ethics

It is not surprising that contractarian business ethics, itself only a decade old, is replete
with unresolved issues. Many difficult and important research issues remain to be
analyzed before social contract theory can live up to its full promise as a critical
theoretical tool for business ethics. Some of the most important issues are identified
briefly below.

Consent

Consent is the justificatory linchpin of any social contract method, whether the contract proposed is hypothetical or real. In the use of hypothetical social contracts, theorists must offer persuasive reasons why rational prospective contractors would agree to the terms of a given agreement. Various strategies have been employed by contractarian theorists, including the use of pre-contractual devices such as a veil of ignorance (Rawls, 1971) and the "state of individual production" (Donaldson, 1982), or the assumption that agreement is the only viable solution to serious non-cooperation problems (Gauthier, 1986). The difficulties in making the case for (nearly) universal acceptability of the terms of a hypothetical agreement tend to lead theorists toward parsimonious assumptions that, in turn, lead to narrowly defined social contracts. In a sense, the more insignificant the agreement, the less the justification required to show that its terms are generally acceptable.

Interestingly, few social contract theorists have presumed that contractors are even moderately altruistic (both Rawls and Gauthier expressly reject the idea), even though there is growing evidence that humans appear to be, by nature, altruistic. This strategy aims to strengthen the persuasiveness of the agreement, as if to say, "If self-interested contractors will agree to these moral principles without supposing any altruistic influence, clearly ordinary humans, who may possess altruistic instincts, will also agree to them."

Many issues pertaining to the vital element of consent in social contracts remain open to further research. One is whether a creative way exists to design a hypothetical agreement appropriate to business ethics that can solve the problems of justifying the agreement. For example, can the new evidence from the fields of behavioral economics and economic psychology provide insights into the nature of human rationality that will be helpful in designing plausible social contracts? Can the limited research concerning universally held values be used in designing a global social contract for economic ethics?

Reliance upon existing or "extant" social contracts is one part of the solution to the justification problem. Such reliance assumes that there is no agreement for existing contracts unless there is evidence of consent. Even though consent fails as a sufficient condition for the justification of a normative agreement (brigands can consent to a conspiracy of murder), it is – from the standpoint of social contract theory – a necessary condition for such justification. In assessing whether consent has occurred in a given extant social contract, the answer cannot lie merely in definition. Rather, the question becomes an empirical one of determining whether members of a particular community have indeed accepted the terms of the agreement. Certain statistical and empirical methods are clearly helpful in making such a determination. If the determination is affirmative, i.e., if evidence shows they have, in fact, consented to the contract, then the first step has been taken towards establishing that an obligation to comply with the norms also exists.

In this context, a different, but vitally important, question arises concerning the manner in which consent is tested. Consent by its very nature is valid only when uncoerced and informed. The issue thus becomes one of how best to identify genuine versus apparent consent in business communities. Norms such as dress codes or participation in corporate blood drives that are forced from the top-down may not involve genuine consent when employees participate only from fear of retaliation. Certainly, the mere fact that an "ethics code" exists is insufficient to establish its status as the consented-to term of a firm-level, social contract.

Yet, a workable and useful contractarian approach to business ethics needs a similarly workable and useful test of genuine consent. If, for example, consent is to be established through survey techniques, what controls are important for identifying genuine consent? Is it necessary to have the surveys done by outside parties in an environment of strict confidentiality? What other restrictions on testing should be employed? And so on.

Empirical foundations

Contractarian approaches inevitably generate a swarm of empirical issues. One important question is the extent to which managers and political leaders accept the contract metaphor as representative of current social approaches. If they are already familiar with and accept the idea, then they may be particularly receptive to the use of contractarian language to translate ethical precepts. An important stream of research in business ethics seeks to determine how business decision makers reason in the context of ethical decisions. For example, is there a general tendency for managers to use a particular ethical theory (Jones, 1991)? If not, then are there other variables, including gender, industry, or decision-context which may influence the ethical theory chosen (Smiley, 1992)? Within this framework, an important open question is: How likely are managers to reason in contractarian terms?

A key research question in business ethics is the extent to which a person's ethical thought, or the mode of that person's ethical thought, influences his or her behavior. In the contractarian context, the question is one of whether individuals who tend to think in terms of unwritten agreements or unspoken promises will be less likely to act unethically. If so, then such a finding would lend further support to the value of the social contract metaphor as a way of thinking about ethical decisions in business.

Contractarianism tends to be a norm-centered approach to ethics. Empirical issues abound concerning how norms come to be created, communicated and accepted within particular business communities, how they change or are purged, and how they are enforced or supported. The issue of how to identify norms accurately within a particular community is vitally important for any contractarian approach relying upon real or extant norms. For example, are there certain proxies for norms within particular communities that can be identified? Consider this question: Under what circumstances can a corporate code of ethics be considered representative of ethical norms within that community? Which of the following, if any, would represent the best method for testing this important issue:

- when employees are required to sign a code and do so;
- when a code is listed as part of the application process to work at a firm; or
- when most employees privately and confidentially state that they agree with the provisions of a code?

Contractarian business ethics and stakeholder management

Earlier, we identified critical issues needing resolution in stakeholder analysis, which we believe to be an important and increasingly well-accepted approach to corporate ethics. These include establishing methods for justifying the claims of particular stakeholders, identifying normative criteria for weighing competing stakeholder interests and for resolving conflicts between stakeholder interests and the financial objectives of the firm. In short, stakeholder analysis requires some normative justification that goes deeper than a mere assertion of the stakeholder idea itself. Evan and Freeman (1988) proposed a Kantian solution to this problem, yet contractarian approaches also have significant potential for resolving core issues. Consider, for example, the fundamental question of whether a plausible justification can be presented for the claim that firm managers have a significant responsibility to stakeholders other than stockholders. Social contract theory can be used as an imaginary heuristic device to develop a persuasive case that management has duties to employees and customers, as Donaldson (1982) has demonstrated. Further, we believe that, empirically, a social contract does exist in the USA and most other developed countries that requires management to recognize certain sets of stakeholder interests. If our assumption is correct, then empirical research capable of isolating the boundaries of general public expectations concerning obligations to stakeholders would contribute significantly to the debate on this topic. The debate engendered by Milton Friedman concerning whether it is socially responsible for managers to seek to do otherwise than maximize profits ultimately reduces to a certain set of empirical claims. The contractarian alternative, also in part empirically based, has the potential to serve as a powerful, legitimate counterpoint to the Friedman position.

We suggest further that context-specificity in contractarian ethics may constitute an ideal source of normative standards for the actual process of stakeholder management. Can, for example, implied social contracts be identified that specify with some precision the tradeoffs that need to be recognized among certain classes of stakeholders and also specifying how firm-stakeholder tradeoffs should be made? Thus, a contractarian approach may have comparative advantages in dealing with the dilemma of choosing between "multi-fiduciary" and "strategic" stakeholder analysis as described by Goodpaster (1991).

Contractarian business ethics and ethical theory

There may be a tendency to see the various ethical theories as competitive, and to suppose that one must either be a utilitarian, a virtue ethics theorist, a deontologist, or so on. This view is losing ground in philosophy (Becker, 1992) and, indeed, we see contractarian approaches as potentially consistent with a number of alternative ethical theories. The possibility of significant ethical "pluralism" has received increasing attention in recent years. In 1992, the journal *Ethics* devoted a special edition of the journal (Vol. 102) to this very issue. Important questions include determining the circumstances in which different theories result in irreconcilable judgments, and understanding the factors generating inapposite results.

Consider an example of such pluralism. Contractarian approaches that incorporate reference to actual implied social contracts are potentially reconcilable with virtue ethics. Concepts of virtue may themselves be part of an extant contract (as when, say, the employees of a corporation internalize the virtue of "integrity" in their corporate roles). Further, certain virtues may be seen as critical in the construction of extant social contracts (as when, say, the virtue of tolerance is important in establishing ethical norms among racially diverse contractors). Important research issues involving the integration of virtue and contractarian ethics approaches include understanding the relationship between the use of the concept of "practices" in the work of virtue theorist Alisdair MacIntyre (1981) and the process by which norms are formed and recognized within communities.

Even Milton Friedman's (1970) conception of the corporation as merely agent for self-interested shareowners, long regarded by many as an amoral agency theory, may be understood as using a contractarian approach. For the Friedman view to obtain legitimacy under a contractarian approach, one of two claims must be established. Either, it must be established that a plausible hypothetical contract, grounded in a realistic account of human rationality, can be defined which endorses single-minded attention to shareholder wealth; or, extant social contracts which support his position, must be identified. At least one of these two is necessary to bestow legitimacy to his theory – although neither is sufficient to bestow such legitimacy. If neither can be established (which is our intuition), then Friedman's claim is merely one of the minority voices in US society advocating an, as yet unendorsed, normative policy position. In such a circumstance, Friedman's theory could not lay claim to imposing ethical obligations on business practitioners.

Contractarian assumptions and moral psychology

A great deal of empirical work has been done in the last few decades concerning how people think generally about ethical issues. Few people apply what Lawrence Kohlberg (1983) identifies as the highest or sixth stage of moral reasoning (either Kantian or Utilitarian reasoning would, according to Kohlberg, qualify as sixth stage). Most people respond to the laws and norms of society (which Kohlberg identifies as stage four) and the expectations of their close colleagues and relatives (stage three). It remains to be seen whether a relationship exists between these findings and the assumptions of contractarian business ethics. Are these findings supportive of, and compatible with, contractarian ethics as opposed to other approaches? Can extant contracts be classified by Kohlbergian stages? In a related vein, can contractarian analysis help in understanding the process of moral reasoning? At the extreme, might more explicit incorporation of contractarian approaches require changes in standard frameworks or testing procedures used in moral psychology?

Managerial utility and contractarian business ethics

Managers often use the terminology of social contract in describing, for example, relationships between their firm and the local community. Employees also frequently speak of the "implied agreements" that surround policies and procedures, including ones affecting downsizing, corporate pensions, and due process. Corporate pensioners may, for example, express belief in a social contract obligation on the part of the firm to take steps to guarantee that their retirement remains secure. Similarly, even politicians sometimes make use of contractarian language when describing business–government relationships.

Thus, the concept and terminology of social contract is, to some extent, already familiar to business managers. Further, new research indicating that managers tend to think in terms of unwritten agreements and unspoken promises (Robertson and Ross, 1995, and sources cited therein) suggests potential far-reaching receptivity to ethical standards grounded in contractarian concepts. Even so, the specific implications need to be put into user-friendly terms. Mangers confronted with urgent ethical dilemmas cannot be expected to pause in the middle of hectic schedules to reflect carefully on the detailed implications of the terms of a hypothetical social contract or to search for microsocial contract norms. Some "translator" concepts, suitable for hands-on application to day-to-day business problems, would be desirable. Can contractarian business ethics be reduced to certain rules of thumb, or sets of questions which can serve as effective, efficient normative guideposts for managers? Can such approaches be devised and tested? What would be the most effective tests for systems which seek to operationalize a particular ethical theory?

These, then, are some of the issues and challenges confronting social contract theory as it enters the next century to examine the norms of modern business. We have seen that, in one sense, the concept is as old as philosophical speculation. Surely, the "compact" with God spoken of in the Old Testament and the imaginary agreement between hypothetical members of the state in Plato's (1968) *The Republic* are influential examples of social contracts in intellectual history. Yet, as we have also seen, the contractarian device promises striking contributions to modern business issues. A growing wave of efforts in the 1980s and early 1990s applied contractarian thinking to a vast range of economic issues. The concept of social contract is clearly here to stay, and we believe it will contribute substantially to the growing sophistication of normative business ethics.

References

Aoki, M. 1984: *The Co-operative Game Theory of the Firm*. Oxford: Clarendon Press.

Aupperle, K. E., Carroll, A. B., and Hatfield, J. D. 1985: An empirical examination of the relationship between corporate social responsibility and profitability. *Academy of Management Journal*, 28(2), 446–63.

Becker, L. C. 1992: Places for pluralism. *Ethics*, 102, 707–19.

Bhat, V. N. 1996: *Do Environmental Regulations Spur Innovations?* Northeast Decision Sciences Institute, 33–5.

Bowie, N. E. 1982: *Business Ethics*. Englewood Cliffs, NJ: Prentice-Hall.

Bowie, N. E. 1988: The moral obligations of multinational corporations. In S. Luper-Foy Boulder (ed.), *Problems of International Justice*. London: Westview Press, 97–114.

Brady, F. N. and Wheeler, G. E. 1996: An empirical study of ethical predispositions. *Journal of Business Ethics*, 15, 927–40.

Brummer, J. J. 1991: *Corporate Responsibility and Legitimacy, An Interdisciplinary Analysis*. New York: Greenwood Press.

Carroll, A. B. 1989: *Business and Society: Ethics and Stakeholder Management*. Cincinnati: South-Western Publishing Company.

Cavanagh, G. F., Moberg, D. J., and Velasquez, M. 1981: The ethics of organizational politics. *Academy of Management Review*, 6(3), 363–74.

DeGeorge, R. T. 1993: *Competing With Integrity in International Business*. New York: Oxford University Press.

Deshpande, S. P. 1997: Managers' perception of proper ethical conduct: The effect of sex, age, and level of education. *Journal of Business Ethics*, 16, 79–85.

DesJardins, J. R. and McCall, J. 1985: A defense of employee rights. *Journal of Business Ethics*, 4, 367–76.

Dill, W. R. 1958: Environment as an influence on managerial autonomy. *Administrative Science Quarterly*, 2, 409–43.

Donaldson, T. 1982: *Corporations and Morality*. Englewood Cliffs, NJ: Prentice-Hall.

Donaldson, T. 1988: Fact, fiction, and the social contract: A reply to Kultgen. *Business and Professional Ethics Journal*, 4, 31–49. Also 1987: *Ethics and Risk Management in Engineering*, 1, 40–7.

Donaldson, T. 1989: *The Ethics of International Business*. New York: Oxford University Press.

Donaldson, T. 1990: Social contracts and corporations: A reply to Hodapp. *Journal of Business Ethics*, 9(February), 133–9.

Donaldson, T. and Dunfee, T. W. 1994: Toward a unified conception of business ethics: Integrative social contracts theory. *Academy of Management Review*, 19(2), 252–84.

Donaldson, T. and Dunfee, T. W. 1995: Integrative social contracts theory: A communitarian conception of economic ethics. *Economics and Philosophy*, 11(1), 85–112.

Donaldson, T. and Dunfee, T. W. 1999: *Ties that Bind: A Social Contracts Approach to Business Ethics*. Harvard Business School Press.

Donaldson, T. and Preston, L. E. 1995: The stakeholder theory of the corporation: Concepts, evidence, implications. *Academy of Management Review*, 20(1), 65–91.

Dunfee, T. W. 1991: Business ethics and extant social contracts. *Business Ethics Quarterly*, 1(1), 23–51.

Dunfee, T. W. and Donaldson, T. 1995: Contractarian business ethics: Current status and next steps. *Business Ethics Quarterly*, 5(2), 173–86.

Dunfee, T. W. and Maurer, V. C. 1992: Corporate attorney whistle-blowing: Devising a proper standard. *Business and Professional Ethics Journal*, 11(3 and 4), 3–39.

Evan, W. M. and Freeman, R. E. 1988: (rpt. 1993) A stakeholder theory of the modern corporation: Kantian capitalism. In T. Beauchamp and N. Bowie (eds), *Ethical Theory and Business*. Englewood Cliffs, NJ: Prentice Hall, 75–93.

Frank, R. H. 1993: A new contractarian view of tax and regulatory policy in the emerging market economies. *Social Philosophy and Policy*, 258–81.

Freeman, R. E. 1984: *Strategic Management: A Stakeholder Approach*. Boston: Pitman.

Freeman, R. E. (ed.) 1991: *Business Ethics: The State of the Art*. New York: Oxford University Press.

Freeman, R. E. and Evan, W. M. 1990: Corporate governance: A stakeholder interpretation. *The Journal of Behavioral Economics*, 19(4), 337–59.

Freeman, R. E. and Gilbert, D. R., Jr 1987: Managing stakeholder relationships. In S. P. Sethi and C. M. Falbe (eds), *Business and Society*, Lexington, MA: Lexington Books, 397–423.

Freeman, R. E., and Reed D. L. 1983: Stockholders and stakeholders: A new perspective on corporate governance. *California Management Review*, 25(3), 88–106.

Friedman, M. 1970: The social responsibility is to increase its profits. *New York Times Magazine*, 32–3.

Gauthier, D. 1986: *Morals By Agreement*. Oxford: Clarendon Press.

Goodpaster, K. E. 1991: Business ethics and stakeholder analysis. *Business Ethics Quarterly*, 1(1), 53–73.

Green, M. K. 1986: A Kantian evaluation of Taylorism in the workplace. *Journal of Business Ethics*, 5(April), 165–9.

Green, R. M. 1991: When is "Everyone's doing it" a moral justification? *Business Ethics Quarterly*, 1(1), 75–94.

Hall, W. D. 1993: *Making the Right Decision*. New York: John Wiley & Sons.

Hobbes, T. 1651: *Leviathan; or, The Matter, Form and Power of a Commonwealth, Ecclesiastical and Civil*. Oxford: Basil Blackwell.

Hodapp, P. F. 1990: Can there be a social contract with business? *Journal of Business Ethics*, 9, 127–31.

Hosseini, J. C. and Brenner, S. N. 1992: The stakeholder theory of the firm: A methodology to generate value matrix weights. *Business Ethics Quarterly*, 2(2), 99–120.

Jones, T. 1991: Ethical decision making by individuals in organizations: An issue-contingent model. *Academy of Management Review*, 16(2), 366–95.

Keeley, M. 1988: *A Social Contract Theory of Organizations*. Notre Dame, IND: University of Notre Dame Press.

Kohlberg, L. 1983: *Moral Stages: A Current Formulation and a Response to Critics*. New York: Karger.

Kuhn, J. W. and Shriver, D. W., Jr 1991: *Beyond Success: Corporations and their Critics in the 1990s*. New York: Oxford University Press.

Kultgen, J. 1986: Comments on Donaldson's corporations and morality. *Business and Professional Ethics Journal*, 5, 28–39.

Levitt, L. 1986: Donaldson's social contract for business. *Business and Professional Ethics Journal*, 5, 47–50.

Locke, J. 1948: *The Second Treatise of Civil Government and a Letter Concerning Toleration*. Oxford: Basil Blackwell.

MacIntyre, A. C. 1981: *After Virtue: A Study in Moral Theory*. Notre Dame, IND: University of Notre Dame Press.

McGuire, J. B., Sundgren, A., and Schneeweis, T. 1988: Corporate social responsibility and firm financial performance. *Academy of Management Journal*, 31(4), 354–72.

Nash, L. L. 1981: Ethics without the sermon. *Harvard Business Review*, (Nov.–Dec.), 78–90.

Orts, E. W. 1992: Beyond shareholders: interpreting corporate constituency statutes. *The George Washington Law Review*, 61(1), 14–135.

Pastin, M. and Hooker, M. 1980: Ethics and the Foreign Corrupt Practices Act. *Business Horizons*, (Dec.), 43–7.

Plato 1968: *The Republic*. Book I. Translated by A. Bloom. New York: Basic Books.

Preston, L. E. and Sapienza, H. J. 1990: Stakeholder management and corporate performance. *The Journal of Behavioral Economics*, 19(4), 361–75.

Preston, L. E., Sapienza, H. J., and Miller, R. D. 1991: Stakeholders, shareholders, managers: Who gains what from corporate performance? In A. Etzioni and P. R. Lawrence (eds), *Socio-economics: Toward a New Synthesis*. Armonk, NY: M. E. Sharpe, 149–65.

Rawls, J. 1971: *A Theory of Justice*. Cambridge: Harvard University Press.

Robertson, D. C. and Nicholson, N. 1996: Expressions of corporate social responsibility in UK firms. *Journal of Business Ethics*, 15, 1095–106.

Robertson, D. C. and Ross, J. W. T. 1995: Decision making processes on ethical issues: The impact of a social contract perspective. *Business Ethics Quarterly*, 5(2), 213–40.

Rousseau, J.-J. 1997: *Rousseau – The Social Contract and Other Later Political Writings*. Cambridge: Cambridge University Press.

Scheppele, K. L. 1993: "It's just not right": The ethics of insider trading. *Law and Contemporary Problems*, 56(3), 123–73.

Smiley, M. 1992: *Moral Responsibility and the Boundaries of Community: Power and Accountability from a Pragmatic Point of View*. University of Chicago Press, 257.

Swinyard, W. R., Rinne, H., and Kau, A. K. 1990: The morality of software piracy: A cross-cultural analysis. *Journal of Business Ethics*, 9, 655–64.

Walzer, M. 1994: *Thick and Thin: Moral Argument at Home and Abroad.* Notre Dame, IND: University of Notre Dame Press, 12.

Werhane, P. 1984: Individual rights in business. In T. Regan (ed.), *Just Business: New Introductory Essays in Business Ethics.* New York: Random House.

Werhane, P. 1991: *Rights, Persons, and Corporations.* New York: Oxford University Press.

Williams, B. 1985: *Ethics and the Limits of Philosophy.* Cambridge, MA: Harvard University Press.

5

Business ethics and the pragmatic attitude

DOUGLAS R. ANDERSON

The relationship between pragmatism and business ethics is a bit vexed. On the one hand, US business culture has often been called "pragmatic," drawing in loose fashion on William James's pragmatic conception of truth. Thus, Gerald F. Cavanagh (1976, p. 172) says: "One of the strengths of American business ideology has been its pragmatism: how to get the job done without much concern for inconsistencies. Simply put, pragmatism says that which works is by that fact good and true."

On the other hand, four central figures in the history of pragmatism – Charles Peirce, William James, John Dewey, and Richard Rorty – offer various criticisms of US business culture. Thus, the "pragmatic" nature of US business has not been endorsed by the pragmatists themselves.

Peirce, in his 1893 essay "Evolutionary Love," resisted what he called the "Gospel of Greed." Specifically, he attacked Simon Newcomb's US rendering of Adam Smith's political economy. He found Newcomb's underlying principle – or gospel – of the redemption of human existence a peculiar one:

> It is this: Intelligence in the service of greed ensures the justest prices, the fairest contracts, the most enlightened conduct of all the dealings between men, and leads to the *summum bonum*, food in plenty and perfect comfort. Food for whom? Why, for the greedy master of intelligence. I do not mean to say that this is one of the legitimate conclusions of political economy, the scientific character of which I fully acknowledge. But the study of doctrines, themselves true, will often temporarily encourage generalizations extremely false, as the study of physics has encouraged necessitarianism. What I say, then, is that the great attention paid to economical questions during our century has induced an exaggeration of the beneficial effects of greed and of the unfortunate results of sentiment, until there has resulted a philosophy which comes unwittingly to this, that greed is the great agent in the elevation of the human race and in the evolution of the universe. (Peirce, 1893, pp. 192–3)

In short, he took the US devotion to greed to be antithetical to a thriving human community.

James, while defending individualism and laying the theoretical groundwork for the conception of "pragmatism" employed by Cavanagh and others, shared Peirce's concern over our culture's support of the wealthy: "See the abuses which the institution of private property covers, so that even to-day it is shamelessly asserted that one of the prime functions of the national government is to help the adroiter citizens to grow rich" (James, 1956, pp. 206–7). Peirce's and James's worries were taken up by Dewey who was the most systematic and persistent critic of US business practices among the pragmatists.

Although he was not a dogmatic opponent of technology or economic development, Dewey worried about the ill effects our method of achieving them might involve. He looked closely at how our business institutions were structured and at what unintended effects our business habits tended to produce. He was, for example, concerned with the alienated distance US workers often have from their own labor (Dewey, 1962, p. 132): "Their hearts and brains are not engaged. They execute plans which they do not form, and of whose meaning and intent they are ignorant – beyond the fact that these plans make a profit for others and secure a wage for themselves."

Although this statement sounds roughly Marxist, Dewey repeatedly distanced himself from Marx, in part because Marx's metaphysics seemed to him inflexible, and in part because he took the practical consequences of Marx's thought to be the constraint, not the liberation, of human life.

Finally, Richard Rorty, although like James he defends a radical version of negative freedom in the private sphere, is, like Dewey, much concerned with cultural practices whose public consequences feel wrong. In a recent essay for the *New York Times Magazine*, for example, he questioned the central role that selfishness plays in US economic practices, saying that a "burst of selfishness had produced tax revolts in the 70's, stopping in its tracks the fairly steady progress toward a full-fledged welfare state that had been under way since the New Deal" (Rorty, 1996, p. 156).

If, as seems evident, the pragmatists do not themselves offer support for the "pragmatic" nature of US business practices, what is to be said of the relationship between pragmatism and business ethics? The tension, I think, itself requires mediation in a pragmatic way; there needs to be some fleshing out of what pragmatists mean by a pragmaticized ethics. We can begin this mediation by recalling James's adoption of the conception of pragmatism offered by another pragmatist (1981, p. 29):

> It has no dogmas and no doctrines save its method. As the young Italian pragmatist Papini has well said, it lies in the midst of our theories, like a corridor in a hotel. Innumerable chambers open out of it. In one you may find a man writing an atheistic volume; in the next some one on his knees praying for faith and strength; in a third a chemist investigating a body's properties. In a fourth a system of idealistic metaphysics is being shown. But they all own the corridor, and all must pass through it if they want a practicable way of getting into or out of their respective rooms.
>
> No particular results then, so far, but only an attitude of orientation, is what the pragmatic method means. *The attitude of looking away from first things, principles, "categories," supposed necessities; and of looking towards last things, fruits, consequences, facts.*

The pragmatic method, as James sees it, involves the adoption of an attitude of openness in dealing with philosophical problems. We must be experimenters in ideas. However, our openness and experimental attitude must also have a cultural setting. If, for James, we "make" truths, we only do so in conjunction with a wealth of "truths" already established. The pragmatic attitude that we bring to our problems must, from the pragmatists' point of view, be anchored in our personal and cultural funded experience. What this attitude can bring to the study and practice of business ethics remains to be seen.

A corollary of James's pragmatic attitude is the need for philosophy – and thoughtful criticism generally – to deal with the everyday problems of human experience. "The whole function of philosophy," James says, "ought to be to find out what definite difference it will make to you and me, at definite instances of our life, if this world-formula or that world-formula be the true one" (James, 1981, p. 27). Dewey (1988, p. 18) makes the same point even more directly:

> A first-rate test of the value of any philosophy which is offered us is this: Does it end in conclusions which, when they are referred back to ordinary life-experiences and their predicaments, render them more significant, more luminous to us, and make our dealings with them more fruitful?

Dewey, perhaps more than James, found in this corollary of the pragmatic attitude the necessity for philosophers to engage in social criticism. This, of course, takes pragmatic philosophy directly into the moral realm and suggests a revision of the modes of moral discourse. "Hence critical questioning of existing institutions and critical discussion of changes," Dewey maintains, "proposed on the theory that they will produce social betterment, are the best means of enforcing the fact that moral theory is more than a remote exercise in conceptual analysis or than a mere mode of preaching and exhortation" (Dewey and Tufts, 1932, p. 349).

This corollary pretty clearly offers a linkage to the development of business ethics – and applied ethics in general – that has taken place in the philosophical community during the last thirty years. That is, pragmatism asks philosophy to address everyday issues and to deal with issues of social consequence; business ethics has been an ongoing attempt precisely for philosophy to deal with specific issues and practices in the world of business. In its basic purpose, then, business ethics appears to be pragmatic. Ironically, however, the business ethics trade was not generated by, nor has it been heavily influenced by, pragmatism. We should note, however, that Dewey and Tufts devoted a section of Ethics to the problem of business. Those involved in professional and business ethics have seldom – other than in the loose fashion indicated at the outset – looked to the pragmatists for insight.

Business ethics as a philosophical discipline has thus developed with a pragmatic aim, but has done so for the most part with an unpragmatic attitude. As most current textbooks in business ethics evidence, the primary method used by philosophers for introducing ethics into the business world is to provide an overview of a limited set of ethical systems: deontology, utilitarianism, egoism, and so forth. These systems are then taken to the world of case studies where they are applied, often somewhat mechanically. Although I believe this method has some merits, I also think it often misses the mark. The theories tend to function as overlays on, not as direct engagements with, living issues. Students and business practitioners often see in philosophical business ethics precisely what the early pragmatists saw in some late nineteenth-century systematic philosophy: a sense that ethics is a game of abstractions and that philosophers are tied to an intellectualism that, despite their insistence on getting down-to-earth, does not address the actual issues in the case studies. This sense, I think, is the ground of the cynicism that is occasionally aimed at philosophers by those who teach and deal with business ethics in schools and departments of business. The rather formal and abstract approach of "applying" ethical systems bears with it, ironically, a sense of remoteness from the very experience it sets out to engage. Here is where pragmatism, understood as a method and attitude, not as a formal ethical system, has something specific to offer the practice of business ethics. In Dewey's way of putting it (Dewey and Tufts, 1932, p. 366), "[i]n questions of social morality [business ethics, e.g.], more fundamental than any particular principle held or decision reached is the attitude of *willingness to reexamine and if necessary revise current convictions, even if that course entails the effort to change by concerted effort existing institutions, and to direct existing tendencies to new ends.*"

As noted above, James and Dewey maintained that philosophy should address issues that arise in our actual cultural practices, among which we find business practices. The usual issues that attract discussion in business ethics are among these – drug testing, whistleblowing, marketing, and so on. As Dewey liked to put it, our problems are "had" or "felt." Whoever has faced the possibility of "blowing the whistle" on an employer knows that there is more involved than an intellectual assessment of a "case." The test is of one's whole character and, as James says (1956, pp. 214–15): "From this unsparing practical ordeal no professor's lectures and no array of books can save us." The job of a pragmatic philosophy is not merely to understand but to make a difference, to bring our intelligence to bear in addressing these living problems. Thus, for Dewey, pragmatism sees philosophy as "criticism" and effecting this criticism requires something like the pragmatic attitude. By "criticism," however, Dewey does not mean an act of negation and confrontation; rather, criticism is experiential assessment. It is, he says (1988, p. 298), "discriminating judgment, careful appraisal . . ." In this, much philosophy may appropriately be an amateur activity; pragmatism is simply asking that problems and issues in business be assessed with intelligence and discriminating judgment. Philosophers are not to become professional arbiters of the case studies from the world of business. Criticism, Dewey (1988, p. 299) argues,

> is not a matter of formal treatises, published articles, or taking up important matters for consideration in a serious way. It occurs whenever a moment is devoted to looking to see what sort of value is present; whenever instead of accepting a value-object whole-heartedly, being rapt by it, we raise even a shadow of a question about its worth, or modify our sense of it by even a passing estimate of its probable future.

What the pragmatists would have us experiment with is the treating of problems in business culture as "philosophers" in their sense: as critics with a pragmatic attitude. It is to some features of this attitude that I now turn.

The leading feature of the pragmatic attitude is a healthy dose of self-aversion: an active willingness to countenance a change in one's own beliefs. The whole notion of experimentalism that lies at the heart of pragmatism requires this feature as a living character trait. Peirce codified this need for self-aversion in his fallibilism, and Rorty, via James and Dewey, has kept this element alive in the pragmatic tradition through his insistence on self-revision. In the realm of business ethics, its effectiveness is to be found in two directions. First, it loosens the grip of dogmatic, philosophical moral systems that would have us answer newly experienced problems with set rules or calculi. If one is a thoroughgoing Benthamist, for example, there is no other way to decide about the present appropriateness of "Joe Camel" advertisements than to calculate the net pleasures and/or pains. The pragmatically oriented Benthamist, on the other hand, is in a position to be open to revision of his or her position. Second, self-aversiveness can be effective for the business "agent" or practitioner directly. Cavanagh (1976, p. 172) cites the virtues and defects of a narrowly aimed pragmatic attitude that in the business world has

> led to flexibility and innovation in search for a better way of providing . . . goods. On the other hand, it has led us to accept values and goals simply because they seem to work, and often regardless of inequities and undesirable by-products.

A more thoroughly pragmatic attitude will bear with it the possibility of aversion to the consequences Cavanagh describes as well. From the pragmatists' point of view, one incapable of truly being averse to one's present beliefs – and corollarial actions – is in no condition for ameliorative change. We should note well, however, that this insistence on self-aversion does not entail for the pragmatists a chaotic flux of lived beliefs. It is not a recipe for moral mayhem.

On the contrary, each of the early pragmatists was careful to insist on the importance of tradition. It is now commonplace that experiment requires a steady background against which to measure and evaluate changes. Experiment involves, as Dewey notes, constant revision; but it is revision constrained by present and past experience. Tradition, including moral tradition, plays a crucial role in our critical assessment of our immediate problems. The success of past practices counts heavily in our current assessment of them. As Dewey (Dewey and Tufts, 1932, p. 366) points out:

> In moral matters there is a presumption in favor of principles that have had a long career in the past and that have been endorsed by men of insight; the presumption is especially strong when all that opposes them is the will of some individual seeking exemption because of an impulse or a passion which is temporarily urgent. Such principles are no more to be lightly discarded than are scientific principles worked out in the past.

Thus, pragmatism's sense of self-aversion is heavily tempered with a regard for tradition. What perhaps appears in formal terms to be a contradiction – the merging of an active willingness to change with a strong regard for past success – becomes, for the pragmatist, a central dimension of the pragmatic attitude.

The regard for tradition makes for an interesting handling of the ethical systems that have appeared and been employed in the history of Western cultures. The pragmatic business ethicist must respect their strengths and successes; they are not to be dismissed wholesale. So far as they pass through the "corridor" of pragmatism, they may be exceptionally useful in dealing with particular moral issues. The criteria of utilitarianism, for example, come into play when one considers shutting down large industries to make life better for a few asthmatics. Likewise, a Kantian sense of duty may effectively temper a particular company's attempts to ride roughshod over the needs and wishes of individual persons. The traditional systems, however, are not *a priori* solutions. For Dewey, as for James, "it is *not* the business of moral theory to provide a ready-made solution to large moral perplexities" (Dewey and Tufts,

1932, pp. 349–50). Rather, "theory can enlighten and guide choice and action by revealing alternatives, and by bringing to light what is entailed when we choose one alternative rather than another" (p. 350). Thus, the pragmatic attitude reveals a strength of the current practice of assessing case studies through formal systems – it opens the possibilities for us to see. Where the practice goes wrong is in assuming that one of the theories must be decisive in all cases. The pragmatist sees the theories as guides – as instruments – in the ongoing process of revision.

The instrumentality of moral theories recalls another of the central features James associated with the pragmatic attitude: a focus on and attentiveness to consequences. What separates pragmatism from "consequentialist" moral theories such as utilitarianism is that it provides no single formula for assessing consequences. As we just noted, the assessment is an act of criticism, of judgment; utilitarian considerations are to be counted and considered, but they cannot substitute for the agent's judgment in a particular situation. The agent cannot retreat to the harbor of dogmatic belief but must actively address the situation. It is what we mean when we say one must "deal with it." Thus, the generic focus on consequences, for the pragmatists, is tied to their belief that the meanings of things – terms and actions – are to be found in the consequences they would produce under any given circumstances. In the moral realm, the agent assesses consequences to see what particular actions mean or would mean.

Presumably, pragmatists can use this general focus on consequences to assess praise and blame, but this has not been where they have spent most of their energies. Although this focus is instrumental to such assessments, pragmatists were, and are, much more interested in projecting consequences to make judgments concerning present actions. What kind of world will we effect if we continue to use Joe Camel advertisements? What are the consequences of the systematic allowance of insider trading? Thus, as several students of Dewey's work have noted, pragmatism is interested in the projection of possibilities. Moral agents should project imaginative aims and the consequences that attend them. The experimentalism of the pragmatists reveals a kinship with Greek moral thought in rejecting formulaic answers to moral questions and in relying on the judgment of the individual moral agent. Dewey occasionally referred to this moral activity of projecting moral aims and consequences as "dramatic rehearsals." Peirce, without using the phrase, discussed the importance of these rehearsals in the practical realm and, on several occasions, used the example of his brother's mental preparation for dousing a fire created by a table lamp and the time this projection of possibilities paid off when an apron caught fire at the table. Thus, in business as elsewhere, moral activity is, for the pragmatists, a creative, not a deductive, endeavor.

The pragmatic attitude, so far, demands a self-aversion tempered by a respect for the successes of traditional beliefs and attended by a focus on consequences of specific actions and habitual behavior. Although both James and Peirce recognized the need for a greater inclusiveness in moral consideration, it was Dewey who gave articulation to this inclusiveness in the focus on consequences. Inasmuch as US business culture has, in the past, seemed little interested in the social "fallout" of its practices, usually because of a narrow conception of rights and duties and, as Peirce suggested, a naive sense of the cost–benefit analysis of the work of the "invisible hand," this feature of pragmatism's moral experimentalism seems an important offering for the world of business ethics.

Dewey (Dewey and Tufts, 1932, pp. 331–2) noted this special significance:

> Since the prevailing individualism was expressed in an economic theory and practice which taught that each man was actuated by an exclusive regard for his own profit, moralists were led to insist upon the need of some check upon this ruthless individualism, and to accentuate the supremacy in *morals* (as distinct from business) of sympathy and benevolent regard for others. The ultimate significance of this appeal is, however, to make us realize the fact that regard for self and regard for others are both of them secondary phases of a more normal and complete interest: regard for the welfare and integrity of the social groups of which we form a part.

In *The Public and Its Problems*, Dewey (1927) pushed this request for a wide sympathy in a more formal, political direction. His aim was to show that the seeing and projecting of consequences requires us to look where we are not initially – at least in US culture – wont to look. In his distinctions between "the private" and "the public," he tried to make clear that we must consider more than the local consequences – what we like to call "private" effects – of our actions and habits. "The public," Dewey maintains, "consists of all those who are affected by the indirect consequences of transactions to such an extent that it is deemed necessary to have those consequences systematically cared for" (Dewey, 1927, pp. 15–16). The business ethicist requires a greater scope of vision and an attention to the need to be more inclusive in assessing the effects of any action. "Public concern" in the realm of business ethics, then, is exemplified in our concern for the social consequences of cigarette advertising, our worry over the sale of dangerous products to uninformed buyers, and, indeed, our concern over the effects of government interference in market activities.

The distinction between pragmatism's and utilitarianism's concerns for consequences leads to the final feature of the pragmatic attitude for my present purpose. We noted that for pragmatism there is no calculus for measuring or projecting consequences. There is no certainty. Indeed, what James and Dewey see as a serious mistake in traditional moral theory is the attempt to make all moral decisions certainties. For James (1965, p. 210), "ethical treatises may be voluminous and luminous . . . but they never can be *final*, except in their abstractest and vaguest features; and they must more and more abandon the old-fashioned, clear-cut, and would-be 'scientific' form." Pragmatists are serious about the experimental nature of moral behavior. This means that the pragmatic attitude must include a willingness to confront one's own beliefs and their consequences. It means the willingness to accept responsibility for challenges to traditional mores. The pragmatic attitude requires the courage to change and the strength to deal with the public consequences of one's own change. The first companies to become proactive in areas of ethical concern, for example, have to be willing to bear not only the financial burden of their activities but the negative responses both from others in their field and from their own stockholders. Lee Iacocca's oft-repeated, and now outmoded, phrase that "safety doesn't sell" is a constant reminder of this fact. This willingness in the pragmatic attitude James calls the "strenuous mood." In the business world, as elsewhere, "it is at all times open to anyone to make the experiment [to break away from established rules], provided he fear not to stake his own life and character upon the throw" (James, 1956, p. 206).

The spirit of a pragmatic business ethics can be found neither in the simple revelling in expedience suggested by Cavanagh nor in a formalized reading of pragmatism as a traditional consequentialist moral theory. Taken in this latter way, it might seem merely an inept version of utilitarianism. My suggestion is that this spirit *can* be found in bringing something like the pragmatic attitude to bear, both in actual business practices and in talk about the morality of business practices – the discourse of business ethics. It is an attitude that understands moral errors and failures and retains the strength to seek their remedy. The pragmatic attitude is essentially melioristic; it looks for possibilities of betterness in any present situation. As Dewey (Dewey and Tufts, 1932, p. 367) puts it: "Against the social consequences generated by existing conditions there always stands the idea of other and better social consequences which a change would bring into being." We do not need to continue to beat the Ford Pinto case to death; we need to find and deal with our present problems, so as to ameliorate our present conditions.

Pragmatism's focus on the development of a pragmatic attitude also serves to bridge what I take to be an ongoing rift between philosophers and others in dealing with ethical issues in the business world. I noted earlier that philosophers in business ethics are often, though not always, viewed as being distanced from actual practices because of their interest in the abstract formalities of ethical theories. The pragmatic insistence on a specific attitude as character trait changes the philosopher's role from that of solver of moral dilemmas to that of partner in the critical thinking requisite for addressing moral issues and in the attempt to make things better. As James (1956, p. 214) insisted: "The ethical philosopher . . . whether he ventures to say which course of action is the best, is on no essentially different level from the common man." The moral philosopher is not required by pragmatism to begin with some dogmatic axe to grind against all business activity. At the same time, the pragmatic attitude does not allow the business practitioner a moral holiday in his or her role as business person. It reveals that we are *all* engaged in the moral experiment of producing our own world and socio-economic environment; it gives us each a stake in the care of the conditions of human flourishing.

Coming at the relation between business ethics and pragmatism in this way, I hope, allows the mediation I sought at the outset. Cavanagh had identified the ordinary person's understanding of pragmatism in business, but had ignored the pragmatists' pragmaticizing of ethics. This pragmaticizing requires us not to learn a set of answers to certain kinds of moral questions, but to prepare ourselves as moral agents for the judgment necessary in handling the everyday world in which we find ourselves. It also pushes pragmatic philosophers to hold true to their demand for philosophical engagement with the everyday world, and not to become isolated in the talk of pragmatic moral theory, however important such talk is in some venues. A focus on the pragmatic attitude, I hope, opens an avenue for seeing business ethics as pragmatic not only in its general purpose, but in its detailed and ongoing practice.

References

Cavanagh, G. F. 1976: *American Business Values in Transition*. Englewood Cliffs, NJ: Prentice-Hall, Inc.

Dewey, J. 1927: *The Public and Its Problems*. Denver: Henry Holt and Co.

Dewey, J. 1962: *Individualism Old and New*. New York: Capricorn Books.

Dewey, J. 1988: *John Dewey: The Later Works, Volume I, Experience and Nature*. Edited by J. A. Boydston. Carbondale: Southern Illinois University Press.

Dewey, J. and Tufts, J. 1932: *Ethics*. New York: Henry Holt and Co.

James, W. 1956: *The Will to Believe*. New York: Dover Publications.

James, W. 1981: *Pragmatism*. Indianapolis: Hackett Publishing.

Peirce, C. S. 1893: *Collected Papers of Charles Sanders Peirce, Vol. V and VI*. Edited by C. Hartshorne and P. Weiss. Cambridge: Harvard University Press.

Rorty, R. 1996: Fraternity: The case for a society based not on rights but on unselfishness. *New York Times Magazine*, September 29, 155–8.

6

An outline of ethical relativism and ethical absolutism

ROBERT E. FREDERICK

If he believes there is no difference between vice and virtue,
well sir, when he leaves our houses, let us count our spoons.
Samuel Johnson

Like Johnson, most of us are convinced that there is a difference between vice and virtue. The problem, especially in a global economy, is figuring out in useful detail exactly what it is. Some believe the problem can be solved by looking to local cultures, because the difference between vice and virtue depends entirely on local cultural beliefs. They take "when in Rome, do as the Romans" as serious ethical advice, rather than as a rule of etiquette. Others argue that there is more to it than local belief, that there is something universal about the difference that we ignore at our ethical peril. The debate between these two groups – the relativists and the absolutists – is the topic of this paper.

Cultural relativism

Cultural relativism is the thesis that different cultures have different beliefs about the morality of particular types of acts. So, an act that counts as right, good, or virtuous in one culture might be considered wrong, bad, or vicious in another. For example, it is frequently alleged that, in some cultures, bribery is a common and accepted way of doing business while, in our culture, bribery is more or less universally condemned and, sometimes, vigorously prosecuted. Thus, they (those *other* folks) seem to believe that bribery is morally permissible, but we do not. (In this chapter, I will use the words "moral" and "ethical" interchangeably. Occasionally, distinctions are drawn between ethics and morality, but I will not follow that practice here.)

Cultural relativism is supposed to be an ordinary empirical claim about the beliefs of people in different cultures. It is not an ethical proposal about what they ought to believe. We are often assured that cultural relativism is a true description of common-place facts about different cultures. Suppose it is. Does anything of interest for business follow from it?

I doubt it. By itself, cultural relativism is a mildly interesting feature of human societies, but no more interesting or significant for business than many other cultural facts compiled by collectors of sociological curiosities. It is only when a long and complex story about ethics is joined to cultural relativism that things really start to become interesting for business, and for everybody else. Let me try to explain.

Ethical absolutism

Consider the following statements, which are presented in no particular order:

1   Mother Teresa was a good person.
2   Hitler was an evil person.
3   Genocide is wrong.
4   It is wrong to torture children just for the fun of it.
5   Sincere promises ought to be kept.
6   Everyone should have the right to freedom of religion.
7   Honesty and generosity are good character traits, and ought to be encouraged.
8   Envy and spite are bad character traits, and ought to be discouraged.

Most of us, I am sure, would be willing to say that 1–8 are all true, and that we are as certain of their truth as we are of anything. Many of us would be still bolder, and claim that anyone who believes that one or more of 1–8 is false is obviously mistaken. For instance, if your friend Smith declares that torturing children for fun is sometimes okay, you might recoil with horror and contemplate informing the authorities, but it is next to inconceivable to suppose that you would think, "Well, he might be right; after all, who am I to say?" The line must be drawn somewhere, and this looks like a good place to do it.

However, here is the rest of Smith's story. It happens that he is one of those *others* from a very different culture, and, sure enough, in his culture, people sometimes do torture children just for fun. Further, no one there finds this practice morally abhorrent or even particularly troubling. What is your response to Smith now?

I suggest that it will depend on the kind of story you are willing to tell about ethics. One popular story goes something like this. There are "universally true" ethical principles that apply to everyone, everywhere, at all times. We know that one of these is that it is wrong to torture children for fun. Therefore, if Smith believes it is permissible to torture children for fun, what he believes is false. And if he or anyone else engages in this practice, then what they do is morally wrong.

This is the story told by advocates of *ethical absolutism* (EA). If EA is the correct story about ethics, i.e., the story we would all tell were we fully informed and rational, then, as Smith's example shows, taken together EA and cultural relativism imply that some of us (maybe all of us) have false beliefs about ethics; and, if we act on such beliefs, we act unethically. What remains to be established is which of us have false beliefs, why we have these beliefs, and whether we can be held morally blameworthy for acting on them.

However, one might wonder, if EA is true, how does one make sense of the enormous variety of ethical belief and practice in the world? No doubt some people have false beliefs about ethics, but is it credible that all ethical differences can be explained away so peremptorily? That the truth about the universal applicability of the one true code of ethics is grasped only by the cognoscenti, and those who have other ideas are ethical boors, boneheads, or blunderers? Surely supporters of EA owe us something better than this.

Advocates of EA typically reply to this challenge in two ways. First, they point out that lots of people think that the ethical principles they accept apply to everyone. People often judge what happens in other cultures according to local standards – a practice that would make no sense unless they thought that their standards apply to those cultures. Thus, (some version of) EA is a common ethical view. It is not reserved to the ethical incrowd. Second, they argue that cultural relativism does not necessarily imply *moral diversity*, i.e., it does not imply that cultures with different moral *practices* accept different and incompatible ethical *principles* or *theories*. A moral practice is a type of act that is believed to be morally permissible. Defenders of EA, though, say that differences in practice may not indicate differences about principle because a difference in practice may be a mere appearance that masks an underlying ethical unity. For example, people who live in different physical environments or economic circumstances may apply the same moral principles very differently. One would expect, for instance, that a rich society would have quite different moral practices from a poor one, even though both societies accept the same ethical principles. So what may seem to be a moral disagreement between these societies, at least at the level of moral practice, on closer inspection may reveal agreement about moral principles.

Furthermore, the EA response continues, a difference in practice may signal a disagreement about facts rather than a disagreement about principles. An example is the story (possibly spurious) of a society in which parents in late middle age are killed by their children because it is thought that one will spend eternity in the body one has when one dies. If one were to die with an aged body racked by pain and disability, one would suffer for eternity. Accordingly, it is a mark of concern, of caring for one's parents, to make sure that they are sent on their way while still in possession a reasonably healthy body. Thus, despite very different practices in that society and ours, there are underlying similarities of principle, such as the principle that one ought to respect and care for one's parents. We can understand and appreciate the moral principles and motives of the children in this culture while, at the same time, we disagree with them about the facts of existence in the hereafter, assuming there is a hereafter.

And that is not all, say defenders of EA. Suppose there are differences in moral practice between two cultures that cannot be explained as differences in environment or disagreements about facts. These differences certainly seem to rest on different beliefs about which ethical principles are acceptable, or what kinds of things are good or valuable. Yet even if this is right, we should not suppose that the differences are irresolvable, or that they represent a deep split in the ethical sensibility of different cultures. For, if we take human fallibility seriously – as we should – then we should take seriously the possibility that some of these differences can be traced to errors made in the *process* of arriving at ethical beliefs and judgments of value. If these errors are eliminated, the disagreement might disappear. For instance, one or both parties to the disagreement might be making a mistake in logic, or an error, according to their own standards, in judging the weight of reasons and evidence. There also could be errors of misinterpretation or misunderstanding, or even a refusal by one side or the other to see something as an ethical problem. All of these possibilities need to be eliminated, say supporters of EA, before we can conclude that there is real moral diversity about principles and theories that cannot be explained within the framework of ethical absolutism.

Finally, defenders of EA argue, the above considerations show why we need not meekly acquiesce in the face of outlandish moral beliefs like Smith's, in spite of those who, as we will see, advise us to do so. After all, why assume his culture (unlike ours, as our history so richly shows) is immune from error? More than likely they are wrong about a fact about children, or have made a logical or epistemic misstep, or some other mistake. It is much more reasonable to assume that something, somewhere, has gone wrong, than to think that Smith and his culture are infallible. What we need to do is find out what went wrong and do our best to convince them of the error of their ways. Otherwise, we are dangerously close to complicity in this terrible practice.

Opponents of EA – and there are many – are, or should be, prepared to admit all of this. Granted that circumstances differ, that disagreements about facts can conceal agreements about principle, and that other kinds of errors can be made, all that follows is that a great deal of sorting out needs to be done before we can be sure that apparent ethical disagreements are really about ethics and not something else. That having been said, it nevertheless remains true, say the opponents, that different cultures have very different values and principles and very different practices based on those values and principles. These differences go all the way down, so to speak. They cannot be eliminated or patched over in any of the ways discussed for the plain reason that they rest on basic, irreducible differences in moral outlook.

Defenders of EA have a response to this which I will call the "epistemic placement thesis." Suppose someone in our culture denies the truth of one of 1–8. The epistemic placement thesis is that even though he is as convinced of the truth of his belief as we are of ours, and even though he has made no error that anyone can discover, we are better placed than he to know the truth because we do not suffer from epistemic handicaps that prevent him from seeing it. For example, as one prominent defender of epistemic placement puts it, "perhaps he is a victim of a bad upbringing that . . . blinds him to what he would otherwise see; or perhaps he suffers from a cognitive glitch that prevents him from seeing the truth" (Plantinga, 1997); see also Harman and Thomson (1996, p. 12). In other words, he has a false belief about ethics that has its origin in something over which he has no control. It might be his upbringing, or a cognitive glitch, or some other factor. His belief is not the result of a mistake on his part; it is just that, by chance, he finds himself in a situation that prevents him from seeing the truth. Since we do not have this handicap, or so we hope, we are in a better position to know the truth of the matter.

The same kinds of considerations can apply to other cultures, defenders of EA argue. For instance, we know that it is wrong to torture children for fun, so we know that members of Smith's culture have a false belief about ethics even though they are convinced that it is true. If we can find no error of fact, reason, or evidence that causes them to have this false belief, then we can appeal to epistemic placement for an explanation. Perhaps it is a cultural glitch, or something in their traditions or circumstances, that prevent them from seeing the truth. Since we do not suffer from this problem, we are better placed to know the truth about the morality of torture than they are.

The epistemic placement thesis is a last line of defense against those who deny the truth of statements like 1–8, whether they live in other cultures or the house across the street. It may seem arbitrary, or excessively ethnocentric, or even more than a bit smug, but supporters of EA would argue that we should resist the temptation to dismiss it on these grounds. Too much is at stake. We know that 1–8 are true, and if we can find no other reason why a person or society rejects one of them, then the best remaining explanation is that we are in a better epistemic situation than that person or society. We may be mistaken about this, but it is not an arbitrary judgment since we have the absolute and universal truth of 1–8 to back us up – or so the story goes.

A cognitive alternative to EA: ethical relativism

As one might imagine, opponents of EA are not much impressed by the epistemic placement thesis, or, for that matter, any of the other moves that EA's advocates employ. They are convinced that (for the most part) cultural relativism is grounded in genuine moral diversity that cannot be explained away. To bolster their view, they point to internal difficulties in the EA project, e.g., the nagging detail that after donkeys' years of discussion there are still red-in-the-face arguments between absolutists about whether utilitarianism or Kantianism is the "universally true" ethical theory. However, they realize that it is not enough to stand at ringside and chuckle at the wild swings absolutists take at each other. They need to provide their own story about ethics.

Those who would tell this tale face a formidable task. They must elude the Scylla of moral nihilism, i.e., the view that moral diversity shows that, morally speaking, nothing matters, while simultaneously steering clear of the Charybdis of absolutism. Yet, in spite of these dangers, many attempts to construct these tales have been made. They divide roughly into those told by *cognitivists* and *noncognitivists*. Unlike cognitivists, noncognitivists deny that moral statements are true or false in any ordinary sense. Instead, when one says something like "lying is wrong" one is expressing an attitude of disapproval, or issuing the command "do not lie!", or something similar. Non-cognitivist stories are much discussed in the philosophical literature, but little known in the wider world. I will not pursue them here, although some of them are important, because to do so would lead down paths that can be properly explored only in a much longer work. I will stick to cognitivist alternatives to EA, with the caution that they are not the only possibilities available. (A sophisticated version of noncognitivism is defended by Alan Gibbard (1990); for some criticisms of noncognitivism, see Thomson (1996) and Nussbaum (1994).)

The most familiar cognitivist alternative to EA is told by *ethical relativists* (ER). According to one of its main proponents, ethical relativism is the best explanation available for moral diversity. As he puts it, "Moral relativism is a plausible inference from the most plausible account of existing moral diversity" (Harman, 1996, p. 63). The basic story line is that, "Something that is good for some people is bad for others, indifferent to yet others. Moral relativism says that the same is true of moral values and moral norms. According to moral relativism whether something is morally good, right, or just is always relative to a set of moral coordinates, a set of values or moral standards, a certain moral point of view" (Harman, 1996, p. 17).

Since the good, right, and just are always relative to a set of moral coordinates, to determine whether a moral judgment is true it must be compared with a particular moral framework: "For purposes of assigning truth conditions, a judgment of the form, *it would be morally wrong of P to D*, has to be understood as elliptical for a judgment of the form, *in relation to moral framework M, it would be morally wrong of P to D*" (Harman, 1996, p. 4).

This assertion about truth marks a major difference between ER and cultural relativism. Cultural relativism merely states that people in different cultures have different beliefs about morality. What ER adds to this is the claim that these different beliefs are *true* provided that they are in accordance with the moral framework of the culture in question. For example, in relation to our moral framework "torture is wrong" is true, and in relation to the framework of Smith's culture, "torture is permissible," is true.

However, in our culture when most of us say "torture is wrong," we do not mean "torture is wrong in relation to our framework." We mean to say that torture is *simply wrong*. We do this because we believe, as defenders of EA would have us believe, that although there may be many frameworks, there is only *one* set of correct or true moral principles and "torture is wrong" is one of them. For supporters of ER, though, there is no one set of true moral principles. There are *only* local frameworks and the rules they contain. "Moral relativism is a thesis about how things are and a thesis about how things aren't! Moral relativism claims that there is no such thing as objectively absolute good, absolute right, or absolute justice; there is only what is good, right, or just in relation to this or that moral framework" (Harman, 1996, p. 17).

Thus something is good, bad, right, or wrong in relation to the rules and principles of some moral framework or other – where a moral framework is understood as a reasonably coherent set of moral beliefs or principles that a distinct group, culture, or society accepts. There are no absolute ethical truths. Nothing is simply good, bad, right, or wrong independent of specific social or cultural frameworks. That is not how things are. (Are there frameworks of the sort Harman envisions? In modern pluralistic societies, it is not clear that there are. There may be many frameworks in a single society. However, more on this later.)

Notice that ER it is not itself relativistic. If it is true that moral truth is relative to frameworks, it is true for all people at all times. Also, it follows from ER that a particular moral framework cannot be judged better or worse than others from a moral point of view. To make this judgment, we would need a way to compare two frameworks concerning the moral worthiness, as it were, of their various rules and principles. That could be done by using a principle of moral comparison such as "other things being equal, moral frameworks that prohibit torture are better, morally speaking, than moral frameworks that do not." Unfortunately, this principle seems to be one of those objective, universal moral truths that relativists deny exist. Further, to make the principle plausible, one would need to construct an argument for it such as:

1   Torture is wrong.
2   Other things being equal, frameworks that prohibit wrong acts are better, morally speaking, than those that do not.
3   Thus . . . .

However, premise 1 of the argument is clearly intended to be an absolute, objective moral truth. It is unacceptable for supporters of ER, so they would reject the argument. Since the same kinds of troubles attend other principles of moral comparison one might try to construct, a moral comparison of moral frameworks is not an option for ER.

This is a sensible result, say defenders of ER. We have our moral framework, other cultures have their frameworks, and that is the end of it. No framework is morally better or worse than another, nor does it make sense to say that one is "truer" or "more correct" than another. Given that, surely the right attitude toward other frameworks, and the practices they endorse, is tolerance. The last thing anyone needs is a bunch of moral meddlers making nonsensical claims about the relative moral worth of the frameworks of different cultures. The world has seen more than enough of that kind of arrogance and pomposity.

External and internal objections to ER

If ER is the correct story of "how things are ... and how things aren't," then we must give up the idea that 1–8 are universal truths. They are true relative to our framework, but may not be true relative to other frameworks. In addition, the epistemic placement thesis becomes relative to frameworks. We know that 1–8 are true relative to our framework, and we can justly claim to be better placed epistemically than persons in our framework who say they are not. However, we cannot claim to be better placed than people in other cultures who do not accept our framework. Since the truth of ethical statements is relative to frameworks, we can no longer appeal to universal ethical truths to justify claims of epistemic placement across frameworks.

The natural question at this point is: Does ER deliver what its defenders promise? Is it the correct story about ethics? Many writers think not. They have raised two kinds of objections against ER. The first – which I will call the external objection – is that, contrary to what ER claims, it is not a sensible result that we can make no true moral judgments about activities in foreign cultures. Torture, genocide, and any number of other appalling practices are wrong regardless of cultural beliefs. Since ER says otherwise, ER is false. End of that story about ethics.

The external objection is very persuasive. How could it not be for any witness of the deliberate cruelty and rapacity characteristic of so many events of the twentieth century? However, defenders of ER would say that it is not conclusive. They would argue it may be an unpleasant truth, but a truth nonetheless, that different cultures judge things by different standards, and we have no cross-cultural basis for condemning them no matter how repugnant we find their moral principles and practices. We are confined to our framework as they are to theirs, and cannot rightfully judge them by our standards no matter how much we may want to do so. (Consider what Harman has to say (1996, p. 61): "But suppose for the sake of argument that Hitler's moral outlook did not require him to respect all people and did not give him reasons to refrain from ordering the extermination of the Jews. Finally, suppose for the sake of argument that Hitler did not have a compelling reason from any source to refrain and, indeed, had a sufficient reason to proceed with his evil plans. Then any moral judgment that implied that Hitler did have a compelling reason to refrain could not be true. . . . So, the claim that Hitler ought morally not to have ordered the extermination of the Jews would not be true . . .")

This leads to the second set of objections, which I will call internal objections. In one way or another, all these objections try to show that ER is unconvincing or unworkable for reasons other than its implications for cross-cultural moral judgments. There are a number of internal objections to ER; I will discuss just three of them.

The first is that ER makes it hard to understand how moral reform and progress are possible. If there are universal ethical truths, then we make moral progress if we replace mistaken ethical beliefs with universally true ones. Thus moral progress is rather like progress in science when mistaken scientific ideas or theories are replaced by true ones. However, this sort of progress is not possible if what counts as ethical is relative to a particular cultural framework. The reason is that there is no standard independent of the framework against which progress can be measured. Within the framework, one can argue that mistakes were made about facts, logic, or the weight of evidence, but there is no way to argue that the principles that constitute the framework are themselves *morally* defective and should be replaced. Since there is nothing outside the framework, there is nothing that can be used to pry apart the connection between the framework and ethical truth.

The problem is that this seems to defy common sense. It certainly seems as if moral progress has been made since bad old days within living memory. For instance, it was once thought morally permissible in this country to discriminate against people based on race or gender. After long discussion and much resistance, we now know that this is wrong, that it was a mistake to think otherwise, and we feel that moral progress has been made to the extent that this kind of discrimination no longer occurs.

If ER is correct, however, and if we assume that no errors of the sort listed earlier were made, then it was not a mistake to discriminate on the basis of race or gender because it was permissible according to the framework generally followed at the time. Those who discriminated were morally right to do so, and those who believed it was morally wrong to discriminate believed a fiction. Moreover, defenders of ER would argue that it is simple conceit to believe that we have progressed since those dreadful times. We have made no progress, have undergone no reform that replaced false moral beliefs with true ones. For whatever reason, our beliefs and attitudes have changed, that is all. There may have been moral evolution since those days, but no moral improvement, at least not in the sense that our present ethical beliefs are *better* because *truer* than our previous ones.

Capacious though ER may be, it has little room for those who believe that an entire culture can be mistaken about the moral principles it holds, that moral criticisms of accepted principles are rational, and that moral progress is something we should strive for. Moral change is possible; change driven by a vision of moral improvement is not.

A second internal objection is that, were everyone to accept ER, there would no longer be ethical disagreements between people in different cultures with different frameworks. When Jackson says "torture is wrong," everyone would know that she is saying it is wrong *relative* to her culture's framework. When Robinson says "torture is not wrong," he would be saying it is not wrong relative to *his* framework. These are statements of fact; there is no moral disagreement here. Yet surely it is odd, as one writer puts it, "that a view that typically begins by insisting on the intractability of disagreements that others might hope could be settled, should conclude that the disagreements were never real to begin with" (Sturgeon, 1994).

A third internal objection begins with the observation that a single person can be a member of a number of different groups, each with its own moral framework. Thus, suppose Jones is a member of the bar, an employee of a large corporation with a code of ethics, an orthodox Jew, a dual citizen of the USA and Israel, and an official of the Socialist party. There is no guarantee that the behaviors morally approved or required by these different organizations and groups are compatible, so when it comes to making a moral judgment concerning, say, some problem at work, which framework does Jones use? And why just that one and not one of the others?

If the choice is not arbitrary, Jones needs a principled way to justify following one framework rather than another. Presumably the principle (P) would be something like: Given frameworks $F_1, \ldots, F_n$, all of which apply to Jones, in situations of types S one ought to follow framework F_i. Now, the difficulty is that P is a substantive moral principle, although of an unusual kind. It does not directly instruct anyone to do this physical act or refrain from that one, but it does have immediate consequences for the choice of moral frameworks. Hence, it has indirect but definite implications about what Jones morally ought to do. However, P is a moral principle we have constructed for choosing between moral frameworks. It is not itself a part of any framework Jones accepts. Thus, according to ER, it does not govern Jones' moral behavior. From Jones' point of view, it is just irrelevant for the decision about the problem at work, no matter what we may think of it. Further, if P is true, it is not true relative to a specific moral framework that has limited application to a particular group. (If it were, exactly which framework would that be?) Rather, it seems to be another of those objective, universal ethical principles that supporters of ER repudiate.

The upshot of this is that ER has nothing to offer just when Jones needs it the most. It cannot help in choosing between conflicting frameworks. Should Jones be in this predicament, e.g., should there be a conflict between the moral requirements of Jones' religion and work, it is inevitable that subsequent actions will be immoral according to one of the frameworks accepted by Jones. This is a moral tragedy, and it is no mark in favor of ER that it can do nothing to prevent it. Note that it is fruitless for supporters of ER to tell us to avoid accepting incompatible frameworks. For one thing, we may not realize they are incompatible until we are faced with the choice, and then it is too late. For another, the reason we should avoid this is to avoid the moral calamity of being put in a situation in which anything we do is immoral by some framework we accept. However, that we should avoid such calamities is a universal, objective moral truth that ER cannot accommodate.

A closely related objection is that ER is in extreme danger of collapsing into ethical subjectivism, which is the view that each individual is the sole authority concerning the selection and applicability of his or her ethical principles. If ethical subjectivism is true, there are no valid public standards of morality, no standards that apply to more than one person except insofar as different people happen to choose the same standards, or freely agree to follow standards devised by others. Informally, it is the idea that "what's right for me may not be right for you."

The reason relativism is in danger of collapsing into subjectivism is that once one abandons absolute ethical truth for truth relative to a framework, the question arises: Which framework, and who is to decide? The Jones case shows, if I am correct, that

ER cannot answer this question. So, for the unreflective, the choice is made for them, by their parents, or their traditions, or something else. For the reflective, who are (allegedly) unconstrained by absolute ethical truth yet unmoved by local habits, by default, the only answer is "I choose! No one else has any say in the matter." From this, we have ethical subjectivism, the hypothesis that *all* ethical authority rests with the individual. (Of course, one may choose to follow cultural traditions, or a guru, or whatever, but subjectivists deny that such a choice is forced by any moral authority that may reside there.)

One of the many criticisms of subjectivism is that it leads either to ethical nihilism or is incoherent. For example, suppose we ask subjectivist Brown why he chose moral principle Q instead of some other principle. Either his choice was arbitrary or made for some reason. If it was arbitrary, then the ethical principles he lives by are selected for no reason at all. Apparently it does not matter to him that he lives one way rather than another. However, this is nihilism, not ethics. If we want a more sympathetic name for it, perhaps we could call it despair.

The other possibility is that he chose for a reason – presumably a good reason rather than a bad one. However, one mark of a good reason in ethics is that it can withstand scrutiny and criticism by other reasonable people. Put another way, the goodness of a good ethical reason is public in the sense that it is open to inspection and evaluation by more than one person. Hence, if Brown claims he has good reason for making the choice he did, he should be willing to make those reasons available for other people to judge. If they are judged good, then his choice is publicly confirmed. If they are not, he has three options. He could try to convince people that his reasons are good after all, or he could try to find better reasons, or he could abandon his choice of principles. What he cannot do, and still maintain that his choice is based on good reasons, is refuse to defend or modify his position. Were he to do so, he would be back to making an arbitrary choice, or one admittedly based on bad reasons.

Brown's problem is that the process of evaluating reasons for choosing ethical principles is incompatible with subjectivism. Subjectivists assert that the choice of ethical standards is entirely personal and private. No one has any legitimate say in the matter other than the person making the choice. However, if subjectivists are committed to having good reasons for their choice, the process cannot be entirely private since in ethics what counts as a good reason is a public affair. Thus subjectivism, if it is not arbitrary, is incoherent. It says both that the choice of principles is completely private, and that the choice has a public component insofar as it is based on good reasons.

Brown could respond to this criticism in two ways. First, he might reject all this talk of good and bad reasons for choosing moral principles as oppressive and hegemonic. He might deny that intersubjective consensus is what makes a reason good in ethics, and say that what makes one good is that it seems good to him. Thus his choice of principles is not arbitrary because it is based on reasons: *his* reasons, and not reasons that others must approve.

An implication of Brown's response is that he cannot choose the wrong ethical principles since any choice will do provided it is for a reason that seems good to him. Hence, anything Brown decides to do is ethically permissible for him, as long as it is authorized by a principle he has chosen for reasons he finds congenial. For example, if, for reasons he finds sufficient, Brown chooses a principle that permits racial discrimination, then according to his standards it is ethically permissible for him to practice racial discrimination.

Brown's second response might be that he does not need a reason for his choice. He just prefers principle Q to other possibilities. That is enough for him, he might say, even if other people do not share his preferences. (An interesting question is whether Brown's two responses really differ from each other. There are those who would argue, persuasively in my view, that they are not because there can be no such thing as a "private" reason in ethics. So Brown's claim that he has reasons that seem good to him is merely an elaborate way of stating his preferences.)

Again, an implication of this second response is that Brown cannot choose the wrong principles as long as he chooses principles he prefers. Anything he decides to do is ethically permissible for him, provided it is in accordance with his preferences. Thus, if he prefers a principle that permits racial discrimination, then it is ethically permissible for him to engage is such behavior.

There are three replies to Brown. The first is a modification of the external objection. It may be true that the ethical principles a person lives by are ultimately chosen by that person, but it does not follow from this that *any* principle a person might choose is rendered ethically acceptable by the mere fact that it was chosen. People can choose evil principles as well as good ones. Since Brown's arguments do not admit this distinction between principles, they fails as a defense of subjectivism.

The second reply is an appeal to the epistemic placement thesis. Suppose Brown is a member of our culture and further suppose one of his principles is incompatible with one of 1–8. We can justly claim to be epistemically better placed than Brown because we know that 1–8 are all true. Thus we know that any principle that implies otherwise is false. Therefore, we know that Brown has chosen the wrong principles, regardless of his reasons or preferences.

The final reply is that, in both of his responses, Brown denies a fundamental characteristic of ethics – its public nature. Ethics *essentially* involves giving reasons, judging arguments, and evaluating outcomes in a public arena. It cannot be based on private reasons, if there are such things, or personal preferences. If it were, all that would be left is a kind of ethical solipsism. The self would be the only substantial ethical reality, and other people would have ethical standing only if permitted by the whims of the subjectivist. Since this is unrecognizable as an *ethical* viewpoint, the conclusion can only be that subjectivism is not an acceptable ethical story, because it is not a story about ethics at all.

I have discussed subjectivism at some length because many people talk as if they believe it. "Who's to say?", is their usual rhetorical question. Of course, the answer is that *we* are to say. There is no one else, but that is just the point. It is *we*, collectively, who must investigate ethical issues in public forums by doing the hard work of giving arguments, weighing reasons, and drawing conclusions. Only in this way – there is no other – can we find ethical truth.

To summarize, I have argued that ER is at risk of collapsing into subjectivism because it can provide no principled way of choosing between moral frameworks. However, subjectivism is completely implausible as an *ethical* view. Therefore, if ER cannot prevent a descent into subjectivism, and it is not clear how it can, it is an unacceptable ethical story.

Finding the middle ground: pluralistic relativism

All these objections against ER claim that it gives away too much. It is too permissive, and too ready to grant ethical status to reprehensible practices and offensive beliefs. On the other hand, EA may seem too restrictive, and not sufficiently respectful of the real differences and possibilities that there are in the world outside its understanding of the right and the good. Thus, the thought occurs: if we could find a mean between these extremes – some way to combine their virtues while avoiding their vices – then we might have something.

Several attempts have been made to find a middle ground between EA and ER, an ethical porridge that is just right. I will briefly discuss one of them called pluralistic relativism (PR).

What seems right about ER is that people in different societies organize their lives around a plurality of diverse and irreducible values and conceptions of a good and worthwhile life. These values and conceptions of the good are both incommensurable in theory and uncombinable in practice. They do not fit together and cannot fit together. Nevertheless, for a large but restricted class of them, none can be judged morally better or worse than the others.

What seems right about EA is that some things are morally good, bad, right or wrong for everyone. For example, whether one lives in Terra Haute or Tierra del Fuego, there are minimum physical, economic, and social conditions necessary for anything remotely resembling a decent human life. To have these things is beneficial for anyone; and it is morally wrong for anyone to be intentionally deprived of them for insufficient reason.

Assume all of this is true. Assume that there are incommensurable values and conceptions of the good, and that some things are good, bad, right or wrong for anyone. The puzzle is to put these two ideas together in an ethical view that makes sense. Advocates of PR try to do it like this. Suppose moral systems or frameworks have the social function of establishing rules or procedures within which people have a reasonable opportunity to achieve their vision of the good life without unjustifiably denying the same to others. On this view, as one defender of PR writes, "morality is partly a system of rules that human beings have evolved in order to work and live together. It therefore serves to regulate cooperation, conflicts of interest, the division of labor, and it specifies the conditions under which some people have authority over others" (Wong, 1996, p. 383). In addition, morality "in the form of character ideals and conceptions of the good life specifies what is worthwhile for the individual to become and pursue" (p. 383). Thus moral frameworks function to regulate social interactions and promote moral ideals.

Understanding moral frameworks in functional terms hints at a non-moral way they can be compared. Consider an ordinary kitchen knife. A kitchen knife has a function. If we say it is a good knife, we give it no moral praise, we only say that it performs its function effectively – it sharpens quickly, holds an edge, handles easily, and so on. To say that one kitchen knife is better than another is just to say that it functions better. It does better what kitchen knives are intended to do. Similarly, if moral frameworks have a non-moral function, a good moral framework is one that performs its function well. If one moral framework is better than another, it performs that function better. There is no apparent moral judgment here, only a practical one about the relative merits of different moral tools.

If PR is the correct story about ethics, then *moral truth* is still relative to moral frameworks. This is the relativistic part of PR, the part that permits people in different frameworks to have true moral beliefs about the different values prevalent in those frameworks. However, if frameworks have a non-moral function, then it might turn out that some moral frameworks are *functionally* better than others. For example, those that effectively regulate cooperation are functionally better than those that do not. This is the absolutist part of PR since it permits judgments of good function across frameworks based on universal criteria of functional goodness.

A purported advantage of PR is that what were once thought to be moral disagreements between cultures can be recast as practical disagreements about how effectively a practice or belief functions in a culture. So, our disagreement with Smith is not about the morality of torture – it remains a moral truth in his culture that torture is permissible – it is about the practical, functional effects of that belief. Consequently, in our discussions with Smith, we do not claim that torture is morally wrong. We argue that it is functionally bad, e.g., it encourages conflict or has other deleterious effects. The hope is that by talking about function, instead of ethics, it will be easier to achieve agreement because functional effectiveness is an empirical matter that can be settled by empirical means once both sides agree on the appropriate criteria for judging good function.

But, that is the rub. It is easy to devise criteria for judging a functionally good knife; it is not so easy to discover criteria for judging functionally good moral frameworks. It seems probable that earlier arguments about what is morally good across cultures will be replicated in arguments about what is functionally good across cultures. Functional relativists will argue that good function is strictly a cultural matter; functional absolutists will claim that it is not. The dance begins again.

We could try to avoid this problem by appealing to the intuition from EA that some things are good or bad for everyone. Unfortunately, it is not clear that this will help us very much. Is human nature so transparent that we can say with confidence what is functionally good or bad for everyone? Even if it is, will it be enough to give us stable functional criteria, or is human nature too ephemeral? Further, might good function be so variable, so tied to time, place, and circumstance that it is essentially useless for the purposes we want it to serve? And are we really willing to say that the only reason genocide and torture are universally wrong is because they are functionally inefficient? These questions, and many others like them, need to be answered before any comparative functional judgments about moral frameworks can be made. It is not an inviting prospect.

As it is presently, PR is little more than a bare schema about how to combine some of the insights of EA and ER into a theory of moral function. Whether it has any prospects of being completed is a matter of some dispute (Rorty, 1989; 1996). Still, it has its attractions. It has affinities with liberal democratic theory and the integrative social contract theory proposed by Tom Dunfee and Tom Donaldson (1994). See also, Galston (1996) and, in the same issue, the reply to Galston by Altman (1996), and the very interesting piece by Xiaorong Li (1996). However, PR has a long way to go before it can be considered a competitor to the other positions discussed in this paper.

Ethics in business

I suspect that those hardy souls who have managed to make it this far are thinking: This is all very nice, but it says nothing about what a business person is to *do* when faced with ethical issues or problems in other societies. *That* is the real question, not the endless spiral of philosophical argument and counterargument.

I am not unsympathetic with this protest. Fortunately, there are other places in this volume where concrete advice about what to do is given, and I am more than happy to leave it to those authors to lend substance to this somewhat abstract discussion of relativism and absolutism. Still, for what it is worth, I will venture this.

For the reasons I gave earlier, I believe that the plain vanilla version of ER presented in this article is not acceptable. More sophisticated versions of ER, and some noncognitivist theories, have responses to some of the internal objections I raised. However, these theories have serious problems of their own – so serious that they are of little practical use. For example, like PR, several of them are scant proposals or sketches. Others rely on highly controversial theories about the meaning of moral words, or the possibility of moral truth, or the role of moral emotions. And, I believe, all of them are vulnerable to the external objection.

When I discussed the external objection – the objection that practices like genocide and torture are simply wrong – I did not respond to the assertion from ER that it may be unpleasant, but it is a fact, that we can make no true moral judgments about these practices so long as they occur in other frameworks. It is time to remedy that omission.

It is not unpleasant that that things like torture and genocide occur in the world, it is a horror. Generally speaking supporters of ER do not deny this; they are as horrified as anybody. What they deny is that we can pass moral judgment on these acts when they occur in other cultures. We can feel as much outrage and revulsion as we like, but we cannot judge, or cannot truly judge, their moral worth.

Yet, what supporters of ER sometimes overlook, and sometimes deny, is that without the judgment, the outrage we feel would soon disappear, to be replaced, possibly, with mild regret. It is the judgment that justifies the outrage. Without it, outrage cannot be sustained. Further, if we convince ourselves that we cannot judge what others do, it is but a short step to cutting ourselves off from their folly, and their agony. We can make no judgments, we would say. It is their business, so let them sort it out. We have our own concerns to attend to.

This sort of moral disengagement – moral cowardice some might say – is, in my view, precisely the wrong way to approach ethics. As I said earlier, ethics is public by its very nature and, in the final days of this century, that public is more and more all of us, wherever we happen to be, whatever culture we find ourselves in. To claim, as ER must claim, that we are a loose confederation of separate publics, each with its own separate moral rules, is a retreat to the moral dark ages. Kant was right at least about this: from the moral point of view, we are all in this together.

Is this an argument? Not exactly. Will it convince those who think otherwise? Not likely. I offer it as a petition – a request – that we consider carefully the full implications of the ethical stories that are told before we make moral commitments that we may later have good reason to repent.

Conclusion

To conclude I would like to mention two things. The first is that we are fortunate that there is much more moral agreement across the world than ER admits. We are as much alike, morally, as we are different. Wilson (1993) argues convincingly that all cultures share certain moral norms, and that such norms are necessary for the survival of any culture. For instance, as far as I know, every culture is repelled by the thought of torturing children for fun. The purpose of the example was to engage a certain kind of moral intuition, not to make a factual claim about practices in distant lands.

The second is this: I do not doubt that the grinding wheels of international capitalism have done more to crush out cross-cultural moral differences than any theory of ethics has ever done. I suspect this is likely to continue. In these times, ethics can, at best, make changes at the margins, as the economists like to say. However, it is only at the margins, if it is anywhere, that we can begin to remake the world as it ought to be.

References

Altman, A. 1996: In defense of enlightenment liberalism. *Report from the Institute for Philosophy and Public Policy*, 16(2), Spring, 13–18.

Donaldson, T. and Dunfee, T. W. 1994: Toward a unified conception of business ethics: Integrative social contracts theory. *Academy of Management Review*, 19, 252–84.

Galston, W. A. 1996: Value pluralism and political liberalism. *Report from the Institute for Philosophy and Public Policy*, 16(2), Spring, 7–13.

Gibbard, A. 1990: *Wise Choices, Apt Feelings*. Cambridge: Harvard University Press.

Harman, G. 1996: Moral relativism. In (Harman and Thomson, 1996, pp. 3–64, 157–187).

Harman, G. and Thomson, J. J. 1996: *Moral Relativism and Moral Objectivity*. Oxford: Blackwell.

Li, X. 1996: "Asian Values" and the universality of human rights. University of Maryland, College Park, MD: Institute of Philosophy and Public Policy, 18–23.

Nussbaum, M. 1994: Skepticism about practical reason in literature and law. *Harvard Law Review*, 103(3), January, 714–44.

Plantinga, A. 1997: Ad Hick. *Faith and Philosophy*, 43(7), July, 297.

Rorty, A. O. 1989: Relativism, persons, and practices. In M. Krausz (ed.), *Relativism: Interpretation and Confrontation*, Notre Dame: University of Notre Dame Press, 418–40.

Rorty, A. O. 1996: The many faces of morality. In P. A. French, T. E. Uehling, Jr, and H. Wettstein (eds), *Midwest Studies in Philosophy Volume XX: Moral Concepts*, Notre Dame: University of Notre Dame Press, 67–82.

Sturgeon, N. L. 1994: Moral disagreement and moral relativism. In Paul et al. (1994, p. 81).

Thomson, J. J. 1996: Moral objectivity. In Harman and Thomson (1996, pp. 67–154, 188–217).

Wilson, J. Q. 1993: *The Moral Sense*. New York: The Free Press.

Wong, D. B. 1996: Pluralistic relativism. In P. A. French, T. E. Uehling, Jr, and H. Wettstein (eds), *Midwest Studies in Philosophy Volume XX: Moral Concepts*, Notre Dame: University of Notre Dame Press, 378–99.

Further reading

Benedict, R. 1934: *Patterns of Culture*. New York: Penguin.

Berlin, I. 1969: *Four Essays on Liberty*. Oxford: Oxford University Press.

Fried, C. 1978: *Right and Wrong*. Cambridge: Harvard University Press.

Hare, R. M. 1969: *The Language of Morals*. London: Oxford University Press.

Herskovits, M. 1972: *Cultural Relativism: Perspectives in Cultural Pluralism*. New York: Vintage.

Ladd, J. 1973: *Ethical Relativism*. Belmont, CA: Wadsworth Publishing.

MacIntyre, A. 1981: *After Virtue*. Notre Dame: University of Notre Dame Press.

Mackie, J. L. 1977: *Ethics: Inventing Right and Wrong*. Harmondsworth: Penguin.

Nagel, T. 1986: *The View From Nowhere*. New York: Oxford University Press.

Parfit, D. 1984: *Reasons and Persons*. Oxford: Oxford University Press.

Paul, E. F., Miller, F. D., and Paul, J. (eds) 1994: *Cultural Pluralism and Moral Knowledge*, Cambridge: Cambridge University Press.

Rorty, R. 1989: *Contingency, Irony, and Solidarity*. Cambridge: Cambridge University Press.

Singer, P. (ed.) 1991: *A Companion to Ethics*. Oxford: Blackwell Publishers.

Stevenson, C. L. 1994: *Ethics and Language*. New Haven: Yale University Press.

Stevenson, L. 1974: *Seven Theories of Human Nature*. Oxford: Oxford University Press.

Walzer, M. 1993: *Spheres of Justice*, New York: Basic Books.

7

Feminist theory and business ethics

ROBBIN DERRY

Feminist theory encompasses a broad range of thinking about the roles and experiences of women. Writers and scholars in the feminist genre share a commitment to valorize the contributions of women, to recognize and reduce the barriers to women's participation in every field, and to promote the emancipation and equality of women. Feminist ethical theories focus on the construction of ethical systems which reflect the experiences of women and address the moral issues confronting women in society. Feminist research draws on the strengths and interests of women to create innovative methods for gathering data and grounding theory.

Contemporary research in business ethics demonstrates little awareness of feminist theory. Two broad areas hold potential for the integration of business ethics and feminist theory: the articulation of ethical theory, and the research methodologies underlying ethical theory and practice. The scholarly literature in business ethics reveals occasional and limited reference to one strand of feminist ethical theory, but virtually no application of feminist research methods. The use of feminist theory and research methods could significantly extend the scope of issues addressed and the depth of learning from research in the field of business ethics.

Feminist ethical theory

Feminist ethical theories are numerous, representing many voices and perspectives. In her useful taxonomy, Rosmarie Tong distinguishes four approaches of feminist theories of ethics: feminine, maternal, feminist, and lesbian (Tong, 1997). Of these, only the feminine approach has been explored in business ethics theory-building. However, each offers a potential contribution to the study of ethics in the institutions and interactions of business.

Femine ethics

Feminine ethics include those theories which explore the behaviors of caring, nurturing, and building close relationships, attributes often ascribed to women. These are contrasted to ethical attributes ascribed to men and to male-centered ethical theories: the concerns for rights, justice, principles, and individual autonomy (Tong, 1993). The underlying assumptions of feminine ethics – that women and men approach moral reasoning from different experiential backgrounds – provide the theoretical grounding for studies of gender differences in ethical and moral decision making. While the feminine approach recognizes and values the experiences of women as distinct from men, it contributes to continued gender stereotyping by emphasizing the differences between men and women, while masking significant differences between women.

Maternal ethics

Maternal ethics are theories which privilege the mother–child relationship, and suggest that this primary relationship be considered as paradigmatic for studying the ethics of social and civic interactions. Virginia Held proposes the term "mothering person" as more gender neutral than mother, and argues that a non-contractual perspective for determining social ethics more realistically reflects and illuminates our important relationships. On these grounds, she suggests that the perspective of the mothering person and child is a worthwhile replacement for the fictional but ubiquitous rational economic man (Held, 1993). The maternal approach to ethics, like the feminine, gives good weight to the real-life experiences of women and men, in this case as parents. It validates the primacy of the parent–child relationship, which virtually everyone shares in some form. Consideration of this relationship as paradigmatic prompts a re-evaluation of the nature and quality of workplace interactions. Critics of the maternal approach argue that the mother–child relationship is inadequate to inform a study of the full range of relationships in our personal and professional lives.

Feminist ethics

In contrast to the ethical approaches which emphasize the differing experiences and characteristics of women and men, feminist ethics focus on the social and political systems which perpetuate the oppression and subordination of women. Those who adopt a feminist approach are generally committed to the goals defined by Alison Jagger (1992):

- To articulate moral critiques of action and practices that perpetuate women's subordination
- To prescribe morally justifiable ways of resisting such actions and practices
- To envision morally desirable alternatives that will promote women's emancipation.

Feminist approaches critique traditional ethics for their lack of attention to gender oppression as an important ethical issue, and for their contribution to repressive systems by undervaluing women's moral experiences and insights. They also critique feminine approaches to ethics for their tendency to put women and men in tidy categories by "what women do" and "what men do" which are often grossly simplified to "women care" and "men make rules." This tendency privileges women who are good carers and devalues women who have other strengths, thereby oppressing all women by limiting the acceptable behavioral options. Critics of the feminist approach argue that ethical systems should not be limited to, or focused on, the particular concerns of one gender. Feminist ethicists agree, pointing out that traditional ethics are flawed by their narrow focus on men's interests and issues. Further, they assert that the emancipation of women should be a concern for ethicists of both genders.

Lesbian ethics

Lesbian approaches to ethics articulate an even greater distance between their goals and those of traditional ethics and the other feminist approaches. Among the lesbian theories, there is a shared interest in the definition and promotion of what is good for women, as distinct from what is good for a heterosexual society. Heterosexuality is seen as inherently repressive to women, so that women's freedom from subordination will be achieved only by exploring new patterns of relationships with other women (Hoagland, 1989). Given the entrenched systems of male power, and the history of domination of women in our civilization, patriarchy pervades even the definitions of what constitutes good and right. Lesbian ethics suggest that women working within the framework of a heterosexual society are working to improve a system that continues to benefit men and harm women. From the lesbian perspective, what is good for women is that which furthers their freedom and self-discovery. Thus, valuable ethical systems should not be concerned with duties and obligations which constrain and control behavior. Rather, ethics should encourage the playfulness and creativity of women, and discourage relationships of power and authority. In this way, lesbian ethicists choose to create their own moral revolution, rebelling against the norms of the patriarchal hierarchy. Critics argue that it is impractical to propose separatist ethics when our society needs systems that all can follow for moral guidance. Indeed, the individual self-improvement aspects of lesbian ethics are at odds with the traditional focus on ethical social systems. The reasons for this variance are found in the differing assumptions about what is good.

Application of ethical theories

Each of these "woman-centered approaches" to ethical theory offers new insights on how ethics can be understood and practiced; nonetheless, these perspectives have had little attention or application in the field of business ethics.

The feminine approach to ethics is most in evidence, as researchers have probed the putative Gilligan thesis that women and men are oriented differently when it comes to moral reasoning (Gilligan, 1982; Derry, 1987). Despite Gilligan's disclaimers about her contribution to this theory, many business ethicists seem to be interested in whether such differences exist, and in the question of whether men or women are measurably more ethical in particular contexts (Khazanchi, 1995; Smith and Oakley, 1997; Schminke, 1997). It has also been argued that the ethics of care could make a valuable contribution to business organizations where relationships are defined primarily in economic and contractarian terms (Wicks et al., 1994; Burton and Dunn, 1996; Liedtka, 1996). Adding the ethics of care to the existing bag of moral reasoning tools used by business ethicists may effectively integrate a theory derived from women's experience. Such an expansion may be worthwhile in the process of organizational analysis and ethical problem solving. However, most of these studies do little to contribute to the goals of emancipation articulated by Jagger. In the terms defined here, this research draws on feminine ethics, not feminist.

Feminist approaches to ethics have been touched on only briefly in business ethics research (Fisher and Fowler, 1995; Derry, 1996), as have maternal ethics (Frederick,

1995). In both cases these approaches have been described in hopeful terms, as offering insights which could alter the role of ethics in the study and practice of management. Lesbian approaches to ethics have not been addressed in the business ethics literature.

The inattention to these ethical approaches is a loss for the field of research and practice of business ethics. The strengths and experiences of women could contribute to a broader range of behavioral models for both men and women in the workplace. Feminine ethics highlights some of those strengths. Similarly, maternal ethics encourages us to reflect on real-life relationships, particularly those which shape primary moral development. As children and as parents, we learn about dividing limited resources, motivating others to achieve common goals, the results of truth-telling and lying, the options for expressing disagreement, and the means of addressing conflict. These lessons are broadly applicable in the business world.

Feminist ethics puts the agenda of liberation and equality on the front burner. As corporations struggle with the issues of diversity and multiculturalism in making the transition to global markets, new ethical approaches are needed to explicitly address these issues. Traditional ethical frameworks, relying on the values of the majority to determine normative standards, are inadequate to resolve pressing questions about the treatment of the "least advantaged" in our society. Without a commitment to recognizing and resisting oppression, these ethical theories are limited in the scope of issues they can effectively address.

Feminist research methods

In addition to the ethical theories articulated by feminist scholars, there are a number of innovative feminist approaches to research methodology that could make significant and interesting contributions to business ethics. Currently, business ethics research reflects the fields of its origins, drawing on the structural discourse of organizational theory, the theoretical constructs of applied philosophy, and the quantitative methods of economics. Each of these embraces the positivist traditions of objectivity and personal detachment as conditions for reliable data gathering and theory building. In contrast, feminists in social research have adopted methods which challenge these traditions, redefining the conditions for "reliable," "valid," and "rigorous" research.

In contrast to feminist ethics which advocate change, these methods themselves are the change from conventional epistemologies. Collectively, they represent alternative ways of knowing, seeing, and gathering data. Using these methods has enabled women and men "to be producers of knowledge without being trapped into the reproduction of patriarchal ways of knowing" (Campbell, 1982, p. 24).

Feminists use many methods of research; in fact, there is disagreement among the researchers themselves about whether there are specific feminist methodologies. Some scholars decry positivist methods as antithetical to feminism, while others insist that feminists must use quantitative as well as qualitative methods so as to demonstrate competence with rigorous scientific standards. The debate illustrates the challenge for women to excel in a system that they are committed to changing. This conflict is described by Marjorie DeVault (1990, p. 701): ". . . the dilemma for the feminist scholar, always, is to find ways of working within some disciplinary tradition while aiming at an intellectual revolution that will transform the tradition."

Shulamit Reinharz (1992) in her book, *Feminist Methods in Social Research*, points out that "... feminists have used all the existing methods and have invented some new ones as well" (p. 4). She takes the broad position that feminist methods are all the methods used by feminists, including interview research, ethnography, case studies, survey research, action research, statistical analysis, cross cultural research, and content analysis. What makes these methods feminist? The answer is found not strictly in the methods themselves, but in how they are used. The methods are adapted, revised, and reconsidered in the process of defining the goals and collecting the data.

To demonstrate, we can imagine a feminist project researching decision making in a large corporation. A topic is derived from the experiences of the researchers who worked in clerical positions before attending graduate school. They choose to study the role of secretaries as decision makers so as to "give voice" to women who have previously been "invisible" in decision-making studies. In the process of interviewing the participants, the researchers may structure the interviews in ways that reduce the power differential between the researchers and the interviewees. The interview questions are more likely to be semi-structured or open-ended, allowing for free interaction between the researcher and interviewee. In this way, the researchers can induce theory from the descriptions of real-life experiences, rather than forcing the responses to fit a pre-determined theory. The researchers are open to discovery and detail, which may alter the direction of the project, but will certainly contribute to the learning about the topic, the subjects, and the method being used.

In writing up their findings, the feminist researchers on this project may reflect on their own experience as secretaries, or perhaps describe how this research experience challenged their stereotypes about organizational roles and assumed competence. They are likely to share their findings as well as their personal learning with the interviewees. They may use this research to rethink their interviewing process, and discuss the level of trust or distrust between the interviewers and interviewees. The researchers may also present their findings directly to the organization managers, proposing concrete steps that could be taken to increase two-way communication with secretaries.

This imaginary interview project, using methods accessible to all social scientists, embraces many of the characteristics found in feminist research. These characteristics are: a research topic derived from personal experience; self-disclosure by the researcher as a way of building trust and establishing a shared commitment; the use of open-ended questions to enable participants to "tell their stories;" consideration of the assumed roles of power and authority in the research process; sharing knowledge (theory and findings) with the participants so as to reduce the distance between the production of knowledge and the use of knowledge; presenting research findings in the first person and engaging in self-reflection about the levels of learning; creating an action component to advocate change; and building theory inductively.

Discussing the characteristics of feminist methods, Shulamit Reinharz (1992, p. 194) suggests that "learning should occur on three levels in any research project: the levels of person, problem, and method ... (T)he researcher would learn about herself, about the subject matter under study, and about how to conduct research." These kinds of learning empower the researcher with self-knowledge, create alternative models of producing knowledge, and contribute multi-faceted data to social theoretical constructs.

Application of research methods

The methods and characteristics of feminist research could be readily integrated with business ethics research. For example, research topics could be selected with more relevance to the lives and personal interests of the researchers. Ethical issues in the workplace are commonly described from an arm's length distance, with little or no connection made to the ethical dilemmas faced by the researcher in her own work-life. Open discussions of ethical conflicts within the field itself are strictly avoided. However, much could be gained by candid investigation and discussion of the ethical issues inherent in such topics as research collaboration, hiring and promotion, the tenure review process, grading disputes, departmental power struggles, obligations for disclosure in consulting, and the balancing of family responsibilities and work productivity.

In the area of research design, business ethicists could also make good use of feminist methods. Open-ended questions and self-disclosure by the researchers could foster a fruitful dialogue, contributing to theory-building based more on experience, and less on philosophical hypotheses. In surveying student populations, attention could be given to issues of authority in research relationships, in particular to the interaction of professors and students in the roles of researchers and subjects. Gained knowledge could be shared with students serving as researcher assistants as well as subjects. The research discussion would reflect on the learning of students at both levels, as well as the process of collaboration between professors and students.

Research articles in business ethics frequently conclude with an articulation of future research questions. In suggesting related research topics, a self-reflective perspective could inform colleagues of critical methodological insights gained in the research process. Rather than ending with vague policy recommendations for unknown decision makers, we should use our research learning as an opportunity to propose specific action strategies: for corporate managers, for researchers, and for individual employees. Rather than simply publishing these strategies in an academic journal, we could find ways to move them toward implementation. The action plan and implementation would be important components of the research project.

Conclusion

The field of business ethics has emerged from the convergence of interests in several disciplines. Researchers have learned to converse in the languages of philosophy and management studies. The corpus of business ethics research generally reflects the conventional methods and limitations of both fields. Yet as a group of innovative, ideologically driven scholars, business ethicists face the opportunity to broaden their skills by engaging in more reflective research. The feminist research methods, discussed above, hold the potential for greatly increased learning on the three levels of "the person, the problem, and the method." If we are willing to explore beyond the positivist process, we may learn about ourselves and the research method as well as the problem under study. If we are willing to admit and discuss that learning in the context of our research presentations and publications, we will be doing the field a much greater service than if we merely write up the numerical or theoretical results of our research.

References

Burton, B. K. and Dunn, C. P. 1996: Feminist ethics as moral grounding for stakeholder theory. *Business Ethics Quarterly*, 6(2), 133–47.

Campbell, M. A. 1982: Creating feminist sociology. *Society for Women in Sociology Network*, 12(1), 23–4.

Derry, R. 1987: Moral reasoning in work-related conflicts. *JAI Research in Corporate Social Performance and Policy*, 9, 25–49.

Derry, R. 1996: Toward a feminist firm: Comments on John Dobson and Judith White. *Business Ethics Quarterly*, 6(1), 101–109.

DeVault, M. L. 1990: Talking and listening from women's standpoint: Feminist strategies for interviewing and analysis. *Social Problems*, 37(1), 701–21.

Fisher, D. K. and Fowler, S. B. 1995: Reimagining moral leadership in business. *Business Ethics Quarterly*, 5(1), 29–42.

Frederick, W. C. 1995: *Values, Nature, and Culture in the American Corporation*. New York: Oxford University Press.

Gilligan, C. 1982: *In a Different Voice: Psychological Theory and Women's Development*. Cambridge, Mass.: Harvard University Press.

Held, V. 1993: *Feminist Morality: Transforming Culture, Society, and Politics*. Chicago: University of Chicago Press.

Hoagland, S. L. 1989: *Lesbian Ethics*. Palo Alto, Ca.: Institute of Lesbian Studies.

Jaggar, A. 1992: Feminist ethics. In L. Becker and C. Becker (eds), *Encyclopedia of Ethics*. New York: Garland Press, 363–4.

Khazanchi, D. 1995: Unethical behavior in information systems: The gender factor. *Journal of Business Ethics*, 14, 741–9.

Liedtka, J. M. 1996: Feminist morality and competitive reality: A role for an ethic of care? *Business Ethics Quarterly*, 6(2), 179–200.

Reinharz, S. 1992: *Feminist Methods in Social Research*. New York: Oxford University Press.

Schminke, M. 1997: Gender differences in ethical frameworks and evaluation of others' choices in ethical dilemmas. *Journal of Business Ethics*, 16, 55–65.

Smith, P. L. and Oakley, E. F. III 1997: Gender-related differences in ethical and social values of business students: Implications for management. *Journal of Business Ethics*, 16, 37–45.

Tong, R. 1993: *Feminine and Feminist Ethics*. Belmont, Ca.: Wadsworth, Inc.

Tong, R. 1997: Feminist ethics. In P. H. Werhane and R. E. Freeman (eds), *The Blackwell Encyclopaedic Dictionary of Business Ethics*. Oxford: Blackwell Publishers.

Wicks, A. C., Gilbert, D. R. Jr, and Freeman, R. E. 1994: A feminist reinterpretation of the stakeholder concept. *Business Ethics Quarterly*, 4(4), 475–98.

8

Business ethics in a free society

TIBOR R. MACHAN

A most serious controversy about capitalism is whether people who manage commerce and business (the professional arm of commerce) may be trusted to use their own judgment concerning how to conduct themselves. One need only look for the topic under the label, "the social responsibility of corporations," – even though this label begs the question by assuming that businesses have basic, binding responsibilities to society and the communities in which they live and conduct their professional tasks – to see whether they have made any commitment to fulfill such responsibilities. While not entirely unreasonable, the idea should not simply be assumed to be correct. Is there a social responsibility for artists, the press, athletes, or writers? Certainly no subdisciplines in ethics developed throughout universities, colleges, and professional schools focus on such issues. Juilliard does not teach such a course, nor do other institutions of higher learning where the various arts are taught. Some would argue, plausibly, that spelling out such standards for (not to mention imposing them on) artists is an infringement on artistic creativity. The same may be said about writers and dancers. (There are no courses in the ethics of scholarship, either, let alone how to teach professional ethics.)

Graduate schools preparing students for teaching positions at universities have no such courses. It is assumed, apparently, that when the students arrive at their jobs, they themselves will make sure that they behave ethically in their classrooms, and as they carry out their scholarly work. Or, perhaps it is assumed that students who embark on degrees in art, philosophy, or literature are already sufficiently moral and require no special courses on ethics? But this assumption is unfounded. Why, then, should we impose ethics courses on those who are obtaining education in the field of business?

Whatever we conclude about the teaching of applied ethics in art, science, and the professions, let us assume for the moment that we need some help in how we think about our ethical responsibilities in various fields of work. Accordingly, we can ask the question, "What are the moral responsibilities, of those who embark upon a career in business?" It is this topic that will explore here by way of considering the views of Milton Friedman, someone who is closely identified with the free market and whose writing on precisely this topic has been widely discussed and criticized.

In the field of business ethics, Friedman's account of the social responsibility of corporations stands out as work that is under extensive scrutiny if not relentless criticism. His basic view – that corporations have the obligation to make a profit within the framework of the legal system, nothing more – is discussed by nearly everyone who writes in this field, and Friedman's own piece is reprinted in virtually all collections of business ethics essays. It is notable that Friedman is usually represented as holding the more radical view that business ought to aim solely at profit rather than the milder version in which the ethics of society ought also be followed in the course of doing business. This is understandable, though, especially in light of the apparent cultural relativism implicit in Friedman's position. In an international and intercultural world of commerce, however, the prescription to strive for profit is far more direct and practicable than that requiring one to follow "law [and] ethical custom." In short, the only genuine ethical position Friedman addresses is that profit ought to be pursued, although he agrees that allowances need to be made to circumstances (Friedman, 1961, 1970; Carson, 1993).

The main complaint about his view is, first of all, that it is basically intolerant of government intervention in economic affairs. However, criticism begins with the lament that Friedman's moral outlook is too thin. The belief that executives in business enterprises are *morally* obligated, primarily if not exclusively, to make a profit is just too incredible, is it not? There surely must be something more to what such executives ought to do in their professional capacity. This skepticism about Friedman's view shows the impact of neo-Kantian moral theory, exhibited in most works in contemporary moral philosophy, including some that deal explicitly with business ethics (Baier, 1958; Etzioni, 1988). According to this theory, nothing can be morally praiseworthy or even significant that enhances only personal or even public objectives, that is directed to the satisfaction of some private or vested interest or inclination.

Despite some recent analytical, as distinct from strictly critical, work on Friedman's ideas, the question can and should be raised as to whether the libertarian economic philosophy Friedman himself embraces might not be compatible with a different, let us say richer, conception of the moral responsibility of corporations. This chapter will argue that it is. In particular, a position called "classical individualism" will be spelled out here, and it will be shown that this position can address the issue of the social responsibility of corporations better than the one that Friedman defends. Yet classical individualism will remain fully compatible with the position that everyone, including people in business, have a basic right to negative liberty. It will not yield to the contention that the freedom of action of corporations should be limited by government in the effort to advance responsible corporate conduct (Galbraith, 1982; Nader et al., 1976; Hessen, 1979).

Classical individualism

Classical individualism (or egoism) is the view that all ought to benefit themselves, first of all (though not exclusively) and that an objective view of human nature provides standards of guidelines on what benefits a person. Furthermore, it is by reference to such standards that private, professional, and political conduct ought to be carried out. According to this form of individualism, contrary to Marx's (1977) claim that "the human essence is the true collectivity of man," the human essence is the true individuality of every human being (Rand, 1961; Norton, 1976; Machan, 1998), without the implication, however, that the human individual is self-sufficient, capable of living a full life cut off from others.

Classical individualism is an ethics of self-development, self-perfection, only with a greater role for individuality than found in similar views, mainly because of the discovery of the fundamental individuality of human nature. Accordingly, whereas it is often argued that a communitarian theory of politics could be inferred from an Aristotelian virtue ethics, classical individualism rejects this and holds that the politics that is justified is libertarian. The reason for this view is that, in classical individualism, the task of self-perfection must be chosen by the individual. There is, here, a greater emphasis on individual choice and responsibility, following the Kantian stress that "ought" implies "can." If a person or group of people ought to act in certain ways, this is of moral significance only if the option of not so acting is actual and not foreclosed, even by the punitive measures of the law. Morally significant conduct cannot be regimented or imposed by force – which raises the perennial issue of freedom of the will, concerning which the classical individualist position takes an affirmative position; see Sperry (1976, 1983) and Machan (1974). This is how classical individualism gives support to the libertarian polity. Yet it is also important that classical individualism provides such a libertarian polity with its distinctive rationale, not with the standard classical liberal or *homo economicus* support that stresses the greater efficiency of free action for purposes of securing public prosperity.

Classical individualism and corporate responsibility

Because the central features of the free market system may be defended on the basis of this more robust individualism, Friedman's position on the social responsibility of corporations could now be amended without entailing any compromise of his libertarianism – that is, his *laissez-faire* economics. Nevertheless, as will be evident presently, corporations have a broader range of responsibilities than Friedman ascribes to them.

The essential task of businesses – firms, partnerships, companies, enterprises, and other establishments – needs to be defensible by reference to the general tenets of whatever turns out to be the ethical theory that is most successful, most suited to the task of guiding us most consistently, coherently, and completely in our conduct. Needless to say, it would be difficult to demonstrate here that classical individualism is this ethical theory. What can be achieved here, I think, is to show that classical individualism is a richer ethical framework from which to identify the ingredients of a system of general and professional ethics than that presupposed in Friedman's often-discussed theory of the social responsibility of corporations. Let me define "professional ethics" as a code of conduct pertaining to a specialized field of activity – law, medicine, education, diplomacy, or business – justified in terms of a sound ethics (Machan, 1988b). Professional ethics, to have any binding persuasive force, must rest on a sound general ethical system, lest it amount to nothing more than a conventional framework that some people prefer and wish to impose on others.

By "business," I have in mind an organized human endeavor that has, as its dominant end, economic enhancement or prosperity, or wealth. That is, businesses are profit-making institutions. (By "profit," I do not have in mind the technical term defined in tax law or even economics in general, but the familiar idea of prospering in one's ability to obtain goods and services for purchase in the market place.) Whereas physicians heal, attorneys make cases before the law, educators develop and impart knowledge, business professionals have as their central task increasing wealth. Business ethics, then, is a branch of professional ethics. It is concerned with how people engaged in commerce and working in the field of business ought to conduct themselves.

Is business morally legitimate?

Any profession, whether very generally conceived (such as medicine) or highly specialized branch of it (such as plastic surgery), can be subjected to ethical scrutiny. Those who embrace the morality of pacifism argue that the military profession is morally misguided, if not outright vicious. Those convinced that Christian Science preaches the moral truth argue that physicians do wrong. Most Roman Catholics argue that abortionists are morally corrupt. Those opposed to euthanasia claim that physicians who assist people in their efforts to commit suicide are violating their professional ethics, based on the Hippocratic oath. Some utilitarians, in turn, condemn the use of animals for purposes that support our pleasures and medical needs because doing so diminishes total welfare.

Whether we judge from a narrow or broad moral perspective, we often hold professions up to such critical scrutiny. From a rather commonsense moral perspective, some professions seem to be on the verge of immorality. Espionage comes to mind here; that aspect of the profession is exploited to full measure by John Le Carré in his numerous novels, most notably *The Spy Who Came In From The Cold*.

In commonsense morality, or the ethics that tend to guide most people within a given culture and that requires philosophical assistance only when dilemmas arise, the profession of business may be viewed as based, ultimately, on the virtue of prudence. Prudence has been identified as the first of the cardinal virtues, and it requires that we take conscientious care of ourselves. It is a virtue to do so, whereas slothfulness, recklessness, carelessness, inattentiveness, etc., are all deemed moral failings. (This is not the place to work out a full ethical system in which wealth pursuit can be seen as morally proper. Nevertheless, it should be hinted that such a system is person-relative about the nature of the good and sees living economically, successfully, or prosperously as a goal that constitutes a significant aspect of the good life for any human moral agent; see Den Uyl (1991, 1992) and Machan (1993a). There is an ontological feature of a moral perspective that would be applicable to evaluating the various professions people embark upon, namely, that there is no basis for precluding the possibility of free will in human living. Indeed, there is both philosophical and special scientific justification, beyond a reasonable doubt, to believe that human beings are facilitated to activate their mental functions, as it were, to initiate their own conduct and, thus, to govern themselves. Instead of the reductionist approach found in much of economics, a pluralistic ontology with different kinds and types of entities in nature would be more sensible. Within such a perspective, the moral dimension of reality arises in connection with living entities that have the faculty of choice and thus can govern their own conduct. This brings into nature the problem of how they ought to act and how their living as the kind of beings they are ought to be carried out.)

The fact that prudence is a virtue does not settle the matter of the moral basis of commerce. Two questions need to be addressed so as to be sure that prudence does indeed give commerce moral support. First, what exactly is the nature of the self of which we must take care? An idealist, and even dualist, idea of the self will lead us to understand prudence as less focused upon prosperity here in life than would a naturalist conception. If human beings are essentially divided into two parts, one tied to this world, the other reaching for a superior, supernatural dimension, prudence will, in this view, have different implications from one that conceives of the self as part of the natural world alone.

The second question is whether we can rank the familiar moral virtues when they seem to be in conflict from the viewpoint of common sense. This is akin to our not understanding the structure of the physical world from simply experiencing it by way of the normal use of our senses. Here we need an ethical theory that places our commonsense ideals and ethics in a coherent framework. Hard cases in ethics cannot be decided without a systematic moral viewpoint. Classical individualism is a candidate for serving this purpose. One point in its favor would be if it managed the hard cases well and could be applied readily within the fields of professional ethics, such as business.

Classical individualism and business ethics

Assuming for now that classical individualism – otherwise referred to as classical egoism, the ethics of individual flourishing, and the ethics of self-perfection – is sound, what are its implications for professional ethics and for business ethics in particular?

A significant part of what a person ought to do in life is to secure economic values: objectives that enable one to obtain worldly goods, pleasures, joys, delights, etc. We may regard this as implied by the virtue of prudence. But unlike the individualism of many textbooks on ethics (Machan, 1982), in classical individualism, one aims to make oneself a good human being as the individual one is, and *that involves many capacities to be realized outside economic ones.*

While it is vital to serve one's economic or, more broadly, prudential goals, even these can extend far beyond the mere satisfaction of one's desires. Thus, given the classical individualist outlook, one's desires should be shaped by the vision one creates of oneself as the human being one can and would ideally or optimally become.

Professional versus social responsibilities

There are – to focus on the distinction between this and Friedman's thesis concerning the social responsibility of corporations – vital community and political dimensions of one's self that may require enhancement even in the course of conducting one's professional tasks. In the case of corporate business, for example, one may be morally responsible not only for reaching one's economic objectives which are moral in their own right – but also various objectives associated with being a member of one's community.

Professional ethics involves determining the responsibilities and restraints one needs to observe in relationship to the profession one has chosen to pursue. Of course, there are preprofessional ethics that guide one in determining what one's profession will be, so it is assumed that the choice of profession is itself capable of being morally justified. Once so justified, the question then left is what that choice implies – mostly conscientiousness in one's professional conduct – and what else ought to be attended to in connection with one's chosen profession.

Friedman's thesis (1970) was that no moral claim may be made on those in corporate business other than to fulfill their implied promise to their clients, namely, to secure for them the greatest possible economic benefits "while conforming to the basic rules of the society, both those embodied in law and in ethical custom." This view is consistent with the radical individualist conception of the human being; beyond the mere imperative of keeping a promise made in the service of one's self-interested goals, there is nothing one ought to do in one's capacity as a business professional.

Critics view this as an impoverished conception of what a human being ought to do in a professional role. Often, they go to the other extreme and argue that business should nearly be sacrificed for whatever alternative need is evident in the community. Furthermore, business is to be tamed so that it is not pursued with the kind of rapaciousness that one associates with an innately selfish drive for profiteering.

The classical individualist position understands professional ethics to require that one's *dominant* yet not *exclusive* objective is the conscientious performance of one's professional tasks, to fulfill one's job description, as it were, to carry out what one has embarked upon in one's capacity as a professional. In business, this amounts, indeed, to what Friedman believes is the exclusive or sole task of business: the pursuit of profit. To the contrary, one's professional responsibilities are not all one is responsible for carrying out. They are fully consistent with paying heed to other goals, including, fulfilling parental duties, being a good friend, enhancing the quality of one's community, improving the environment, and developing and maintaining sound political institutions. First, one has obligations to achieve goals other than those one takes up professionally, and some of these take priority over one's job. Second, even in the course of fulfilling one's professional responsibilities one might have to pay attention to goals that do not directly bear on profit maximization. Thus, the totality of one's moral tasks, combined with those arising from the fulfillment of professional tasks within the physical and political setting of one's place of work, oblige one who is in the world of business to go beyond what Friedman claims he ought to pay exclusive heed to (Miller and Ahrens, 1988). It is worth noting that Carson (1993) faults Friedman for not including as a requirement of the social or ethical responsibility of business to "warn the public about all serious hazards or dangers created by the firms which they represent." (p. 20) One might think that the current position also falls prey to this flaw. Yet, arguably, neither Friedman nor I can be so faulted. Friedman is, after all, a defender of an individual – including private property – rights-based free-market economy, including privatization in all possible means of production, trade, transportation, etc. In such a system, exposing customers to known hazards and dangers that pose risks (beyond what is reasonable, i.e., significantly above the normal prevailing hazards and dangers of their lives) without informing them about these constitutes legally actionable misrepresentation or deception. Product and service liability law suits are entirely consistent with, indeed native to, a *bona fide* free-market system. A socialist system, for example, cannot make theoretical room for such an individual rights-based legal action. It is even doubtful that a government-regulated legal system can escape the force of the charge that, in view of such regulation of business, liability action might have to be significantly circumscribed. Responsibility for hazards and dangers would, in such a system, be shared between the business and the regulatory agent (the public!) ultimately complicit in the hazardous or dangerous behavior; see also Machan (1987, 1989a, 1995).

Ethics and choice

One dimension to classical individualism recalls a certain feature of deontological ethics. This is the importance of moral sovereignty, the role of the choices of the moral agent in the determination of conduct. This is where fundamental individuality or selfhood enters the moral situation, by recognizing that it is the person who chooses morally significant conduct for himself, not others for him. Instead of atomistic individualism, this view embraces moral individualism, which is the view that the individuality of human beings is central, and emerges through everyone's moral agency, in being the initiator of morally significant conduct.

Accordingly, the scope of legally enforceable moral responsibility within classical individualist ethics is respect for others' moral agency, nothing more. This framework does not identify individuals as being naturally *connected* to society, in the fashion in which a team member is tied to the team or a business partner is tied to the partnership. Social ties in adulthood, even if they are essential and proper, must – in classical individualism – be left to choice, not imposed by law. Law enters *only* when citizens' sovereignty is intentionally or negligently infringed upon.

Hence, while the moral demands of classical individualism on those in various professions, including business, are greater than those advanced in Friedman's position, the political framework of business conduct implicit in this ethics is close to that advocated by Friedman. For example, although businesses ought to support neighborhoods to improve their quality, they may not be coerced to do so (Machan, 1983, 1984, 1987, 1989b, 1990, 1991a, 1991b, 1992, 1993b).

Business ethics: some issues in focus

Now that we have explored the ethical foundations of business and the main tenets of business ethics, we can now take a brief look at some of the implications of this viewpoint for certain frequently raised concerns within business ethics. Although many of those concerned are actually focused upon public policy – i.e., what governments ought to or ought not to do about business – there are others that are indeed *bona fide* ethical concerns. Among these, we find such issues as these:

- Is racial discrimination in conducting trade, employment, and promotion morally wrong?
- What should advertisers do, or not do, in their endeavors to attract buyers to their products or services?
- Ought those in the financial professions to engage in insider trading?
- How should one deal with laws and customs when doing business abroad?
- Should employees be treated as subordinates in a firm?
- Is it morally wrong to hire non-union employees when one's employees have gone on strike?
- Is nepotism always morally objectionable?

- Is there moral merit to any type of affirmative action?
- And, finally, is it always a form of morally objectionable bigotry to hire or fire on the basis of the prospective employee's beliefs?

We will look at these matters briefly here, merely to suggest the implications of classical individualism for these and other concerns that arise in business ethics proper. We will not concern ourselves here explicitly with broader issues of public policy and law. Let us take some of these issues under consideration:

Is racial discrimination in conducting trade, employment, and promotion morally wrong?

It is nearly always wrong, unless race has a direct bearing on advancing the business. Thus, a casting agency for movies would have a concern with employing people who can indeed be cast in parts that the motion picture industry needs in its films, and paying attention to race in such a business would be morally legitimate. Otherwise, it would be wrong because

- race is no indicator of any kind of talent or skill, and
- paying attention to race distracts from the responsibility of those engaged in business, namely, to generate profit, that is, to prosper.

Generally, racial discrimination is unjust and unproductive.

Despite this, no general prohibition of racial or any other type of discrimination can be justified. What can be legally actionable, in the systems of laws of a free society, is the failure to disclose racial or similar irrelevant criteria for engaging in trade, when the reasonable assumption is that no such criteria are invoked (as when one walks into a restaurant designated only as "restaurant," whereas, in fact, it is a restricted place of business).

What should advertisers do, or not do, in their endeavors to attract buyers to their products or services?

Advertising involves, in essence, calling attention to one's products and services, not mainly conveying information. Thus, advertising is necessarily a partisan, promotional activity, wherein only some of the truth about products or services is of relevance. (One does not have to promote possible liabilities – e.g., the high cost of one's wares relative to competitors, just as a resume need not contain unfavorable information.) Advertising ought to involve gimmicks, if these achieve the goal of gaining customers' attention – celebrities, jingles, and humor. Where, however, information is being utilized for advertising purposes, honesty is required, mainly because honesty is generally required in human relationships and also because dishonesty distorts one's business processes and undermines the prospects of business success. Advertising is not a creator of desires, but a means of turning those who already desire something to one's products and services in hope of having these achieve the satisfaction of those desires. Of course, potential customers may learn from advertising – but that is true of anything regardless of whether teaching is its central purpose (entertainment, adventure). Advertisers do need not to concern themselves about the vulnerability of adult consumers – that is the responsibility of the consumer, except in some cases where advertisers know that a significant segment of their target group has special deficiencies that may distinguish it.

Ought those in the financial professions to engage in insider trading?

Unless a fiduciary duty is violated or information is illegally obtained, insider trading is sound business practice. Getting a jump on others is part of doing good business. One would not demand that people forgo important opportunities solely to benefit total strangers. Insider trading is merely prudent and entrepreneurial trading, and it is to the credit of traders to embark on it (Chesher and Machan, 1999).

How should one deal with laws and customs when doing business abroad?

Doing business is not mainly proselytizing or advancing causes, but promoting one's economic well-being. If the basic individual human rights of potential trading partners are respected, and if one's own integrity need not be compromised, one ought to do business wherever profitable. However, contributing to the torture of innocent people so as to make money is morally wrong, as is the facilitation of slavery or other types of oppression. Yet things may not be what they appear – doing business in a country with oppressive practices could help to ease those practices, depending on the business policies employed. However, sending a black to head a division in a country that practices apartheid would be bad business and not required by justice, as long as it is understood that, aside from business objectives, it is morally decent to promote racial justice as well. Sending a woman to head a division in a country in which sexual discrimination against women is the rule would have to be considered imprudent. When one tolerates morally objectionable practices, one does not necessarily condone them; one is not guilty of any moral wrongdoing.

Should employees be treated as subordinates or partners within a firm?

Employees are not owners. They are trading partners who join a business on certain mutually agreed-to terms. If those terms require subordinating one's judgment to that of others, that is what the employee will be asked to do. A manager should manage those who are hired with the understanding that this is what will be going on. However, subordination has its proper scope – it may not be extended to areas that do not fall under the purview of the enterprise. Thus, managers or other leaders and "bosses" would act immorally in utilizing their job-specific position of superiority for irrelevant purposes. (This is where sexual and other exploitation would be morally wrong.) It may be a controversial issue of public policy, yet, employees have no special rights outside those everyone has and ones that have been created through honest negotiation.

Is it morally wrong to hire non-union employees when one's employees have gone on strike?

This depends on the employee agreement. If people walk away from a job, to hire others to work is sound business policy, and morally unobjectionable. "Scabs" are competing employees who demand less from the employer than others. It may well be their best chance at employment. In a free society, no one can be made to work for others, and this applies also to employers – they may not be forced to work for the employees.

Is nepotism always morally objectionable?

Nepotism, favoring kin in hiring, promotion, and trade in general, is usually morally objectionable because it tends to undermine the purposes of the business and to deceive others to whom it has been indicated that the employment relationship depends on merit, not blood. However, there are many exceptions – when some family members are in dire need, and business objectives might have to give way to more important ones, or when the business itself would improve by way of family cooperation, (in which case nepotism is merely apparent).

Is there moral merit to any type of affirmative action?

Affirmative action, when not a public mandate and thus an intervention in freedom of trade, is often morally unobjectionable. People from some ethnic, racial, religious or national group may have succeeded to the point where they are in a position to help those who are just starting, and if the policy does not undermine business, following it can be generous and charitable.

Is it always a form of morally objectionable bigotry to hire or fire on the basis of the prospective employee's beliefs, etc.?

Sometimes what people believe and would act on is so repulsive morally that even if they are best qualified for a job, they should not be hired. A very skilled engineer or manager who happens also to be a Nazi should not be hired, since the business objective that might be enhanced by employing the person would not outweigh the betrayal of one's values. A private firm owned by a Roman Catholic cannot reasonably be expected to give economic support to someone who despises Roman Catholicism. Freedom of association is well-founded on the need to trust people's judgments, especially when it comes to something that is a matter of choice, namely, what people believe and use for guidance in their lives.

Conclusion

The purview of professional ethics, as any area of applied ethics – indeed, of ethics itself – is in constant flux. While some very broad principles can be identified - and this is what gives the field of ethics its standing and constant relevance – it is not possible to tell just what the results of ethical judgment will be in the constantly developing world around us. This is what makes writing codes of ethics so difficult – no sooner does one spell out how people ought to act, for example, in the computer industry or telecommunications, than the variables change and adjustments are needed.

It is, thus, always important to keep in mind that professional ethics depends mainly on constant vigilance, on sustained discretion and prudence, and on wisdom, rather than on certain set rules. It is true here as elsewhere that character is destiny.

References

Baier, K. 1958: *The Moral Point of View*. Ithaca, NY: Cornell University Press.

Carson, T. 1993: Friedman's theory of corporate social responsibility, *Business and Professional Ethics Journal*, 12(Spring), 3–32.

Chesher, J. E. and Machan, T. R. 1999: *The Business of Commerce; Examining an Honorable Profession*. Stanford, CA: Hoover Institution Press.

Den Uyl, D. J. 1991: *The Virtue of Prudence*. New York: Peter Lang.

Den Uyl, D. J. 1992: Teleology and agent-centeredness. *The Monist*, 75(January), 14–33.

Etzioni, A. 1988: *The Moral Dimension*. New York: The Free Press.

Friedman, M. 1961: *Capitalism and Freedom*. Chicago: University of Chicago Press, 133–6.

Friedman, M. 1970: The social responsibility of business is to increase its profits. *New York Magazine*, 13 September, 33.

Galbraith, J. K. 1982: *The Affluent Society*, 3rd edn. New York: Houghton Mifflin.

Hessen, R. 1979: *In Defense of the Corporation*. Stanford, CA: Hoover Institution Press.

Machan, T. R. 1974: *The Pseudo-Science of B. F. Skinner*. New Rochelle, NY: Arlington House.

Machan, T. R. 1982: Recent work in ethical egoism. In K. J. Lucey and T. R. Machan (eds) *Recent Work in Philosophy*. Totowa, NJ: Rowman & Littlefield, 185–202.

Machan, T. R. 1983: Should business be regulated? In T. Regan (ed.) *Just Business: New Introductory Essays in Business Ethics*. New York: Random House, 202–34.

Machan, T. R. 1984: Pollution and political theory. In T. Regan (ed.) *Earthbound: New Introductory Essays in Environmental Ethics*. New York: Random House, 74–106.

Machan, T. R. 1987: Corporate commerce vs. government regulation: the state and occupational safety and health. *Notre Dame Journal of Law, Ethics, and Public Policy*, 2, 791–823.

Machan, T. R. (ed.) 1988a: *Commerce and Morality: Alternative Essays in Business Ethics*. Totowa, NJ: Rowman & Littlefield.

Machan, T. R. 1988b: Ethics and its uses. In Machan (1988a).

Machan, T. R. 1989a: Bhopal, Mexican disasters: what a difference capitalism can make. In T. R. Machan (ed.) *Liberty and Culture*. Buffalo: Prometheus Books, 180–1.

Machan, T. R. 1989b: *Individuals and Their Rights*. LaSalle, IL: Open Court Publishing.

Machan, T. R. 1990: *Capitalism and Individualism*. New York: St Martin's Press.

Machan, T. R. 1991a: Pollution, collectivism and capitalism. *Journal des Economists et des Etudes Humaines*, March, 83–102.

Machan, T. R. 1991b: Do animals have rights? *Public Affairs Quarterly*, 5(April), 163–73.

Machan, T. R. 1992: Between parents and children. *The Journal of Social Philosophy*, 23(Winter), 16–22.

Machan, T. R. 1993a: Applied ethics and free will: some untoward results of independence. *The Journal of Applied Philosophy*, 10, 59–72.

Machan, T. R. 1993b: Environmentalism humanized. *Public Affairs Quarterly*, 7(April), 131–47.

Machan, T. R. 1995: *Private Rights and Public Illusions*. New Brunswick, NJ: Transaction Books.

Machan, T. R. 1998: *Classical Individualism*. London: Routledge.

Marx, K. 1977: *Selected Writings*. Oxford: Oxford University Press, 126. Edited by David McClellan.

Miller, F. D. Jr and Ahrens, J. 1988: The social responsibility of corporations. In Machan (1988a), 140–60.

Nader, R., Green, M. and Seligman, J. 1976: *Taming the Giant Corporation.* New York: W. Norton.

Norton, D. L. 1976: *Personal Destinies: A Philosophy of Ethical Individualism.* Princeton, NJ: Princeton University Press.

Rand, A. 1961: *The Virtue of Selfishness: A New Concept of Egoism.* New York: Signet Books.

Sperry, R. W. 1976: Changing concepts of consciousness and free will. *Perspectives in Biology and Medicine,* 9 (Autumn), 9–19.

Sperry, R. W. 1983: *Science and Moral Priority.* New York: Columbia University Press.

9

Nature and business ethics

WILLIAM C. FREDERICK

Naturalist business ethics describes the natural forces, processes, and scientific laws that influence human conceptions of morality and ethics, and their operationalization in the business firm. The naturalist approach goes beyond descriptive explanations of nature-influenced business behavior to hypothesize normative implications of work-related behaviors of business managers, employees, and corporate stakeholders.

To some extent, a nature-based concept of ethical–unethical workplace behavior competes with alternative explanations given by social, behavioral, and organizational scientists, and by philosophers. The former emphasize social, psychological, cultural, and organizational forces as the main determinants of normative behavior, with explanations couched in empirical terms, while philosophers work to identify normative principles, rules, and concepts distilled from the long traditions of philosophical thought, with explanations defended through abstract logical reasoning. However, neither of these two scholarly approaches is immune from the influence of the other's preferred methods. The same cannot be said regarding naturalist business ethics whose emphasis on nature as a prime explanatory variable is often at odds with sociocultural theory and with philosophy's abstract logic; and these differences will be revisited at a later point in the discussion. For now, it will be helpful to explain the spillover into the business arena of a naturalist ethics approach that has had a long history in other areas of scholarly inquiry.

The evolutionary background

Naturalist business ethics is a spin-off from Charles Darwin's theory of evolution through natural selection and the neo-Darwinian emphasis on genes as an agent of evolutionary change. The last half of the twentieth century has been especially fruitful in many branches of natural science but none more so than research into genetics, along with the prospect of producing genetic effects beneficial to humans either directly (as in health and medicine) or indirectly (as in genetically engineered plant and animal forms). The Human Genome Project whose goal is to provide a map of the entire human genome, holds great promise as well as considerable threat to current conceptions of human nature. Cloned animals raise the prospect of cloned humans, thereby alarming the general public and posing potential ethical and moral issues for business firms whose genetic research and commercial incentives are heavily implicated.

Before Darwin, though, Western philosophy from the time of Aristotle and earlier has sought to understand the relationship of nature and ethics, an effort that has clearly continued into the twentieth century, as such notable philosophers as William James, John Dewey, Karl Popper, W. V. O. Quine, and others have grappled with the normative implications of human evolution. Economists too, from Adam Smith to Thomas Malthus and David Ricardo, and on to the English utilitarians and contemporary ecological economists, have assigned a central role to nature. Eastern philosophies are well known for the diverse pictures of nature woven into human meaning, human behavior, and human fate generally. While nature has long been a factor in moral conceptions of humans and human activity, the current emphasis placed on nature in theories of business ethics is due almost entirely to neo-Darwinian hypotheses and the biological explanations spawned by them.

Genes: Selfish? Altruistic? Or both?

A central premise of neo-Darwinian thought is that the physical and behavioral traits of all organisms are a function of the organism's genome, which is its entire set of genes. Metaphorically, it is said that genes send directives or instructions to the physical organism that houses them, which is called a phenotype, thus producing the distinctive characteristics and behavioral patterns of plants, animals, bacteria, fungi, etc. However, as Darwin had earlier proposed, an organism's environment is constantly intruding on it, sometimes supportively and at other times in threatening ways. Thus, the mechanism of evolutionary change – the factor that accounts for modifications, in the forms and functions of plants and animals over time – is the interactions between organism and environment. Darwin labeled these interactions "natural selection," meaning that the pressures of an organism's environment have the effect of "selecting" those physical and behavioral traits that sustain the organism's life and enable it to reproduce and, by default, "rejecting" all features with negative effects on life and reproductive ability. (Modern genetic theory was, of course, unknown to Darwin, and there is no evidence that he was familiar with or made any use of Gregor Mendel's pioneering work on genetics.)

Darwin's twentieth-century successors, who are known as neo-Darwinians, have extended his evolution-by-natural-selection idea by incorporating genetic theory into it and arguing that genes are "selfish" (Dawkins, 1976). By "selfish genes," neo-Darwinians mean that the directives and instructions sent by genes promote the genes' own survival and reproduction; otherwise the genes and their host phenotypes would be eliminated by natural selection pressures. This picture shifted attention from the whole organism, which feels the direct effects of environmental pressures, to the organism's genes which determine the organism's ability to "fit" into its environment. So, in this view, "fitness" is a direct outcome of genetic function. It implies that no organic trait will survive unless it contributes to the genes' survival and reproduction.

It was soon realized that this neo-Darwinian canon contained the seeds of its own destruction when biological and ethological research revealed a wide range of helping behaviors that involve one organism risking or sacrificing its own survival and reproduction on behalf of others. A prime example is infertile worker and soldier members of ant, bee, wasp, and termite colonies who serve the survival and reproductive interests of the colony's queen and their own brothers and sisters, rather than reproducing their own genes and transmitting them to future generations. By sacrificing their own genes' future, they appear to act not selfishly but selflessly; see Wilson (1975) for other examples.

Clearly, this finding posed a grave threat to one of the central tenets of Darwinian theory, because how might one explain the survival of such an unselfish behavioral trait that otherwise would be expected to have been eliminated by natural selection? "Fitness" seemed to be turned on its head in these cases. Darwin himself spoke of the sterile insect castes as "one special difficulty, which at first appeared to me insuperable, and actually fatal to my whole theory" (quoted by Wilson, 1975, p. 117).

The answer came in two major forms, but both were different versions of what biologists call "altruism." One of these is "kin selection," the other "reciprocal altruism." It is important to note that biological altruism is not the same as the more generous and subtle philosophical concept of altruism, although arguably the former can be seen as a more austere rendition of the latter. To biologists, altruism means that an organism sacrifices its own chance to extend its genes into the future by helping another organism to do so. The altruist here is acting under the control of its genes, and its altruistic behavior is, in that sense, unconscious and nondeliberative. Philosophers, on the other hand, mean by altruism that a conscious, intentionally motivated act of benevolence toward others has occurred, one that is not limited to a single purpose such as reproductive success but may extend to a large range of human goals, purposes, and motives (Blum, 1997).

Neo-Darwinians met this crisis by arguing that those insect altruists – the sterile workers and soldiers – are, after all and in spite of appearances to the contrary, acting selfishly in the biological sense of extending their genetic heritage to future generations. They do so vicariously or by proxy through the genetic calculus of gene transmission from parent to offspring. (In the present account, the mathematics of the proof are left aside, for lack of space.) By feeding the queen and protecting their brothers, sisters, and cousins, who carry at least partial sets of identical genes (in varying proportions, depending on degree of kinship), the sterile workers and soldiers are, in a sense, working on behalf of the greater genetic future of the entire hive or colony, including themselves. Copies of genes like theirs are passed along after all, and that is what is required by Darwinian natural selection theory. They are selfish altruists; the closer the kin, the more altruistic they will be. They needn't consciously know or compute the degree of relationship; their genes impel them to act as if they know. The practice is called "kin selection" and produces "inclusive fitness," meaning that natural selection favors individual organisms that act not only in their own interest but, in doing so, also produce fitness benefits for their kin. (However, inclusive fitness should not be confused with group selection. Whether natural selection acts on groups or individuals has generated an intense, continuing debate among evolutionary theorists, with the majority favoring selection at the level of individual organisms.)

A broader, and more morally profound, kind of behavior is "reciprocal altruism" – broader because altruistic acts go beyond kith and kin to include non-kin strangers, and more profound because it implies that this kind of altruism is favored by natural selection and will win out over strictly selfish attitudes and motives. The idea is the brainchild of biologist Robert Trivers (1971) but now vastly elaborated by an entire generation of game theorists, Prisoner's Dilemma enthusiasts, and sociobiologists. (Through one of those fortuitous linkages of disparate but related inquiry, game theory became a vehicle tying together biologists, economists, mathematicians, and evolutionary theorists in an effort to explain the logic of altruistic thinking and cooperative behavior between self-interested parties. The favorite analytic device was the Prisoner's Dilemma which revealed that a strategy of reciprocal behavior called "tit-for-tat" would emerge and tend to dominate within a given population. The main proponents of this approach were geneticist Maynard Smith, biologists William Hamilton and Robert Trivers, and political scientist Robert Axelrod. For the story and references, see Ridley (1997, pp. 53–66).)

Reciprocal altruism is evident in thinking organisms – this includes at least the higher primates as well as humans. These organisms help others with an expectation of return favors, even if helping puts one in danger or imposes costs. Those who do not return favors are soon found out and may suffer a variety of punishments. A moral code of helpful, supportive behavior evolves, building social bonds that strengthen the group. Natural selection favors this kind of group cooperative behavior over fractious, spiteful, vengeful attitudes. Here, then, is a biological impulse to extend kinship caring and morality into the larger society where even genetic strangers may learn that it pays to treat one's fellows altruistically. Even so, the impetus remains a self-interested one, which accords with Darwinian doctrine.

Sociobiologists argue that kin selection and reciprocal altruism apply not just to insect societies but to the human realm as well. Caring and concern for family members is stronger than for strangers, as reflected in the kinship systems of many different peoples. However, reciprocal altruism, along with the trust implicit in it, is the glue that binds larger social groups into a moral community.

The hunter-gatherer mind and before

The Darwinian preliminaries leading up to naturalist business ethics include two other gripping, even dramatic perspectives on the evolution of morality.

Primatologist Frans de Waal's (1996) observational research on bonobos, a smaller and perhaps more intelligent version of the chimpanzee, reveals that these close evolutionary cousins of ours behave in ways strikingly parallel to what we humans recognize as morality. They seem to favor close relatives over strangers from other groups – which would be kin selection at work – and they engage in several kinds of helpful, cooperative behaviors, such as grooming, food sharing, and protecting the young, where reciprocation is expected and non-reciprocation is punished – an instance of reciprocal altruism.

Other scientists and scientific observers reinforce de Waal's contention, Lyell Watson (1995) maintaining that "evil," especially in violent and aggressive forms, is a normal part of animal biology but can be offset by the altruistic actions induced by kin selection and, in a limited number of species, by reciprocal altruism. Another group (Wrangham et al., 1994) has explored the question of whether chimpanzees have minds capable of reason, language, and culture, cautiously concluding that social learning within chimpanzee groups leads to behavior that resembles but does not duplicate human moral actions.

Hence, long before humans emerged as a recognizable species, their closest animal kin displayed a moral potential, a kind of proto-morality based on the neo-Darwinian traits of kin selection and reciprocating altruistic acts. As author Robert Wright (1994, p. 201) says in *The Moral Animal.* "These and other elements of altruism were part of the ape mind, ready to be wired together in a new way."

But how do we get from ape morality to human morality? Wright helps to answer this question by pointing out that present-day human psychology is Pleistocene psychology. The "ancestral environment" in which the human psyche was formed, with all of its built-in impulses and urges, was that of the Ice Age hunter-gatherer peoples. They lived in small groups or clans consisting of close relatives, the very conditions necessary for both kin selection and reciprocal altruism to emerge, and that is a reassuring thought. But since genetic change which occurs very slowly, and randomly, over long time periods has produced no discernibly new neurological traits or capabilities since those ancient times, it follows that we confront today's remarkably different environment and the moral problems it generates with a 50,000-year-old Pleistocene brain. As Wright (1994, p. 38) says, "[T]he ancestral environment . . . wasn't much like the environment we're in now. We aren't designed to stand on crowded subway platforms, or to live in suburbs next door to people we never talk to, or to get hired or fired, or to watch the evening news."

The resultant disjunctions are stark, if not staggering, in their normative implications:

- Old brain/new environment
- Ice Age mentality/Electronic Age challenges
- A Pleistocene psyche honed to promote self-interest and limited altruism, paired with complex modern institutions that promote their own goals, some group-oriented, others individualistic and self-centered
- A Stone Age business mind seeking profits through a narrow cost–benefit lens, contrasted with the diverse and insistent claims of multiple corporate stakeholders; in other words, Darwinian self-interest pitted against neo-Darwinian reciprocal altruism

What hope then for morality in an Electronic Age? The answer came from some unexpected quarters, from scholars who detected a core of "moral sentiments" embedded in that ancient brain.

Nature's moral sentiments

Economic philosopher Robert Frank (1988) in *Passions within Reason* accepts the classic neo-Darwinian idea that people are genetically programmed to act in self-interested ways, but he believes that this behavioral impulse is only part of the story, and probably the least important part for anyone wanting to know why people, in spite of that self-regarding impulse, act altruistically.

According to Frank, Darwinians have omitted or overlooked the way emotions shape human attitudes, inclinations, and decisions. Rational, self-prudential considerations are always, and necessarily, moderated by an emotional concern for others and especially for what others will think of them. Frank argues that most people can't help but act altruistically because their emotions impel them toward behaviors that are simultaneously self-prudential and other-regarding. Human memories are long (thanks to that Pleistocene brain); people remember both good deeds and bad ones. They will have a fond regard for those who can be trusted to act benevolently toward others but a very guarded attitude about the less trustworthy or the malevolent.

These attitudes, and the behavior they induce, lead to the emergence of a range of biologically based moral sentiments:

- *Sympathy* toward others
- A sense of *fairness* in social transactions
- *Trust* in dealing with others
- *Love* in close personal relationships
- *Decency* as a widespread trait in most societies

Where these moral sentiments come into play, people are responding to their emotional feelings (the "passions" of the book's title) rather than to their cognitive perceptions alone (the "reason" of the title). These moral impulses toward altruism outperform purely self-centered traits and will become dominant throughout any given human population, driving out the selfish – well, not completely, but largely so – and favoring the altruist. The emotional component of decision making then has survival value and will be favored by natural selection.

An even more remarkable theoretical initiative was launched by political scientist-sociologist James Q. Wilson (1993) in *The Moral Sense*. It is remarkable because, like Frank, this *social* scientist traces altruism's rise and persistence to innate human qualities selected for in evolution. These qualities assume the form of moral sentiments – sympathy, fairness, self-control, and duty – each one taking the selfish edge off human interactions. He argues, as any good Darwinian would, that these moral sentiments would not have survived had they not contributed positively to the needs of human populations.

They are an outgrowth of the even more basic trait that Wilson calls a "moral sense." People are naturally, innately affiliative creatures, inclined to sociability. This leads them to develop a *sympathetic* outlook, to seek *fairness* for themselves and others, to be willing to curb selfish inclinations by exerting *self-control* within social groups, and to accept the *duties* and responsibilities toward one's fellows that are expected in social exchanges and transactions.

The human moral sense that underlies and supports these sentiments or behavioral predispositions originated within familial, kinship relations, specifically from the nurture and protection of the newborn and immature offspring by parents plus similar supportive sympathies extended to and reciprocated by other close kin. Proto-altruism here is clearly perceived to derive from the survival necessities of the nuclear family and its network of extended kin. "At some stage in the evolution of mankind – probably a quite early one – [this kind of kin-based] cooperative behavior became adaptive. . . . And so by natural selection and sexual selection, individuals with prosocial impulses had greater reproductive success" (Wilson, 1993, p. 70).

By emphasizing that moral sentiments activate and sustain human altruism, both Frank and Wilson have continued a long-established Enlightenment effort to explain moral behavior in naturalist, or natural law, terms. The eighteenth century's David Hume and Adam Smith made nature-based moral sentiments a central part of their philosophies of human action (Ruse, 1986, pp. 182–4; 266–9), with Smith then proposing an economic mechanism (the market) to link self-regarding impulses with societal well-being. Nature, in attenuated form, though not specifically conceived as moral sentiments, continued to be given a strategically important role in accounting for economic and societal well-being (or ill-being) in the works of nineteenth-century political economists such as Thomas Malthus, Karl Marx, Jeremy Bentham, John Stuart Mill, and others.

Clearly, these older inquiring traditions along with their modern counterparts that rely on natural forces to explain human altruism pose a central challenge to today's student of business ethics. Is nature relevant on the job? In the office? In the factory? In a work group? In Internet commerce?

Nature in the workplace

It is odd that Darwin/neo-Darwin altruistic explanations are found so seldom in theories of business ethics, all the more so since other-regarding behavior is so frequently invoked by business ethicists as a workplace ideal. The general discipline of philosophy, from whose ranks many ethicists are regularly recruited, long ago either came to terms with naturalism – Quine (1992, 1995); Hahn and Schlipp (1986) being a good example – or accepted them provisionally as less than the whole story (O'Hear, 1997). None of the widely used anthologies or standard business ethics textbooks refer students to Darwinian sources, although there is little hesitancy in invoking Social Darwinism as an orientation to be avoided.

The explanations for this scientific void are not far away. Business ethicists are not educated in science, nor do they read science with any grasp of its philosophical significance. Within those business schools where ethics has secured a curricular foothold, the subject is normally taught by faculty with social science backgrounds, i.e., economics, political science, sociology, and/or psychology, or those with derivative social science credentials such as organization behavior and business environment, or the occasional legal scholar and philosopher. The dread fear of crossing disciplinary lines and chancing the clarity of one's academic qualifications holds many back from looking into the natural sciences, and little wonder since careers are at stake. Of larger, though less immediately threatening, personal import is the strong culturological bias of twentieth-century social science. Here the *tabula rasa* orientation reigns supreme, where culture not only writes the message of human learning in bold strokes, but supports a belief in almost infinite flexibility and diversity in human affairs, and posits freedom and individuality as potentialities within the grasp of each and every person (Degler, 1991). For their part, philosophers have brought along their own self-imposed disciplinary albatross as they moved out of philosophy into business ethics. They balk when confronted with evolutionary theory that seems to them to derive normative meanings from evolutionary observations, i.e., finding "oughts" where there are only "is-es" – the dreaded "naturalistic fallacy," which is closely related to, if not identical with, the (equally dubious) "fact-value" distinction. However, it might be noted that one philosopher, well versed in Darwinian thought has questioned the validity and reach of the Hume–Moore "naturalistic fallacy" doctrine (Ruse, 1985, pp. 200–201; 1986, pp. 86–90; 256–8). Nor are philosophers helped in grasping nature's normative significance by the disciplinary habit of avoiding empirical studies in favor of abstract speculative thought.

The rather peculiar result is that an entire body of theory, research, and empirical data in the natural sciences, much of it rich in potential relevance to questions of workplace ethics, dangles and twists in an intellectual void as if it is not there, virtually ignored by the great majority of business ethicists. Only the occasional macro-economist (Boulding, 1978) or institutional economist (Hodgson, 1993, 1995) has grappled with the normative complexities of Darwinian thought, but none has focused specifically on the ethical dimension of managerial behavior within the modern corporation.

Two business school ethicists who have ventured directly into the naturalist realm are William C. Frederick (1995) and Timothy L. Fort (1997a, 1997b, 1997d). Frederick's academic credentials are in institutional economics and anthropology, while Fort's degrees are in theology, law, and government. Neither background hints of an orientation toward Darwinian thought. In fact, their uses and interpretations of naturalist forces are less reliant on neo-Darwinian theories of altruism than one might expect.

Frederick has laid out a comprehensive theory of the origin and operation of business values which he believes to be the outcome of thermodynamic energy flows. The modern corporation is driven by two primary nature-based value clusters: self-centered *economizing values* and self-promoting *power-aggrandizing* values. In business operations, these values intersect and clash with a third value cluster, community-building *eco-logizing values*. The resultant tensions among these natural forces create the normative problems that arise in the workplace, including on-the-job fairness, justice, and rights.

In addition to the physics of thermodynamics, Frederick summons research findings from *ethology* to explain the aggressive-dominance behavior of business executives, from *ecology* to explain ecosystem dynamics and communal behavior, from *genetics* to explain human symbolic attributes and cooperative organizational behavior, and from *cognitive development theory* to explain on-the-job personal values. Thus, his natural science platform is considerably broader than the altruistic focus of the neo-Darwinians who, it will be recalled, stumbled almost by accident and certainly by necessity on the issue of other-regarding behavior by supposedly self-regarding organisms.

Moreover, Frederick draws extensively on cultural and sociological explanations of both individual and organizational behavior found in the business workplace, thereby avoiding the highly controversial sociobiological constraints on individual flexibility and societal pluralism. Because of the central role assigned to thermodynamics – as the originator and operator of the core values of the business order – this view of business values could well be called "sociophysical" as contrasted with a sociobiological approach, a label Frederick explicitly rejects (Frederick, 1995, p. x).

Frederick also proposes a synthesis of nature-based normative behavior, socio-cultural norms, and the philosophic concepts of rights, justice, and fairness found so frequently in business ethics literature. He appears to believe that these three intellectual traditions might be conjoined to form a more effective way to understand corporate operations and to promote greater ethicality in the business workplace.

107

Timothy Fort's naturalist bent is at once original as well as emergent from a trend among some of today's theologians to incorporate scientific findings into theology, especially Darwinian evolution, neo-Darwinian genetics, and astrophysical cosmology (Harris, 1987, 1991, 1992; Kaufman, 1993). Fort grounds his naturalist ethics in an idea developed by James Q. Wilson (1993) that individuals learn what it is to be moral in small groups, beginning with an infant's early experiences within the family. For Wilson, it will be recalled, such a familial practice proved to be evolutionarily adaptive. However, Fort takes the approach even further by citing three telling bits of scientific research: primatologist Frans de Waal's (1996) observations about the reciprocating affectionate, caring behavior within bonobo kin groups; psychologist Robin Dunbar's (1996) finding of a correlation between size of the neocortex (where conscious thought occurs) and both the degree of reciprocal supportive behavior among chimpanzees and the expected size of such groups; and Robert Wright's (1994) contention that the modern mind is a mirror of the more ancient hunter-gatherer brain. Bonobos' proto-moral inclinations suggest the presence of an innate precursor to the more fully developed human notion of morality, while Dunbar's hypothesis linking size of social group to reciprocating supportive behavior interfaces well with Wright's propositions about hunter-gatherer mentality and the typical size of such early societies.

Fort argues that individuals necessarily learn moral behavior within the family, extended kinship groups, and close-knit clans, where group size and moral comprehension are constrained by the neocortex-group size correlation. It is there that people acquire their social and moral identity. Therefore, if morality is to find meaningful expression in the modern business firm, there must be organizational structures compatible with the size and familiarity of one's early moral experiences. These structures he calls "mediating institutions" because they provide a link between a person's moral identity and the work they perform for the firm. Examples would be small work teams who "own" their piece of a firm's assembly process, or empowering employees with new responsibilities, or apportioning work in relation to available decentralized information, and similar organic work schemes based on close contacts among co-workers. Business thus incurs a moral responsibility to organize itself in the spirit and methodology of a mediating institution, to make ethical behavior an achievable reality on the shop floor and in the executive suite (Fort, 1997e, 1998).

Fort takes a strong stand regarding nature's role, saying that "moral reasoning and culture are manifestations of nature itself [and that] the capability for moral reasoning, caring for others, being aware of one's impact on others is indeed hard-wired in the human species." The emotional component or "affect . . . may be the link – an evolutionary adaptation – necessary for us to translate our need for mutual support into moral reasoning" (Fort, 1997c). Nature then is seen as a "transcendent reality" of eschatological proportions, which imposes moral responsibilities on individuals and business firms alike because all are subject to its reach.

A fair summation of the views of these two business ethicists reveals both convergence and distinctiveness in how nature is related to everyday business activities. Fort's naturalist theology leads him to discover universal transcendent meaning in both nature and religion, with the two linked yet distinct, but each providing grounds for normative analysis of business operations, decisions, and policies (Fort, 1997b).

Frederick's sociophysics approach, though grounded in neurological cognitive processes and experiential problem solving in an entropic universe, also acknowledges that individuals, including business practitioners, seek a transcendant, cosmic meaning for their lives (Frederick, 1998a). Moreover, he uses complexity theory to argue that business and community relationships evolve along largely unpredictable pathways set by self-organizing biological impulses (Frederick, 1998b).

The rest of the story and more

Much more, both pro and con, could be said about the prospects for an ethics grounded in nature. Ecologists, particularly those who focus on the ecologically negative practices of business, industry, and high-consumption societies, have in a sense been pioneers and advocates of using the natural sciences, especially biology, to take normative positions regarding business operations. Their story is told elsewhere in this volume and in many others too numerous to cite here; however, see *Academy of Management Review* (1995) for several examples.

Another business school ethicist, Diane Swanson (1992, 1995), builds an entire model of corporate social performance on naturalistic values and argues that only a systems analysis that incorporates both biological and cultural factors can provide normative clarity. Her work, inspired in part by Gregory Bateson, is a clear step beyond current treatments of ecological sustainability by organizational theorists; see for example Egri and Pinfield (1996). Other recent uses of natural science are Bella (1997) and Brockett and Tankersley (1997).

These scholarly affirmations of Darwinian natural science are by no means the whole story, and perhaps the recent statement by philosopher Anthony O'Hear (1997), *Beyond Evolution: Human Nature and the Limits of Evolutionary Explanation* can symbolize the unease with which Darwinians and Darwinian analysis are still regarded. O'Hear's impressive, if not entirely persuasive position, is that human self-consciousness is the unique component that separates humans from the remainder of nature, making possible a reasoning power and rationality that seems to stand above and beyond science's search for empirical explanations. This mental capability drives a desire to discover the true, the good, and the beautiful which are depicted as qualities not easily sensed by limiting oneself to the scientist's objective world. Truth here emerges as having a dimension that causes it to stand above mere empirical truth, and it is sought for its own sake rather than for instrumental purposes alone. Morality then is not an outcome of organismic striving for survival, as the Darwinians would have it. "[T]he very essence of morality is its unconditional nature and its non-relativity to circumstance" (O'Hear, 1997, p. 141). In what he calls "a quasi-Darwinian approach to tradition, custom, and morality," O'Hear believes that sociocultural rules and conventions, not biology or scientific rationality, provide normative direction to human affairs and can explain the survival and evolutionary success of human societies (1997, pp. 145–6). Well-read in Darwinian theory, O'Hear provides clear evidence that doubts remain in some quarters about the viability of relying exclusively on post-Darwinian accounts of morality's emergence and meaning. Whether this skepticism is more than the last gasp of a moribund anti-Darwinist philosophy remains an open question.

References

Academy of Management Review 1995: Special topic forum on ecologically sustainable organizations, 20(4), 873–1089.

Bella, D. A. 1997: Organized complexity in human affairs. *Journal of Business Ethics*, 16, 977–99.

Blum, L. A. 1997: Altruism and benevolence. In P. H. Werhane and R. E. Freeman (eds), *The Blackwell Encyclopedic Dictionary of Business Ethics*. Oxford: Blackwell.

Boulding, K. 1978: *Ecodynamics*. Beverly Hills, CA: Sage.

Brockett, P. L. and Tankersley, E. S. 1997: The genetics of revolution, economics, ethics, and insurance. *Journal of Business Ethics*, 16, 1661–76.

Dawkins, R. 1976: *The Selfish Gene*. Oxford: Oxford University Press.

Degler, C. N. 1991: *In Search of Human Nature: The Decline and Revival of Darwinism in American Social Thought*. Oxford: Oxford University Press.

de Waal, F. 1996: *Good Natured: The Origins of Right and Wrong in Humans and Other Animals*. Cambridge, MA: Harvard University Press.

Dunbar, R. I. M. 1996: *Grooming, Gossip, and the Evolution of Language*. London: Faber & Faber.

Egri, C. and Pinfield, L. T. 1996: Organizations and the biosphere: Ecologies and environments. In S. R. Clegg, C. Hardy, and W. R. Nord (eds), *Handbook of Organization Studies*, Thousand Oaks, CA and London: Sage Publications, 459–83.

Fort, T. L. 1997a: Naturalism and business ethics: Inevitable foes or potential allies? *Business Ethics Quarterly*, 7(3), 145–55.

Fort, T. L. 1997b: *Business and naturalism: A peek at transcendance?* Conference on Value Inquiry, Appalachian State University, Boone, NC, April 17–19.

Fort, T. L. 1997c: Personal communication to author, August 30.

Fort, T. L. 1997d: How relationality shapes business and its ethics. *Journal of Business Ethics*, 16, 1381–91.

Fort, T. L. 1997e: The corporation as a mediating institution. *Notre Dame Law Review*, 73, 101–32.

Fort, T. L. 1998: Goldilocks and business ethics: A paradigm that fits "just right." *Journal of Corporation Law*, Winter Issue, 245–76.

Frank, R. H. 1988: *Passions within Reason: The Strategic Role of the Emotions*. New York: Norton.

Frederick, W. C. 1995: *Values, Nature, and Culture in the American Corporation*. Oxford: Oxford University Press.

Frederick, W. C. 1998a: Moving to CSR4: What to pack for the trip. *Business & Society*, 37(1)(March), 40–59.

Frederick, W. C. 1998b: Creatures, corporations, communities, chaos, complexity: A naturological view of the corporate social role. *Business & Society*, 37(4)(December), 358–89.

Hahn, L. E. and Schlipp, P. A. (eds) 1986: *The Philosophy of W. V. Quine*. LaSalle, IL: Open Court.

Harris, E. 1987: *Formal, Transcendental, and Dialectical Thinking*. Albany: State University of New York Press.

Harris, E. 1991: *Cosmos and Anthropos*. Atlantic Highlands, NJ: Humanities Press.

Harris, E. 1992: *Cosmos and Theos*. Atlantic Highlands, NJ: Humanities Press.

Hodgson, G. M. 1993: *Economics and Evolution*. Cambridge, UK: Polity Press.

Hodgson, G. M. (ed.) 1995: *Economics and Biology*. UK: Elgar.

Kaufman, G. D. 1993: *In Face of Mystery: A Constructive Theology*. Cambridge, MA: Harvard University Press.

O'Hear, A. 1997: *Beyond Evolution: Human Nature and the Limits of Evolutionary Explanation*. Oxford: Clarendon Press.

Quine, W. V. O. 1992: *Pursuit of Truth*. Cambridge, MA: Harvard University Press.

Quine, W. V. O. 1995: *From Stimulus to Science.* Cambridge, MA: Harvard University Press.

Ridley, M. 1997: *The Origins of Virtue.* London: Penguin Books. First published by Viking in 1996.

Ruse, M. 1985: *Sociobiology: Sense or Nonsense?* 2nd edn. Dordrecht: R. Reidel. First published in 1979.

Ruse, M. 1986: *Taking Darwin Seriously: A Naturalistic Approach to Philosophy.* Oxford: Basil Blackwell.

Swanson, D. L. 1992: A critical evaluation of Etzioni's socioeconomic theory: Implications for the field of business ethics. *Journal of Business Ethics,* 11, 545–53.

Swanson, D. L. 1995: Addressing a theoretical problem by reorienting the corporate social performance model. *Academy of Management Review,* 20(1), 43–64.

Trivers, R. 1971: The evolution of reciprocal altruism. *Quarterly Review of Biology,* 46, 35–57.

Watson, L. 1995: *Dark Nature: A Natural History of Evil.* London: Hodder & Stoughton.

Wilson, E. O. 1975: *Sociobiology: The New Synthesis.* Cambridge, MA: Belknap Press, Harvard University Press.

Wilson, J. Q. 1993: *The Moral Sense.* New York: Free Press.

Wrangham, R., McGrew, W.C., de Waal, F. B. M., and Heltne, P. G. (eds) 1994: *Chimpanzee Cultures.* Cambridge, MA: Harvard University Press.

Wright, R. 1994: *The Moral Animal: The New Science of Evolutionary Psychology.* New York: Pantheon.

10

Toward new directions in business ethics: some pragmatic pathways

SANDRA B. ROSENTHAL AND ROGENE A. BUCHHOLZ

Classical American pragmatism offers a unique normative frame for rethinking several key features which are embedded in traditional theories of business ethics and which are proving to be problematic at best. By classical American pragmatism is intended that position incorporating the works of its five major contributors: Charles Peirce, William James, John Dewey, C. I. Lewis, and G. H. Mead. That these philosophers provide a unified perspective is assumed in this essay, but this claim is defended at some length by Rosenthal (1986, 1990).

Here are five key features which will provide the focal points for a turn toward new directions:

1 An implicit moral pluralism with all the problems this involves
2 An atomic individualism which pits the individual against the community and requires a choice between communitarianism and libertarianism
3 The understanding of moral decision making as involving "top-down" rule application and fixed-end reasoning, and the resulting turn toward the study of irrationalism
4 The fact–value distinction and the resulting separation of empirical and normative business ethics
5 The lack of a business ethics framework which can incorporate an environmental ethic to clarify an area that is rapidly becoming one of its major concerns.

With these various focal points in mind, the ensuing discussion will first turn to the issue of moral pluralism.

The usual approach to ethical theory in business ethics texts is to present – either in cursory form or sometimes in greater detail – the theory of utilitarianism based on the writings of Bentham and Mill as representative of a more general class of teleological ethics, and Kantian ethical theory related to the categorical imperative as representative of the deontological approach to ethical decision making. These texts then go on to present as well certain notions of justice, usually going into the egalitarianism of John Rawls and the opposing libertarianism of Robert Nozick. They also generally include a discussion of rights, and at times, some variation of virtue theory.

What we are left with is a kind of an ethical smorgasbord where one has various theories from which to choose that will hopefully shed some light on the ethical problems under consideration and lead to a justifiable decision. However, we are never told to any extent exactly how we are to decide which theory to apply in a given situation, what guidelines we are to use in applying these different theories, what criteria determine which theory is best for a given problem, and what to do if the application of different theories suggests totally different courses of action. Furthermore, what implications does switching back and forth between theories and their corresponding principles have for the ethical enterprise as a whole?

The litany of conflicting theories and principles – each of which was initially meant as a universal approach to ethical problems – gives conflicting signals to people in positions of responsibility in business and other organizations and can, at times, allow them to pick principles at will to rationalize what, from another perspective, may be unethical activity in concrete situations. Shifting between utilitarianism and Kant's categorical imperative or between theories of justice and rights involves at best an unreflective or shallow commitment to ethics and to a moral point of view. These theories cannot be applied at will as the situation may seem to dictate, for each of them involves commitment to the philosophical framework on which it is based, and which provides for its richness and rationale. Unfortunately, these frameworks are often in conflict.

The philosophical foundations on which Kant's deontological ethics is based are radically different from the philosophical foundations on which either act or rule utilitarianism is based. To be Kantians at one time and Benthamites at another is to shift philosophical frameworks at will and results in what has been quite aptly called "metaphysical musical chairs" (Callicott, 1990; Weston, 1991). Attempts to avoid this type of philosophical schizophrenia have led some philosophers to claim that moral principles can be divorced from their philosophical underpinnings (Wenz, 1993). Thus one can hold to a single moral theory which claims that there are a variety of moral principles which cannot be reduced to or derived from a single master framework. What this view seems to be saying is that to think morally and to think philosophically are no longer compatible endeavors.

What we are really dealing with, in all the above instances, is moral pluralism, and are thus involved in all the problems this poses for the field. Moral pluralism is the view that no single moral principle or overarching theory of what is right can be appropriately applied in all ethically problematic situations. There is no one unifying, monistic principle from which lesser principles can be derived. According to moral pluralism, the right act is the one which is subsumed under the proper balance of rules or principles or theories, but in none of these theories can there be guidance in deciding when to use a particular theory, for each theory is self-enclosed or absolute; no principle or rule can provide any guidance for the moral reasoning that underlies the choice among the various principles or rules. The basis for this choice, which now becomes the heart of moral reasoning, the very foundation for moral decision making, remains mysterious and outside the realm of philosophical illumination.

For example, actions done with the best of intentions by virtuous people may nonetheless be misguided and can only be so judged by something other than intentions, and the application of a moral rule to a specific case can be used by ill-intentioned individuals to justify all sorts of behavior which common sense judges to be immoral.

113

Rules seem to judge intentions, yet bad intentions can misuse rules. Moreover, in spite of the seemingly radical difference between the monistic theories of Bentham and Kant, for example, there is a striking similarity. For Kant and Bentham alike, the value of an act is to be found solely in its exemplification of a rule, be it the categorical imperative or the greatest happiness for the greatest number. On further reflection, it becomes evident that not only is there no mechanical way to decide the proper balance among principles for moral pluralism, but for neither moral pluralism nor monism is there a mechanical way to decide if a particular act falls under a rule in a given situation. When one has to deal with a radically new kind of situation, where one cannot call on old decisions, this problem is even more pronounced. The end result – of moral learning which is not learning to deal with the novel in situations and to reconstruct both rules and traditions accordingly – is moral sterility.

It is not surprising that a broad study of the field of business ethics has concluded that there is a persistent unwillingness to grapple with tensions between theories of ethical reasoning, and that this, in turn, hampers an understanding of ethical decision making (Derry and Green, 1989). Moreover, the inability of a tradition of conflicting rules to account for concrete ethical decision making has led, in turn, to the focus on, and study of the so-called irrationality inherent in actual decision making in the business context. A deeper, unifying level must be reached to explain why and how we reconstruct rules and traditions, and choose among various principles in an ongoing process of dealing with change and novelty.

An adequate moral pluralism, like any adequate moral theory, requires a solid philosophical grounding, but it requires a philosophical grounding that is, itself, inherently pluralistic. With such a pluralism, there must conjointly be a radically new understanding of what it is to think morally. A philosophical theory forms a coherent whole, a world vision, and thus in the process of rethinking the nature of moral reasoning other key elements undergo rethinking as well.

While the various traditional positions conflict with each other in what they explicitly espouse, there are underlying assumptions which render groups of them similar in certain ways. One of the key assumptions in traditional theories concerns the nature of the self; the long-standing view of the individual as an atomic unit – as an isolatable building block of community – dominates the ethical tradition. Indeed, views of justice as diverse as that of Rawls and Nozick both presuppose the individual as an atomic unit that can be considered theoretically in isolation from, and prior to, a community. Similarly, the conflict between individual and community, which manifests itself in the conflict between Kant and Bentham, presupposes the individual as an atomic building block of community. The pragmatic understanding of the moral situation involves a rejection of all vestiges of atomic individualism in favor of a relational theory of the self.

Turning to virtue ethics, while the virtue theory of Aristotle is, in certain ways, quite distant from later virtue ethics that denies the closure of Aristotelian teleology, yet virtues result from the inculcation of tradition, and there is offered in virtue ethics no understanding of the self as a creative agent that eludes or outstrips the inculcation of roles and habits of behavior so as to evaluate and reconstruct the very tradition which engendered these roles and habits. Thus, again, we return to a rethinking of the nature of the self, this time to elicit its strain of radical creativity. It may, at this point, be objected that the view of the self as both relational and creative sounds somewhat contradictory, but it is precisely these two features which are operative in the pragmatic rethinking of the self – a view which is intertwined with its understanding of the nature of experience.

Selfhood and community

The pragmatic position holds that all knowledge and experience are infused with interpretive aspects, funded with past experience, and stem from a perspective, i.e., a point of view. In being inherently perspectival, experience and knowledge are at once experimental, for this perspectivalism involves a creative organization of experience which directs our anticipatory activity and which is tested by its workability in the ongoing course of experience. In the adjustments and coordinations needed for co-operative action in the social context, individuals take the perspective of the other in the development of their conduct and, in this way, there develops the common content which provides community of meaning.

In incorporating the perspective of the other, the developing self comes to take the perspective or standards and authority of others in terms of the group as a whole. There is a passive dimension to the self. Yet, the individual as a unique center of activity responds to this common perspective; there is a creative dimension to the self. Any self thus incorporates, by its very nature, both the conformity of the group per-spective and the creativity of its unique individual perspective. Selfhood is derivative from communicative interaction; individuals exist in their social relations.

Because of the very nature of the self, the individual is neither an isolatable discrete element in, nor an atomic building block of, a community. Rather, community is con-stituted by the dynamics of adjustment between the individual and the common other, which involves neither assimilation of perspectives, one to the other, nor the fusion of perspectives into an indistinguishable oneness, but an accommodation in which each creatively affects, and is affected by, the other through accepted organs of adjudication. Pragmatic community is constituted in its very nature by the ongoing dynamics of socializing adjustment. The social dynamic lies in this continual interplay of adjustment of attitudes, aspirations, and factual perceptions between the common other as the condition for the novel emergent perspective, and the novel emergent, as it conditions the common other.

Thus, a community of any kind is a community of ongoing socializing adjustment between the creative activity constitutive of the novel individual perspective and the common perspective, and each gains its meaning, significance, and enrichment from this process of adjustment. A community reflects the ongoing dynamics of the two poles of creativity and conformity, liberation and constraint, manifest above as two poles in the dynamics of selfhood. The development of the ability both to create and to respond constructively to the creation of novel perspectives, as well as to incorporate the perspective of the other, not as something totally alien, but as something sym-pathetically understood, is at once growth of the self and growth of community. Thus, to contribute to the growth of community is at once to contribute to the growth of the selves involved in the ongoing dynamics of adjustment.

This view of community does not imply that differences should be eliminated or melted down, for these differences provide the necessary materials by which a society can continue to grow. Yet, an authentic community does involve a shared value or goal. The overreaching goal of a community is precisely the control of its own evolving growth. Thus, the ultimate "goal" of a community is growth or development, not final completion; a self-controlled process, not a self-imposed fixed content. Authentic reconstruction in cases of incompatibility must be based on the problem situation and the history within which it has emerged. Yet, reconstruction cannot be imposed from on high by eliciting the standards of a past which does not contain the organs of resolution, but must be developed by calling on a sense of a more fundamental and creative level of activity. The very relation of individual selves to the generalized other requires the openness of perspectives. Also, the adjustment of perspectives through rational reconstruction requires not an imposition from "on high" but a deepening to a more fundamental level of human rapport. The deepening process frees intelligence from the bonds of rigidities, rule applications, and procedural steps, allowing us to grasp different contexts, to take the perspective of "the other," to participate in dialogue with "the other," and to utilize liberated possibilities.

Such a deepening does not negate the use of intelligent inquiry, but rather opens it up, frees it from the products of its past in terms of rigidities and abstractions, and focuses it on the dynamics of concrete human existence. In the literature today, there is growing interest in what is called "irrationality" in management decisions. This is based on the perception – becoming ever more widespread – that decisions are not based on the weighing of abstract, "objective," calculative alternatives, that the process of reasoning in concrete situations is not understandable as the application of abstractly grasped rules, nor can it be subjected to step-by-step analysis. What this calls for, however, is not a turn to the irrational but a new understanding of rationality. Pragmatism does not destroy reason but brings it down to earth, so to speak. Reason, brought down to earth, is concrete, imaginative, deepened to operate with possibilities which have been liberated from the confines and rigidities of abstract rules and procedural steps or the confines of inculcated tradition.

Value

It is within the dynamics of community that value arises, and all of the above ingredients permeate the moral situation. The ensuing discussion will turn to the emergence of the experience of value and the development of moral norms, as well as to the way in which this incorporates moral reasoning as both deepened and embodying the process of experimental method.

For the pragmatist, value is a real emergent property of the relational contexts of organism–environment interaction, a qualitative dimension of concrete human existence. Humans have a plurality of values emerging from their organic embeddedness in a natural and social world. Further, the experience of value emerges as both shared and unique, as all experience is both shared and unique. The adjustment between these two aspects, the shared and the unique, gives rise to the novel and creative aspects within moral community. Finally, value situations, like all situations, are open to inquiry and require the general method of scientific experimentalism by which to progress from a problematic situation to a meaningfully integrated one.

In this way, pragmatism undercuts the various ethics of rule application in favor of a moral creativity in decision making which focuses on contextual reconstruction of problematic situations in a process of ongoing moral growth. Moral decision making is no longer a merely rule-driven activity but rather involves the ongoing dynamic interplay between rule development and rule application. Our moral claims are about something that requires experimental integration: the emergence of concrete valuings of humans in their specific situational concrete interaction with their world. Just as scientific hypotheses emerge as ways of organizing the diversity of physical data and must be judged by their workability in organizing the data into an integrated, meaningful whole, so we create and utilize norms or ideals in the moral situation as working hypotheses by which to organize and integrate the diversity of concrete valuings. However, where the scientist deals with abstractions, the moral realm is one of concrete situations, and what works is dependent upon the emergent but real domain of valuings which need integration and harmonizing. Workability cannot be understood in terms of one fixed end, but rather workability involves the enrichment of experience in its entirety.

In this view, moral reasoning involves an enrichment of the capacity to perceive moral dimensions of situations rather than a way of simplifying how to deal with what one does perceive. It involves sensitivity to the rich, complex value ladenness of a situation, and to its interwoven and conflicting dimensions, the ability to utilize creative intelligence geared to the concrete situation, and an ongoing evaluation of the resolution. Also, decisions which change a situation will give rise to new problems requiring new integrative solutions. One cannot just "put the problem to bed" and forget about it. The goal is not the most unequivocal decision, but the richest existence for those involved.

In this process, we are often reconstructing moral rules. Principles are not directives to action but are rather suggestive; they are tools for grasping the diverse strands operative in complex situations. Just as hypotheses in the technical experimental sciences are modified through ongoing testing, moral principles are hypotheses which require ongoing testing and allow for qualification and reconstruction. Moral reasoning is not the inculcation of a past – either in terms of rules or dispositions – but, it is inherently historical, for moral reasoning involves a creative reorientation of the present toward the future in light of the past. It involves dealing with a changing world which manifests stabilities and possibilities to be utilized. It does not ignore the lessons of the past, or past theory–data relations, but reinterprets and reappropriates them in light of an imaginative grasp of what might be, based on possibilities operative in the present. One grasps a situation historically, not just in terms of the past but in terms of the future.

This position, of course, rules out absolutism in ethics, but what must be stressed is that, equally, it rules out subjectivism and relativism, for normative hypotheses are rooted in, and ultimately judged by, the conditions and demands of human living and the desire for meaningful, enriching lives. We create and utilize norms or ideals in the moral situation, but which ones work is dependent upon the emergent but real domain of valuings which need integration and harmonizing. Also, while the experience of value arises from specific, concrete contexts shaped by a particular tradition, this is not mere inculcation, for the deepening process offers the openness for breaking through and evaluating one's own stance.

This view cannot tell us what position to take on specific issues, but then no theory can supply – to ordinary people – unambiguous, practical prescriptions in all situations where moral choices must be made. It does, however, clarify what is at issue in moral decisions and gives a directive for making intelligent choices and for engaging in reasoned debate on the issues. What must be mediated is not a conflict among abstract moral principles; rather, a plurality of conflicting interests must be integrated, and that can only be done by the morally perceptive, creative, individual operating in a specific context in response to specific conflicts.

Understanding moral action as adherence to pre-established rules encourages rigidity and lack of moral sensitivity. Understanding moral action as the development of a good character or a good will encourages the self-engrossed concern with meaning well or of having good intentions. Each of these provides a comfortable substitute for the difficult task of bringing about good consequences in concrete situations. Morality is more than following rules and more than manifesting a set of inculcated virtues. At no time can one say, "The consequences turned out to be terrible, but at least I know I did the morally right thing." Such a statement is, from the pragmatic process perspective, a contradiction. The most important habits we can develop are habits of intelligence, sensitivity, and flexibility, for neither following rules nor meaning well can suffice. Bringing about good consequences in concrete situations through moral decision making helps to develop, as by products, both good character traits as flexible, creative habits of acting and good moral rules as working hypotheses needing ongoing testing and revision.

Morality is not postulated in abstract rules to be followed or virtues to be inculcated, but is discovered in concrete moral experience. The vital, growing sense of moral rightness comes from concrete moral attunement, and it is this which gives vitality to the diverse and changing principles as working hypotheses embodied in concrete moral activity and guides the ongoing creative development of ways of acting. The pluralism involved is far from immune to hazardous pitfalls and wrenching clashes. What will change factionalism into community diversity engaged in an ongoing process of growth, and what is needed for the moral reasoning that will allow the flourishing of such growth, is the development of the reorganizing and ordering capabilities of creative intelligence, the imaginative grasp of authentic possibilities, the vitality of motivation, and a deepened sensitivity to the sense of concrete human existence in its richness, diversity, and complexity. Humans cannot assign priority to any one basic value, nor can their values be arranged in any rigid hierarchy, but they must live with the consequences of their actions within concrete situations in a process of change. With the above points in mind, the focus can now turn to the issue of scientific or experimental method, and the implications this has for rethinking the normative–empirical split in business ethics and the related fact–value distinction.

The normative–empirical split

Scholars who are interested in business ethics seem for the most part to have split into two camps in talking about two kinds of business ethics – the normative and the empirical – and each of these two domains are considered to be guided by different theories and assumptions, which often results in misunderstanding or lack of appreciation for the other's endeavors. The empirical approach is rooted in the social sciences, and scholars here tend to devalue the normative interests of philosophers because moral judgments cannot be understood in empirical terms and cannot be verified by empirical test nor be used to predict or explain behavior. On the other hand, the social scientist's statements about morality tend to be seen as of little value to the philosopher because they do not address the essential questions of right and wrong (Treviño and Weaver, 1994).

This split between the two approaches to business ethics is another manifestation of a problem that has existed between philosophy and science for several centuries and of the fact–value distinction with which it is intertwined. The pragmatic understanding of science and scientific method, along with its rethinking of the fact–value distinction, offers a new way of understanding the normative business ethics–empirical business ethics issue. The ensuing discussion will turn first to the pragmatic understanding of scientific method and then to its understanding of the fact–value controversy. While these two issues are intertwined, they offer distinct dimensions of the general problematic.

Although the issue of the empirical–normative split in business ethics, along with the fact–value split with which it is intertwined, has been a subject of much debate in recent years, what has not been so explicitly the object of focus is the pervasive understanding of scientific method which seems to both underlie and emanate from such a split. Pragmatism arose in part as a reaction against the modern or Cartesian world view understanding of the nature of science and of the scientific object. This understanding resulted from the general fact that the method of gaining knowledge which was the backbone of the emergence of modern science was confounded with the content of the first "lasting" modern scientific view – the Newtonian mechanistic universe. Such a confusion, based largely on the presuppositions of a spectator theory of knowledge, led to a naively realistic philosophic interpretation of scientific content. Scientific knowledge provided the literal description of objective fact, and excluded our lived qualitative experience as providing access to the natural universe. This resulted in a quantitatively characterized universe, the alienation of humans and nature, and a radical dehumanizing of nature. Nature as objectified justified nature as an object of value–free human manipulation. It is precisely the pragmatic refocus on science in terms of method, rather than content, which provides the key to its radical correction of modernity.

What, then, does pragmatic philosophy find when it focuses on the lived experience of scientists rather than on the content they put forth as their findings. The very first stage of scientific inquiry requires human creativity. We are not mere passive spectators gathering ready-made data, but rather we bring creative theories which enter into the very character and organization of the data grasped. Second, there is directed or goal-oriented activity dictated by the theory. The theory requires that certain activities be carried out, certain changes brought about in the data to see if anticipated results occur. Finally, the test for truth is in terms of consequences. Does the theory work in guiding us through future experiences in a way anticipated by its claims. Truth is not something passively attained, either by the contemplation of absolutes, or by the passive accumulation of data, but by activity shot through with the creative theory that guides it. This role of purposive activity in thought and the resultant appeal to relevance and selective emphasis which ultimately must be justified by workability are key pragmatic tenets. Such creativity involved in scientific method implies a radical rejection of the "passive-spectator" view of knowledge and an introduction of the active, creative agent who, through meanings, helps to structure the objects of knowledge, and who cannot be separated from these objects.

These dynamics of scientific or experimental method are operative in science and common sense alike. As indicated earlier, for pragmatism all experience is experimental, manifesting the above features. Here it is important to clarify the point of the comparison of scientific method with the dynamics of everyday experience. This is in no way an attempt to assert that perceptual experience is really a highly intellectual affair. Rather, the opposite is more the case. Scientific objects are highly sophisticated and intellectualized tools for dealing with experience at a "second level," but they are not the product of any isolated intellect. Rather, the total biological organism in its behavioral response to the world is involved in the very ordering of any level of awareness, and scientific knowledge partakes of the character of even the most rudimentary aspects of organism–environment interaction.

Further, the scientific purpose of manipulation of the environment, and its use of scientific concepts as an instrument of such manipulative control, are not technological maneuvers into which human activity is to be absorbed. Rather, again, the opposite is more the case. All human activity, even at its most rudimentary level, is activity guided by direction and noetically transformative of its environment. As such, it is instrumental, and the abstractly manipulative and instrumental purposes attributed to science have their roots at the foundation of the very possibility of human experience in general. Moreover, human activity and the concepts which guide it are permeated by a value-laden value-driven dimension, and this dimension pervades the activity of the scientist, just as it pervades all human activity.

To be scientific does not mean to be inhumanly free of all biases, assumptions, and preconceived notions and convictions. However, being scientific does require that one be aware of these and to understand how they influence the way one structures one's research and the very way one perceives the resulting data, for observations are neither theory free nor value free. Indeed, no theory is itself value free, but one can become aware how the values and theories operative affect the type of data that emerges as well as the way one interprets the data. Observational and normative analysis, facts and values continually interact. Even this way of stating the situation is misleading, however, for facts and values are not ontologically disparate in kind, brought together through interaction. This point can be further clarified by turning to the pragmatic rethinking of the fact–value distinction from another direction.

It has been seen that nature is rich with contextually emergent qualities, including value as a real emergent property in the interactive context of organisms within nature. Value need not be, nor can it be, reduced to some experienced quality other than itself, for it is among the contextually emergent qualities which pervade our experience of nature. The occurrence of the immediate experience characterized by value is a qualitative dimension of a situation within nature, on an equal footing with the experiencing of other qualitative aspects of nature. Further, any experienced fact within the world can have a value dimension, for the value dimension emerges as an aspect of the context within which the fact functions as value relevant. Indeed, the experience of value is itself a discriminable fact within our world.

Claims about the valuable – about what *ought* to be – are about the enrichment of value, about creative ways of organizing the real value qualities of experience in ways which will direct activity toward what works in enhancing experienced value for all those involved over the long haul. There is, of course, a difference between normative and descriptive claims, but the difference is a difference based on contextual and functional considerations, not on ontologically distinct types of data, facts and values. Whether a statement is descriptive or normative depends on its function in a problematic situation. Moreover, normative judgments involve the facts relevant to the potential production of valuing experiences. It is not fact versus value but facts about values and their potential enhancement, about discriminating them and constructing them in ongoing experience. This requires not only knowledge of cause and effect relations operative in the non-human environment, but also an understanding of the probable type of effect particular actions will have on other participants in a situation given the factors which contour their ongoing activity.

Thus, normative conclusions, though not reducible to factual dimensions, cannot be understood even abstractly in separation from more factual dimensions. Unless one has some awareness of how human and environmental factors interrelate in concrete situations to give rise to value qualities within experience then normative claims are not possible. The diversity of immediately "had" values, because they are original qualitative emergents, within the context of our natural interactions with an environment, are real emergent facts within nature. The move to "ought" statements is not a move from facts to values, an attempt to pull an "ought" from an "is." Rather, it is a move to a claim about how to integrate originally conflicting data of problematic situations in ways which will organize, integrate, and enhance further value relevant qualitative experiences within nature.

The pragmatic understanding of value qualities (as naturally occurring, irreducible contextual emergents) and of normative claims (as experimental hypotheses about ways of enriching and expanding the value relevant dimension of concrete human existence) undercuts the entire problematics of the fact–value distinction. Facts and values emerge as wedded dimensions of complex contexts which cannot be dissected into atomic bits. The entire fact–value problem – as it has emerged from the past tradition of moral philosophy – is wrong-headed from the start. The problem of how values can exist in a world composed of facts – or how normative claims about what ought to be can be derived from descriptive statements of what is – is based on philosophical starting points which are alien to pragmatic thinking.

The development of normative principles is guided by experience, just as empirical studies are guided by values, and they both proceed via one general method, the method of experience as experimental, the method of experimental inquiry developed above. When one operates with the specific experimental tool of mathematical quantification and the "rigor" this allows, one tends to forget that this tool, in the very process of quantifying, leaves behind all of the richness of reality which cannot be caught by a quantitative net. The use of the tool of quantification within experimental method predetermines the type of content which is apprehended as being inherently mathematizable, and the exclusive mathematizable type of content apprehended reinforces the belief that quantification is the tool for observational truth.

The recognition that one methodology – the methodology of experimental inquiry – guides the development of normative principles and empirical research alike need not result in collapsing the two fields into a single entity, for they each use experimental method to abstract out different dimensions of concrete situations because of their different areas of focus, their different goals, and their different contextual interests. Nor does the recognition that the fact–value distinction is neither existentially nor ontologically rooted mandate such a collapse of the two fields. Indeed, this should not be the attempt, for one cannot study everything at once, nor can one grasp the world other than creatively and perspectively. Trying to do everything at once would result in a conceptual morass, and would be ultimately self-defeating to pursue. Rather, the methodology that unites the two areas of interest demands the reflective awareness in each area – that its perspectival approach not only cannot substitute for the other, but in fact gains its full significance only within the context of the other – and incorporates the dimensions of experience focused upon by the other in the essential structure of its own ongoing inquiries.

Moreover, there is demanded a recognition that each area of interest is highlighting a dimension of a unified concretely rich complexity from which both draw their ultimate intelligibility and vitality. The recognition of the common concrete context within which their respective frames of reference take shape, and which binds each to the other – along with a recognition of the common experimental method which unites their respective endeavors – should allow for ongoing dialogue which, in turn, reinforces this intertwining. The problem is not to figure out how to unite two ontological discretes – facts and values – but rather how to distinguish the two dimensions for purposes of intellectual clarity and advancement of understanding through experimental method without viewing the resultant "products" in ways which distort both the concrete reality they are intended to clarify and the process by which these products are obtained.

All of the above features of pragmatism combine to make it a unique framework for business ethics and provide, at the same time, an environmental ethics that can be part and parcel of it.

Environmental ethics

When it comes to the environment, business ethics is confronted with another field of ethics that has a separate body of literature, different professional organizations, and disparate scholars and educators. Attempts are being made to overcome this chasm through the establishment of new groups, through sessions at various organizational meetings, through special conferences, and through books and papers, all concerned with environmental issues both from managerial and ethical perspectives, however, some better bridge needs to be formed to allow dialogue to begin at a deeper, theoretical level. For, most importantly in understanding the chasm involved, the field of environmental ethics, by and large, rests on theories and conceptual foundations quite disparate from those of business ethics. This separation poses numerous problems – both practical and pedagogical – for the field of business ethics, and while the concern for the natural environment gains in importance, these problems can only multiply.

It has been seen that one presupposition underlying Kant, Bentham, and Mill and social contract theories alike is that of atomic individualism. Various attempts to overcome this external individualism cannot succeed; while peripheral ties may be established, when antecedent individuals enter into contract with one another or come together through other means of collection so as to secure their own individualistic goals more readily, these bonds cannot root them in any ongoing endeavor which is more than the sum of their separate selves, separate wills, separate egoistic desires, much less bond them to anything beyond contractually established social structures. Further, these positions lead to problems with the understanding of communities of any sort, for a community can be no more than the collective sum of the parts, with the individual in some sense pitted against, or set over, the collective whole in an external relationship.

Such positions are not congenial to the needs of environmental ethics, for there is no philosophical structure for providing an inherent relatedness of the individual and the broader natural environment. Neither are the virtue ethics approaches of Aristotle and McIntyre conducive for work in environmental ethics, for the self is now rooted in the cultural traditions of self-enclosed societies, and there is no philosophical structure available for moving beyond this impasse. Moreover, for all of the above position, the source of ethical action lies either in the application of abstract rules to cases or in the inculcation of tradition, neither of which incorporates the type of attunement to experience in nature which is required for a environmental consciousness. It is small wonder, then, that in the environmental literature one finds little application of these theories to the natural environment. Individual philosophers of the tradition utilized by business ethics, such as Kant and Aristotle, etc., are at times being used in theoretical discussions of environmental ethics in ways geared toward overcoming the above features that have pervaded moral thinking in industrial societies. However, the dominating drive in environmental ethics is to move beyond traditional positions to the development of other approaches to deal with problems that the natural environment poses for ethical thinking. Thus, the theoretical paths of the two fields are quite disparate.

The following discussion will briefly highlight the way in which pragmatism naturally lends itself to providing a unifying theoretical foundation for both business ethics and environmental ethics, as well as the way in which this perspective, in casting the theoretical problems of business ethics in a new light, at the same time reshapes many of the theoretical tensions of environmental ethics in a constructively new manner which is more "business-ethics friendly."

It has been seen that a proper understanding of the lessons of scientific method reveals that the nature into which the human organism is placed contains the qualitative fullness revealed in lived experience, and that the grasp of nature within the world is permeated with the action-oriented meaning structures by which the human organism and its world are interactionally bound, both at the level of scientific reflection and commonsense experience. The nature of everyday human experience is inherently experimental, reflecting the major features of scientific method developed above.

It is only within this context that the pragmatic focus on the human biological organism and organism–environment adaptation can be understood. The human being is within nature. Neither human activity in general nor human knowledge can be separated from the fact that this being is a natural organism dependent upon a natural environment. However, the human organism and the nature within which it is located are both rich with the qualities and values of our everyday experience. Distinctively human traits such as mind, thinking, and selfhood are emergent characteristics of nature, and part and parcel of its richness. They refer to ways in which the lived body behaves. For none of the pragmatists is the self understood as a self-enclosed entity. Rather, it is viewed as a body-self which is "located," if one speaks of location, throughout the biological organism with its reflexive ability as this emerges from, and opens onto, the relational contexts in which it functions. Humans are concrete organisms enmeshed in an environment with which they are continuous. Human development is ecologically connected with its biological as well as its cultural world.

From the backdrop of the non-spectator understanding of human experience, humans and their environment – organic and inorganic – take on an inherently relational aspect. To speak of organism and environment in isolation from each other is never true to the situation, for no organism can exist in isolation from an environment, and an environment is what it is in relation to an organism. The properties attributed to the environment belong to it, in the context of that interaction. What we have is interaction as an indivisible whole, and it is only within such an interactional context that experience and its qualities function.

It has been seen that growth cannot be understood in terms of mere accumulation. Rather growth, for the pragmatist, involves the deepening and expansion of perspective to include ever-widening horizons of the cultural and natural worlds to which we are inseparably bound. Moreover, though not independent of intelligent inquiry, growth is not merely a change in an intellectual perspective but rather is a change which affects, and is affected by, the individual in its total concreteness, allowing one to become more attuned to the fullness of existence in its concreteness and hence more appreciative of its qualitative richness and value-laden contexts. In this way, it can be seen again that growth is best understood as an increase in the moral–esthetic richness of experience.

Such a deepening involved in attunement allows us to "rise above" the divisiveness we impose through arbitrary and illusory in-group out-group distinctions by "delving beneath" to the sense of the possibilities of a deep-seated harmonizing of the self with the totality of the conditions to which it relates. For all the pragmatists, this involves the entire universe, for their emphasis on continuity reveals that, at no time, can we separate our developing selves from any part of the universe and claim that it is irrelevant. Indeed, while environmentalists may seek to describe "objective" relationships among interacting individuals – human, non-human, organic, and inorganic, that make up the biosphere – yet the properties attributed to the individuals are not possessed by them independently of the interactions in which they exhibit themselves. Nature cannot be dehumanized, nor can humans be denaturalized.

Humans exist within and are part of nature, and any part of nature provides a conceivable relational context for the emergence of value. The understanding of "human interests," of what is valuable for human enrichment, has to be expanded, not just in terms of long range versus short range and conceivable versus actual, but in terms of a greatly extended notion of human interest or human welfare. Further, to increase the experience of value is not to increase something subjective or within us, but to increase the value ladenness of relational contexts within nature. While every situation or context is in some sense unique, no situation or context is outside the reaches of moral concern. Pragmatic ethics, properly understood, is an environmental ethics.

Such an ethics cannot be called an anthropocentrism, a position from which environmental ethics is concerned to distance itself. True, only humans can evaluate; and, without evaluation as a judgment concerning what best serves the diversity of experienced value, the normative could not emerge. Further, humans can speak of non-human types of experience only analogically in reference to their own. However, though the concept of what ought to be emerges only through judgments involving human intelligence, value emerges – either positively or negatively – at any level of environmental interaction involving sentient organisms.

Yet, neither can this position be considered a biocentrism which faces the problem of devaluing human life in favor of the biotic community as a whole. For, while value is an emergent contextual property of situations as long as and whenever there are sentient organisms experiencing, yet the value-level emergent in organism–environment contexts increases with the increased capacity of the organism to experience in conscious and self-conscious ways. Though some may question the claim that a distinction in levels of value-emergence can be made, when push comes to shove, when all the abstract arguments are made, is it not the case that claims of the valuable must be seen in light of its promotion of, or irrepressible harm to, human welfare, actual or potential? Does anyone really think that the preservation of the spotted owl and the preservation of the AIDS virus have equal moral claim? The biological egalitarianism of biocentrism can perhaps be thought consistently, but it cannot be maintained in practice. Surely one is not willing to move from the theoretical egalitarianism of humans and the AIDS virus to an implementation of such theory in practice. Yet, this does not mean that humans can ignore the value contexts of sentient organisms within nature. To do so is not to evaluate in terms of the weighing of conflicting claims, but to exploit through egocentric disregard for the valuings of other organisms. We must make judgments which provide protection for the welfare of humans, yet such judgments must consider the value-laden contexts involving other sentient organisms to the largest degree consistent with this goal.

This pragmatic position, then, cuts beneath the either–or of anthropocentrism/biocentrism. In fact, both–and is closer to the position intended, but even this is inadequate, for it fails to capture the radical conceptual shift which, in making the conjunction, changes the original extremes of the positions brought together. There is no "all or none" involved. It is not the case that all value is such, only in relation to humans. Yet, neither is it the case that all value has equal claim, irrespective of its relation to the welfare of humans. It has been seen that if evaluations are to be about anything, they must be about the way experiences of value, actual or conceivable, are to be organized. Only contexts involving sentient organisms yield the emergence of value, but, while this position does not allow for the emergence of value in non-sentient contexts, yet neither does it allow for the exploitation of non-sentient contexts. For, is it possible to envision any aspect of nature, any relational context in nature, any thing in nature that cannot be the object of a conceivable experience of sentient organisms?

It may be further questioned as to whether the pragmatic ideal of "fully attained growth" in the union of self and universe merges into an ecocentrism in which value is given to the system rather than to the individual. Here again, these alternatives do not hold within the pragmatic context. Sometimes, the system is more important, sometimes the individual, and this is dependent on the contexts in which meaningful moral situations emerge and the conflicting claims at stake. Further, no absolute break can be made between the individual and the system, for each is inextricably linked with the other and gains its significance in terms of the other. The whole notion of an isolated individual is an abstraction, for diversity and continuity have been seen to be inextricably interrelated. Neither individuals nor whole systems are the bearers of value, but rather value emerges in the interactions of individuals, and wholes gain their value through the interactions of individuals, while the value of individuals cannot be understood in isolation from the relationships which constitute their ongoing development. When we slide over the complexities of a problem, we can easily be convinced that categorical moral issues are at stake. Also, complexities of a problem are always context dependent or relational.

The conflict of business ethics and environmental ethics is brought into sharp focus in what has been seen as the fundamental choice of environmental policy: whether our relation to nature is ethical or economic, whether we will see nature as having intrinsic value or instrumental value. The pragmatic answer is that our relation to nature is at once moral and economic. The protection of the environment and the enhancement of quality of life are inextricably joined through the esthetic–moral nature of concrete growth as involving the ongoing integration and expansion of concrete contexts in their qualitative richness, and this concrete growth involves economic dimensions as part and parcel of its moral nature.

Further, from the pragmatic perspective, the entire debate concerning instrumental versus intrinsic value is wrong-headed from the start. Everything that can conceivably enter into experience has the potential for being a relational aspect of the context within which value emerges, and any value, as well as any aspect of the context within which it emerges, involves consequences and is therefore instrumental in bringing about something further. There is an ongoing continuity in which the character of the means enters into the quality of the end, which in turn becomes a means to something further. Moreover, interaction is an indivisible whole, and it is only within such an interactional context that experience and its qualities function. The intrinsic–extrinsic dichotomy is again a remnant of the fact–value distinction rooted in the illicit reification of abstractions which dominated the modern world view.

In conclusion, it can be seen that the new directions offered by pragmatic thinking involve inextricably intertwined pathways. The understanding of the relational nature of the self – and the ongoing socializing accommodations of self and other in the dynamics of community – undercuts atomic individualism and the false alternatives to which this gives rise. The deepening process which goes beneath the abstract principles embodied in diverse and often conflicting perspectives to a more fundamental level of human rapport, thereby allowing for ongoing growth of self and community, includes a deepening attunement to the value-laden richness of concrete human existence and the diversity of concrete valuings which must be reconstructed and harmonized in problematic contexts. This involves a rejection of top-down fixed-end reasoning in favor of concrete contextual decision making as the matrix from which experimental hypotheses and novel habits of acting take their shape, and by which they are judged. A new understanding of rationality emerges which is not that of abstract, calculative rule-driven activity but concrete, imaginative, attunement to situational complexities. These features, in turn, involve ever-expanding relational contexts and the inclusion of the natural environment as part and parcel of the relational matrixes within which the concrete richness of human existence is embedded and which provide the very fiber for the esthetic–moral richness of concrete human growth.

New directions in business ethics are not going to be found in a forced choice between traditional alternatives but in a recognition of the way in which these traditional alternatives distort the very nature of the concrete reality they must ultimately serve. This recognition requires a clear rejection of the modern world view with its separation of facts and values, instrumental goods and intrinsic goods, its atomic individualism and fascination with the products of quantification, its resulting understanding of growth as the quantifiable accumulation of individual things and, what underlies it all, its persistence in giving independent status to discriminable dimensions of concrete human existence, resulting in the need for us to engage, ceaselessly, in destructive choices among false alternatives or in the futile endeavor of trying to put together that which a long philosophical tradition has illicitly pulled asunder in the first place. The above discussion has attempted to provide a sketch of the way in the which the normative frame offered by pragmatic philosophy provides viable new directions out of this quagmire.

References

Callicott, J. B. 1990: The case against moral pluralism. *Environmental Ethics*, 12, 115.

Derry, R. and Green, R. M. 1989: Ethical theory in business ethics. *Journal of Business Ethics*, 8, 521.

Rosenthal, S. B. 1986: *Speculative Pragmatism*. Amherst, Massachusetts: The University of Massachusetts Press.

Rosenthal, S. B. 1990: *Speculative Pragmatism* (paperback edn). Peru, Illinois: Open Court Publishing Co.

Treviño, L. K. and Weaver, E. R. 1994: Business ETHICS/BUSINESS ethics: One field or two? *Business Ethics Quarterly*, 4, 113–28.

Weston, A. 1991: Comment: On Callicott's case against pluralism. *Environmental Ethics*, 13, 283–6.

Wenz, P. S. 1993: Minimal, moderate, and extreme moral pluralism. *Environmental Ethics*, 15, 61–74.

11

Business ethics: pragmatism and postmodernism

R. EDWARD FREEMAN AND ROBERT A. PHILLIPS

Introduction

For the first fifty of so years of its life, business ethics has developed primarily along two lines of thought. The first – encapsulated in the phrase "business and society" or "social issues in management" – tries to situate business conceived as primarily economic activity into a larger social matrix. The scholars who have taken this approach have resided primarily in business schools, and have adopted many of the methods of their colleagues particularly from the social sciences. The second approach, encapsulated in the phrase "business ethics" comes primarily from philosophers working in the Kantian or analytic tradition. "Business ethics" has come to be seen by these scholars as one more realm in which ethicists can apply their mostly Kantian theories. In principle, business ethics is no different from medical ethics, whereby general ethical principles are deduced from the categorical imperative or some modern version of it, and then applied to the context of business.

Recently, some scholars have adopted a different approach. Perhaps this new approach will bring together both strands of business ethics, or perhaps it will make them irrelevant. We want to describe some features of this new approach and how it dovetails with some broader intellectual trends that go under politically charged names like "postmodernism" and "pragmatism."

It is presumptuous to attempt in the span of a single chapter to discuss the concepts of business ethics, postmodernism, and pragmatism. First, as the name suggests, postmodernism is a response to the method of inquiry characterized as "modern" (or "Enlightenment") thinking. Hence, in order to make any sense out of postmodernism, it will be necessary to give a thumbnail sketch of the Enlightenment project to which it is a response, and this alone is an effort that is guaranteed to include vast overgeneralizations and incomplete descriptions. Interestingly, the effort to *define* postmodernism without reference to modernism (and other contextual features) is a remnant of modernism itself. Any postmodern description or definition of anything would have to refer to the context and practice of which it is a part. On a postmodern account, there is no such thing as "the thing-in-itself," so it should come as no surprise that it would be necessary to describe the context that gives rise to postmodernism so as to fully describe both the postmodern critical and affirmative projects.

The second reason the project at hand is presumptuous is the existence of a rather large and wide-ranging canon of work that is characterized variously as postmodern or "the new pragmatism." In philosophy and critical theory alone, the works of Lyotard (1984), Foucault (1972), Gadamer (1975), Rorty (1979, 1982, 1991), Nietzsche (1969a), and Heidegger (1962), among many others, provide enough intellectual raw material from which to fashion an academic career. And, this is before we look at the emerging scholarship on postmodern organization studies and business ethics more specifically. Therefore, in this chapter, we are forced to limit ourselves to broad characterizations of modernism, postmodernism and pragmatism. We invite the reader to examine more closely the works cited herein for a better understanding of topics discussed.

In the following sections, we will move from the rather broad notion of postmodernism as a response to the Enlightenment project (modernism) to the more specific instantiation of this postmodern response in the area of organization studies. We will then suggest that postmodernism and pragmatism have both a deconstructive and a reconstructive task. We show how these tasks have been carried out by a number of scholars working in business ethics.

Postmodernism and pragmatism as a response to the Enlightenment

Both approaches to business ethics that we mentioned above share a common tradition: the Enlightenment Project of the triumph of reason over the world. While there are many ways, all of them controversial, of stating this project, the basic idea is that humans can use their reason to dominate and control the world. Science and the language of science is at the forefront of this battle, from Da Vinci to Feynman. And, we should understand science as foundational, as providing certainty to our knowledge and hence our place in the world. Certainly, the majority of scholars in business ethics, trained either as philosophers or social scientists, have been influenced by the masters of Western intellectual thought from Plato through Kant, Bentham, Mill, Hobbes, Locke, etc. They share a belief in the inevitable forward march of science and philosophy towards knowledge of the objective truth. That is, there is a notion of the truth in-itself (which we will designate "Truth") and, if humans could only see through their own biases and cognitive shortcomings, they would be able to rationally see Nature for what it is and come to know the Truth.

The Enlightenment project has provided the world with many scientific and cultural advantages. Knowledge in the natural and social sciences is increasing at an unprecedented rate, and the uses to which humans have been able to put this knowledge are nothing short of wondrous. We do not dispute the usefulness of Enlightenment thinking. The challenge posed by postmodernism concerns the relative importance of the search for knowledge over the Truth that is sought. The postmodernist argues that there is no Truth to be known. There are no "foundations" to be found. Rather, Truth is the compliment we pay to ideas upon which there is relatively more agreement among intelligent creatures. The search for "foundations" is a search for a level of abstraction and generalization in our ideas that can meet with the highest possible level of agreement among intelligent creatures (and thus lay claim to the accolade

"Truth"). That is, objectivity is merely a very high degree of intersubjectivity among relevant parties. As postmodernists and pragmatists, we applaud the search for "Truth" because it helps us to live better, not because there is some Truth out there waiting to be discovered.

Richard Rorty has spent the last several years crafting in detail the linkage between postmodernism and pragmatism. He has argued that Dewey's experimentalism has roughly the same starting point as Derrida and Foucault. The antifoundationalism of the postmodernist and the attitude of "everything being up for grabs" of the pragmatist unite both in a search for better ways to live. In Rorty's (1989) words, the pragmatist has twofold project of "community and self redescription."

For the most part, postmodernism has adopted a critical stance, a questioning and tearing down of the received edifices of modern thought. Postmodernists have developed a method, or perhaps an "anti-method" known as "deconstruction" by which texts are shown to collapse into self-reference, contradiction or become exposed as insensitive to the human matrix of race, gender, sexuality, and class. Those who bear the label "postmodern" have come to be seen as radical, as suggesting that systems of thought have to be ruptured, torn down, and undermined in a wholesale way.

On the other hand, the pragmatists like Rorty are reformers. They seek to describe and redescribe the best and worst of human experience in hopes that better ways of living and interacting with each other can be invented. Such a program is no Pollyanna affair, as the human condition requires that description and redescription take a careful look at the matrix of race, gender, class, authority, and the like. However, for the most part pragmatists have come to designate those who are more hopeful and reconstructive rather than deconstrutive.

Sandra Rosenthal and Rogene Buchholz have recently taken a very different approach to pragmatism from the one described here. Their book (1999) eschews the connection between pragmatism and postmodernism, and relies on a more traditional interpretation of the American pragmatists, John Dewey and Herbert Mead. They fall squarely into the reconstructionist camp.

The postmodern response in organization studies

As we attempt to narrow our subject down from the most general notions of postmodernism as a response to the Enlightenment project toward our goal of assessing the role of postmodern thought on the field of business ethics, a reasonable focal point is the role of postmodernism in organizational studies. (The assumption in this instance is that business ethics is a branch of organization studies. This should not be taken as implying exclusivity of lineage. That is, business ethics is (rightly in our estimation) a child of many disciplinary parents. Organization studies is merely the one on which we have chosen to focus – though the effect of postmodernism on other disciplines is similar to the effects described herein upon organization studies.)

Alvesson and Deetz (1996) have provided a helpful assessment of the emerging role of postmodernism in the study of organizations. Though recognizing the multiplicity in the use of the term "postmodern," Alvesson and Deetz suggest some "common themes" in the postmodern organization studies literature:

In postmodernism as a philosophically based research perspective . . . the following, on the whole interrelated, set of ideas is often emphasized: (a) the centrality of discourse – textuality – where the constitutive powers of language are emphasized and "natural" objects are viewed as discursively produced; (b) fragmented identities, emphasizing subjectivity as a process and the death of the individual, autonomous, meaning-creating subject where the discursive production of the individual replaces the conventional "essentialistic" understanding of people; (c) the critique of the philosophy of presence and representation where the indecidabilities of language take precedence over language as a mirror of reality and a means for the transport of meaning; and (d) the loss of foundations and the power of grand narratives where an emphasis on multiple voices and local politics is favored over theoretical frameworks and large-scale political projects.

It should prove helpful for our purposes to describe some of the effects of postmodernism on one of more general fields upon which business ethics is based.

First there is the matter of the centrality of discourse. The postmodern approach operates on the notion that ideas – including our conceptions of objects in the physical world – are dependent upon the language used to describe them. Indeed, ideas just are the words by which they are described. This is consistent with the so-called linguistic turn in philosophy (Wittgenstein, 1968; Habermas, 1984, 1987). The world cannot be "carved up at the joints," because there are no joints prior to humans discursively creating them. The language that we use is the primary means by which humans interact with the world and, hence, influences how the world is perceived. Knowledge is dependent on language for its description and, therefore, for its reality.

Another commonality among postmodern organization studies is, according to Alvesson and Deetz, the move toward a "fragmented" view of the person. This notion is in contrast to the modernist assumption of the unitary person. This assumption, attacked by Freud, tended toward the suppression of conflict and the privileging of "masculinity, rationality, vision, and control." The postmodernist departs from such assumptions and, instead, views the person as complex. Persons are inevitably situated in a matrix of race, gender, sexuality, power, and other complex notions that have moral content.

Another commonality among postmodern discourses of organization studies is the view taken of objects in the external world. Postmodernism denies the existence of any attainable "Objective Truth." Rather, objects are seen as bundled up with and inseparable from their context. According to Alvesson and Deetz (1996, pp. 207–208): "The questions 'What is a worker really?', 'What is the essence of a worker?', 'What makes one a worker?' are not answerable by looking at the something that can be described as a worker, but are the products of the linguistic and nonlinguistic practices that make something into an object . . . The focus on the object and object properties is the mistake; the attention should be to the relational systems which are not simply in the world but are a human understanding of the world, are discursive or textual."

All objects are mediated by human perceptions, and human perceptions are dependent upon language and context. An object's meaning is not contained in the object "in itself." Rather, we know something "by the relations that make it like and unlike other things."

The postmodern response is also generally characterized by a disbelief in "grand narratives" and ahistorical "foundations." Rather, on the postmodern account, truth is local. While many have suggested that this commits postmodernists to a kind of relativism, Rorty and other pragmatists have responded that one has to start one's narrative from where one is, and that is situated in time, in place, in the human matrix. Narratives stand or fall, not because they correspond to the world, but because they are useful.

Boje, Gephart, and Thatchenkery (1966b) provide an entire volume dedicated to postmodernism in organization studies. Whereas many articles on the subject simply present an overview of the postmodernist affect on whatever the particular field may be (rather like the chapter you are reading), their volume tries to "advance the field by offering essays that not only review and explain postmodern perspectives and concepts but that also actually apply these postmodern concepts and ideas to emerging managerial and organizational issues that characterize the postmodern era" (Gephart et al., 1996).

Toward this end, Boje, Gephart, and Thatchenkery have assembled essays concerning the relationships between early modem, late modem and postmodern organizations (Gephart, 1996) as well as organization theory (Hassard, 1996), a postmodern deconstruction of how the scientific stories among the "administrative science subcommunity" have served to squelch postmodernism (Boje et al., 1996a), as well as essays on gender, the natural environment, pedagogy, and globalization. Wicks and Freeman (1998) have recently argued that a more thoroughgoing pragmatism can serve to better build theories of organization. They seek to put a reconstructive spin on what has largely become a deconstructive project.

These are but a few examples of the growing literature on postmodernism in organization studies. Having now (too briefly) discussed postmodernism in general and some of its specific uses in organization studies, we may proceed to a discussion of these ideas in the study of organizational ethics.

Postmodern and pragmatist organizational ethics

In parallel with the previous, more general discussions, postmodernism in organizational ethics has manifested as, among other instantiations, deconstructionist, reconstructionist, feminist, and multi-culturalist critiques. Richard Nielsen's recent work on action learning is an important example of both the deconstructionist and reconstructionist varieties of postmodernism employed in the context of organizational ethics. As such, we begin with a discussion of this work followed by some analyses of the role of gender and multiculturalism in business ethics.

Nielsen's theory of action learning

Nielsen's theory of action learning includes ways in which several varieties of postmodernism may be useful in thinking about organizational ethics. He begins by suggesting a categorization of postmodern scholarship (Nielsen, 1993, 1996). He distinguishes between "unfriendly, friendly, and experimental postmodernism." He describes "unfriendly deconstruction" as "adversarial, sometimes mocking, criticism of negative biases-oppressions in 'dominant' cultures/systems." Examples of such unfriendly postmodernists are Nietzsche (1969a, b), Heidegger (1962), Derrida (1981), and Foucault (1972). Most, if not all, of the writings of these authors are aimed toward the destruction (or deconstruction) of all notions of metaphysics and the entire Enlightenment project. To these authors, all mainstream thought is bankrupt. Further, they make few suggestions for modes of thought with which to replace the mainstream ways of thinking except difference, pluralism and diversity for their own sakes. There is little in the way of a goal for either humans or society, except the multiplication of diversity. This is the most nihilistic variety of postmodernism.

Nielsen's second category of postmodernism is what he terms "friendly reconstruction" characterized by "friendly upbuilding upon shared commonalties, positive prejudices, and friendly criticism of negative biases / oppressions in cultures / systems." Exemplars of this variety of postmodern thought include (according to Nielsen) Kirkegaard (1938) and Gadamer (1975). Like the deconstructionists, these thinkers also perceive little in the way of universal foundations for knowledge and objective Truth. On their accounts, we still have nothing to rely upon but our own biases and prejudices. However, contrary to the unfriendly deconstructionists, the friendly reconstructionists do perceive the possibility of overlap among variously held prejudices. It is this overlap that may allow for some (temporary) progress and improvement in the human condition. That is, while there is no objective Truth, there may nonetheless be adequate coincidence of views to allow people to work together.

The final category suggested by Nielsen is that of the experimental pragmatist. The pragmatist focuses on "civil consensus-building experimentation that continues, evolves, and can result in at least temporary improvements." Rorty (1998) stands out as the most prolific and eloquent defender of neo-pragmatism and a recent essay applies his general pragmatism to business ethics.

After suggesting this taxonomy, Nielsen employs the various techniques described to demonstrate how these different styles of postmodern thought may be of use in the case of an international child worker safety dilemma. The three styles of postmodernism correspond with three "moments" in a solution-generating discourse between two managers on the opposite horns of a dilemma involving profound cultural and political disagreements. In this way, Nielsen is able to fashion, from postmodernism a potential positive solution from an otherwise intractable situation. Even the most nihilistic and critical variations of postmodernism are put to positive use in this way.

Some feminist analyses

There is no one univalent theory called "feminism". Rather there are many "feminisms" which offer different analyses of both postmodernism and business. We want to look at two recent approaches to apply some feminist thinking to business ethics: one by Calas and Smircich (1997), and another by Wicks, Gilbert and Freeman (1994).

In a recent essay, Calas and Smircich (1997) argue that business ethics has developed as an apology for business. They outline three tasks for a feminism intent on revising the role of morality in organizations.

1 The record needs to be completed and corrected, since it often leaves out the role of the silent other, the woman or other oppressed groups.
2 Bias in current knowledge must be assessed.
3 There needs to be "new theorizing" an opening of the discipline to diverse often silent points of view.

They begin this task in business ethics by showing, in detail, how some of the utilitarian arguments need to be understood in light of a feminist revision of utilitarianism that assesses the importance of Harriet Taylor in addition to Mill. They suggest that current bias be acknowledged in the Kantian portion of business ethics by focusing on a contextualization of Kant and his view of women. This critique has much in common with Seyla Benhabib's idea that Kant's idea of the "generalized other" does not allow for the particularity of women's experience. Finally, they suggest a wholesale revision of the texts of business ethics to include other voices such as Chodorow, Gilligan, Harding, Dewey, Sartre, and others.

Showing how the language of patriarchy pervades business ethics is an important critical task – one that is "postmodern" in spirit and execution – but Calas and Smircich go further to recommend how we can revise business ethics to make it more useful, to empower the disempowered, and to give voice to large silences. In this reconstructive project, they show how business ethics can be enriched and how it can regain its profoundly critical stance, which is necessary if we are to redescribe business in more human terms.

In another recent paper, Wicks et al. (1994) suggest that feminist standpoint theory – the idea that women are equal to and different from men – can be used to reconstruct some of the basic ideas in business ethics and, in particular, stakeholder theory. They show how masculinist assumptions are present in the development of stakeholder theory and suggest a revision so that it is more in line with what Carol Gilligan and others call "different voice feminism." The basic idea is to see corporations as networks of relationships built on caring and connection, rather than as bubbles of autonomy threatened by interaction. Stakeholder management on this reconstruction is "about creating value for an entire network of stakeholders by working to develop effective forms of cooperation, decentralizing power and authority, and building consensus among stakeholders through communication to generate strategic direction" (Wicks et al., p. 493).

So, both Calas and Smircich, writing from the outside of business ethics, and Wicks, Gilbert, and Freeman, writing from the inside of business ethics, come to similar conclusions: that seeing business ethics in more inclusive and more critical terms invites a more useful analysis for the project of reconstruction. (The next section is based on Freeman (1997) and we wish to thank the editors for their permission to reprint some paragraphs here.)

Some multicultural analyses

What pragmatists and postmodernists agree upon is a view often called "multiculturalism." Multiculturalism starts with the premise that most of our "knowledge" is fixed in the sense that the 1919 World Series was fixed. Whether something is knowledge largely depends on the race, gender, sexual orientation and culture of the author with the winners all "just happening" to be white, Western males. Multiculturalism seeks to address what we might call "monoculturalism" by a politics of inclusion, by including others' work who are explicitly not white, Western males. Thus both of the articles discussed above move for a multiculturalism in business ethics.

Henry Louis Gates, Jr suggests that we adopt a "minority culture view" that explicitly recognizes that the standpoint of a minority culture, in particular African American culture, is in fact multicultural. Gates (1992) reminds us: "For whatever the outcome of the culture wars in the academy, the world we live in is multicultural already. Mixing and hybridity are the rule, not the exception. As a student of African American culture, of course, I've come to take this kind of cultural palimpsest for granted. Duke Ellington, Miles Davis, and John Coltrane have influenced popular musicians the world over. Wynton Marsalis is as comfortable with Mozart as with jazz. Anthony Davis writes in a musical idiom that combines Bartok with the blues. In the dance, Judith Jameson, Alvin Ailey, and Katherine Dunham all excelled at 'Western' cultural forms, melding these with African American styles to produce performances that were neither, and both. In painting, . . . and in literature, . . . African American culture, then, has been a model of multiculturalism and plurality. It is this cultural impulse, I believe, that represents the best hope for us, collectively to forge a new, and vital, common American culture in the twenty-first century."

Freeman (1997) goes on to show how we might define a multicultural firm from the standpoint of such a minority culture, and suggests that most of the major terms of the debate of business ethics are in fact from the standpoint of monoculture. Thus, we can read Gates as inspiring yet another critical and reconstructive view in business ethics much in the spirit offered by Calas and Smircich. It is worth noting that most business ethics conversations are simply silent about the role of race.

In *Race Matters*, philosopher Cornell West (1993) suggests that race places a critical role in our understanding of the human condition. Like many theorists before him, he laments the current conversation about race, and suggests that until we escape the debate between liberals (who want more structural solutions) and conservatives (who want more individual initiative), we are unlikely to make much progress.

Liberals assume that the causes are structural in nature and that the solution is better structures; conservatives assume that the problem is internal to the character of poor people with the only hope to be better people. While West believes that we certainly need better structures and that we need more people to bootstrap their way out of poverty, he identifies a different alternative for our discourse. Because he sees poverty and hopelessness as intimately connected, he calls for a politics of conversion within a prophetic framework to restore hope and to offer the possibility of creating some meaningful future. A politics of conversion offers hope that people can struggle together to find meaning, and a prophetic framework builds in moral assessment from the beginning. Now, West is proposing such a framework as necessary to address the African American experience in the USA, but we want to suggest that it has a broader application. (We want to do this without minimizing the differences between the problems of racism and poverty, and certainly without suggesting that the African American experience is solely or even essentially defined by poverty.) It is ironic that West sees no role for capitalism in this prophetic framework, for we want to suggest that, if we can retell the story of capitalism in a particular way, we can see how the prophetic framework can gain even more power and applicability.

Retelling the story of capitalism in a prophetic framework should be one of the central tasks of a postmodern and pragmatist approach to business ethics, and there are multiple retellings available. R. Edward Freeman and several colleagues have suggested one such project of redescription – coming to see the very idea of capitalism as a co-operative enterprise among firms and their customers, suppliers, employees, financiers and communities. The resulting view known as "values-based capitalism" or "stake-holder capitalism" is a retelling of the narrative of business that gives a central role to ethics and to the cultural and even biological matrix that is the human condition. Freeman and his colleagues suggest that the role of business ethics scholar is neither to prescribe nor describe business, but one of putting together narratives which describe and redescribe the best and worst of business as we know it.

Conclusion

We would like to conclude with some general comments on the relationship between postmodernism and business ethics. It bears mention how closely intertwined are the goals of business, business ethics, and postmodernism. That is, business brings people into closer and more frequent contact with those of other nationalities, cultures, back-grounds, and assumptions than would otherwise be the case. This is increasingly true as business becomes an increasingly global practice. Business *is* the commonality sought by the reconstructionists; see for example Nielsen, (1996). The only contact that some people have with those of different meta-narratives is through economic exchange. Business and trade since ages past – at least since Marco Polo, Columbus, and the great expeditionists – has forced the margins down the throats of foundationalists. While immanent critique may be possible from within the various traditions, the demands of economic interactions with other cultures provide a more stark and im-mediate call for assessment of similarities and differences. Historically, encounters with such differing traditions demanded war rather than reconciliation. This made it easier for both sides to remain convinced of the Truth of their own traditions. The imperat-ives of economic trade and the continuance of commercial interaction for mutual benefit make such narrow-minded conviction a great deal more difficult.

Another commonality of the work described herein as postmodern business ethics is an emphasis not only on *de*construction, but more importantly on *re*construction. Postmodernism, especially when considered of a piece with critical theory, may be considered as merely a critical project decrying the current state of affairs with little explication of what should replace it. This is not so with the postmodernist business ethics work considered here. Nielsen, Calas and Smircich, Rorty, Wicks, Gilbert and Freeman, Gates, and West all suggest a positive replacement for the conditions they find wanting. This is the necessary next step for postmodernism. It is time to move beyond treatises on the death of Western metaphysics and put more work into prag-matically and optimistically figuring out ways to help us live (and work) better.

Finally, to embrace postmodernism is to obviate the need for the facile distinction between science and the humanities. We freely admit that the tools and knowledge with which the Enlightenment has provided us are invaluable and it would be foolish to abandon them. We whole-heartedly advocate the use of the tools of social science (e.g., the methodologies and theories of economics, sociology, psychology, etc.) in dis-cussions of business ethics. Such tools are invaluable. An earlier quote from Alvesson and Deetz (1996) mentioned that to look at objects and object properties is a mistake.

We find this to overstate the matter somewhat. The search for object (and objective) properties is a (pragmatically) valid and useful search, and one that will likely continue in the advancement of knowledge. However, especially in the fields of organization studies and business ethics, the tools of social science should be employed with full knowledge of their limitations as well as the discursive and intersubjective nature of the subject matter being pursued. That is, social scientists should operate with full awareness of the nature of their quarry, and with a more robust understanding of the nature of "truth" (with a small "t"). Although the goal of perfect objectivity is an impossible one, the fact remains that the search for more objective knowledge will tend toward the expanding of human knowledge. While quantum physics may not be perfectly objective – the Heisenberg uncertainty principle suggests that the act of investigation affects the quanta studied – it is more useful (it allows human beings to do more things) than the Aristotelian, Ptolemaic, Copernican, and Newtonian theories that preceded it (Kuhn, 1970) and the last thing we want to advocate is the cessation of such basic research.

However, the usefulness of scientific approaches and the advances of the Enlightenment should not blind us to the value of other methods of rendering knowledge. The exclusivity in organization studies of social scientific approaches is unwarranted and unduly limiting. Even on a modernist account of knowledge, management and organization scholars have failed to use all of the tools at their disposal to best advance our wisdom on the subject of people in organizations through the systematic exclusion of anything "non-scientific" from the conversation. That is, the desire for scientific legitimacy has caused many business scholars to discount the usefulness of humanities-based accounts of business. Given the nature of truth and objectivity that postmodernism exposes, there is now even less reason (and there was not much before) to exclude non-scientific contributions to our knowledge of organizations and organizational ethics more specifically.

References

Alvesson, M. and Deetz, S. 1996: Critical theory and postmodernism approaches to organizational studies. In S. Clegg, C. Hardy and W. Nord (eds), *Handbook of Organization Studies*, London: Sage Publications, 197–217.

Boje, D. M., Fitzgibbons, D. E. and Steingard, D. S. 1996a: Storytelling at *Administrative Science Quarterly*: Warding off the postmodern barbarians. In Boje et al. (1996b, pp. 60–92).

Boje, D. M., Gephart, R. P. Jr, and Thatchenkery, T. J. (eds) 1996b: *Postmodern Management and Organization Theory*. Thousand Oaks, CA: Sage Publications.

Calas, M. and Smircich, L. 1997: Predicando la moral en calzoncillos. In A. Larson and E. Freeman (eds), *Women's Studies and Business Ethics: Towards a New Conversation*, New York: Oxford University Press, 50–79.

Derrida, J. 1981: Three questions to Hans-Georg Gadamer. Interpreting signatures (Nietzsche/Heidegger): Two questions. In D. P. Michelfelder and R. E. Palmer (eds) 1989: *Dialogue and Deconstruction: The Gadamer–Derrida Encounter*, Albany: SUNY Press, 52–5.

Foucault, M. 1972: *Power-Knowledge*. New York: Pantheon.

Freeman, R. M. 1997: Managing in a global economy: From relativism to multiculturalism. In B. Toyne and D. Nigh (eds), *International Business: An Emerging Vision*, Columbia, SC: University of South Carolina Press, 131–9.

Gadamer, H.-G. 1975: *Truth and Method.* New York: Seabury Press.

Gates, H. L. Jr 1992: *Loose Canons.* New York: Oxford University Press, xvi–xvii.

Gephart, R. P. 1996: Management, social issues, and the postmodern era. In Boje et al. (1996b, pp. 21–44).

Gephart, R. P., Boje, D. M. and Thatchenkery, T. J. 1996: Postmodern management and the coming crises of organizational analysis. In Boje et al. (1996b, pp. 1–18).

Habermas, J. 1984/1987: *The Theory of Communicative Action, Vols. 1 and 2.* Translated by T. McCarthy. Boston: Beacon Press.

Hassard, J. 1996: Exploring the terrain of modernism and postmodernism in organization theory. In Boje et al. (1996b, pp. 45–59).

Heidegger, M. 1962: *Being and Time.* New York: Harper & Row. First published in 1932.

Kirkegaard, S. 1938: *Purity of Heart.* Translated by D. Steere. New York: Harper and Row. First published in 1846.

Kuhn, T. S. 1970: *The Structure of Scientific Revolutions,* 2nd edn. Chicago: University of Chicago Press.

Lyotard, J.-F. 1984: *The Postmodern Condition: A Report on Knowledge.* Translated by G. Bennington and B. Massumi. Minneapolis: University of Minnesota Press.

Nielsen, R. P. 1993: Varieties of postmodernism as moments in ethics action learning. *Business Ethics Quarterly,* 3(3), 251–70.

Nielsen, R. P. 1996: *The Politics of Ethics.* New York: Oxford University Press.

Nietzsche, F. 1969a: *Ecce Homo.* Translated by W. Kaufman and R. J. Hollingdale. New York: Random House. First published in 1878.

Nietzsche, F. 1969b: *The Genealogy of Morals.* Translated by W. Kaufman and R. J. Hollingdale. New York: Random House. First published in 1887.

Rorty, R. 1979: *Philosophy and the Mirror of Nature.* Princeton: Princeton University Press.

Rorty, R. 1982: *Consequences of Pragmatism.* Minneapolis: University of Minnesota Press.

Rorty, R. 1989: *Contingency, Irony and Solidarity.* New York: Cambridge University Press.

Rorty, R. 1991: *Objectivity, Relativism, and Truth.* New York: Cambridge University Press.

Rorty, R. 1998: Can American egalitarianism survive in a globalised economy? *Business Ethics Quarterly,* Supplemental Volume. The Ruffin Lectures, 1–6.

Rosenthal, S. and Buchholz, R. 1999: Rethinking Business Ethics: A Pragmatic Approach. New York: Oxford University Press.

West, C. 1993: *Race Matters.* Boston: Beacon Press.

Wicks, A. C. and Freeman, R. E. 1998: Organization studies and the new pragmatism: Positivism, antipositivism, and the search for ethics. *Organization Science,* 9(2), 123–40.

Wicks, A., Gilbert, D. and Freeman, E. 1994: A feminist reinterpretation of the stakeholder concept. *Business Ethics Quarterly,* 4(4), 475–98.

Wittgenstein, L. 1968: *Philosophical Investigations.* Translated by G. E. M. Anscombe. Oxford: Blackwell.

PART II

BUSINESS ETHICS AND THE BUSINESS DISCIPLINES

12

Ethics in management

ARCHIE B. CARROLL

Managers in organizations face ethical issues every day of their working lives. There is seldom a decision they face that does not have an ethical dimension or facet to it. In addition to facing ethical aspects in their decision making, they confront ethical issues as they carry out their leadership responsibilities. Whether they be engaged in planning, organizing, motivating, communicating, or some other management role, they face the fact that matters of right and wrong, fairness and unfairness, and justice or lack of justice creep into their decisions, actions or behaviors. Furthermore, it does not matter what level of management is under consideration – top, middle, or lower; managers at all levels, and in all functions, face situations wherein ethical considerations play a major role. The topic of ethics in management is a crucial one with which managers today must be informed. Therefore, it is the purpose of this article to survey some of the special topics about management ethics that may help the academic and practitioner alike to be more knowledgeable about this vital topic.

In this quest to provide insights into the topic of management ethics, or ethics in management, we shall first provide an overview of the topic, and then discuss a number of important themes such as: why managers should be ethical, ethical issues managers face, models of management morality, ethical decision making, and the manager's role in shaping the ethical climate of his or her organization. Some of these topics may touch upon others discussed in this volume, but we will strive to keep the overlap to a minimum.

Overview of management ethics

Management, or managerial, ethics as a broad subject matter deals with the situations managers face in their worklives that are imbued with ethical content. By ethical content, we are referring to issues, decisions or actions which contain matters of right versus wrong, fair versus unfair, or justice versus injustice. That is, these situations are ones with which there may be some disagreement about what is the correct – or ethical – course of action or decision.

When we speak of management ethics, we also need to distinguish between what we are observing managers do today and what they should be doing as ethical managers. The former is often termed descriptive ethics; that is, we would be describing what managers are actually doing in terms of their ethics or their actions and decisions with respect to their ethicality. By contrast, when we speak of what managers "ought" to be doing, or "should" be doing, this is typically referred to as normative ethics. In this chapter, we will be concerned both with descriptive and normative ethics; however, our foremost concern is with what managers should be doing to enhance their own ethics and the ethical climates in their organizations.

Management ethics may be seen as a component of corporate social responsibility (CSR). In the past fifty years, there has been an unrelenting call for businesses to be more socially responsible. That is, there has been a blossoming expectation that business not only be profitable and obey the law, but that it be ethical and a good corporate citizen as well. Thus, it may be asserted that the four social responsibilities of business are as follows: be profitable, obey the law, engage in ethical practices, and be philanthropic, or be a good corporate citizen (Carroll, 1979, 1991). To be sure, these other responsibilities (profitability, legal obedience, and philanthropy) contain ethical content, but we think it is important to single out the ethical component as one part of what an organization does beyond the minimum. Though society expects business organizations to be profitable, as this is a precondition to their survival and prosperity, profitability may be perceived as "what the business does for itself," and obeying the law, being ethical and being a good corporate citizen may be perceived as "what the firm is doing for others (society or other stakeholders)." In this discussion, we sharpen our focus to the ethical component of CSR and dwell on what this means for managers in organizations today.

Why should managers be ethical?

One might rightly ask "Why should managers be ethical?" Using the frame of reference mentioned above, the short answer would be that society *expects* managers to be ethical and that managers should be responsive to the expectations of society and stakeholders if they wish to maintain their legitimacy as agents in society. From a moral philosophy perspective, managers should be ethical because it is the right thing to do. We should go beyond these simple, but appropriate, answers, however, and point out some other reasons why ethical behavior and practice is warranted. Some of the reasons often given as to why managers should be ethical include the following that are set forth by Rushworth Kidder (1997). Kidder suggests that, in at least ten ways, managers are finding that sound ethics can have a practical impact on the bottom line:

- Shared values build trust.
- Consistency leads to predictability in planning.
- Predictability is essential for crisis management.
- Confidence in such rewards builds loyalty.
- Companies are as good as their people.
- Consumers care about values.
- Shareholders also care about values.
- Ethical leadership forestalls oppressive regulation.
- Effective partnerships depend on common values.
- Ethics is a form of insurance.

An examination of these reasons suggests two broad categories of justification:

1   Society and stakeholders *expect* managers to do what is right, fair and just.
2   It is in organizations' and managers' best interests to be ethical.

Regarding the first reason, it has been clearly documented by studies and surveys that business and its agents – managers – are expected to be ethical. For example, a Lou Harris, *Business Week* survey of adults found that 95 percent of the 1,000 adults surveyed felt that US corporations owe something to their workers and the communities in which they operate, and that they should sometimes sacrifice some profit for the sake of making things better for their workers and communities (*Business Week*, 1996).

It has also been well established that it is in the best long-term interests of organizations and managers to be ethical. At a minimum, ethical management practices keep organizations and managers out of trouble. The threats of expensive, prolonged litigation or the likelihood of more significant governmental intervention in the form of regulations, are strong, practical reasons for ethical behavior. Furthermore, the ethical climate created by the management group may have a significant bearing on the actions and behaviors of employees and may, indeed, lead to unethical practices that are costly to management and the organization.

One company's experience in this regard is worth mentioning. According to a major *USA Today* article, Prudential Insurance was a victim of an ethical breakdown which was quite costly to it (Jones, 1997). The large insurance company may end up paying $1 billion to policyholders who were coaxed by Prudential agents into buying more expensive life insurance than they needed. Prudential replaced more than 1,000 of its agents and managers due to the high-profile scandal (Jones, 1997, p. 1A). Prudential's experience, however, is not an isolated case. In a major study by the Ethics Officer Association and the American Society of Chartered Life Underwriters & Chartered Financial Consultants, costly violations resulting from ethical and legal lapses are common at all levels of the American workforce. With 48 percent of workers surveyed admitting to unethical or illegal acts, management groups everywhere have a serious problem on their hands (Jones, 1997, p. 1A).

Thus, it may be concluded that there are strong and persuasive reasons for managers to engage in and promote ethical behavior within their organizations. The reasons range from normative ones (managers are *expected* to be ethical and *ought* to be ethical) to the pragmatic or instrumental (it is in their *self-interest* to be ethical).

Ethical issues managers face

When does a manager face an ethical issue? According to Ferrell and Fraedrich (1991, p. 35), "an ethical issue is a problem, situation or opportunity requiring an individual or organization to choose among several actions that must be evaluated as right or wrong, ethical or unethical." Josephson helps us to understand an ethical issue when he states that conduct has a significant ethical dimension if it involves dishonesty, hypocrisy, disloyalty, unfairness, illegality, injurious acts, or unaccountability. These represent at least two ways of thinking about ethical issues managers face.

Managers today face many such ethical issues and these issues may be grouped according to different levels at which they occur. Managers experience ethical issues at the personal, organizational, trade/professional, societal and global levels (Carroll, 1996, pp. 145–8).

Furthermore, ethical issues may be categorized in a number of different ways. Vitell and Festervand identify conflicts between companies' or managers' interests and personal ethics. In their study, these issues arise between managers and their conflicts with such stakeholder groups as customers, suppliers, employees, competitors, law and government, superiors, wholesalers, and retailers. In terms of specific issues, these same researchers see ethical conflicts arising in these situations: the giving of gifts and kickbacks, fairness and discrimination, price collusion and pricing practices, firings and layoffs, and honesty in communications and executing contracts with investors (Vitell and Festervand, 1987, p. 114).

According to a major report from The Conference Board, there is widespread agreement that the following constitute ethical issues for managers: employee conflicts of interest, inappropriate gifts, sexual harassment, unauthorized payments, affirmative action, employee privacy, and environmental issues (Berenbeim, 1987, p. 3). In this same report, CEOs reported specific topics which constituted ethical issues for them, which were categorized as follows:

- *Equity*: Executive salaries, comparable worth, product pricing
- *Rights*: Corporate due process, employee health screening, privacy, sexual harassment, affirmative action/equal employment opportunity
- *Honesty*: Employee conflicts of interest, security of employee records, inappropriate gifts, unauthorized payments to foreign officials, advertising content
- *Exercise of corporate power*: Political action committees, workplace/product safety, environmental issues, disinvestment, corporate contributions, closures/downsizings

Finally, Waters, Bird and Chant (1986) provide us with insights into what managers consider to be ethical issues based on their research using open-ended interviews with managers in a variety of organizational positions. In response to the question "What ethical questions come up or have come up in the course of your work life?" the following ethical, or moral, issues (p. 375) were identified most frequently:

- With respect to *employees*: feedback about performance and standing; employment security; appropriate working conditions
- With respect to *peers* and *superiors*: truth-telling, loyalty and support
- With respect to *customers*: fair treatment, truth-telling, questionable practices, collusion
- With respect to *suppliers*: fair/impartial treatment, balanced relationship, unfair pressure tactics, truth-telling
- With respect to *other stakeholders*: respecting legal constraints, truth-telling in public relations, stockholder interests

To be sure, managers face many situations in which ethical issues arise. These situations may occur at a multitude of levels, they involve multiple stakeholders, and they may be categorized or perceived in a variety of ways. What do they have in common? Virtually all ethical issues managers face may be characterized as a conflict of interest. The conflict usually arises between the manager's own values or ethics and those of his or her employer, employees, or some other stakeholder group which has an interest in the decision.

Models of management morality

It can often be difficult to discern whether managers are being ethical or unethical, moral or immoral. In our discussion here, we are equating the terminology of ethics with that of morality, though there might be subtle differences that philosophers or theorists would want to make. In thinking about management behavior, actions, or decisions, it is often impossible to clearly categorize these actions as moral or immoral. In a quest to understand management behavior, a third category is usefully added, that of amorality. Carroll has presented three models of management morality that help us to understand better the kinds of behavior that may be manifested by managers. These three models, or archetypes – immoral management, moral management, and amoral management – serve as useful base points for discussion and comparison (Carroll, 1987, 1996).

The media has focused so much on immoral or unethical management behavior that it is easy to forget or not think about the possibility of other ethical types. For example, scant attention has been given to the distinction that may be made between those activities that are immoral and those that are amoral; similarly, little attention has been given to contrasting these two forms of behavior with ethical or moral management.

A major goal in considering the three management models of morality is to develop a clearer understanding of the full gamut of management behavior in which ethics or morality is a major dimension. Further, it is helpful to see through description and example the range of ethical behavior that management may intentionally, or unintentionally, display. Let us consider the two extreme positions first.

Immoral management

Let us start with immoral management as this model is perhaps most easily understood and illustrated. Immoral management is a style that not only is devoid of ethical principles or precepts, but also implies a positive and active opposition to what is ethical. Immoral management is discordant with ethical principles. This view holds that management's motives are selfish and that it cares only about its own or its organization's gains. If management activity is actively opposed to what is regarded as ethical, this implies that management can distinguish right from wrong, and yet chooses to do wrong.

According to this model, management's goals are purely selfish (if the individual is acting on his or her own behalf), or focused only on profitability and organizational success (if the individual is acting as an agent of his or her employer). Immoral management regards the law or legal standards as impediments it must overcome to accomplish what it wants. The operating strategy of immoral management is to exploit opportunities for organizational or personal gain. An active opposition to what is moral would suggest that managers would cut corners anywhere and everywhere it appeared useful to them. The key operating question of immoral management would likely be: "Can I gain from this decision or action, or can we make money with this decision or action, regardless of what it takes?"

Examples of immoral management   Examples of immoral management are easy to identify as they frequently involve illegal actions or fraud. The Frigitemp Corporation, a manufacturer of refrigerated mortuary boxes, provides an example of immoral management at the highest levels of the corporate hierarchy. In litigation, criminal trials, and federal investigations, corporate officials, including the president and chairman, admitted to having made millions of dollars in payoffs to get business. They admitted taking kickbacks from suppliers, embezzling corporate funds, exaggerating earnings, and providing prostitutes to customers. One corporate official said that greed was their undoing. Records indicate that Frigitemp's executives permitted a corporate culture of chicanery to flourish. The company eventually went bankrupt because of management's misconduct.

Another example of immoral management was provided by a small group of executives at the Honda Motor Co. Federal prosecutors unraveled a long-running fraud in which a group of Honda executives had pocketed in excess of $10 million in bribes and kickbacks paid to them by car dealers. In exchange, the executives gave dealers permission to open lucrative dealerships and they also received scarce Honda automobiles, which were in short supply at the time. Eight executives pleaded guilty and many others were indicted.

Moral management

At the opposite extreme from immoral management is moral management. Moral management conforms to high standards of ethical behavior and professional standards of conduct. Moral management strives to be ethical in terms of its focus on, and preoccupation with, ethical norms and professional standards of conduct, motives, goals, orientation toward the law, and general operating strategy. In contrast to the selfish motives of immoral management, moral management aspires to succeed but only within the confines of sound ethical precepts – that is, standards predicated on such norms as fairness, justice, and due process. Moral management would not pursue profits at the expense of the law and sound ethics. Indeed, the focus would be not only on the letter of the law but on the spirit of the law as well. The law would be viewed as a minimal standard of ethical behavior because moral management strives to operate at a level well above what the law requires.

Moral management requires ethical leadership. It is an approach which strives to seek out the right thing to do. Moral management would embrace what Lynn Sharp Paine (1994) has called an "integrity strategy." An integrity strategy is characterized by a conception of ethics as the driving force of an organization. Ethical values shape management's search for opportunities, the design of organizational systems, and the decision-making process. Ethical values in the integrity strategy provide a common frame of reference and serve to unify different functions, lines of business and employee groups. Organizational ethics, in this view helps to define what an organization is and what it stands for.

Examples of moral management   A couple of examples of moral management are illustrative. When McCullough Corporation, maker of chain saws, withdrew in protest from the national Chain Saw Manufacturer's Association because the association fought mandatory safety standards for the dangerous saws, this illustrated moral management. McCullough knew its industry's products were dangerous and had put chain brakes on its saws years before, even though it was not required to do so by law. Later, it withdrew from the association because this group fought government regulations to make their products safer.

Another well-known case of moral management occurred when Merck and Co., the pharmaceutical firm, invested millions of dollars to develop a treatment for river blindness, a third world disease affecting almost 18 million people. Seeing that no government or aid organization was agreeing to buy the drug, Merck pledged to supply the drug free forever. Merck's recognition that no effective mechanism existed to distribute the drug led to its decision to go far beyond industry practice, and to organize and fund a committee to oversee the distribution.

Amoral management

There are two kinds of amoral managers: unintentional and intentional. Unintentional amoral managers are neither immoral nor moral but are not sensitive to, or aware of, the fact that their everyday business decisions may have deleterious effects on other stakeholders (Carroll, 1995). Unintentional amoral managers lack ethical perception or awareness. That is, they go through their organizational lives not thinking that their actions have an ethical facet or dimension. Or, they may just be careless or insensitive to the implications of their actions on stakeholders. These managers may be well intentioned, but they do not see that their business decisions and actions may be hurting those with whom they transact business or interact. Typically, their orientation is towards the letter of the law as their ethical guide.

Intentional amoral managers simply believe that ethical considerations are for our private lives, not for business. These are people who reject the idea that business and ethics should mix. These managers believe that business activity resides outside the sphere to which moral judgments apply. Though most amoral managers today are unintentional, there may still exist a few who simply do not see a role for ethics in business or management decision making (Carroll, 1987). Fortunately, intentional amoral managers are a vanishing breed.

Examples of amoral management   An early example of amoral decision making occurred when police departments stipulated that applicants must be 5' 10" and weigh 180 pounds to qualify for being a police officer. These departments just did not think about the unintentional, adverse impact their policy would have on women and some ethnic groups who, on average, do not attain that height and weight. This same kind of thinking spilled over into the business context when firms routinely required high school diplomas as screening devices for many jobs. It later became apparent that minority groups were adversely impacted by this policy and, therefore, was unintentionally unfair to many of them who otherwise would have qualified for the job.

The liquor, beer and cigarette industries provide other examples of amorality. Though it is legal to sell their products, they did not anticipate that their products would create serious moral issues: alcoholism, drunk driving deaths, lung cancer, deteriorating health, and offensive secondary smoke. A specific corporate example of amorality occurred when McDonald's initially decided to use polystyrene containers for food packaging. Management's decision did not adequately consider the adverse environmental impact that would be caused. McDonald's surely did not intentionally create a solid waste disposal problem, but one major consequence of its decision was just that. To its credit, the company responded to complaints by replacing the polystyrene packaging with paper products. By taking this action, McDonald's illustrated how a company could transition from the amoral to the moral category.

There are two possible hypotheses regarding the three models of management morality that are useful for ethics in management.

- One hypothesis concerns the distribution of the three types over the management population, generally. This *population hypothesis* suggests that, in the management population as a whole, the three types would be normally distributed with immoral management and moral management occupying the two tails of the curve, and amoral management occupying the large middle part of the normal curve. According to this view, there are a few immoral and moral managers, given the definitions stated above, but that the vast majority of managers are amoral. That is, these managers are well intentioned, but simply don't think in ethical terms in their daily decision making.
- A second hypothesis might be called the *individual hypothesis*. According to this view, each of the three models of management morality may operate at various times and under various circumstances within each manager. That is, the average manager may be amoral most of the time but may slip into a moral or immoral mode on occasion, based on a variety of impinging factors.

Neither of the above two hypotheses has been empirically tested. However, they provide food for thought for managers striving to avoid the immoral and amoral types.

It could well be argued that the more serious social problem in organizations today is the prevalence of amoral, rather than immoral, managers. Immoral management is headline grabbing, but the more pervasive and insidious problem may well be that managers have simply not integrated ethical thinking into their everyday decision making, thus making them amoral managers. These amoral managers are basically good people, but they essentially see the competitive business world as ethically neutral. Until this group of managers moves toward the moral management ethic, we will continue to see businesses and other organizations criticized as they have been in the past several decades (Carroll, 1996).

Ethical decision making

We have alluded to the importance of ethical decision making, but it is useful to treat it briefly as a distinct topic. Decision making is at the heart of the management process.

If there is any act or process that is synonymous with management, it is decision making. Though there is a need for improved managerial performance in the private and public sectors, there is a special need for improved ethical decision making by managers (Petrick and Quinn, 1997). Petrick and Quinn (pp. 24–5) state five reasons for managers to improve their ethical decision making:

1 The costs of unethical workplace conduct
2 The lack of awareness of ethically questionable, managerial, role-related acts
3 The widespread erosion of integrity and exposure to ethical risk
4 The global corruption pressures that threaten managerial and organizational reputation
5 The benefits of increased profitability and intrinsically desirable organizational order.

In the academic literature, there is much written about ethical decision making, including the use of models of ethical decision making. Most business ethicists would advocate the use of ethical principles to guide organizational decision making. A principle of business ethics is a concept, guideline, or rule that, if applied when you are faced with an ethical dilemma, will assist you in making an ethical decision. There are many different principles of ethics, but an extensive coverage of them is outside the scope of this chapter. Suffice it to say here that such useful principles include the principles of justice, rights, utilitarianism and the golden rule (Buchholz and Rosenthal, 1998). The basic idea behind the principles approach is that managers may improve the quality of their ethical decision making if they factor into their proposed actions, decisions, behaviors and practices, a consideration of certain principles of ethics.

A very practical approach to ethical decision making has been suggested by Laura Nash (1981) who argues that there are twelve questions managers should systematically ask in a quest to make an ethical decision:

1 Have you defined the problem accurately?
2 How would you define the problem, if you stood on the other side of the fence?
3 How did this situation occur in the first place?
4 To whom and what do you give your loyalties as a person, and as a member of the corporation?
5 What is your intention in making this decision?
6 How does this intention compare with the likely results?
7 Whom could your decision or action injure?
8 Can you engage the affected parties in a discussion of the problem, *before* you make your decision?
9 Are you confident that your position will be as valid over a long period of time as it seems now?
10 Could you disclose without qualms your decision or action to your boss, your CEO, the board of directors, your family, or society as a whole?
11 What is the symbolic potential of your action if understood? If misunderstood?
12 Under what conditions would you allow exceptions to your stand?

Another set of useful questions to aid ethical decision making has been offered by Blanchard and Peale (1988). They recommend that managers ask these questions before making a decision, and they call these three questions the "ethics check."

1   *Is it legal?* Will I be violating either civil law or company policy?
2   *Is it balanced?* Is it fair to all concerned in the short term as well as the long term? Does it promote win-win relationships?
3   *How will it make me feel about myself?* Will it make me proud? Would I feel good if my decision was published in the newspaper? Would I feel good if my family knew about it?

Obviously, the "wrong" answers to the above questions should move the manager into reconsidering his or her decision.

Shaping the organization's ethical climate

In addition to striving towards moral management and fully integrating ethical considerations into management decision making, managers have another major responsibility: shaping the organization's ethical climate. As we shift our attention away from the manager's personal actions and decision making, it is imperative that managers, as leaders, consider carefully the context in which decision making and behavior occurs – the organization. To manage ethics in an organization, the manager needs to appreciate that the organization's ethical climate is just one part of its overall corporate culture. This point is effectively illustrated in the now classic Tylenol case. When McNeil Laboratories, a subsidiary of Johnson & Johnson, voluntarily withdrew Tylenol from the market immediately after the reported incidents of tainted, poisoned product, some people wondered why they made this decision as they did. Johnson & Johnson's often cited response was "It's the J & J way." This statement conveys a significant message about the role of a firm's ethical climate. It also raises the question of how organizations and managers should deal with, understand, and shape business ethics through actions taken, policies established, and examples set. The organization's moral climate is a complex phenomenon, and it is greatly shaped by management's actions, policies, decisions, and examples. Aguilar (1994, p. 15) goes so far as to say that an ethical corporate climate can "supercharge" a well-managed and well-positioned business by helping to release creative ideas and by fostering collaborative follow-though.

Important components of an organization's ethical climate or culture include, but are not limited to: top management leadership, codes of conduct, ethics programs, realistic objectives, processes for ethical decision making, effective communication, disciplining of ethics violators, ethics training, ethics audits, and the use of whistle-blowing mechanisms (Carroll, 1996). Several research studies have concluded that the behavior of superiors is the most important factor contributing to the organization's ethical climate; therefore, this point needs to be fully understood and embraced by all managers.

Summary and conclusions

Management ethics has become a vital concern to organizations and society over the past several decades. Polls indicate that the public does not have a high regard for business and management ethics. For the management community to turn this situation around, significant efforts are required. Part of the challenge is coming to understand what management ethics means, why it is important and how it should be integrated into decision making. Principles of ethics from moral philosophy and management theory are available to inform interested managers.

One of the most formidable challenges is avoiding immoral management, and transitioning from an amoral to a moral management mode of leadership, behavior, decision making, policies and practices. Moral management requires ethical leadership. It entails more than just "not doing wrong." Moral management requires that managers search out those vulnerable situations in which amorality may reign if careful, thoughtful reflection is not given by management. Moral management requires that managers understand, and be sensitive to, all the stakeholders of the organization and their stakes. If the moral management model is to be achieved, managers need to integrate ethical wisdom with their managerial wisdom and to take steps to create and sustain an ethical climate in their organizations. If this is done, the desirable goals of moral management are achievable.

References

Aguilar, F. J. 1994: *Managing Corporate Ethics.* New York: Oxford University Press.

Berenbeim, R. E. 1987: *Corporate Ethics.* New York: The Conference Board.

Blanchard, K. and Peale, N. V. 1988: *The Power of Ethical Management.* New York: Fawcett Crest.

Buchholz, R. A. and Rosenthal, S. B. 1998: *Business Ethics: The Pragmatic Path Beyond Principles to Process.* Upper Saddle River, NJ: Prentice-Hall.

Business Week March 11, 1996: Lou Harris & Associates Survey, 65.

Carroll, A. B. 1979: A three-dimensional conceptual model of corporate social performance. *Academy of Management Review*, 4(4), 497–505.

Carroll, A. B. 1987: In search of the moral manager. *Business Horizons,* March/April, 8.

Carroll, A. B. 1991: The pyramid of corporate social responsibility: Toward the moral management of organizational stakeholders. *Business Horizons,* July/August, 39–48.

Carroll, A. B. 1995: Stakeholder thinking in three models of management morality: A perspective with strategic implications. In Jusa Nasi (ed.), *Understanding Stakeholder Thinking,* Helsinki, Finland: LSR-Publications, 47–74.

Carroll, A. B. 1996: *Business and Society: Ethics and Stakeholder Management,* 3rd edn. Cincinnati: South-Western Publishing Co./International Thompson Publishing.

Ferrell, O. C. and Fraedrich, J. 1991: *Business Ethics: Ethical Decision Making and Cases.* Boston: Houghton Mifflin Company.

Jones, D. 1997: Doing the WRONG thing: 48% of workers admit to unethical or illegal acts. *USA Today,* April 4–6, 1A–2A.

Kidder, R. 1997: Ethics and the bottom line: Ten reasons for businesses to do right. *Insights on Global Ethics,* Spring, 7–9.

Nash, L. L. 1981: Ethics without the sermon. *Harvard Business Review,* November–December, 79–90.

Paine, L. S. 1994: Managing for organizational integrity. *Harvard Business Review*, March–April, 106–17.

Petrick, J. A. and Quinn, J. F. 1997: *Management Ethics: Integrity at Work*. Thousand Oaks, CA: Sage Publications.

Vitell, S. J. and Festervand, T. A. 1987: Business ethics: conflicts, practices and beliefs of industrial executives. *Journal of Business Ethics*, February, 114.

Waters, J. A., Bird, F., and Chant, P. D. 1986: Everyday moral issues experienced by managers. *Journal of Business Ethics*, 5, 373–84.

13

Finance ethics

JOHN R. BOATRIGHT

Although many business ethics problems are common to every functional area, finance involves some distinctive ethical issues that require separate treatment. Because financial activity is closely regulated, these issues are often addressed as matters of law rather than ethics, but the basis of regulation in finance includes some fundamental ethical precepts, such as fairness in financial markets and the duties of fiduciaries. The law is an uncertain regulator, though, and much financial activity presupposes unwritten rules of ethical behavior. People trained in finance enter many different lines of work, and so finance ethics is necessarily diverse; ethical conduct is not the same for bond traders, mutual fund managers, and corporate financial officers, for example. Moreover, finance ethics is concerned not only with individual conduct but also with the operation of financial markets and financial institutions. Finally, the financial management of corporations, with its objective of maximizing shareholder wealth, raises yet different ethical issues.

Despite this complexity, the field of financial ethics can be organized under the three major headings of financial markets, financial services, and financial management.

- *Financial markets* are vulnerable to unfair trading practices (fraud and manipulation), unfair conditions (an unlevel playing field), and contractual difficulties (forming, interpreting, and enforcing contracts). The main aim of federal securities laws and the self-regulation of exchanges is expressed in the phrase "fair and orderly" markets, which reflects the need in financial markets to balance the twin goals of fairness and efficiency.
- Many individuals and institutions serve as financial intermediaries, providing *financial services* on behalf of others. Financial intermediaries commonly make decisions as agents for principals in an agency relation, and they often become fiduciaries with fiduciary duties. Agents and fiduciaries have an obligation to act solely in the interests of other parties and, especially, to avoid conflicts of interest. Although financial services providers are often merely sellers in a buyer–seller relation, they still have the obligations of any seller to avoid deceptive and abusive sales practices.
- *Financial Management*: Business firms are legally structured as the financial instruments of shareholders, and officers and directors are agents of firms, and have a fiduciary duty to manage the firms with the objective of maximizing shareholder wealth. Ethical issues in financial management concern the actions that violate the duties of financial managers and the discretion of financial managers to serve the interests of nonshareholder groups, commonly called "stakeholders."

All financial activity takes place in a larger economic, political, and social setting, and so ethical issues arise about the overall impact of financial activity. Although financial decision making is generally limited to the financial factors of risk and return over time, ethics includes a consideration of the ethical treatment of everyone affected by a decision, and the consequences for the whole of society.

Financial markets

The fundamental ethical requirement of financial markets is that they be *fair*. Fairness may be defined either *substantively* (when the price of a security reflects the actual value) or *procedurally* (when buyers are enabled to determine the actual value of a security). In the USA, some state securities laws aim at substantive fairness by requiring expert evaluation of new securities (so-called "blue-sky" laws), but the federal Securities Act of 1933 and the Securities Exchange Act of 1934 attempt to secure fairness procedurally by requiring adequate disclosure. The rationale for mandatory disclosure is that securities transactions are more likely to be fair when material information must be disclosed, and investors have easy access to information.

Unfair trading practices

Fraud, manipulation, and other unfair trading practices lead not only to unfair treatment in securities transactions but to a loss of investor confidence in the integrity of financial markets. Speculative activity also produces excess volatility, which was blamed for the stock market crashes of 1929 and October 1987.

Both fraud and manipulation are defined broadly. Section 17(a) of the 1933 Securities Act and Section 10(b) of the 1934 Securities Exchange Act prohibit anyone involved in the issue or exchange of securities to make a false statement of a material fact, to omit a fact that makes a statement of material facts misleading, or to engage in any practice or scheme that would serve to defraud. Whereas fraud generally involves the disclosure or concealment of information that bears on the value of a security, manipulation consists of trading for the purpose of creating a misleading impression about a security's value.

Fraud is obviously committed by an initial stock offering that inflates the assets of a firm or fails to disclose some of its liabilities. Insider trading has been prosecuted as a fraud on the grounds that nonpublic material information ought to be disclosed before trading. In the 1920s, the stock market was manipulated by traders who bid up the price of stock in order to sell at the peak to unwary investors. In recent years, concern has been expressed about a form of program trading known as index arbitrage, in which traders are able to create volatility in different markets, solely for the purpose of trading on the resulting price differences.

Fair conditions

Fairness in financial markets is often expressed by the concept of a level playing field. A playing field may be unlevel because of inequalities in information, bargaining power, resources, processing ability, and special vulnerabilities.

Unequal information, or *information asymmetry*, may refer either to the fact that the parties to a transaction do not possess the same information or that they do not have the same *access* to information. The possession of different information is a pervasive feature of markets that is not always ethically objectionable. Indeed, investors who invest resources in acquiring superior information are entitled to exploit this advantage, and they perform a service by making markets more efficient. The unequal possession of information is unfair only when the information has not been legitimately acquired or when its use violates some right or obligation. Other arguments against insider trading, for example, are that the information has not been acquired legitimately but has been misappropriated from the rightful owner (the "misappropriation theory") and that an insider who trades on information that has been acquired in a fiduciary relation violates a fiduciary duty. Equal access to information is problematical because accessibility is not a feature of information itself but a function of the investment that is required to obtain information. To the objection that an inside trader is using information that is inherently inaccessible, some reply that anyone can become an insider by devoting enough resources.

Similarly, inequalities in bargaining power, resources, and processing ability – which are pervasive in financial markets – are ethically objectionable only when they are used in violation of some right or obligation and especially when they are used coercively. The main ethical requirement is that people not use any advantage unfairly. For example, American stock markets permit relatively unsophisticated investors with modest resources and processing ability to buy stocks on fair terms, and some changes, such as increased use of program trading or private placements, are criticized for increasing the advantages of institutional investors. (The growth of mutual funds has served to reduce the adverse consequences of inequalities among investors.) Vulnerabilities, such as impulsiveness or overconfidence, create opportunities for exploitation that can be countered by such measures as a "cooling off" period on purchases and loans, and the warning to request and read a prospectus before investing.

Financial contracting

Some financial instruments, such as home mortgages and futures options, are contracts which commit the parties to a certain course of action, and many financial relations, such as being a trustee or corporate officer, are contractual in nature. Contracts are often vague, ambiguous, or incomplete, with the result that disagreements arise about what is ethically and legally required.

First, beyond the written words of *express contracts* lie innumerable tacit understandings that constitute *implied contracts*. Financial affairs would be impossible if every detail had to be made explicit. However, whatever is left implicit is subject to differing interpretations, and insofar as implied contracts are not legally enforceable, they may be breached with impunity. Not only financial instruments but the relations of corporations with employees, customers, suppliers, and other stakeholders consist of implied contracts, from which each party receives some value. One objection to hostile takeovers is that raiders are able to finance such deals by capturing the value of the implied contracts that the target firm has made with its stakeholders.

Second, contracts are sometimes imperfect because of limitations in our cognitive ability, especially incomplete knowledge, bounded rationality, and future contingencies.

In addition, some situations may be too complex and uncertain to permit careful planning. As a result, the parties may fail to negotiate contracts that produce the maximum benefit for themselves. Disputes in contractual relations also arise over what constitutes a breach of contract and what is an appropriate remedy.

Agency and fiduciary relations are one solution for the problems of imperfect contracting because they replace specific obligations with a general duty to act in another's interests. In particular, the fiduciary relations of managers to shareholders has arisen because of the difficulties of writing contracts for this particular relation. Similarly, supplier relations are not easily reduced to contractual terms. The term *relational contracting* has been coined to describe the building of working relations as an alternative to rigid contracts.

Financial services

The financial services industry – which includes commercial banks, securities and investment firms, mutual and pension funds, insurance companies, and financial planners – provides a vast array of financial services to individuals, businesses, and governments. Financial services firms act primarily as financial *intermediaries*, which is to say that they use their capital to provide services rather than to trade on their own behalf. In providing financial services, these firms sometimes act as agents or fiduciaries with respect to clients; at other times, they act as sellers in a typical buyer–seller relation. Thus, a broker who is authorized to trade for a client's account is an agent, but a broker who makes a cold call to a prospect is merely a salesperson. Many ethical disputes result from misunderstandings about the nature of a financial service provider's role.

Fiduciaries and agents

A fiduciary is a person who is entrusted to act in the interests of another. Fiduciary duties are the duties of a fiduciary to act in that other person's interest without gaining any material benefit except with the knowledge and consent of that person. Similar to the fiduciary relation is the relation of *agent* and *principal*, in which one person (the agent) is engaged to act on behalf of another (the principal). Whereas fiduciary relations arise when something of value is entrusted to another person, agency relations are due to the need to rely on others for their specialized knowledge and skill. In both relations, the specific acts to be performed are not fully specified in advance and fiduciaries and agents have wide latitude.

A major source of unethical conduct by fiduciaries and agents is conflict of interest, in which a personal interest of the fiduciary or agent interferes with the ability of the person to act in the interest of the other person. Fiduciaries and agents are called upon to exercise judgment on behalf of others, and their judgment can be compromised if they stand to gain personally by a decision. For example, a conflict of interest is created when a brokerage firm offers a higher commission for selling in-house mutual funds. The conflict arises because the broker has an incentive to sell funds that may not be in a client's best interests. Whether mutual fund managers should be permitted to trade for their own account is a controversial question because of the perceived conflict of interest. Fiduciaries and agents also have duties to preserve the confidentiality of information and not to use the information for their own benefit. Thus, "piggyback" trading, in which a broker copies the trades of a savvy client, is a breach of confidentiality.

Agency relations are subject to some well-known difficulties that arise from the inability of principals to monitor agents closely. These difficulties are opportunism, moral hazard, and adverse selection. Opportunism, or shirking, occurs because of the tendency of agents to advance their own interests despite the commitment to act on behalf of another. In agency theory, which is the study of agency relations, whatever a principal loses from opportunism is known as agency loss. The total of the agency loss and expenditures to reduce it are called agency costs. Moral hazard arises when the cost (or risk) of an activity is borne by others, as when a person seeks more medical care because of insurance. Moral hazard can be reduced in insurance by requiring deductibles and copayments, which provide an insured person with an incentive to lower costs. Insurance companies can also seek out better insurance prospects, but this leads to the problem of adverse selection. Adverse selection is the tendency, in insurance, of less suitable prospects to seek more insurance, which increases the risk for insurers who cannot easily identify good and bad insurance prospects. More generally, principals are not always able to judge the suitability of agents, and agents have an incentive to misrepresent themselves.

Many ethical problems, ranging from churning of client accounts by stockbrokers to the empire-building tendencies of CEOs, result from the difficulties inherent in agency relations. These problems can be addressed by closer monitoring and by changes in the structure of the relation. For example, the incentive for brokers to churn could be reduced by basing compensation more on the performance of clients' portfolios and less on the volume of trades. In addition, compensating executives with stock options aligns their interests more closely with those of the shareholders and thus prevents empire building. The most effective solutions for ethical problems in agency relations are twofold: first, there must be a strong sense of professionalism accompanied by professional organizations with codes of ethics; second, a high degree of trust must be present. Trust is essential in the financial services industry, and companies generally pay a heavy price for violating the public's confidence.

Sales practices

In the selling of financial products, such as mutual funds, insurance policies, and loans, the ordinary standards for ethical sales practices apply. Thus, the financial services industry, like any business, has an obligation to refrain from deception and to make adequate disclosure of material information. A mutual fund prospectus, for example, is screened by regulatory authorities, but personal sales pitches and mass-media advertising sometimes contain false and misleading claims. For example, figures in an advertisement may exaggerate the fund's past performance or omit sales charges. Whether an advertisement is deceptive is often a matter of dispute. The generally accepted standard for disclosure is materiality, which refers to information about which an average prudent investor ought to be informed or to which a reasonable person would attach importance in making a decision.

For many financial products, the degree of risk is material information that ought to be disclosed. Thus, some clients of investment firms have attributed large losses in derivatives to inadequate disclosure of the risks involved. Brokers and insurance agents have an obligation to recommend only products that are *suitable*. Risk and suitability are closely related because whether an investment is suitable generally depends on the level of risk that is appropriate for an investor. Suitability is often difficult to determine, and investments may be unsuitable for many different reasons. Thus, a security might be unsuitable because it does not offer sufficient diversification or it is not sufficiently liquid, or because it involves inappropriate trading techniques, such as the use of margin.

Financial products are susceptible to abusive sales practices, such as "twisting," in which an insurance agent persuades a client to replace an existing policy merely for the commission, and "flipping," which is the practice of replacing one loan with another in order to generate additional fees. The poor are frequent targets of abuses by loan providers who offer high-interest loans and add on various "options" of little value. Finally, financial products should meet certain standards of integrity. Just as automobiles and houses can be shoddily made, so too are there shoddy financial products. The sale of limited partnerships, for example, has been criticized in recent years for dubious valuation of assets and questionable practices by developers.

Victims of fraud or abuse by financial services firms generally have recourse to the courts, but the securities industry in the USA requires most customers (and employees) to sign a predispute arbitration agreement (PDAA) that commits them to binding arbitration of disputes. Mandatory arbitration is spreading to the holders of credit cards, insurance policies, and other financial products. Although arbitration has many advantages over litigation, critics charge that the process is often unfair and denies investors adequate protection. The controversy over compulsory arbitration in the securities industry focuses on three issues: the requirement that investors sign a PDAA as a condition of opening an account, the alleged industry bias of arbitration panels, and the permissibility of punitive damages. In addition, the requirement that employees submit complaints about such matters as discrimination and harassment to arbitration denies them of the right to sue in court, a right that employees outside the securities industry take for granted.

Financial services firms

Financial services firms are themselves businesses, and the management of such a business raises some ethical issues, especially in the treatment of institutional clients. For example, underwriters of municipal bonds have been criticized for making political contributions in city elections in order to gain access. Firms as well as individuals encounter conflicts of interest, such as the reluctance of brokerage firms to issue a negative analysis of a client company's stock. In recent years, rogue traders have caused great losses at some firms, including the collapse of a major bank.

The managers of large investment portfolios for mutual funds, insurance companies, pension funds, and private endowments face two important ethical questions.

1   Should they consider social factors in making decisions, such as how a corporation treats its employees or its record on the environment?
2   Should they vote the stock that they hold, and if so, what criteria should they use to evaluate the issues that are submitted to a vote?

Some large institutional investors take a hands-off approach, while others are becoming actively involved as shareholders in a movement known as relationship investing.

Financial management

Financial managers have the task of actively deploying assets rather than investing them. Unlike a portfolio manager who merely buys stocks of corporations for a client, a corporate financial manager is involved in the running of a corporation. Investment decisions in a corporation are concerned not with which securities to hold but with what business opportunities to pursue. These decisions are still made using standard financial criteria, however. Finance theory can be applied to the operation of a corporation by viewing the various components of a business as a portfolio with assets that can be bought and sold. Option pricing theory, in particular, suggests that all of the possibilities for a firm can be regarded options to buy and sell assets. Bankruptcy, for example, is exercising an option to "sell" the corporation to the debtholders. (However, one critic has called this a "thoroughly immoral view of finance.")

The ethical issues in financial management are twofold.

- Financial managers, as agents and fiduciaries, have an obligation to manage assets prudently and especially to avoid the use of assets for personal benefit. Thus, managers, who have preferential access to information, should not engage in insider trading or self-dealing. For example, management buyouts, in which a group of managers take a public corporation private, raise the question whether people who are paid to mind the store should seek to buy it.
- Financial managers are called upon to make decisions that impact many different groups, and they have an obligation in their decision making to balance some competing interests. For example, should the decision to close a plant be made solely with the shareholders' interests in mind or should the interests of the employees and the local community be taken into account?

Balancing competing interests

In finance theory, the objective of the firm is shareholder wealth maximization (SWM). This objective is reflected in corporate law, according to which officers and directors of corporations are agents of the corporation and have a fiduciary duty to operate the corporation in the interests of the shareholders. Despite the seemingly unequivocal guide of SWM, financial managers still face the need, in some situations, to balance competing interests. In particular, decisions about levels of risk and hostile takeovers reveal some difficulties in the pursuit of SWM.

The level of risk   Maximizing shareholder wealth cannot be done without assuming some risk. A critical, often overlooked, task of financial management is determining the appropriate level of risk. Leveraging, for example, increases the riskiness of a firm. The capital asset pricing model suggests that, for properly diversified shareholders, the level of risk for any given firm, called *unique* risk, is irrelevant and that only market or *systemic* risk is important. Finance theory treats bankruptcy as merely an event risk that is worth courting if the returns are high enough. If a firm is in distress, then a high risk, "bet-the-farm" strategy is especially beneficial to shareholders, because they will reap all the gains of success, while everyone will share the losses of failure (the moral hazard problem). Consequently, a financial manager should seek the highest return adjusted for risk, no matter the actual consequences.

However, a high-risk strategy poses dangers for bondholders, employees, suppliers, and managers themselves, all of whom place a high value on the continued operation of the firm. Employees, in particular, are more vulnerable than shareholders to unique, as opposed to systemic, risk because of their inability to diversify. Is it ethical for financial managers to increase risk in a firm so as to benefit shareholders, at the expense of other corporate constituencies? Does the firm, as an ongoing entity, have value that should be considered in financial decision making? Some have argued that managing purely by financial criteria, without regard for the level of risk, is immoral.

Hostile takeovers   Hostile takeovers are often epic battles with winners and losers. For this reason, the rules for acquiring controlling interest should be fair to all parties involved. Managers of target companies feel entitled to a fair chance to defend their jobs; shareholders who sell their shares, and those who do not, have a right to make a decision in a fair and orderly manner; bondholders often lose in takeovers because of the increased debt; and employees and residents of local communities, who usually have no say in the decision, are generally the groups most harmed.

Insofar as a takeover is conducted in a market through the buying and selling of shares, there exists a "market for corporate control." Critics of hostile takeovers question whether such an important decision should be made in the marketplace. Does a market for corporate control provide adequate protection for all of the parties whose interests are affected? Incumbent managers have many defenses. Collectively called "shark repellents," these include poison pills, white knights, lockups, crown jewel options, the Pac-Man defense, golden parachutes, and greenmail. These are frequently criticized for being self-serving and for giving management an undue advantage in thwarting shareholder desires for change.

The directors of a target company, whose approval is often necessary for a successful takeover, have a fiduciary duty to act in the best interests of the firm itself, which may not be identical with the interests of either the preexisting shareholders or those who seek control. A majority of states have adopted so-called "other constituency statutes" that permit boards of directors to consider other constituencies, such as employees, suppliers, customers, and local communities, in evaluating a takeover bid. Many other laws govern the conduct of raiders and defenders alike, so that the market for corporate control is scarcely a pure market. In general, courts and legislatures have created rules for takeovers that seek both fairness and efficiency.

The financial theory of the firm

The financial argument for SWM, and the legal argument for the fiduciary duties of corporate officers and directors, are each built upon a conception of the business firm as a nexus of contracts between a firm and its constituencies, including shareholders, debtholders, employees, suppliers, and customers. This nexus-of-contracts view of the firm is employed in law and finance as a descriptive model for explaining the legal and financial structure of firms as well as a normative model for justifying fiduciary duties and SWM. The normative adequacy of the nexus-of-contracts view has been challenged, especially by those who contend that corporations have ethical obligations to various nonshareholder constituencies which are not accounted for in the model. Stakeholder theory is offered by some as a more adequate descriptive and normative model of the modern corporation.

Fiduciary duties in corporate law were originally founded on the role of shareholders as the owners of the corporation who had entrusted their assets to management. With the separation of ownership and control in the modern corporation, shareholders ceased to be owners in any meaningful sense, and the fiduciary duties of corporate managers to shareholders are now based on the premise that serving the shareholders' interests maximizes total wealth creation. The aim of corporate governance structures is to restrain managers, who have *de facto* control, from using corporate assets for their own benefit and to give them incentives to apply these assets to their most productive uses. In terms of agency theory, this end can be achieved at the lowest agency cost by imposing a fiduciary duty on managers to maximize shareholder wealth.

In finance theory, shareholders are residual risk bearers, which is to say that they are entitled only to the earnings that remain (the residue) after all other obligations (such as wages to employees and payments to suppliers) are met. The argument, then, is that people with capital would agree to become residual risk bearers only if a firm is operated in their interests. Without this protection, investors would seek other contractual arrangements, such as the guaranteed returns of a bondholder. In the nexus-of-contracts firm, bondholders' returns, employees' wages, and suppliers' payments are assured by fixed-term contracts, but the interests of shareholders can be protected only if management agrees to serve their interests. Furthermore, residual risk bearers have the greatest incentives to ensure that the firm is operated so as to create the maximum amount of wealth. The primacy of shareholder interests thus benefits society as a whole.

Stockholders vs stakeholders

The shareholder-centered financial theory of the firm is criticized for giving inadequate recognition to the rights and interests of nonshareholder constituencies. Critics make four related points concerning ethical standards, externalities, abuses in contracting, and distribution.

Ethical standards Corporations ought to treat all corporate constituencies or stakeholder groups according to certain minimal ethical standards. Agents and fiduciaries do not have a right to advance the interests that they are pledged to serve in ways that violate fundamental rights or inflict wrongful harm. Thus, to expose workers and consumers to hazardous substances, or to exploit labor in lesser-developed countries, is unjustified.

Externalities Business activity imposes great social costs in the form of externalities or spillover effects. When pollution or urban blight, for example, is a direct result of corporate investment decisions, then critics contend that they have an obligation to address these problems.

Abuses in contracting Contracting provides an opportunity for one party to take unfair advantage of the other party. Such advantage-taking occurs in many forms. For example, downsizing may involve breaking an implicit understanding of job security for loyal employees. Some solvent corporations have sought bankruptcy protection so as to avoid paying product liability claims to injured consumers or to renege on collective bargaining agreements. In agency theory, principals are assumed to be vulnerable to shirking by agents, but agents can abuse principals by predatory behavior that has been called "sharking."

Distribution The financial theory of the firm takes no account of the inequalities that result from contracting in the nexus-of-contracts firm. In the USA, the widening gulf between low- and high-wage employees, and the high levels of executive compensation are causes for concern. In general, markets achieve efficiency, not equity; hence the need to attend to the equity/efficiency trade-off.

Stakeholder theory

These four sources of ethical problems are acknowledged in the finance literature, and disagreements occur primarily over their solution. Proponents of the financial theory of the firm generally argue that other constituencies should either protect themselves (workers can bargain for safer working conditions, for example) or seek regulatory protection by means of occupational safety and health laws. On the financial theory of the firm, the responsibility for upholding ethical standards, forcing the internalization of costs, and so on, belong ultimately to government, not to corporate managers. The main argument for this position is that corporate managers have neither the right nor the ability to pursue multiple, nonfinancial goals.

By contrast, stakeholder theory contends that the list of corporate constituencies includes all those who have a legitimate interest in the activities of a firm, regardless of any interest that the firm takes in them. Furthermore, the interests of these stakeholder groups merit consideration for their own sake, not because of their usefulness to the firm. Stakeholder theory has not been developed as a full-fledged alternative to the financial theory, and it is questionable whether it is necessarily incompatible with it. SWM is justified on the financial theory for its benefits to the whole of society, which includes all stakeholder groups. Corporate managers need not consider the interests of all stakeholders as long as these interests are adequately protected by some means, such as government regulation. In addition, managing a corporation with attention to stakeholder interests may be an effective means for maximizing shareholder value. Some very successful companies are driven by philosophies that put employees or customers first.

Finally, the concept of shareholder wealth is problematical. The existence of different kinds of securities blurs the distinction between equity and debt, and creates multiple classes of shareholders with divergent interests. Even holders of ordinary common stock may differ in their risk preferences or time horizons. Some finance research indicates that managing to maximize short-term stock price may not result in maximum shareholder value in the long run. Thus, SWM is not a wholly objective guide for financial managers, and the decisions about the shareholders' interest may themselves involve some value judgments.

Further reading

Bear, L. A. and Maldonado-Bear, R. 1994: *Free Markets, Finance, Ethics, and Law*. Englewood Cliffs, NJ: Prentice Hall.

Blair, M. M. 1995: *Ownership and Control: Rethinking Corporate Governance for the Twenty-first Century*. Washington, DC: The Brookings Institution.

Boatright, J. R. 1996: Business ethics and the theory of the firm. *American Business Law Journal*, 34, 217–38.

Boatright, J. R. 1999: *Ethics in Finance*. Oxford: Blackwell Publishers.

Cornell, B. and Shapiro, A. C. 1987: Corporate stakeholders and corporate finance. *Financial Management*, 16, 5–14.

Dobson, J. 1997: *Finance Ethics: The Rationality of Virtue*. Lanham, MD: Rowman and Littlefield.

Donaldson, T. and Preston, L. E. 1995: A stakeholder theory of the corporation: Concepts, evidence, and implications. *Academy of Management Review*, 20, 65–91.

Hoffman, W. M., Kamm, J. B., and Frederick, R. E. (eds) 1996: *The Ethics of Accounting and Finance: Trust, Responsibility, and Control*. Westport, CT: Quorum Books.

Horrigan, J. O. 1987: The ethics of the new finance. *Journal of Business Ethics*, 6, 97–110.

James S. A. (ed.) 1993: Forum on financial ethics. *Financial Management*, 22, 32–59.

Malkiel, B. and Quandt, R. E. 1971: Moral issues in investment policy. *Harvard Business Review*, March–April, 37–47.

Markowitz, H. M. 1992: Markets and morality: Or arbitrageurs get no respect. *Journal of Portfolio Management*, Winter, 84–93.

Prindl, A. R. and Prodhan, B. (eds) 1994: *The ACT Guide to Ethical Conflicts in Finance*. Oxford: Basil Blackwell.

Shefrin, H. and Statman, M. 1993: Ethics, fairness and efficiency in financial markets. *Financial Analysts Journal*, November–December, 21–9.

Twentieth Century Fund 1990: *Abuse on Wall Street: Conflicts of Interest in the Securities Markets*. Westport, CT: Quorum Books.

Williams, O. F., Reilly, F. K. and Houck, J. W. (eds) 1989: *Ethics and the Investment Industry*. Notre Dame: University of Notre Dame Press.

14

Ethics in the public accounting profession

MOHAMMAD J. ABDOLMOHAMMADI AND
MARK R. NIXON*

> I know only that what is moral is what you feel good
> after and what is immoral is what you feel bad after.
> Ernest Hemingway

Introduction

The American Heritage Dictionary defines profession as "the body of qualified persons in an occupation or field." A major characteristic of a "qualified person" is the specialized knowledge of the profession: medical knowledge for medical doctors, accounting knowledge for certified public accountants (CPAs). Professionals have an ethical responsibility to have acquired the specialized knowledge before offering their professional services. Professionals are also expected to keep abreast of the knowledge enhancements through continuing professional education. Another characteristic of professionals is that they possess the mental attitude of serving the public with the best of their ability so as to earn the public trust. How does a profession enforce these ethical responsibilities? By self-monitoring, supported by a viable code of conduct. In fact, the existence of a code of professional conduct is considered a hallmark of any profession.

The Code of Professional Conduct of the American Institute of Certified Public Accountants (AICPA) is the primary source of guidance for accountants in public practice. Similar codes, issued by the Institute of Management Accountants (IMA) and the Institute of Internal Auditors (IIA), govern accountants and auditors in private practice. In recent times, the accounting profession has developed several recognized subspecialties, such as Certified Personal Financial Planner, or Certified Fraud Examiner. Each of the subspecialties have also adopted professional codes of conduct that are consistent with AICPA's Code of Professional Conduct. The focus of this chapter is on professional accountants in public practice. Consequently, we limit our discussion to the CPAs who are obliged to adhere to the Code of Professional Conduct of the AICPA. The AICPA Code (hereafter, the Code) is designed to serve a multitude of purposes:

- A message that the professional CPA has a duty to serve the public (Collins and Schulz, 1995, p. 32)

---

* We appreciate research assistance provided by Lynette Greenlay at Bentley College.

- A means of conferring legitimacy upon the professional body, i.e., the AICPA (Preston et al., 1995, p. 509)
- Protecting public interest or a client where the professional delivers a specialized service which cannot be easily measured or judged as to its quality (Preston et al., 1995, p. 508; Neale, 1996, p. 223)
- Providing a filtering mechanism to limit the number of professionals to those who are willing and capable of adhering to the Code and unattractive to those who do not abide by it (Neale, 1996, p. 223).

In the remainder of this chapter, first, we briefly discuss the types of services that are provided by CPAs. Of particular importance to the discussion of ethics is ethics audit services as an emerging area of assurance services that major public accounting firms have begun to offer in recent years. Second, we provide a brief discussion of the AICPA's Code of Professional Conduct with a focus on its principles, but also examples of its rules. Third, the elaborate professional ethics enforcement program is discussed, where illustrative cases and descriptive statistics about the AICPA's disciplinary actions over a 20-year period are provided. The chapter ends with a concluding section where some observations about controversial ethical issues facing the profession are discussed.

Public accounting services

The AICPA has approximately 350,000 members, all of whom are CPAs. To be a CPA, most states require that an individual have had some experience in public accounting. The most distinguishing characteristic of a public accounting practice is to provide audit services for financial statements of various businesses. These financial statements are normally used by the CPA's clients to provide information to stockholders, potential investors, creditors, and regulatory agencies. However, not all CPAs remain in public practice. A large number of members of the AICPA are in industry, such as those working in accounting departments of private or public companies. Others are in private practice (provide clients with unaudited financial statements, tax and business consulting), government or education. While there are some minor differences in the ways in which these members keep their AICPA membership in "good standing," they all are required to adhere to the provisions of the Code. (For example, members in public practice are generally subject to more stringent continuing professional education requirements than those in industry or education.) However, due to the importance of the public trust to the profession, those in public practice are scrutinized more closely than others. For this reason, it is important to identify various areas of services provided by the CPAs in public practice with some emphasis on those in ethics audit services.

CPAs in public practice provide these services:

- Audit services
- Compilation and review services
- Attestation services
- Management advisory services, including internal audit services
- Tax services
- Assurance services, including ethics audit services

The purpose of an *audit service* is to add credibility to financial statements of clients by issuing a report on the fair presentation of the financial statements taken as a whole. A vast majority of clients receive a standard three paragraph audit opinion (called an "unqualified" opinion) which is essentially a bill of health. Variations of this opinion indicate that the auditor is either taking some exceptions (called "modified wording" or a "qualified opinion" depending on the extent of the exception), or states that the financial statements are not presented fairly (called an "adverse opinion"). If the auditor finds that he/she is not independent of the client, then a "disclaimer of opinion" is issued. The Auditing Standards Board of the AICPA is responsible for developing the *Statements on Auditing Standards* that must be followed by auditors in the conduct of their audits. It is important to note that the issuance of an independent audit opinion can *only* be made by a CPA. The other services listed below can be provided by individuals that are not CPAs.

A *compilation* is the presentation of financial information, in the form of financial statements, without the CPA expressing any opinion on them. A *review* is where a CPA has conducted only limited procedures and can give only limited assurance that the financial statements require no material modification. Compilation and review services are normally for non-public companies that may not require full audited statements, but do want some limited assurance about the reliability of their financial statements.

The Statement of Standards for Attestation Engagements, *Attestation Standards* (AT Section 100) defines an attest engagement as "one in which a practitioner is engaged to issue or does issue a written communication that expresses a conclusion about the reliability of a written assertion that is the responsibility of another party." If the written communication is about historical financial statements, then the attestation is the same as an audit. However, a client may want an opinion on its representations related to its own internal controls, or investment performance history, or remaining reserves in an oil field. In these types of engagements, the CPA will still be held to the same level of professional standards as if they were auditing financial statements.

Management advisory services, including internal audit services, are often referred to as *consulting services*. Most of the consulting is related to the internal operations or planning for a client. A practitioner has developed an expertise in a client's affairs and is probably also an expert in the client's industry. This background makes the practitioner a logical choice to consult on matters related to accounting information systems (including hardware and software choices), inventory planning and flows, executive compensation arrangements, or designing pension and profit-sharing plans.

Tax services relate to corporations, other businesses, and individuals. The services can be limited to only the preparation of federal, state, and local tax returns, but frequently include advice on merger and acquisition, tax planning for current tax minimization or estate planning, and representation in tax audits from the Internal Revenue Service. The tax services area is an example where a practitioner is not required to be strictly independent from the client. The practitioner is expected to be an advocate for the client and to minimize the client's total tax liability.

Assurance services, including ethics audit services are defined by an AICPA special committee as "independent professional services that improve the quality of information, or its context, for decision makers" (Pallais, 1996, p. 16). Assurance services can include audit and attestation, but also includes other non-traditional services. Assurance services are centered on improving the quality of information, and frequently involve situations when one party wants to monitor another, even when both parties work for the same company (Pallais, 1996). Ethics audit services would be an example of the latter service and will be discussed further in a later section.

A recent meeting of the National Association of State Boards of Accountancy concluded that regardless of the type of service provided, CPAs are required to have seven "competencies" (Haberman, 1998, p. 17): four of these competencies are technical in nature (e.g., the ability to assess the achievement of an entity's objectives); one relates to decision making, problem solving, and critical thinking; and another one concerns the ability to communicate the scope of work, findings and conclusions; but the one that is most relevant to ethics is "an understanding of the Code of Professional Conduct." Also, in a National Future Forum held in January 1998, five core values were identified for CPAs: continuing education and life-long learning, competence, integrity, attunement with broad business issues, and objectivity (CPA Vision Project, 1998). Of particular importance to this chapter are integrity and objectivity that are part of the Code as well. This Code is discussed in the next section.

Among the services identified above, assurance services have gained much attention in recent years as an area of significant growth for the accounting profession. These services are provided to improve the quality of information or its context, for decision makers. An example of these assurance services is the CPA *WebTrust*[sm] service by which CPAs assess the reliability of information in company web sites, and if the information is found to be reliable, the *WebTrust*[sm] seal is stamped on the client's web site.

The AICPA's Special Committee on Assurance Services (also known as the Elliott Committee after its chairman, Robert Elliott) has proposed many areas of assurance services. Of special interest to ethicists is "assessment of ethics-related risk and vulnerabilities" (Elliott and Pallais, 1997, p. 63). Some accounting firms (e.g., Arthur Andersen, KPMG Peat Marwick) have already begun offering ethics audit services. According to KPMG Peat Marwick, the ethics audit has four components (KPMG, 1997).

- An assessment of the ethical climate of the client encompassing culture, environment, motives, and pressures
- An assessment of performance incentives – the issue is whether the performance incentives provide a motivation to behave outside the moral norm
- The communication of the message about what is acceptable or unacceptable ethical behavior – this communication covers issues of ethical policies, procedures, and training downstream from management to employees; it also covers the nature of upstream communication from employees to management
- Compliance where the policies, procedures, and offices involved in the enforcement of the client's ethics program are assessed

Although an ethics audit is designed for a company's internal purposes, it is clear that there could be external ramifications. The fact that a company has conducted an ethics audit may have positive implications with outside regulatory agencies, suppliers, customers, or prospective employees.

Ethics audit services are partly governed by *Statements on Auditing Standards* promulgated by the Auditing Standards Board (1997). However, there are significant differences between ethics audits and financial audits. For example, an ethics audit is used to identify a client's areas of vulnerability in comparison with its industry benchmarks. This is different from comparison of a company's ethical performance with absolute ethical philosophies. It is also different from a financial audit where the fairness of financial statements is assessed against generally accepted accounting principles. KPMG Peat Marwick LLP states that an ethics audit is a "positive confirmation of the existence and effective implementation of best ethical practices" (KPMG, 1996).

A concern about the multitude of services provided by CPAs is that conflict of interest may arise from an auditor performing the financial audit as well as other services. This is said to threaten auditor independence. As discussed in the next section, independence is one of the major rules in the Code. In the past, it was not uncommon for auditors to decline engagements or not provide additional services if there was any threat, real or perceived, to their independence. We will return to a discussion of the magnitude of this issue in the final section. Suffice it to say here that, today, it is common for CPAs to avoid this problem by offering various services from separate divisions of the audit firm so as to minimize issues of conflict of interest. In one case, the accounting firm split into two separate entities: Andersen World-wide split into Arthur Andersen to provide audit and tax services and Andersen Consulting to provide management advisory services. Recently, however, Andersen Consulting has alleged that Arthur Andersen is also providing management advisory services to its big clients against the contract that resulted in the split of Andersen in the first place.

AICPA's code of professional conduct

The AICPA's mission statement charges its CPA members with the responsibility to "serve the public interest in performing the highest quality of professional services" (AICPA, 1988, p. vii). The Code calls for honorable behavior, even at the sacrifice of personal interest. Various steps are necessary to prepare the CPA for these services. These steps include education, certification, licensing, and practice, but also a mental ability and commitment to discharging one's responsibility with care and diligence. (Note that all states require that CPAs in public practice to be licensed. A CPA may choose *not* to be a member of the AICPA, and thus not subject to the AICPA Code. However, most state licensing authorities have adopted the AICPA Code as their ethical and professional standards.)

The AICPA's Code of Professional Conduct states, in its preamble, that being a member is voluntary, but by accepting membership one assumes an obligation to the public, clients, and colleagues. To guide behavior, the AICPA has instituted a Code that has four components:

- Principles of professional conduct
- Rules of conduct
- Interpretations of rules of conduct
- Rulings by the Professional Ethics Division of the AICPA and its Trial Board.

Table 14.1   AICPA's Principles of Professional Conduct

Principle	AICPA Directive
1 Responsibilities	In carrying out their responsibilities as professionals, members should exercise sensitive professional and moral judgments in all their activities.
2 The public interest	Members should accept the obligation to act in a way that will serve the public interest, honor the public trust, and demonstrate commitment to professionalism.
3 Integrity	To maintain and broaden public confidence, members should perform all professional responsibilities with the highest sense of integrity.
4 Objectivity and independence	A member should maintain objectivity and be free of conflicts of interest in discharging professional responsibilities. A member in public practice should be independent in fact and appearance when providing auditing and other attestation services.
5 Due care	A member should observe the profession's technical and ethical standards, strive continually to improve competence and the quality of services, and discharge professional responsibility to the best of the member's ability.
6 Scope and nature of services	A member in public should observe the Principles of the Code of Professional Conduct in determining the scope and nature of services to be provided.

Source: AICPA (1988)

There are six principles in the Code. These principles and the AICPA directives related to them are listed in table 14.1. They provide the basic foundation of ethical and professional conduct that is expected of the CPA. However, due to their conceptual nature, these principles are not enforceable. Nevertheless, they point to the importance of public interest (Principles 1 and 2) and the requisite moral characteristics of CPAs in public practice (Principles 3–6).

The Rules of Conduct and the Interpretations of the Rules of Conduct are more specific in nature than the Principles, and as such, they are enforceable. A detailed discussion of these rules and their interpretation is beyond the scope of this chapter but may be found in the AICPA publications and standard auditing texts. To show the general tenet of the rules, we provide a summary here:

- Section 100: Independence, Integrity, and Objectivity (e.g., Rule 102-2 prohibiting conflict of interest)
- Section 200: General Standards and Accounting Principles (e.g., Rule 201-1 requiring competence)
- Section 300: Responsibilities to Clients (e.g., Rule 301-1 prohibition of dissemination of any confidential client information obtained during the course of an audit)
- Section 500: Other Responsibilities and Practices (e.g., Rule 501-1 forbidding retention of client records)

Section 400 that related to responsibilities to colleagues no longer has any rules at this time. However, concurrent with the issuance of the new Code in 1988, the AICPA also approved a mandatory quality peer review program where CPA firms provide reviews of the quality of practice in other CPA firms and present recommendations for improvement. The AICPA also established a number of practice-monitoring committees to facilitate these peer reviews for CPA firms.

The final component of the Code, Rulings by the Professional Ethics Division and the Trial Board of the AICPA, relates to the AICPA's activities to enforce the rules and their interpretations. These issues are discussed in the next section.

Enforcement of the Code of Conduct

Violations of the Code can be diverse and numerous. A detailed listing and discussion of these violations is beyond the scope of this chapter. Here are several examples:

- A CPA was engaged to prepare the financial statements of a company and then audited those same financial statements – a violation of the rule of independence.
- A practitioner prepared a fraudulent tax return on a client's behalf.
- A practitioner did not have the necessary technical skills to perform required work for an engagement – a violation of competence.
- A CPA did not release documents to a client – a violation of Rule 501-1 requirements.

These violations result in disciplinary actions by the AICPA such as admonishment, termination or suspension of membership in the Institute. Since 1975, the Joint Trial Board of the AICPA has been the source of disciplinary action with the participation of some state societies. This cooperation has recently been expanded to include virtually all 50 states and has resulted in the establishment of the Joint Ethics Enforcement Program (JEEP) since 1995. JEEP maximizes the resources for investigation and eliminates duplication (News Report, 1995).

Penalties for violation of the Code range from a recommendation that a member take remedial or corrective action, to a permanent expulsion from the AICPA. For example, a member who has violated the Code may be recommended by the Professional Ethics Division to take a continuing professional education course. If the member does not comply with the recommendation, the Ethics Division may refer him/her to the Trial Board for a hearing. The Trial Board may suspend a member for up to two years or expel him or her for violating the Code. In cases where a crime punishable by imprisonment for more than one year has occurred the member is automatically suspended or terminated from AICPA membership. A similar penalty can be imposed for filing a false income tax return on a client's behalf.

The disciplinary actions of the Joint Trial Board are publicized in the AICPA's newsletter, *The CPA Letter*. Generally, this means that a similar action has been taken by the professional state society of CPAs in the state where the violator has membership. (Note that a CPA can have membership in more than one state society. Furthermore, a CPA can get licensing from various state boards of CPA for practice in multiple states.) These state societies have codes of professional conduct for their membership that are identical with, or similar to, the AICPA Code (AICPA, 1997, p. 6).

On the surface, the actions taken by the AICPA and/or state societies of CPAs may appear to be insignificant in nature since membership in these associations is voluntary and one can resign at any time. In reality, an action such as termination of membership, may indeed tarnish one's reputation as a CPA to the extent that one would voluntarily leave the profession altogether. Also, consider the fact that the practice of public accounting requires licensing by governmental regulatory agencies such as state boards of public accountancy. The AICPA and/or state society actions to terminate or suspend membership may precede or succeed revocation or suspension of practice licenses by state boards of accountancy. Thus, the CPA may be barred from practice, involuntarily, for a period of time or forever, depending on the nature of the violation.

State boards of public accountancy have been set up to enforce state accounting laws. These boards are generally charged with the responsibility of overseeing the accounting profession in their states. Consequently, they have mechanisms by which complaints against CPAs are documented, investigated, and adjudicated. These complaints "can come from a variety of sources, including clients, third parties such as federal, state and local governments; and other CPAs, especially successor accountants and auditors. The state board must investigate each complaint to assess its merit and, if necessary, determine the appropriate corrective action" (Ruble, 1997).

The disciplinary actions taken by state boards of accountancy and state societies of CPAs may also be the result of court action against a member. For example, a criminal conviction in a court of law may automatically result in suspension or termination of membership in state societies and the AICPA, as well as loss of practice license by the state board of public accountancy.

As stated earlier, violations of the AICPA Code may require a hearing by the Ethics Division of the AICPA or its Trial Board. State societies of CPAs have similar mechanisms, and they cooperate closely with the AICPA. Virtually all states boards have joined with the AICPA to create the Joint Ethics Enforcement Program (JEEP). This program has developed a detailed manual for effective and efficient treatment of code violations. According to the AICPA professional standards and the provisions of the JEEP manual (AICPA, 1997), there are two distinct methods of dealing with member violations. The first is suspension or termination of membership without a hearing, i.e., automatic disciplinary actions. The second is the AICPA disciplinary action process where provisions are made for a hearing.

The automatic sanctions are generally the result of court actions or other governmental (e.g., Securities and Exchange Commission) actions against CPAs. As soon as notification is received by the secretary of the AICPA, a suspension or termination notice is automatically mailed to the member via registered or certified mail. If the member does not appeal, then the action is viewed as final and publicized in *The CPA Letter*. However, if the member appeals in writing, then the Trial Board forwards the appeal to an *ad hoc* committee for a decision. If the appeal is granted, then the case is forwarded to the Ethics Division for appropriate action. Otherwise, the automatic decision is affirmed and publicized in *The CPA Letter*. The disciplinary action is termination in cases of:

- crime punishable by imprisonment for more than a year;
- willful failure to file an income tax return when required by law;

- filing false or fraudulent income tax return on own or client behalf; and
- willful aid in preparation and presentation of a false and fraudulent income tax return of a client.

Membership will be revoked or suspended without a hearing if the member's practice license is suspended or revoked as a disciplinary action by a governmental agency.

The cases that do not result in automatic suspension or termination of membership are Code violations that have been brought to the attention of state societies or the AICPA through complaints made by individuals, clients, or other CPAs. JEEP processes these cases. The member can plea guilty and/or resign from the AICPA and state society membership. In this case, the Trial Board may recommend acceptance of the member's resignation, but require that the member appear for a hearing by the Trial Board at a later date. If the member does not plead guilty or the Trial Board does not accept the member's resignation, a panel is set up by the Trial Board for investigation of the case. The Trial Board may choose not to accept a member's resignation due to the seriousness of a violation. They may feel that, to serve the public interest, the member needs to be publicly expelled. The panel may decide that no action is necessary or may schedule a hearing. The result of the hearing may be that no action is necessary or that the member must be admonished, suspended, terminated, or must perform some activity such as taking x hours of continuing professional education. The member can appeal this decision within thirty days, and if granted, the Trial Board will review the decision and will uphold it, change it, or find the member innocent and inform the member of its decision. If the decision is that a violation had occurred for which disciplinary action is taken, then the decision is publicized in *The CPA letter*.

Illustrative disciplinary actions

To illustrate the disciplinary actions against CPAs, we first present the facts about an individual who was found to have violated the AICPA Code. We will then present descriptive data to show the extent of the disciplinary actions taken over a 20-year period. This information is extracted from a disciplinary action database we have compiled from an examination of *The CPA Letter* published from 1977 till 1996.

Case 353 occurred in 1990. The individual was found to have violated the AICPA Code by having assisted in the preparation of a false tax return and having obstructed justice by lying about it (i.e., perjury). The information came from conviction in the court of law and automatically resulted in termination of AICPA membership.

A summary of the 20-year data is presented in table 14.2. The data are classified by the type of disciplinary action (termination, suspension, and other) and by the source of action (automatic or hearing). Also provided are the averages per year. These averages are calculated by dividing the raw numbers by 20 years (1977–1996). Finally, we have divided the average yearly disciplinary actions by the average number of members in the AICPA over the 20-year period to find the average number of disciplinary actions per 10,000 AICPA members.

Several observations from table 14.2 are interesting to note. First, a majority of cases were automatic disciplinary actions. Of the 488 terminations, 330 were automatic as compared with 158 that resulted from the Joint Trial Board hearings. Similarly, of

Table 14.2   AICPA's disciplinary action statistics 1977–1996

| Disciplinary action | Source | | | Average per 10,000 |
	Automatic	Hearing	Total	
Termination	330	158	488	
	(16.5/year)	(7.9/year)	(24.4/year)	1.1
Suspension	138	112	250	
	(6.9/year)	(5.6/year)	(12.5/year)	0.5
Other (e.g., admonish	0	65	65	
or censure	(0/year)	(3.25/year)	(3.25/year)	0.1
Total	468	335	803	
	(23.4/year)	(16.75/year)	(40.15/year)	1.7
Average per 10,000	1.0	0.7	1.7	
Membership size:	1977	130,331		
	1996	324,938		
Average		227,634		

Source: Disciplinary Action Database compiled by the authors from *the CPA Letter*.

the 250 cases of suspension, 138 were automatic as compared with 112 that resulted from hearings. The exception was "other" cases that resulted in admonishment, censure or other types of disciplinary actions. None of these cases was the result of an automatic disciplinary action. Thus, overall, of the 803 cases, 468 were subjects of automatic action as compared with 335 hearings by the Joint Trial Board.

Second, a related observation is that a majority of the cases, automatic or hearing, resulted in the termination of the violator from the AICPA membership. Of the 468 automatic cases, 330 resulted in termination of membership. Similarly, 158 of the 335 hearing cases resulted in termination of the violator. Suspension was next followed by "other" disciplinary actions.

Third, the average per 10,000 membership indicates that overall, only 1.7 persons (1 automatic and 0.7 from hearing) were disciplined per year. Of these 1.1 were terminated, 0.5 were suspended, and 0.1 were subjected to other disciplinary actions.

A conclusion from this data is that violations of the Code by the AICPA members are rare. The assumption is that all major cases are detected and adjudicated by the AICPA, state boards of accountancy, and state societies of CPAs. There are, of course, unreported or undetected violations of the Code as well. Thus, the true level of ethical behavior is not possible to observe. However, it is in the best interest of a self-regulating profession to expose unethical behavior. With this in mind, there are several significant overall ethical controversies facing the profession and these are discussed in the next section.

Controversial ethical issues in the accounting profession

As discussed in the previous sections, the accounting profession has developed a code of conduct and has an elaborate disciplinary program in place to enforce the Code.

Surveys of CPAs (e.g., Cohen and Pant, 1991) indicate that the Code and its enforcement are viewed as effective for the professional body. This does not, however, mean that the profession has been free from criticism. While CPAs, in general, do not believe that unethical behavior leads to success, they do perceive that opportunities exist in the accounting profession to engage in unethical behavior. This is because surveys of CPAs indicate that some clients request fraudulent alteration of tax returns or financial statements (Finn et al., 1988).

Critics allege that these client pressures, causing ethical problems for the profession, are partly due to the professionals having abandoned the legitimacy of ethical character that was the norm in the early 1900s. Critics support this allegation by noting that, in the early 1900s, there were virtually no general auditing or accounting standards, while today there is a large complicated set of standards and rules. Critics claim that today's CPAs rely on "following the rules" rather than focusing on what is the best, fairest, or clearest presentation of accounting information. As technical expertise has become the cornerstone of the CPA practice, the legitimacy of technique has replaced the legitimacy of character (Abbott, 1988, p. 190). Even within this technical expertise, critics argue that some CPAs have ignored their clients' creative accounting in which earnings have been manipulated in some cases. For example, Lomas Financial Corporation has filed a $300 million lawsuit against its auditors, alleging that two audit partners collaborated with the management of Lomas Financial Corporation to conceal risky financial practices that contributed to the company's failure (MacDonald, 1997).

Similarly, a large potential area of concern for CPA firms is the exposure to lawsuits from consulting engagements. The largest lawsuit yet filed against a CPA firm ($4 billion) was related to a consulting engagement by an accounting firm to develop and implement a "turnaround plan" for Merry-Go Round Enterprises (MacDonald, 1997). The suit alleges fraud, fraudulent concealment, negligence, and lack of independence. These are issues that are normally raised in an audit engagement lawsuit. William Brewer, an attorney, states "It's an unusual suit. Big Six accounting firms have generally not been sued for their consulting work. However, it's a sign of the times. You'll see many more of these cases in the future as accountants hold themselves out as business consultants" (MacDonald, 1997, p. 312).

In other cases, rapid changes in the information technology have brought the CPA's knowledge under question. The new information technology has also changed the public need for CPA services. For example, whereas traditional audited financial statements were issued three or four months after the closing of the client's fiscal year, the new technology has made it possible to provide the information on line and in real time. As mentioned earlier, the profession has responded by developing the *WebTrust*[sm] service to respond to this need.

Perhaps the most significant ethical challenge to the profession is the question of independence. It has been alleged that auditors systematically violate the Code's independence rule. The Code is clear in its direction of the need for independence, not only in fact which is unobservable, but also in appearance which can be observed by third parties. The auditor may, in fact, exercise independence from the client even if he or she has financial interest in the company. However, to assure independence in appearance, the auditor is prohibited from having any direct interest such as stock ownership in the client, or significant indirect interest such as ownership of stocks in the client by the CPA's close relatives.

Critics argue that independence rules must also be addressed in cases of providing conflicting services to the client. For example, how can an auditor be independent of his or her client in conducting a financial audit if the auditor is also the one who had provided advice in the development or purchase of the client's accounting system? Similarly, the profession has been criticized for taking inadequate responsibility for detecting fraudulent financial reporting by clients in situations where auditor's self interest has been on the line. These allegations have resulted in Congressional invest-igations of the profession. For example, Senator Metcalf investigated the profession in 1976 (US Senate, 1976) while Senators Moss did the same in 1978 (US Senate, 1978). (A detailed discussion of these investigations and the profession's response to them is beyond the scope of this chapter; they are stated here to show the significance of the issues.)

The profession's response has been to set up commissions to investigate these issues, and to provide recommendations, based on which new pronouncements could be issued. For example, in response to Senators Metcalf and Moss investigations, the AICPA established The Commission on Auditors' Responsibilities in the mid-1970s (The Cohen Commission, 1978). The recommendations from this commission led to the establish-ment of another commission later to investigate fraudulent financial reporting (The Treadway Commission, 1987) and later to yet another commission (COSO, 1992) that made a long list of recommendations. As a result of the recommendations of these commissions, the profession has taken significant steps to enhance its guidance for practitioners by issuing new pronouncements. The revised Code of Conduct issued in 1988 (AICPA, 1988) tightened the Code requirements by eliminating some ambigu-ous and controversial sections. Specifically, the new Code allows for advertising by CPAs that was prohibited by the earlier code. In the same year, the Auditing Stand-ards Board issued a package of nine new *Statements on Auditing Standards* (dubbed expectation gap standards) to provide better guidance to the auditors in their conduct of the financial audit. More recently, the Auditing Standards Board responded to the Treadway Commission (1987) and COSO (1992) reports by issuing a new *Statement on Auditing Standards No. 82* that requires auditors to plan the audit so that if fraud exists, it can be detected (Auditing Standards Board, 1997). In the past, the profession steadfastly denied responsibility to plan the audit for the purpose of detecting fraud although it maintained that if fraud was indicated in the course of the normal audit, it would be investigated.

Other contemporary ethical issues confronting the profession include confidentiality, public confidence, and serving the public interest.

Confidentiality

The CPA is entrusted with a large amount of information from the client. The auditor is prohibited to share this information with others, except in response to court order and other exceptional situations. For example, the auditor can provide financial ratios to industry trade groups so long as specific client information is not revealed. However, the auditor cannot use confidential information for self or other financial interests such as trading stocks based on the insider information gathered in the course of the audit.

Public confidence

The profession allows CPAs to advertise, but through its ethics rulings limits the type of advertising to those that enhance public confidence. For example, contingent fees and commissions are not allowed for referral of attest function services (i.e., audits, compilation and reviews), but allowed for management advisory services. Contingent fees and referral commissions were prohibited altogether until 1988 when under pressure from the Federal Trade Commission, the AICPA council voted to change the rule (Mintz, 1990, p. 3). Nevertheless, critics argue that advertising has helped change public accounting from a profession to a business (Mason, 1994).

Serving the public interest

As stated earlier, the profession only recently has begun to accept responsibility for planning the audit for detection of fraud and other illegal acts (Auditing Standards Board, 1997). More needs to be done to clarify the CPA's responsibility to the public. For example, should the CPA engage in whistle-blowing when an illegal act or fraud is detected to have been committed by a client? As critics argue, at the present time, "the resolution of conflicts between an accountant's client, on the one hand, and the general public, on the other, is usually balanced in favor of the client. The legal system supports this outcome, at least for the time being" (Epstein and Spalding, 1993, p. 271). Others argue that the source of this problem is the weight that is placed on confidentiality at the expense of public interest (Collins and Schulz, 1995).

Conclusion

The accounting profession has developed an elaborate Code of Conduct complete with a continuing education and an effective enforcement program. However, more needs to be done to make accountants more responsive to public expectations to enhance public trust. While the profession has been forthcoming in its responses to Congressional hearings and private commission recommendations in the past two decades, more is needed to continue building a more trustworthy profession. This is especially urgent in light of the speedy change that is fostered by the age of information technology.

References

Abbott, A. 1988: *The System of Professions: An Essay on the Division of Expert Labor*. Chicago, IL: University of Chicago Press.

AICPA 1988: *Code of Professional Conduct*. New York: AICPA.

AICPA 1997: *Joint Ethics Enforcement Program (JEEP): Manual of Procedures*. New York: AICPA.

Auditing Standards Board 1997: *Statement on Auditing Standards No. 82: Consideration of Fraud in a Financial Statement Audit*. New York: AICPA.

Cohen, J. R. and Pant, L. W. 1991: Beyond bean counting: Establishing high ethical standards in the public accounting profession. *Journal of Business Ethics*, 10, 45–56.

Collins, A. and Schulz, N. 1995: A critical examination of the AICPA Code of Professional Conduct. *Journal of Business Ethics*, 14, 31–41.

COSO (Committee of Sponsoring Organizations of the Treadway Commission) 1992: *Internal Control: Integrated Framework*. Harborside, NJ: AICPA.

CPA Vision Project 1998: CPA vision project identifies top five core values. *The CPA Letter*, 1(June), 9.

Elliott, R. K. and Pallais, D. M. 1997: First: Know your market. *Journal of Accountancy*, (July), 56–63.

Epstein, M. J. and Spalding, A. D. 1993: *The Accountant's Guide to Legal Liability and Ethics*. Boston, MA: Irwin.

Finn, D. W., Chenko, L. B., and Hunt, S. D. 1988: Ethical problems in public accounting: The view from the top. *Journal of Business Ethics*, 7, 605–15.

Haberman, L. D. 1998: Regulatory reform at NASBA. *Journal of Accountancy*, (February), 16–17.

KPMG 1996: *Innovating Best Ethical Practices*. Montvalle, NJ: KPMG Peat Marwick LLP.

KPMG 1997: Creating the moral organization. *KPMG Internet Web Site*. Montvalle, NJ: KPMG Peat Marwick, LLP.

MacDonald, E. 1997: Trustee files $4 billion lawsuit against Ernst & Young. *The Wall Street Journal*, December 2, 240, B12.

Mason, E. 1994: Public accounting: No longer a profession? *The CPA Journal*, 64(6) July, 34–7.

Mintz, S. 1990: *Cases in Accounting Ethics and Professionalism*. New York: McGraw-Hill.

Neale, A. 1996: Conduct, misconduct and accounting. *Journal of Business Ethics*, 15, 219–26.

News Report 1995: New era in ethics enforcement. *Journal of Accountancy*, August, 13.

Pallais, D. 1996: Assurance services: Where we are; where we're going. *Journal of Accountancy*, 182(3) September, 16–17.

Preston, A. M., Cooper, D. J., and Scarbrough, D. P. 1995: Changes in the code of ethics of the US accounting profession, 1917 and 1988: The continual quest for legitimization. *Accounting, Organizations and Society*, August, 507–46.

Ruble, M. R. 1997: Letter from the state board: What should you do next? *Journal of Accountancy*, 183(5) May, 75.

The Cohen Commission 1978: *Report, Conclusions, and Recommendations*. New York: AICPA.

The New York Times December 27, 1997: 147, B147.

The Treadway Commission 1987: *Report of the National Commission on Fraudulent Financial Reporting*. New York: AICPA.

US Senate Subcommittee on Reports, Accounting and Management of the Committee on Governmental Affairs; the Metcalf Committee 1976: *The Accounting Establishment*. Washington DC: US Government Printing Office.

US Senate; the Moss Committee 1978: *Report of the Committee on Auditors' Responsibilities*. Washington DC: US Government Printing Office.

15

Marketing ethics*

GEORGE G. BRENKERT

Marketing and ethics

Marketing raises some of the most widely and hotly disputed ethical issues regarding business. Whether it be advertising, retailing, pricing, marketing research, or promotion (to name just a few marketing areas), marketing has been charged with engaging in practices that involve dishonesty, manipulation, invasion of privacy, creating unsafe products, as well as the exploitation of children and vulnerable consumers. Two general studies which refer to these (and other) criticisms of marketing are John Tsalikis and David J. Fritzsche (1989) and Bol et al. (1991).

It should be noted that, in the preparation of this chapter, I have drawn primarily on articles and books which are to be found within the "marketing ethics" literature. This means that there are numerous other articles and books outside of marketing (so defined), which have implications, both direct and indirect, for the topics and issues discussed here on which I did not draw. I adopted this approach to give yet a further sense of the state of marketing ethics itself today. Whether this limitation best serves the topics discussed, the reader must decide for him or herself. However, because some sort of marketing activities are necessary in any society beyond the most undeveloped, the elimination of marketing is not the answer to the problems listed above. Rather, we must look to the formulation and implementation of an ethical theory for marketing.

In the past several decades, a great deal has been written about the ethics of marketing. This article attempts both to provide a brief overview of the main currents of this literature and to participate in the development of marketing ethics. I do the latter, in part, by suggesting a framework according to which present work in marketing ethics might better be understood and areas of future work identified. The aim of such work must be twofold: to develop an evaluative response to present ethical challenges to marketing, and, proactively, to create an ethical theory to tell us how marketing activities ought morally to be constituted so as to avoid those charges. Such an ethics must avoid the Scylla of irrelevant idealism, but also the Charybdis of an unwarranted defense of the status quo. Accordingly, an ethical theory for marketing cannot limit itself simply to current assumptions about present capitalist markets. It must examine

* The final preparation of this paper was greatly helped by the suggestions of Robert Frederick and Craig Smith.

these assumptions as well as the activities which take place within their confines. (This view contrasts with that of Robin and Reidenbach (1993, p. 104) who seek to measure the ethical or unethical nature of basic marketing functions "within our understanding of their history, the times in which they are applied, the context in which they are applied, the expectations of society, the requirements of capitalism.")

The creation of an ethics of marketing is not simply a matter of theoretical interest, but also one of practical concern. This has been demonstrated by the creation, in the past century, of significant regulations and regulatory bodies to oversee marketing activities, e.g. the Food and Drug Administration, the Federal Communications Commission, and the Federal Trade Commission. The development of these agencies has been, in part, a response to concerns about the ethics of marketing. A marketing ethics will provide a basis whereby the actions (or omissions) of such agencies and regulations may be appraised. It will also, however, furnish the grounds upon which those in marketing, those who are the targets of marketing, and society more generally may morally judge the activities and relations marketing engenders.

Ethics and marketing: initial distinctions

A marketing ethics will not be a simple thing. To emphasize this, some initial distinctions concerning both ethics and marketing will be useful. When people speak of the ethics of marketing, they refer, most generally, to the principles, values and/or ideals by which marketers (and marketing institutions) ought to act. Arguable, these "norms" are the core of a marketing ethics, since we are interested in how marketing ought morally to be organized and undertaken. As such, a marketing ethics is a normative ethics. It tells marketers how they morally ought to act. However, this leaves empirical and analytical (or meta-ethical) discussions of marketing ethics, which are crucial to its normative ethics, without a home. It would be better then to use the rubric "marketing ethics" more broadly to encompass:

- *descriptive (or empirical) studies* of the moral values, beliefs and practices of marketing,
- *analytical studies* of the nature of ethically relevant marketing concepts and the kinds of justifications which can be offered for normative ethical marketing claims, as well as
- *normative studies* of the values, principles, and ideals to which marketers should be held.

Though descriptive and analytical studies can be engaged in for their own sakes, ultimately they should serve to enhance our development of a normative ethics. "Marketing ethics," then, refers to this comprehensive study of the ethics of marketing from these three different directions. To develop such a marketing ethics would be to respond to the call by Murphy and Laczniak (1981, p. 262) for a "global theory of ethics." Unfortunately, these distinctions are not often made, with the result that the same discussion may move seamlessly from one approach to marketing ethics to another. The article by Laczniak and Murphy (1991) nicely illustrates the seamlessness by which discussions of marketing ethics may move from descriptive marketing ethics, to normative and analytical marketing ethics without particular notice being given of the transitions involved. The danger is that the criteria which are appropriate for one area may not be similarly appropriate to discussions in other areas of marketing ethics. Thus, for example, the standards by which we would judge a discussion of what we mean (or should mean) by "honesty," "confidentiality," "privacy," or "vulnerability," will differ from those we would use in judging whether a marketing researcher who secretly codes survey forms so as to identify respondents has done something morally permissible or morally wrong.

Since we are interested in the ethics of marketing, it is also appropriate to say something, briefly, about the nature of marketing. The nature of marketing was the source of considerable dispute, particularly during the 1960s and 1970s. Battles raged over whether marketing must necessarily be linked simply with market exchanges (Luck, 1969), as opposed to whether it may be conceived to include transactions and exchanges of a much broader nature (Kotler and Levy, 1969). What is clear is that those in favor of broadening marketing to include the marketing of traditional non-business activities, such as religion, education and politics, have prevailed. As such, the American Marketing Association has defined marketing to refer quite broadly to activities involved in conceiving, pricing, promoting and distributing ideas, goods and services so as to create exchanges that satisfy individual and organizational objectives; For the American Marketing Association's definition of marketing, see Assael (1993, p. N-1).

Two ethical implications of this development are worth noting. First, the ethics of marketing today encompasses a much wider range of activities than previously. When religion, politicians and education (among other traditional non-market arenas) are viewed as products or services to be marketed, the range of ethical questions regarding the ways in which marketers' skills and knowledge may benefit (or harm) its objects is greatly extended. Accordingly, marketers must address standard ethical questions regarding (for example) manipulation, truth-telling and freedom over a much wider and more diverse area than in the past. Second, the broadening of marketing's reach also raises ethical questions concerning whether these areas, heretofore outside of marketing, are themselves being transformed through marketing into forms of markets, subject to the values, standards and expectations of markets. Thus, questions concerning the "selling" of ideas, the "packaging" of politicians, and the commercialization of religion raise significant ethical issues in their own rights about the moral integrity of these domains. In short, the nature or scope of marketing may not simply raise particular moral questions regarding the instrumental support that marketing may give to other areas, but also important ethical questions about the transformation of the areas to which marketing is extended.

Descriptive marketing ethics

A complete marketing ethics, I have indicated above, would include a descriptive, a normative and an analytical ethics. Normative moral discussions of marketing depend, either directly or indirectly, on empirical matters. Consider the following hypotheticals. Suppose that it is morally wrong to advertise to children, if they are unable to discern the nature and purpose of the advertising directed at them. Suppose also that, if various marketing activities unnecessarily promote environmental degradation or cause the poor to pay more for their products and services, those activities are morally wrong.

The hypotheticals in these claims involve empirical questions. It is of no small importance, then, for marketers to address such crucial empirical issues as follows.

- In what ways do advertisements influence people?
- What cognitive conditions are required for an individual to discern the purpose(s) of advertisements?
- What moral problems do marketers and consumers believe they face?
- What are the effects of marketing on economic development, the environment and the poor?
- What processes do marketers go through when they seek to make ethical decisions?
- How do customers or marketers morally rationalize unethical behavior in the market?
- What different moral beliefs regarding marketing do societies such as the US and India maintain?

It should be obvious that a wide range of marketing descriptive studies may fall within this category. Such studies empirically investigate either a moral value, belief or principle people hold, or they investigate empirical conditions which bear directly on the realization of moral values or principles. Accordingly, a brief summary of such studies is impossible to provide.

However, there is one area of descriptive marketing ethics which is particularly worthy of more detailed consideration, due to the attention it has received within the last twenty years. This is the empirical study of ethical decision making in marketing. These studies take two major forms, which are not always distinguishable. On the one hand, some have investigated various influences on the ethical decision-making behavior of marketers. On the other hand, researchers have tried to devise models which will describe and/or explain the ethical decisions marketers make.

Among the former, the influences on individual ethical decision behavior have been divided into two rough catgories: individual and situational. The individual category includes variables associated with the individual decision maker such as sex, nationality, education, religion, age, employment, personality, attitudes, and values. The results of these studies are many times mixed. For example, some find that there is no distinction between men and women when it comes to various modes of moral reasoning in organizations (Derry, 1989; Schminke, 1997), while others find that gender is a significant factor (Fritzsche, 1988; Konovsky and Jaster, 1989). Fritzsche, for example, reported that male respondents are less likely to pay a bribe than female respondents, but more likely to ask for a bribe than female respondents (Singhapakdi et al., 1996, p. 638). Chonko and Hunt (1985) found that female marketers are more likely to perceive ethical problems than male marketers. However, Singhapakdi and Vitell (1991) found no relationship between the gender of a sales professional and his or her perception of an ethical problem. The role of gender in moral decision making remains one of the more hotly contested disputes regarding influences on individual ethical decision behavior.

Situational factors include peer group influence, organizational climate and/or culture, top management influence, codes of ethics, corporate ethical values, rewards, sanctions, organization size and level, and various industry factors such as industry type and competitiveness (Ford and Richardson, 1994; Akaah, 1996, p. 605). For example, Akaah (1996, p. 605) looked at organizational rank and role as ethics correlates, and found (p. 612) that "marketing professionals of lower organizational rank do not differ significantly from marketing professionals of upper organizational rank in ethical judgments." However, he also found that "marketing professionals of executive role reflect higher ethical judgments than marketing professionals of research role" (p. 612).

One concern in such studies is that the factors whose correlations are examined are truly empirically separate, rather than conceptually linked. It is not obvious that this point is always recognized. It is the distinction between descriptive ethics and analytical ethics. Thus, when Singhapakdi et al. (1996, p. 641) claim that "our survey results generally indicated that professional values do influence a service professional's ethical perceptions in a positive way as hypothesized," one might wonder whether an individual's having certain professional values necessarily or conceptually (rather than empirically) involves having certain ethical perceptions. Suppose, for instance, that the individuals in this study had not had the appropriate ethical perceptions. Would the investigators conclude that they nevertheless had those professional values but simply did not see the scenarios as involving ethical problems, or (instead) that they did not have those professional values?

The other kind of study of individual ethical decision making involves the development of explanatory models and frameworks of ethical decision making which seek to identify the various steps involved in arriving at ethical decisions. One of the more elaborate accounts is that of Hunt and Vitell (1993), who take a cognitive, multi-staged perspective:

1   An individual must, first, perceive an ethical problem.
2   The individual seeks to identify various alternative actions that might solve the problem and what their consequences would be.
3   Two kinds of evaluations take place: one looks to the inherent rightness or wrongness of each alternative (deontological considerations); and, one considers the probability and desirability of the consequences of each alternative as well as the importance of the relevant stakeholders (teleological considerations).
4   These two evaluations are merged to form a single ethical judgment.
5   Such ethical judgments impact on a person's behavior through the intervening variable of his or her intentions, which may, however, differ (due to other preferred consequences) from what he or she judged to be ethical.
6   The resulting behavior may vary from the individual's prior intentions and ethical judgments, depending on "the extent to which the individual actually exerts control in the enactment of an intention in a particular situation" (Hunt and Vitell, 1993).
7   Personal characteristics, as well as organizational, industrial, professional and cultural environments directly influence steps 1–3 above.

While the Hunt and Vitell model encompasses many, if not most, of the factors which are included in models of moral decision making, others theorists emphasize some steps more than others or introduce them at different stages. In addition, other models inject various decisions rules (Fritzsche, 1991), ideological frameworks, or interpretations of moral development not part of the preceding model. In general, all such theories move from the recognition of an ethical problem, to the search for alternatives, evaluation, choice and behavior. However, the devil is in the details and here they go their separate ways.

The descriptive studies of marketing ethics noted above and empirical studies of ethical decision making are useful for a marketing ethics in a variety of ways. The former help us to understand the effects of marketing on various groups of people, as well as what excuses are used to deflect moral criticism. The latter help us to see more clearly how ethical marketing decisions might actually be made. The upshot of models of actual ethical decision making may lead to the redesign of organizational and strategic mechanisms for improving ethical decision making (Laczniak and Murphy, 1985). Ferrell and Gresham (1985) claim that in making these changes, individual, organizational and opportunity variables will require attention. Further, these models may reveal ethical conflicts and tendencies which marketers would not have otherwise suspected. As such, descriptive marketing ethical studies can play a significant role in directing the attention and research of normative marketing ethical studies.

However, these studies do not always recognize their own limitations. For example, some descriptive studies conclude from the diversity of moral decisions they survey, that it is impossible to say what is right or wrong (Ferrell and Fraedrich: 1997, p. 105). Similarly, on the basis of his empirical decision model, Fritzsche (1991, p. 851) speculates that decision makers are practicing situational ethics rather than absolute ethics. However, these conclusions do not follow simply from such descriptive studies. Instead, they are conclusions which can only follow from an analytical marketing ethics, i.e. a study of the forms of justification available to marketing ethical judgments. In short, though descriptive marketing ethics plays a vital role in any general theory of marketing ethics, its relation to normative and analytical studies requires close attention.

Normative marketing ethics

Two broad streams of discussion – the applied and the theoretical – address the normative ethics of marketing. The former uses various moral (and non-moral) values and principles to evaluate marketing and to engage in efforts to change those practices. These accounts tend to mix, sometimes uncritically, descriptive and normative considerations regarding marketing.

Four basic sets of values are prominently appealed to in these discussions – truth, freedom, well-being, and justice – although some marketers still speak of the main ethical issues facing marketers as the "key values of trust, honesty, respect and fairness" (Smith and Quelch, 1993, p. 11). Most often, in applied accounts, the values – truth, freedom, well-being and justice – are used to criticize marketing for various ethical failures. Accordingly, with regard to truth, advertisements, purchase agreements, and promotions have been attacked for dishonesty or misleading customers (Carson et al., 1985; Jackson, 1990). The nature and limits of puffery (hyperbole) in advertising has been a constant source of concern (Preston, 1975; Pollay, 1986). Marketing researchers have been criticized for using hidden codes to identify supposedly anonymous response questionnaires, for sending undercover investigators into stores to observe the behavior of customers and employees, and for not revealing the nature of their research to their informants (Crawford, 1970; Tybout and Zaltman, 1974; Akaah and Riordan, 1989). Studies of the ways and occasions on which marketers have provided their customers with correct information about their products are much less frequently part of the normative marketing ethics literature.

The value of freedom lies behind criticisms of forms of promotion which pressure or coerce vulnerable, as well as ordinary, consumers (Beauchamp, 1993). Morally unscrupulous marketers are said not to value the freedom of choice of the elderly, the grieving, and the young, when they manipulate them into buying what they do not need or understand (Paine, 1983; Gentry et al., 1994). In channels of distribution, large retailers are sometimes accused of coercing small suppliers to accept agreements they would not otherwise accept. And since freedom is usually understood in terms of lack of constraint, the intrusiveness of some marketing activities (e.g. telemarketing during the evening) has increasingly raised moral questions of freedom as well as privacy (Morris-Lee, 1996).

In particular, the development of new technologies (computers, scanners, monitoring devices) have become a threat to freedom and are one reason that privacy has become a paramount concern. Thus, many have raised normative ethical questions concerning the nature and amount of information that can today be gained through scanning devices, computer records of credit card purchases, and Internet purchasing. Once again, normative studies of the ways in which current marketing practices involving such technologies might enhance the freedom of their customers are relatively rare.

The well-being of people is partially captured by concern about the quality and safety of products, e.g., the Ford Pinto, drugs, pesticides, food, breast implants. Various motorized vehicles, such as the Suzuki Samurai, All Terrain Vehicles, etc., have been criticized due to their performance features as well as the ways in which they have been promoted and advertised (Smith and Quelch, 1993). The marketing of tobacco both in the US and in developing countries (where the percentage of women smokers and lung cancer in women has greatly increased) has been attacked for its lack of concern for the well-being of its users. In addition, marketers are criticized for encouraging people to acquire new products, go more deeply into debt, collect new experiences and participate in rampant forms of consumerism (Korten, 1995; Jacobson and Mazur, 1995). Their accumulation of information on consumers, through the various sources noted above, has been said to threaten individual privacy (Fost, 1990).

Finally, justice (or injustice) has underlain criticisms of the prices of products, debt arrangements, and the targeting of children. The marketing of alcohol (e.g., PowerMaster) to inner-city residents and of tobacco through the use of Joe Camel have occasioned strong justice-based objections. Various forms of marketing are said to constitute forms of exploitation, such as the target marketing of certain alcoholic beverages to inner-city blacks and the use of women in the Swedish Bikini Club commercial. Exploitation of a very different form has been the charge in developing countries where marketers have been accused of paying very low wages to workers, even though these companies frequently pay above the average wage in those countries. Disney, the Gap, Nike and many other businesses have been criticized for their policies in the use of foreign labor and suppliers. These objections raise difficult questions regarding what is a just wage and the role that local conditions should play in such a determination. On the other hand, marketing has been praised for bringing efficiency and economic progress to developing countries.

The moral appeal in these cases is both to mid-range and fundamental values or principles. In each of the above cases, the charge is that marketing has either failed to safeguard these values or has given one an unjustified priority over another. The value of competition, for example, which might be captured under freedom, is less frequently heard in these accounts (Nelson, 1978). The importance of efficiency, which might be brought under well-being, is also infrequently heard when it comes to the wages of employees or the use of greater amounts of information so as to be able to tailor products to various specific customers (Maitland, 1997). Rightly or wrongly, the pressures that marketers are under are often not taken into account. Accordingly, many times the criticisms focus on individual instances, rather than address the systems within which those cases arise. To this extent, they appear to accept a market system but chide marketers for ethical failures within it.

Theoretical normative discussions have sought to formulate the values and standards to which people ought to appeal in marketing. They also attempt to provide normative guidelines for managers to follow in resolving moral disputes as well as in moral investigations of functional areas of marketing, e.g., marketing research, advertising, and retailing. These normative studies come in two main types. On the one hand, there are normative models of the substantive steps which individuals should take in making moral decisions. Articles on this topic have become much more prominent in the last couple of decades. On the other hand, some normative accounts, apparently despairing of identifying any small set of moral principles, simply list a number of normative questions which marketers should ask when making moral decisions.

Examples of the former approach include the limited relativist theory of Robin and Reidenbach (1993). In their view, moral issues in marketing are to be decided by which actions and policies promote a "well-structured and happy life" within the constraints of a society's history, capitalist objectives and human psychological limitations (p. 102). Robin and Reidenbach suggest such a marketing ethics is a form of moral relativism, inasmuch as it is constrained by the preceding limitations and relies heavily on descriptive ethics. As such, they reject the tradition of grand narratives and overarching moral principles such as utilitarianism and Kantianism. Nevertheless, it would appear that their view has strong sympathies with utilitarian moral philosophy.

A rather different approach is taken by Smith and Quelch, who offer a continuum of moral decision making criteria (from caveat emptor to caveat venditor) which may provide benchmarks for marketing managers. However, they maintain that one criterion on this continuum is superior to others for ethical decision making: consumer sovereignty test (Smith and Quelch, 1993, pp. 20–34; Smith, 1995). This normative guide is composed of three sub-criteria: the consumer's capabilities regarding understanding the product and purchase decision, the information provided, and the consumer's ability to choose among products. This normative guide is, however, of limited usefulness. As Smith (1995) notes, it can only be applied in a narrow band of issues which arise for marketers and consumers. It does not extend more broadly to other normative issues marketers might face in marketing research, channels of distribution, environmental questions, etc. Further, how much consumer sovereignty (capability, information and choice) is required? Must the sub-criteria of this test be maximized in some manner or other? Smith and Quelch provide some tentative suggestions for determining how adequately these criteria are fulfilled by referring to various consumer expectations and preferences. Thus, they ultimately say that the answer is "likely to change as society's expectations of business change" (Smith and Quelch, 1993, p. 34). But then the consumer sovereignty test provides no means to judge the expectations of society, which may be unreasonable or even unethical themselves. Further, it derives the moral criterion for marketers simply from the fact of social expectations, an "ought" derived from a fact, something which requires further explanation and justification.

The second normative approach noted above is followed by those who do not propound a single or small number of general principles, but instead turn to a list of norm-laden questions which they would have marketers ask in order to arrive at justified moral judgments. This kind of approach has affiliations with casuistry, i.e., the attention to "the concrete circumstances of actual cases, and the specific maxims that people invoke in facing actual moral dilemmas" rather than an emphasis on "universal rules and invariant principles" (Jonsen and Toulmin, 1988, p. 13). Nevertheless, no one has explored this connection.

Laczniak and Murphy (1991), for example, defend what might be called a multiple responsibilities test which involves a "sequence of questions" that each marketer should use to determine whether a contemplated action is ethical. This test includes questions which ask whether the action is: legal; contrary to widely accepted moral obligations; violates any special obligations; has a harmful intent; imposes major damages on people or organizations; is the alternative that produces the best consequences for affected parties; does not infringe on inalienable rights; or does not leave others less well off (Laczniak and Murphy, 1991, p. 267; 1993, pp. 48–51). They do not claim that if an action passes all these questions it is moral, only that the action "is quite likely to be ethical" (Laczniak and Murphy, 1991, p. 268). Crucial for this test is that the implications and effects on all stakeholders be weighed. However, they do not say how these multiple considerations are to be weighted, whether some ought to have greater weight than others, or what one is to do when answers conflict. It is exactly these difficulties that have driven other marketing ethicists to take the first approach above, which seeks basic normative principles by which to make these determinations.

Several general observations regarding the above normative ethical studies are appropriate. First, it is striking that many applied normative studies of marketing offer ethical criticisms with little reflection on the system within which marketers are operating. It is also noteworthy that many marketers are more concerned with consumer complaints from the standpoint of how to identify and control them so as to enhance the bottom line, rather than satisfy them in an ethically appropriate manner. If there is to be normative ethical progress, both groups need to consider their cases more broadly.

Second, a large number of the scholarly studies of marketing ethics in the US occur at the meso level (the marketing institution) and the micro level (individual manager and customer) – which contrasts with the more systematic (or macro-level) approach of many European business ethicists. For example, many US marketing texts take the view point of the marketing manager. Numerous articles examine the ethical beliefs of managers, as well as attempt to develop practical guidelines and theoretical statements regarding ethical decision making by managers. However, not everyone in, or affected by, marketing is marketing manager. If moral reflection is to consider one's action in light of the full circumstances and the moral point of view, micro- and meso-level studies carry an important limitation. Thus, for example, if a marketer claims that the use of "push money" to retail sales associates "to present the manufacturer's products to the store's customers" is a legitimate form of sales promotion, we might wonder whether they have overlooked the view point and interests of others, e.g. customers. In short, one might regard "push money" differently depending upon whether one saw the retailer as a selling agent for manufacturers or as a buying agent for customers (Langrehr, 1994). Accordingly, it would benefit the development of a marketing ethics if scholarly studies took a broader view, while the practical critics of marketing ethics would find their accounts deepened if they considered the specific contexts or situations within which the issues they discuss arose.

Analytical marketing ethics

Though marketers rarely characterize their work under the heading of "analytical marketing ethics," this is a distinct area, properly so identified, for their discussions of such topics as the nature of various marketing concepts, the kind of justification that can be given to basic marketing moral judgments, whether marketing ethics is a separate ethics from ordinary ethics, and why marketers ought to be worried about being moral. Clearly these kinds of studies are more theoretical than applied, but, as others have said, (normative) marketing ethics has suffered from the lack of a theoretical basis (Laczniak, 1983). (It might be noted that Andrew Stark (1993) has criticized business ethics as being too theoretical (and impractical) and Craig Smith (1995, p. 86) has suggested, in reply, that by focusing on ethical issues as they relate to the various functional areas of business, e.g. marketing, one ". . . is more likely to produce theory useful to marketing decision makers.")

The topic of the justification of basic marketing ethical norms has received attention in a number of recent accounts. The options here include skeptical, relativist, objectivist and absolutist views. For example, Chonko (1995, p. 39) rejects ethical relativism, which he interprets (in an analytical, rather than a normative, sense) as the view that "no ethical guideline has any greater claim to objectivity and universality than any other." He understands this to mean that one cannot justify any value judgments at all. Since he apparently thinks that this is so obviously false, he does not argue against it.

Nevertheless, he maintains that "there are no universally accepted absolute standards . . ." (p. 23). Accordingly, he accepts some form of descriptive ethical relativism (i.e., people in fact accept different basic moral norms), but not analytical relativism (all justifications are equally valid). As such, he maintains that ethics requires absolutes (p. 20). How then are these "absolutes" justified? Chonko says little on this, though he refers to his own Christian religious preferences and seems to suggest that the justification of absolute standards derives from this religious source.

Other marketers have advocated a more relativist or contextualist approach to the justification of moral beliefs. Drawing on MacIntyre, Robin and Reidenbach (1993) defend a view of marketing ethics which is bounded by the constraints of history, time, and context. Such an account tells us how to justify normative moral standards, rather than defends any particular standard. So characterized, theirs is clearly a relativist

187

account. It is for this reason that they speak of "boundaries", rather than principles or values. Indeed, they reject the use of deontological and utilitarian principles, as well as all grand narratives (Robin and Reidenbach, 1993, p. 97).

However, to make their account more realistic, they introduce four other boundary conditions in addition to history, time and context (p. 101):

1   The constraint of morality viewed as having the basic purpose of ameliorating the negative outcomes of life
2   Societal constraints of laws and the satisfaction of consumers' needs
3   Constraints relating to capitalism including meritarian justice, the reward of risk taking, creativity, and industriousness
4   Constraints related to human capacities and limitations, such as psychological egoism.

Unfortunately, these additions undo their relativist marketing ethics. First, by invoking as the purpose of morality the aim of creating conditions so that individuals may "pursue a well-structured and happy life," Robin and Reidenbach (1993, p. 100; p. 102) provide a non-relativist touchstone for the justification of moral beliefs. And, second, their invocation of one form of justice and advocacy of certain values (e.g., industriousness) amount to the identification of certain normative bases which any marketing ethics must adopt. As a consequence, their analytical ethics is not relativist in the standard sense that an objective justification cannot be given of moral beliefs, but only in the sense that the justification of moral beliefs is relative to the features they identify. But given these values and purpose of morality, this would permit a non-relativist justification of moral beliefs. In effect, Robin and Reidenbach have restricted their relativism out of existence. Nevertheless, their paper is an explicit and sophisticated effort on behalf of an analytical marketing ethics. Where other accounts of marketing ethics simply assume or briefly mention their relativistic views on justification, Robin and Reidenbach have looked much more closely.

A somewhat similar approach has been taken by Thompson (1995, p. 183), who argues that "a person's moral viewpoint . . . [is] fundamentally entwined with cultural belief and value systems; that is, a person's understanding of ethical dilemmas ensues from a socialized perspective rather than from a detached perspective of society." Now this might be the case in a causal sense, in which case those who reject ethical relativism could agree. However, Thompson further claims that our moral reasoning and its justification are logically tied to the contexts in which they are situated. Accordingly, our assessment of the moral reasoning of marketers should be made "in relation to the more context specific influences that are exerted by corporate culture." And this leads to this acceptance of the view that "significant disparities may arise between the logic of moral reasoning used in private and professional contexts." Thompson's contextual view thus rejects not only the absolutist or objectivist views of Chonko, but also the bounded relativism of Robin and Reidenbach.

The upshot is that there is little agreement among marketers on what kinds of justification can be offered for normative moral judgments made regarding marketing. There is also considerable disagreement on whether marketing ethics is (or should be) separate from the rest of business ethics – or, indeed, from the ethics of (non-business) society. Again, Chonko (1995, p. 24) holds that "marketing professionals do not operate under an ethical code different from those of us in society," a position that Peter Drucker (1981) strongly defended years ago. However, the result of Thompson's view is that the logic of the two is different. Robin and Reidenbach (1993, p. 103) claim that a separate marketing ethics must be developed which takes into account the "mission, constraints, and directives created for it [marketing] by others . . ." At the same time, marketing's "own" ethical philosophy must recognize "the history, time and context of its pronouncements." The upshot of their view seems to be that the logic of ordinary and marketing ethics may be the same, but the results diverge due to the boundary conditions. Accordingly, the justification of basic marketing ethics norms clearly requires considerable more attention.

Why should marketers bother about morality? Why should marketing organizations attempt to foster ethical behavior? Laczniak and Murphy have responded by noting the various significant personal, organizational and societal costs involved if they do not do so (Laczniak and Murphy, 1991, p. 262; 1993, p. 6). They also note that "the obvious answer [is] that being ethical is simply the proper thing to do" (Laczniak and Murphy, 1993, p. 6). Like all others, however, marketers continue to struggle to find answers as to why they or marketing organizations ought to do the morally right thing, rather than simply the expedient or profitable thing. Clearly, one of the difficulties faced by those seeking to answer this question is the primacy of self-interested justifications which marketing (and all of business) tends to assume. Only if this assumption is successfully challenged, will answers to the present question seem defensible.

These studies in analytical marketing ethics are particularly important if marketers are to understand the moral situations and dilemmas that face them, not only in national but also in international marketing. They need to have formulated a theory which tells them when (and which) moral principles or standards are justified, and whether the domain of that justification is restricted to particular societies or extends to all societies. Do such principles hold, for example, simply for developed (capitalist) nations or do they hold cross-culturally? Do they hold regardless of what people believe or only because of what they believe? These are, admittedly, theoretical questions of the first order, but they are also questions which carry direct practical implications for marketing ethics. For example, answers to these problems will affect the positions marketers take on the cross-cultural role of human rights, the treatment of women, nepotism, gift-giving and bribery. Marketing ethicists must face these issues in one manner or another.

New directions and challenges

Both the ethics of marketing itself and ethical theorizing about marketing will be challenged, in the coming years, from a number of different directions. Many for the ethical challenges for marketing will come from three present sources. Prominent among these has been the development of various technological innovations involving, for example, computers, systems which monitor customers' purchases, the Internet, pagers, faxes, e-mail, etc. Electronic marketing of books, music, medical and legal advice, and education are among many of the developments which will provide increasingly more complex ethical challenges to marketing. Low-cost television screens will advertise goods and services in new and unexpected places. New technologies may be developed to permit monitoring of what shoppers look at while visiting a store and to alter their moods while shopping. What ethical limits should marketers adopt regarding the ways in which they should reach customers and how much they should know about the customers they seek to reach? Additional technological developments will only increase the need for answers to these already important questions.

A second important source will be the increasing influence of global competition. Product development, pricing strategies, and advertising programs will raise, with greater intensity, questions about the ethical propriety of products produced, the prices charged and the ways in which they are advertised and promoted. The homogenization of life styles, the sustainability of forms of production, and the justice of using sophisticated marketing techniques on those in developing nations who lack experience and training regarding such forms of marketing are important ethical challenges which will be increasingly heard.

Third, the continued expansion of marketing activities into non-traditional business areas will serve as an additional source of ethical challenges. For example, secondary schools are increasingly an arena for marketing. Principals and teachers have been involved in marketing efforts. Marketers now reach into churches, not only on behalf of religious institutions but also political campaigns. Further, marketing efforts are undertaken to gain support for legislation which has yet to come before the Congress. The expansion of marketing efforts will continue throughout society – we may become the "marketed' society – on school buses, in schools, embedded in movies, cartoons, and television, on the Internet, wherever people may be reached. Some marketers wish to buy the right to name streets after their companies or products. As these efforts and the techniques of persuasion they use become more subtle, powerful and pervasive, we can be confident that ethical questions regarding marketing will continue to arise.

Challenges to the further development of a marketing ethics will involve continued studies on the interrelation of descriptive and normative marketing claims. The effort here is to develop a normative ethics that is realistic in the sense that it can be applied to practical situations and yet not simply be a stamp of approval of present affairs. Towards this end, some have urged that efforts be made to expand the range of theories relevant to questions of marketing ethics. Laczniak (1993, p. 94) has urged the application of more diverse theories: deconstructionism, feminism, Eastern Religions, humanistic criticism, and non-Kohlbergian models of moral development. He also has advocated greater cross-cultural explorations and evaluations. These would involve descriptively comparing and contrasting the beliefs and practices of a wide spectrum of culturally diverse managers and companies. Marketers might also look to the implications of postmodern philosophy (Robin and Reidenbach, 1993). These challenges might fruitfully expand the vision of marketing ethical theorists.

These efforts might have salutary effects on overcoming some of the limitations of current marketing ethics. For example, there has been a strong individualistic bias shared by those doing research in marketing ethics. Marketing ethicists have tended to focus on the ethical decision making of individuals (usually managers) in marketing. Though this is clearly an important area of marketing ethics, the emphasis on individuals has led to the neglect of moral evaluations of marketing as an institution or activity, as well as neglect of collective forms of moral responsibility. Indeed, some moral problems at the individual level can only be solved by moving to a higher organizational or system level, a move that De George (1993, pp. 97–9) calls "displacement."

The introduction of a wider range of theories might also expand the amount of effort that is expended on international marketing ethics. Though there have been a number of discussions of international marketing ethics, these remain fairly modest in light of the increasing amount of marketing which has international implications and impacts.

Finally, marketing ethics is due for some self-reflection on whether, and to what extent, it has been successful. Has it had any significant effects on the ethics of marketing? (Thompson, 1995, p. 177; Laczniak and Murphy, 1993). In short, an important area of empirical and analytical research in marketing ethics might be to identify those moral changes which have occurred in marketing over the years, and attempt to determine what factors led to their occurrence. If it turned out that important changes have been primarily due to external moral forces in society, e.g. monitoring by private watchdog groups, rather than internal developments of moral codes, ethics workshops, or ethics ombudsmen within productive organizations engaged in marketing, this would have significant implications for future work in marketing ethics. In any case, such a self-critical turn is appropriate if marketing ethics is to know whether it has helped to respond to the many current ethical challenges to marketing noted at the outset of this article.

References

Akaah, I. P. 1996: The influence of organizational rank and role on marketing professionals' ethical judgments. *Journal of Business Ethics*, 15(6), 605–13.

Akaah, I. P. and Riordan, E. A. 1989: Judgments of marketing professionals about ethical issues in marketing research: a replication and extension. *Journal of Marketing Research*, 26, 112–21.

Assael, H. 1993: *Marketing: Principles & Strategy*, 2nd edn. Fort Worth, Texas: The Dryden Press.

Beauchamp, T. L. 1993: Manipulative advertising. In T. L. Beauchamp and N. E. Bowie (eds), *Ethical Theory and Business*, 4th edn. Englewood Cliffs, NJ: Prentice Hall, Inc.

Bol, J. W., Crespy, C. T. Stearns, J. M., and Walton, J. R. 1991: *The Integration of Ethics into the Marketing Curriculum*. Needham Heights, MA: Ginn Press.

Carson, T. L., Wokutch, R. E., and Cox, J. E. Jr 1985: An ethical analysis of deception in advertising. *Journal of Business Ethics*, 4, 93–104.

Chonko, L. B. 1995: *Ethical Decision Making in Marketing*. Thousand Oaks, CAL: Sage Publications.

Chonko, L. B. and Hunt, S. D. 1985: Ethics and marketing management: An empirical investigation. *Journal of Business Research*, 13, 339–59.

Crawford, C. M. 1970: Attitudes of marketing executives toward ethics in marketing research. *Journal of Marketing*, 34(April), 46–52.

De George, R. T. 1993: *Competing with Integrity in International Business*. New York: Oxford University Press.

Derry, R. 1989: An empirical study of moral reasoning among managers. *Journal of Business Ethics*, 8, 855–62.

Drucker, P. 1981: What is business ethics? *The Public Interest*, 63(Spring), 18–36.

Ferrell, O. C. and Fraedrich, J. 1997: *Business Ethics: Ethical Decision Making and Cases*, 3rd edn. Boston: Houghton Mifflin Company.

Ferrell, O. C. and Gresham, L. G. 1985: A contingency framework for understanding ethical decision making in marketing. *Journal of Marketing*, 49(Summer), 87–96.

Ford, R. C. and Richardson, W. D. 1994: Ethical decision making: A review of the empirical literature. *Journal of Business Ethics*, 13(March), 205–21.

Fost, D. 1990: Privacy concerns threaten database marketing. *American Demographics*, 12(May), 18–21.

Fritzsche, D. J. 1988: An examination of marketing ethics: Role of the decision maker, consequences of the decision, management position and sex of respondent. *Journal of Macromarketing*, 8(Fall), 29–39.

Fritzsche, D. J. 1991: A model of decision-making incorporating ethical values. *Journal of Business Ethics*, 10(November), 841–52.

Gentry, J. W., Kennedy, P. F. Paul, K., and Hill, R. P. 1994: The vulnerability of those grieving the death of a loved one: Implications for public policy. *Journal of Public Policy & Marketing*, 13, 128–42.

Hunt, S. D. and Vitell, S. J. 1986: A general theory of marketing ethics. *Journal of Macromarketing*, 6(Spring), 5–16.

Hunt, S. D. and Vitell, S. J. 1993: The general theory of marketing ethics: A retrospective and revision. In N. C. Smith and J. A. Quelch (eds), *Ethics in Marketing*, Burr Ridge, ILL: Richard D. Irwin.

Jacobson, M. F. and Mazur, L. A. 1995: *Marketing Madness*. Boulder, CO: Westview Press.

Jackson, J. 1990: Honesty in marketing. *Journal of Applied Philosophy*, 7, 51–60.

Jonsen, P. R. and Toulmin, S. 1988: *The Abuse of Casuistry*. Berkeley: University of California Press.

Konovsky, M. A. and Jaster, F. 1989: "Blaming the victim" and other ways business men and women account for questionable behavior. *Journal of Business Ethics*, 8, 391–8.

Korten, D. C. 1995: *When Corporations Rule the World*. West Hartford, Conn.: Kumarian Press, Inc.

Kotler, P. and Levy, S. J. 1969: Broadening the concept of marketing. *Journal of Marketing*, 33(January), 10–15.

Laczniak, G. R. 1983: Framework for analyzing marketing ethics. *Journal of Macromarketing*, 3(Spring), 7–18.

Laczniak, G. R. 1993: Marketing ethics: Onward toward greater expectations. *Journal of Public Policy & Marketing*, 12(1), Spring, 91–6.

Laczniak, G. R. and Murphy, P. E. 1985: *Marketing Ethics: Guidelines for Managers*. Lexington, MA: Lexington Books.

Laczniak, G. R. and Murphy, P. E. 1991: Fostering ethical marketing decisions. *Journal of Business Ethics*, 10(April), 259–71.

Laczniak, E. R. and Murphy, P. E. 1993: *Ethical Marketing Decisions: The Higher Road*. Upper Saddle River, New Jersey: Prentice-Hall, Inc.

Langrehr, F. W. 1994: Review of *Ethical Marketing Decisions: The Higher Road*, by G. R. Laczniak and P. E. Murphy. *Journal of Marketing*, 58(January), 158–9.

Luck, D. 1969: Broadening the concept of marketing – too far. *Journal of Marketing*, 33(July), 53–5.

Maitland, I. 1997: The great non-debate over international sweatshops. *British Academy of Management Annual Conference Proceedings*, September, 240–65.

Morris-Lee, J. 1996: Privacy: It's everyone's business now! *Direct Marketing*, 58(April), 40–3.

Murphy, P. E. and Laczniak, G. R. 1981: Marketing ethics: A review with implications for managers, educators, and researchers. In B. M. Enis and K. J. Roering (eds), *Review of Marketing*, Chicago: American Marketing Association.

Nelson, P. 1978: Advertising and ethics. In R. T. De George and J. A. Pichler (eds), *Ethics, Free Enterprise, and Public Policy*, New York: Oxford University Press.

Paine, L. S. 1983: Children as consumers. *Business and Professional Ethics Journal*, 3, 119–46.

Pollay, R. W. 1986: The distorted mirror: Reflections on the unintended consequences of advertising. *Journal of Marketing*, 50(April), 18–36.

Preston, I. L. 1975: *The Great American Blow-Up: Puffery in Advertising and Selling*. Madison: University of Wisconsin Press.

Robin, D. P. and Reidenbach, R. E. 1993: Searching for a place to stand: Toward a workable ethical philosophy for marketing. *Journal of Public Policy & Marketing*, 12(Spring), 97–105.

Schminke, M. 1997: Gender differences in ethical frameworks and evaluation of others' choices in ethical dilemmas. *Journal of Business Ethics*, 16(1), 55–65.

Singhapakdi, A. and Vitell, S. J. 1991: Analyzing the ethical decision making of sales professionals. *Journal of Personal Selling & Sales Management*, 11(4), 1–12.

Singhapakdi, A., Rao, C. P. and Vitell, S. J. 1996: Ethical decision making: An investigation of services marketing professionals. *Journal of Business Ethics*, 15(6), 635–44.

Smith, N. C. 1995: Marketing strategies for the ethics era. *Sloan Management Review*, (Summer), 85–97.

Smith, N. C. and Quelch, J. A. 1993: *Ethics in Marketing*. Burr Ridge, Illinois: Richard D. Irwin.

Stark, A. 1993: What's the matter with business ethics? *Harvard Business Review*, May–June, 38–48.

Thompson, C. J. 1995: A contextualist proposal for the conceptualization and study of marketing ethics. *Journal of Public Policy & Marketing*, 14(Fall), 177–91.

Tsalikis, J. and Fritzsche, D. J. 1989: Business ethics: A literature review with a focus on marketing ethics. *Journal of Business Ethics*, 8, 695–743.

Tybout, A. M. and Zaltman, G. 1974: Ethics in marketing research: Their practical relevance. *Journal of Marketing Research*, 11(November), 357–68.

Further Reading

Levitt, T. 1970: The morality of advertising. *Harvard Business Review*, (July–August), 84–92.

16

Law, ethics, and managerial judgment*

LYNN S. PAINE

The question of how best to understand the relationship between law and ethics is a perennial one in Western jurisprudence. It is a topic addressed by many leading thinkers in that tradition – Aquinas, Bentham, Holmes, Kelsen, Fuller, Hart, and Dworkin – to name some of the best known. However, my plan is not to examine the issue as an abstract question of jurisprudence, but as a practical matter of crucial importance for executives and managers of business organizations, and for management educators. Certain ways of conceiving the relationship between law and ethics hinder a useful and effective approach to educating managers for responsible business leadership, both in the business school setting and in the corporation.

Many of the incidents which have fueled the movement for business ethics education in the USA, and more recently in Europe, have involved unlawful conduct. Examples that come to mind are criminal or tortious insider trading on Wall Street, fraud and bribery in defense contracting, and fraud and breach of fiduciary obligation in the thrift industry. So, one might reasonably ask, "Why have business schools created new courses to teach ethics rather than courses to teach law?" Indeed, speaking directly to this point, many corporations have responded to the call to better ethics by setting up legal compliance programs.

While an understanding of law and the legal process is essential to responsible management, a legal compliance approach – whether to building responsible organizations or to preparing students for responsible business leadership – is very misguided. An ethics-driven approach is far better; and attention to law should be an integral part of any program of ethics education. Most important of all, though, the approach to teaching ethics and law should set aside the academic and disciplinary boundaries that divide the fields, and focus on the ultimate objective: preparing students for responsible, fulfilling, and socially beneficial careers in business. This starts with a framework for managerial judgment that brings the ethical point of view to bear on choice and action, as well as on the design of organizational systems and processes. Attention to law, as an important source of managers' rights and responsibilities, is integral to, but not a substitute for, the ethical point of view – a point of view that is attentive to

* This paper has been adapted from Paine (1994b), and is based on a presentation made to the Academy of Legal Studies in Business, Annual Meeting, Colorado Springs, August 19, 1993.

rights, responsibilities, relationships, opportunities to improve and enhance human well-being, and virtue and moral excellence.

There are, however, a number of barriers that stand in the way of this integrated approach. Some are institutional or political, but the focus of this chapter involves conceptual barriers: in particular, the barriers created by two different models of the relationship between law and ethics. Though both are common among managers and management educators, they are, nevertheless, incompatible with one another.

The first model might be called the "separate realms view;" the second, the "congruence" or "correspondence view." Each of these views captures a fragment of a complex reality, but both are inaccurate in important ways. Perhaps more critically, both are dysfunctional for managers. This chapter examines these two views to see what is plausible, and implausible, about each and then sketches out a third alternative which is much truer to the situation as well as more useful for managers. The chapter concludes with some of the implications of this analysis for management and for business ethics education.

To illustrate the separate realms view, consider a recent talk. The speaker's thesis was that company codes of conduct should clearly distinguish between behavioral standards required by law and those that are only matters of ethics. The speaker argued that many codes of conduct are very confusing because they mix up law, which is obligatory, with ethics, which is nice, but optional. Though the speaker's thesis had merit, assumptions underlying it are problematic.

Interlaced with the argument was a familiar picture of law as hard and ethics as soft. Law is obligatory, while ethics is aspirational. Law is rigorous; ethics is a matter of intuition. Law is determinate; ethics is vague. Law is social; ethics is personal. Infringements of law result in external sanctions; ethical lapses are sanctioned only by conscience. According to this picture, ethics is whatever is "not law."

Though this model has several noteworthy features, two are fundamental. The first is the strict separation of law and ethics. This view envisions the class of actions and behavioral standards required or prohibited by law as mutually exclusive of those praised or condemned by standards of ethics. Within this conceptual world, an issue is either a matter of law, or it is a matter of ethics, and anyone who thinks otherwise is confused. This is the sort of view animating comments one often hears, such as "Insider trading is a legal issue, not an ethical issue." Or, "Why are you teaching that case in the ethics course? It involves a clear violation of law."

The lawyer's version of the separate realms thesis usually elevates law over ethics and endows law with all the "good" characteristics of a field of study: hard, rigorous, objective, and important. Consistent with the dualism inherent in the thesis, ethics is left with all the "lesser" qualities: it is soft, intuitive, subjective, and of little importance.

This conceptualization leads fairly directly to the conclusion that managers must be concerned with law, but they need only concern themselves with ethics if they feel personally so inclined. Ethics is a frill, an optional part of management practice. What business schools should teach, and hard-headed managers should pay attention to, is law.

The ethicist's version of the separate realms thesis typically preserves the underlying duality, but reverses the ranking and characterizations of law and ethics. Law is made to seem trivial, as in "But that is *merely* a legal matter. Morally, the company must treat all employees as ends in themselves." The ethicist's picture tends to depict ethics as required and law as optional; ethics as fundamental and enduring, while law is adventitious and contingent; ethics as a realm of rigorous and objective reasoning, while law is a realm of politics, power, and ultimately irrational compromise.

To the non-lawyer ethicist, law is a technical detail, better left to another time and place. Translated into educational practice, the separate realms view often means that students in ethics courses are spared discussion of relevant legal considerations. Students are permitted to discuss topics such as honesty, fair-dealing, employer responsibilities, and the duties of corporate executives as if the legal framework did not exist or was unimportant. The potential concerns of a court or legislature are never mentioned or explored. Unless they have prior knowledge, students remain ignorant that their choices may have serious legal consequences.

The correspondence view

Standing in sharp contrast to the separate realms view is the correspondence or congruence view. The correspondence view, also common among managers and management educators, regards the prescriptions of law and ethics not as constituting separate and distinct realms, but as more or less coextensive. According to this school of thought, a useful rule of thumb is "If it's legal, it's ethical." Whatever is legally permissible is ethically okay; whatever is legally prohibited is ethically unacceptable. Ethics is treated as a shadow cast by the law, of little importance in its own right.

The correspondence thesis does not suppose a perfect match between ethics and law. Most adherents would readily point to laws calling for actions which are, in themselves, ethically neutral. These are laws establishing, for example, the filing date for taxes or the rules of the road, or laws laying out the procedures necessary to make a valid will, establish a corporation, or appeal the judgment of a court. With respect to actions which are ethically significant, the law is seen as a sufficient guide. To simplify, the correspondence thesis regards the class of ethical actions as corresponding with some subset of the class of lawful actions, and the class of unethical actions as corresponding with the class of unlawful actions.

The correspondence view is quite common among managers. When asked how they decide on an ethically appropriate course of action, many say they look to the law. However, actual working knowledge of the law is far rarer. In one company, for example, twelve managers were interviewed about ethical issues in competitor intelligence gathering. When asked whether they understood the law relevant to the area, eight said they did not, including one who expressed surprise that there was any relevant law and another who claimed always to use the law as his guide to ethical behavior. Of the four who claimed to understand the legal framework, my personal experience is that only two were able to demonstrate a working knowledge when discussing hypothetical cases.

The correspondence thesis, like the lawyer's version of the separate realms thesis, leads directly to the view that managers should focus on law, not on ethics. Ethics, they seem to imply, is not something that managers need to be seriously concerned about.

Accounting for the two theses

Both these views capture some important aspects of a complex situation. To a certain extent, the strengths of one view are the weaknesses of the other. Let us look at the strengths of each in turn.

The impulse to define ethics and law as separate domains is not just the product of academic turf wars, though there is an element of that. The separate domains tradition has a venerable heritage within legal history originating in the attack on Natural Law theory and transcendent conceptions of morality. Legal philosophers like Bentham were keen to destroy the idea that positive law mirrored an enduring and unchanging morality or Natural Law. As Professor Lon Fuller (1940) has observed, numerous theorists with a positivist cast of mind have sought to develop a conception of law that is totally independent of morality. This tradition has had great influence on legal education and popular thought about law.

While the goal of totally disengaging law from morality seems misguided and, in any event, hopeless, there are compelling reasons to insist on a distinction between law and ethics in certain circumstances and for certain purposes. There are matters of ethics about which the law has nothing to say. Law, in general, is concerned with conduct which is wrongful, which results in relatively serious harm, and which is not an everyday occurrence. The legal system does not address trivial matters, especially those which can be rectified in other ways and by other authorities. In such cases, we may want to say that certain behavior is "ethically or morally wrong," but not "legally wrong."

Consider the case of the unreliable dinner guest. (This case was the subject of discussion in a course on the legal process taught by Professor Albert M. Sacks at the Harvard Law School when I was a student.) When David, the invitee, fails to show up for dinner, should the distraught host have a remedy at law? Didn't David, who said he would come, have a duty to show up? And wasn't his failure a breach of his duty that caused harm? The host has, after all, expended effort and money to prepare for the event. He has suffered great embarrassment and loss of face before the other guests who came to meet David. Perhaps, this means the end of a profitable business arrangement for the host.

Most of us would want to say that David's duty was a moral or ethical one, not a legal one, to indicate that there is not, and probably should not be, a legal remedy for David's lapse. A distinction between law and ethics is very useful in this situation to differentiate wrongs for which there is a remedy at law from those which are subject only to the sanction of social disapproval.

Of course, what is trivial in this sense and thus properly outside the legal system reflects social judgment and is subject to change and variation across societies. Moreover, a wrong that is trivial from the perspective of the legal system may be extremely serious from the perspective of the individuals involved. David's gaffe may cost him a friend or an opportunity, even if he cannot be successfully sued.

This way of putting things tends to cast ethics as the domain of the socially trivial and unimportant. A very different impulse toward distinguishing the domain of law from the domain of ethics starts from the observation that the law, unlike ethics, has nothing to say about moral excellence. Ethics, on the other hand, addresses itself not only to misconduct or unethical behavior, but also to outstanding conduct which is morally praiseworthy, endorsed by social ideals, exemplified in good practice, but not required by law. Merck's decision to donate its river blindness drug, Mectizan, in the Third World (The Business Enterprise Trust, 1991), Johnson & Johnson's recall of Tylenol (Harvard Business School, 1989), AT&T's leadership of the Industry Cooperative for Ozone Layer Protection (*Industry Week*, 1989), and Stride-Rite's assistance with employee and elder care (Laabs, 1993) are just a few examples of morally exemplary conduct which seems to have nothing whatsoever to do with legal requirements.

Some who favor a strict separation between law and ethics want to emphasize the importance of ideals, aspirations, good will, and human sympathy in defining the quality of our lives and communities. They do not want to stress the social importance of law, as contrasted with ethics – just the reverse: they want to highlight the poverty of an excessive reliance on law as a guide to right conduct.

The law does not generally seek to inspire human excellence or distinction. There is no legal sanction for failing to be the best we can be or for failing to make a positive contribution to society. The law, instead, is concerned with defining and upholding basic rights and duties among members of the social community, and with preventing and punishing serious forms of misconduct. The standards of law apply to everyone. When law invades the realm of "ethics" as defined in this conceptual world, it deprives us of moral imagination, of opportunities to exhibit exemplary conduct, and opportunities to praise and take inspiration from the moral leadership of others.

This point seems to be what Alexander Solzhenitsyn had in mind in his 1978 speech at the Harvard Commencement. He urged, "Whenever the tissue of life is woven of legalistic relations, there is an atmosphere of moral mediocrity, paralyzing man's noblest impulses." (Solzhenitsyn, 1978). As Boston lawyer Frederic G. Corneel (1983) observed in his commentary on this speech, "Perhaps this must be so. After all, since it is the virtue of the law to apply uniformly to all alike, it must set a standard that all can reasonably meet, the weak, as well as the strong, the ignorant, as well as the educated. Such a standard cannot demand more than mediocrity."

Yet another impulse behind the separate realms thesis is the insight that the demands of law and ethics do not always coincide. There are situations in which what is legally permissible, or even legally required, is morally wrong. Classic examples are the 1935 Nuremberg laws stripping Jews of their rights as German citizens and denying them admission to German universities; or South African apartheid laws which required that blacks be denied certain rights, privileges, and opportunities. Many other examples could be cited to show the divergence between what law permits and what ethics approves.

Companies engaged in international business often discover that conduct which infringes common standards of human rights and decency is nevertheless legally permissible in some jurisdictions. Sometimes such conduct is not prohibited or punishable by law, nor is it even discouraged through systems of taxation or licensure. One example is the reported use of forced prison labor in China. Detainees, including political prisoners, whose official sentences have been served, are reportedly required to work in unsafe, unpaid, and exhausting conditions (Billenness and Simpson, 1992; Barnathan, 1991).

198

Presumably discrepancies of this sort prompted Justice Holmes (1920), a great proponent of the separation of law and morals, to insist that "[M]any laws have been enforced . . . which are condemned by the most enlightened opinion of the time. . . ." He went on to add, "[N]othing but confusion of thought can result from assuming that the rights of man in a moral sense are equally rights in the sense of the Constitution and the law." Even in our own society, with its highly developed – some say over-developed – legal system, conduct which is ethically problematic may nevertheless be entirely lawful. The export of hazardous chemicals without appropriate health and environmental warnings, the marketing of violent films as entertainment, and the use of cigarette advertising which appeals to children are examples. It is important to preserve the distinction between law and ethics, to highlight such differences, and to maintain a critical standpoint from which to evaluate the law.

Finally, if we consider law and ethics, not as defining classes of permissible and impermissible actions, but as methods of reasoning and justification, there are similarities as well as important differences. Both legal thinking and some forms of ethical thinking involve the interpretation and application of general principles. However, legal reasoning, or more precisely, judicial reasoning, is constrained and channeled by the concept of authoritative sources, by the doctrine of precedent, by numerous principles and rules of interpretation and construction, and by the content of the actual cases that come before the courts.

The principles that guide ethical reasoning are, arguably, found in our collective consciousness – our conceptions of freedom, responsibility, well-being, justice, truth, rights, and wrongs. While many philosophers have made careers putting forth proposals for a single principle to guide ethical thinking, most practical people operate with a somewhat inchoate set of principles setting out their rights, responsibilities, and ethical ideals. They move readily between an intuitive level of moral thinking and a critical level of morality. From the perspective of methodology, legal and ethical reasoning have different starting points and different procedural characteristics.

Given these compelling reasons to regard law and ethics as separate domains, we might well ask how anyone could possibly endorse the correspondence thesis. What could lead someone to say that whatever is lawful is ethical? Those inclined toward the correspondence view are likely to be impressed by the wide area of overlap between the requirements of law and those of ethics. Not only do law and ethics share a common syntax of rights, wrongs, and duties, but they share a lexicon of common terms and precepts. Both law and social morality frown upon deception, promise-breaking, theft, overreaching, unfairness, injustice, and imposing unjustifiable harm on others. Many acts falling within these categories give rise both to social disapproval and to legal sanctions.

This should not be surprising. The law is, in part, a mechanism for reinforcing and enforcing, through the coercive power of the state, those moral obligations regarded as critical to social life. As the court noted in *Blachly v. US* (380 F.2d 665, 671 (5th Cir. 1967)), a case involving the interpretation of the mail and wire fraud statutes: "Law puts its imprimatur on the accepted moral standards and condemns conduct which fails to match the reflection of moral uprightness, of fundamental honesty, fair play and right dealing in the general and business life of members of society."

Consider the cartoon in the *Wall Street Journal* (June 16, 1993, A3) of a lawyer entering his client's plea before the judge. Says the lawyer, "My client pleads not guilty to the murder charges, Your Honor, on the grounds that you can't legislate morality." The humor, of course, reflects our understanding of the obvious – the vast area of overlap between the commands of law and the commands of morality.

Those who are taught to regard law and ethics as entirely different realms, and who have no training in the law, may easily neglect this area of overlap. For example, Oliver North is quoted as saying, "I was raised to know the difference between right and wrong. I knew it wasn't right not to tell the truth about those things. But I didn't know it was unlawful" (Hodgson, 1992).

North's understanding is not idiosyncratic. Many business students are shocked to discover, after a detailed discussion about the merits of deliberate deception in a negotiating session, that the proposed course of action constitutes criminal fraud. Operating with the "separate realms" view of law and ethics, and lacking any know-ledge of the law, they assume that ethical questions concerning truthfulness have nothing to do with the law.

Law may be described as "an island floating on a sea of ethics." This metaphor is suggestive in emphasizing the priority of ethics and its role in supporting the legal system, as well as the far greater scope of ethics. The vitality and social importance of the law depends fundamentally on the strength of the obligation people feel to obey it. Unfortunately, the metaphor does not fully capture the extent to which moral ideas are internal to the legal system itself, nor the extent to which both law and ethics are dynamic social systems.

Neither the separate realms thesis nor the correspondence thesis accurately capture the complex and multifaceted relationship between law and ethics, between legal and moral judgment, between the legal and moral status of the various actions and policies managers may consider or undertake. Neither is very helpful for the practicing manager. In fact, taken at face value, either one can be downright disastrous, as the following examples illustrate.

Example I

In the mid-1980s, a subsidiary of a major US company began work on developing a business to collect, analyze, package, and sell information about consumer purchasing behavior. The initial effort focused on collecting consumer purchase data using scanner technology. From a legal point of view, there were no apparent difficulties with this business concept, provided the information was accurate. Judicial authority, though scant, indicated that consumers have no legal claim against companies for selling their names along with data about their purchasing behavior.

Nevertheless, from day one, this business was plagued with ethical questions concerning the propriety of collecting purchase data, the role of consumer consent in legitimizing the practice, and the propriety of packaging and selling the information in various ways. For example, in the latter category, the company had to consider whether to provide a list of beer purchasers to opponents of a proposed state beer tax. Another issue was whether to sell lists of contraceptive users to abortion foes.

These and other ethical questions came from many directions. They were voiced by executives and employees who wanted to ensure that their company acted responsibly and ethically, by retailers concerned about consumer reaction to the collection of data, and by privacy advocates and lawmakers. Company management set up a special committee to address the ethical questions on an ongoing basis. However, some retailers balked, concerned that the consumer privacy issue was not being adequately addressed.

For a variety of reasons, this business floundered. According to senior managers, one of the main stumbling blocks was the privacy issue and ethical concerns about the collection and use of consumer purchase data. In the past several years, there have been numerous legislative proposals, both in the USA and in Europe, to give consumers certain legal rights to prevent the collection, sale, or use of data about their purchases without their consent, for example the *Consumer Credit Reporting Reform Act of 1991*, (H.R. 3596, 102d Cong., 1st Sess. (1991)), and the *Council Directive on the Protection of Individuals with Regard to the Processing of Personal Data and on the Free Movement of Such Data* ((COM 92) 422 final, O.J. EUR. COMM. (No. C311) (1992)).

Example 2

In 1985, E. F. Hutton, a now-defunct brokerage house, pled guilty to 2000 counts of wire and mail fraud when its cash management practices were challenged by federal prosecutors. Through large one- or two-day overdrafts of its local bank accounts, Hutton secured for itself regular interest-free loans. The overdraft amounts were completely arbitrary, sometimes as much as several millions on accounts with less than $100,000 on deposit. With interest rates hovering at 18%, interest on these "borrowings" gave Hutton's bottom line a significant boost.

Today, it is widely believed that Hutton's practices were clear violations of the federal criminal law. At the time, the government had real doubts about the likelihood of a successful prosecution (*E. F. Hutton Mail and Wire Fraud Case: Hearings Before the Subcomm. on Crime of the House Comm. on the Judiciary*, 99th Cong., 1st Sess. 1640ff. (1985) – hereafter *E. F. Hutton Hearings*). *Fortune* (1985) published an editorial taking the position that the overdrafters "probably didn't violate any [laws]." Given prevailing judicial interpretations and statutory definitions, it was not clear that Hutton had violated federal statutes or that the company could be prosecuted by federal authorities for "check-kiting" (*E. F. Hutton Hearings*, pp. 1752–3). A comprehensive bank fraud statute was subsequently enacted as part of the Comprehensive Crime Control Act of 1984 to remedy this problem. Moreover, Hutton's checks did not actually bounce, since the overdrafts were usually paid within a few days. Clearly, Hutton had the means and the intent to pay the banks, thus, arguably vitiating any alleged criminal intent.

Nevertheless, prosecutors and many other informed observers viewed the practices as ethically problematic because they were deceptive, unfair, and harmful in a variety of ways. Indeed, the search for a legal theory of the case was driven by such concerns. The prosecution's legal theory, which focused on Hutton's misrepresenting the function of its depository accounts, was never tested because Hutton chose to settle with a plea of guilty. The plea bargain included a civil injunction which set strict new standards for cash management practices and gave notice that federal authorities would be

201

reviewing such practices in the future (Donnelly, 1985). After the plea, Hutton faced a barrage of investigations and charges from state and federal government and self-regulatory authorities; for a summary, see *Committee on Federal Regulation of Securities, Report of the Task Force on SEC Settlements*, 47 Bus. Law. 1136–1140 (1992).

Hutton never fully recovered and was eventually bought by another financial services company.

Example 3

In April 1991, four top executives of Salomon Brothers, an international securities firm, learned that the head of the government trading desk had submitted an unauthorized bid in a customer's name at a US Treasury auction two months earlier. The bid permitted Salomon to circumvent a Treasury auction rule limiting each bidder's bid and award to 35 percent of the issue. The executives discussed whether they should report the impropriety to the Treasury or other government officials. They decided that the irregularity should be disclosed, but none of them took steps to implement the decision.

Four months later, when the failure to report the improper bid became public knowledge, the company faced a serious crisis of confidence among its creditors, customers, employees, shareholders, and the public. Within a week, the company's stock declined in value by some $900 million, nearly a quarter of the firm's market capitalization. Having lost the ability to lead, the four executives were forced to resign, and new leaders were propelled into top positions. Though research was not entirely conclusive, Salomon's lawyers were unable to say that the company's former executives had an affirmative legal obligation to report the bidding irregularities. They had an ethical obligation to disclose, perhaps, but it was not clear they had a legal one.

As a result of the incident, Congress began to consider new legislation for the government securities market (Conner, 1993); the Treasury began to take a new look at the primary dealer system (Murray, 1991); and the SEC undertook discussion of the disclosure and supervisory responsibilities of individuals serving as corporate general counsel (Moses, 1992; Spiro et al., 1992).

Lessons

What can we learn from these examples? All three show, in quite different ways, the practical inadequacy of both the correspondence and the separate realms views.

In all three cases, we see that the law is an important but insufficient guide to ethical conduct. A clean bill of health from the legal department does not ensure the absence of serious ethical problems, as managers at the consumer data business and E. F. Hutton discovered. In an inter-office communication titled "E. F. Hutton Money Management Procedures," dated March 7, 1980 (Bell, 1985, Appendix), Hutton's general counsel had declined to render a written opinion affirming the legality of Hutton's cash management practices on the grounds that there was "no question as to the propriety of such transactions." And the prosecution seemed to think that the practices might arguably pass legal muster, at least as the law stood in early 1982 when the practices occurred. The Salomon case, too, shows that law is an inadequate guide to appropriate conduct. Even though the executives' failure to report the Treasury auction improprieties was not clearly unlawful, it was inconsistent with the standard of public responsibility expected of the company's management.

These three examples also illustrate the dynamic and interrelated nature of law and ethics, a point entirely neglected by both the separate realms and the correspondence views. In truth, the relationship between the two is in flux: the prescriptions of law and the prescriptions of ethics coincide to different degrees at different times, and in different societies. As all three examples suggest, what is legally permissible but ethically questionable today may be legally restricted or prohibited tomorrow. The legislative, regulatory, and judicial processes are dynamic, and they are driven by a number of forces. One of those is the force of social morality.

In the Hutton case, the lead prosecutor was prompted to search for a legal theory to condemn Hutton's cash management practices because they seemed unfair, misleading, and possibly harmful to the banking system. Anyone who has practiced law knows that cases often originate in this way. People seek redress through the legal system when they feel they have been wronged. Rarely do they know whether a constitution, statute, regulation, or common law principle has been infringed, but they feel an injustice has been done. The creative lawyer tries to find or develop a theory making the wrong legally actionable. This is only one way in which social morality influences the development of judge-made law.

Ethics is also an important factor driving the legislative process. For example, legislative and regulatory proposals to curb the collection and sale of consumer purchase data reflect a widespread sense that this practice threatens an important social interest in personal privacy. Calls for new legislation cannot be understood without appreciating this underlying ethical concern.

Finally, these three examples also show that ethics is not a frill – something to be treated as an afterthought – but something which can be quite integral to sound decision making and organizational success. The examples all belie the idea that ethics is "soft, personal, optional, and subject only to the internal sanction of conscience." The consequences of neglecting, or failing to deal adequately with ethical issues can be very hard indeed, prompting not only social concern but serious external sanctions.

The sanctions of public opinion and the marketplace can be much more costly than the damages and fines imposed by the legal system. Salomon Brothers executives have referred to prior management's handling of the Treasury auction improprieties as the "billion dollar error in judgment," taking into account $290 million in legal fines and damages paid to the federal government, other legal expenses and damages paid to private parties, as well as lost business, increased funding costs, and other management costs.

By the same token, conduct that is ethically exemplary can contribute to managerial effectiveness as well as personal well-being. Warren Buffett's handling of the Salomon crisis is a striking example. His forthrightness and candor, his commitment to make amends where appropriate, and his waiver of the attorney-client privilege, earned the respect of government regulators and gave the firm the foundation it needed to earn back its integrity in the face of a massive loss of confidence.

Does good ethics always pay? Of course not! Neither does good marketing, good technology, nor good analysis. So long as the criteria for goodness are independent of wealth enhancement, the link between what is good and what pays cannot be assured.

The point is not that ethics always pays, but that ethics, whether it pays or not, should not be thought of as a purely personal matter between individuals and their consciences. Ethics is about human relationships and the norms, principles, and ideals that govern them. To the extent that individuals have internalized ethical principles and ideals, they will suffer the pangs of conscience when their behavior departs from those ideals. How a person acts – how a person treats others – is a matter of concern not only because of the actor's personal well-being, but because the actor affects other people's lives as well. Thus, managers are accountable not only to their consciences but to their companies and to the society from which they derive their authority.

As this analysis suggests, responsible and effective management must rest not on a broad conception of ethics, but one which is supplemented and filled out with an understanding and appreciation for law and the legal system. After all, an obligation to obey the law is a *prima facie* moral duty of all who live under a legitimate government. The law is an important source of managers' rights and responsibilities. However, the relationship between law and ethics is much more complex than either the separate realms or correspondence models suggest. Law is one of several dynamic subsystems that a society may use for regulating authority and social relationships. The legal system serves to reinforce and uphold certain norms of right, wrong, justice, and responsibility, though as discussed, the law is far from exhausting the whole of ethics, even in a highly legalistic society such as ours.

Moreover, as a subsystem, the law may be well, or poorly, aligned with the society's prevailing ethical norms and with the more universal ethical norms expected of all societies. As noted, the degree of correspondence between the class of unlawful and unethical acts varies from time to time. Law is most often a lagging indicator of social ethics, especially in dynamic societies characterized by rapid technological change. In a society with a strong legal system, most citizens will respect the law, feel they have an obligation to obey it, and expect others to obey it. That is an aspect of their morality.

Even though it is useful to use the words "law" and "ethics" as parallel and contrasting terms in certain contexts, we must not be lulled into treating them as independent and unrelated domains or into collapsing one into the other.

Implications

What are the implications of recognizing the ethics–law relationship as presented here? Here are two: one for educators and one for managers. First, education for responsible management should be ethics-driven, while including some familiarity with law and the legal process. "Ethics-driven" means the educational program should prepare students to deal with the broad range of issues they will encounter relating to their responsibilities as managers: those that flow from their obligation to obey the law, as well as those that flow from their role as managers, trustees of society's resources, and members of the human community. The notion that law is a mere technicality or detail not worthy of serious attention, should be abandoned. By the same token, educators should avoid a legalistic approach to responsible management which treats ethics as the domain of the trivial or a concern of the soft-hearted.

An effective approach requires greater cooperation and teamwork among law and ethics professors, as well as faculty members trained in social psychology, management, political science, and economics. Like managers who are redesigning their company's core processes to achieve their performance objectives, business school faculty members must ensure that the educational process is properly designed and implemented to develop the knowledge, skills, and attitudes required of effective and responsible business managers. According to historian James Willard Hurst (1970), the social legitimacy of US business has rested historically on twin pillars: on efficiency in utilizing resources to produce goods and services, and on social responsibility. Surely, the role of management educators is to prepare managers to address the latter as well as the former?

This analysis of the relation between law and ethics has important implications for corporate managers as well. Many companies have, in recent years, set up corporate ethics programs. This activity has accelerated recently with the enactment of the 1991 Federal Sentencing Guidelines for organizations. Broadly speaking, company initiatives tend to fall into one of three categories. Some are law and lawyer-driven compliance programs closely allied with the correspondence thesis: if it's legal, it's ethical. Others are ethics or values programs which focus on very broad company aspirations. The aspirational programs tend to have little, if any, legal content and to assume the separate realms view of law and ethics.

A few initiatives, however, take a third approach, one which reflects an ethics-driven but law-inclusive view of corporate responsibility based on organizational integrity (Paine, 1994a). In these organizations, senior managers lead the initiative, but engage the involvement of the general counsel and legal staff, along with human resources, audit, and other appropriate personnel. An integrity-based program recognizes the complex relationship between law and ethics, and is far more likely to achieve the objective of responsible and effective organizational conduct. A purely aspirational effort runs the risk of overlooking important legal obligations; and a compliance-based effort, especially one narrowly targeted to preventing criminal misconduct, is much too limited. As former SEC Chairman Richard Breeden observed, "It is not an adequate ethical standard to aspire to get through the day without being indicted." (Salwen, 1991). Surely managers must be law-abiding, but, just as surely, they must envision responsible management as involving far more than that.

References

Barnathan, J. 1991: It's time to put screws to China's gulag. *Business Week*, Dec. 30, 1991–Jan. 6, 1992, 52.

Bell, G. 1985: *The Hutton Report*, Atlanta, Spaulding.

Billenness, S. and Simpson, K. 1992: *Thinking Globally, Franklin's Insight Study of International Corporate Responsibility*. Boston, MA: Franklin Research and Development Corporation, Sept., 12.

Conner, J. 1993: Senate panel clears bill on marketing of US securities. *Wall Street Journal*, May 28, A5A.

Corneel, F. G. 1983: The role of law: Musings on Solzhenitsyn, *Boston Bar Journal*, June, 9.

Donnelly, B. 1985: Cash management: Where do you draw the line? *Institutional Investor*, Sept., 69.

Fortune (editorial) 1985: Up from Aristotle. Oct. 14, 197.

Fuller, L. 1940: *The Law in Quest of Itself.*

Harvard Business School 1989: *James Burke: A Career in American Business (A)-(B)*, 9-389-177, 9-390-030, Harvard Business School Publishing.

Hodgson, K. 1992: A *Rock and a Hard Place*.

Holmes, O. W. 1920: *Collected Legal Papers 171–172*.

Hurst, J. W. 1970: *The Legitimacy of the Business Corporation in the Law of the United States 1780–1970*.

Industry Week, 1989: What's a company to do? *Industry Week*, November, 42.

Laabs, J. 1993: Family issues are a priority at Stride Rite. *Personnel Journal, 72*, 48.

Moses, J. M. 1992: SEC spotlight role of in-house counsel in Salmon report. *Wall Street Journal*, Dec. 7, B3D.

Murray, A. 1991: Salmon scandal calls for auction overhaul. *Wall Street Journal*, Aug. 28, A1.

Paine, L. S. 1994a: Managing for organizational integrity. *Harvard Business Review*, March–April, 106.

Paine, L. S. 1994b. *The Journal of Legal Studies Education*, 12(2), Summer/Fall, 153–69.

Salwen, K. V. 1991: SEC Chief's criticism of ex-managers of Salomon suggests civil action is likely. *Wall Street Journal*, Nov. 20, A10.

Solzhenitsyn, A. 1978: The exhausted West. *Harvard Magazine*, July–Aug., 21–6.

Spiro, L. N., Galen, M., and Foust, D. 1992: Pinning the blame of Wall Street's lawyers. *Business Week*, Aug. 17, 93.

The Business Enterprise Trust 1991: *Merck & Co., Inc. (A)-(D), case nos.* 90-013–90-016.

17

Business ethics and economics

DIANE L. SWANSON

Readers of this volume are undoubtedly familiar with the proclamation, often posed as a question: "Isn't 'business ethics' an oxymoron?" This cynical query persists despite the fact that ethics is required in most US business schools, often as part of coursework that pertains to business and society issues. This chapter addresses some reasons for the perception among many students and practitioners that "ethics" and "business" are contradictory even in theory, by analyzing how deontological philosophy and economic utilitarianism are typically applied to business. As this analysis suggests, the notion that " 'business ethics' is an oxymoron" actually, if accidentally, illuminates the fundamental tension between these two theoretical orientations. The logic under-girding them tends to forge a dichotomy between ethics as duty and business based on economic self-interest. Further, it will be argued that neither perspective, as conventionally understood, is adequate for theory-building which addresses the normative aspects of business in society.

First, a few caveats, This chapter does not describe a hard and fast dichotomy, but rather a marked *tendency* for ethics and economics to be in conflict. Moreover, since the antagonism results from competing theories, it does not necessarily represent the state of affairs faced by practicing managers. Nor can it be assumed that those who refer to business ethics as a contradiction in terms are actually hostile or indifferent to normative matters. As discussed below, students of business have long been indoctrinated with explanations and justifications of economic activity based on a particularly narrow kind of self-interest. This primacy of self-interest is very difficult to reconcile with a morality of "duty to others" (meaning in this instance those not directly benefiting from the economic activity itself). As a result, practicing managers have no widely accepted theory to invoke for fully integrating moral dimensions into their decisions, beyond those which are associated with their institution's self-interest.

Although this chapter addresses several problems of theory, it ends on a constructive note. Identifying the obstacles to reconciling the described perspectives can be an important step towards finding and developing a coherent normative theory for business. (For related arguments, see Swanson (1995, 1999).)

The application of deontological ethics to business

Of the many theoretical systems of moral philosophy, deontology has most influenced business ethics and the affiliated notion of corporate social responsibility. Theorists who adopt this outlook typically propose rules for corporate behavior, often deriving these rules from standards of human rights and social justice. Applied to business, these rules are ultimately expressed as managerial responsibilities, obligations, or *duties*. Hence, in the following analysis, terms like "duty-aligned," "duty-centered," and "duty-bound" are used to describe the overall manner by which deontology has influenced inquiry into the moral dimensions of business. (Many normative theories have influenced inquiry into the ethics of business, including virtue ethics, feminist theory, contractarianism, communitarianism, and the postmodern critique. As implied in the Introduction, it is beyond the scope of this chapter to elaborate on these many normative theories. Instead, the two dominant approaches to business which perpetuate a conflict between ethics and economics are outlined.)

Most moral philosophy begins with the proposition that certain duties adhere to decision makers by virtue of their humanity. Although the duty-aligned perspective addresses many managerial and economic issues, it never loses sight of its overriding interest in identifying moral rules for individual choice. A theoretical prerequisite for such rules is to establish the moral status of a corporation. The argument is that if corporations are moral agents, they should, like people, assume moral burdens. Otherwise, to identify corporate responsibilities or obligations is, from a philosophic viewpoint, a moot exercise. (For examples of different kinds of moral agency arguments, see Tom Donaldson, 1982.)

Once the moral agency argument is accepted, business ethicists use moral reasoning to deduce moral rules from well-argued axioms, such as those proposed by Kant, whose work constitutes one of the most influential canons in moral philosophy. Kant argues that rationality is a distinct and valuable human attribute. From this axiom, Kantian ethics deduces consistent, logical rules for dutiful behavior, applicable to all situations. Certainly, the majority of rules formulated by business ethicists are congruent with Kant's second categorical imperative, which advocates respect for the moral personhood of others. Accordingly, one ought to treat others as having intrinsic value in themselves, and not merely as means to achieve one's ends. This rule is a prescription for both moral motivation and for the subsequent enactment of duties. When applied to the business sector, it means that managers are moral agents, and as such, they have basic moral duties to other members of society.

Such moral obligations include those affiliated with human rights. Rights-based reasoning is concerned with rules which protect individual entitlements. Individual rights can, in this view, be negative or positive, which in turn require negative or positive duties from others. (For a discussion of negative and positive rights, see Werhane, 1985). Negative (or passive) rights include the right to be free from harm and from that which prevents the pursuit of one's good. Kantian respect for moral personhood is the motivation for actions that protect these freedoms. In contrast to negative rights, positive rights support positive freedoms, as in providing persons with a standard of living adequate to the exercise of freedoms otherwise prohibited by poverty, such as freedom of movement.

Even though deontology is conventionally understood to be an ethic of duty, lately many philosophers have used it to emphasize rights. It can be seen that rights usually require duties because for one person's right to be meaningful, another person typically must have a duty to respect that right by not violating it. Negative rights require that, as a duty, individuals not interfere with others, based on respect for their moral personhood. This ease of interchangeability demonstrates the logical compatibility of rights and duties in ethics reasoning.

Standards of social justice are also used by ethicists who are interested in analyzing moral obligations or duties. Justice-based reasoning identifies rules for establishing and preserving liberty, equality and fairness of opportunity for members of society. These standards are motivated by respect for the moral autonomy of personhood and the right of individuals to pursue their own good (Rawls, 1971). Because justice theorists are interested in fairness, they insist that an unfair distribution of benefits and harms be explained and defended on logical grounds. The standard of rights often provides the logic, because it establishes the conditions that determine which harms and benefits should be distributed. Consequently, justice is commonly measured by the extent to which entitlements or rights exist and are upheld.

The social contract framework illustrates how moral reasoning in applied ethics research can formulate justice and rights standards as rules for duty. Because social contract logic asks what conditions justify society in conferring legitimacy on productive organizations, it provides useful insights into the moral obligations of corporations. Tom Donaldson (1989), for example, uses the social contract to frame his theory of international business ethics, reasoning that society expects corporations to adhere to the terms of social justice which are upheld and measured by individual rights. From this, he deduces a list of corporate duties that also respect the rights of corporate stakeholders under the terms of the social contract.

In sum, business ethicists seek to identify consistent moral rules for individual choices, and, for the most part, these rules align rights and justice standards with duties. This alignment takes place for three mutually supportive reasons: rights require duties, rights and justice are logically affiliated, and the motivation upholding both is the respect for moral personhood required by a deontological or duty-centered ethic. The importance placed on moral obligations by the duty-aligned approach contrasts sharply with the narrow focus on self-interest in economic utilitarianism, discussed next.

The application of economic utilitarianism to business

While there are many variants of economic inquiry, neoclassical economics is the one most influential in US business schools, which serve as the professional training ground for corporate managers and business leaders. (Economic theory represents a vast body of knowledge with numerous variants ranging from the radical Marxist paradigm, to Keynesian revisionism, to the more cultural approaches of institutionalism and socioeconomics. This chapter does not address the many theories of economics. Nor does it address all the facets of utilitarian economics. The point is to identify the ways in which economic orthodoxy is at odds with the logic of duty-centered ethics.)

It is the neoclassical economic model that is most often invoked to elevate the prerogatives of narrow self-interest, and to justify a laissez-faire or "hands off" policy on ethical matters for the business sector and its corporate managers. A representative claim derived from this view is Milton Friedman's (1962, 1979) assertion that there is no such thing as corporate social responsibility, and managers should not act as moral agents. Discussed later, conservative economists like Friedman do accept some social restraints to economic activity, despite their emphasis on the importance of autonomy and freedom for the business sector and its managers.

Friedman's stance is a contemporary articulation of neoclassical economic utilitarianism. This model provides the organizing logic for two types of economic efficiency: allocative and output. Allocative efficiency posits that individuals, motivated solely by self-interest, will make exchanges of reciprocal advantage in competitive markets that will lead to the greatest social satisfaction. Allocative efficiency assumes a specific kind of calculated, rational choice, i.e. that individuals know how to rank their preferences, and that they seek to maximize satisfaction or utility. Hedonism is deeply rooted in this economic logic, propelled to theoretical acceptability in the late nineteenth century by Francis Edgeworth (1881), who applied mathematical reasoning to utility theory. Edgeworth offered logical proof that the greatest social happiness or good is the consequence of pleasure-driven, acquisitive economic choices by individuals. At the same time, avarice, ill-will and predatory power seeking were ruled out of self-interest.

In contemporary form, the "greatest good" outcome is expressed as Pareto optimality – an analytical device that allows economists to separate efficient resource use from the more controversial problem of its distribution. In effect, Pareto optimality says that a given economic arrangement is efficient or optimal if it cannot make someone better off without worsening the situation of others. This arrangement is for the "greatest good" because it prevents scarce resources from being exhausted (to the detriment of all), given human wants and needs that axiomatically are considered inexhaustible.

From Adam Smith to contemporary proponents, orthodox theorists analytically separate markets from politics, or business from government. For them, only self-interested pecuniary gain is expressed in markets and business, while power-seeking and ceremonial behaviors are expressed in other arenas, such as politics and government. As a result of this *ideal-type* of logic about markets, an inherent compatibility between self-interest and the greater social good in economic activity is assumed. As a consequence, orthodox economists see no reason to advocate a strong role for government in business, or for any other institution or principle of restraint. Instead, managers are assigned the role of agents for the self-interested owners of capital, and tasked with pursuing pecuniary gain for them in the form of dividends and capital gains. (This formulation of management's role has spawned a large body of literature on the agency problem, i.e., the possibility that managers will shirk their responsibilities to pursue the financial concerns of the owners of capital in favor of their own self-interest. Berle and Means (1921) give an authoritative statement on the nature of this problem.)

At this point, it is important to note the different ways in which ethicist-philosophers and orthodox economists use the "greatest good" concept of utilitarianism. Traditional ethical philosophy emphasizes that the greatest happiness is a moral principle that requires people to consider not only themselves when choosing a course of action, but to try to maximize the good for all. In this case, utilitarianism is used as a moral precept or rule that is universally applied to all situations *prior to choice*. This rule requires that individuals place their self-interest no higher or lower than the interests of others. To assign such importance to universalized reason and other-interest is consistent with the philosophy of duty, previously described. In contrast, neoclassical utility theory provides a *post hoc* rationalization for the good produced by self-seeking actions, because it associates the greatest good outcome with choices that have *already been made* on the basis of narrow self-interest.

The second form of economic efficiency is output efficiency from the private sector. This efficiency is equivalent to a favorable ratio of output to resource inputs and their costs, and accrual of profit on the resultant output. It is traditionally assessed by cost–benefit analysis. Like allocative efficiency, output efficiency is possible only if avarice, ill-will towards others, and power-seeking are factored out of human behavior in business. The search for output efficiency under conditions of resource scarcity constitutes the core problem addressed by the science of management. Congruent with the Pareto principle of utilitarian economics, management science focuses on the value of outcomes rather than those of the means chosen. Both allocative and output efficiency were prompted by economists' long-standing concern about the fundamental problem of resource scarcity, given unlimited human wants and needs. Both kinds of efficiency are consequentialistic in that they stress the importance of outcomes.

It is evident that the utilitarianism underlying neoclassical economics does not encourage the inclusion of moral dimensions, other than self-interest, in explanations of economic choice. The combination of utilitarian and Pareto principles means that exchanges in markets are viewed as mutually beneficial and socially integrative, and that self-interest and the greater social good are largely accordant. Most importantly, the condition of Pareto optimality seemingly resolves the problem of scarce resource allocation. Consequently, standard economists see no compelling reason to impose rules about specific duties to others on economic behavior, or to include such considerations in economic choices, although these theorists do accept some external restraints to economic activity based on self-interest. These restraints are in the form of social controls, such as the law, public policy, and ethical customs. Such controls or negative duties are not thought to be numerous because, again, conservative economists do not advocate a strong role for government in business. The *minimal* application of the law, public policy, and ethical customs is believed to be sufficient external check on the harmful spillover effects of business activity, such as pollution.

To summarize, utilitarian economists characteristically elevate the importance of self-interest and then address any of the adverse consequences of this kind of choice with social control. They acknowledge that social harms can result from *laissez-faire* business activity. The proposed solution is to rectify such adverse outcomes with social policy as the harmful impacts become apparent, rather than to promote the inclusion of moral factors in managerial choice, which might minimize or preclude the harm in the first place. This dealing with the moral implications of choice somewhat "after the fact" is very different from advocating moral reflection prior to choice, which is the position of theorists who adopt the deontological approach to ethics.

Problems of reconciling deontological and economic perspectives

According to the above analysis, the vernacular "business ethics is an oxymoron" actually represents penetrating insight into the fundamental tension between deontology and economic utilitarianism. These two orientations, as typically applied to business,

211

face obstacles to theoretical integration. The impasse is traceable to three interrelated but antagonistic tenets shared by the perspectives.

The first and most obvious impediment to reconciliation is that both perspectives employ reasoning that prizes fixed-ended value standards that are seemingly disparate. Standard economics focuses on gain for self. It employs a cost–benefit rule to measure whether a desirable net gain accrues to individuals in markets, or to stockholders vis-à-vis corporate efficiency and profits. Focused on this self-centered end, the economic orientation de-emphasizes standards of rights and justice for others. In contrast to this self-fixation, the duty-aligned method grants primacy to duty to others and, despite an emphasis on moral motivation, it weighs morality by the extent to which others are treated dutifully by criteria of rights and justice. This antagonism between self-interest and other-concern takes the form of a tradeoff problem. That is, when compliance with duty criteria appears costly, a tradeoff is invoked between economic goals (of stockholder or firm-interested gain) and duty to others (as standards of rights and justice).

Even in those instances where profits and duty seem to be compatible, another problem is encountered, that of moral justification. (The tradeoff and moral justification problems in Business and Society literature were identified by Frederick (1987).)

This moral justification problem stems from the second tenet shared by the perspectives: both use formal logic to support dissimilar stances on the roles that rationality and morality play in choice. The economic view holds that, if duty pays off, then it is strategically justifiable as a byproduct of rational self-interest. However, ethicists never justify morality solely by economic criteria, even when the two coincide. For them, morality is not a byproduct or "spillover" effect of rational choice. Instead, deontologists place human rationality in the service of morality. Hence, the moral justification problem is a manifestation of the immutable, bedrock disagreement between utilitarian economics and deontological philosophy over whether economic consequences formulated as the greatest good – motivated by self-seeking gain – or dutiful motives – that prompt dutiful actions for the greatest good – constitute legitimate moral reasons for choice.

The third shared tenet that poses obstacles to integration is related to the first two (fixed-ended reasoning and the reliance on formal logic). This third tenet consists of a narrow or myopic conception of value. It has two dimensions. First, both perspectives formulate values singularly. The economic focus prizes primarily gain, while the duty-aligned approach prizes primarily duty. Second, both emphasize individual choice in the expression of these singular values. The first part of the value myopia problem reinforces the tradeoff problem. That is, the two perspectives tend to force a choice between the single values of gain or duty. Then, given their respective fixed-ended reasoning, these singular values seem incompatible. However, if theorists who rely on these perspectives were to acknowledge value pluralism in choice, then gain and duty would become part of a broader and more complex matrix of value relationships. In such cases, a simple tradeoff in choice between gain and duty would be unlikely or unnecessary. The second part of the value myopia problem reinforces the moral justification problem. Because both research orientations emphasize the individual level of analysis, their concepts of the greatest social good can be traced to the logic of individual choice, as if individuals were "freestanding" apart from their social contexts. From this individualistic logic, the perspectives embody their own unique morally justifiable rules for choice.

It is evident that reconciliation difficulties stem from the way in which the tenets shared by the duty-aligned and economic perspectives are employed. Broadly speaking, they are used to formulate two conflicting, value-myopic systems of logic. Yet, beyond problems of logic lies an even deeper reason for the reconciliation dilemma. The crux of the matter is that two disparate concepts of self are assumed. Deontologists conceive of a self willing and capable of considering how the concerns of others can be incorporated into choices aimed at the broader social good. This type of self engages in moral reflection and, through this inner mechanism, is able to factor the concerns of others into choices. In contrast, orthodox economists view the impulses of self as justifiably driven towards the pleasures provided by the outer world of gain and material goods. Since an *ideal-type* of market logic is used to correlate the interests of self with the concerns of others, utilitarian economists see no compelling reason to elaborate on the inner moral character of decision makers.

Because the perspectives rest on such divergent concepts of self, they portray the relationship between choice and negative duty quite differently. This creates a dichotomy between the "inner" and the "outer" realms of human affairs. Standard economists formulate restraint to self-interest as external to the firm, or coming from society in the form of social control. Obversely, deontologists stress that a moral agent can utilize rationality and, through reflection, identify circumstances which require self-controlled restraint. Between these two poles of reasoning, a chasm is created between an interior world constituted by moral awareness and an exterior world in which reflexively rational pleasure-seeking is justifiable. In both cases, the greatest social good is claimed as a logical implication of theoretical assumptions. Taken together, the two perspectives enforce the perception that the interior and exterior realms of human affairs are separate, with other-oriented morality associated with the former and self-seeking satisfaction with the latter.

It is important to stress that this gulf between ethics and economics is a theoretical construction. For instance, the fundamental tenets of deontology and economic utilitarianism were codified long before the advent of the large-scale corporation. This means that the tension between duty-centered reasoning and self-interested economics is not necessarily based on collective human experience with business in contemporary societies. Nor is the described dichotomy consciously created and purposefully perpetrated by theorists. The truth of the matter lies in an evolutionary interpretation. Two distinct systems of thought have evolved into well-entrenched traditions of inquiry. Currently, these two doctrines co-exist uneasily in US business school curricula, each in an advanced stage of theoretical maturation, and each with normative biases which are often taken for granted. Notably, standard economists do not place a high value on intentional moral agency for corporations and managers. At the same time, deontologists do not have a strong tradition of prizing the market as a social vehicle for allocative and output efficiency. (Because it deals with general social principles, the social contract approach can be used to acknowledge the vital role of corporate economic efficiency in society. Still, because this method is a subset of deontological reasoning, it is more aptly employed to prize duties based on rights and justice. For example, Tom Donaldson (1989, pp. 47–64) starts with social contract reasoning to construct a theory of international business ethics which ultimately emphasizes the alignment of human rights and justice with corporate

213

duties.) Given different normative priorities, it is not surprising that duty and economics collide. What is surprising is that these two orientations commingle in business curricula without calling into question the whole philosophic foundation of management coursework.

The perspectives' problems of theoretical scope and relevance

It is now possible to identify some of the missing or flawed elements of the two research orientations that make them inadequate for comprehensive and relevant theorizing about business. Three interrelated theoretical biases will be outlined – all implied by or embodied in the above obstacles to integrative theory-building. All the biases stem from the propensity of these orientations to favor the logic of individual choice over the knowledge based on social experience and collective social action. This shared propensity means that both orientations face the same kinds of limitations in theoretical scope and relevance.

The first bias is that both approaches emphasize guidelines for individual choice which are extrapolated to "greatest good" outcomes. As a result, the organization is underrepresented as a level of analysis. Consequently, many contemporary developments in organizational studies are ignored, downplayed, or marginalized by theorists who adopt either the deontological or economic viewpoints. This limitation of scope is not insignificant. Social scientists in the twentieth century have added much to explanations of business phenomena, and they have done so by placing the individual within the context of group processes in organizations. This method has provided many useful research agendas, including those related to organizational dynamics, corporate culture, organizational learning, information systems and the psychological and political factors of decision-making processes. A major insight of such research is that the logic of rational individualism does not necessarily explain collective action in organizations. Organizational processes very often yield unintended consequences, as well as the illogical separation of means from ends, and decision makers from the consequences of their actions. Such disruption can sometimes be traced to political processes marked by managerial power-aggrandizing behaviors. These power-seeking behaviors can derail the socially desirable implications of both deontology and utilitarian economics. (For example, a corporation might restructure its departments for economic reasons. If such restructuring serves mostly the political ambitions of certain managers, then the means (restructuring) can become separated from the putative economic goals. Some theorists, in examining such organizational circumstances, describe choices made in organizations as sometimes so irrational that it seems as if they are pulled out of "garbage cans." For this garbage can view, see Cohen et al. (1972). For a theoretical accounting of disruptions of rationality due to executive power-aggrandizing, see Swanson (1996).)

On another level of analysis, business organizations themselves represent systems of power which can interfere with efficient market outcomes or, through political representation in public policy, influence their *own* social control. All this suggests that business organizations can affect the social good in ways not realistically addressed by either the duty-aligned or economic-focused viewpoints. Quite simply, neither perspective comes fully to terms with *power*.

The second bias is that the emphasis on individualistic logic means that neither approach is compelled to address fully the role that sociocultural values play in the relationship of business and society. This oversight, manifested by the value myopia problem, is significant, since values are thought to motivate actions and influence what humans define as their needs, wants and goals. Furthermore, what society expects from business institutions is largely determined by sociocultural values, which can change over time or be subject to different interpretation and articulation. These sociocultural values, in turn, can affect individual choices made within business organizations. Neither the duty-aligned nor economic focus gives a broad accounting of the social values that can influence these choices. Thus, both approaches are too narrow for a social ethic of business.

The third bias is that both perspectives adopt theoretical traditions that highly prize freedom and autonomy for individuals. Both utilitarian economics and Kantian deontology associate individual freedom and autonomy with rationality. Neoclassical economics does so explicitly, in what has come to be known as Milton Friedman's "free-to-choose" ideology. This ideology holds that the business sector should be restrained only minimally by government directives and by ethical customs. Since standard economics does not identify the social values on which government directives and ethical customs might be based, they are largely unspecified. Lacking in normative specificity, economic theory is used to grant the individual manager a great deal of autonomy from morality. As the argument goes, managers do not have explicit moral obligations to others, beyond adhering to social control and performing their fiduciary responsibilities to stockholders.

That the Kantian philosophy inherent in the duty-aligned perspective also prizes individual freedom and autonomy is evident from the formulation of the categorical imperative. This imperative holds that autonomous individuals would freely subordinate themselves to the moral principles that they would rationally choose for themselves. In Kantian philosophy, individual free will in choice is of utmost importance. Indeed, normative philosophers generally assume that ethical actions are performed with autonomy and free choice (Selznick, 1992).

Such prizing of individual liberty and autonomy is very entrenched in Western thought. Amitai Etzioni (1988) describes this prizing of individual freedom as so interwoven with the concept of rationality that many political and ethical theorists seem to be unaware of the normative association between the two. At some point in theory construction, the elevation of individual liberty leads to the idealization of the individual as freestanding or independent from a socializing other. A significant theory-building limitation of such formulation of the individual is that positive duty to others is marginalized or downplayed. It simply does not enjoy the same approval as negative duty in theory construction. To grant it more importance would seemingly violate the prerogatives of individual freedom and autonomy. An illustrative example of this state of affairs is the theory of justice set forth by John Rawls (1971, p. 70). Exhibiting a logic strikingly similar to that of economic Pareto optimality, Rawls does not advocate improving the lot of the disadvantaged if this comes at the cost of liberty for others. Analogously, Pareto logic does not advocate a rearrangement of economic value if it worsens anyone's position. These status-quo renditions of the social good reflect a thinking among many philosophers that positive duty infringes on individual autonomy, and that only ethical theories built on negative duty provide the greatest freedoms for all (Werhane, 1985, p. 10).

As a result of the perspectives' shared emphasis on individual freedom, a considerable body of evidence on other-affirming human behavior is held at bay. Such evidence suggests that humans can be psychologically motivated to help others in positive ways, and that people often make choices by considering the interests of others over their own narrow self-interest (Etzioni, 1988, pp. 51–88). Arguably, a theory which seeks to describe a constructive role for business in society would take positive duty as seriously as negative duty (Swanson et al., 1997).

To recapitulate, reconciliation difficulties are compounded by a related, perhaps more serious dilemma. Neither perspective, as generally understood, is adequate for addressing the magnitude and complexities of business and society interactions. Favoring the logic of individualism over the knowledge of social experience, both approaches have immunized themselves from research which is highly relevant to understanding how business functions in society, including the dynamics of group processes in organizations, the relevance of sociocultural values to these dynamics and the bearing these dynamics could have on the enactment of a corporation's positive duty to society.

Conclusion

This chapter has identified some reconciliation and adequacy problems of duty-aligned and economic-focused approaches to business. Given the described difficulties, it would be futile to skew a social theory of business toward either perspective as currently formulated. While both offer insights into life-affirming aspects of human association (such as the importance of economic efficiency as well as duties to others based on standards of rights and justice) neither is wholly adequate for theorizing about a constructive role for business in society.

This shared limitation is a product of theoretical dissonance. As long as this state of affairs persists, a serious interest in ethics on the part of business theorists and practicing managers will be stymied.

Although this chapter has not gone so far as to offer a strategy for integration, it is possible to make some general statements about the direction such an endeavor would take. Necessarily, it must come to terms with how typifications of *self* are relevant to business and society interactions vis-à-vis organizational decision processes. For it is in this context that moral reflection and self-seeking impulses become bound up with group-based decision processes which have market and nonmarket impacts. At times, these impacts are related to corporate power-aggrandizing, a subject which needs to be fully confronted in attempts to revise duty-aligned and economic-focused approaches so that theory-building problems are rectified. Notably, any claim that managerial choices driven by unreflective hedonism are in the best interests of society needs to be expunged from economic logic. Finally, it is important that the full range of values relevant to corporations' negative and positive duties to society be identified and incorporated into theory.

In the final analysis, both the duty-aligned and economic-focused viewpoints need to be reconsidered for their relevance to business and society issues. Whether an expanded theoretical synthesis is possible remains to be seen. One thing, however, is clear. In attempts to rectify these theory-building problems, what is ultimately at stake is a coherent understanding of how contemporary business activity is related to the social good.

References

Berle, A. and Means, O. 1921: *The Modern Corporation and Private Property.* New York: Macmillan.

Cohen, M., March, J., and Olsen, J. 1972: A garbage can model of organizational choice. *Administrative Science Quarterly,* 17, 1–25.

Donaldson, T. 1982: *Corporations and Morality.* Englewood Cliffs, NJ: Prentice Hall.

Donaldson, T. 1989: *The Ethics of International Business.* New York: Oxford Press.

Edgeworth, F. Y. 1881: *Mathematical Psychics: An Essay on the Application of Mathematics To the Moral Sciences.* Republished in 1953 by New York: Kelley.

Etzioni, A. 1988: *The Moral Dimension: Toward a New Economics.* New York: The Free Press.

Frederick, W. C. 1987: Theories of corporate social performance. In S. P. Sethi and C. M. Falbe (eds), *Business and Society: Dimensions of Conflict and Cooperation,* New York: Lexington Books, 142–61.

Friedman, M. 1962: *Capitalism and Freedom.* Chicago: University of Chicago Press.

Friedman, M. 1979: The social responsibility of business is to increase its profits. *New York Times Magazine,* September 13, 122–6.

Rawls, J. 1971: *A Theory of Justice.* Cambridge Mass: Harvard University Press.

Selznick, P. 1992: *The Moral Commonwealth: Social Theory and the Promise of Community.* Berkeley and Los Angeles: University of California Press.

Swanson, D. L. 1995: Addressing a theoretical problem by reorienting the corporate social performance model. *Academy of Management Review,* 20, 34–64.

Swanson, D. L. 1996: Neoclassical economic theory, executive control, and organizational outcomes. *Human Relations,* 49, 735–56.

Swanson, D. L. 1999: Toward an integrative theory of business and society: A research strategy for corporate social performance. *Academy of Management Review,* 25(July).

Swanson, D. L., Calton, J. M., and Jones, R. E. 1997: Reconstructing positive duty: Theory-building exercises. In J. Weber (ed.), *The International Association For Business and Society Proceedings,* 275–90.

Werhane, P. H. 1985: *Persons, Rights, and Corporations.* Englewood Cliffs, NJ: Prentice Hall.

18

Business ethics and the social sciences

LINDA KLEBE TREVIÑO

The social science perspective on business ethics

The study of business ethics has been approached from two very different perspectives: a normative perspective and a social science perspective. My purpose in this chapter is to differentiate the social science perspective from the normative perspective and then to focus on the important knowledge that has been gained from applying a social scientific approach to the study of business ethics. The reader should be aware that this representation of the two approaches is necessarily simplistic because of its brevity.

In earlier work with my colleague, Gary Weaver (Treviño and Weaver, 1994), I outlined several key differences in the normative and the social science perspectives. Although the two perspectives share their interest in the moral aspects of business practice, they differ in significant ways and along multiple key dimensions. The first dimension is the different academic paradigms which drive the training, and guide the thinking and work of philosophers and social scientists who study business ethics. The normative approach has its academic home in philosophy and the liberal arts. The perspective is explicitly value driven, focusing on questions of *should* and *ought* – how individuals and/or businesses ought to behave. Alternatively, the social scientist who studies business ethics is likely to be trained in management and/or one of its root social science disciplines (e.g., psychology, sociology). The dominant paradigm guiding social scientists teaches that scientists should be objective and that science should be value free. Social scientists are interested in answering questions of *what is* rather than *what ought to be*. They focus on the world as it exists and attempt to understand and predict how it works using research designs and methodologies designed to eliminate researcher bias. Thus, social scientists are interested in answering questions such as: "Why do people and/or organizations behave ethically or unethically?", "Why do corporations develop ethics programs?", and "What effects do these programs have on employees?"

Differences in training contribute to differences in the vocabulary members of these two groups use for talking about the phenomenon they study. These language differences can contribute to disagreements and communication difficulties. For example, the phrase "ethical behavior" can mean different things depending upon one's perspective. To the philosopher, "ethical behavior" simply means right action; but, the social scientist is likely to use the phrase more generally and descriptively to refer to the behavior of individuals or organizations facing ethical decisions. To the social scientist, "ethical behavior" can be influenced in a complex manner by both internal (e.g., cognitive moral development) and external (e.g., reward systems) forces.

The different vocabularies are linked to important underlying assumptions about human agency. The normative approach generally assumes human autonomy and individual responsibility. Individuals are assumed to act based upon free choice. They are ethical or unethical simply because they choose to be. Social scientists, on the other hand, make no such assumption. The dominant social science paradigm assumes that human behavior is influenced by a combination of individual and contextual factors. Individual factors are stable traits that predispose individuals to behave in particular ways. The contextual factors are likely to be organizational characteristics such as ethical climate or culture, reward systems, and leadership. These contextual factors are particularly interesting to management scholars because managers have some control over the context within which people work. Thus, the assumption is that managers can influence their subordinates' ethical conduct.

Thus, the goals of the two perspectives are also quite different. The philosopher seeks to prescribe and to provide tools that can be used to analyze and critique ethical behavior in business. The social scientist, on the other hand, seeks to describe actual behavior, and to uncover the factors that influence ethical and unethical conduct in business settings.

Finally, the guidelines for theory evaluation differ significantly. Guidelines for philosophical theory evaluation are not clear cut. Regan's (1984) guidelines for constructing the "ideal moral judgment" called for rationality, impartiality, calm, and reasoning based upon valid moral principles. For a social science theory to be evaluated as good, it must be logical as well, but it must also contribute to the two goals of social science. It must be able to predict and/or explain behavior, and to solve problems. Social science theories are validated through a series of empirical tests, based upon the natural science model of empirical confirmation and disconfirmation.

In sum, Weaver and I concluded that, despite their common interest in morally significant business practice (e.g., lying, cheating, stealing, whistleblowing, corporate crime), the differences cited above remain a source of confusion and conflict. Confusion can arise primarily from differences in language. The potential for conflict exists in different underlying assumptions and purposes, and bases of theory evaluation.

A number of scholars have expressed concern about the lack of integration between these two very different perspectives (Fleming, 1987; Kahn, 1990). In response to this concern, Weaver and I (Weaver and Treviño, 1994) proposed three very different conceptions of the potential relationship between normative and empirical business ethics. The first, which we termed parallelism, explicitly rejects attempts to link the two perspectives, suggesting instead that the self-conscious separation of the two perspectives should be maintained. This conception acknowledges the deeply entrenched differences outlined above and argues that the barriers between them are impenetrable. The second conception, symbiosis, suggests that a more collaborative relationship is possible in which scholars from the two perspectives communicate with each other, recognizing the potential relevance of each other's work for their own. The most extreme and difficult to achieve form of integration – referred to as theoretical hybridization – would seek to create a new kind of theory that commingles the two disciplines. We concluded that symbiosis was the most likely to occur, at least in the near future. I view this chapter as a contribution to symbiosis, as I communicate knowledge of business ethics gained from a social science perspective to an audience that will include many philosopher colleagues.

In the remainder of the chapter, I will focus on major knowledge in the field of business ethics. This perspective is gaining in influence as more well-trained social scientists turn their attention to theory development and as they conduct carefully designed empirical research that answers important questions about ethical decision making and conduct in organizations.

What is unethical conduct in organizations?

Much of the theorizing and research on ethical/unethical conduct in organizations has talked about unethical conduct in general terms, or has focused on specific types of conduct such as lying, cheating or theft. Research is needed to categorize ethical and unethical conduct in ways that are empirically valid and useful. For example, in related work, Robinson and Bennett (1995) defined "workplace deviance" as voluntary behavior that violates significant organizational norms and, in so doing, threatens the well-being of the organization and/or its members." They determined empirically that deviant workplace behaviors vary along two dimensions (minor versus serious and interpersonal versus organizational) and that these behaviors fall into four categories:

- *Property deviance* refers to situations where employees "acquire or damage the tangible property or assets of the work organization without authorization."
- *Production deviance* refers to employees doing less than the minimum in terms of quality or quantity of production.
- *Political deviance* is defined as "engaging in social interaction which puts other individuals at a personal or political disadvantage."
- *Personal aggression* is defined as "behaving in an aggressive or hostile manner toward other individuals."

Obviously, this categorization scheme does not incorporate *all* possible unethical conduct, but it does provide an empirically-based framework for thinking about workplace deviance. Such a framework can influence future research by suggesting that different antecedents might influence different categories of deviance. For example, organizational factors may influence deviance directed at the organization while individual difference factors may be more important for deviance aimed at persons. Similar work is needed in the area of ethical and unethical workplace behavior.

Influences on ethical decisions and conduct in organizations

Conceptual models of ethical decision making in organizations (e.g., Jones, 1991; Treviño, 1986) have been developed to propose relationships and to guide the conduct of empirical research. Jones' model, based upon Rest (1986), proposed that individuals' ethical decision making occurs in four stages (Jones, 1991; Rest, 1986):

1   Recognize the moral nature of the situation.
2   Make a moral judgment.
3   Establish moral intent.
4   Engage in moral action.

Most empirical research has focused on the second and fourth steps, moral judgment (e.g., Derry, 1987; Weber, 1990) and moral decision making and action (e.g., Treviño and Youngblood, 1990), although researchers are beginning to attend to the first step as well, moral issue recognition. Researchers have proposed that characteristics of individuals, issues, roles, and organizations influence thoughts and behavior at each stage.

Individual difference factors

The individual differences approach to understanding ethical decision-making behavior suggests that persons bring something of themselves to situations. It is based upon research in psychology which has clearly demonstrated that individuals can be differentiated in terms of psychological characteristics that guide their behavior across situations. I will focus here on two important individual characteristics that have been linked to moral judgment and action in organizations – cognitive moral development and locus of control.

Cognitive moral development   One of the best explanations for ethical judgment and action based on an individual differences approach comes from thirty years of moral psychology research by Lawrence Kohlberg (1969), his students and colleagues. Moral psychology research provides insight into how people think when confronted with ethical dilemmas. Kohlberg's theory, built on earlier work by Piaget (1932) has spawned hundreds of carefully designed empirical studies on ethical decision making and action, and the theory has been effectively applied in the context of business ethics.

Kohlberg's cognitive moral development theory is concerned with how people judge what is morally right. The theory developed out of a seminal study in which 58 males (10–16 years old) were interviewed at 3-year intervals over a 12-year period. Based upon an analysis of their responses to systematic questioning about hypothetical moral dilemmas, Kohlberg found that individuals' moral reasoning abilities develop through an invariant sequence of hierarchical stages. Development through the six stages (which are classified into three levels) results from cognitive disequilibrium that occurs when an individual's current thinking is challenged. According to the theory, reasoning becomes more autonomous as individuals advance through the stages, and at higher reasoning stages, decisions will be more ethical because thinking at these higher stages is more consistent with normative ethical principles of justice and rights.

At level I (labeled the preconventional level and including stages 1 and 2), a person views rules as imposed from outside the self. Stage 1 individuals are interested primarily in avoiding punishment. Something is thought to be wrong if the individual is likely to be caught and punished. At stage 2, concern for personal satisfaction also becomes important and a sense of duty develops. Further, a kind of reciprocity in relationships is considered in which, for example, the individual might consider the need to repay a favor.

At level II (labeled the conventional level and including stages 3 and 4), the individual begins to internalize the moral norms of important social groups. Social approval is particularly important at stage 3. At stage 4, the perspective broadens to consider society and its laws. The individual is concerned about fulfilling agreed-upon duties and following rules or laws that are designed to promote the common good. Kohlberg's research placed most American adults at this level and research in business ethics has found that most business managers reason at this level as well (Weber, 1990).

Finally, at level III (postconventional, sometimes called principled reasoning – stages 5 and 6), the individual has progressed beyond simply identifying with others' expectations to make decisions more autonomously. These decisions are carefully reasoned and based upon principles of justice and rights. Stage 5 thinking goes beyond stage 4 in that a stage 5 individual would consider the possibility of breaking the law or changing it if such a decision would create the greatest societal good. Very few adults actually reach stage 5, and stage 6 is thought to be a theoretical stage represented by a select few moral leaders.

Kohlberg's research has been criticized because of its focus on males. Gilligan (1982) claimed that females were more likely to use a "morality of care" that emphasizes relationships and caring for others than a morality based upon justice and rights. However, subsequent empirical research has found that Gilligan's claim does not apply to adult women in organizational settings. Her own research on male and female medical students found no significant differences in moral reasoning between the genders. Similarly, Derry's (1987) interview study of male and female business managers found no gender differences in moral reasoning. Finally, a large number of more general studies based on Kohlberg's theory have found only trivial gender differences. When differences were found, females generally scored higher in cognitive moral development than men.

Kohlberg has also been criticized by both philosophers and psychologists (Modgil and Modgil, 1985) because his work, falling somewhere between the two fields, does not completely satisfy either. Although it is more psychology than it is philosophy, Kohlberg reached beyond moral psychology to incorporate moral philosophy. He claimed that higher stage judgments are "better" because they are cognitively more complex *and* because they are most consistent with formal normative criteria derived from moral philosophy. In fact, his theory represents one of the very few examples of the integration category, theoretical hybridization, discussed above. The many criticisms of his work over the years, despite strong empirical support, attest to the difficulty faced by theorists who attempt to cross paradigmatic boundaries.

Research has found that cognitive moral development theory applies across cultures (Snarey, 1985), making it useful for cross-cultural studies, and that a moderate statistical relationship exists between cognitive moral development and actual behavior (Blasi, 1980). In my own research, I found that cognitive moral development significantly influenced ethical decision making in the context of a simulated in-basket exercise (Treviño and Youngblood, 1990). Individuals higher in cognitive moral development were more likely to make ethical decisions.

Research has also found that moral development continues at least through young adulthood and that specific types of training can contribute to increases in cognitive moral development. The common mythology continues to assert that ethics cannot be taught and that young adults in colleges and work organizations are fully formed adults whose ethics can not be influenced. However, research based upon cognitive moral development theory has found that young adults in carefully designed moral education programs advance in moral reasoning even more than younger individuals (Rest and Thoma, 1986).

Perhaps the most important finding of cognitive moral development research is that, consistent with other adults, most business managers reason at the conventional level of cognitive moral development (Weber, 1990). This means that their decisions about what is morally right are highly influenced by what significant others think, say, and do. Thus, business managers are not autonomous decision makers who look inside themselves to decide what is right. Rather, they look to relevant others in the social context (e.g., peers, leaders) for cues.

Thus, empirical research based upon cognitive moral development theory helps to explain much of the moral behavior we observe in organizations. For example, people who are caught engaging in unethical conduct in organizations frequently claim that they were simply doing what they were told to do by an authority figure, or that they were simply doing what everyone else does. Doing what one is told to do by an authority figure is likely related to level I thinking. The level I individual will simply do as he or she is told, because failing to do so is likely to result in punishment. Besides, this level I person may think, if the boss said to do it, it is probably okay. In fact, variations on Stanley Milgram's (1974) infamous obedience to authority experiment found that people at lower levels of cognitive moral development were more likely to obey an authority figure and deliver painful electric shocks to the learner in the experiment, while research subjects who were higher in cognitive moral development were more likely to refuse to obey. Doing something because everyone else is doing it is likely related to level II thinking. A level II individual will think that significant others in the environment are doing it, so it must be all right.

Although much ethical decision making is carried out by individuals, research has also considered what happens when ethical decision making occurs in a group setting (Dukerich, et al., 1990). This research found that the cognitive moral development of the leader was important. When less principled individuals were selected to lead a group, the group's ethical decision-making performance decreased. However, groups with leaders higher in moral reasoning either improved or stayed the same.

Research on cognitive moral development has clear implications for business ethics. It tells us that we should not expect the large majority of employees to be autonomous ethical decision makers. In fact, most employees are cognitively incapable of such high-level reasoning. They are at the conventional level of cognitive moral development, meaning that they will look to significant others and to the social system for guidance. This knowledge has important implications for the fields of business ethics and management. It means that attention should turn toward preparing managers and leaders for their role as ethical leaders, and to the development of organizational structures and systems that support ethical conduct.

Locus of control Locus of control (Rotter, 1966) is another individual characteristic that has been found to influence ethical behavior. Locus of control refers to an individual's perception of how much control he or she exerts over the events in life. Locus of control ranges along a single continuum from a high internal locus of control to a high external locus of control. An individual with a high internal locus of control believes that outcomes are primarily the result of his or her own efforts, while an individual with a high external locus of control believes that life events are primarily determined by fate, luck, or powerful others.

Empirical research has demonstrated that internal locus of control is positively related to cognitive moral development, helping behaviors, whistleblowing, and resistance to social pressure. External locus of control has been related to cheating and willingness to harm another individual if told to do so by an authority figure. These relationships are likely due to perceptions of causality and responsibility. Individuals with a high internal locus of control see the relationship between their behavior and its outcomes clearly. They see themselves as in charge of their fate and responsible for their actions. Therefore, they are more likely to take responsibility for the consequences of their actions. In my own research on ethical decision making, locus of control was significantly correlated with cognitive moral development, and internals were more likely to make ethical decisions.

Issue-related factors as influences on moral awareness and moral judgment

Jones (1991) proposed that characteristics of ethical issues influence all stages of the ethical decision-making process. He created a construct he called "moral intensity" which is comprised of multiple dimensions:

- *Magnitude of consequences*: the sum of the harms or benefits done to victims or beneficiaries of the moral act in question
- *Social consensus*: the degree of social agreement that a proposed act is evil or good
- *Probability of effect*: a joint function of the probability that the act will actually take place and the act in question will actually cause the harm or benefit predicted
- *Temporal immediacy*: the length of time between the present and the onset of consequences
- *Proximity*: the feeling of nearness . . . that the moral agent has for victims
- *Concentration of effect*: an inverse function of the number of people affected by an act of given magnitude

Jones (1991) proposed that issues of higher moral intensity would be associated with recognition of moral issues, more sophisticated moral reasoning, and more frequent moral intent and moral behavior. Empirical research has begun to provide support for these propositions, although magnitude of consequences is the only moral intensity dimension studied thus far. My colleagues and I found that moral issue recognition was associated with higher magnitude of consequences (Butterfield et al., 1998). Further, Weber (1996) found that moral judgments were higher in response to situations of greater magnitude of consequences.

Role-based factors as influences on ethical decisions

Grover (1993) proposed that role conflict theory could help to explain why professionals lie in situations where their professional standards conflict with organizational requirements. In a scenario-based empirical study of nurses, Grover supported this proposition. Nurses facing situations in which professional standards and organizational requirements conflicted experienced more emotional distress and were more likely to lie when reporting their behavior on a patient's chart and when discussing their behavior with other nurses. Grover suggested that, in attempting to reduce role conflict for nurses, hospitals could provide formal voice mechanisms for nurses to discuss and resolve such role conflicts.

Organizational factors as influences on employee attitudes and behaviors

Models of ethical decision making in organizations have also proposed that organizational factors can influence individuals' ethical decisions and actions (e.g., Treviño, 1986). Recall that cognitive moral development theory tells us that the majority of adults look outside themselves for ethical guidance. Therefore, the organization has an important role to play in guiding individuals' ethical decision making and action. For example, research based upon the notion that ethical and unethical conduct result from self-interested behavior has found that reward systems can influence ethical and unethical conduct. Hegarty and Sims (1978) found that individuals were more likely to pay bribes when rewarded for doing so, and Treviño and Youngblood (1990) found that individuals were more likely to make ethical decisions when rewarded for doing so. Greenberg's (1990) field experiment based upon equity theory found that employees were more likely to steal from their employer when they believed that they had been unfairly treated in a pay cut situation.

Research has also explored questions of whether and how broader organizational contexts influence employees' ethical conduct. Victor and Cullen (1987, 1988) proposed a construct they called "ethical climate" which they defined as "the prevailing perceptions of typical organizational practices and procedures that have ethical content" or "those aspects of work climate that determine what constitutes ethical behavior at work." Their proposed nine ethical climate types were grounded in three classes of philosophy (principle, benevolence, and egoism) and three levels of analysis (individual, local, and cosmopolitan). Victor and Cullen later tested for the empirical existence of these theoretical climate types. They were able to validate the existence of five climate types they labeled caring, law and code, rules, instrumental, and independence. They also found relationships between climate types and employees' organizational commitment. Employees who perceived a benevolent climate were more highly committed to the organization; employees who perceived an egoistic climate were less committed.

In 1990, I proposed a construct I referred to as ethical culture (Treviño, 1990). I conceptualized ethical culture as a subset of organizational culture composed of multiple formal and informal systems of behavioral control that can support either ethical or unethical behavior. Formal systems include formal ethics initiatives such as codes and training programs while informal systems include informal organizational norms, organizational stories, and rituals.

In a field survey (Treviño et al., 1998), my colleagues and I investigated the relationship between ethical climate and ethical culture and the relationships between these constructs and employee commitment and ethical conduct in the firm. The findings suggested that ethical climate and ethical culture are related, but somewhat different constructs. The most important influence on employee commitment and ethical conduct was an ethical culture dimension we labeled "ethical environment" which incorporated top management commitment to ethics and a reward system supportive of ethical conduct. Where respondents perceived the overall ethical environment in the firm to support ethics through top management commitment, and a reward system that rewarded ethical behavior and disciplined unethical behavior, they reported higher commitment to the organization and lower observed unethical conduct. Obedience to authority was another important ethical culture dimension. In organizations that respondents perceived to demand unquestioning obedience to authority, organizational commitment was lower and observed unethical conduct was higher. The most important ethical climate dimension was "self-interest." In organizations in which respondents perceived people to be mostly out for themselves, they reported more observed unethical behavior and lower organizational commitment.

In another study (McCabe et al., 1996), my colleagues and I found that company codes of conduct were associated with lower self-reported unethical behavior. In survey responses, individuals who reported that their company had a code also self-reported less unethical behavior. Interestingly, the least unethical behavior was reported by individuals who had attended an honor code college and who were working for an organization with a code at the time of the survey. This finding suggests that code environments may have an additive effect, meaning that the corporate code environment serves to reinforce and build on the earlier collegiate honor code environment.

This research on the relationship between organizational context and employee attitudes and behaviors is important because it demonstrates the important role played by the organization. Organizations can no longer attribute unethical conduct solely to "bad apples" alone (Treviño and Youngblood, 1990). Organizations need to also look at the organizational context they have created and its role in shaping employee behavior.

Managing ethics and legal compliance in US corporations

Given the importance of the organizational context, it would be helpful to understand what organizations are doing to support ethical conduct in their firms. In a study of *Fortune* 500 manufacturing and service firms, my colleagues and I investigated the extent to which these firms have formal ethics programs (Weaver et al., 1998). The study found that 98 percent of responding firms claimed to address ethics in some kind of formal document. Of those, 78 percent had separate codes of ethics and most of those codes have been introduced in the last twenty years. 515 of the firms reported having some kind of telephone system for responding to employees' ethical concerns. Management employees were most likely to receive some form of ethics training, at least every few years, but, such training was less likely for lower rank employees. CEOs of these firms rarely communicated with employees about ethics; 84 percent sent out some kind of company-wide written communication on ethics only once a year or every few years. CEOs rarely attended meetings that had ethics as their primary focus. These findings suggest that the top management of large US firms are either unaware of the importance of their role as ethical leaders, or uninterested in playing such a role in their firms. These survey findings are disturbing given the finding reported earlier that ethical leadership is an important element of a firm's ethical environment that influences employees' ethical conduct.

Given the variation in formal ethics activity across a sample of large US corporations, we were also interested in understanding why some firms engage in a wide range of formal ethics management efforts while others do relatively little, and why these programs take various forms. Conventional wisdom has attributed much formal ethics activity to the requirements of the US Sentencing Commission guidelines for organizational defendants. These guidelines, which were released in late 1991, provide an incentive for firms to be proactive in managing ethics and legal compliance. Firms convicted of criminal misconduct face reduced fines and penalties if they can demonstrate that they made an effort to manage employee legal compliance by assigning responsibility for ethics/legal compliance management to high-level managers, developing and communicating policies, and instituting reporting and disciplinary mechanisms. Data from our study (Weaver et al., 1998) suggest that management's awareness of these guidelines had the most powerful influence on ethics program "scope"– the sheer size of the ethics/legal compliance management effort. Firms whose top managers were aware of the guidelines and its requirements were more likely to have developed multiple ethics and legal compliance initiatives. However, the orientation of the ethics/compliance management effort toward values and/or legal compliance was due primarily to management's own commitment to ethics. Firms with executives who expressed commitment to ethics had ethics/compliance programs that were both more values-based and more legal compliance-based.

Corporations should be interested in preventing unethical and illegal conduct because research has found a relationships between corporate crime and firm performance. Firms' stock prices have been found to drop in the short term in response to announcements of allegations of corporate crime and in response to announced penalties (Strachan et al., 1983; Wier, 1983). Further, a recent study (Baucus and Baucus, 1997) found that firm financial performance suffers significantly over the five years following a conviction.

Firm social responsibility and financial performance

Over the years, researchers have attempted to document a relationship between corporate social responsibility and firm financial performance. One difficulty in conducting this research is that social responsibility can be defined and measured in many ways. A recent empirical study (Waddock and Graves, 1997) found significant positive and negative relationships. The study used an index of eight attributes of corporate social responsibility as rated by the firm Kinder, Lydenberg, Domini, an independent service that assesses corporate social performance of companies in the Standard & Poor's 500, based upon firms' responses to key stakeholder interests. The findings suggest, first, that firms with strong financial performance were later rated higher on corporate social performance. Thus, the authors argued that companies that do well financially allocate more resources to social concerns – they "do good by doing well." Those that do not have strong finances may not be able to engage in philanthropy or other discretionary corporate social performance activities. The study also found that financial performance depends upon good social performance, suggesting that firms also "do well by doing good." The authors termed this the "good management theory." They reasoned that good social performance is related to other good managerial practices. The authors also proposed that these relationships are linked in a "virtuous circle" in which good corporate social performance feeds financial performance and good financial performance then feeds good corporate social performance. Clearly, this research has found that being socially responsible does not harm the financial bottom line as many economists have suggested in the past. In fact, the study's findings suggest that a firm's relationships with key stakeholders (e.g., employees, community, natural environment) are definitely tied to its financial performance.

Conclusion

In this brief chapter, I have highlighted what I believe to be some of the most significant social science research related to business ethics. This research has been carefully designed and conducted, and has contributed to our understanding of individual and organizational ethical conduct. It has pointed to the importance of both individual characteristics and organizational contexts for understanding ethics-related attitudes and behaviors. We have also begun to understand what drives organizations' approaches to ethics management and the relationship between social responsibility and firm financial performance. Although these studies have taught us a lot, they often raise as many questions as they answer. In addition, there are important areas that remain relatively unexplored from the social science perspective. For example, ethical leadership in organizations seems important, but we know very little about it. I hope that social scientists will continue to contribute in important ways to our understanding of individual and organizational ethical behavior.

References

Baucus, M. S. and Baucus, D. A. 1997: Paying the piper: An empirical examination of longer-term financial consequences of illegal corporate behavior. *Academy of Management Journal*, 40(1), 129–35.

Blasi, A. 1980: Bridging moral cognition and moral action: A critical review of the literature. *Psychological Bulletin*, 88, 1–45.

Butterfield, K. D., Treviño, L. K., and Weaver, G. R. 1998: Moral awareness in business: Influences of issue-related and social context factors. Working paper.

Derry, R. 1987: Moral reasoning in work-related conflicts. *Research in Corporate Social Performance and Policy*, 9, 25–50.

Dukerich, J. M., Nichols, M. L., Elm, D. R., and Vollrath, D. A. 1990: Moral reasoning in groups: Leaders make a difference. *Human Relations*, 43(5), 473–93.

Fleming, J. 1987: A survey and critique of business ethics research. *Research in Corporate Social Performance and Policy*, 9, 1–24.

Gilligan, C. 1982: *In a Different Voice*. Cambridge, MA: Harvard University Press.

Greenberg, J. 1990: Employee theft as a reaction to underpayment inequity: The hidden cost of pay cuts. *Journal of Applied Psychology*, 75L, 561–8.

Grover, S. 1993: Why professionals lie: The impact of professional role conflict on reporting accuracy. *Organizational Behavior and Human Decision Processes*, 55, 251–72.

Hegarty, W. J. and Sims, H. P. Jr 1978: Some determinants of unethical decision behavior; an experiment. *Journal of Applied Psychology*, 63, 451–7.

Jones, T. M. 1991: Ethical decision making by individuals in organizations: An issue-contingent model. *Academy of Management Review*, 16, 366–95.

Kahn, W. A. 1990: Toward an agenda for business ethics research. *Academy of Management Review*, 15, 311–28.

Kohlberg, L. 1969: Stage and sequences: The cognitive-developmental approach to socialization. In D. A. Goslin (ed.) *Handbook of Socialization Theory and Research*, Chicago: Rand-McNally, 347–480.

McCabe, D., Treviño, L. K., and Butterfield, K. 1996: The influence of collegiate and corporate codes of conduct on ethics-related behavior in the workplace. *Business Ethics Quarterly*, 6, 441–60.

Milgram, S. 1974: *Obedience to Authority*. New York: Harper & Row.

Modgil, S. and Modgil, C. 1985: *Lawrence Kohlberg: Consensus and Controversy*. Philadelphia and London: Falmer Press.

Piaget, J. 1932: *The Moral Judgment of the Child*. London: Kegan Paul.

Regan, T. 1984: *Just Business: New Introductory Essays in Business Ethics*. New York: Random House.

Rest, J. 1986: *Moral Development: Advances in Research and Theory*. New York: Praeger.

Rest, J. and Thoma, S. J. 1986: Educational programs and interventions. In Rest (1986).

Robinson, S. L. and Bennett, R. J. 1995: A typology of deviant workplace behavior: A multi-dimensional scaling study. *Academy of Management Journal*, 2, 555–72.

Rotter, J. B. 1966: Generalized expectancies for internal versus external control of reinforcement. *Psychological Monographs: General and Applied*, 80, 609.

Snarey, R. 1985: Cross-cultural universality of social-moral development: A critical review of Kohlbergian research. *Psychological Bulletin*, 97, 202–32.

Strachan J. L., Smith, D. B., and Beedles, W. L. 1983: The price reaction to (alleged) corporate crime. *Financial Review*, 18(2), 121–3.

Treviño, L. K. 1986: Ethical decision-making in organizations: A person–situation interactionist model. *Academy of Management Review*, 11, 601–17.

Treviño, L. K. 1990: A cultural perspective on changing and developing organizational ethics. *Research in Organizational Change and Development*, 4, 195–230.

Treviño, L. K. and Weaver, G. R. 1994: Business ETHICS/BUSINESS ethics: One field or two? *Business Ethics Quarterly*, 4, 113–28.

Treviño, L. K. and Youngblood, S. A. 1990: Bad apples in bad barrels: A causal analysis of ethical decision-making behavior. *Journal of Applied Psychology*, 75, 378–85.

Treviño, L. K., Butterfield, K. D., and McCabe, D. L. 1998: The ethical context in organizations: Influences on employee attitudes and behaviors. *Business Ethics Quarterly*, 8(3), 447–76.

Victor, B. and Cullen, J. B. 1987: A theory and measure of ethical climate in organizations. In W. C. Frederick (ed.), *Research in Corporate Social Performance and Policy*, Greenwich, CT: JAI Press, 51–71.

Victor, B. and Cullen, J. B. 1988: The organizational bases of ethical work climates. *Administrative Science Quarterly*, 33, 101–25.

Waddock, S. A. and Graves, S. B. 1997: The corporate social performance-financial performance link. *Strategic Management Journal*, 18, 303–19.

Weaver, G. R. and Treviño, L. K. 1994: Normative and empirical business ethics: Separation, marriage of convenience, or marriage of necessity? *Business Ethics Quarterly*, 4, 129–43.

Weaver, G. R., Treviño, L. K. and Cochran, P. L. 1999: Corporate ethics practices in the mid-1990s: An empirical study of the Fortune 1000. *Journal of Business Ethics*, 18(3), 283–94.

Weber, J. 1990: Managers' moral reasoning: Assessing their responses to three moral dilemmas. *Human Relations*, 43, 687–702.

Weber, J. 1996: Influences upon managerial moral decision making: Nature of the harm and magnitude of consequences. *Human Relations*, 49, 1–22.

Wier, P. 1983: The costs of antimerger lawsuits. *Journal of Financial Economies*, 11, 207–24.

PART III
ISSUES IN BUSINESS ETHICS

19

International business ethics

RICHARD T. DE GEORGE

International business ethics, as the name implies, is that part of business ethics that deals with international issues. It encompasses moral judgements made about these issues, as well as the various theoretical considerations connected with explaining and/or justifying such judgments. Beyond this, the term has no precisely defined agreed upon meaning, and it is used in many different ways to refer to a variety of topics. For some people, it refers to the ethical dimension of any business relation involving two or more countries. Thus the NAFTA treaty among the USA, Canada and Mexico, when considered from an ethical point of view, is a topic in international business ethics. Yet the ethical issues concerning NAFTA that were raised in editorials and in journals prior to the adoption of the agreement were very different in the USA than they were in Mexico or Canada. Some in the USA questioned the morality of an agreement that would lead to the transfer of US jobs to Mexico, while some Mexicans questioned the morality of an agreement that would lead to greater dominance of US business in Mexico. In both instances, international business ethics was an extension of national approaches to business ethics issues. For this reason, other people prefer to think of international business ethics as the attempt to transcend national viewpoints and to look at international business from an ethical viewpoint that is internationally neutral.

According to this position, one would not consider NAFTA from any national point of view but from a purely ethical point of view, transcending all national interests and borders. Whether attaining such a neutral point of view is possible is a disputed question.

Multinationals are at the heart of most discussions of international business ethics. Critics either attack multinational corporations in general, making such charges as the claim that US multinationals exploit less developed countries (Barnet and Mueller, 1974); or they investigate particular instances of unethical conduct by multinationals, such as the investigation of the infant milk formula marketing practices of Nestlé in Africa and a subsequent boycott of its products for eight years until international guidelines were agreed upon and followed (Dobbing, 1988; Nestlé, 1985; Sethi, 1994).

Multinationals in turn have sought to counter such claims and defend their positions. In some instances, they have acknowledged the legitimacy of the attacks and changed their practices.

The set of issues concerning multinationals is related to such questions as the ethics of bribery or of child labor or of pollution. These questions raise the related general questions of ethical relativism and of whether there are any universal norms that businesses everywhere should follow if they are to act ethically, and they also form part of the literature of international business ethics. Although such general questions are of interest to academic writers in the area, individual multinational corporations are primarily concerned more concretely and pragmatically with what they must do to operate ethically in the many and diverse countries in which they find themselves.

They typically do not seek to determine how all companies should act, but only how they should act, given their values, commitments, and constituencies. Acting in accordance with their values and principles constitutes their acting with integrity. For a development of this approach, see De George (1993).

In addition, international business ethics is sometimes taken to encompass such broad issues as the ethics of the present rate of use of natural resources; the obligations, if any, of rich countries to poor countries; and the justice of the international economic system, to the extent that one can be described. Also included are global issues such as the depletion of the ozone level and global warming.

There is little reason to privilege any one of these meaning or approaches or topics and all of them appropriately fall under the general heading of international business ethics.

International business ethics mirrors the division of general ethics. It thus includes descriptive ethics, which consists in describing ethical practices in different parts of the world; comparative ethics, which compares and contrasts both ethical theories and practices in different countries or cultures; normative ethics, which attempts to state and justify norms, principles, and values that should be followed by businesses in international dealings and operations; and metaethics, which considers the meaning of ethical terms and such questions as whether human rights are universal or a Western philosophical position based on an individualistic view as opposed to a communal view of the human being and human society. Although it seems contradictory to speak of a US or a Japanese approach to international business ethics, the alternative is not clear. Some claim that the best we can do is to try to achieve an overlapping consensus on issues (John Rawls (1993) uses the term in a somewhat different context); others claim that there are indeed universal principles that transcend national and cultural boundaries; and still others attempt combinations of the two. Various groups have proposed sets of principles for multinationals of all nations to follow. The UN Commission on Transnational Corporations has been working on a general code for many years (Dell, 1990). A group of US, European, and Japanese corporations joined together at Caux in Switzerland and developed a set of guidelines known as the Caux Principles, based on the notions of human dignity and the Japanese concept of *kyosei*, which means "living and working together for the common good" (Caux Round Table, 1994). Other codes have also been proposed and adopted by some firms. No code has yet attained broad international adherence.

Comparative ethics, cultural relativism and metaethical issues

Just as any non-domestic news is considered international in most countries, so descriptions of ethical practices, norms, and cases in a country other than one's own are often considered part of international business ethics. Studies that compare practices or responses by, for instance, managers in different countries to similar questions form a large part of the academic literature of international business ethics. Much of this is descriptive.

Related to these descriptive studies, a focus of continuing discussion in the literature on international business ethics is the general issue of ethical relativism. Although the existing differences in moral customs pose practical problems for multinationals operating in diverse cultures, the simplistic claim of ethical relativism (which says that because there are diverse moral customs in different cultures, therefore there are no generally valid moral norms) has been shown in the philosophical literature not to be valid, among others, see Stace (1937), and Wellman (1963), and for a more recent useful collection of articles on relativism, see Krauz and Meiland (1982). The more philosophically subtle forms of moral relativism play little role in the discussions of international business ethics. Hence for practical reasons and despite the theoretical arguments, many firms from the USA, Japan, Germany and other industrially developed countries conduct their business on the principle of "When in Rome, do as the Romans do;" for a fuller discussion of this position, see De George (1993, pp. 9–15). If this means following the apartheid laws in South Africa during the apartheid period, or paying bribes in some developing countries where this is the practice, or using suppliers who utilize child labor, then that is what they do. They claim that their job is not to transmit or impose their own moral and cultural norms on others. That would be moral imperialism. Although, in their own countries, they would not bribe or employ children or practice discrimination, in countries in which these are the practices they will follow local custom, and they claim they are justified in doing so.

This line of argument and justification is coming under heavier and heavier attack. Although the theoretical arguments against it have long been known, the attacks are now coming from the general populations of many countries. Bribery is a case in point.

The theoretical argument says that bribery everywhere is unjust, even though it is widely practiced in some countries; for a history of bribery and an extended argument showing it is unethical, see Noonan (1984). Recently the people of countries such as Korea (Brull, 1995), Indonesia (TI, 1996) and Japan (Baum et al., 1995), among others, where high-level governmental bribery has been exposed, have voiced their disapproval of government corruption and bribery, indicating that the practice is not held to be ethical, but merely tolerated in those countries. In fact, there is no country in which bribery of public officials is openly and publicly defended as ethical. In 1977, the USA passed the Foreign Corrupt Practices Act, which forbids US corporations from paying bribes to high-level government officials of any country in the world. In 1997, the OECD countries, under public pressure, recommended that member countries follow the US example.

Other metaethical issues besides relativism still remain. The meaning and status of human rights is still debated and challenged in some parts of the world. Here, again, public pressure rather than theoretical argument seems to be bringing about universal recognition of human rights; for a discussion and defense of the role of human rights in international business ethics, see Donaldson (1989).

The meaning of "justice" in international relations is a continuing topic of dispute, and affects such discussions as the justice of the international economic order, defended by some in the name of justice and attacked by others in the name of justice differently conceived.

Whether there is a universal meaning of justice, or whether the best we can hope for is consensus and agreement on particular issues, practices and structures, is one of the questions that remains open at the present time.

The international economic system and background conditions

Business ethics, as it has developed in the USA and the countries of Western Europe, and as it is emerging in Japan and other countries of the world, has been primarily nationally oriented.

What is ethical in business is a function not only of general ethical norms but also of the legal structure of the country; its customs, traditions, and expectations; the presence and role of non-governmental organizations; the presence or absence of pressure groups and of a critical and investigative press and media; and other factors that form the background in which business carries on its activities. Laws generally provide the framework for what a business can or cannot do. The relation of government to business varies from country to country. In some countries, such as Japan, the relation is comparatively close, and government and some big corporations are interlinked in a way that is very different from the relation of government to business in the USA. In Germany, by law, workers have representation on corporate boards, which is not the case in the USA. Nations differ in the way they handle unemployment and the benefits they give to workers. Whether health care is provided by the government or paid for by employers or handled by each individual will make a difference in what is considered ethical for a business to provide or not provide in the way of health benefits.

Because of differing background conditions, business practices that are ethical in one country may not be considered ethical in another. A difficulty with international business with respect to ethics is that, on the one hand, it functions to some extent in a vacuum with respect to background conditions and restraints, and on the other hand, to the extent that businesses operate in different countries they face a great variety of different background conditions. Since national laws typically cover only the territory over which the government has jurisdiction, multinational corporations can, in some instances, act without legal restraint when operating between countries. Multinational corporations may also take advantage of laws that are more favorable to some of their activities and carry on those activities there, while moving other kinds of activities to countries more tolerant of these other activities. What is the ethics of such practices, and what ethical judgments can one make in contexts that are underdetermined by adequate background conditions, institutions and constraints? This is a pressing question in international business ethics.

The second set of ethical difficulties for international business, related to the first, comes from the absence of any international government or governing body that can adequately and fairly handle issues of international justice and the redistribution of wealth. In most countries, a system of taxation provides for the nation's common goods and by transfer payments helps those who are not able to take part in the economic activity of the country. Welfare payments or systems of various sorts help those in need. Among nations, no such system of taxation or of transfer payments exists.

Gross exploitation of workers that is prohibited by law in some countries is not prohibited in others. And the exploitation of countries – especially less developed countries – and their people and resources by multinational businesses remains both a possibility and a fact of international business.

The absence of adequate background conditions and restraints for business is clear, for instance, in the countries of the former Soviet Union which are in a transition period between socialism and some form of free enterprise. The dissolution of the Soviet regime, in Russia, brought with it a relatively weak government that is only slowly passing the legislation necessary to provide an adequate background for reliable business transactions and enforceable business contracts. In addition, the government has not been notably successful in enforcing the laws it has, with the result that the criminal element (the mafia) has a very strong presence in the business world. Not only are bribery and extortion rampant, but the murder of business people reached over 500 in 1994, double that of the previous year (Arvedlund, 1997; Mellow, 1995; Stanley, 1995). In addition, since the system is still very inefficient and misallocates resources, it is very difficult for local entrepreneurs to carry on their businesses without paying bribes and extortion, and obtaining goods where and how they can. To the extent this is an accurate description of the situation, operating ethically is almost impossible, and paying bribes and extortion (which is unethical) may be seen as the lesser of two evils for local businesses, the alternative being to leave all business to the criminal element. Yet that type of excuse, possibly available to the local entrepreneur, is arguably not available to the large multinational. The foreign multinational operating in Russia is not forced to pay bribes or extortion. It can forego locating in Russia in the first place, an option which the local entrepreneur does not have. The multinational has hard currency which is in great demand; it has the ability to protect itself if the local authorities are unable to do so; and it is able to attract and deal with the legitimate business people present in the society. Doing so under present conditions takes more time and effort than the multinationals would like; and some multinationals have decided to wait for more favorable background conditions and laws before venturing into Russia. Nonetheless, from an ethical point of view, the multinationals are not in the same circumstances as the local entrepreneur, even though they both are conducting business in the same geographical location. Does this mean that there is a double standard and that the multinational is held to a higher ethical norm than the local entrepreneur? Most observers agree that the answer is no. What makes the difference from an ethical point of view, is that the two are in different circumstances and the excusing condition that applies to the local entrepreneur does not apply to the multinational. A similar type analysis can also be made with respect to multinationals operating in what can be called corrupt environments, where that means either that the government is corrupt or that the government is ineffective in controlling gangs, drug lords, or other criminal elements; for a fuller analysis of this, see De George (1993, ch. 7). Differing background conditions and institutions affect the ethical evaluation of particular practices; but they do not make wrong actions, such as murder or bribery, right.

When multinationals from one developed country operate in another developed country, typically the laws of the host country are sufficient to prevent any gross exploitation of the host country or its people. This is not typically the case in less developed countries, which often have high rates of unemployment, low standards of living, below subsistence wage levels, and inadequate laws controlling business or protecting workers, consumers, or the general public. Under such conditions multinationals are nonetheless bound by ethical norms to respect the human rights of all, to pay a living wage to their employees, and to avoid doing harm, directly or indirectly, to the country or its people. Exactly what this means in particular countries and with respect to specific practices is one of the areas being explored in international business ethics. Thus, there are discussions of the ethical requirements of multinationals in exporting hazardous industries to less developed countries, controlling toxic wastes, converting prime arable land to cash crops, extracting minerals, and the like. Case studies of exemplary behavior as well as of unethical behavior on the part of multinationals form an important part of the international business ethics literature. One exemplary case is that of Merck & Co. and its development and gratis distribution in Africa of Mectizan, a drug that helps to prevent river blindness, a disease that afflicts millions of people. For this Merck received a Business Enterprise Trust Award. For some negative cases, see Barnet and Mueller (1974).

Some normative ethical issues

To some extent international business carries with it a set of norms that are necessary for business to function. Respect for life is basic to a functioning society and essential for business to be carried on with any sense of security. This goes together with a basic trust that is also essential if there is to be a transfer of goods, services and money, and if orders are to be accepted and filled. Similarly, honoring contracts and agreements made is also necessary for continuing relations and repeat transactions between parties. The absence of any of these makes business transactions extremely unstable, problematic, expensive and inefficient. Three issues are of broad concern and are widely discussed in the literature on international business ethics: bribery, child labor, and human rights.

Bribery is not essentially an issue in international business ethics. The immorality of bribery does not depend on its being practiced internationally. We have already noted that bribery is nowhere defended as being an ethical practice, although it is widely practiced in some countries. Bribery becomes an especially pressing ethical issue for multinationals that refuse to pay bribes and are faced with other multinational competitors that are willing to do so to win contracts or business. From a business point of view, bribes are inefficient allocators of goods and resources. Recipient countries do not necessarily receive the best products for their money, and sellers do not receive the best price. Government officials are the beneficiaries, and seldom pass on any of the benefit to their countries and their people. Petty bribery, or the making of facilitating payment to lower level government employees, such as customs clerks, to encourage them to perform their legal functions or to perform their functions expeditiously rather than after a long time delay, is a related prevalent problem. Such payments are legal under the US Foreign Corrupt Practices Act as amended. A group called Transparency

International has been organized as a "coalition against corruption in international business transactions." It has national chapters in over 40 countries, it reports on bribery in countries throughout the world, and it lobbies for legislation against bribery. It has helped to focus attention on the problem and has helped to mobilize popular opinion in a variety of countries in seeking legislation against bribery.

The issue of child labor has been the focus of consumer pressure groups in the USA as they have learned of US multinationals involved in such practices in some developing countries in Asia and Latin America. The pressure is on US firms and distributors not to use suppliers who use child labor, which is defined as the full-time employment of children under the age of fourteen. Most countries have laws prohibiting such employment – a few do not – but even in some countries in which it is illegal, the law is not enforced. The normative ethical issue is whether such employment is unethical in cultures in which it has been the practice for long periods of time and in which it is accepted. Schools are not available for the children if they do not work, and the supplemental income provided by children is often necessary to help a family to survive. If the alternative is to leave the children on the street or to have young girls turn to prostitution, perhaps keeping them employed is the lesser of two evils. The argument has not been accepted by most consumers in the West, and has not publicly been endorsed by any Western multinational, but how much effort the multinational should expend in investigating the practices of its suppliers, and what it should do if it finds violations of anti-child labor laws are questions with which multinationals are struggling.

The issue of human rights is found on three levels. On the first level, we can consider the multinational and its direct relations with its employees, suppliers, customers, and neighbors. Recognition of human rights requires that no one and no corporation or government violate the human rights of others. This prevents them from engaging in slavery, from employing child labor (which violates the child's human right to an education), and from grossly exploiting people, for instance, by paying them less than a living wage. The second level is once removed and consists of multinationals utilizing suppliers or others who directly violate human rights. The case of using suppliers that utilize child labor is an instance of this. The third level, in which the multinational is twice removed from the human rights violation, involves a multinational's choosing to operate in a country whose government is guilty of extensive violations of human rights.

With respect to the first, there is little controversy, at least among those who accept the ethical claim that human rights should be respected. There is more controversy about the second, and it hinges on how much is required of a buyer with respect to suppliers. How much are corporations required to learn of their suppliers and what means must they use to be sure that what the supplier tells them is, in fact, the case? The third level is the most contentious. The most dramatic case was South Africa under apartheid. Many US groups – church organizations, universities, student groups, cities, and others – protested against apartheid and put pressure on the US firms located in South Africa to withdraw. Some of the firms claimed that they could do more to break down apartheid by remaining than by leaving South Africa. Leon Sullivan, a member of the Board of Directors of the General Motors Corporation, proposed a set of principles according to which US corporations would not follow the apartheid laws

239

and so would not directly violate the rights of their employees or anyone else's. They would put pressure on the South African government to rescind the apartheid laws. Sullivan advocated following his principles for a test period of ten years to see whether doing so would, in fact, undermine apartheid. In 1987, when that time was up and apartheid was still enforced, a number of firms left, including General Motors, IBM, Coca-Cola, Exxon, Proctor and Gamble, and others. Other corporations remained, claiming they could do more good by working internally than by disinvesting. In 1994, apartheid officially ended in South Africa. Whether those companies that left or those that stayed did more towards helping to end apartheid is still debated. Nonetheless, many critics claim that multinationals should not continue operations in countries that grossly violate the human rights of their citizens. In 1993, Levi Strauss decided that it should no longer use Chinese suppliers who produced its jeans, and started a three-year withdrawal (Carlton, 1993). Other companies have decided to stay in China, or to enter that market, despite the government's abysmal record on human rights. The government of Burma similarly has come under very strong criticism, and popular boycotts of Heineken beer caused that company to withdraw, as did PepsiCo. The conditions under which multinationals may ethically operate in such countries is an area of debate and disagreement.

Some approaches to international ethics issues

Self-regulation by industries is also taking place. Following the Bhopal disaster in which a Union Carbide subsidiary suffered a release of toxic chemicals that killed over 3,000 people and injured more than 200,000, the Chemical Manufacturers Association adopted a "Responsible Care" program and a set of Guiding Principles. The Principles list norms of safety to which the member firms worldwide agree to adhere, and they agree to apply peer pressure on violating firms to ensure compliance.

Some corporations that wish to act ethically in the international arena have developed special codes, consistent with their general corporate ethical codes, guiding how they will behave in various international contexts. Yet more and more companies are discovering that they do not have to act alone, and that there are many other companies facing similar problems and searching for acceptable ethical answers. The experience of South Africa shows that when companies act together, they are both more likely to achieve their ends and less likely to suffer adverse consequences for standing by their principles. For details on apartheid and the Sullivan Principles, see Williams (1986).

The South African government chose to ignore the fact that the 172 US corporate signatories of the Sullivan principles were breaking the apartheid laws. Had any company violated those laws by itself, it might well have suffered some penalty from the South African government, but the government did not wish to take on 172 US corporations. Whether this shows that the government felt it gained more by allowing the US companies to break the apartheid laws than it would if it forced them to leave is debatable. Nonetheless, the lesson that has been learned and that companies are using in other areas to protest bribery, for instance, is that they are more likely to succeed when they join forces than when they act alone.

Another lesson from South Africa is that consumer and other groups have a great deal of power if they organize to protest a practice. The protests against companies that did business in South Africa were the most widespread. The boycott against Nestlé, which we noted earlier, was one of the most successful. Similar protests against retailers and other businesses have also been successful, if less well publicized, and the threat of boycotts has effected changes in the way some multinationals do business. Those that value their reputations are much more conscious of the possibility of any shady actions being reported in the media and becoming the target of consumer watchdog groups.

Thus international business ethics is not only an area of academic discussion and research. In fact in many ways, there is less academic activity and research in this area of business ethics than there is corporate concern and popular activism. If followed, international codes, such as those of the UN and the Caux Principles, may help to provide a background for ethical corporate behavior, help to provide a level playing field for all competitors, and help to give people everywhere a standard against which to measure the performance of multinationals.

Global issues

The global issues of international business ethics remain largely unsolved. The destruction of the rain forest in some developing countries affects not only those countries and their people but also other countries and the world climate. Some countries, like Brazil, argue that the forest is theirs, that the developed countries have for the most part destroyed their own forests to build cities and develop, and that Brazil has the right to do whatever it deems best with its own resources. The counter is that the forest is being depleted in ways that are shortsighted, that cause more problems in the way of floods and unusable land than the good produced for the multinational lumber companies, and that the effect on the climate of other countries is not something that affects only Brazil.

The control of pollution in developing countries, especially when the pollution affects neighboring countries, is another bone of contention. Multinationals are often involved in both issues, although local companies are also. How to control pollution worldwide, how to lessen the use of chloroflurocarbons (CFCs) that deplete the ozone level, and how to equitably balance the right of countries to develop as they please with the right of other countries not to be harmed are all issues that have brought together representatives of multinationals, government bodies and heads of state, environmentalists, and leaders of many non-governmental organizations. These are large issues of international business ethics but they are issues of geopolitics as well. Businesses are major contributors to the problems, but individual businesses cannot solve them on their own. Governments as well must take some responsibility, and must be willing to pass and enforce appropriate legislation.

Conclusion

International business ethics cannot be simply the extension of any nation's business ethics. The issues with which it deals are diverse and involve practices in many parts of the world. As business becomes more and more international, some believe that the ethical and other values necessary for its efficient development will emerge with time, just as it has on the national level of most of the developed countries of the world. Whether this is the case remains to be seen.

In the meantime, various corporations, industries, groups, academics, governmental organizations, and international organizations of many kinds are working to clarify applicable ethical norms for international business, to provide incentives to ethical behavior on the part of multinationals, and to help form and implement background conditions necessary to support and sustain the ethical development of international business.

References

Arvedlund, E. 1997: Murder in Moscow. *Fortune*, March 3, 128–34.

Barnet, R. and Mueller, R. 1974: *Global Reach: The Power of Multinational Corporations*. New York: Simon & Schuster.

Baum, J., Jae, H. S., and Smith, C. 1995: Grease that sticks. *Far Eastern Economic Review*, March 23, 54–5.

Brull, S. 1995: Running scared in Seoul. *Business Week*, November 27, 52.

Carlton, J. 1993: Ties with China will be curbed by Levi Strauss. *Wall Street Journal*, May 4, A3.

Caux Round Table 1994: Principles for Business. Reprinted in 1995: *Business Ethics*, 9(3), May/June.

De George, R. T. 1993: *Competing with Integrity in International Business*. New York: Oxford University Press.

Dell, S. (ed.) 1990: *Draft United Nations Code of Conduct on Transnational Corporations as of Mid-1989. The United Nations and International Business*. Durham and London: UN Institute for Training and Research.

Dobbing, J. (ed.) 1988: *Infant Feeding: Anatomy of a Controversy, 1973–1984*. London: Springer-Verlag.

Donaldson, T. 1989: *The Ethics of International Business*. New York: Oxford University Press.

Krauz, M. and Meiland, J. W. (eds) 1982: *Relativism: Cognitive and Moral*. Notre Dame, Ind.: University of Notre Dame Press.

Mellow, C. 1995: Russia: Making cash from chaos. *Fortune*, April 17, 145–51.

Nestlé 1985: *The Dilemma of Third World Nutrition: Nestlé and the Role of Infant Formula*. Report prepared and distributed by Nestlé.

Noonan, J. T. Jr 1984: *Bribes*. New York: Macmillan.

Rawls, J. 1993: *Political Liberalism*. New York: Columbia University Press.

Sethi, S. P. 1994: *Multinational Corporations and the Impact of Public Advocacy on Corporate Strategy: Nestlé and the Infant Formula Controversy*. Boston: Kluwer Academic Publishers.

Stace, W. T. 1937: *The Concepts of Morals*. New York: Macmillan, chs 1 and 2.

Stanley, A. 1995: Russia's deadly business climate: To the many risks, add poisoning. *The New York Times*, August 9, A7.

TI (Transparency International) 1996: *Newsletter*. March, 1.

Wellman, C. 1963: The ethical implications of cultural relativism. *Journal of Philosophy*, 60, 169–184.

Williams, O. F. 1986: *The Apartheid Crisis: How We Can Do Justice in a Land of Violence*. San Francisco: Harper & Row.

20

Corporate moral agency

JOHN R. DANLEY

The problem of corporate moral agency is one aspect of a much broader set of concerns about the role of collectivities in explanations and descriptive models, in logic, in metaphysics, in law, and in ethical theory and social-political philosophy.

Collectivities include loosely assembled groups such as the passengers on the bus, a mob, a group of conspirators, the people of the USA, as well as more formally organized groups such as teams, the medical or legal profession, labor unions, churches, social clubs, corporations, and various forms of government. Although ordinary language involves frequent references to these entities, what we mean when we make judgments about collectivities is often far from clear. There are, for example, metaphysical, semantic and methodological perplexities.

- In what sense do these groups exist?
- To what do we refer when we speak of a collectivity, such as a corporation?
- Is there really an entity to which we refer, or is this noun merely some kind of placeholder which could be replaced by a list of the names of individuals?
- In explanations and descriptive models, what role will be played by references to collectivities?
- Do "real" explanations refer only to individual actors?

Lurking behind all these is the question of how to categorize different kinds of collectivities. Are there different kinds? How are they to be distinguished? Making normative judgments complicates matters even further. Does it make sense, for example, to blame "Germany" for the Holocaust during World War II, or "the German people," or a particular German citizen who opposed Hitler? (Martin Niemoller (1892–1984), for example, a minister in the Evangelical Church, became convinced of the collective guilt of Germans based on his experience during World War II. The Evangelical Church declared this in the "Stuttgart Confession of Guilt," 1945. Karl Jaspers (1947) also argued for collective guilt of the German people, in some sense, in *The Question of German Guilt*.) If it does make sense to lay blame, what does this mean? Or does it make sense to blame Corporation X for an oil spill? And if a collectivity is blamed, does the blame sometimes or always extend to the individual members of the group?

Disputes over four issues are particularly salient. One revolves around questions of the nature of and conditions for the ascription of moral rights, duties and responsibilities. Most of the concern has revolved around ascribing responsibility and blame.

Second, since most contend that to be held responsible for an event or state of affairs (usually an untoward one) an agent must have caused the event or state of affairs, the issue of corporate agency *per se* has been one important component of the larger discussion. This issue involves the question of the nature of agency or the nature of action. These two issues lead immediately to a third, which involves the question of the nature of the agent itself. Is the corporation the kind of thing which can act and be held responsible? Finally, a fourth issue involves the question of the nature of moral personhood. Is the corporation a moral person? Does the ascription of responsibility require as a subject a moral person?

Over the past two decades, debate in the field of business ethics has been shaped largely by the views of Peter French (1974, 1975, 1976, 1979, 1982a, 1982b, 1983a, 1983b, 1984a, 1984b, 1984c, 1985, 1991). French has vigorously defended the position that corporations are intentional actors, which is, he contends, necessary and sufficient for them to be held morally responsible; see also French et al. (1992). He claims, since they can be held morally accountable, they count as "full-fledged moral agents," i.e., moral persons. Even those who have attempted to defend an alternative, such as Manuel Valasquez (1982, 1983), Thomas Donaldson (1982) and Patricia Werhane (1985), have felt compelled to begin with criticisms of French's views.

Although French's views have been widely discussed, this should not be taken to mean that they are therefore the most widely held. On the contrary, French developed his views in opposition to what he describes as methodological individualism, one or another variant of which probably remains the orthodox or traditional view. French is not very clear about the precise nature of methodological individualism, and the target of his attacks seems to vary. At times, he appears to challenge those descriptive theories which attempt to explain events or states of affairs entirely in terms of the actions of individuals. At other times, French challenges moral or meta-ethical positions. For our purposes here, methodological individualism will not be associated with any particular view about explanation, but will be understood as any view which denies that corporations are moral persons. Some methodological individualists may claim that moral rights, duties and responsibilities may be ascribed to corporations or other collective entities, while others deny this.

As a backdrop against which to discuss and situate French's views, it will be useful to briefly develop the views of one very prominent theorist in social-political philosophy, Joel Feinberg, as an example of a methodological individualist (Feinberg, 1968, 1970, 1980a). Regrettably, the debate in business ethics has largely ignored the details of Feinberg's analysis.

Feinberg's "methodological individualism"

Reflecting on ordinary language, Feinberg (1970, pp. 129–39) notes that there are at least six different things which we might mean in ascribing responsibility, i.e., in saying "Jones is responsible for . . ." (Both Donaldson (1982) and Werhane (1985) develop views which would count as methodological individualism on this account. Werhane describes her position as ontological individualism, meaning that only individuals are moral persons, but methodological collectivism, asserting that we can legitimately ascribe to collectivities agency and moral predicates, such as responsibility. Werhane distinguishes primary and secondary actions, relying upon a distinction which is captured in the notion of vicarious agency or vicarious responsibility.) Of Feinberg's list of six, French focuses only upon a narrow subset of these. The first three involve various forms of ascribing agency or causation, as when we say, for instance, "A variation in the jet stream is responsible for the drought," "Jones is responsible for the door being closed," or "Corporation X is responsible for the bridge being built." There are at least three other senses of responsibility, two involving imputations of fault, the other ascriptions of liability. These three reflect different stages in the logic of holding agents responsible. All "ascribe agency, simple or (more commonly) causal, for a some-how defective or faulty action" (French, 1984c, p. 136). But in the first stage, "we simply note that the act is Jones's [Corporation X's] and that it was in some way faulty or defective." In this sense, however, the agent is not necessarily faulted or blamed. Thus, in some contexts, to say that "Jones is responsible for dropping the ball" is to say nothing more than "Jones dropped the ball," with no fault or blame attaching to the agent (French, 1984c, p. 128). Similarly, one can imagine saying that "Union Carbide is responsible for the destruction and death at Bhopal," but asserting no blame, only identifying Union Carbide (as opposed to Corporation Y) as the agent involved in the defective act. In the second stage, however, we move toward laying fault with Jones when we assert that Jones is responsible for dropping the ball in the sense of saying "Jones fumbled the ball." The same move can be made with corporations. In these instances, we are resorting to the language of defeasible ascriptions, akin to defeasible claims in law. Defeasible claims are claims which can be defeated by providing relevant evidence of sufficient strength. Thus, in ascribing responsibility in this sense, it is as if we are bringing charges against someone. It is as if one is "registering the defective performance on the actor's record" or marking it against one's reputation (French, 1984c, p. 128). In the language of baseball, for instance, this is the difference between merely stating that the shortstop dropped the ball, and judging that the shortstop committed an error.

In the third stage, assuming that we can make the charge stick that the agent was not capable of defeating our charge, Feinberg claims that "we may put the record or reputation, with the fault being duly registered, to any one of a great variety of uses, including among other things, overt blame" (French, 1984c, p. 128). This is the sense of responsibility as the ascription of liability. To claim that one is liable is to claim that one is properly subject to particular kinds of responses. If the charge of liability is not defeated in some way (e.g., mental incompetency, some kind of justification), the ascription of responsibility in this sense may open the door to yet further moves in which we require the responsible party to be punished, to pay compensation, and so forth. Determining responsibility is important insofar as it may constitute a prolegomena to these other steps.

Our motivation in determining whether something is "charged against our record" (i.e., whether an agent is to be held responsible) arises, Feinberg emphasizes, from very practical considerations. First of all, we only initiate the process of determining respons-ibility if something has attracted our attention; usually, only after something quite bad has happened. Second, we have practical motives for determining why something has happened. In baseball, we keep records to appraise the strengths and weaknesses of players and teams, to make predictions about behavior, and to develop strategies to best respond. Similarly, in our social lives, we need to appraise certain characteristics and traits of entities in our environment, determining, for example, whether an infliction of harm was the result of lack of skill or ability, improper care or effort, or improper intention, and we need to be able to make predictions about future behavior and to develop appropriate strategies. Thus, and third, depending upon the nature of the defective behavior, we will respond in appropriate ways – another very practical consideration. Namely, we are concerned, in large measure, with discouraging certain behaviors, traits and characteristics. Generally, we judge intentional harm severely, since this would suggest an agent needing special attention. Hence, holding an agent responsible is a critical institution serving important practical social purposes. No less is involved when we attempt to ascribe liability to corporate entities.

When dealing with collective responsibility, Feinberg's (1968) model is relatively simple. There is no need to posit additional moral agents to make sense of such ascriptions of responsibility. Feinberg begins with what he calls "the standard case" of holding someone responsible (French, 1984c, p. 674), involving contributory fault. Briefly, we ascribe contributory fault when an agent did the harmful thing, the action was faulty (deviated from some standard for behavior), and the faulty action really did cause the harmful outcome. Intentional harm is only a species of contributory harm.

Beyond the standard cases in which we ascribe responsibility (and blame), Feinberg extends his analysis to include cases of "strict liability," where one or the other of the conditions for establishing contributory fault is weakened or absent. In these cases, even though we use the language of responsibility, the meaning of the locutions is interpreted slightly differently. Vicarious and collective liability are considered as species of strict liability. Vicarious responsibility is when contributory fault, or some element of it, is properly ascribed to one party, but liability is ascribed to a different party (e.g. principal and agent relationship, employer and employee relationship). Vicarious responsibility is the model for many (perhaps most) cases in which we ascribe responsibility to corporations. Larry May (1983) follows this line in analyzing ascriptions of responsibility. In May's words (p. 69) "corporations have the peculiar property of only being able to act vicariously."

However, there are instances in which we use ascription of responsibility to collectivities which do not fit. Rather than ignore these, or to claim that they are without real meaning, Feinberg also examines three kinds of ascriptions of responsibility which do not conform to these standard and derivative cases:

1 Liability with noncontributory fault
2 Contributory fault: collective and distributive
3 Contributory fault: collective and non-distributive

Feinberg gives as an example of the first: a case in which a friend, driving home from a party after having a little too much to drink, injures a pedestrian as a result of impaired skills. We might say that "We are as guilty [responsible] as he is," which sounds extravagant, but this probably means only that we share the same defective behavior, even though we did not contribute to the harm, perhaps because of our good fortune. This is not a vacuous concern, and such defective behavior should be registered, because it is productive of harm. One might make a similar claim of corporate entities in certain situations. "Corporation X is as guilty [responsible] as Corporation Y for . . ." It is much like saying "There is an accident waiting to happen."

Regarding the second kind of collective responsibility, Feinberg discusses three different kinds of cases. One of most interesting is the case in which "harm is to be ascribed to some feature of the common culture consciously endorsed and participated in by every member of the group" (French, 1984c, p. 683). If the culture of a group is racist, and this racism contributes to harmful action, Feinberg says "wouldn't it make sense to say that the group was collectively responsible for this?" (p. 683). At least some talk about corporations being responsible for this or that may fit this model.

The third case is noteworthy because it involves what Feinberg claims to be a model "for a thousand crises in history of our corporate lives" (p. 687). Feinberg has in mind cases in which some harms arise as a result of group faults, perhaps as a result of the way in which a group or corporation is organized, but the blame cannot be distributed to all members. Perhaps some members, however, with the power or opportunity to overcome the defective organization, would be ascribed responsibility.

The point of this rather lengthy discussion of Feinberg is to illustrate how at least one prominent theorist handles collective and corporate responsibility without invoking the idea that corporations are moral persons, and without venturing far into discussions of intentionality and *mens rea*. In a later piece, Feinberg (1980a, p. 172) makes the point explicitly, claiming that "when an institution has a duty to an outsider, there is always some determinant human being whose duty it is to do something for the outsider." Hence, he concludes, "there is no need to posit any individual superperson named by the expression 'the State' (or for that matter, 'the company,' 'the club,' or 'the church')" (p. 173).

French and his critics

Although French rails against methodological individualism, he fails to demonstrate the inadequacy of an analysis like Feinberg's. Nor is French's foundational theory without serious difficulties. His position involves at least four key claims. His first claim is about the nature of the corporate entity, identified by and distinguished from other collectivities by having a corporate internal decision structure (CIDS). The CIDS contains two important elements:

- An organizational or responsibility flowchart that "delineates stations and managerial levels, and plots the lines of authority, subordination, and dependence among and between such stations with the organization"
- Corporate decision recognition rules, i.e., the procedural rules and the policies structure (French, 1984c, p. 41)

His second claim is that decisions can be described as corporate intentional acts if (and only if) they arise in accord with the CIDS (French, 1984c, pp. 39, 46). His third claim is that there are only two necessary and sufficient conditions for ascription of moral responsibility (and blame):

- An agent must have caused some untoward event or state of affairs to come about.
- The agent must have intended the event or state of affairs to occur.

Given French's second claim, that corporations can act intentionally, it follows that moral responsibility can be ascribed to corporations but not to more loosely organized collectivities (French, 1984c, p. 7). However, even if one were to agree that we can ascribe intentional actions to corporations, and even if one were to agree that this is all that is required to ascribe moral responsibility, why would French claim that corporations are moral persons? This move is by definition fiat. His fourth key claim is that a moral person is "the subject of a right," that a moral person is defined as "the referent of any proper name or of any noneliminable nature of a subject in an ascription of moral responsibility" (French, 1984c, p. 38). This amounts to saying that any entity which is an intentional actor is not merely a subject of a responsibility ascription but also a moral person. Thus, and surprisingly, French leaps from ascribing responsibility to the corporation to the idea that a corporation is a moral person. Not surprisingly, criticisms have developed along most of the major lines of French's analysis.

Corporations and other collectivities

Even the first claim is not entirely without controversy, though many, even Feinberg, appeal to something like CIDS in attempting to distinguish among different kinds of collectivities. French explicates the CIDS in terms of H. L. A. Hart's discussion of how to recognize law, and French's account has clear parallels in the way the law, in some cases, recognizes corporate acts (French, 1984c, pp. 56–66). However, French's failure to reference specific organizational theorists makes it difficult to understand with which organizational models French's view is consistent. French's views might be construed to be consistent with what Herbert Simon (1965) called "formal organizations," in contrast with much more loosely connected collectivities. Others, such as Peter Drucker (1946), might scoff at this notion of a formal organization as idealistic, though French invokes Drucker's account as if he believes that it is consistent with his own. Donaldson sees Drucker's account as a competing one. The issue here is not merely how to distinguish between different kinds of collectivities, but how to best to model the corporation. Both Donaldson (1982, pp. 23–30) and Werhane (1985, pp. 40–6) provide brief but useful overviews of alternative accounts of the nature of the corporation.

Problems with the CIDS

Difficulties in interpreting the CIDS is a serious problem for French because of its central role. Difficulties reverberate through all other aspects of French's theory, because in the second claim, for instance, French links the notion of intentional action with one arising in accord with the CIDS, and, in the third, he links the conditions for ascription of moral responsibility to intentional action. "Link" is too weak; an outcome of the corporate CIDS, intentionality, and moral responsibility are coextensively equivalent. Critics can challenge each concept, as well as French's attempt to link these as he does.

In "Corporate moral agency: The case for anthropological bigotry," by focusing on the CIDS, John Danley (1980) attacked both claims and attempted to place French on the horns of a dilemma. On the one hand, Danley claimed, if French strictly adheres

248

to the claim that corporate actions must arise in accord with the CIDS, then many of the decisions which we would like to include as actions of the corporation could not be included on French's account. Danley urged a less idealistic and more "positivistic account," one which accords more with the reality of corporate decision making. One clear example of this general problem concerns the corporate charter, an important component of the CIDS. While corporate charters are extremely permissive, allowing actions "for any lawful purpose," any decision which produced an unlawful action would therefore violate the CIDS and could not count as an intentional action of the corporation. Thus, it is not clear that French's angelic corporation can do anything illegal! Yet, on the other hand, Danley claims, if French relaxes his account, then it becomes increasingly difficult to know just which decisions should be counted as corporate decisions. Too many decisions could be countenanced as corporate actions.

While French devotes substantial attention to addressing this problem (French, 1984c, pp. 54–66), the adequacy of his response is arguable. French is quite correct in claiming that his account cannot become too positivistic, because it would lose its normative force (p. 55); clearly, not all decisions can be licensed as descriptions of corporate intentional actions. French claims that, even within organizations which are "loosely" non-hierachially organized (French uses the example of Gore Associates), there are sufficiently precise recognitors to determine what will count as a corporate decision (p. 65). In attempting to respond to the problem arising from the corporate charter's reference to "any lawful purpose," French moves to briefly discuss the *ultra vires* and business judgment rule, and then appeals to the Ford Pinto case in which Ford was charged with criminal reckless homicide. In the end, though, French offers no solution, and without a way of clearly determining which decisions will count as corporate actions, the entire enterprise falters.

There is a certain irony in French's exclusive reliance upon the CIDS in ascribing intentional actions because it reveals that French is following a line of analysis of action sentences which was rejected by H. L. A. Hart (1948), even though French adopts Hart's account of identifying law in explicating the CIDS. For Hart, and for Feinberg, who modifies Hart's account, not only should some ascriptions of responsibility be understood as defeasible, but ascriptions of action should be as well. Statements ascribing actions are not descriptive statements like "This is a piece of earth," Hart suggests, but defeasible statements, such as the legal claim "This is my property." Action statements are ascribed to agents for very practical reasons, and just as property claims, they are defeasible. Ascribing an action to an agent, like ascribing responsibility or blame, is tantamount to bringing a charge against someone. In law, there is an elaborate set of institutionalized moves one makes to determine whether, indeed, "This is my property" is true. Yet, French treats "This is an intentional action of the corporation" as if were is a descriptive statement, and all one needs to do is to determine whether, in fact, the CIDS was followed; and if one takes that line, one must carefully and precisely delineate the CIDS, which French has not.

The law does not rely exclusively upon anything like the CIDS in determining whether to count something as a corporate act. In ordinary cases, it might. For example, the law takes as a corporate criminal action the action of an employee who, when using a particular procedure to flush out a barge, spills petroleum into the river, even though the corporation has a written policy against using this procedure, has trained and warned employees to use other procedures, has reprimanded those employees who have failed to comply, and even though the corporation has previously warned and reprimanded this employee. The law may take as actions of the corporation things which are of legitimate public policy considerations, though these actions may have little relevance to whether there has been adherence to decision procedures. Indeed, one purpose of beginning to count a certain class of actions as corporate actions may well be to modify the decision procedures of corporations, even when the corporation could not be faulted for the existing CIDS. In this way, the law attempts to modify behavior and to bring about changes in the corporate internal decision procedures themselves.

This discussion suggests two other problems for French. First, if French gives full reign to the law in determining the nature of the CIDS, then his moral person is nothing more than a superfluous shadow of the legal entity created by law. Second, there are limits to what the law can legitimately do when dealing with competent adult moral persons by virtue of the fact that they are moral persons. What limits would French impose on the law's treatment of corporations? One of the reasons most of us have no qualms about manipulating what will count as liable actions of the corporation is because we view corporations in a purely instrumental fashion, not as moral persons. Any objection to implementing a policy which imposes new liabilities on a corporation is rooted in our concern that the policy might unfairly harm the interests of particular human moral persons or the interests of a class of human persons (e.g. stockholders, employees, debt holders, etc.). Claims that regulation might have an adverse indirect impact on the economy have force because that also involves jeopardizing the interests of human moral persons. However, without identifying some such interest, the objection would be without merit. To paraphrase Meir Dan-Cohen's (1986) theory of organizational rights, we use "utilitarianism for corporations, Kantianism for people;" see especially Dan-Cohen (1986, ch. 5). If corporations are moral persons, then there should be some limits to our treating them in purely instrumental ways. French provides none; there is no basis for drawing any limits, since being a moral person for French amounts to nothing more than being an entity which acts intentionally, and anything can count as an intentional action as long as some procedure is followed.

Morality, formal organizations and other external constraints

Writing prior to French, John Ladd (1976), in "Morality and the ideal of rationality in formal organizations," argues from premises very similar to those later developed by French, but draws a radically different conclusion. Ladd appears to agree with the first two, if not the first three, of French's key claims. By building upon the model of a formal organization developed by Herbert Simon (1965) in his classic *Administrative Behavior*, Ladd's account of the corporation appears quite consistent with French's. Further, Ladd seems to agree that it makes sense to describe corporations as intentional actors, although Ladd's concern is with corporate rationality, not intentionality as such. Organizational rationality consists in achieving certain goals efficiently and effectively. Ladd may even share with French his view of the conditions for ascribing moral responsibility, but, Ladd argues, there is no room for moral considerations in the deliberations of these organizations. Hence, formal organizations cannot be expected to act in accord with ordinary moral principles. By implication, Ladd may be claiming that corporate behavior cannot even be judged in terms of moral concepts. In other words, they are not morally responsible, and it is not appropriate to either blame or praise their behavior.

The locus of the dispute between French, Ladd and others appears to be over the sorts of things which formal organizations may take into consideration, rather than disputes about the nature of ascription of responsibility, or moral personhood. Donaldson (1982, pp. 30–35), Werhane (1985, pp. 49–59), Kenneth Goodpaster (Goodpaster and Matthews, 1982) and others emphasize the extent to which moral considerations can and should become a part of the corporation's reasoning. Goodpaster ascribes moral responsibility to corporations on the basis of their ability to manifest rationality and treat others with respect, but sees no reason to posit personhood. For Donaldson, a corporation is not a moral agent unless it structures itself to have this capacity.

One possible weakness of these views is that they tend to focus only upon constraints which are internal to the organization and give little consideration to factors in the environment of the corporation. By shifting the focus, others have defended the conclusion reached by Ladd from a different perspective. If one emphasizes external constraints, such as those in a competitive market, then one might argue that corporations can do little other than to respond to economic threats and opportunities (at least in the long term). In that environment, there is no discretion to act otherwise, and it would be unrealistic to expect nonmarket considerations (such as moral considerations) to play any role at all in the decisions of the corporation. There is a growing consensus that this is an increasingly accurate description of the climate in the USA and in global markets today. Kaysen (1996) makes the point (in his introduction) that the consensus is that the so-called large modern corporation today has little discretion given market forces at work. In fact, in such an environment, it may make no sense even to bring moral judgments to bear on organizations. As many have noted, before it makes sense to allege that an agent ought to do something, it should be possible for the agent to discharge the duty.

Problems with the concept of intentional

In general, two lines of criticism have evolved in relation to the concept of intentionality. On the one hand, Danley (1984, pp. 143–4), Donaldson (1982, p. 22), Werhane (1985, pp. 36–40) and Velasquez (1983) have all raised questions about the application of the concept of intentionality to corporations in particular, and to organizations in general. Danley, for example, suggested that the sense of intention used in connection with corporate behavior may well be different than that used when assessing the actions of moral persons. For instance, the sense in which I intend P-K4 in a chess match would seem to be a quite different sense than the sense in which a computer intends P-K4, or a corporation intends something (French, 1984c, p. 144). If so, French may be involved in equivocating in the second and third claims.

On the other hand, Donaldson notes that we also speak of animals acting intentionally, but Donaldson claims that he would not hold his cat morally responsible for intentional actions (nor would he consider his cat to be a moral agent merely because it can be said to be have acted intentionally). Werhane develops this line of criticism most extensively, noting that Daniel Dennett defines an intentional system as one whose behavior "can be – at least sometimes – explained and predicted by relying on ascriptions to the system of beliefs and desires ..." In short, we ascribe intentional behavior to such systems. Werhane's point is that being an intentional system, in this sense, is not the same sense as that required for ascribing moral responsibility to agents (or systems) or for claiming that these are moral persons (French, 1984c, p. 38).

French does not respond to the objection that the sense of "intentional" involved in intentional systems and organizations may be quite different than that involved in discussing other agents. This remains a serious problem for him. French does attempt to respond to the challenge posed by Donaldson's cat, but his very brief retort appears to introduce, in an *ad hoc* fashion, two additional necessary conditions for the ascription of responsibility. Donaldson's cat and other lower animals should be excluded from the class of moral persons, French claims, because, while they may behave intentionally, "they can neither appreciate that an event for which their intentional or unintentional behavior has been causally responsible is either untoward or worthy nor intentionally modify their way of behaving to correct the offensive actions or to adopt the behavior that was productive of their worthy results" (French, 1984c, p. 166). French does not discuss the requirement that ascription of moral responsibility involves that an agent "appreciate" an event in any other place, nor does it seem to follow as a corollary to his CIDS. While individuals in the corporation may appreciate events, it is not clear that the CIDS licenses descriptions of self-awareness to the corporation. Donaldson's objection stands.

The requirement that an entity be capable of modifying its behavior is discussed below, in the context of French's "principle of responsive adjustment." Suffice it to say here, Donaldson's cat might be said to modify its behavior as well. More importantly, this modification creates other difficulties for French, detailed below.

Linking responsibility and intentionality

While Feinberg's treatment of collective responsibility begins with the standard case of contributory fault, of which intentional wrongdoing would be a subset, French and many others begin with intentional wrongdoing as the standard case. For some reason, treating of *moral* responsibility tempts many to the assumption that this must be the standard case, as if we should not be held morally responsible for nonintentional contributory harm! Velasquez (1983) makes this assumption, holding up the importance of the *mens rea* in common law criminal cases. Velasaquez then concludes that corporations cannot be intentional actors in the requisite sense of having intentionality or *mens rea*.

One of the most serious problems associated with making intentional wrongdoing the standard case for moral responsibility is that actors are not morally responsible for a broad range of classes of wrongdoing which do not involve intentionality. What of criminal negligence or recklessness, for instance, or civil negligence or recklessness? Apparently sensitive to this problem, French modifies his view to accept what he calls the "extended principle of accountability (EPA)," which would hold an agent responsible for unintended effects of actions, provided the agent knew or should have known the consequences of the act (French, 1984c, p. 132). This is an attempt to extend, belatedly, the ascription of responsibility to reincorporate many of the kinds of cases which Feinberg includes within contributory fault. In another place, French moves to further extend the ascription of responsibility by developing what he calls the "principle of responsive adjustment," which contends that we are to hold agents responsible (in a rather strange backward sense) for untoward events if the agent fails to make adjustments for harm causing behavior (French, 1984c, p. 154). It is as if we could undo our past liability by mending our ways.

French will doubtlessly need to develop other modifications, otherwise he will not be able to explain why we hold corporations responsible (in ordinary language, law, and morality) for a wide range of nonintentional contributory faults which cause harm. However, it is not merely a matter of arriving at the same position from a different starting point. French must insist on first identifying corporations as moral persons and intentional agents, and only then extend responsibility toward nonintentional actions. One consequence of this is that he will be unable to make any sense of ascribing responsibility to collectivities which do not possess a CIDS.

Responsibility and other collectivities

Rather than attempting a sympathetic understanding of the meaning of rather frequent ascriptions of responsibility and blame to collectivities which do not possess a CIDS, French merely claims that moral "responsibility predicates cannot be legitimately ascribed to aggregate collectivities" (French, 1984c, p. 10). This is a strength of Feinberg's analysis, as explained earlier, and Larry May (1983, 1989, 1990, 1992, 1994) has done much to add to our understanding of such ascriptions in a way which is not inconsistent with Feinberg's suggestions. Using the notion of "solidarity," for example, May relies upon the model of vicarious responsibility to attribute responsibility to mobs and members in the mob. (May still seems to feel the need to find something to allow ascription of an intention to a mob, however.)

Corporations as moral persons

There are at least two kinds of objections which can be raised against French's view that the conditions for the ascription of moral responsibilities are the same as the conditions for ascription of moral personhood. One is that his position leads to counterintuitive consequences. The second is that French's conception of a moral person is inarticulated and undefended. These are not unrelated. When French responds to critics who draw implications, French's responses ring hollow and *ad hoc*, precisely because he says nothing about moral personhood.

Danley, Donaldson, Werhane and others, for instance, follow the first line, claiming that French's view leads to counterintuitive consequences. Danley (1980, pp. 145–7) argued that ascribing responsibility to corporations and pretending that they are moral persons disrupts the logic of moral discourse, threatening to reduce human moral persons to second-class citizens in the expanded moral community. The language of responsibility is a part of the broader logic which is often a prelude to praising or blaming. However, Danley argues, attempting to extract compensation or to punish corporations creates difficulties unlike those associated with ordinary moral persons. Indeed, punishing corporations involves punishing individuals (e.g., employees, stockholders). Hence, corporations may benefit from being given the status of moral personhood, but human moral persons are left with the costs.

Donaldson (1982, pp. 22–3) claims that if corporations are moral persons, then they should be entitled to vote, and to receive social security benefits. Indeed, do they have a right to worship as they please and to pursue happiness? French claims that any theory which would have that as a consequence would not only be "implausible" but "stupid" (French, 1984c, p. 170). French claims that twelve-year-olds may be moral persons but that they neither have the right to vote nor to draw social security benefits. French claims that the right to vote and to draw social security benefits are instances of legislated rights, and that rights are always specific to a particular institutional context. Decisions regarding ascription of such rights are made in accord with the rules of the relevant institutions. As French notes, beings incapable of intentional action may even receive benefits. French also claims that it makes no sense to claim that corporations have any natural rights since they are not natural persons.

While French's response may be correct, insofar as it goes, he seems to have missed the deeper point. When an entity enjoys the status of moral personhood in a country, we expect that the law will make appropriate accommodations. The problem with French's account is that we have no idea what kind of accommodations would be appropriate. (This is the flip side of the problem of not knowing what kind of limits to impose on intrusions into the corporate moral person.) Of course, we do not give social security benefits to twelve-year olds, but we do give them to 70-year-olds, provided that they meet certain other qualifications. Why not seventy-year-old corporations? If corporations are moral agents, should we not require that they pay into the system for themselves, making them eligible at 62 or 65? This raises the more general issue that French really has not referenced any literature on the concept of moral persons, nor has he given us any guidance about what is involved in the concept of moral person. French's contention that being an intentional actor is a necessary and sufficient condition for moral personhood is extreme, in comparison to most other criteria. Feinberg (1980b), for example, identifies the notion of personhood in ordinary language, what he calls commonsense personhood. An entity is considered a commonsense person if it possesses a number of characteristics, such as being capable of experiencing pain and pleasure, has emotions, has a concept of self, is self-conscious, can plan and can act on a plan. Feinberg then defends the idea that this is the concept which we should adopt for moral personhood, against four other proposals. No other plausible proposal resembles French's.

Conclusion

While the debate over corporate moral agency, responsibility and personhood initiated by French has done much to call attention to important issues which might have otherwise gone unexplored, the evidence does not suggest that his view provides a viable alternative to the traditional conceptions of methodological individualism.

References

Dan-Cohen, M. 1986: *Rights, Persons, and Organisations*. Berkeley, California: University of California Press.

Danley, J. R. 1980: Corporate moral agency: The case for anthropological bigotry. In M. Bradie and M. Brand (eds), *Action and Responsiblity*, Bowling Green State University Conference in Applied Philosophy, Bowling Green, Ohio: Applied Philosophy Program: 140–9.

Donaldson, T. 1982: *Corporations and Morality*. Englewood Cliffs, NJ: Prentice-Hall, Inc.

Drucker, P. 1946: *Concept of a Corporation*. New York: John Day.

Feinberg, J. 1968: Collective responsibility. *The Journal of Philosophy*, 65, 674–88.

Feinberg, J. 1970: Action and responsibility. In J. Feinberg (ed.), *Doing and Deserving*, Princeton, NJ: Princeton University Press, 119–51.

Feinberg, J. 1980a: *Rights, Justice, and the Bounds of Liberty: Essays in Social Philosophy*. Princeton, NJ: Princeton University Press.

Feinberg, J. 1980b: On Abortion. In T. Regan (ed.), *Matters of Life and Death*, 2nd edn. New York: Random House, 256–93.

French, P. A. 1974: Morally blaming whole populations. In V. Held, S. Morgenbesser, and T. Nagel (eds), *Philosophy, Morality, and International Affairs*. London: Oxford University Press: 266–85.

French, P. A. 1975: Types of collectivities and blame. *Personalist*, 56(Spring), 160–9.

French, P. A. 1976: Senses of "blame." *Southern Journal of Philosophy*, 14(Winter), 443–52.

French, P. A. 1979: The corporation as a moral person. *American Philosophical Quarterly*, 3, 207–15.

French, P. A. 1982a: What is Hamlet to McDonnell-Douglas or McDonnell-Douglas to Hamlet: DC-10? *Journal of Business & Professional Ethics*, 1(Winter), 1–14.

French, P. A. 1982b: Crowds and corporations. *American Philosophical Quarterly*, 19(July), 271–8.

French, P. A. 1983a: Individual and corporate responsibility. *Business & Professional Ethics Journal*, 2(Summer), 89–93.

French, P. A. 1983b: Kinds and persons. *Philosophy and Phenomenological Research*, 44(December), 241–54.

French, P. A. 1984a: A principle of responsive adjustment. *Philosophy*, 59, 491–504.

French, P. A. 1984b: The principle of responsive adjustment in corporate moral responsibility: The crash on Mount Erebus. *Journal of Business Ethics*, 3(May), 101–11.

French, P. A. 1984c: *Collective and Corporate Responsibility*. New York: Columbia University Press.

French, P. A. 1985: The Hester Prynne sanction. *Business and Professional Ethics Journal*, 4(Winter), 19–32.

French, P. A. 1991: *The Spectrum of Responsibility*. New York: St Martin's Press.

French, P. A., Nesteruk J., and Risser D. T. 1992: *Corporations in the Moral Community*. New York: Hartcourt Brace Janovich.

Goodpaster, K. E. and Matthews J. B. Jr 1982: Can a corporation have a conscience? *Harvard Business Review*, (January–February).

Hart, H. L. A. 1948: The ascription of responsibilities and rights. *Proceedings of the Aristotelian Society*. New Series, 49, 171–94.

Jaspers, K. 1947: *The Question of German Guilt*. New York: Dial Press.

Kaysen, C. (ed.) 1996: *The American Corporation Today: Examining the Questions of Power and Efficiency at the Century's End*. New York: Oxford University Press.

Ladd, J. 1970: Morality and the ideal of rationality in formal organizations. *The Monist*, 54, 488–516.

255

May, L. 1983: Vicarious agency and corporate responsiblity. *Philosophical Studies*, 43(January), 69–82.

May, L. 1989: Mobs and collective responsibility. In C. Peden and J. P. Sterba (eds), *Freedom, Equality, and Social Change*, Lewiston, NY: Edwin Mellen Press, 300–11.

May, L. 1990: Collective action and shared responsibility. *Nous*, 24(April), 269–77.

May, L. 1992: *Sharing Responsibility*. Chicago: University of Chicago Press.

May, L. 1994: Men in groups: Collective responsibility for rape. *Hypatia*, 9(Spring).

Simon, H. A. 1965: *Administrative Behavior* (2nd edn). New York: Free Press.

Valasquez, M. G. 1982: *Business Ethics: Concepts and Cases*. Englewood Cliffs, NJ: Prentice-Hall, 20–33.

Valasquez, M. G. 1983: Why corporations are not morally responsible for anything they do. *Business & Professional Ethics Journal*, 2(Spring), 1–18.

Werhane, P. H. 1985: *Persons, Rights, & Corporations*. Englewood Cliffs, NJ: Prentice-Hall.

21

Employee rights

RONALD DUSKA

Does drug testing violate an employee's right to privacy? Should companies be able to fire employees without cause? Is there a right to a safe workplace? All of these questions revolve around the notion of employee rights, one of the most important in business ethics. Much recent legislation has been passed which specifies employees' rights and which regulates working conditions, hiring and firing procedures, harassment and a host of other areas. There has been so much regulation and so many assertions of rights, recently, that some critics bemoan what they see as an unwarranted proliferation of rights. Sometimes, rights seem to be created out of thin air. Opponents of those critics, however, are not concerned about a proliferation of rights, but rather see the articulations of new rights as an inevitable product of a society's concern for preserving and protecting human dignity. Defenders of the expansion of rights follow the lead of Judge Blackstone (1941) who in Book I of his famous *Commentaries on the Law*, asserts that "The principal aim of society is to protect individuals in the enjoyment of those absolute rights, which were vested in them by the immutable laws of nature, but which could not be preserved in peace, without the mutual assistance and intercourse of social communities. The primary end of human laws is to maintain and regulate these absolute rights of individuals."

From Blackstone's perspective, our human laws, rather than proliferating rights arbitrarily, are doing exactly what they are supposed to be doing – identifying and specifying human rights which were never before articulated, particularly in the workplace and particularly for the employee.

The purpose of this essay is to examine the nature of rights and their application in the workplace.

A right can be defined as either a capacity, possession, or condition of existence which entitles either an individual or group to the enjoyment of some object or state of being. For example, the right to free speech is a condition of existence which entitles one to express one's thoughts as one sees fit. Of course, if someone has a right, someone else must have an obligation to respect that right. Hence, a right is a relational entity. In the case of employee rights, there are correlative employer obligations. However, employers have rights too, so that there are also employee duties. However, in this essay we will concentrate on employee rights, rather than the rights of other groups. First, though, we need a clearer idea about what rights are.

Quite simply, rights are entitlements by virtue of which one person justifiably lays claim to an object or state of being against another person, who has an obligation to respect that claim. One respects a claim either by providing the object claimed, assisting in the achievement of the state of being claimed, or, at the very least, not standing in the way of the obtaining of the object or the achieving of the state of being. We add the qualification that the claim is justified, for one could claim a right that was not justified, and, in that case, it would not be a right. Thus, asserting a right carries with it the belief that the entitlement claim is justified. Thus, if an employee has a right to a safe workplace, that employee is justified in claiming that right, and in expecting and demanding that his or her employer meet certain standards in setting up the employee's work area.

Rights are secured either by nature, human laws or societal conventions, including a grant or a purchase. That being so, we can distinguish between three possible types of rights: natural, conventional or civil (legal). Philosophers and jurists split on the issue of whether nature secures any rights. Positivists who deny the existence of natural rights and reduce moral law to the ethos and customs of various societies, necessarily claim that there are only customary (conventional) rights or legal rights, rights which are the result of legislation. Hence, rights apply only to those whom the laws or traditions designate. The difficulty with this positivist position is that, if it were true, every system of rights would be self-legitimating and there could be no claims of natural rights or objective moral rights by which one can evaluate the soundness of the laws or the conventions. Hence, there would be no framework of rights with which to criticize a regime that took away rights from one or another group, e.g. gays, women, Jews.

Those who claim that there are universal rights and that some legal systems such as those which permit slavery are immoral and violate moral rights, must maintain that rights are grounded somehow in the nature of things, or in some sort of objective moral code. Most people implicitly recognize or appeal to such a higher set of rights, called moral rights or natural rights.

But what would those natural rights be grounded in? The most basic grounding would be in the needs of human beings. One is entitled, or has a right, to those things which are necessary for a quality existence. This was the method of philosophically grounding rights in western cultures from the time of Socrates to the modern era, called Natural Law theory. For example, Aquinas, in the thirteenth century, with respect to the right of property asserted that "Whatever is held in superabundance is owed by natural right to those in need." John Locke (1960) in the seventeenth century echoed Aquinas, and argued for the natural rights to life, liberty and property. In line with the theories of Locke, the writers of the American Declaration of Independence claimed basic rights to life, liberty and the pursuit of happiness. For them, as for Locke, these rights were grounded in the fact that our dignity arises from our being children of God. Further, the existence of these rights, and the equality of all men, was thought to be a self-evident truth.

However, Locke added to the right to property argument a consideration of fairness. It is only fair that people be entitled to that for which they work. The notion of a right to property based on need begins to fade with the development of Capitalism, and the later enlightenment figures such as David Hume are skeptical of the self-evidence claim and attempt to ground rights without an appeal to God or Nature. This leads to a more modern approach from either a deontological or utilitarian perspective. Either rights flow from the basic equality and dignity of humans – Immanuel Kant grounds them in the fact that rational beings are ends in themselves – or they flow from the natural needs of humans which must be met to maximize happiness (John Stuart Mill).

Of course, the Utilitarian, Jeremy Bentham (1941) refers to rights as "nonsense on stilts," since from his point of view, the word "right" is just shorthand for securing those actions which will bring about that greatest happiness. From Bentham's perspective one finds rights, not by consulting a catalogue of rights, but by examining whether behavior such as respecting peoples' property leads to more pleasure than pain. His successor, John Stuart Mill grounds rights in the same way. Mill defends the existence of a right to liberty by demonstrating that a society which allows its members to express themselves freely will be a society that is better off (happier) than a society which does not allow such self expression.

Deontologists, following Kant, would maintain that the difficulty with this position is that it makes the rights of individuals susceptible to revocation if they no longer serve the needs of the society. This is incompatible with the notion of inalienable or indefeasible rights, where inalienable means those incapable of being surrendered or transferred, and indefeasible means not capable of being annulled, voided or undone. Of course, Marx, critiquing Kant's individualism maintained that rights are egoistic since they give the individual predominance over the community. Sides of this debate can be seen in contemporaries such as H. L. A. Hart (1955) and Ronald Dworkin (1978).

Whatever the grounding of rights, there are certain other aspects of rights theory that must be mentioned. It is often held that for every right there is a correlative duty. Hence, if I have rights to life and liberty, others have a duty to respect that right and not interfere with my life and liberty.

Since rights is a relational concept, the elucidation of the rights will reflect the view of the relationship. So while in England and Europe, the predominant view of the employer–employee relationship was that of master–servant, with its consequent rights and obligations, in the USA the predominant view of the relationship was as a quasi contractual or implied contractual relationship. Some Pacific Rim countries, of course, have their own cultural version of some sort of quasi familial relationship, with their consequent rights and obligations. Thus, the list of employee rights will vary according to the predominant image of the relationship. For example, if one views the relationship in feudal terms such as lord and serf, then while the serf has few claims to private property and independence, he has large claims to protection and sustenance.

The reciprocity of rights and duties leads to a distinction between positive and negative rights, for if every right has a corresponding duty and rights are based on needs, the question arises who has the duty to provide those goods? Positive rights are rights of recipience. They are claims to entitlement to receive certain goods or services. For example, the right to an education is a positive right. The right to employment is a positive right. Whether such rights exist is a subject of debate, for given the law of reciprocity of rights and duties, if I have a right to education, someone has a correlative obligation to provide the education. If I have a right to employment, someone has the obligation to provide the employment. The last is a difficult kind of claim in a free market society, for how can it be claimed that anyone has an obligation to start a business so that others have employment? If one lays the obligation on the state, then the free market is compromised.

Some argue that it makes sense to claim such rights only when there are facilities to provide the goods available. What sense would it make to claim a right to health care in a society that had no health care delivery systems? It certainly would make sense to claim a need for health care, but that underscores the difference between a right and a need.

Given the above difficulties with the notion of positive rights, some claim that there are only negative rights, for negative rights do not require others to provide the goods or the needs. They are rights that protect those goods or needs. Hence the rights to life, liberty and property are negative rights, for no one has the obligation to provide those goods, only an obligation to respect them which means in essence, not to violate them.

Still, as Stanley I. Benn (1967) says, the positive rights are different, a more modern concept that is the corollary of the equally modern notion of social justice.

> Rights of this kind are different in that though they appear to make a very definite claim, the correlative duty seems to rest neither on individuals at large (as with freedoms) nor on anyone in particular. To say, as does the 1948 UN Universal Declaration of Human Rights, that "everyone as a member of society, has the right to social security" (article 22) and "to a standard of living adequate for the health and well-being of himself and his family, including food, clothing, housing" (article 25), is not to say that his government has a duty to provide these things; many who subscribe to this declaration would deny that such services were a government's proper business. Rather, statements of this kind provide, in the words of the Preamble, "a common standard of achievement for all peoples;" that is, they are canons by which social economic, and political arrangements can be criticized. Human rights, in short, are statements of basic needs or interests. They are politically significant as grounds of protest and justification for reforming policies. They differ from appeals to benevolence and charity in that they invoke ideals like justice and equality. A man with a right has no reason to be grateful to benefactors; he has grounds for grievance when it is denied. The concept presupposes a standard below which it is intolerable that a human being should fall – not just in the way that cruelty to an animal is not to be tolerated but, rather, that human deprivations affront some ideal conception of what a human life ought to be like, a conception of human excellence. It is on the face of it unjust that some men enjoy luxuries while others are short of necessities, and to call some interests luxuries and others necessities is implicitly to place them in an order of priorities as claims. Upsetting that order then demands to be justified.

Are rights inalienable? Is not some interference justifiable? The classic case against free speech is that one is not free to shout fire in a crowded theater if there is no fire. Issues of killing in self-defense and in war, and issues of capital punishment, require working out the limits of the indefeasibility. It is helpful to remember that the modern working out of rights was for the purpose of securing a justification for rebelling against governmental authority. Since, one of the primary functions of government was to secure the rights of its citizens, if the government, for no good reason, violated those rights, it failed in its primary task as a government, thereby losing its legitimate authority.

Besides the traditional doctrines on rights, the number of rights articulated have expanded. For example the UN declaration of human rights in article 22, claims that everyone has a right "to a standard of living adequate for the health and well-being of himself and his family, including food, clothing, housing." (This echoes the "right to a living wage" enunciated in the Papal Encyclical *Rerum Novarum*, in 1891.) Others claim rights such as a right to adequate health care. There are contemporary concerns for animal rights. In such contexts, we see clearly that these rights claims are statements of basic needs or interests, either of humans or animals, which rest on criteria for the good life which become a standard by which to judge existing governments and policies.

Employee rights

Given the above we can now sort out various claims about employee rights. Legal rights of employees are simply those that exist through legislation or government regulations. However, claims made about natural rights, or conventional rights of employees will be based on how one views the relationship between employer and employee. The supposed "proliferation of rights" that is taking place in the latter part of the twentieth century, can be best understood as what results from new ways of viewing the employer–employee relationship.

There are philosophers who view the employer–employee relationship as reciprocal relationships where moral obligations exist by virtue of those relationships. The primary example of reciprocal relationships are those found in a family. For example, parents are in a relationship with their children where they are obliged to provide for the children's food, shelter, clothing and education. Consequently, the children have rights to receive those things. However, this relationship also gives the parents the right to lay down rules without consultation with the children, a kind of paternalism. Of course, reformers of the nuclear family wish to invest the children with a right to participate in family decisions. Attributing such rights to children, however, alters the view of how the family should operate – and, consequently, what the family is – since, in one sense, a family is described by its nexus and relationships, and the obligations and rights that go with those relationships. Hence, some sets of relationships are in essence moral, since they specify rights and obligations in describing the relationship.

Different views of what the employer–employee relationship is, and ought to be, will yield different claims of rights and obligations on the part of the employer and employee. So, depending on the way the relationship is viewed, different rights will be claimed.

One of the earliest views of the employer–employee relationship was of the master–servant view. That was the successor to the feudal dependency relationship of lord–serf. If we look at the lord–serf relationship, we see that the lord had the obligation to provide for the serf's safety. The serf owed his allegiance and first fruits of his labor to the lord. That means the lord had a right to those first fruits, but the lord, in return, owed to the serf safety and protection. Thus the serf had rights that the lord needed to respect. There were, of course, unscrupulous lords who did not respect those rights, but they are considered evil, or at least some sort of moral slackers. Further, there was a bond of loyalty that was expected. Paternalism was justified and, although there was equality among lords and among serfs, there was no equality between lord and serf. As a matter of fact, it was commonplace for the serf to bow down to the lord in an expression of fealty.

The master–servant relationship, which was an operative paradigm at the beginning of the industrial revolution, was severely critiqued by Marx on the one hand and enlightenment utilitarians on the other. To break the feudal mode, the view of the employer–employee relationship had to be revised away from the master–servant view.

It was replaced by the implied contractual view, which simply views the relationship as a contractual relationship of two self-sufficient individuals, agreeing to engage in commerce with one another. One claim against the implied contractual view is that it does not take enough note of the complexity of the relationship between employer and employee.

Since each of these views are analogies to the real situation, the analogies sometimes fit and sometimes do not. A master–servant or slave view is more accurate to the extent that it reflects more the asymmetry of power inherent in some contractual relationships, particularly involving those employees with no marketable skills. An implied contractual relationship reflects more the equality relationship that is a political desiderata since the enlightenment. Contractual relationships do not carry the baggage of loyalty, which is a virtue, and obligation more in accord with master–servant. Hence, the rights claimed will usually reflect the model of the relationship developed.

The most recent and useful model of the employer–employee relationship in business ethics, superseding the master–slave and implied contract views, that has been developed in recent years is the stakeholder model, according to which the various constituencies of the business as having a stake in the business. In the light of our subject, that means the business will impact on some of the interests of the stakeholders, be they members of the community where the business is located, potential hires, customers, other businesses with whom the company does business, stockholders or employees. If those interests are important, those stakeholder constituencies can make a rights' claim against the business. For example, vendors can claim a right to be paid for their services, but they can do that on the contract view. The consumer movement has claimed that consumers have a right to truthful advertising and a safe, quality product. The government claims a right to taxes. Communities make claims to rights to protection against environmental impurities, and last but not least, employees claim a plethora of rights. Rights expand and multiply as certain things are seen as necessary for a sufficient quality of life, or for the maintenance of one's dignity. We would expect those rights' claims to change as the view of the relationship of employer–employee changes.

Some rights are basic and some are derivative. Some philosophers have claimed that all human rights can be derived from Kant's second Categorical Imperative, "Act so as never to treat another rational being merely as a means to an end." Marx uses this as a moral critique of Capitalism. It reduces the worker to a commodity, a thing. Using someone as a thing is the height of immorality. Note though that Marx had no use for the notion of rights; neither, for that matter, did Jeremy Bentham. Kant's rule requires us to respect other human beings as fellow members of the Kingdom of ends. It is Kant's way of asserting basic human dignity.

Let us look at what specific rights have been claimed for employees in recent times. Such a list, of course, will not be exhaustive; no list of rights is. Nor will this list attempt to order the rights in terms of which are derived from which. To do that would require settling an issue in ethical theory of whether rights are derived from basic necessities for the good life or from the basic requirements necessary to achieve human dignity. In either case, as society changes and life adapts to new circumstances, newly perceived necessities will become candidates for rights. As the employer–employee relationship evolves, new rights will be asserted.

The right to work

Clearly, one cannot be an employee unless one is employed, so it seems somewhat odd to talk about the right to work as an employee's right. One can talk of a potential employee's right, but even, in that case, since there is no actual employer, who would have the corresponding obligation to provide a job. However, since having a job is currently an "essential need" or requirement for most people, it can be argued that all able-bodied individuals have a right to a job. So, the right to work would be a right of recipients that leaves it unspecified who has the obligation to provide the work. We cannot require a particular employer to provide a job for a particular individual. What can be claimed is that, if a particular employer has a job to offer, perspective employees, with proper qualifications, have a right to an equal opportunity to attain the job.

Does the person who is "most qualified" have a right to the job? The condition of qualified has force only within the context of a business which has as one of its primary goals, the maximization of productivity. In a family-owned private business, set up for the security of the family, the owner is perfectly within his or her rights to hire any of the children they wish without regard to qualifications, since the owner may have started the business for the specific purpose of providing jobs and financial security for members of the family.

Hence, if there are rights to work, they seem to be delimited by circumstances. It seems the claim that every able-bodied person has a right to work can only make sense if a consequent obligation to provide jobs falls primarily on the state to set up an environment that encourages job creation, and enforces equal opportunity for hiring. This would mean there would seem to be more force to the claim of a right to work within the context of a more socialist state than in a more free market oriented state. Certainly, one of the motivations behind socialism is the feeling of the necessity of providing jobs to the unemployed based on a belief that everyone who is able has a right to a job.

The right to meaningful work

A corollary to the right to work, is the claim of some that there is a right to meaningful work, i.e. a moral claim that tedious, repetitive, and boring work is dehumanizing. As John Ruskin (1968) said, "It is a good and desirable thing, truly, to make many pins in a day; but if we could only see with what crystal sand their points were polished – sand of human soul, much to be magnified before it can be discerned for what it is – we should think there might be some loss in it also." All agree it is a good thing to create jobs that do not alienate or dehumanize, but is the creation of jobs, that have meaning and purpose (whatever that might mean beyond the fact that they provide, through the division of labor a desired good for society), really an obligation of anyone? Is it even possible? There are some jobs that are tedious and distasteful by their very nature. Yet they need to be done.

There is an analogy here with the right to property. Most people want to claim property as their own, as long as it is beneficial for them, but any right to property should carry with it an obligation to protect the rest of society from that property which turns obnoxious. Not all property is beneficial. There is garbage, old cars, junk,

263

and old deserted buildings. Does the right to property entail a right to dispose of it without any obligation, if it is undesirable property? One would think not. There needs to be more attention paid to the downside of property.

Just as there is undesirable property, similarly there are tedious jobs in the world. Society needs someone to do them. The issue of distributive justice must focus on how this burden of the world is to be distributed, as well as the goods of the world. Since some jobs are burdensome, a view that claims a right to meaningful work and equates meaningful work only with jobs that are not burdensome, is seriously flawed in facing reality. At most, what can be claimed is a right of a worker to a job which is made as meaningful as possible. The correlative duty would be for the employers to do what they can to alleviate tediousness, burdensome, and dehumanizing working conditions.

The rights of the employee

Once hired, an employee certainly can claim rights such as:

- The right to a safe and healthy work environment
- The right to job security and due process in firing and promoting
- The right to privacy
- The right to compensation for injury
- The right to participation or voice in matters affecting workers
- The right to equal treatment without regard to race or gender
- The right to pension protection
- The rights to collective bargaining such as those established by the National Labor Relations Board
- The right to be free from harassment
- The right to a living wage

We will examine each to see what the claim is based on and to what extent it is justified.

The right to a safe and healthy work environment   One can defend the claim that employees have a right to a safe and healthy environment on the grounds that an employer like everyone else is obliged to do no harm. However, such a claim is challenged by some defenders of a free market view which sees the employment relationship as simply a contractual arrangement, wherein both parties are free to accept or reject the terms of the contract. From such a perspective, the worker is seen as free to choose to do the job under whatever circumstances it occurs. If workers desire a safe and healthy environment, then they can refuse to work under those unsafe conditions. If enough workers refuse, there will be a short supply of workers and the employer will be forced either to develop safer work environments or to pay higher wages to reflect the higher safety risk. Defenders of the right to a safe work environment counter that the employment relationship must be seen in a more realistic light. It is clear that in an urbanized market economy where there are more workers than desirable jobs, there are severe asymmetries of power between employer and employee. Given that fact, the employee is forced to take certain jobs to survive, so that the conditions of a contract – two free and autonomous individuals making an uncoerced choice – are difficult to meet.

Consequently, a claim that it is not incumbent on an employer to provide a safe and healthy work environment if the worker chooses to accept a job under such circumstances is disingenuous. Such an attitude justified the sweatshops of the late nineteenth and early twentieth century, but it seems no longer tenable.

Even if the free market contractual approach were tenable, the requirements of the free contract would make it imperative that the prospective employee knows the safety and health risks before going into the situation. So, the perspective employee could claim a right to the knowledge of the *conditions* of the job, as well as a right to some later choice if new and unforeseen health and safety factors come to light. There seems to be no way under either model that an employer can justify withholding such vital information from employees.

Given the realities of the asymmetries of power in the employer–employee relationship, it seems reasonable to assume that there should be a right to a safe and healthy work environment. Further, such a right would necessarily override the right of shareholders to profit maximization. All profit maximization is trumped by other stakeholder rights so the goal of business which is to maximize profits becomes limited to as much profit as possible while respecting the rights of other stakeholders.

The right to job security and due process in disciplining, demoting, promoting, and firing It was long held that the employer had a right to fire employees at will – the core of the doctrine euphemistically named, "employment at will." The arguments were: for the sake of efficiency (a utilitarian argument) and to respect the property rights of owners (a deontological argument), owners were free to fire workers as they wished. The business was the owner's property and the owner had the right to do what he or she willed with that property, including firing employees for whatever reason or no reason.

This view, of course, fails to recognize that the employment relationship is a reciprocal relationship which involves interdependencies between an employer and an employee. Implied or explicit agreements and promises are entered into when a job is offered and accepted. No prospective employees, in their right mind, would *freely* accept a job on the condition that they could be let go on the whim of the employer. The operative word here is *freely*. If one has little or no choice, one accepts to work under conditions that would not otherwise be endured. Reasonable people expect that others have justifiable reasons for what they do. Hence, there is a right to job security which means the person, once hired, has a right to hold that job as long as there are no good reasons for terminating the employment.

Given the right to job security, it is incumbent on the employer to give the employee the right to due process when decisions are made concerning his or her welfare. Such decision involve a renegotiation of the implied understanding. The insistence on due process is made because employers who hold power over the employee is analogous to the US government which holds power over its citizens. Since, to avoid the abuse of power, governments cannot act against its citizens without giving due process and since the employee is in the same subservient relationship to the employer, as the citizen to the government, similar protections need to be given. Hence, there should be right to due process, a right to procedures, including notice and a hearing or process where good reasons for firing or demotion need to be presented. Of course, given that most states in the USA are still employment-at-will states, the right to due process can be no more than a moral right, since it is not recognized as a legal right, except, of course, where it was negotiated into a contract. However, as we know, provisions in contracts that give power to one or the other party are only negotiated from strength.

The right to privacy   The right to privacy is also argued for by drawing an analogy of the employee to the citizen. The right to privacy is not specifically mentioned in the US constitution, but is asserted in the rulings of supreme court justices. Justice Brandeis (1890), one of the first to assert privacy rights, maintained that the right to privacy was "the right to be let alone." The claim to a right to privacy springs from an individualism which asserts that no one has the right to tell another what to do in his or her personal and private life, and also asserts that other people do not have the right to know what goes on in a person's private life if that person does not wish to disclose it. A derivative of the general right to privacy, is of course, the right to freedom in one's off hours, as long as what one does not hurt the employer. Privacy rights, of course, are negative rights. The employer need not do anything except respect an employee's privacy.

There are arguments against privacy rights or, at least, arguments that there are times when those rights can be overridden. Specifically, privacy rights can be overridden when private action *harms* others. That, of course, means the actions are no longer private. Such a stance, however, respects privacy rights much more than an earlier view which held an employer had a right to tell an employee what they could or could not do in his or her private life. Here, we have the question of how much an employer is entitled to demand from an employee which is not job relevant. What are the rights of the employer vis-à-vis the employee?

Defenders of procedures which seem to violate privacy, such as polygraphs and drug testing, defend this invasion of privacy on the grounds that it conflicts with others' rights to a safe workplace. However, that would not be a denial of the right to privacy, only a claim that it conflicts with other rights.

The right to privacy, of course, implies a right to freedom in one's off hours and relates to a different and more controversial rights' claim, the claim that employees have a right to freedom of speech. Now, few contest the right to free expression of opinions, but what if those opinions, possibly gained in working for a company, when publicly expressed, are harmful to that company. The complexity of such issues indicate that a great deal of work needs to be done in resolving the public/private distinction and how it relates to the employer–employee relationship.

The right to compensation for injury   A rather compelling case can be made for a right to compensation for injury, on the basis of economic harm. There are good reasons to believe in compensatory justice. When one person suffers economic harm from another person's activity, the injured party is entitled to compensation. It is the principle that makes parents tell their child to fix or pay for the neighbor's window that the child broke. If I suffer harm in your service, fairness would seem to dictate that you reimburse me for that harm. There is, of course, an exception in the case where the harm was expected and compensation initially took the risk of harm into account, so that the employee was paid more for participating in a high risk job. As in other cases we have seen, the strength of the rights' claim here will rest on the characteristics of the contract or agreement, explicit or implied, between the employer and employee.

The right to participation or voice in matters affecting workers   This is a recently articulated and much more controversial right, but it is a right that flows out of the temper of the times that call for solidarity and total quality control management. As the view of the relationships between owners, managers and employees changes, and as the notion of stakeholder gains ascendancy, the employee is seen as a more and more important player in the corporate culture. Accordingly, in those matters which seriously affect workers, participation in deciding their own fate is seen not so much as a desideratum, but more as a right. The existence of such a right becomes tenable, if one recognizes the asymmetry of power between employer and employee, and how that affects employment agreements. The right is asserted as a foil to ward off the potential abuse of power that can arise from such asymmetry. Existing agreements, to be morally binding, need to be the result of informed mutual consent. If existing implied and explicit contracts or established relationships need to be changed, those affected by the result of the changes ought to have a voice in renegotiating the revisions.

The right to equal treatment without regard to race or gender   Since violations of equal treatment occur in the workplace, it seems obvious that one assert a right to equal treatment without regard to race or gender, where race or gender are irrelevant, as they usually are. This is a general human right, derived from the principle of justice which can be applied to workers specifically.

The right to pension protection   This right is a much more specific right and does not seem too problematic. Given the beliefs in a right to one's own property, or to what one worked for, and granting that the pension is the property of the workers, promised by the employer, it would seem that good stewardship would oblige the companies to protect the pension and not to put it at risk in speculative business projects.

The right to organization bargaining and the right to strike   These are, of course, legal rights and established by legislation and regulation in the USA by the NLRB, but there is a moral basis for the NLRB regulations. The US bishops remind us that human nature being what it is, one way to overcome power is to confront it with equal power. In modern industrialized societies with most of the power on the side of corporations, organizations of workers or consumers are indispensable to redress the balance of power. Hence, to gain the power to secure their rights, workers need to be able to organize. To attack the ability to organize is to attack a right essential to human dignity.

The right to be free from harassment   This right, like the right to equal treatment is a human right, that should not be violated anywhere, let alone in the workplace. Emphasis lately has been on the right to be free from *sexual* harassment, but it is imperative to note that there are other forms of harassment.

The right to a living wage   This is the last employee right we wish to consider. As far back as 1891, Pope Leo XIII, in an encyclical entitled *Rerum Novarum* (Of New Things), articulated a number of employee rights. Among these was the right to a living wage. For him, a living wage was enough to support a family with children, so that the children were adequately cared for. It is debatable how many jobs today pay a living

267

wage. At any rate, the Pope's call for rights was reiterated by the US bishops in 1986. The bishops not only argued for a living wage, they articulated a set of rights. The argument was simple and familiar.

According to the bishops, asymmetry of power presses workers into choosing between an inadequate wage and no wage at all. Justice demands minimum guarantees. "The provision of wages and other benefits sufficient to support a family adequately is a basic necessity to prevent (the) exploitation of workers. The dignity of workers requires adequate health care, security for old age or disability, unemployment compensation, healthful working conditions, weekly rest, periodic holidays for leisure and reasonable security against arbitrary dismissal" (National Council of Catholic Bishops, 1986).

We do not claim that this list is exhaustive, even if it is exhausting. For, if we ground rights on necessity, then as society articulates the new necessities required for living well in a new technologically advanced age, it will also articulate newly discovered goods which will become candidates for rights.

References

Aquinas, T., *Summa Theologica*, II–II. Q. 66, a.7.

Benn, S. I., 1967: Rights. *Encyclopedia of Philosophy*, Vol. 7&8*, 199.

Bentham, J. 1941: *Introduction to the Principles of Morals and Legislation*. Blackstone. First published in 1798.

Blackstone, W. 1941: *Commentaries on the Law*. Abridged edn, edited by B. C. Gavit. Washington, DC: publisher?. 26, 68.

Brandeis, Justice and Warren, S. 1890. *Harvard Law Review*.

Dworkin, R. 1978: *Taking Rights Seriously*. New Impression with a Reply to Critics. London: Duckworth.

Hart, H. L. A. 1955: Are there any natural rights? *Philosophical Review*, 64, 212–13.

Locke, J. 1960: *Two Treatises of Government*. Cambridge. Edited by P. Laslett. First published in 1690.

National Council of Catholic Bishops 1986: Economic Justice for all. *Origins*, 16(24), November 27. Washington DC: US Catholic Conference.

Ruskin, J. 1968: Stones of Venice. In M. Abrams et al. (eds), *The Norton Anthology of English Literature*, Vol. 2. New York: W. W. Norton, 1295.

22

Business ethics and work: questions for the twenty-first century

JOANNE B. CIULLA

If you know nothing about work in a corporation, business ethics texts would give you a very strange view of a place rife with racism, sexism, danger, drugs and disease – not a pretty picture. The bulk of business ethics literature on work focuses on discrimination, affirmative action, comparable worth, whistleblowing, sexual harassment, and right to privacy issues such as drug testing and AIDS. Discussion of work as a human experience is elusive in business ethics. One reason for this is that we business ethics scholars tend to be ambulance chasers. We go after the latest scandal or disaster, whether it is insider trading, sexual harassment, cigarette advertising or pollution. Another reason is that topics in business ethics often shadow legal cases concerning situations where there are charges of serious wrongdoing and harm. The law treats overt problems in the workplace, but does not usually look at broader ethical questions related to work.

At the close of the twentieth century, a century dominated by the clash between capitalism and communism, the ethical problems of work are not about particular incidents in the workplace, but fundamental questions about how people think about work and how the workplace is managed. Business ethics scholars need to examine some of the basic assumptions about the relationship between employers and employees and how work affects people's lives. The primary ethical questions about work are, "Is work morally better today?" and "What does this question mean?" To answer these, I first examine how business ethics texts cover work. Then I look at the criticisms of management in the mid-twentieth century that foreshadow the problems that confront us about work and life at the beginning of the twenty-first century.

Work in business ethics texts

The best way to understand how a field of study discusses a topic is to look at its textbooks. An informal survey of the contents of twelve popular business ethics texts offers a snapshot of what business ethics scholars talk about when they talk about work in the corporation. The criterion for a popular text is one that has been published in more than one edition by an author or authors well-known in the field. All of the texts, except for the two most recent ones, were published in at least two editions. I randomly reviewed one edition of each text. The chart indicates the first year the book was published and then the edition that I consulted. I ordered the texts according to

Table 22.1 Work issues in business ethics texts

Text surveyed	Dates	Hiring	Firing	Wages	Rights	Loyalty	Capitalism	QWL	Meaning
Steiner and Steiner *Business Government and Society*	1971 1991	X			X		X		X
Vincent Barry *Moral Issues in Business*	1979 1986	X	X	X	X	X	X	X	X
Beauchamp and Bowie *Ethical Theory and Business*	1979	X				X	X		
Donaldson and Werhane *Ethical Issues in Business*	1979 1988	X	X	X	X		X		
Richard T. De George *Business Ethics*	1982 1986	X	X	X	X	X	X	X	
Manuel G. Velasquez *Business Ethics: Concepts and Cases*	1982 1992	X		X	X	X	X		
Hoffman and Moore *Business Ethics*	1984 1990	X		X	X		X	X	
Desjardins and McCall *Contemporary Issues in Business Ethics*	1985 1990	X	X			X		X	
Matthews and Goodpaster *Policies and Persons*	1985 1991	X			X	X			
William H. Shaw *Business Ethics*	1991	X	X	X	X	X	X	X	
John R. Boatright *Ethics and the Conduct of Business*	1993	X	X		X	X			
Robert C. Solomon *Above the Bottom Line*	1985 1994	X			X	X	X	X	X

the first dates that they were published, because subsequent editions of texts usually follow the same general section format as first editions. Usually authors and editors either update the cases or add new topics in later editions.

The twelve texts surveyed offered a fairly consistent picture of what business ethics has said about work, and they support my contention that the treatment of work in business ethics tends to parallel legal discussions. All of the texts discussed hiring, but all did so in sections on affirmative action, discrimination and/or reverse discrimination. Half of the books talk about firing with five out of six doing so in sections on the employment at will doctrine or due process. Barry (1986) and Shaw (1991) are the only exceptions. They both discuss conditions of fairness in firing without specific reference to legal notions. (Since Shaw's (1991) book is an update of Barry's (1986), it takes the same general approach to most topics listed.) Wages were also treated in half of the texts. Barry (1986), Shaw (1991) and De George (1986) talk about the idea of a fair wage, whereas Velasquez (1992), Hoffman and Moore (1990), and Donaldson and Werhane (1988), discuss wages in sections on comparable worth.

Workers' rights was the second most discussed topic, found in ten of the twelve books. Texts usually used cases or articles on the right to privacy or the right to freedom of speech. Seven out of ten texts cover right to privacy in sections on polygraphs and/or drug tests. These issues dominate, partly because textbooks tend to replicate each other, and partly because scholars find some issues more fun to write about than others. Nonetheless, given the limited amount of text space set aside for work issues and the small proportion of the work force affected by drug tests and polygraphs, the amount of attention paid to these issues seems out of proportion. The treatment of loyalty in nine of the twelve texts is also very narrow. Eight out of nine texts discuss loyalty in terms of whistleblowing. Beauchamp and Bowie's (1979) text is the only one that does not focus on whistleblowing; it includes an article on the loyal agent's argument. Today loyalty is one of *the* major topics of discussion in corporate America and the issues go far beyond the whistle-blowing situations frequently discussed in business ethics texts.

Another way to examine the ethical problems of work is by tapping into the standard Marxist criticisms of capitalism. Marx's critique of alienated labor lays out some of the basic ethical questions about the meaning of work, its place in life and the relationship of employer to employee. Seven of the nine books that talked about Marx, contained sections on alienated labor. Hoffman and Moore (1990) and Steiner and Steiner (1991) concentrated more on Marx's economic critique of capitalism. Today, you do not hear managers talking about alienated workers, but you do hear them talk about commitment, which has become a great concern in the corporate workplace. Since this sample of texts is small and unsystematic, it is dangerous to make any other generalizations from this chart. However, it is noteworthy that fewer texts, originally published after 1984, had sections on Marx or critiques of capitalism. It would be a real pity if the fall of communism meant the elimination of critiques of work under capitalism in business ethics texts. Without challenging the nature of work under capitalism, the field risks losing sight of the fundamental ethical tensions in the employer–employee relationship, i.e., exploitation and abuse of power.

The last two categories are quality of worklife (QWL) and the meaning of work. Here I was hoping to find discussion of some of the root ethical questions that underlie work as a human experience. The term QWL emerged in the late 1960s and early 1970s, and gained currency in the 1980s. The term referred to "the degree to which members of a work organization are able to satisfy important personal needs through their experiences in the organization" (Suttle, 1976). The dimensions of QWL include some elements that are not part of the other categories, such as a safe and healthy work environment, opportunity to use and develop human capacities, future opportunities for growth and security, integration of work and life, social relevance of work life, participation, and job design (Walton, 1973). These areas all have rich ethical implications. Some areas of QWL are particularly important today, such as job security, participation, and the integration of work and life. Half of the books surveyed either had sections on QWL or discussed two or more of the QWL issues listed above. Under meaning, I specifically looked for readings that examined the social and personal meanings of work. Three of the texts talked about these issues. Steiner and Steiner (1991) has almost two pages on the nature and meaning of work. Barry (1986) has two pages on changes in attitudes towards work. Solomon (1994) titles a 33-page chapter of his text "The meaning of work;" this section also includes one of my own articles on the meaning and ethics of work (Ciulla, 1990).

All of these texts take a problem-based and somewhat legalistic approach to work in corporations. Nonetheless, through their writing and consulting, business ethics scholars have influenced the ways that businesses think about issues such as sexual harassment and discrimination, but clearly not as much as law suits. Business ethics is about more than just problem solving; it is a field of critical study that should help people to think in new ways about business and its responsibilities to employees, society and other stakeholders. The present and future questions about work require a reassessment of the relationship of employees to the corporation. Business ethics scholars will have to pay more attention to the areas least covered in the texts surveyed. Those areas include QWL, particularly in relation to job security, the allocation of time between home and work, loyalty and commitment in the employment relationship, the meaning of work, and manipulative and deceptive management practices. These are the pressing ethical issues of work. Unlike many other topics in business ethics, they are philosophic questions about work and life, not questions about particular business practices. Some of these ethical questions about work and life surfaced in the mid-twentieth century and have come to a head in the workplace today.

Work from the 1950s through the 1980s

Over the past 100 years, consultants and management theorists have sought out new ways to organize work that increase productivity and quality. In contrast to Taylor's (1967) physically harsh and mentally demeaning articulation of scientific management, kinder gentler management techniques emerged. The human relations approach seemed more humane and ethically sensitive. Organizational and industrial psychologists sought to create workplaces that satisfied human needs. Managers went from being engineers to sociologists and therapists, from muscle men to holy men. But, did this mean that work in corporations was morally better?

In the early 1950s, sociologist C. Wright Mills (1956) expressed concern about social engineering and the psychological approach to corporate management. He said:

"The moral problem of social control in America today is less the explicit domination of men than their manipulation into self-coordinated and altogether cheerful subordinates." Mills believed that management's real goal was to "conquer the problem of alienation within the bounds of work alienation" (Mills, 1951). By this, he meant that the problems of the workplace had to be defined, and solved, in terms of the values and goals of the workplace itself. By controlling the meanings and the terms under which alienation was conquered and satisfaction found, employers could maintain control without alienating workers.

William H. Whyte (1956) echoed Mills' concern about psychological manipulation, but focused on people's need to belong. The corporate workplace of the late 1950s is both radically different from, and strikingly the same as, today's workplace. Whyte criticized the social ethic that makes morally legitimate the pressure of society against the individual. The social ethic rationalizes the organization's demand for loyalty and gives employees who offer themselves wholeheartedly a sense of dedication and satisfaction. The social ethic includes a belief that the group is a source of creativity. A sense of belonging is the ultimate need of the individual, and social science can create ways to achieve this sense of belonging (p. 6–7). The same ideas are bantered around in corporations today, under the guise of loyalty, commitment and team membership.

Whyte feared that psychologists and social engineers would strip people of their creativity and identity. He attacked the use of personality tests to weed out people who do not fit in and challenged the idea that organizations should be free from conflict. The critique of the workplace in Whyte's book is similar to the critiques that liberals have of communitarianism. Community-oriented life looks good, but it is ultimately oppressive and authoritarian. In the 1950s, social critics worried about the conformity of people to institutions and the values of suburban life. Today, we worry about lack of consensus about values and the breakdown of urban and suburban communities. The increasing effort in the workplace is to build teams and to emphasize the value of the group over the individual. No one seems worried about loss of creativity and submission of individual identity to group identity. Managers care more about the problem of the individual who is not a team player and a majority of management theorists today believe that groups and teams are the foundation of all that is good and productive.

Whyte says, "The most misguided attempt at false collectivization is the attempt to see the group as a creative vehicle" (p. 51). Contrary to popular management thinking today, Whyte does not believe that people think or create in groups. Groups, he says, just give order to the administration of work. Whyte describes an experiment done at the National Training Lab on leaderless groups. Theoretically, when the group "jelled," the leader would fade into the background, to be consulted for his expertise only. These groups resulted in chaos but as Whyte puts it, the trainers hoped that the resulting "feeling draining" of the group would be a valuable catharsis and a prelude to agreement (p. 54). According to Whyte, the individual has to enter into the process somewhere. If everyone wants to do what the group wants to do, and nothing gets done, then the individual has to play a role in the process. However, Whyte wonders if we should openly bring individuals into the process or "bootleg" it in an expression of group sentiment. Basically, he sees the leaderless group as intellectual hypocrisy. The power and authority of groups simply mask the real power and authority of leaders.

273

Whyte urges people to cheat on all psychological tests given during job interviews and at the workplace. He takes a strong stance against the organization and what he sees as the social scientist's coercive idea of belongingness.

Another famous illustration of the struggle against the organization is in Sloan Wilson's (1955) novel *The Man in the Gray Flannel Suit*, published a year before Whyte's book. In the novel, a personnel manager asks the main character, Tom Rath, to write an autobiography in which the last line reads, "The most significant thing about me is . . ." Rath, disgusted by the exercise, debates whether to say what the company wants to hear or to write about his most significant memory, concerning a woman he met during the war. Caught between truth and fiction, Rath holds on to his dignity by stating the facts – his place of birth, his schooling, and the number of children in his family. He writes that the most significant thing about him is the fact that he is applying for the job. He also says that he does not want to write an autobiography as part of his application (p. 14).

Rath draws a fine line between himself and the organization. Whyte misses the moral message of the first scene of Wilson's book – telling the truth strikes a much stronger blow for individual dignity than beating the organization at its own game. The beginning of Wilson's novel resonates with students today because all of them at some time will have to decide how truthful they have to be in a job interview or with an employer, and how much of themselves they are willing to give to an organization. It is hard to tell the truth when you are afraid of not getting the job. The thin line is not about the amount of hours or work one does. It is the boundary that people draw between their inner self and the parts of them needed to do their job. It is the line that allows a person to be both an individual and part of a group. In the modern workplace, it is not always easy to draw this line. Over the years, various management programs have either consciously – or unconsciously – attempted to erase the line between the two parts.

In *The Triumph of the Therapeutic*, Philip Rieff (1966, p. 137) says that truth has become a highly personal matter which he calls "psychic truth;" see also Bellah et al. (1985). Rieff thinks that therapeutic effectiveness has replaced the value of truth in our culture. Truth in the workplace became therapeutic truth designed to make people feel better and help them to adjust and fit. This kind of truth was far more desirable than truth that might rock the boat. Many of the management programs implemented over the past 50 years have shown greater concern for therapeutic effectiveness than truthfulness. They were geared toward making people feel better about work, not on truthfully articulating the moral agreements of the workplace. That is why none of the management fads have lasted long. The corporate workforce has been jump started time and time again by the latest management program.

The state of work in the 1990s

In the 1960s, the centralized bureaucratic organization of the 1950s gave way to the sensitive approach to management. The National Training Labs developed sensitivity training and T-Groups to transform bossy managers into participative ones. After much crawling around on the floor together and getting in touch with their inner feelings, few managers were transformed. During the 1970s and 1980s, management programs designed to capture the souls of workers bombarded the workplace. Whereas the 1960s had managers crawling on the floor, the 1990s had them hanging from ropes to build teams. Fueled by competitive pressures to downsize, the challenge of management in the 1990s was to get more work out of fewer people. Total Quality Management (TQM) was the answer to their prayers.

The twentieth century began with scientific management with its physical control over production. It ends with TQM and its social control over production. They are two sides to the same coin. Scientific management separated the mind from the body of the worker to mass produce goods. TQM puts workers together in teams to produce quality goods and services. Both systems assert a high level of control at all phases of production (albeit using different means of control), and both systems have been extremely successful at improving production of goods and services.

Teams are a powerful form of social control. Peer pressure from the group keeps everyone in line, and pulling his or her weight. Teams affect the individual more directly than the larger culture of the organization does. If the group puts out a measurable product it can "keep score," which makes it accountable, and allows for direct feedback and reinforcement. Hence, it is not surprising that along with excitement over teams some businesses engender a religious fervor for TQM. Originating from statistical quality control, TQM pieced together quality circles, team approaches, and leadership into a new philosophy that required leaders "to accept TQM as a way of life" (Johnson, 1993).

One book on leadership and TQM advises front-line supervisors to act like leaders and to become "more participatory and less authoritarian." Participatory means listening to employees' ideas and, when appropriate, implementing their ideas. The author goes on to say that employees, too, have to change. They need to know "that improved quality performance on their part, while vital, may bring no added compensation ('what's in it for me?'), but in the long run, productivity and quality improvement are necessary for survival" (Pierce, 1991). Behind TQM is the idea of reinstating a craft ethic in workers, which includes pride in workmanship and the intrinsic value of a job well done. While this is a positive and rewarding model of work, it cannot be isolated from the context in which a job is done and the kind of work that is done. In this setting, the manager does not want employees to behave as if they are engaged in an economic transaction. Yet, the employer bases most of his or her decisions regarding the employee on economic considerations. This is a good example of a therapeutic fiction: everyone pretends that work is not guided by the values of instrumentalism and economic efficiency.

A great attraction of TQM is that it gives the impression that managers are giving up control and being democratic, while they actually have more control. True believers assume that TQM is intrinsically ethical because employees are empowered to participate in decisions, and management listens to their employees. This is a fairly thin description of an ethical arrangement. The key issue here is: What is the relationship of employees to management? Listening to employees and allowing them to participate in decisions does not mean that their relationship to management or to each other has changed, especially if the listening and participation takes place between parties of unequal power. Furthermore, TQM says that managers should treat employees like customers. This is a nice idea, but it breaks down in practice.

In a recent book documenting the wonders of teamwork in various organizations, Fisher (1993) emphasizes the importance of authenticity. He says that the key values of a team leader are belief in the importance of work, a belief that work is life, a belief in the "aggressive" development of team members, and a conviction to "eliminate barriers to team performance." He quotes a manager who says: "The distinction between the work person and the family person is unhealthy and artificial" (pp. 105–109). In today's volatile economic environment, rhetoric like this rings false because, as Robert Frost (1979) said, "Home is the place where, when you have to go there, /They have to take you in." We don't have many workplaces that do that. Throughout the twentieth century, Marxists and management scholars believed that alienation from work and home was a bad thing. Maybe they were wrong. Perhaps a strong fence between the two is the best way for a person to maintain control of his or her life.

Today's problem of work and life

One of the saddest places to be is in a company that implements a quality program at the same time as it is downsizing (and this often happens). Managers in these companies emphasize teamwork and empowerment, and use the moral language of trust, loyalty, and commitment. Employees are confused and they work more because they are scared. In a seminar for mid-level managers at a Fortune 500 company that was going through downsizing and a quality process, I asked participants to make up stories that characterized a major ethical problem in the workplace. One group told the story of Harry and Mary. Harry worked twelve hours a day and had little life outside of work. Mary worked eight hours a day and was actively involved with her family and church. Both did the same quality work only Harry did more. Mary did not want to live like Harry, but wondered if that is what it would take to keep her job. Her manager says no, but her experience tells her otherwise. Mary raises two fundamental questions about work: What is its proper place in the context of her life? Is her employer telling her the truth? Corporate downsizing in the 1990s reminded people that work in corporations is precarious. Nonetheless, it also made work more precious to them. For many people, work provides the basis of their identity, self-esteem, friendships and community. In a time of exceptionally low unemployment in America, people are working longer and harder, often at the expense of their family life and health. Even the most progressive corporate workplace is laced with fear of layoffs. In her book, *Time Bind*, sociologist Arlie Russell Hochschild (1997) studied a company listed in *100 Best Companies to Work for in America* (Levering and Moskowitz, 1993) and in other books on companies with excellent family policies. She discovered that, despite the fact that this company had some of the best policies for giving working parents time to fill their family needs, few employees took advantage of them. The people she studied were actually putting in more hours at work than ever before. Even employees with managers who encouraged them to use these policies, did not use them. During the time of her study, the company was implementing a quality program, but not downsizing. The people she studied told her that they were not worried about being fired, still put in more time at work, often to the detriment of their marriages and children.

There are three ways to understand this and all are problematic. Hochschild suggests that the company made work so enjoyable that the people she studied preferred being there than being at home. At work, they could solve problems and were praised for their efforts, whereas, at home, the family is not always appreciative and the problems less finite. We have never had to ponder the question: What would happen if we designed a corporation in which work was so enjoyable that people preferred it to home? If the answer is that this kind of workplace ruins people's family lives then we are faced with a very curious social and ethical problem. Employers and spouses can both divorce you. When people choose to work more on their job than their marriage, it raises a second set of issues. Can you give total commitment to both an employer and a spouse? Does the culture of the company force you to choose? Do the demands of the employer cause people to lose perspective on their lives? The third interpretation of Hochschild's study is that people work longer hours because they were scared. They like the corporation, but deep down in their hearts, they do not believe the company when it says there will be no lay-offs in the future. This is likely, because Hochschild reports that, after she finished her study, the company did indeed lay people off, including the manager in charge of the family policies.

Business leaders know they cannot promise much to employees. To be competitive, they need to get as much as they can out of the smallest workforce possible. They cannot enjoy loyalty and commitment from employees if they are not loyal and committed to them. In some organizations, managers and employees are supposedly empowered to do their work, but no one appears to be in control. When an economic downturn occurs, business leaders put their hands in their pockets and whistle at the sky. Layoffs and "redundancies" are the result of stiff competition, the market, Wall Street, or perhaps even the workers themselves – the team was just not good enough. Often this stance allows for management to have control without accountability, whereas employee teams have accountability without real control (Ciulla, 1998a). When workers are laid off, they shake their fists as if some primitive god of fate governs them or, worse yet, they blame themselves. Companies desperately seek ways to secure loyalty, trust and commitment from employees who are afraid that they will receive the next pink slip.

Business ethics and work in the twenty-first century

We have reached the limits of the psychological approach to management. In the twenty-first century, business ethics scholars should help business to think creatively about a moral approach to management. The popularity of the cartoon *Dilbert* illustrates the cynicism that employees have for the latest management program, especially quality initiatives. By introducing the language of trust, loyalty and commitment to the workplace, managers upped the moral stakes and many corporations cannot live up to these principles. As a result of this, employees feel manipulated and betrayed. Managers are discovering that the moral values of trust and commitment are central to work. What they have not understood is that both of these are reciproal values. You can not expect commitment from employees without giving it to them, and the same is true for trust. The best way for corporations to begin developing trust is by keeping their promises and telling the truth. The best way to keep promises, is to make promises that they can keep. In a volatile business environment, people do not need therapeutic truths. They need to be told where they stand, so they can have some control over their lives (Ciulla, 1998b).

This leads us back to the two questions posed at the beginning of this paper. Is work morally better today? What does "morally better" mean? It is easy to list the ways in which work is better today than it was in the past. Innovations in technology and job design, programs geared towards developing employees, benefit packages, on-site daycare, etc., certainly improve life at work in some ways. Legislation and the threat of law suits make businesses more hesitant to fire without due process, to discriminate, to tolerate sexual harassment and to persecute whistleblowers, but morally better means more than solving these problems. It also means the moral relationship between employers and employees has improved. I would argue that it has not improved. The demise of unions in America led to a demise in the voice and autonomy of employees. Work has improved for employees on management's terms, not on employees' forms. Unions are the only institution that give employees an independent voice and some employment security. Today, the only recourse employees have are the courts. The level of distrust and bad faith between employers and employees is high. We might also question whether the "new improved" workplace has helped people to live better lives. They may have improved their material lives, but what about its impact on people's social and personal lives?

If we can say anything about the moral relationship between employer and employee at the close of the twentieth century, we can say it is confusing. The social contract is changing; at the same time, managers emphasize trust and loyalty. Stories are often the best way to develop moral imagination in business people. Consider, for example, the case of Malden Mills. On December 1, 1995, the factory burnt down. Owner Aaron Feuerstein distributed Christmas bonuses and continued to pay his employees their full salaries for the next three months, while the factory was being repaired. This is more than a Christmas story about corporate benevolence. If job security is related to commitment, then Feuerstein's workers are probably among the most loyal and committed in America. One can write this off as old-fashioned paternalism, but I doubt that any management initiative could produce in employees the trust, commitment, and self-esteem of the employees at Malden Mills. While many companies try psychological and social interventions, moral action is stronger and longer lasting than therapeutic intervention. The challenge for business ethics in the twenty-first century is to examine the moral relationship of employers to employees critically, to design new approaches to management, based on ethical commitments, and to explore how work in corporations enhances – and deters – a person's ability to lead a good life.

References

Barry, V. 1986: *Moral Issues in Business*, 3rd edn. Belmont, CA: Wadsworth. First published in 1979.

Bellah, R. N., Madsen, R., Sullivan, W. M., Swidler, A., and Tipton, S. M. (eds) 1985: *Habits of the Heart*. Berkeley, CA: University of California Press, ch. 2.

Beauchamp, T. L. and Bowie, N. E. (eds) 1979: *Ethical theory and Business*. Englewood Cliffs, NJ: Prentice Hall.

Boatright, J. R. 1993: *Ethics and the Conduct of Business*. Englewood Cliffs, NJ: Prentice Hall.

Ciulla, J. B. 1990: Honest work. *Benchmark Magazine*. Reprinted in R. C. Solomon (1994, pp. 437–9).

Ciulla, J. B. 1998a: Leadership and the problem of bogus empowerment. In J. B. Ciulla (ed.), *Ethics as the Heart of Leadership: Essays on the Ethics of Leaders and Followers*, Westport, CT: Quorum Books.

Ciulla, J. B. 1998b: *Honest Work*. New York: Times/Random House.

De George, R. T. 1986: *Business Ethics*, 2nd edn. New York: Macmillan Publishers. First published in 1982.

DesJardins, J. R. and McCall, J. J. 1990: *Contemporary Issues in Business Ethics*, 2nd edn. Belmont, CA: Wadsworth. First published in 1985.

Donaldson, T. and Werhane, P. H. (eds) 1988: *Ethical Issues in Business*, 3rd edn. Englewood Cliffs, NJ: Prentice Hall. First published in 1979.

Fisher, K. 1993: *Leading Self-Directed Work Teams*. New York: McGraw-Hill.

Frost, R. 1979: The death of the hired man. In E. C. Lathem (ed.), *The Poetry of Robert Frost*, New York: Holt, Rinehart and Winston, 38.

Hochschild, A. R. 1997: *Time Bind*. New York: Metropolitan Books.

Hoffman, W. M. and Moore, J. M. 1990: *Business Ethics*, 2nd edn. New York: McGraw-Hill. First published in 1984.

Johnson, R. S. 1993: *TQM: Leadership for the Quality Transformation*. Milwaukee: ASQC Quality Press.

Levering, R. and Moskowitz, M. 1993: *100 Best Companies to Work for in America*. New York: Penguin Books.

Matthews, J. B. and Goodpaster, K. E. 1991: *Policies and Persons: A Casebook in Business Ethics*, 2nd edn. New York: McGraw-Hill. First published in 1985.

Mills, C. W. 1951: *White Collar*. New York: Oxford University Press, pp. 232–7.

Mills, C. W. 1956: Crawling to the top. *New York Times Book Review*, Dec. 9.

Pierce, R. J. 1991: *Leadership. Perspective and Restructuring for Total Quality*. Milwaukee: ASQC Quality Press, 11.

Rieff, P. 1966: *The Triumph of the Therapeutic*. New York: Harper & Row.

Shaw, W. H. 1991: *Business Ethics*. Belmont, CA: Wadsworth.

Solomon, R. C. 1994: *Above the Bottom Line*, 2nd edn. Fort Worth: Harcourt Brace. First published as Solomon, R. C. and Hanson, K. 1985: *It's Good Business*. New York: Harper & Row.

Steiner, G. A. and Steiner, J. F. 1991: *Business Government and Society*, 6th edn. New York: McGraw-Hill. First published in 1971.

Suttle, J. L. 1976: Improving life at work – Problems and perspectives. In J. R. Hackman and J. L. Suttle (eds), *Improving Life at Work: Behavioral Science Approaches to Organizational Change*, Santa Moncia, CA: Goodyear, p. 4.

Taylor, F. W. 1967: *The Principles of Scientific Management*. New York: W. W. Norton & Co.

Velasquez, M. G. 1992: *Business Ethics: Concepts and Cases*, 3rd edn. Englewood Cliffs, NJ: Prentice Hall.

Walton, R. E. 1973: Quality of working life: What is it? *Sloan Management Review*, 15, 11–21.

Whyte, W. H. Jr, 1956: *The Organization Man*. New York: Simon & Schuster.

Wilson, S. 1955: *The Man in the Gray Flannel Suit*. New York: Arbor House.

23

Business's environmental responsibility

JOSEPH R. DESJARDINS

Even under the most laissez-faire system, business can be said to have ethical responsibilities concerning the natural environment. Traditional categories of liability and
negligence can be readily applied to business activities that cause environmental
harm. Familiar environmental issues such as air and water pollution and toxic waste
disposal, as well as the infamous cases of Love Canal, Bhopal, and the Exxon Valdez,
speak to a wide range of environmental responsibilities for business.

While there is a strong consensus that business has ethical responsibility *concerning*
the natural environment, a more controversial claim is that business might have
ethical responsibility to the natural world. On the former view, environmental responsibilities are indirect. Business has direct responsibilities only to human beings, but
fulfilling these responsibilities sometimes requires certain action concerning the environment, e.g., do not pollute water, do not dump toxic wastes, etc. On the latter model,
business would be said to have *direct* moral responsibility to the natural world. If
animals, plants, or ecosystems have moral standing, then business ethics must address
business's moral responsibility to such natural objects.

Environmental issues also pose significant challenges to mainstream economic
thinking, particularly the commitment to economic growth central to neoclassical economics. Since much thinking about corporate social responsibility is connected to
neoclassical economics, these environmental issues will also have important implications for business ethics.

This chapter examines the environmental responsibilities of business along three
dimensions: responsibility for environmental harms to humans caused by business;
responsibility to the non-human natural world; and business ethics in the age of
sustainable economics.

Responsibility for environmental harm to humans

We can begin the analysis of business's environmental responsibility with familiar
categories from ethics and philosophy of law: business has a responsibility not to intentionally or negligently cause harm to others. When such harms do occur, business
has a responsibility to compensate individuals who are harmed by its intentional or
negligent acts.

In this way, both law and ethics have always recognized business's environmental responsibility. A firm that dumps toxic chemicals into a river upstream from a

community's drinking water can be held liable for any illness that results. Like many cases of liability, however, debates develop over the details: what counts as a "harm?" What constitutes "causing" the harm, and how can it be proven? What makes an act "negligent?" How far, and to whom, does liability extend?

Many well-known environmental disasters fit this general pattern. In the Love Canal, Bhopal, and the Exxon Valdez cases, environmental controversies arose over the details of business's liability. Were provable harms caused by business? Who decides this, and on what grounds? Were companies negligent, or were these unavoidable accidents? What are the limits of corporate liability? What sort of compensation is appropriate once harm is established?

Development of environmental policy beyond this liability model is helpfully explored by examining the Reserve Mining controversy; see Bartlett (1980) for an extended analysis, and Newton and Schmidt (1996), and for helpful descriptions of many environmental ethics cases, including Love Canal, Bhopal, and the Exxon Valdez, see Newton and Dillingham (1994). Reserve Mining Company was located along the northern shore of Lake Superior in Silver Bay, Minnesota. Reserve Mining processed low-grade iron ore, called "taconite," into a form suitable for use in steel production. Processing involves crushing taconite rock into fine-grain dust, mixing this dust with large quantities of water, and then flushing this through a series of magnets that separate out most of the iron particles. The remaining dust and rock, approximately two tons for every ton of iron retrieved, was discharged, with the waste water, back into Lake Superior. Tons of these "tailings" and millions of gallons of waste water were discharged daily into the lake.

When the company began operation in the late 1940s, it met with little controversy. There was no evidence that the tailings were directly or indirectly harmful to humans, and the lake itself seemed big and deep enough to absorb the discharge. The company received the appropriate licenses and began a twenty-year period of relatively trouble-free operation as a firm that was contributing to the local economy, meeting the demands of the marketplace, and causing no demonstrable environmental harms. In this sense, Reserve Mining met its environmental responsibilities, at least according to the standards of the 1950s.

By the late 1960s, however, all this changed. Some scientific studies suggested that the tailings were harming fish and other lake life. Some local residents objected, mostly on aesthetic grounds, to the discoloration of the lake water. Some studies found trace amounts of a form of asbestos in area water systems and suggested that Reserve Mining's discharge was its source. In 1969, several environmental groups filed lawsuits to stop the discharge of tailings into Lake Superior.

In the initial liability stage, the burden of proof was on those harmed by business activities. Individuals could recover compensatory damages only if it could be proven that an identifiable harm was caused by the negligent conduct of business. Absent that proof, business was free to continue its pursuit of profit. This was the context in which Reserve Mining operated for decades.

During the years of litigation that followed, business' environmental responsibilities were being expanded. This was the decade that witnessed the creation of the EPA (1970), and passage of the federal Clean Air (1970), Clean Water (1972), and Pesticide Control (1972) Acts. Public policies developing during this period shifted the focus from liability and compensation to regulation and prevention. By the early 1970s, business was required to meet a wide range of regulatory standards aimed at preventing environmental harms and the burden of proof for meeting these standards was shifting on to business.

A number of ethical considerations support this shift away from an exclusive reliance on liability and compensation. First, there is the general principle that preventing harm is preferable to providing compensation after the fact. As the Ford Pinto case illustrated, the threat of compensatory damages is an insufficient deterrent when companies use cost–benefit analysis to decide if the benefits outweigh the potential liability. Second, the liability model works best in cases of financial harm since legal compensation is typically monetary. However, in many environmental controversies, people suffer harms to their health and safety, and this cannot adequately be compensated through financial payments. Third, environmental harms can often be long term, and intervening events can make compensation impossible. Such was the case with Love Canal where seepage of toxic chemicals occurred years after their burial and the resultant diseases even years later. Proof of liability in this case was difficult, and the firm that disposed the waste was no longer in business at that site. Finally, the application of the liability model was restricted to provable harms (e.g., physical injuries or financial loss) to identifiable individuals. This omitted a wide range of potential victims and potential harms, including aesthetic, ecological, and health harms to future generations of humans, as well as present and future animals, plants, and ecosystems.

This shift from liability, with its goal of compensation, to the regulatory model, with its goal of prevention, represented a dramatic change in environmental responsibility. This shift was essentially complete by the end of the Reserve Mining litigation. At the start of this case, the burden of proof was on the environmental groups to show that the discharge was harmful to humans. During the litigation, however, especially after a form of asbestos was identified in the wastes, the burden shifted on to the company to prove that the tailing were safe. The scientific evidence was ambiguous. In light of this, the courts allowed Reserve Mining to continue operating at the start of the case; within a year, the court issued an injunction to close the plant. The evidence had not changed, but the burden of proof had.

By the mid-1970s, a wide-ranging environmental regulatory system was in place. These standards restricted the manufacture and use of pesticides, fertilizers and other chemical products; they controlled what could be discharged into air and water; they established norms for waste disposal; they protected wetlands and wilderness areas; they controlled land use and fish and wildlife management; they set limits to noise pollution; they conserved energy sources and open spaces.

The philosophical ethics implicit in this approach fits the standard utilitarian/individual rights model. The assumptions seem to be that business serves the utilitarian goal of maximizing happiness when it seeks to satisfy consumer demand in an open and competitive marketplace. However, this utilitarian goal is constrained by the rights of individuals. Business has an obligation to respect the rights of individuals and activities that threaten these rights should be restricted, even if they advance the overall good. Environmental harms violate the rights of individuals and thus business has an obligation to refrain from causing such harms, even at the cost of increased consumer satisfaction (and therefore profits). While there is a widespread consensus on this general framework, resolutions of these specific questions remain at the center of many contemporary environmental debates.

Responsibilities to the natural world

Many ethicists have criticized the application, if not the appropriateness, of the utilitarian/individual rights approach to environmental concerns. Some, for example Peter Singer and Tom Regan, argue that this framework has been inappropriately restricted to humans. These philosophers argue – Singer (1990) on utilitarian grounds and Regan (1983) in terms of individual rights – that animals have moral standing and that, consequently, humans have moral responsibilities to them. Others, for example Holmes Rolston (1988) and Mark Sagoff (1990), argue that environmental concerns raise broader questions of value than those raised by the more narrow utilitarian and rights perspectives. Thus, human responsibility to the natural world should be based upon a wide range of values, including aesthetic, symbolic, spiritual, historical, as well as moral values.

Many of these issues were first raised for the business community in the well-known Mineral King Valley dispute. In the late 1960s, the US Forest Service solicited proposals for development of Mineral King Valley, a publicly owned wilderness area adjacent to Sequoia National Park. Walt Disney Enterprises submitted a plan to develop this area as a ski resort, complete with hotels, restaurants, a rail line and other facilities to accommodate an estimated 14,000 daily visitors. The Sierra Club objected to these plans and filed a lawsuit to prevent the commercial development of the area.

The case made its way to the US Supreme Court, where it was decided in favor of Disney and the Forest Service. The Court argued that the Sierra Club lacked the necessary legal standing to file suit. Nevertheless, the case explicitly raised two critical issues seldom before considered as part of business's social responsibilities. The Sierra Club argued that the well-being of animals, plants, rivers, and the valley itself should have been considered in the decision to develop the land. They also argued that the Forest Service failed to give aesthetic and ecological considerations equal weight with economic considerations.

To support the Sierra Club's case, Christopher Stone (1974) wrote his well-known book, *Should Trees have Standing?*, in which he argued that trees and other natural objects should be granted legal standing. Arguing by analogy with corporations and other social institutions, Stone claimed that trees, animals, and other natural objects have interests that can and should be legally recognized and protected. Thus, business should be legally constrained from harming the interests of natural objects.

While Stone was making the legal case for animal rights, Singer and Regan were making the philosophical case that animals deserve moral consideration. Singer argued, as had Bentham in the nineteenth century, that the capacity for suffering is sufficient for moral standing. Thus, we have ethical responsibilities to all sentient creatures. Regan argued that being a "subject of a life," essentially the cognitive capacity for self-consciousness, was sufficient for moral standing. On these grounds, at least mammals can be said to have rights that entail obligations on the part of all moral agents.

These views have significant implications for the ethical responsibility of any business that relies on other living creatures. If these arguments are sound, the compensatory and regulatory framework described above should be extended to include harm to other living creatures. Businesses involved in farming, agriculture, food service, recreation, logging, medical and commercial research, to mention just a few, would have to radically alter their practices to avoid causing harm to animals.

However, extending moral standing to individual animals and other living things fails to address numerous other environmental issues. Many think that the focus on individual animals overlooks, and perhaps conflicts with, important environmental issues such as land development, resource use, wilderness preservation, and global warming. In addition, environmentalists influenced by ecology often support policies that conflict with the animal welfare perspective. Ecological science emphasizes ecological systems as opposed to individual members of the system. Thus, a more ecocentric (or "holistic") approach to environmental concerns will focus on the well-being of an ecosystem rather than the well-being of individual animals that are a part of the ecosystem. An ecocentric ethic is willing to pursue policies that may actually harm individual animals, including thinning herds of overpopulated species, introducing predators, and exterminating non-native species.

One alternative perspective is to argue for moral standing for such things as ecosystems and species. This approach seeks to extend the language of utilitarianism and rights to objects other than individual living beings, but this ethical extensionism is controversial. Applying such concepts as "rights," "welfare," and "interests" to wetlands, lakes, prairies, mountains, and wilderness areas requires quite a stretch. Instead, a shift to discussions of intrinsic value provides an alternative way to talk about responsibilities to the non-human natural world.

Environmental responsibilities arising out of this perspective differ significantly from the more individualistic approach of the animal welfare view. For example, wilderness areas and wetlands should be protected not just because they provide habitat for animals (as the animals welfare movement would claim), nor just when they provide instrumental goods for humans (as the more traditional anthropocentric ethics would claim). Rather than granting moral standing to ecosystems, a more promising approach emphasizes the intrinsic value of natural ecosystems. We have responsibilities to them because of their aesthetic, spiritual, historic, or symbolic value. It is these values which sometimes conflict with the more narrow financial interests of business.

This framework can be helpful in understanding many common local disputes often characterized as "environmental." Zoning controversies, for example, raise ethical conflicts between property rights and other important values. Local developers seeking to build a strip mall on the remaining native prairie in a community pits property rights against aesthetic, symbolic and historical values. A real estate company building a housing development along a scenic river or within an endangered oak savanna raises similar value conflicts. Urban sprawl offends a variety of values that make human life meaningful and worth living. On the national level, a proposal by the Disney Company in the early 1990s to develop an amusement park on the site of a Civil War battlefield was cast as an environmental dispute in which historical and symbolic values conflicted with the interests of business and consumers.

Distinct philosophical issues are implicit in this approach to environmental ethics. Some of the earliest environmental controversies, such as air and water pollution, fit the common applied ethics framework. Widely accepted ethical principles were applied to novel environmental issues. Even the novel issues of responsibilities to future generations of humans and to animals only extended the utilitarian/rights language. However, the shift to discussions of intrinsic value raises many questions seldom asked under the applied ethics framework.

In many ways, this shift can be seen as a return to a more traditional understanding of ethics. Greek ethics, for example, focused ethical responsibilities on the pursuit of the good, in all its forms. It was only in the modern period that "ethics" took on a more narrow scope in which responsibilities extend only to other individual human beings, or "rights-bearers." This alternative approach requires that we return to discussions of the good, in all its forms: moral, aesthetic, spiritual, symbolic, etc.

Many challenges face those who would defend environmental responsibilities in terms of the intrinsic value of non-human natural objects. Epistemological challenges are perhaps the most serious. Aesthetic, symbolic, and spiritual values are thought vague and subjective. They seem to speak more about us as subjects than about anything factual or objective. Values are thought personal, a matter of mere feelings or emotions, and therefore an inadequate basis for ethical or legal responsibilities. Beauty is, so the saying goes, in the eye of the beholder.

One implication of this critical view would be that non-human natural objects are valuable only insofar as they serve human interests. Unused or "undeveloped" land is wasted if not worthless. Nature is equated with "resources," and has no value unless used. On this view, nature has only instrumental value and ethics is narrowly anthropocentric. Thus, those who wish to defend the intrinsic value of nature face serious hurdles. Policies aimed at preserving wilderness areas, seashores, native prairies, and woodlands are challenged to articulate and defend the claims that such areas are more valuable and more meaningful than strip malls, housing developments, farmland, and, in general, property rights.

It is fair to say that, when such issues are raised, environmental ethics has expanded into something more accurately described as environmental philosophy. As we have seen, environmental issues raise important questions not only of morality, but epistemological, aesthetic, religious, social, and even metaphysical issues as well.

Business ethics in the age of sustainable economics

A final area of overlap between business ethics and environmental issues involves neoclassical economics and the value of economic growth. Virtually all discussions of corporate social responsibility within business ethics fit one of three general models, each operating against a backdrop of neoclassical economics and the assumed value of economic growth. There are good reasons, however, for thinking that economic growth is ecologically and ethically deficient. If this is so, then most theories of corporate social responsibility must be significantly revised.

A variety of social responsibilities for business are derived from the neoclassical model of economics. In general, business managers have a responsibility to maximize profits. By doing this, business contributes to an efficient allocation of resources (they go to produce those goods that people most value) and an optimal satisfaction of consumer demand. To meet this demand, a successful business creates jobs, which puts more income into the hands of consumers, which increases consumer demand, which begins the process all over again. Within the neoclassical model, a healthy economy is a growing economy – more people are continuously receiving more of what they want – and business is the engine that powers this growth.

However, a variety of environmental issues pose profound challenges to the assumption of economic growth that lies at the heart of neo-classical economics. Some thinkers argue that environmental issues should operate not simply as side-constraints upon the economic activity of business, but must be used to redefine the very nature of economic activity.

To understand this claim, consider several economic, population, and ecological facts. First, the 25 percent of the world's population that live in industrialized countries (mostly North America, Europe, and Japan) consume 80 percent of the world's goods. Producing these goods has already put a significant strain on the natural world, ranging from ozone depletion and global warming to air, water, and soil pollution, to loss of such resources as forests, wetlands, and topsoil, to the extinction of countless species of plants and animals.

The remaining 75 percent of the world's population live not only in relative poverty (relative to the industrial nations), but many live in absolute poverty as well. Literally, hundreds of millions of human beings live at barely minimal levels of subsistence. The majority of the world's population lacks the nutritional, medical, and housing resources that the industrialized world takes as given. In light of this tremendous inequality, human beings face overwhelming humanitarian concerns, if not basic questions of justice.

Economic growth is widely seen as the answer to this inequality and misery. The World Bank, the International Monetary Fund, most governments, and certainly the majority of economists, believe that so-called "undeveloped" economies can follow the same path as the "developed" economies and grow themselves out of poverty. As the undeveloped economies (mostly in the South) grow, they provide jobs and income for their citizens. This income is used to satisfy the needs of the population and creates more demand, more growth, and more income. Of course, the developed economies in the North also must grow to provide markets and investments for the South. Thus, worldwide economic growth is the means for achieving a more decent and just world. Business serves this ideal simply by fulfilling the responsibilities established for it by neoclassical economics.

However, let us consider the amount and type of growth that would be necessary to achieve such goals. One estimate claims that a fivefold increase in energy use, and a five-to-tenfold increase in general economic activity would be necessary over the next fifty years to bring the standards of living for the present population of developing countries into line with the standards of living in the industrialized world. Even by conservative estimates, the world's population in fifty years will be nearly double what it is now. Thus, bringing the standard of living of the less developed economies into line with that presently enjoyed by the developed world would require perhaps a ten-to-twentyfold increase of economic activity. Further, given the amount of capital investment that would be required to support that growth, and given the fact that most accessible and highest grade resources have already been used, the ten-to-twentyfold increase estimate is likely very conservative. (For the five-to-tenfold increase claim, see MacNeill (1989). Population growth during the early 1990s is estimated to be between

1.7 percent and 2 percent. A 2 percent growth rate would double the world population in 34 years. At 1.7 percent, the world population would increase to 27.5 billion people within one hundred years. For the greater capital investment claim, see Daly (1993).)

Consider what a ten-to-twentyfold increase would mean for such issues as carbon dioxide emissions, the extraction of fossil fuels and minerals, rainforest destruction, fish harvest, pesticide and fertilizer use, the diversion of water from lakes, rivers, and aquifers, the generation of nuclear wastes, and plant and animal extinction. Consider also that orthodox economists and politicians consider a 3 percent growth rate for the economy as healthy. That would double the size of the US economy, for example, in less than twenty-five years.

Most importantly, we need to acknowledge that there are biophysical limits to such growth. As economist Herman Daly convincingly argues, the world economy is but a subsystem of a fixed-size ecosystem. It depends on that ecosystem for resources ("input") and as a repository for wastes. With the exception of solar energy, the worldwide supply of resources is already under stress. Given the second law of thermodynamics, there are also real limits to our ability to recycle wastes. The world's economy cannot, biologically and physically, grow indefinitely. For the most recent statement of Daly's views, see Daly (1996).

One implication of this is that business cannot continue to operate in ways that ignore these biophysical limits to growth. Business ethics cannot continue to assume that a major portion of business's social responsibility is met by contributing to continuous economic growth. While, perhaps, not every business at all times needs to operate in a sustainable manner, it is clear that every business at all times cannot continue to grow indefinitely.

If the economic model that most theories of corporate social responsibility presuppose is ecologically deficient, then these theories must be recast in terms of an acceptable economic model. In recent years, the outlines of that alternative theory have begun to emerge. This alternative theory is variously called "sustainable," "steady-state," or "ecological" economics.

The alternative to economic growth is not economic stagnation or decline as some critics would claim. Clearly substantial economic activity will be required to meet the basic needs of the world's growing population. The alternative is best understood through a contrast between economic "growth" and economic "development."

Daly refers to "growth" as a quantitative increase in the economy's physical scale; growing economies become bigger. "Development" refers to a qualitative improvement in the economy; developing economies become better. Sustainable economies, what Daly calls the "steady-state economy," can develop indefinitely but they cannot grow indefinitely. Thus, sustainable development ought to be the goal of the world's economy and a primary ethical standard for business activity. Sustainable growth, on the other hand, is an oxymoron.

To the two fundamental norms of neoclassical economics, efficient allocation and efficient (or just) distribution, Daly adds a third: efficient scale. Economies should operate at a scale that can meet the needs of the present generation, without jeopardizing the ability of future generations to meet their needs.

We can now begin to sketch some of the implications that this norm would have for business ethics. One important test focuses on the rate at which resources are being taken from the ecosystem and wastes are being disposed back into the ecosystem. Business should not, and over the long term cannot, use renewable resources at rates that exceed the ecosystem's ability to replenish itself. Business should not and cannot use non-renewable resources at rates that exceed the development of alternatives. Business should not and cannot generate wastes at rates that exceed the ecosystem's capacity to assimilate them.

These general conditions can be understood as side-constraints upon how business operates in meeting consumer demand. Business ought to respond to the market only in ways that are ecologically sustainable. However, we should recognize that business does not merely respond to markets, business activity influences markets as well. There would thus be marketing implications of the shift to steady-state economics. Business should stop promoting products that are unsustainable, and help to educate consumers to the need for ecologically benign, if not beneficial, choices.

The shift to steady-state economics also has implications for strategic planning, finance, and accounting. Throughout the reign of neoclassical economics, labor and human-made capital were the limiting factors of production. Economic rationality directed business to invest in the most scarce factor. Thus, in times of high unemployment, investing in factories yields greatest returns; in times of idle factories and low unemployment, investing in worker training or wages would yield greatest returns. So, what if, as some evidence already suggests, we are in an age in which natural resources, "natural capital," is the limiting factor? The same economic (and ethical) rationality directs business to invest in natural capital.

Daly uses the example of the oceanic fishing to highlight this point. Until the 1990s, the limiting factor on fish harvest was either labor or human-made capital (e.g., fishing boats). In this situation, responsible managers would invest in fishing boats (labor not being an issue) so as to optimize their returns. Since the early 1990s, the limiting factor on worldwide fish harvest has been the dwindling population of fish. Workers and boats lie idle because there simply are no fish to catch. We have reached the limits of growth for the fishing industry (at least in many sections of the Atlantic, the Mediterranean, and Bering); but we have not reached the limits of development.

One implication of this is that business management should, on economic, ecological, and ethical grounds, begin investing in natural capital. This can be done through cultivation of resources, investment in research and development of alternatives, and in reducing present use of resources to a level of use that could be sustained indefinitely.

There would also be financial and accounting implication of this shift. Again under the neoclassical model, natural resources were typically treated as income, something that could be freely and indefinitely consumed without cost. (The classic "Hicksian" definition of income (Hicks, 1946) is the maximum value which people can consume during a period of time and still be as well off at the end as they were at the beginning.)

Steady-state economics argues that natural resources should be treated as capital, not as income. While it is always possible to liquidate one's resources, i.e., treat capital as income, in a world of biophysical limits doing so is neither economically, ecologically, nor ethically right. Incorporating this shift into accounting, banking, and finance would involve a major rethinking of the social responsibilities of these professions.

Much work is yet to be done on the social responsibilities of business under a steady-state model of economics. International investments and trade, wage differentials within a firm, research and development, engineering, plant location, and energy use are just some of the areas that would need to be revisited with an eye towards the ecological implications of present practice. However, the combination of economic growth, population growth and poverty coming up against the ecological limits to growth make this work imperative.

References

Bartlett, R. 1980: *The Reserve Mining Controversy*. Indianapolis: Indiana University Press.

Daly, H. 1993: Sustainable growth: An impossibility theorem. In H. Daly and K. Townsend (eds), *Valuing the Earth*, Boston: MIT Press, 267–73.

Daly, H. 1996: *Beyond Growth*. Boston: Beacon Press.

Hicks, J. 1946: *Value and Capital*, 2nd edn. Oxford: Oxford University Press.

MacNeill, J. 1989: Strategies for sustainable development. *Scientific American*, 155–65.

Newton, L. and Dillingham, C. 1994: *Watersheds: Classic Cases in Environmental Ethics*. Belmont, Ca.: Wadsworth Publishing.

Newton, L. and Schmidt, D. 1996: *Wake Up Calls: Classic Cases in Business Ethics*. Belmont, Ca.: Wadsworth Publishing.

Regan, T. 1983: *The Case for Animal Rights*. Berkeley: University of California Press.

Rolston, H. 1988: *Environmental Ethics*. Philadelphia: Temple University Press.

Sagoff, M. 1990: *The Economy of the Earth*. New York: Cambridge University Press.

Singer, P. 1990: *Animal Liberation*, 2nd edn. New York: New York Review of Books Press.

Stone, C. 1974: *Should Trees Have Standing? Toward Legal Rights for Natural Objects*. Los Altos, Calif.: William Kaufmann.

24

Business ethics and religion

RONALD M. GREEN

On the night of December 11, 1995, fire destroyed a century-old factory complex in Methuen, Massachussets, belonging to Malden Mills, manufacturer of Polartec fabric. Within days of the fire, Malden's CEO and President, Aaron Feuerstein, made a dramatic announcement: he pledged to rebuild his textile operation in Methuen and to continue to pay the full salaries of employees for 30 days. This pledge was later extended several times. As a result of this and other decisions, Feuerstein's handling of the crisis has come to be regarded as a classic instance of ethically responsible business management. (For a fuller presentation of the facts of this episode, see the unpublished case by Penelope Washbourn.)

Feuerstein's decisions were substantially shaped by his Orthodox Jewish faith. In speeches, interviews, and writings, Feuerstein repeatedly refers to biblical and rabbinic teachings to explain his conduct. For example, Feuerstein (1997) began a recent address before a national society of business ethicists by reciting the *Shema*, the ancient prayer uttered daily by Jews: "Hear, O Israel, the Lord, our God, is One." This ritual testimony to monotheism, Feuerstein observed, underlay his refusal to separate his private ethics from his business ethics, and led him to bring his concern for his employees into his business decision making. The separation of personal and professional responsibility that is evidenced in so many corporate business decisions, Feuerstein explained, seems to him to be a form of "polytheism" because it divides the moral world into discreet and independent spheres.

The insistence that one's business life be governed by religiously informed ethical values is not unique to Feuerstein or his Jewish faith. Virtually every major religious tradition emanating from the Bible insists that one's business life is an important dimension of one's faith and a central area of religious expression. Judaism, Islam and Christianity all have long and developed traditions of teaching about business and ethical life.

Despite this, the fact that Feuerstein has been lauded as an "exceptional" businessman shows how infrequently today managers appear to bring their personal religious and ethical values to bear on their workplace decisions. Indeed, the fact that Methuen, Lawrence and other towns where Feuerstein took his stand, though situated at the heart of Protestant New England, had been devastated for decades by the flight of textile mills to lower wage environments, provides dramatic evidence of how unusual this kind of religiously informed, value-laden thinking has been among many ostensibly religious business owners and managers.

The Malden Mills story thus deserves mention at the start of a discussion of religion and business ethics for two seemingly contradictory reasons. First, because it illustrates how important religious ethics can be in shaping conduct in business life. Second, because it also illustrates how unusual it is for American business managers to bring their faith tradition to bear on their business decision making. A single exemplary instance of business conduct provides testimony both to the importance and the irrelevance of religion to business ethics.

In what follows, I want to explore both sides of this paradox. First, I want to develop some of the themes in the Western religious heritage that affirm the importance of ethical conduct in business and that refuse to see business life as a sphere separate from believers' religiously informed ethical responsibilities. Historically, these teachings have had a powerful effect on the conduct of business persons, just as they have in the life of Aaron Feuerstein. Second, I want to offer some explanations of why these teachings have become increasingly irrelevant to the practice of business. Ironically, aspects of these same religious traditions – especially early Christian asceticism and later Protestant concepts of election – played a role in helping to separate the sphere of business conduct from one's personal religious and ethical life. Finally, I will suggest that this separation of religion and business ethics should be reconsidered. Religious values are major shapers of people's conduct. Business ethics, whether as an academic discipline or as a part of management practice, cannot afford to ignore "the religious factor."

Historical perspectives on business ethics and religion

Biblical teachings

The religions that have most influenced American culture – Judaism, Catholicism, and Protestantism – all take as their point of departure the Hebrew Bible, which possesses a rich tapestry of teachings about both social justice and business conduct. Characteristically, social justice and business conduct are not treated as distinct matters: the larger norms and structures governing economic distribution are reflected in the specific practices expected of business persons. Thus, the Bible's concern for the poor finds expression in such specific matters as the requirement that farmers leave gleanings of the harvest in their fields for the poor and day laborers, and the requirement that they pay their workers promptly (Leviticus 19:9–10; 23:22; Deuteronomy 24:10–14, 19–21). Despite sharp criticisms of economic injustice, greed, and commercial chicanery in the law codes and prophetic writings, the Hebrew Bible clearly accepts business itself as a legitimate sphere of human endeavor. The market economy, commerce, and the profit motive are all accepted as natural facts of life. Although some Jews and Christians in the modern period interpret the Bible's compassion for the poor as requiring radical social re-engineering and the replacement of capitalism by socialism or communism, there is little support for this in the Bible itself. From the biblical perspective, the task before the righteous is not to replace business with some religiously inspired utopian order, but to conduct business ethically within the confines of a righteous community.

As a rule, the Bible imparts to all the traditions that derive from it – including Islam (Abeng, 1997) – a series of basic business ethics norms. As stated explicitly in the law codes of Exodus, Leviticus, and Deuteronomy, these include the following:

- Fulfillment of promises (pacts and contracts, verbal and written), a requirement based on God's own faithful covenental behavior (Deuteronomy 23:21–23)
- Exactness in weights and measures in all business related matters (Leviticus 19:35–36; Deuteronomy 25:13–16)
- Truthfulness, sincerity and honesty – lying and cheating are condemned (Exodus 22:10; 23:1–3; Leviticus 19:11–12)
- The safe conduct of business and commercial activities (Exodus 21:28–35)
- Condemnations of bribery and corruption, especially efforts to corrupt government or judicial officials for commercial gain (Exodus 23:6; Deuteronomy 16:18–20; Deuteronomy 27:25)
- Protection and respect for those who are powerless or especially vulnerable to harm (Exodus 22:25; 23:10–12; Leviticus 19:9–10) – this embraces strict norms for the fair treatment of labor and extends, as well, to the humane treatment of working animals (Deuteronomy 25:4; cf. Deuteronomy 22:6)
- Respect for the environment as God's property and as the enduring legacy of the holy community (Deuteronomy 11:14; 20:19–20)

Judaism

The Jewish faith, which arose in the first centuries of the common era from this biblical foundation, largely continues and develops this point of view. For many reasons (not least of all their forced exclusion from landowning), Jews became active participants in trade and commerce. Jewish law and ethics were forged by rabbinic teachers in diverse diaspora environments in an effort to apply biblical norms to emergent problems and challenges. The result was a body of teachings compiled in texts collectively known as the Talmud, a large part of whose normative content – some estimate up to a third – deals with matters of trade and commerce. As Elliot Dorff (1997) notes, the importance these teachings had in the lives of Jews is summarized by the rabbinic comment that when a person is ultimately brought before the Heavenly Throne for judgment, the *very first* question he or she will be asked is, "Did you transact your business honestly?" Recently, Jewish and other business ethicists have begun to publish English-language studies of this long tradition and have sought to apply classical norms found there to modern business conditions. These texts deal with issues such as truth in sales and advertising; product safety and liability; workplace safety and the environmental responsibility of firms; employee obligations of service and employee rights to privacy in the workplace; and the ethics of bankruptcy; see, for example, Levine (1987), Tamari (1987, 1990, 1997), Schnall (1993) and Green (1997).

Catholicism

In many respects, it appears that the early Christian community continued the themes found in the Hebrew Bible. Although many Christians were poor and some were slaves, there is no evidence that trade and commerce were forbidden or condemned. At least some members of the early community were wealthy (Matthew 27:57) and all who lacked independent means (including apostles) were expected to work for a living in useful trades (II Thessalonians 3:7–11). However, the New Testament's acute sensitivity to the needs of the disadvantaged, a sensitivity sharpened by Christ's own sacrificial commitment to the poor and socially outcast, added a critical edge to Christian teaching where wealth and the pursuit of private economic gain are concerned. Christ's overturning of the tables of the money changers in the temple (Matthew 21:12–13; Mark 11:15; Luke 19:45–46) and his sharp denunciations of excessive preoccupation with wealth or financial security (Matthew 6:19, 24; 20–23; Mark 10:23–25; Luke 12:16–21; 17:28–30; 18:22–25) sharpened this edge. An ideal of mutual sharing of possessions inscribed in the Book of Acts (4:32) also established an alternate economic vision that continued to influence Christian thought. Finally, early eschatological expectations of the imminent end of the world and repeated bouts of persecution fostered the sense that existing forms and institutions were marked by sin and doomed to soon pass away.

These sentiments were not entirely hospitable to commerce and business life. In time, as the earliest Christian efforts to provide an alternate society were replaced by worldly accommodation, they helped to stimulate development of ascetic forms of world denial at the margin of a thinly Christianized Roman society. This eventually gave rise to the complex and multi-faceted monastic movement of the medieval Catholic Church. The monasteries sustained the early ideal of community of possessions. Although they often innovated in agriculture and technology, and there were even singular instances of saintly Christians who conducted large business enterprises, the monastic ideal was not a model for business life. The predominance of ascetic motifs in Catholic Christianity and the prestige of this ideal contributed to Catholicism's relative disengagement from the kind of normative regulation of business conduct that continued to characterize Judaism and Islam. (For an interesting exception to the rule that Catholic religious leaders were not involved in business, see McKenna (1997).)

As Catholicism developed and became more integrated in the medieval social world, business and commerce eventually came to be regarded as an acceptable (if less meritorious) lifestyle for the laity. The critical edge of earlier Christian attitudes now found expression in the effort to protect poorer members of society from economic exploitation. This took form in the strong reaffirmation of biblical condemnations of usury and development of the doctrine of just price. However, both efforts eventually ran counter to powerful market forces. Over time, they were modified to express greater acceptance of market realities and the ban on usury was eventually phased out as an anachronism in the modern period (Nelson, 1949; Noonan, 1957).

It is thus fair to say that for much of its history, Catholic Christianity devoted its ethical energies in the economic sphere to questions of social justice rather than business ethics per se. The focus of concern was on the just distribution of economic resources rather than the ethical conduct of business by owners, managers, and employees. This remained true well into the modern period. Major papal encyclicals and Episcopal documents dealing with economic life – which together compose what is called the tradition of Catholic Social Teaching – focus on broad questions of social and economic justice. Some issues, such as the rights of workers and the dignity of work, have bearing on the ethical choices before business owners and managers, but, until recently, there was relatively little attention in this literature to addressing the kinds of managerial decisions and stakeholder conflicts that are staples of the modern discipline of business ethics. In this sense, it can be said that there is a side to Roman Catholic economic teachings – its preference for larger scale economic transformation in the name of social justice and its historic discomfort with capitalism – that is inimical to "business ethics." At the same time, however, it should be noted that the long history of Catholic attention to economic justice and the constant insistence that faith cannot be separated from one's conduct in the economic sphere provide important resources for contemporary business ethics. (For a discussion of this tradition and its relationship to business ethics, see Velasquez and Brady (1997).)

As Naughton and Laczniak (1993) observe, many features of the Catholic tradition of social thought have bearing on key issues of contemporary business ethics. Foremost among these is the centrality given to human dignity as the foundation and goal of economic life. The primacy of human dignity underlies other basic aspects of contemporary Catholic teaching, including such matters as the importance of work for the ethical formation of persons; the requirement that workers receive a just wage; the need to preserve the human nature of the productive process; and the requirement that business offer services and products that enhance, rather than erode, the ethical quality of human life. It is also worth noting that the tradition of Catholic social thought may have indirectly contributed to the emergence of modern business ethics through the stimulus it provided to the work of leading business ethicists who were formed in the Catholic tradition or who began their careers teaching ethics in the philosophy or business departments of Catholic universities. The writings of John Boatright, Gerald Cavanagh, Thomas Donaldson, Al Gini, Kenneth Goodpaster, John Houck, Dennis McCann, Manuel Velasquez, Patricia Werhane, and Oliver Williams are examples.

Protestantism

No religious tradition has had greater impact in shaping this culture's attitudes toward business and ethics than Protestantism. In part, this is because of the sheer size of the Protestant community, which, spread among many separate confessions and denominations, has been a majority religion for most of American history. In part, it is because from its inception, Protestantism forged a powerful set of ethical and religious teachings bearing on economic and business life.

The most important of these teaching is the concept of "worldly calling" developed by Luther and Calvin. Reacting against Catholic monasticism and perhaps reflecting their base of middle class or business support, both reformers insisted that it is the obligation of each Christian to work out his or her salvation in the world. Henceforth, Protestant Christians were called to serve God on the farm, in the bank, the marketplace, or factory. Among Calvinists, as Max Weber (1958) has brilliantly shown, this teaching fused with earlier notions of mistrust for worldly luxury and led to the pattern of "inner-worldly asceticism" that fostered prodigious capital accumulation. The ascetic Calvinist Protestants wanted to do good and they did very well indeed. Calvinist doctrines of predestination and the notion of "signs of election" also led to an intense scrutiny of one's life to determine one's salvational status. Although the early Calvinists were very hesitant to take worldly success or failure as unambiguous evidence of salvation or damnation, in later, more popular Calvinism, this hesitancy receded. Economic success became a sign of blessedness and poverty was associated with moral and spiritual failure, especially with the unwillingness to work.

From the perspective of business ethics, these Protestant ideas had several diverse, and sometimes contradictory, implications. At the level of individual conduct, most ethical attention was given to individual personal integrity, especially disciplined labor, thrift, and personal sobriety – the famous "work ethic." An upright employee, manager, or owner was one who worked hard, maintained personal integrity (including reasonably honest business practices), and who gave zealous devotion to the goals of the firm. Less attention was paid to the question of how well business practices or the business system as a whole served the needs of other stakeholders: employees, customers, clients, or communities. During the earliest phases of Protestant capitalist development, it was assumed that Christian businessmen would treat others according to the established Christian ideals of respect and compassion, but as early capitalism gave way to the great business enterprises of the Gilded Age, there was a lessening of ethical restraints and increased emphasis on economic success as the sole end of business life. Great Protestant business barons of this period like Andrew Carnegie sought to salve their uneasy consciences by justifying rapacious business practices as a necessary means to achieving personal fortunes that could then be used in monumental acts of philanthropy. This normative abandonment of business life was further accelerated by the development, on Protestant soil, of classical liberal economic ideas espousing the autonomy of economics. As Adam Smith and others suggested, it was important to make economic decisions, not primarily in accordance with Christian ethics, but with the laws of the market.

This conceptual environment was inhospitable both to the close-grained moral regulation of business life that marks the Jewish tradition or the larger concern for social justice that characterizes Catholicism. It was also not propitious for the kind of complex assessments and negotiation of stakeholder claims that occupy business ethicists today. If "business ethics" has been widely regarded as an oxymoron in our culture, therefore, and if many otherwise deeply committed religious people believe that business life must be kept separate from their personal ethical and religious commitments, this is at least partly the result of a religious history that has shaped and yielded these ideas.

Nor is this history altogether behind us. Earlier in this century, many progressive Protestant denominations, growing uncomfortable with the excessive individualism of Protestant economic ethics, began to look anew at the relationship between Christian faith and the business system. One result of this was the Social Gospel movement whose founders and contributors made various contributions to Protestant thinking in this area. Some, like Walter Rauschenbusch, sought to apply older individualized notions of sin to social structures and urged a thoroughgoing reevaluation of the capitalist business system (Rauschenbusch, 1912, 1917). Others, like Charles Monroe Sheldon (1935), whose book, *In His Steps*, imaginatively portrayed Jesus as a modern businessman, sought to bring older Christian ethical ideals into the workplace. These liberal Protestant efforts helped to pave the way for many progressive economic and social reforms in the course of this century and fostered the inclusion of "social ethics" courses in the curricula of most liberal Protestant seminaries. More recently, the liberal Protestant impulse has turned to business practices and business ethics per se. Individual scholars have tried to apply traditional Protestant economic ideas, such as vocation, covenant, and *agape* (or Christian love) to business issues such as the ethical conduct of downsizing (Stackhouse, 1987; Stackhouse et al., 1995; Childs,

1997). Organizations like the Investor Responsibility Research Center have emerged through which liberal Protestant denominations (and other Christian communities) have tried to encourage investment in socially responsible corporations. (For example, the IRRC, publishes the serial *News for Investors* that is widely used by universities, pension and mutual funds and other institutions and individuals concerned with socially responsible investment.) The IRRC played a major role in encouraging adoption by many American corporations of the Sullivan Principles governing corporate involvement in South Africa during the apartheid years, and in efforts to change the marketing practices of infant formula manufacturers in third world countries (McCoy et al., 1995).

However, liberal denominations no longer form the cutting edge of American Protestantism. Numerically, and in terms of cultural impact, their place is being taken by Evangelical groups. With their emphasis on biblical inerrancy in matters of faith and morals and personal piety in ethics, these groups hark back to the more indi- vidualistic witness of traditional Protestantism. In some cases, this results in a focus on individual piety and integrity (industriousness, self-discipline, churchgoing, and traditional family values) and a relative lack of concern with questions of social justice or the moral quality of corporate business practices themselves. As Shirley Roels (1997, p. 116) observes, "Evangelicals are adamant about their belief in moral absolutes, based in the Ten Commandments, but seem less worried about spelling out detailed implications of these absolutes in the workplace." Sometimes, as well, evangelicalism supports a crass "prosperity theology" in which material success is seen as a token of divine blessedness (p. 113). The worst excesses of discredited televangelists like Jim and Tammy Bakker or Jimmy Swaggert – whose business practices were often as corrupt as their piety – are evidence of this tendency.

More recently, some evangelicals have given renewed attention to the relationship between their faith commitments and business life. Inspired by the application of Gospel ideals to management in books like Robert Greenleaf's (1977) *Servant Leadership*, outspoken "Christian" business managers have emerged who try to bring Christian teachings, as they understand them, to bear on daily life. People like Max De Pree (1989, 1992), retired CEO of Herman Miller, a large furniture manufacturing firm in Zeeland, Michigan, or C. William Pollard (1992, 1996), Chairman of the home and industrial cleaning firm, ServiceMaster, exemplify this development. In some cases, these efforts may point the way to new styles of management in which attention to human values is integrated with older ideals of efficiency and diligence. Based on her study of more than eighty-five evangelical CEOs and top executives from the next management tier, Laura Nash (1994) has argued that many of these evangelicals bring a new, more personal style to management that fits well in the modern relationship-oriented business environment, and addresses some leading issues of business ethics. The personal concern for colleagues and employees that mark many evangelical executives' business life, says Nash, not only corresponds to more participative styles of management but also helps to create a more compassionate and humane work environment. On the other hand, Nash and others acknowledge that, in some cases, evangelical managers' focus on personal piety can mask indifference to more systemic and challenging ethical issues, including such matters as racism and sexism in the workplace (Nash, 1994, pp. 40–45; Roels, 1997, p. 119; Horan, 1995). It can be said, therefore, that the Protestant tradition continues to bring to contemporary business ethics the whole spectrum of its historic responses.

Current issues and challenges

This review of the ways in which business and religion have been related to each other in our cultural past sheds light on the more basic question of the place of religion in the study and practice of business ethics today. It tells us, for example, that religion has always been intimately connected with the ethical conduct of business life, even when that conduct was perceived in only the most limited terms as personal virtue and hard work. It also tells us that many business people are far more influenced in their ethical conduct and attitudes by their religious background than may seem to be the case. It is a mistake to interpret the resistance of many business people to the ethical review of business practices as simply indifference to religious and ethical norms. In many cases, this resistance springs from a religiously informed understanding of righteous conduct that focuses more on personal morality and on the achievement of economic success than on a full range of ethical responsibilities for business managers. There are a small number of empirical studies trying to determine whether there is an association between professed religious commitment and ethical conduct in business environments. These studies reveal no clear pattern and they appear to be flawed in many ways. Most focus on business students possessing little or no practical experi- ence. Most, also, do not consider that competing religious and ethical values, such the unwillingness to report cheating by a peer or the belief that one must give one's full loyalty to one's firm, make it hard to measure the overall impact of religious beliefs and formation. (For the most important of these studies, see Ford and Richardson (1994), Clark and Dawson (1996), Kennedy and Lawton (1996), Barnett et al. (1996).)

Since religion can have such powerful impact on the conduct of business people, the challenge for those concerned with improving the ethical performance of business firms is to integrate religious perspectives into their analyses of business issues and into the training and formation of business managers – not to neglect "the religious factor" in business ethics but to refine and apply it to business problems. In responding to this challenge, however, several practical and conceptual problems must be faced.

At a practical level, it can be asked whether the pluralistic nature of our society, and the religious diversity that marks most large business organizations, permit us to bring religion into corporate decision making. How can CEOs of large public firms employ religious considerations in their decision making when many of the stakeholders of the firm may not share their religious views? Does not the American political doctrine of separation of church and state have its counterpart at the business level in a require- ment of religious neutrality that makes the firm largely a "religion-free" zone?

The answer to this question is quite complex. First of all, it is important to remember that the legal doctrine of separation of church and state has, as its counterpart, citizens' right to the free expression of their religious beliefs. So long as other legal requirements are respected, this certainly includes acting on personal, religiously informed ethical convictions in any context. The official exercise of religion is not permitted in govern- mental organizations, but there is no constitutional bar to what can be done in non- governmental contexts. Although it would be ethically inappropriate for corporate managers to impose their religious views on others, this does not preclude an active role for religious beliefs in managerial decision making. For example, within the forum of their conscience, managers may utilize the resources of their tradition in arriving at decisions that they are prepared to justify on independent, business-related grounds. Aaron Feuerstein's handling of his firm's crisis reflects this pattern, since he was prepared to argue that his employee-regarding policies enhanced the firm's long-term profitability.

When a firm is privately held, and owners and managers make their religious commitments clear in advance, they can go further than this, subordinating business considerations to specific religious goals. For this reason, Robert Van Kampen (1989), a Chicago-based bond trader, tries to express his Christian beliefs by maintaining control over the firms he has established. ServiceMaster is an example of one such firm whose Christian purposes are part of its mission. Of course, even religiously motivated firms and managers must respect US laws and values: first, they may not discriminate against employees on the basis of religion; and second, they must be careful about enacting religiously guided policies that contravene laws (such as barring employment of homosexuals in jurisdictions where such discrimination is prohibited) or that violate employees' religious sensibilities. On this second point, note that some public corporations have provoked regulatory intervention or litigation for trying to use controversial forms of spirituality in their executive education programs; see Chris and Zemke (1993).

Finally, they are well advised to show respect for the diverse religious sensibilities of their many stakeholders. It follows from this that secular business managers must also take the religious sensitivities and values of their stakeholders into account in making business decisions. For example, whatever their personal views on controversial issues like abortion or homosexuality, managers buying advertising time on television are well advised to consider the programming content associated with their advertisements (Green et al., 1991).

For individuals and organizations actively seeking to incorporate religious values into their business life, we can imagine the development of specialized sub-fields of business ethics – Muslim, Jewish, Catholic, or Protestant business ethics – that would seek to provide understanding and guidance to those who try to live their business life in conformity with their faith ideals. This possibility has a parallel in medical ethics where there are extensive bodies of literature and teaching on Jewish, Catholic or Protestant medical ethics designed for use by religiously motivated medical practitioners or specialized religious health care organizations.

A further question is whether, outside this specialized context, the existing discipline of business ethics needs to take religious or theological ethics into account in research and teaching. Richard De George (1986a, 1986b) has forcefully argued against any kind of theological business ethics. According to De George, because their ultimate appeal is to one sort or another of revealed truth, theologically grounded business ethics lack the kind of universal basis and appeals to reason needed in the diverse modern business climate. De George concedes that religions can bring powerful motivational resources to business ethics, but he argues that normative moral reasoning, which he regards as the center of a research-based discipline of business ethics, should not proceed from religious premises.

De George is probably right to insist that a discipline which seeks to understand and provide responses to the ethical problems facing most business organizations must employ standards of reasoning and evidence that can be appreciated independently of one's personal religious beliefs. The parallel here is to the need to employ religiously neutral "public reason" in settling contested matters of public policy in a pluralistic democracy (Rawls, 1993; Fort, 1997). Nevertheless, De George oversimplifies by characterizing theologically derived positions as "revelational" only. As critics of his view point out, many religious traditions incorporate appeals to reason in the development of their ethical views (Kreuger, 1986). The rich Roman Catholic tradition of natural law, Protestant appeals to "right reason," and Jewish understandings of the norms applicable to all the offspring of Noah are examples. Thus, for most religious traditions, it is not possible to say that a specific set of teachings lack universal value merely because they appeal to one or another revealed source for their ultimate authority.

De George recognizes that religious traditions sometimes employ rational tools of analysis, but he contends that, when they do, they essentially resort to the philosophical method that he feels is the only one appropriate to business ethics. However, this puts matters too simply. Patterns of moral justification are complex and multifaceted. In developing a policy to minimize the harm of downsizing, a Protestant business manager may draw on an understanding of the Golden Rule or biblically informed concepts of servant leadership; a Catholic may be informed by the teachings of a papal encyclical on work; a Jew may be informed by an ancient Talmudic source requiring fair treatment of employees; and a secular manager may invoke a form of philosophically developed contract reasoning. Each of these positions has a rich logic of its own and each shares many points of contact with the others. In the words of David Schmidt (1986): "A close reading of actual arguments on business ethics would not discern clear boundaries between philosophical and theological considerations but would detect instead a complex network of similarities and contrasts."

Certainly, a discipline like business ethics should not exclude a conversation about these patterns of justification that form such an important part of the life of actual business managers. These modes of reasoning merit critical attention and review as ethicists try to develop their own positions on business responsibility. A similar point is made in response to De George's position by Gerard Magill (1992) and Williams (1986).

Nor should business ethicists ignore the specific ethical teachings of diverse traditions whose norms, arrived at in complex ways, can help to illuminate new questions of ethical conduct. Again, the parallel to medical ethics is illuminating. In this field, the teachings of the very extensively developed traditions of Catholic and Jewish medical ethics are frequently invoked by even non-religious ethicists as they try to develop approaches to difficult new ethical problems posed by medical technology. In doing this, non-religious ethicists do not assume that these teachings have final authority. However, they accept them as reflecting rich traditions of ethical and clinical experience. In the same way, "religious business ethics" deserve a place within the broader discipline of business ethics, not just as specialized sub-fields for believers, but as sources of ethical wisdom that need to be understood, and critically appreciated, in the effort to arrive at sustainable contemporary positions on questions of business practice.

Conclusion

From its inception, biblical faith has refused to separate decision making in the business environment from other faith commitments. This is perhaps the most important implication of religion for business ethics. In the words of Elliot Dorff (1997, p. 31),

> [R]eligion will not allow the attitude, "Business is business," for that asserts that business exists in an isolated realm, free of any ties imposed by other aspects of our life. Religion attests to exactly the opposite view of the world; as the Latin etymology of the word "religion" indicates, religion proclaims the *connections* that we all have to each other and that every part of our being and activity has to every other.

One consequence of this abiding connection between religion and business is that all the religious traditions stemming from the Bible have significant bodies of thought about the norms governing the conduct of both business and economic life. It is also true, however, that, in its historical development, Christianity has sometimes evidenced a less-than-accepting view of business, the market economy, and the profit motive. In other cases, it has been *too* accepting, allowing commercial life to proceed with inadequate normative scrutiny. These tendencies have worked, in different ways, to separate business from ethics and to lead business practitioners to distinguish their religious commitments from their daily workplace practices.

It is unfortunate that religion and ethics should be separated in this way because this runs counter to some of the deepest impulses of religious life. Separation of this sort can lead to a disturbing moral schizophrenia where the individual is pulled intensely by two competing sources of loyalty. Because religion provides one of the most important sources of guidance and motivation for ethical conduct, this separation is also not conducive to the ethical practice of business. To separate religious ethics from business ethics is to impoverish both.

The challenge before religious and non-religious business ethicists is to understand the ways that different religious teachings can be brought to bear on this discipline. As we have seen, there is room for the development of confessional business ethics that could provide insight and guidance to religiously committed individuals and firms. In addition, even secular business ethicists and managers can learn from religious teachings in this area. Religions have always insisted on the social nature of the self and they have struggled with the special ethical demands of economic life for centuries. Their conclusions about specific issues, their modes of reasoning, and the ethical encouragement they offer are resources to be critically assessed and understood by all who are concerned with the ethical conduct of business.

References

Abeng, T. 1997: Business ethics in Islamic context: Perspectives of a Muslim business leader. *Business Ethics Quarterly*, 7(3), 47–54.

Barnett, T., Bass, K., and Brown, G. 1996: Religiosity, ethical ideology, and intentions to report a peer's wrongdoing. *Journal of Business Ethics*, 15, 1161–74.

Childs, J. M. 1997: Lutheran perspectives on ethical business in an age of downsizing. *Business Ethics Quarterly*, 7(2), 123–31.

Chris, L. and Zemke, R. 1993: The search for spirit in the workplace. *Training*, June, 21–8.

Clark, J. W. and Dawson, L. F. 1996: Personal religiousness and ethical judgements: An empirical analysis. *Journal of Business Ethics*, 15, 359–72.

De George, R. T. 1986a: Theological ethics and business ethics. *Journal of Business Ethics*, 5, 421–42.

De George, R. T. 1986b: Replies and reflections on theology and business ethics. *Journal of Business Ethics*, 5, 521–4.

De Pree, M. 1989: *Leadership is an Art*. New York: Dell.

De Pree, M. 1992: *Leadership Jazz*. New York: Currency Doubleday.

Dorff, E. N. 1997: The implications of Judaism for business and privacy. *Business Ethics Quarterly*, 7(2), 31–44.

Feuerstein, A. 1997: Keynote address delivered to the meeting of the Society of Business Ethics, Boston, Mass., Park Plaza Hotel, August 8.

Ford, R. C. and Richardson, W. D. 1994: Ethical decision making: A review of the empirical literature. *Journal of Business Ethics*, 13, 205–21.

Fort, T. L. 1997: Religion and business ethics: The lessons from political morality. *Journal of Business Ethics*, 16, 263–73.

Green, R. M. 1997: Guiding principles of Jewish business ethics. *Business Ethics Quarterly*, 7(2), 21–30.

Green, R. M., Donahue, J. A., and Van Wensveen Siker, L. 1991: Does religion make a difference in your business ethics? The case of Consolidated Foods. *Journal of Business Ethics*, 10(11), November, 819–32.

Greenleaf, R. 1977: *Servant Leadership: A Journey into the Nature of Legitimate Power and Greatness*. New York: Paulist Press.

Horan, K. 1995: The Christian capitalists. *US News and World Report*, March 13, 54.

Kennedy, E. J. and Lawton, L. 1996: The effects of social and moral integration on ethical standards: A comparison of American and Ukrainian business students. *Journal of Business Ethics*, 15, 901–11.

Krueger, D. 1986: The religious nature of practical reason: A way into the debate. *Journal of Business Ethics*, 5, 511–19.

Levine, A. 1987: *Economics and Jewish Law*. New York: Ktav & Yeshiva U. Press.

Magill, G. 1992: Theology in business ethics – appealing to the religious imagination. *Journal of Business Ethics*, 11, 129–35.

McCoy, C. S., Evers, S., Dierkes, M., and Twining, F. 1995: *Nestlé and the Controversy over the Marketing of Breast Milk Substitutes*. Columbus, Ohio: Council for Ethics in Economics.

McKenna, T. F. 1997: Vincent DePaul: The saint who got his worlds together. *Journal of Business Ethics*, 16, 299–307.

Nash, L. 1994: *Believers in Business*. Nashville: Thomas Nelson.

Naughton, M. and Laczniak, G. R. 1993: A theological context of work from the Catholic social encyclical tradition. *Journal of Business Ethics*, 12, 981–93.

Nelson, B. N. 1949: *The Idea of Usury, from Tribal Brotherhood to Universal Otherhood*. Princeton: Princeton University Press.

Noonan, J. T. Jr 1957: *The Scholastic Analysis of Usury*. Cambridge: Harvard University Press.

Pollard, C. W. 1992: Corporate performance: ServiceMaster: Piety, profits, and productivity. *Fortune*, June 29, 84–5.

Pollard, C. W. 1996: *The Soul of the Firm*. Grand Rapids, Michigan: Zondervan Corporation.

Rauschenbusch, W. 1912: *Christianizing the Social Order*. New York: Macmillan.

Rauschenbusch, W. 1917: *A Theology for the Social Gospel*. New York: Abingdon Press. Republished in 1960.

Rawls, J. 1993: *Political Liberalism*. New York: Columbia University Press, 212–54.

Roels, S. J. 1997: The business ethics of evangelicals. *Business Ethics Quarterly*, 7(2).

Schnall, D. J. 1993: Exploratory notes on employee productivity and accountability in classic Jewish sources. *Journal of Business Ethics*, 12, 485–91.

Schmidt, D. P. 1986: Patterns of argument in business ethics. *Journal of Business Ethics*, 5, 501–509.

Sheldon, C. M. 1935: *In His Steps*. New York: Grosset & Dunlap.

Stackhouse, M. 1987: *Public Theology and Political Economy*. Grand Rapids, Michigan: Eerdmans Publishing Co.

Stackhouse, M., McCann, D. P., and Roels, S. J. (eds) 1995: *On Moral Business*. Grand Rapids, Michigan: Eerdmans Publishing Co.

Tamari, M. 1987: *With All Your Possessions: Jewish Ethics & Economic Life*. New York: The Free Press.

Tamari, M. 1990: Ethical issues in bankruptcy: A Jewish perspective. *Journal of Business Ethics*, 9, 785–9.

Tamari, M. 1997: The challenge of wealth: Jewish business ethics. *Business Ethics Quarterly*, 7(2), 45–56.

Van Kampen, R. 1989: Let not the rich man boast of his riches. *Forbes*, 400/October 23, 44–46.

Velasquez, M. and Brady, F. N. 1997: Natural law and business ethics. *Business Ethics Quarterly*, 7(2), 83–107.

Washbourn, P. (unpublished) When all is moral chaos, this is the time for you to be a Mensch: Reflections on Malden Mills for the teaching of business ethics. St Mary's College.

Weber, M. 1958: *The Protestant Ethic and the Spirit of Capitalism*. Translated by T. Parsons. New York: Scribner's.

Williams, O. F. 1986: Can business ethics be theological? What Athens can learn from Jerusalem. *Journal of Business Ethics*, 5, 473–84.

25

Social responsibility and business ethics

ROGENE A. BUCHHOLZ AND SANDRA B. ROSENTHAL

This essay will trace the evolution and eventual intertwining of the fields of social responsibility and business ethics, interweaving historical and philosophical approaches in discussing the issues involved. It is believed that this approach will be of more interest to readers, many of whom may not be acquainted with the development of social responsibility and how it relates to business ethics in an historical sense or a philosophical sense. An appropriate place to begin this discussion is thus with the emergence of the concept of social responsibility as a concern for business.

Corporate social responsibility

While the subject of social responsibility received some attention prior to the 1960s, it was society's concern with social issues in those years that made the concept of social responsibility of major importance to business organizations (De George, 1985). The years from 1960 to 1970 were years of sweeping social change that affected businesses and management. The concern about civil rights for minorities, equal rights for women, protection of the physical environment, safety and health in the workplace, and a broad array of consumer issues has had far-reaching impacts on business organizations. The long-term effect of this social change has been a dramatic change in the "rules of the game" by which business is expected to operate.

The concept of social responsibility thus came into its own during this period of time as a response to the changing social values of society. Business executives began to talk about the social responsibilities of business, and to develop specific social programs in response to problems of a social, rather than economic, nature. Schools of business implemented new courses in business and society, or in the social responsibilities of business. Some schools even developed doctoral programs in the area. Many articles and books were written exploring the meaning of social responsibility and its importance to business organizations.

There are many definitions of social responsibility but, in general, it means that a private corporation has responsibilities to society that go beyond the production of goods and services at a profit. It involves the idea that a corporation has a broader constituency to serve than that of stockholders alone, and, in more recent years, the term stakeholders has been widely used to express this broader set of responsibilities. The concept also means that corporations relate to society through more than just marketplace transactions and serve a wider range of values than the traditional economic values that are prevalent in the marketplace. Corporations are more than economic institutions; they have a responsibility to help society to solve pressing social problems, many of which corporations helped to cause, by devoting resources to the solution of these problems.

The concept of social responsibility is, fundamentally, an ethical concept. It involves changing notions of human welfare, and emphasizes a concern with the social dimensions of business activity that have to do with improving the quality of life. The concept provided a way for business to concern itself with these social dimensions and pay some attention to its social impacts. The word responsibility implies some kind of obligation to deal with social problems that business organizations were believed to have towards the society in which they functioned. It is thus a normative concept dealing with the behavior and policies business ought to adopt.

The debate about social responsibility reflected many ethical or moral dimensions. Proponents of the concept argued these seven points:

1 Business must accommodate itself to social change if it expects to survive.
2 Business must take a long-run view of self-interest, and help to solve social problems so as to create a better environment for itself.
3 Business can gain a better public image by being socially responsible.
4 Government regulation can be avoided if business can meet the changing social expectations of society.
5 Business has enormous resources that would be useful in solving social problems.
6 Social problems can be turned into profitable business opportunities.
7 Business has a moral obligation to help to solve social problems that it has created or perpetuated.

The opponents of social responsibility developed many persuasive arguments against the concept. There are some of their arguments:

1 The social responsibility concept provides no mechanism for accountability as to the use of corporate resources.
2 Managers are legally and ethically bound to earn the highest possible rate of return on the stockholder's investment.
3 Social responsibility poses a threat to the pluralistic nature of our society.
4 Business executives have little experience, and little or no incentive to solve social problems.
5 Social responsibility is fundamentally a subversive doctrine that would undermine the foundations of a free enterprise system.

After the smoke began to clear from this debate, it was obvious – to many proponents and opponents of corporate social responsibility – that there were several key issues that had not, and perhaps could not, be settled. One concerned the operational definition of social responsibility. The traditional marketplace provided little or no information to the manager that would be useful in making decisions about solving social problems. However, the concept of social responsibility in itself did not make up for this lack and provided no clearer guidelines for managers. Given this lack of precision, corporate executives – those who wanted to be socially responsible – were left to follow their own values and interests or generalizations about changing social values and public expectations. What this meant in practice, however, was difficult to determine.

Another key problem with the concept of social responsibility was that it did not take into account the competitive corporate environment. (This problem is perhaps best expressed by Chamberlain: ". . . every business . . . is, in effect, "trapped" in the business system that it has helped to create. It is incapable, as an individual unit, of transcending that system . . . the dream of the socially responsible corporation that, replicated over and over again can transform our society is illusory . . . Because their aggregate power is not unified, not truly collective, not organized, they [corporations] have no way, even if they wished, of redirecting that power to meet the most pressing needs of society . . . Such redirection could only occur through the intermediate agency of government rewriting the rules under which all corporations operate" (Chamberlain, 1973).)

Many advocates of social responsibility treated the corporation as an isolated entity that had almost unlimited ability to engage in unilateral social action. Eventually, it came to be recognized that corporations are severely limited in their ability to respond to social problems. If a firm unilaterally engages in social action that increases its costs and prices, it will place itself at a competitive disadvantage relative to other firms that may not be concerned about being socially responsible.

Concerted action to solve social problems is not feasible in a competitive system unless all competitors pursue roughly the same policy on these problems. Since collusion among competitors is illegal, however, the only way such concerted action can occur is when some other institution, such as government, makes all competitors pursue the same policy, and this is, in fact, what happened. While the debate about social responsibility was going on and corporate executives were asking for a definition of their social responsibilities, government was rewriting the rules under which all corporations operate in society by developing a vast amount of legislation and regulation pertaining to the physical environment, occupational safety and health, equal opportunity, and consumer concerns.

The last issue that remained unresolved in the debate about social responsibility concerns the moral underpinnings of the notion. The term "responsibility" is fundamentally a moral one that implies an obligation to someone or something. It is clear to most people that business has an economic responsibility to produce goods and services, and to perform other economic functions for society. These economic responsibilities constitute the reason for having something like a business organization. But why does business have social responsibilities? What are the moral foundations for a concern with its social impacts?

The proponents of social responsibility produced no clear and generally accepted moral principle that would impose upon business an obligation to work for social betterment (Frederick, 1978). Ascribing social responsibility to corporations does not necessarily imply that they are then responsible for their social impacts. However, various moral strictures were used to try to impose this obligation on business, and various arguments were made to try to link moral behavior to business performance. Little was accomplished, however, by way of developing solid moral support for the

305

notion of social responsibility. Thus the debate about social responsibility was very moralistic in many of its aspects, a debate that often generated a good deal of heat but very little light.

Corporate social responsiveness

The intractability of these issues, according to Frederick (1978), "posed the dreadful possibilities that the debate over corporate social responsibility would continue indefinitely with little prospect of final resolution or that it would simply exhaust itself and collapse as a viable legitimate question." However, beginning in the 1970s, a theoretical reorientation began to take place regarding the corporation's response to the social environment. This new approach was labeled "corporate social responsiveness," and while, initially, it appeared that only semantics was involved, it gradually became clear that the shift from responsibility to responsiveness was much more substantive. (In his paper, Frederick (1978) referred to corporate social responsibility as CSR1 and corporate social responsiveness as CSR2. In later work, he developed a CSR3 which he called corporate social rectitude.)

This shift from responsibility to responsiveness represented an attempt to escape the unresolved dilemmas of the social responsibility debate. This new concept of social responsiveness was defined by Frederick (1978, p. 6) as refering "to the capacity of a corporation to respond to social pressures. The literal act of responding, or of achieving a generally responsive posture, to society is the focus of corporate social responsiveness . . . One searches the organization for mechanisms, procedures, arrangements, and behavioral patterns that, taken collectively, would mark the organization as more or less capable of responding to social pressures. It then becomes evident that organizational design and managerial competence play important roles in how extensively and how well a company responds to social demands and needs."

Thus attention shifted from debate about a moral notion, social responsibility, to a more technical, or at least morally neutral, term: social responsiveness. Research in corporate responsiveness reflected this same shift, and focused on internal corporate responsiveness to social problems, examining the ways in which corporations responded to such problems. Attempts were made to identify key variables within the organization that related to its responsiveness, and to discover organizational and personnel changes that would enable a corporation to respond more effectively. The important questions asked in this research were not moral, related to whether a corporation should respond to a social problem out of a sense of social responsibility, but more practical and action oriented, dealing with the ability of a corporation to respond and the changes that were necessary to enable it to respond effectively.

An advantage of this approach is its managerial orientation. The approach ignores the philosophical debate about responsibility, and focuses instead on the problems and prospects of making corporations more socially responsive. One of the reasons for research into response patterns is to discover those responses that have proven to be effective in dealing with social problems. The approach also lends itself to more rigorous analytical research in examining specific techniques related to corporate social performance to improve the response process. Such research can also discover how management can best institutionalize social policy in the organization.

Given these advantages, however, the concept of social responsiveness was still plagued with the same key problems that faced the concept of social responsibility. The concept of social responsiveness does not clarify how corporate resources shall be allocated for the solution of social problems. Companies respond to different problems in different ways, and to varying degrees, but there is no clear idea as to what pattern of responsiveness will produce the greatest amount of social betterment. The philosophy of responsiveness does not help the company to decide what problems to tackle and what priorities to establish. In the final analysis, it provides no better guidance to management than does social responsibility on the best policies to be adopted to produce social betterment. The concept seems to suggest that management itself decides the meaning of the concept and what social goods and services will be produced (Frederick, 1978, pp. 12–13).

The concept of social responsiveness does not take the institutional context of business into account any more seriously than did social responsibility. Research in social responsiveness did not deal very thoroughly with the impact that government regulation was making on the corporation, nor how the corporation was responding to this change in the political environment. Individual corporations were again treated as rather isolated entities that could choose a response pattern irrespective of their institutional context. There was not enough concern with business–government relations, nor with the role government played in the social response process. Finally, while the question of an underlying moral principle or theory is ignored in the research dealing with corporate social responsiveness in favor of more action-oriented concerns, this turns out to be a dubious advantage. Social pressures are assumed to exist, and it is believed – as an article of faith – that business must respond to them. This places business in a passive role of simply responding to social change. The concept of social responsiveness provides no moral basis for business to become involved. It contains no explicit moral or ethical theory, and advocates no specific set of values for business to follow (Frederick, 1978, pp. 14–16).

Public policy

In the mid-1970s, academics and business managers began to realize that a fundamental change was taking place in the political environment of business. Government was engaged in shaping business behavior and making business respond to a wide array of social problems by passing an unprecedented amount of legislation and writing many new regulations. The political system responded to the social revolution of the 1960s and 1970s by enacting over a hundred laws regulating business activity. Many new regulatory agencies were created, and new responsibilities were assigned to old agencies. These agencies issued thousands of new rules and procedural requirements that affected business operations.

The regulatory role of government continued to expand until the 1980 election of the Reagan administration, when a serious effort was made to cut back on regulations affecting business, but has picked up again in later years. The new type of social regulation, as it came to be called, affected virtually every functional area within the corporation and every level of management. The growth of this new type of regulation was referred to as a second managerial revolution, involving a shift of decision-making power and control over the corporation from managers to a vast cadre of government regulators who were influencing and, in many cases, controlling managerial decisions in the typical business corporation (Weidenbaum, 1977).

During the late 1970s, more and more attention was paid to the changing political environment of business. Books were written that provided a comprehensive overview of the impacts government regulation was making on business (Weidenbaum, 1979). Studies were completed that attempted to measure the costs of social regulation (Weidenbaum and De Fina, 1978; Anderson, 1979). This activity drew attention to the political environment of business, and showed that it had become increasingly hostile, giving rise to legislation and regulation that interfered with the ability of business to perform its basic economic mission. Largely because of this activity, a national debate on regulation was initiated that culminated in the election of an administration in 1980 that promised to reduce the regulatory burden.

Thus began a serious concern with public policy as a new dimension of management. Many business leaders recognized the importance of public policy to business and advocated that business managers become more active in the political process. The motivation for this concern with public policy is clear. If the rules of the game for business are being rewritten through the public policy process and business is being forced to respond to social values through complying with laws and regulations, then business has a significant interest to learn more about the public policy process and to become involved in writing the rules by which business must live. These rules should not be left solely up to public interest groups, Congressional representatives, or agency employees. Business has since come to adopt a more sophisticated approach to public policy, by attempting to influence the public and the legislative and regulatory process with regard to specific laws and regulations.

The public policy approach has some distinct advantages over the corporate social responsibility and social responsiveness concepts. For the most part, there is no question about the nature and extent of management's social responsibilities. Once regulations are approved, these responsibilities are spelled out in excruciating detail. The government becomes involved in specifying technology that can be employed, publishing labeling requirements, developing safety standards for products, specifying safety equipment, and hundreds of other such management responsibilities. Where questions arise about regulations, the court system is available to settle disputes. Management is thus told in great detail what social problems to be concerned with, and to what extent it has to respond.

Obviously, the public policy approach treats business in its institutional context and advocates that managers learn more about government and the public policy process so that they can appropriately influence the process. Government is recognized as the appropriate body to formalize and to formulate public policy for society as a whole. Some form of response by government to most social issues is believed to be inevitable, and no amount of corporate reform is going to eliminate some form of government involvement. Government has a legitimate right to formulate public policy for corporations in response to changing public expectations. According to Buchholz (1977, pp. 12 & 16):

Society can choose to allocate its resources any way it wants on the basis of any criteria it deems relevant. If society wants to enhance the quality of air and water, it can choose to allocate resources for the production of these goods and put constraints on business in the form of standards . . . These nonmarket decisions are made by those who participate in the public policy process and represent their views of what is best for themselves and society as a whole . . . It is up to the body politic to determine which market outcomes are and are not appropriate. If market outcomes are not to be taken as normative, a form of regulation which requires public participation is the only alternative. The social responsibility of business is not operational and certainly not to be trusted. When business acts contrary to the normal pressures of the marketplace, only public policy can replace the dictates of the market.

There is also, at least on the surface, no need for a moral underpinning for a business obligation to produce social betterment. Society makes decisions about the allocation of resources through the public policy process based on its notions about social betterment. The result is legislation and regulation that impinges on business behavior. Business, then, has a moral obligation to obey the law as a good citizen. Failure to do so subjects business and executives to penalties. The social responsibility of business is thus to follow the directives of society as expressed in, and through, the public policy process.

The public policy approach seems to offer a more democratic basis for judging business performance than can be had either by relying on a vaguely formulated notion of social responsibility or by leaving corporate responses in the hands of a managerial elite. Initially, it seemed possible that, by using the public policy approach, scholars and students could escape the values and ethics that underlie these efforts and substitute a more objective and value-neutral basis by which to measure business's social performance. If business adheres to the standards of performance expressed in the law and existing public policy, it can be judged to be socially responsive.

When one digs beneath the surface of this approach, however, one finds public policy questions plagued by the same kinds of ethical dilemmas that have plagued earlier attempts to address the social responsibilities of business. Those who confront social issues in the public policy context cannot ignore the normative dimensions of these issues, because public policy issues are saturated with value-laden phenomena. Public policy is about values and value conflicts, and public policy solutions to these problems are built on a conception of ethics that concerns the promotion of human welfare.

As business becomes more involved in writing the rules of the game – or preventing new ones from being written – the question of managerial guidelines and principles again becomes relevant. What criteria, other than self-interest, are relevant to guide the corporation in the development of its political strategies? Again, the nagging question of defining social betterment or, in a public policy context, of defining the public interest, reappears. Regarding the institutional context, there is the question of the appropriate role for government to play in shaping business behavior. On the other side of the coin, what is the appropriate role for business to play in the political process?

Finally, the absence of a clear moral underpinning for public policy involvement still presents a problem. Does the involvement of business in the public policy process simply mean that business attempts to minimize the impact of social change on itself?

Does not business have more of an obligation to society than is evident in self-serving attempts to manipulate the political environment for its own advantage? Does not business have a moral obligation that goes beyond obeying law and regulation? If business does have social and political responsibilities, what is the moral basis of these responsibilities?

Ethics is thus an important component of the social–political context in which public policy is formulated. Ethical concerns and ideals interact in a very complex fashion with other components of the social–political environment and thus help to determine the public issues that are given attention by a society and the eventual outcome of the debate about issues that reach the public policy agenda.

Public policy issues, from equal opportunity to the physical environment, involve questions about fairness, equity, justice, and rights. Resources are allocated through the public policy process, and costs and benefits are distributed on some ethical basis, even if unrecognized. Management has a responsibility to participate in the public policy process, and this participation must involve more than self-interest to be considered ethical. Some concern must exist for the public interest and the good of the community. For regulations to work, management must show some commitment to implement the law effectively, and must even go beyond what the law requires to solve problems not covered by public policy.

The development of business ethics

All of these fundamental questions about social responsibility, social responsiveness, and public policy are difficult because they are fundamentally moral and ethical questions having to do with the contribution of business to human welfare and fulfillment, the meaning and purpose of business activity in society, nature of human community and the place of business in that community, and similar questions that are basic to human existence. These questions cannot be answered by appeal to an economic calculus such as profit and loss, nor can they be answered satisfactorily through a political process based on power and influence.

For business to respond effectively to social and political issues, these moral and ethical dimensions of the issues must be explicitly recognized and addressed. Ethical questions are fundamental to an institution such as business, because society allows institutions to be developed and to continue operating, based on conceptions of human welfare that are operative in society and the way institutions in society should behave so as to promote human fulfillment. When society's notions of these ethical concepts change, institutions in society have to change accordingly. Business does not exist apart from society.

These moral concerns surfaced in the early 1980s, as the subject of business ethics received a great deal of increased attention in schools of business and management around the country as well as in corporations themselves. Ethical issues were given explicit attention, not subsumed under the topic of social responsibility, social responsiveness, or public policy. These trends have continued into the 1990s as business ethics has become a field of study in its own right with an extensive body of literature, several journals devoted to the subject, and a number of professional bodies both national and international consisting of scholars and practitioners in the field who are concerned to advance teaching and research and the application of business ethics to the business world. More chairs have been established and more conferences held on the subject. Most large corporations have written ethics codes for their companies and many have established some institutional means for addressing ethical concerns within their company.

In general, it can be said that this increased interest reflects some fundamental changes in society regarding a consensus on ethical standards and the conduct of institutions including business organizations. The debate about business ethics reflects the confusion that has resulted from a breakup of the notions previously held about how a business ought to act in a market economy. This broader view of the problem is held by Powers and Vogel (1980):

> In our view, the new concern for corporate ethics and managerial ethics is the logical culmination of a series of social transformations through which the connecting tissues that make up the "organic" connection between management, institution, and society have eroded. What constitutes "ethical custom" is evaporating. The ability of the market mechanism to carry the normative freight between corporations and society is deteriorating as the society increasingly turns to other ways to try to connect its changing values to corporate practice.

The emergence of this concern about business ethics is thus consistent with the emergence of public concern about business policies and practices. As long as there is a consensus as to the appropriateness of the market mechanism in allocating the great majority of society's resources, the ethical notions embedded in the market concept are also accepted as appropriate with respect to business and managerial conduct. Concern about ethics is limited to situations where the accepted standards are violated. However, as that consensus begins to crumble and management is pressured to respond to concerns that are not reflected in market transactions, ethical notions increasingly come to the surface and are the subject of intense debate.

Business ethics involves an effort to confront the normative issues that were a part of the social responsibility debate, but were not handled very effectively, and that tended to be ignored by advocates of social responsiveness and public policy. These normative issues are at the heart of concerns about the future of the corporation and the appropriate roles for business in society. Normative concerns can provide a foundation for continuing managerial efforts to respond to public pressures in an effective manner and learning to balance different interests in corporate activities appropriately. Managerial activities must be based on ethical principles that are acceptable in society at large and consistent with accepted notions of human welfare and fulfillment.

To support this normative effort, business ethics initially drew on traditional ethical theories for purposes of analysis and discussion of ethical issues in business. These theories are still very much in vogue and are used by many scholars in the field. The usual approach to ethical theory in business ethics texts is to present the theory of utilitarianism based on the writings of Bentham and Mill as representative of a more general class of teleological ethics, and Kantian ethical theory related to the categorical imperative as representative of the deontological approach to ethics. These texts then go on to present as well certain notions of justice, usually going into the egalitarianism of John Rawls and the opposing libertarianism of Robert Nozick. They also generally include a discussion of rights, and at times, some variation of virtue theory.

One problem with this approach is that we are left with a kind of ethical smorgasbord where one has various theories from which to choose that will hopefully shed some light on the ethical problems under consideration and lead to a justifiable decision. However, we are never told to any extent exactly how we are to decide which theory to apply in a given situation, what guidelines we are to use in applying these different theories, what criteria determine which theory is best for a given problem, and what to do if the application of different theories results in totally different courses of action.

The authors of these textbooks usually recognize the problem but do not deal with it to any great extent. Tom Donaldson and Particia Werhane (1993), for example, after presenting the theories of consequentialism, deontology, and what they call human nature ethics, state: "Indeed, the three methods of moral reasoning are sufficiently broad that each is applicable to the full range of problems confronting human moral experience. The question of which method, if any, is superior to the others much be left for another time. The intention of this essay is not to substitute for a thorough study of traditional ethical theories – something for which there is no substitute – but to introduce the reader to basic modes of ethical reasoning that will help to analyze the ethical problems in business that arise in the remainder of the book." Perhaps more instructive are the words of Manuel Velasquez (1982):

> Our morality, therefore, contains three main kinds of moral considerations, each of which emphasizes certain morally important aspects of our behavior, but no one of which captures all the factors that must be taken into account in making moral judgments. Utilitarian standards consider only the aggregate social welfare but ignore the individual and how that welfare is distributed. Moral rights consider the individual but discount both aggregate well-being and distributive considerations. Standards of justice consider distributive issues but they ignore aggregate social welfare and the individual as such. These three kinds of moral considerations do not seem to be reducible to each other yet all three seem to be necessary parts of our morality. That is, there are some moral problems for which utilitarian considerations are decisive, while for other problems the decisive considerations are either the rights of individuals or the justice of the distributions involved . . . We have at this time no comprehensive moral theory capable of determining precisely when utilitarian considerations become "sufficiently large" to outweigh narrow infringements on a conflicting right or standard of justice, or when considerations of justice become "important enough" to outweigh infringements on conflicting rights. Moral philosophers have been unable to agree on any absolute rules for making such judgments. There are, however, a number of rough criteria that can guide us in these matters . . . But these criteria remain rough and intuitive. They lie at the edges of the light that ethics can shed on moral reasoning.

These statements seem to be making a virtue out of a necessity and really beg the questions posed earlier. These different theories and principles, all of which were initially meant as a universal approach to ethical problems, give conflicting signals to people in positions of responsibility in business and other organizations and can, at times, allow them to pick principles at will to rationalize what from another perspective may be unethical activity in concrete situations. Shifting between utilitarianism and Kant's categorical imperative or theories of justice and rights involves at best an unreflective commitment to ethics. These theories cannot be applied at will as the situation may seem to dictate, for each of them involves commitment to the philosophical framework on which it is based, and which provides for its richness and rationale. Unfortunately, these frameworks are often in conflict.

The philosophical foundations on which Kant's deontological ethics is based are radically different from the philosophical foundations on which either act or rule utilitarianism is based. To be Kantians at one time and Benthamites at another is to shift frameworks and results in what has been quite aptly called "metaphysical musical chairs" (Callicott, 1990; Weston, 1991). Attempts to avoid this have led some philosophers to claim that moral principles can be divorced from their philosophical underpinnings (Wenz, 1993). Thus one can hold to a single moral theory which claims that there are a variety of moral principles which cannot be reduced to or derived from a single master principle. What this view seems to be saying is that to think morally and to think philosophically are no longer compatible endeavors.

What we are really dealing with, in all the above instances, is moral pluralism, and are thus involved in all the problems this poses. Moral pluralism is the view that no single moral principle or overarching theory of what is right can be appropriately applied in all ethically problematic situations. There is no one unifying principle from which lesser principles can be derived. Different moral theories are possible depending upon which values or principles are included. Moral pluralism generally advocates two different approaches to an ethical problem:

- that each relevant principle be considered in every instance, or
- that one principle be operative in one type of domain or sphere of interest, and another principle be operative in another type of domain or sphere of interest.

An adequate moral pluralism, like any adequate moral theory, requires a solid philosophical grounding, but it requires a grounding that is itself inherently pluralistic. Recent efforts to address with this problem will be mentioned later, but dealing with this pluralistic nature of ethical theory raises a second problem with traditional approaches to business ethics. Along with the development of an adequate grounding for moral pluralism, there must be an understanding of what it is to think morally that is radically different than the application of a rule to a concrete situation. In brief, the switch from monism to pluralism cannot be accomplished by a synthesis of existing theoretical alternatives for acting in the moral situation but through a radical reconstruction of the understanding of the moral situation.

In spite of the seemingly radical difference between the monistic theories of Bentham and Kant, for example, there is a striking similarity. For Kant and Bentham alike, the value of an act is to be found solely in its exemplification of a rule, be it the categorical imperative or the greatest happiness for the greatest number. Moral pluralism does not provide a rule for the balancing of principles, but the right act is nonetheless the one which is subsumed under the proper balance of rules or principles. However, on reflection it becomes evident that not only is there no mechanical way to decide the proper balance, but for neither moral pluralism nor monism is there a mechanical way to decide if a particular act falls under a rule. When one has to deal with a radically new kind of situation, where one cannot call on old decisions, this problem is even more pronounced.

Furthermore, any moral view is dependent, at least implicitly, on a particular view of the nature of the individual and of the community within the individual functions – and the long standing view of the self as an atomic unit, as an isolatable building block of a community, dominates the ethical tradition. Indeed, views of justice as diverse as that of Rawls and Nozick both presuppose the individual as an atomic unit that can be considered theoretically in isolation from, and prior to, a community. Similarly, the conflict between individual and community, which manifests itself in the conflict between Kant and Bentham, presupposes the individual as the atomic building block of community. This atomic individualism constitutes a third problem with traditional approaches to ethical theory.

New developments in business ethics

There has been an explosion of new developments in ethical theory in recent years, partly based, it seems safe to say, on an increasing dissatisfaction with these traditional approaches. These newer approaches attempt to develop theories that are more directly relevant to business institutions than traditional approaches, and are attempting to link the field of business and society, where issues related to corporate social responsiveness and public policy are discussed, with the field of business ethics itself. These newer approaches include feminist theory, stakeholder theory, social contract theory, ethics and nature, and pragmatism.

Feminist theory

Feminist philosophy as it relates to business ethics is sometimes called the ethics of care. (The term "feminist philosophy" can be misleading and in its own way divisive if taken too literally. For, it would seem to pit better "feminine ways of thinking" against more objectionable "masculine ways of thinking." Yet what the movement is intended to capture is a better understanding of the nature of human thinking in general, one that gets beyond the understanding of human thinking as that of a detached intellect.)

Feminist philosophy focuses on traits of character that are valued in close relationships; traits such as sympathy, compassion, fidelity, friendship, and so forth. Along with this focus, this philosophy rejects such abstractions as Kant's universal moral rules and Bentham's utilitarian calculations, for these abstractions separate moral decision makers from the particularity of the individual lives, and separate moral problems from the social and historical contexts in which they are embedded. Moreover, such abstractions involve rationally grasped rules and/or rational calculations, and ignore the role of sensitivity to concrete situations and to the attitudes and inter-relations of those involved. This process, according to feminist philosophy, leads to a so-called "moral impartiality" that, instead of fostering respect for all individuals, in fact negates respect for concrete individuals by impersonally viewing them as anonymous and interchangeable.

This concern for the individual in feminist philosophy is not a focus on the individualism of atomic agents, but rather on relationships and the caring, compassion, and concern these relationships should involve. This philosophy points out that the feminine "voice" or perspective is, by and large, radically different from the male voice of abstract rights and justice which has dominated the development of moral theory (Gilligan, 1982). Feminist thought rejects the notion of rights involving contracts among free, autonomous, and equal individuals in favor of social cooperation and an understanding of relationships as usually unchosen, occurring among unequals, and involving intimacy and caring. The model used to describe this kind of relationship is often that of the parent–child relationship and communal decision making. The focus on relations leads feminist philosophy to the importance of the need to be attuned to other perspectives and to enter sympathetically into them.

Stakeholder theory

Freeman (1984) is usually given credit for doing the seminal work on the stakeholder concept, even though Abrams (1951) urged business leaders to pay attention to their corporate constituents, a theme that was continued – twenty years later – by the Committee for Economic Development (CED, 1971). Since Freeman's work, however, the stakeholder concept has been widely employed to describe and analyze the corporation's relationship to society. At least one conference has been held that dealt exclusively with the concept and was reported in a major journal (Clarkson et al., 1994).

While each scholar may define the concept somewhat differently, each version generally stands for the same principle, namely that corporations should heed the needs, interests, and influence of those affected by their policies and operations (Frederick, 1992). A typical definition is that of Carroll (1996) which holds that a stakeholder may be thought of as "any individual or group who can affect or is affected by the actions, decisions, policies, practices, or goals of the organization." A stakeholder, then, is an individual or group that has some kind of stake in what business does and may also affect the organization in some fashion.

The typical stakeholders are considered to be consumers, suppliers, government, competitors, communities, employees, and of course, stockholders, although the stakeholder map of any given corporation with respect to a given issue can become quite complicated. Stakeholder management involves taking the interests and concerns of these various groups and individuals into account in arriving at a management decision, so that they are all satisfied at least to some extent, or at least that the most important stakeholders with regard to any given issue, are satisfied.

This theory originally assumed that stakeholders are isolatable, individual entities that are clearly identifiable by management, and that their interests can be taken into account in the decision-making process. Thus stakeholder theory, at least as initially formulated, is plagued by the same problem of atomic individualism as are traditional theories, a problem that is only now beginning to be recognized by some scholars of stakeholder theory, including Freeman himself. According to Wicks, Gilbert and Freeman (1994, p. 479):

> One of the assumptions embedded in this world view is that the self is fundamentally isolatable from other selves and from its larger context. Persons exist as discrete beings

315

who are captured independent of the relationships they have with others. While language, community, and relationships all affect the self, they are seen as external to and bounded off from the individual who is both autonomous from and ontologically prior to these elements of context. The parallel in business is that the corporation is best seen as an autonomous agent, separate from its suppliers, consumers, external environment, etc. Here too, while the larger market forces and business environment have a large impact on a given firm, it is nonetheless the individual corporation which has prominence in discussions about strategy and preeminence in where we locate agency.

In an effort to reinterpret some of these traditional ways of thinking housed in stakeholder theory, Freeman, along with Gilbert and Wicks, has turned to feminist theory as the vehicle for such a reinterpretation. They point out some important short-comings of the earlier versions of stakeholder theory, principally that they rely too much on an "individualistic autonomous-masculinist mode of thought to make it intelligible and discount many of the feminist insights" which can be utilized to "better express the meaning and purposes of the corporation" (Wicks et al., 1994, pp. 476–7).

These insights involve moving away from a view of the corporation as an auto-nomous entity confronting an external environment to be controlled; an entity which is structured in terms of strict hierarchies of power and authority and in which management activities are best expressed in terms of conflict and competition; one in which strategic management decisions result from an objective collection of facts via empirical investigation and a rationally detached decision maker distanced from leanings, biases, and emotion-laden perceptions.

Feminist insights involve, instead, an understanding of the corporation as a web of relations among stakeholders; a web which thrives on change and uncertainty in establishing ongoing harmonious relations with its environment; one whose structure is contoured by radical decentralization and empowerment; one in which activities are best expressed in terms of communication, collective action, and reconciliation, and management decisions result from solidarity and communicatively shared understanding rooted in caring and concrete relationships (Wicks et al., 1994, pp. 479–93).

The criticism of stakeholder theory that it cannot define what or who is or is not a stakeholder, as well as attempts to delimit stakeholders, is perhaps misplaced. In spite of the atomistic nature of early definitions, stakeholder theory embodies, in its very nature, a relational view of the firm, and its power lies in focusing management decision making on the multiplicity and diversity of the relationships within which the corporation has its being, and on the multipurpose nature of the corporation as a vehicle for enriching these relationships in their various dimensions. Moreover, what will count as stakeholder claims is context dependent, and any decision can be only as good as the moral vision of the decision maker operating within the contours of a specific problematic context.

Stakeholder theory contours the direction of the vision; it cannot simplify the con-crete contexts by delimiting, in the abstract, those upon whom the vision should gaze in the diversity of concrete contexts. Moral development here lies not in having rules to simplify situations, but in having the enhanced ability to recognize the complex moral dimensions of a situation. Thus stakeholder theory seems to house, in its very nature, not only a relational view of the corporation, but also an understanding of the situational nature of ethical decision making as operative in concrete contexts.

Social contract theory

The emerging social responsibilities of business have also been expressed in terms of a changing contract between business and society that reflected changing expectations regarding the social performance of business (Anshen, 1974). The old contract between business and society was based on the view that economic growth was the source of all progress, social as well as economic. The engine providing this economic growth was considered to be the drive for profits by competitive private enterprise. The basic mission of business was thus to produce goods and services at a profit and, in doing this, business was making its maximum contribution to society and being socially responsible (Friedman, 1970).

This changing contract between business and society was based on the view that the single-minded pursuit of economic growth produced detrimental side effects that imposed social costs on society. The pursuit of economic growth, some believed, did not necessarily lead automatically to social progress but, instead, led to a deteriorating physical environment, an unsafe workplace, discrimination against certain groups in society, and other social problems. This contract between business and society involved the reduction of these social costs of business through impressing upon business the idea that it has an obligation to work for social as well as economic betterment. This idea was expressed by the Committee for Economic Development (CED, 1971, p. 12):

> Today it is clear that the terms of the contract between society and business are, in fact, changing in substantial and important ways. Business is being asked to assume broader responsibilities to society than ever before and to serve a wider range of human values. Business enterprises, in effect, are being asked to contribute more to the quality of American life than just supplying quantities of goods and services.

The changing terms of the contract are found in the laws and regulations that society has established as the legal framework within which a business must operate, and through shared understanding that prevails as to each group's expectations of the other (Carroll, 1996, p. 19). The social contract is a set of two-way understandings that characterize the relationship between business and society, and the changes in this contract that have taken place over the past several decades are a direct outgrowth of the increased importance of the social environment of business. The "rules of the game" have been changed, particularly through the laws and regulations that have been passed relating to social issues such as pollution and discrimination.

More recent formulations of the social contract notion have emphasized a broad range of responsibilities related to consumers and employees (Donaldson, 1982) and the responsibilities of multinational corporations to home and host countries (Donaldson, 1989). Thus, social contract theory has a long and rich history in business and society thought. It is also found in business ethics literature, particularly in the work of John Rawls (1971) with respect to the concept of justice. The principles of justice that Rawls advocates are based on a social contract agreed to by members of society in a so-called original position. This original position is something of an intellectual exercise to show how principles of justice could be derived that can be defended on grounds of impartiality and unbiased decision making. (In this exercise, these principles are worked out behind a so-called veil of ignorance, where the members of society do not know their race, social standing, economic resources, gender, or anything else about themselves. Without this kind of knowledge, they are then supposedly free from particular kinds of interests. Since they do not know their station or role in society, it is assumed that they can come to a more just agreement regarding the rules they want to live by when they step out from behind the veil. This agreement is worked out by atomic individuals prior to their membership in any kind of society. Thus Rawls' position is rooted in the self-interest driven principles of abstract justice formed by atomic, pre-social individuals operating behind a veil of ignorance. This position emphasizes the primacy of the individual.)

Recent work by Donaldson and Dunfee (1994, 1995) focuses on the development of integrative social contracts theory which among other things, attempts to deal with the issue of taking a pluralistic approach to business ethics without falling into the problem of relativism. In Donaldson and Dunfee (1994), they are concerned to advance the interconnection between empirical and normative research in business ethics, but in the 1995 paper, they develop the theory without reference to the issue of empirical and normative research. They hold that pluralism, and the "moral free space" it involves, is embodied in the diversity of microcontracts that represent agreement or shared understandings concerning the moral norms governing specific types of economic interactions. This freedom to specify more precisely the norms of economic interaction is, in turn, guaranteed by the macrosocial contract to which all contractors, regardless of specific microcontracts, would agree. When a microcontract for a given community has been grounded in informed consent and allows for the right of exit, the norm is authentic. As the authors note, at this point the macrocontract allows for moral free space, but sets no limits.

What results if one stops here is cultural relativism. What the macrocontractors must do is authorize limits that are not microcommunity relative. These limits are embodied in hypernorms, defined as entailing principles so fundamental to human existence that they serve as a guide in evaluating lower level moral norms. Donaldson and Dunfee do not take any specific stand on the fundamental question concerning the epistemological basis of hypernorms, viewing this as unnecessary to the process of identifying hypernorms. The task of indentifying and interpreting a comprehensive list of hypernorms is open-ended, since there is no way to determine when a proposed list is complete. Moreover, our understanding of hypernorms may change over time, resulting in an ongoing and changing list. The macrosocial contract would include a means of arbitrating and resolving conflicts among various microsocial contracts by the use of rules based on priorities consistent with the macrosocial contract. The macrosocial contract, then, sets moral constraints and bestows moral legitimacy on microsocial contracts. The two levels of contracts together provide for pluralism without falling into relativism.

The natural origin of business values

A novel and comprehensive understanding of the origins of the ethical dimensions of business in its social context is found in a recent work by William C. Frederick (1995), who develops the thesis that the original values of business, which include economizing,

growth, and systematic integrity, are rooted in the first and second laws of thermodynamics. These values which constitute his first cluster of values are listed under the
general category of economizing values, or those values which support prudent and
efficient use of resources. This value cluster is, in turn, intertwined with two other sets
of value clusters, called ecologizing and power-aggrandizing respectively. The tensions
and conflicts between and among these three sets of value clusters – economizing, eco-
logizing, and power-aggrandizing – are seen as evolutionarily inevitable. As Frederick
(1995, p. 14) summarizes, "This is tantamount to saying that the values by which
humans gain a living, allocate and wield power, and establish communal relations
with each other are anchored partially in nature and partially in sociocultural
processes."

Through the development of this position, Frederick focuses on the emergence of
value from the ground up, in opposition to the traditional approach of abstract rule
application of so-called universal moral principles. Moreover, his development of the
intimate and inextricable interrelation between economizing and ecologizing values
roots business in a social context with which it is inextricably interwoven. Frederick's
position incorporates the important distinction between expansion and authentic
growth, and negates the notion of profit as a primary business value while stressing
the moral legitimacy of the economizing function.

Pragmatism

Rosenthal and Buchholz have recently been utilizing classical American pragmatism
as a new approach to business ethics that incorporates and systematizes the various
trends to be found in contemporary business ethics perspectives. Pragmatic philosophy develops a deeper, unifying level for moral pluralism to explain why and how we
reconstruct rules and traditions and choose among various principles in an ongoing
process of dealing with change and novelty, thus providing a philosophical grounding
that is itself inherently pluralistic and offering, as well, a radically new understanding
of what it is to think morally.

In place of the traditional understanding of moral reasoning as abstract and discursive, it is now understood as concrete and imaginative and, as such, does not work
downward from rules to their applications, but works upward from concrete moral
experience and decision making toward guiding moral hypotheses. Normative claims
are hypotheses grounded in the domain of the diversity of contextually emergent
valuings, and established, guided and revised by concrete, imaginative reason utilizing
experimental method. Normative claims can take hold of various dimensions of a rich
concrete attunement, but as abstractions from a concrete attunement, no number of
normative claims can adequately capture, much less exhaust, the richness of concrete
situations.

Pragmatism also rules out absolutism in ethics without falling into relativism. The
vital, growing sense of moral rightness comes not from the indoctrination of abstract
principles but from sensitivity to concrete situations and the demands of human
valuings in their diversity and underlying commonness as human qua human confronting a common reality within which they must learn to flourish. This philosophy
offers an epistemic basis for norms of any kind as based not in abstract rationality but

in the rich, elusive primal sense of our embeddedness in communal life. This sense of communal life in turn is rooted in the novel understanding of self and community as inherently relational and dynamic, consisting of an ongoing accommodation between creativity and conformity, self and other, change and tradition, and analogously, the corporation and the manifold relational contexts which are part and parcel of its existence.

Within this pragmatic context, growth cannot be understood in terms of a fixed end, but rather involves the enrichment of experience in its entirety. Thus, growth is ultimately answerable to the moral dimensions of concrete human existence, whether this be growth of self, growth of community, or growth of the corporation. In sum, then, Rosenthal and Buchholz have argued that pragmatism is inherently pluralistic thus providing a foundation for a pluralistic approach to business ethics that does not fall into relativism, that it involves attunement to concrete situations in contrast to rule application, and that it overcomes atomic individualism within relational view of the self and community. For a complete discussion see chapter 10 of this volume.

Conclusion

These new developments in business ethics are, as stated previously, more directly related to business organizations themselves because they have largely been developed for this kind of application. With the exception of feminism and pragmatism, they are less ethical theories in general than ethical theories related specifically to business organizations and their specific problems. They, in different ways, address some or all of the problems associated with traditional theories of ethics that were utilized almost exclusively when the field of business ethics first developed as a field of study in its own right. There has been, and continues to be, a wealth of interesting and creative efforts to develop the normative dimension of social responsibility, which was beginning to drop out of consideration with the focus on corporate social responsiveness and public policy, and make it a central concern in dealing with social issues by, in some sense, redefining them as ethical issues and analyzing them with normative frameworks. There will undoubtedly be further efforts of this nature as ethical issues continue to be raised about the practices and policies of business organizations.

References

Abrams, F. 1951: Management's responsibilities in a complex world. *Harvard Business Review*, 24(3), 29–34.

Anderson, A. 1979: *Cost of Government Regulation.* New York: The Business Roundtable.

Anshen, M. 1974: *Managing the Socially Responsible Corporation.* New York: Macmillan.

Buchholz, R. A. 1977: An alternative to social responsibility. *MSU Business Topics*, Summer, 12 & 16.

Callicott, J. B. 1990: The case against moral pluralism. *Environmental Ethics*, 12, p. 115.

Carroll, A. B. 1996: *Business and Society: Ethics and Stakeholder Management*, 3rd edn. Cinicinnati: South-Western Publishing, p. 74.

CED (Committee for Economic Development) 1971: *Social Responsibilities of Business Corporations.* New York: CED.

Chamberlain, N. W. 1973: *The Limits of Corporate Responsibility.* New York: Basic Books, p. 486.

Clarkson, M. et al., 1994: The Toronto Conference: Reflections on stakeholder theory. *Business and Society*, 33, 83–131.

De George, R. T. 1985: *The Status of Business Ethics: Past and Future*. Business Ethics Research Workshop, Stanford University, August 14–17.

Donaldson, T. 1982: *Corporations & Morality*. Englewood Cliffs, NJ: Prentice Hall.

Donaldson, T. 1989: *The Ethics of International Business*. New York: Oxford University Press.

Donaldson, T. and Dunfee, T. 1994: Toward a unified conception of business ethics: Integrative social contracts theory. *Academy of Management Review*, 19(2), 252–84.

Donaldson, T. and Dunfee, T. 1995: Integrative social contracts theory: A communitarian conception of economic ethics. *Economics and Philosophy II*, pp. 85–112.

Donaldson, T. and Werhane, P. 1993: *Ethical Issues in Business: A Philosophical Approach*, 4th edn. Englewood Cliffs, NJ: Prentice Hall.

Frederick, W. C. 1978: From CSR1 to CSR2: *The Maturing of Business and Society Thought*. Graduate School of Business, University of Pittsburgh, Working Paper No. 279, p. 5.

Frederick, W. C. 1992: *Social Issues in Management: Coming of Age or Prematurely Gray?* Paper presented to the Doctoral Consortium of the Social Issues in Management Division, The Academy of Management, Las Vegas, Nevada, August, p. 5.

Frederick, W. C. 1995: *Values, Nature and Culture in the American*. New York: Oxford University Press, p. 14.

Freeman, R. E. (1984) *Strategic Management: A Stakeholder Approach*. Boston: Pitman.

Friedman, M. 1970: The social responsibility of business is to increase its profits. *New York Times Magazine*, Sept. 13, 122–6.

Gilligan, C. 1982: *In A Different Voice*. Cambridge: Harvard University Press.

Powers, C. W. and Vogel, D. 1980: *Ethics in the Education of Business Managers*. Hastings-on-Hudson, NY: The Hastings Center, p. 7.

Rawls, J. 1971: *A Theory of Justice*. Cambridge: Harvard University Press.

Velasquez, M. G. 1982: *Business Ethics: Concepts and Cases*. Englewood Cliffs, NJ: Prentice-Hall, pp. 104–106.

Weidenbaum, M. L. 1977: *Business, Government and the Public*. Englewood Cliffs, NJ: Prentice-Hall, p. 285.

Weidenbaum, M. L. 1979: *The Future of Business Regulation*. New York: AMACOM, p. 34.

Weidenbaum, M. L. and De Fina, R. 1978: *The Cost of Federal Regulation of Economic Activity*. Washington, DC: American Enterprise Institute.

Weston, A. 1991: Comment: On Callicott's case against pluralism. *Environmental Ethics*, 13, 283–6.

Wenz, P. S. 1993: Minimal, moderate, and extreme moral pluralism. *Environmental Ethics*, 15, 61–74.

Wicks, A. C., Gilbert, D. R. Jr, and Freeman, R. E. 1994: A feminist reinterpretation of the stakeholder concept. *Business Ethics Quarterly*, 4(4) (October).

PART IV

BUSINESS ETHICS: ORIGINS AND CONTEMPORARY PRACTICE

26

Business ethics and the origins of contemporary capitalism: economics and ethics in the work of Adam Smith and Herbert Spencer*

PATRICIA H. WERHANE

The origins of capitalism in the form of commerce and free enterprise can be traced to a prehistoric era when people began trading with each other. Ethical issues in business arose simultaneously or soon after. As early as 1800 BC, for example, we find worries about the ethics of traders and merchants in the Code of Hammurabi. However, I shall not begin there. Rather, in this paper I shall dwell on the work of two more recent thinkers, the eighteenth-century Scottish economist and philosopher, Adam Smith, and the later nineteenth-century English thinker, Herbert Spencer. I have chosen these two for focus, because, as I shall demonstrate, their thinking has influenced much of what today we take to be the relationship between economics and ethics. What I shall call the "popular views" of their writings do not represent the full body of their texts; yet these popular views have had profound implications in economics and in applied ethics. At the same time, if one carefully reads their work, each has something importantly new to contribute to contemporary analyses in applied ethics.

Adam Smith has been called the father of the Industrial Revolution, the first neo-classical political economist, and one of the earliest defenders of private free enterprise. Yet, interestingly, almost since his death there has developed a caricature of his best-known treatise on political economy, the *Wealth of Nations (WN)*. Beginning in the early nineteenth century, Smith has been read as having promulgated Thomas Hobbes' allegedly egoistic picture of human motivation in the *WN*, and as having solved the problem of the dichotomy between the so-called natural selfish passions and public interests. When individual human beings are granted what Smith calls the "natural liberty" to pursue their own interests, where "all systems . . . of restraint, therefore, being thus completely taken away" (Smith, 1976b, iv.ix.51) the harmony of these

* A previous version of this paper will appear in the *Journal of Business Ethics*, 1999. Reprinted by permission of that journal. An earlier and more lengthy version of the Adam Smith portions of the paper appeared in Werhane (1991) and in Werhane (1997). Research on Herbert Spencer was completed while I was the Arthur Andersen Distinguished Visiting Scholar at the Judge Institute of Management, Cambridge University.

individual pursuits will, unintended by the actors, often produce social and economic good. This is because, according to this reading of Smith, self-interested, economic actors in free competition with each other unintentionally create a self-constraining system. This system, the "invisible hand" which governs market transactions, functions both to regulate these self-interests and to produce economic growth and well-being such that no one actor or group of actors can take advantage of other actors or take advantage for very long (Hildebrand, 1848; Knies, 1853; von Skarzynski, 1878); see also Buckle (1861).

Interestingly, a number of late twentieth-century scholars including Amatai Etzioni (1988), Robert Frank (1988), Milton Friedman (1962, 1976), Albert Hirschman (1977), and George Stigler (1971) have adapted this reading of Smith as well. A. O. Hirschman (1977, p. 100) declared that "the main impact of *The Wealth of Nations* was to establish a powerful *economic* justification for the untrammeled pursuit of individual self-interest." This view is nicely summarized by George Stigler (1971, p. 265), the late Nobel Prize Chicago economist who writes, "*The Wealth of Nations* is a stupendous palace erected upon the granite of self-interest."

How did what I take to be a misreading of the *WN* occur? It may have been, in part, a confusion of Smith with his predecessor, Bernard Mandeville, who was famous for arguing that private vices could be turned into public virtues. Mandeville (1988, pp. 23–4) writes,

> So Vice is beneficial found,
> When it's by Justice lopt and bound; . . .
> Bare Virtue can't make Nations live
> In Splendor; they, that would revive
> A Golden Age, must be as free,
> For Acorns, as for Honesty.

However, such an interpretation may also have arisen from reading Smith through a certain understanding of the writings of Herbert Spencer. Spencer's social Darwinism has influenced some of the more libertarian twentieth-century thinking about free enterprise in this century and may have tainted the reading of the *WN* as well.

In what follows, I shall spend some time delineating Spencer's thinking. I shall then present a non-Spencerian interpretation of Smith's work that more closely resembles the original text. I shall conclude with some speculations concerning how Spencer and Smith have influenced modern economic theory and applied ethics. Neoclassical economists appealed to Smith for a justification for laissez-faire capitalism, and to Spencer for grounding a "night watchman" theory of the state. However, we can appeal to another reading of Smith to tell a different story about commerce and free enterprise. Surprisingly, too, we can look to Spencer's libertarianism and evolutionary social Darwinism for a model of workplace democracy in mature capitalist economies.

Herbert Spencer, the great British nineteenth-century radical liberal, sociologist, and political philosopher, is usually referred to as the father and founder of social Darwinism. In nineteenth-century Europe, evolutionary theory was not the monopoly of Charles Darwin, but was part of speculative thinking of the time. It was Darwin (1996) who gave biological proof for a theory of biological evolution, but the theory, albeit unproved, predates the voyage of the Beagle and his publication of *On the Origin of Species*. Spencer was one of its most articulate proponents, and it was Spencer, not Charles Darwin, who coined the term, "survival of the fittest." Spencer depends on Lamark rather than Darwin for the basis of his system, and a number of his books and essays were published before Darwin's work came out. According to one sympathetic interpreter, it is not that Spencer was a social Darwinist; rather one should more properly say that Darwin was a "biological Spencerian" (Turner, 1985, pp. 107ff).

Spencer is a systemic thinker who conceives the universe, in all its diversity, as constructed from one set of principles, in his case, the principles of evolution. He calls this set of principles and his depiction of this system as the "System of Synthetic Philosophy"; see, for example, Spencer (1862). Spencer outlines the basic principles of natural selection: the evolution of natural phenomena from the very simple to the increasingly complex. According to Spencer, evolution is "a continuous change from indefinite incoherent homogeneity to definite coherent heterogeneity of structure and function, through successive differentiation and integration" (Hudson, 1996, p. 88). For example, we find the universe evolving from a simple homogenous mass to a highly complex solar and galactic system. Similarly, biological evolution begins with simple single-cell amoebae and evolves to a collection of increasingly complex organisms where those species that can best adapt to changing environmental and global conditions survive. The weak, less fit, and least flexible die off. In this process of complexification, organisms evolve from simple, fairly undifferentiated phenomena to highly differentiated, specialized, heterogeneous organisms. "The development of society, as well as the development of man and of life generally, may be described as a tendency to individuation – *to become a thing*" (Spencer, 1851, p. 408). Because of differentiation and specialization, individual species become dependent on other species, and later, individual human beings become dependent on other human beings.

This process is neither simple nor linear. Despite the indestructibility of matter and the fact that it is continually in motion, at various stages there are periods of devolution and regression in the development of organisms. As new species evolve, others devolve, and with each iteration the most adaptable species, and the fittest individuals in each species, survive the increasing complexification of their surroundings and the increasing interdependence. In this spontaneous process of evolution and devolution is exhibited the law of the survival of the fittest. According to Spencer (1872, II: pp. 379–80):

> The law is the survival of the *fittest*. . . . [T]he law is not the survival of the "better" or the "stronger," if we give to those words anything like their ordinary meanings. It is the survival of those which are constitutionally fittest to thrive under conditions under which they are placed . . .

The ideal is a state of equilibrium where each organism, each species, each planet, each star and each galaxy is in stasis with its surroundings and other phenomena. For example, in the evolution of the universe, the revolution of the planets around the sun has reached a state of fairly stable equilibrium and, for the time being at least, is no longer subject to drastic change.

This evolutionary process is not merely a natural or biological one. Rather, in accordance with Spencer's System of Synthetic Philosophy, the principles of evolution apply to all phenomena including human beings and their social interactions.

The evolution of individuals in their social and political relationships, and of cultures, societies, and social systems is as much a part of the evolutionary process as are biological and natural phenomena. Spencer analogizes society to an organism, and traces the history of humankind as an evolutionary process from simple informal arrangements between hunters and gatherers to hierarchical military or military-like political systems, then thence to more complex political and economic systems. Private enterprise introduces the notion of economic liberty as well as industrialization, and eventually, the idea of democratic political development. As societies become more complex, there is evidence of increased differentiation parallel to species differentiation, and at the same time greater mutual dependence exhibited by increasingly complex interrelationships between highly differentiated and specialized individuals, institutions, and society, and, sometimes, between societies. Like natural evolution, these social processes are spontaneous unless tampered with, and like natural evolution these processes are not linear; there are periods of devolution as well, when particular societies revert to simpler social, political, and economic arrangements (Spencer, 1857, pp. 8–62).

Spencer applies the term "survival of the fittest," alternately to particular political economies or societies and to individuals (Spencer, 1886, pp. 389–466). A society is most likely to survive if it is constantly developing more complex economic systems, and adapting itself to whatever changes it encounters. The society that is independent – that is allowed to evolve in its own way – is most likely to develop its own survival and adaptability mechanisms so that, Spencer thought, it is immoral to interfere with this process. Spencer writes (1851, pp. 290–91),

> [t]o interfere with this process [of spontaneous evolution] by producing premature development in any particular direction is inevitably to disturb the true balance of organization by causing somewhere else a corresponding atrophy.

A particular society should look after itself, but not come to the aid of its neighbor for two reasons. First, such aid reduces the strength, capital, or resources of the aiding society, thus diminishing its own chances for evolutionary development. Second, each society should be left alone to make its way. Interfering with that process of evolution may be harmful to that society or make it less independent, or it may assist a weak, devolving society to continue, again interfering with the principles of evolution. War is an interesting anomaly for Spencer. Our aggressive nature is obviously evolutionary, inherited from other animal species, and, he writes, "in the earlier states of civilization, war has the effect of exterminating the weaker societies, and of weeding out the weaker members of the stronger societies" (Spencer, 1873, p. 346). Still, as civilizations evolve, industrialize, and democratize, there develops a strong sense of individual morality including the principle that it is wrong to interfere with others. War depletes capital and cultivates antisocial immoral behavior. Thus, as societies evolve, "wars" will be industrial competitions rather than physical battles. The result will be similar without the accompanying negative financial and moral side effects.

Spencer's synthetic philosophy appears holistic, and he often uses the term "social organism" to refer to society or societies. Nevertheless, Spencer is a methodological individualist. The primary unit out of which social organisms are made up is the individual human being. Societies evolve, they develop complex interrelationships, and they affect, and are affected by, individual relationships. However, societies are merely aggregates – albeit complicated aggregates – often constructed out of impossibly complicated interrelationships. It is the individual, in this case, the individual human being, that is the basic unit and at the core of Spencer's synthetic system. It is, of course, difficult to envision how the principles of evolution drive social evolution of societies that are merely aggregates of individuals, and Spencer does not fully answer that criticism. Despite this problem, Spencer never relinquishes his individualism to the general principles of social evolutionary theory (Simon, 1960, pp. 294–99).

In the *Social Statics* and in his political writings Spencer applies his synthetic system with its evolutionary principles to individual human development. Spencer parallels individual development to natural development and social development, adding one more factor. Like every organism, according to Spencer, we seek our own pleasure or happiness and try to avoid pain. However, the evolution of the human being entails the development of complex mental abilities. Along with this mental development, we have developed a notion of free will, thus we are able to direct our own individual destinies. If particular societies should be left alone to evolve or devolve as they are fit, so too, the individual, who makes up the basic unit of any society, should be left alone to develop his or her resources and strengths. This conclusion is based upon what Spencer calls the "Law of Equal Freedom," stated as, "[e]very man may claim the fullest liberty to exercise his faculties compatible with the possession of like liberty by every other man," (Spencer, 1851, p. 35), or, "[e]very man is free to do that which he wills, provided he infringes not the equal freedom of any other man" (Spencer, 1892b, II: p. 46).

The ideal just society grants and protects equally these negative rights, and indeed, the Law of Equal Freedom forms the basis for Spencer's commutative theory of justice. Every individual has the equal natural right to be left alone; the right not to be harmed or interfered with by others or by society. As a result, individuals have the equal liberty to pursue their own ends as they are able and desirous of doing, so long as they do not interfere with others' pursuits. Importantly, freedom is the absence of restraints, not self-determination. Thus the natural right not to be interfered with allows, but does not require, the right to pursue one's own ends (Doherty and Gray, 1993, p. 484). If left alone, some of us will develop, mature, and contribute; others will atrophy or wither away. Thus the strongest and most adaptable, both physically and mentally, will and should survive and flourish. As a result of noninterference, a collection of the fittest individuals will create the fittest society. This is not quite radical individualism, because Spencer recognizes that – as complex highly differentiated individuals – we live in, and must work within, social structures. This is always a struggle because we have not yet reached a stage in evolution where private and social interests coincide. It is hard not to interfere with others while at the same time interrelating in a community.

One of the issues raised by Spencer's preoccupation with the natural right to be left alone is whether or how the Law of Equal Freedom makes sense within Spencer's naturalistic hedonism. Spencer finds that each biological species seeks its happiness or pleasure and tries to avoid pain. Spencer agrees with Mill that only happiness is valued for its own sake (Spencer, 1904, II: pp. 88–9). At the same time, he argues, because human beings are fallible, we cannot always maximize utilities nor be sure that we are, or can orchestrate, even our own happiness, much less the greatest happiness for the greatest number. Thus, by granting the greatest equal freedom, each individual is free to pursue his or her own ends and achieve (or fail to achieve) happiness. Thus the Law of Equal Freedom allows the "greatest happiness of each and everyone" (Spencer, 1851, pp. 60–62, 409; 1892b, II: pp. 62–3); see also Weinstein (1990, pp. 140–2).

Spencer adopts Lamark's theory that, along with inherited characteristics, human beings pass on acquired traits as well. So children of smart, strong, adaptable parents will inherit those traits. However, children of a lazy or slothful person, for example, would most likely inherit those traits as well as parental biological characteristics. Thus, if those of us less able to adapt reproduce, we will add to the number of devolving individuals, and eventually affect the development of society. To protect those who cannot independently pursue their own ends or protect themselves, then, like aiding another community, is antithetical to evolutionary principles and interferes with its spontaneity. Future generations will suffer both because capital was deflected from productive means to help those who could not help themselves, and because future generations will have to deal with increasingly large numbers of individuals who are incapable. Thus that society will eventually devolve and disappear (Spencer, 1851, pp. 59–65).

Spencer is outspoken against vaccinations, prevention of cattle disease, sewers, municipal fire fighters, community hygiene laws, and safety regulations for factories. He rails against labor laws that restrict days or hours of work or proscribe women or children from laboring. He fights against compulsory education, orphanages, poor houses, libraries, or any sort of public institution that requires government funds, government intervention, and helps people who should be helping themselves. He also questions taxation, particularly of the poor, arguing that the deserving poor should be given an opportunity to work and support themselves, and he argues against inheritance since that abets sloth in children and grandchildren of the rich. Note that Spencer is not in favor of genocide; rather, Spencer argues, it is imperative that each of us should have to try to survive, both physically and in the economy, on our own. Those who cannot, will wither away, neither helped nor abetted in their demise. However, social interference either in the form of governmental charity or taxation should not be tolerated. Government intervention and regulation interfere with natural selection, they are a costly and unfair tax burden to the rich and the working poor, depriving the rich of earned capital for reinvestment and the working poor of opportunities to improve.

> The quality of a society is lowered morally and intellectually, by artificially preserving those who are least able to take care of themselves and to behave well. For if the inferior are helped to increase, by shielding them from that mortality which their inferiority would naturally entail, the effect is to produce, generation after generation, a greater inferiority. From diminished use of self-conserving faculties already deficient, there must result, in posterity, still smaller amounts of self-conserving faculties. (Spencer, 1873, p. 339)

At the same time, Spencer claims that private charity is fine so long as the donors selectively choose deserving poor as their recipients. The result of noninterference and personal altruism with be that the strongest and most fit will survive, achieve, and reproduce resulting in a society of strong, adaptable, entrepreneurs and a healthy industrial and technical economy (Spencer, 1851, pp. 278–363; 1982, pp. 31–70).

Spencer concludes that the best society is a laissez-faire private enterprise political economy with almost no government except to protect us from deliberately harming or interfering with each other. A laissez-faire economy best permits individual entrepreneurial economic development where each individual can control his or her economic life and receive the full benefits of that individual's labor, and industrialization, as Smith pointed out, creates economic growth and contributes to the positive social evolution of a political economy. Indeed, he argues, community priorities supersede those of individuals only when rights are violated or in times of war. Roads, schools, money, mail services, land, parks, and utilities should all be private; taxes should be the minimum possible, and, to borrow a phrase from Robert Nozick, government should be in the form of a "night watchman" (Spencer, 1982, pp. 31–70; Nozick, 1974).

In Spencer's early writings, in particular, in *Social Statics*, Spencer argued for universal suffrage, thinking that a participatory democracy protects the rights of each individual and allows each of us a voice. In his later writings, he retracts the idea of universal suffrage. He was worried that if propertyless workers were able to vote, we would have the rule of the majority which itself could decide against private enterprise or equal liberty. He was afraid that women were not fully developed or educated to be able to exercise proper judgment in voting. These worries were based on his view that economic liberty is the best means for equal freedom and thus the foundation of political liberty. Spencer did believe that as women became more educated, they should be able to vote. His theory about workers' rights to vote is more complicated, as we shall see in the next paragraphs (Doherty and Gray, 1993, pp. 475–90; Paul, 1982, pp. 499–514; Francis, 1978, pp. 317–28).

Given his night watchman theory and a strong criticism of any form of socialism, Spencer does not envision his ideal industrial state to be that of late nineteenth-century England. This is not merely because of active governmental and legislative processes that were in place nor the existence of complicated governmental bureaucracies that mimicked military structures. More importantly, Spencer sees industries – and in particular the joint-stock company that was to become the modern corporation – as iterations of earlier military hierarchies. Spencer (1892a, III: pp. 52–3) writes,

> [a]s devised by Act of Parliament, the administrations of our public companies are almost purely democratic. . . . Shareholders elect their directors, directors their chairman . . . Yet . . . the very form of government, while remaining nominally democratic, is substantially so remodeled as to become a miniature of our national constitution. The direction . . . falls under the control of some one member of superior cunning, will, or wealth, to whom the majority becomes so subordinate, that the decision on every question depends on the course he takes . . . thus, a mixture of the monarchic, the aristocratic, and the democratic elements is repeated . . .

Democratic practices are nonexistent in joint-stock companies, and the mix of monarchy and hierarchical bureaucracy better describes a military form of governance that precedes democratic industrialization in the social evolutionary process. Only in a democracy can each individual explore his or her freedom without interference, both politically and within economic enterprises.

331

Worse, Spencer argues, the British factory system depreciates the workers' ability to think for themselves.

> The wage-earning factory-hand does, indeed, exemplify entirely free labor, in so far that, making contracts at will and able to break them after short notice, he is free to engage with whomsoever he pleases and where he pleases. But this liberty amounts in practice to little more than the ability to exchange one slavery for another; since, fit only for his particular occupation, he has rarely an opportunity of doing anything more than decide in what mill he will pass the greater part of his dreary day. The coercion of circumstances often bears more hardly on him than the coercion of a master does on one in bondage. (Spencer, 1896, III: part 8, p. 516)

Trade unions are attempts to ameliorate these conditions, but they are not universally effective. This is because their claims to be democratic are usually untrue, and union leaders tend to control, rather than consult with, workers.

Spencer concludes that we have not yet reached a high stage of social development. If evolutionary development includes individual right not to be interfered with or coerced, the next stage will be that of cooperative communal enterprises governed by worker committees with democratic decision making, and where pay is assigned according to ability and difficulty, and profits are shared among the workers. Each worker will cooperate with the others, productivity will increase, and individuals will actually exercise their natural liberty at work (Spencer, 1896, III: part 8, pp. 504–9, 559–563). Although Spencer is not specific, it surely follows that if workers control joint-stock companies, they will both become educated into democratic processes and antisocialists. From this exercise of economic liberty, universal suffrage makes sense. Thus economic liberty and political liberty are not two distinct principles, but rather they are mutually dependent concepts where, because of the Law of Equal Freedom, economic liberty precedes.

Spencer (1851, p. 417; 1896, III: part 8, p. 601) concludes,

> [t]he ultimate man will be one whose private requirements coincide with public ones. He will be the manner of man, who, in spontaneously fulfilling his own nature, incidentally performs the functions of a social unit; and yet is only enabled so to fulfill his own nature, by all others doing the like.

The influences of Spencer are subtle, because almost no one reads or refers to him any more, yet they are clearly important. Whether evolution is, or should be, spontaneous, Spencer's theory of social evolution has had an enormous influence in the social sciences as a framework to describe social development and devolution. Social Darwinism is often equated, wrongly, with genocide, but correctly with the argument that a welfare state is immoral, that it encourages poverty, and that it is unfair to tax those who can support themselves and must bear the burden of those who cannot. Spencer's critique of bureaucracies is still apt today in describing government or large organizations. North American individualism surely has its roots in Spencer's thought. Along with this individualism Spencer is sometimes attributed what is called "Cowboy Capitalism" – that the best society is one in which each of us, on our own horse, so to speak, works for his or her own ends. This is partly an accurate attribution, but Spencer also argues that one can only succeed as part of a society even though that society is merely an aggregate of individuals. In any society, when there is an absence of interference, the best will succeed and be rewarded; a true meritocracy will be established where the best should be the most successful, and thus the most deserving. Sometimes this is translated to imagine that those who have succeeded *are*, in fact, the most deserving. The weakest, laziest, and least adaptable should, deservedly, remain unrewarded and fade away.

Echoes of Spencer are reverberated by those who decry welfare, worry about regulation and government involvement in business, and question taxation. The themes that taxation is a form of slavery and that those who work should not have to bear the burden of those who do not are reiterated today. Arguments abound that government interference and regulation only deflect economic development and destroy incentives. The recent transformation of the national welfare system in the USA to a workfare system is justified on grounds Spencer would admire. Even though a pure Spencerian laissez-faire political economy has never been established, the "night watchman" idea is not dead, and indeed, is celebrated by leading intellectual libertarians.

What is less celebrated is Spencer's critique of industrial hierarchies and his idea that cooperative self-managed industrial enterprises best exemplify true evolutionary social progress. To be consistent, libertarians and others who question the role of government in economic and private affairs, need to think carefully about the lack of democratization and the prevalence of coercion in private institutions such as the church and the corporation. Spencer is suggesting a truly revolutionary form of self-management that is decoupled from socialism and Marxism.

Because of Spencer's influence and that of other liberals of his ilk, one tends to read Smith in the way I described earlier: as an egoist, a *laissez-faire* economist, and as at least as implying that a night watchman political economy is the ideal. As a result, there are a number of influences from Spencer's work and from this reading of Smith that have trickled down into neoclassical economics and into twentieth-century thinking about markets and morality. First, there is sometimes a preoccupation with the individual economic actor both in economic theory and in business ethics. In business ethics, we sometimes focus on dilemmas of individual managers as if they operated in autonomous vacuums rather than in corporations; see, for example, Donaldson and Werhane (1977). Second, at least some neoclassical economic theory appears, now and again, to be preoccupied with the individual non-tuistic or self-interested rational utility maximizer as the paradigm of economic choice and purveyor of economic value, where economic value is often linked to preferences, however qualified or defined. (Sen, 1987; Hausman and McPherson, 1996) Thus the individual, as if acting on his or her own, without social, cultural, religious or corporate influences, is naturally and primarily motivated by self-interests; in cool rational moments, this individual is a non-tuistic utility maximizer of preferences, or considered preferences. Third, Smith appears to separate the economic actor in the *WN* from the ordinary moral person to whom he devotes his earlier work, *The Theory of Moral Sentiments* just as Spencer focuses on the individual as the primary actor in an evolving political economy. Government should be minimal, and ethical issues arise only when one individual (or the government) is interfering with another individual or government. So, too, it would appear, one can separate ethics, politics, and economics (as we have done in academia) such that not only are these three fairly Balkanized disciplines, but more importantly, that they are different mental models and create distinct approaches. Such distinct approaches result in The Separation Thesis – the view that politics, economics and ethics (or, translated, public policy, ethics and business) are three separate endeavors. Therefore, one needs moral philosophers and public policy to straighten out managers and companies when they go astray. Conversely, one needs managers and management theory to tell us how it "really is" so that the practicalities of doing business are not lost in a Kantian or Aristotelian ideal world of what should be, nor are undermined by regulation (Freeman, 1994).

What I want to suggest in what follows is that the popular interpretation of the *WN* is a misreading of Smith. At least one careful reading of Smith's texts can paint a different picture of Smith's idea of political economy. Smith is not a *laissez-faire* economist. Economic exchanges occur and markets are efficient, according to Smith, precisely because we are not merely non-tuistic, and economic growth depends on what today we call the rule of law. Individual utility maximization is not the only criterion for rational choice. Indeed, Smith is not a pure utilitarian, and values are not merely individual preferences, nor even individual *considered* preferences. Moreover, Smith was the Professor of Moral Philosophy at Glasgow, and argues precisely against, and may not have even imagined, a separation of ethics from economics, ethics from commerce, or ethics from his idea of a viable political economy. So a careful reading of Smith, or, at least, one kind of careful reading, finds Smith at odds with Spencer, and such a reading can produce some insights into how to approach ethical issues in business that avoid forms of radical individualism, a preoccupation with egoism, and the Separation Thesis.

Let us now turn to Smith's work and examine Smith's notion of self-interest, a notion developed in Smith's earlier work, *The Theory of Moral Sentiments (TMS)*. The first thing that is striking in the *TMS* is Smith's emphasis on the social nature of human beings. Early on he proclaims (1976a, II.ii.3.1),

> [m]an, who can subsist only in society, was fitted by nature to that situation for which he was made. All the members of human society stand in need of each others assistance, and are likewise exposed to mutual injuries.

Thus it is hard to portray Smith as a radical individualist as some of his later readers such as Hirschman (1977) do. Smith begins the *TMS* with this statement (Smith, 1976a, I.i.1.1):

> [h]ow selfish soever man may be supposed, there are evidently some principles in his nature, which interest him in the fortune of others, and render their happiness necessary to him, though he derives nothing from it except the pleasure of seeing it . . .

At the same time, Smith (1976a, II.ii.2.1) argues, "Every man is, no doubt, by nature, first and principally recommended to his own care." Smith explains what appear to be contradictory statements through his analysis of motivation. While recognizing that all one's motivations are self-interested in a trivial sense that they originate in, and are interests *of* the self, he goes on to claim that not all our interests are interests *in* the self. That is, the self is the subject, but not the object, of all our passions and interests. Smith is highly critical both of Hobbes and Smith's infamous predecessor, Bernard Mandeville. (Smith, 1976a, VII.iii.i) Indeed, it was Mandeville

(1988), *not* Smith, who argued that private vices could be transformed into public virtues.

According to Smith, human beings are motivated by three sets of passions or natural affections, each with its own set of objects:

- the *selfish passions*, whose object is interests, pleasures, and pains of the self,
- the *social passions* such as altruism and compassion which are directed to others, and
- the *unsocial passions* such as hate and envy which are negative reactions to others.

Importantly, for Smith, none of the passions dominates others so that most of us are as naturally interested in others as we are in ourselves.

Interests are derived from, but are not identical to, the passions. Passions are akin to natural drives; interests are cognitively and emotionally developed from the passions. Like the passions, each of us has self-interests and social interests; unlike the passions, we assign virtues and vices to the operations of each of the sets of interests. Since self-interest has distinct objects (the self or others), egoism and altruism are not opposites for Smith. Egoists are individuals whose interests are all of the self as object, but this is not necessarily evil. Virtuous self-love is prudence; its vice is avarice or greed. So one can be a virtuous, i.e., a prudent, egoist. Even a selfish person is not necessarily evil unless he or she harms others or treats others unfairly in the pursuit of his or her interests. Social interests can be exhibited in the excellences or virtues of benevolence, altruism, and/or justice or in the vices that include harming others in the forms of malevolence or injustice.

Although Smith spends some time explaining passions and interests, values are not created merely from interests or preferences, Smith argues, because we distinguish between what we prefer, what we approve of, and what *ought to be approved of.* The criteria for either of the latter do not consist merely of one's own considered preferences. One may prefer what one does not approve of, and one constantly tests one's own values against both what I and others approve of and what society deems ought to be approved of, that is, what society values. So, at a minimum, values are what a society finds admirable and praiseworthy.

Smith also grounds many of his conclusions in an appeal to warmed-over natural law theory. In the *TMS*, Smith sometimes uses expressions such as, "men by nature . . .". In both the *TMS* and the *WN*, Smith uses terms such as "the natural order," "natural liberty," and "natural jurisprudence;" he appeals to natural jurisprudence as justification for his theory of justice, and, in the unpublished *Lectures on Jurisprudence*, he explicitly adopts Pufendorf's notion of natural rights (Smith, 1978, [A] pp. 1–16, [B] pp. 1–10). So, Smith appears to appeal to some nonrelative basic principles, although how those relate to societal values is unclear in his writings.

In the *WN*, self-interest is usually equated with the natural desire to better one's condition and look after one's own welfare. So, at least one commentator contends that "[in the *WN*] Smith gave new dignity to greed and a new sanctification to the predatory impulses" (Lerner, 1937, p. ix). Part of the difficulty in reading Smith is that he is both descriptive and normative, and despite the fact that he was a student of David Hume, famous for instigating the fact–value distinction, Smith is notoriously slipshod in making that distinction. So, Lerner may have confused Smith's description of self-interest in commerce with his admonitions concerning greed and avarice. Smith repeatedly argues that avarice interferes with competition, hoarding capital slows down economic growth, and greed is antithetical to the ideal of a free political economy as Smith envisions it; see for example, Smith (1976b, II.iii.25–26, II.ii.36). So, even as we strive to "better our condition," the demands of morality and the ideal of a free exchange political economy require prudence and parsimony of one's economic desires.

But what is the role of the social passions and interests in the *WN*? One of the most famous quotations in the *WN*, of course, is (Smith, 1976b, I.ii.2):

> [i]t is not from the benevolence of the butcher, the brewer, or the baker, that we expect our dinner, but from their regard to their own interest. We address ourselves, not to their humanity but to their self-love, and never talk to them of our own necessities but of their advantages.

Indeed, he says further, "[n]obody but a beggar chooses to depend chiefly upon the benevolence of his fellow-citizens" (Smith, 1976b, I.ii.2). Has Smith divided "economic man" from ordinary mortals who have a variety of passions, interests, and virtues? Dealing with these quotations out of context, one might be led to that conclusion. However, such a conclusion ignores two important notions that play central roles in commerce and in any political economy: cooperation and justice.

Economic exchanges, even between the most selfish parties, are not merely competitive nor purely adversarial, according to Smith. We have a natural "propensity to . . . truck, barter, and exchange" and indeed, "The division of labour . . . is a necessary, though very slow and gradual consequence of [this] certain propensity in human nature" (Smith, 1976b, I.ii.1, I, ii.5). Our natural desire to cooperate motivates us to work together by dividing and specializing our labor. It also motivates us to barter, where the appeal to self-interest of others as well as to their good will in honoring the exchange results in "mutual and reciprocal" gains (Smith 1976b, II.i.1). Do we participate in cooperative ventures because it is our self-interest to do so, or does cooperation arise out of our social passions? For Smith, these two cannot be separated. It is both natural and an advantage to cooperate in economic affairs. Our friends, the butcher, brewer, and baker, do not give away meat, beer, or bread, but they depend on mutual respect, fair play in business, the honoring of contracts, and indeed, even cooperation to stay in business together in the same town.

What about benevolence, and the poor beggar? One will remember that there are two virtues of the social interests: benevolence and justice. It will turn out that justice is the most essential virtue both in the *TMS* and in the *WN*, and it will also turn out that justice, as natural jurisprudence, will play a critical role in Smith's ideal of a political economy as well.

According to the TMS, the notion of justice arises from the social passions and is the virtue of what Smith calls impartial social interests. Justice is the "consciousness of ill-desert" (Smith, 1976a, II.ii.3.4). It is what an impartial spectator would classify as unfair in social relationships even among strangers. It is both a negative principle that proscribes deliberately harming another and includes the positive notion of fair play. In the TMS Smith (1976a, II.ii.2.1) writes,

[If one is just] he would act so as that the impartial spectator may enter into the principles of his conduct. . . . In the race for wealth, and honours, and preferments, he may run as hard as he can, and strain every nerve and every muscle, in order to outstrip all his competitors. But if he should justle, or throw down any of them, the indulgence of the spectators is entirely at an end. It is a violation of fair play, which they cannot admit of.

In the *TMS*, justice is both a personal virtue and, as natural jurisprudence, "the main pillar that upholds the whole edifice [of human society]" (Smith, 1976a, II.ii.3.4). "Society may subsist, though not in the most comfortable state, without beneficence; but the prevalence of injustice must utterly destroy it" (Smith, 1976a, II.ii.3.3).

In his unpublished *Lectures on Jurisprudence*, Smith is careful to clarify his notion of justice. By justice he means commutative, not distributive justice. According to Smith, it is always wrong to harm others deliberately, to violate their personal rights to liberty, property (however societally defined), and reputation, not to honor promises and contracts, or to act unfairly. Thus one has perfect duties, always to be just; that is, it is always wrong to violate the principles of commutative justice. While other virtues such as benevolence are desirable, they are not enforceable since one need not be benevolent to be moral. Justice, Smith argues, is the only virtue for which one may use force to ensure. While the beggar has no claim on our benevolence, he does have a claim on equal opportunity and fair treatment. Principles of distributive justice like benevolence, are not enforceable, since there is conceptual disagreement about the extent and fairness of such principles.

Because economic exchanges are often between strangers, justice plays a central role in a viable political economy. Laws of justice are essential not only to restrain overindulgent self-interests, but also because we often unfairly cooperate or collude with each other. Thus, Smith writes (1976b, IV.ix, 51, my italics),

[e]very man, *as long as he does not violate the laws of justice*, is left perfectly free to pursue his own interest in his own way. . . .

But there remains the *invisible hand* question. Smith wrote (1976b, IV.ii.9),

[The man of commerce] generally, indeed, neither intends to promote the public interest, nor knows how much he is promoting it. . . . By directing industry in such a manner as its produce may be of the greatest value, he intends only his own gain, and he is in this, as in many other cases, led by an invisible hand to promote an end which was no part of his intention. Nor is it always the worse for the society that it was no part of it. By pursuing his own interest he frequently promotes that of the society more effectually than when he really intends to promote it.

Smith is obviously arguing that people in commerce tend to act in their own self-interest, i.e., to seek personal economic gain. However, this neither means that people of commerce are, or should be, necessarily selfish or greedy, nor is Smith proposing purely laissez-faire markets. Putting this quotation in the context of the rest of the *WN*, Smith (1976b, I.x.a.1) is arguing that "markets (the famous invisible hand) work best under conditions of economic liberty grounded in commutative justice, (the 'rule of law') when people are parsimonious and prudent, and cooperative as well as competitive. Markets work best when embedded in political economy that enforces human rights, contractual agreements, and fair play." Smith goes so far as to claim that the ideal is a "level playing field" – a climate where "[t]he whole of the advantages and disadvantages of the different employments of labour and stock . . . be either perfectly equal or continually tending to equality."

This is neither to conclude that economic actors consciously or intentionally are always prudent, fair, cooperative, nor that markets act independently. Rather, the market works most efficiently and competitively when prudent parsimonious actors act fairly in competitive and cooperative ventures, whether or not they deliberately intend to do so.

Still, could we not conclude that we are prudent, fair, and cooperative because it is in our self-interest, at least long-term self-interest, to be so? Smith's answer would be "yes" and "no." Of course, it is in my interest, thus rational, to act accordingly. On the other hand, according to Smith each of us is naturally interested in others, thus it is also rational to be cooperative. "Consciousness of ill-desert" is part of human nature, even though some of us do not play fairly all the time. Prudence and parsimony are virtues many of us try to emulate; sloth and greed are not admired. So for Smith, a rational person is prudent, cooperative, and fair "by nature," because this is admirable, and because it is to one's advantage to be so.

Smith was not a purist, nor was he naive about agency problems. He was highly critical of "joint-stock companies," writing (1976b, V.i.e.18),

> [t]he trade of a joint stock company is always managed by a court of directors . . . The directors of such companies, however, being the managers rather of other people's money than of their own, it cannot well be expected, that they should watch over it with the same anxious vigilance with which the partners in a private copartnery frequently watch over their own . . . Negligence and profusion, therefore, must always prevail, more or less, in the management of the affairs of such a company.

Yet, at least part of this criticism is leveled because there were few corporations in Smith's time, the most notorious being the East India Company which, despite mercantile regulations, exemplified managerial greed to perfection.

On a macro level, Smith argues that the ideal political economy is one that protects its citizens, creates conditions for well-being, including economic growth, and provides public services in the context of personal liberty, protections of rights, and enforcement of laws of justice (Smith, 1976b, Introduction, IV.vii.c.44 and IV.ix.51 and 1762–64; 1978, [A] i.9). This is hardly a "night watchman" theory of the political economy, a position sometimes traced to Smith. A viable political economy cannot exist for long without justice, and it cannot prosper without economic development in the form of free commerce. Thus, in the Smithian well-functioning political economy, ethics (as prudence and personal fairness), economics (the enhancement of economic well-being of each citizen) and politics (in the form of protection of rights and commutative justice through the laws and guardians of the system) are all interrelated, inseparable, and necessary for a well-functioning, just, political economy.

What can be concluded from this reading of Smith is that the "popular view" of Smith creates a questionable paradigm and is not the only way to think about politics, economics, and ethics. Just as one set of political economists, in particular, neoclassical economic theory, appealed to Smith for some ground for their conclusions, so too, we can appeal to Smith to tell another story about commerce and free enterprise. This story might include: questioning the range and scope of rational choice theory and agency theory, pointing to the normative aspects of positive and welfare economics, raising questions about the alleged autonomy of markets (e.g., the "market for corporate control"), and exploring what kinds of stories one can tell about free enterprise if ethics, economics and politics cannot be neatly compartmentalized.

Much of this critical project is already under way. Since 1989, we have seen examples of "cowboy capitalism" where, without a rule of law, new capitalist economies flounder. Agency theory and rational choice theory are objects of a number of attacks, some by eminent economists such as Robert Frank and Amartya Sen. Sen, in his book, *On Ethics and Economics* (1987) and David Hausman and Michael McPherson (1996), in a newer book, *Economic Analysis and Moral Philosophy*, focus on the normative aspects of positive economics and, in the case of Sen, of welfare economics. Criticizing the Chicago School reading of Smith, Sen points out the limitations of rational choice theory, and Hausman and McPherson argue that the modeling criteria one uses in economics function normatively to frame the kinds of outcomes a particular model will produce.

What has been given less attention is the Separation Thesis. If ethics and economics are not easily compartmentalized, that is both good news and bad news. The good news is that, as Oliver Williamson (1985, p. 170) has recently noticed, if managers behave ethically, transaction costs go down. The bad news is that management cannot use the excuse, "We did it for business reasons, even though, on moral grounds, the behavior raised some questions." That is almost a direct quotation from the former CEO of Lockheed when, in 1977, he paid $12 million in extortion to Japanese government agents to win the Lockheed 1011 contract; he wrote, "From a purely ethical and moral standpoint I would have declined such a request. However, in this case, I would most certainly have sacrificed commercial success" (Kotchian, 1977, p. 11).

If ethics and economics are mutually dependent constructs, then a morally "good" company that fails in the market (e.g., IBM in the late 1980s) is really no better than the unethical behavior of a manager (e.g., Ivan Boesky), a morally questionable company (e.g., Bre-X), or a questionable activity of a company (Shell Oil's behavior in Nigeria) that is economically successful. On a practical level, the challenge is to tell a new story about business, to create a new mental model wherein the interrelationships between commerce, ethics, and public policy are formulated as a positive construct that makes sense to management as part of their competitive advantage.

Spencer's challenge is even more difficult. Corporate democratic self-management has seldom been conceived as part of libertarian democracy, and even employee ownership is usually decoupled from employee control. Will we see the growth of truly cooperative employee managed democratic economic enterprises as we move into the next century? Or will monarchies and aristocracies prevail in the world's corporations, despite political democratic tendencies to the contrary?

Rereading Smith and Spencer forces us to question some traditional assumptions about democratic free enterprise. Such analyses help us to envision democratic capitalism not as a static well-defined system but rather as an evolving set of political economies where a particular prevailing view is not, and should not be, the sole model.

Smith and Spencer, each in quite different ways, suggest how free enterprise can work to create viable, fair, or democratic economic institutions that protect and even enhance human liberty. While we may not agree with all their conclusions, we are at peril not to take them seriously.

References

Buckle, H. T. 1861: *History of Civilization in England, Volumes. I and II.* London: Williams and Norgate.

Darwin, C. 1996: *On the Origin of Species.* Edited by G. Beer. New York: Oxford University Press. First published in 1859.

Doherty, G. and Gray, T. 1993: Herbert Spencer and the relationship between economic and political liberty. *History of Political Thought*, 14, 475–90.

Donaldson, T. and Werhane, P. H. (eds) 1977: *Ethical Issues in Business*, 1st edn. Englewood Cliffs, NJ: Prentice-Hall.

Etzioni, A. 1988: *The Moral Dimension.* New York: Free Press.

Francis, M. 1978: Herbert Spencer and the myth of laissez faire. *Journal of the History of Ideas*, 21, 294–9.

Frank, R. 1988: *Passions Within Reason.* New York: Norton.

Freeman, R. E. 1994: The politics of stakeholder theory: Some future directions. *Business Ethics Quarterly*, 4, 409–22.

Friedman, M. 1962: *Capitalism and Freedom.* Chicago: University of Chicago Press.

Friedman, M. 1976: *Adam Smith's Relevance for 1976.* Chicago: University of Chicago Graduate School of Business Occasional Papers # 50.

Hausman, D. M. and McPherson, M. S. 1996: *Economic Analysis and Moral Philosophy.* Cambridge: Cambridge University Press.

Hildebrand, B. 1848: *Die Nationaloekonomie der Gegenwart und Zukunft.* Frankfurt. Quoted in the Introduction to Smith (1976).

Hirschman, A. O. 1977: *The Passions and the Interests.* Princeton: Princeton University Press.

Hudson, W. H. 1996: *An Introduction to the Philosophy of Herbert Spencer.* London: Routledge/ Thoemmes Press. First published in 1895.

Knies, C. G. A. 1853: *Die Politisch Zoekonomie vom Standpunkte der Geschichtlichen Methode.* Braunschweig. Quoted in the Introduction to Smith (1976).

Kotchian, C. 1977: The payoff: Lockheed's today mission to Tokyo. *Saturday Review*, July 9, 7–12.

Lerner, M. 1937: Preface. In E. Cannan (ed.), *Adam Smith, The Wealth of Nations*, New York: Modern Library.

Mandeville, B. 1988: *The Fable of the Bees.* Edited by F. B. Kaye. Oxford: Clarendon Press. First published in 1732.

Nozick, R. 1974: *Anarchy, State, and Utopia.* New York: Basic Books.

Paul, J. 1982: The socialism of Herbert Spencer. *History of Political Thought*, 3, 499–514.

Sen, A. 1987: *On Ethics and Economics.* Oxford: Basil Blackwell.

Simon, W. M. 1960: Herbert Spencer and the social organism. *Journal of the History of Ideas*, 21, 294–9.

Smith, A. 1976a: *The Theory of Moral Sentiments.* Edited by A. L. Macfie and D. D. Raphael. New York: Oxford University Press. First published in 1759.

Smith, A. 1976b: *The Wealth of Nations.* Edited by R. H. Campbell and A. S. Skinner. New York: Oxford University Press. First published in 1776.

Smith, A. 1978: *Lectures on Jurisprudence [A] and [B].* Edited by R. L. Meek, D. D. Raphael, and P. G. Stein. New York: Oxford University Press. First published in 1762 and 1764.

Spencer, H. 1851: *Social Statics*. London: John Chapman.

Spencer, H. 1857: Progress: its law and cause. *The Leader*, March 20. Reprinted in Spencer (1892a, I: pp. 1–59).

Spencer, H. 1862: *First Principles*. London: Williams and Norgate.

Spencer, H. 1872: Mr. Martineau on evolution. *The Leader*, October 23. Reprinted in Spencer (1892a, II: pp. 371–88).

Spencer, H. 1873: *The Study of Sociology*. London: Williams and Norgate.

Spencer, H. 1886: The factors of organic evolution. *The Nineteenth Century*, April–May. Reprinted in Spencer (1892a, I: pp. 389–466).

Spencer, H. 1892a: *Essays: Scientific, Political and Speculative*. Volumes I, II and III. New York: D. Appleton and Company.

Spencer, H. 1892b: *The Principles of Ethics*. Volumes I, II and III. London: Williams and Norgate.

Spencer, H. 1896: *The Principles of Sociology*. Volumes I, II and III. New York: D. Appleton and Company.

Spencer, H. 1904: *Herbert Spencer: An Autobiography*. Volumes I and II. London: Williams and Norgate.

Spencer, H. 1982: *Man versus the State*. Indianapolis: Liberty Classics. First published in *Contemporary Review* (Feb, May, June, July) 1884.

Stigler, G. 1971: Smith's travels on the ship of state. *History of Political Economy*, III.

Turner, J. 1985: *Herbert Spencer: A Renewed Appreciation*. Beverly Hills, CA: Sage Publications.

von Skarzynski, W. 1878: *Adam Smith als Moralphilosoph und Schoepfer der Nationaloekonomie*. Berlin. (Quoted in the Introduction to the 1976 edition of *The Theory of Moral Sentiments*.)

Weinstein, D. 1990: Freedom, rights, and utility in Spencer's moral philosophy. *History of Political Thought*, 11, 119–42.

Werhane, P. H. 1991: *Adam Smith and His Legacy for Modern Capitalism*. New York: Oxford University Press.

Werhane, P. H. 1997: *Adam Smith's Legacy for Ethics and Economics*. Judge Institute for Management Studies Working Paper 143, University of Cambridge.

Williamson, O. 1985: *The Economic Institution of Capitalism*. New York: Free Press.

Bibliography

Bellamy, R. and Gray, T. 1990: *Herbert Spencer's Liberalism*. London: Routledge.

Cropsey, J. 1977: *Polity and Economy*. Westport, Conn: Greenwood Press.

Gray, J. N. 1982: Spencer on the ethics of liberty and the limits of state interference. *History of Political Thought*, 3, 465–82.

Gray, T. S. 1988: Is Herbert Spencer's law of equal freedom a utilitarian or rights-based theory of justice? *Journal of the History of Philosophy*, 26, 259–78.

Morrow, G. R. 1926: *The Ethical and Economic Theories of Adam Smith*. New York: Augustus M. Kelley.

Peel, J. D. Y. 1972: *Herbert Spencer on Social Evolution*. Chicago: University of Chicago Press.

Spencer, H. 1854: Railway morals and railway policy. *Edinburgh Review*, October. Reprinted in Spencer (1892a, III: pp. 2–112).

Spencer, H. 1860: The social organism. *Westminister Review*, January. Reprinted in Spencer (1892a, I: pp. 265–307).

Viner, J. 1926: Adam Smith and laissez faire. In J. M. Clark et al. (eds), *Adam Smith, 1776–1926*. New York: Augustus M. Kelley.

Werhane, P. H. 1989: The role of self-interest in Adam Smith's *Wealth of Nations*. *Journal of Philosophy*, 669–80.

27

A brief history of American business ethics

THOMAS F. MCMAHON

The history of American business ethics may be viewed in six successive stages:

1   The religious underpinnings and underlying ideologies of English origins (1700–1776)
2   The early American business ethics in development (1777–1890)
3   A mature concept of business ethics (1891–1963)
4   The rise of social issues in business ethics (1962–1970)
5   Perceiving business ethics as a specific discipline
6   Recognizing American business ethics as global

Some of these phases overlap because the time frames are not exact. At best, they are approximations, so some divisions are not distinctly marked off from others. However, for purposes of presenting an overview of ethics in American business, in this article they will be treated separately.

Origins and underlying ideologies 1700–1776

As a result of the USA's status as a British colony, American business ethics in its earliest stage reflected English law and business practices. An example was accepting monopolization of certain products, such as tobacco and textiles. During most of the 1700s, businessmen were primarily brokers and wholesalers since industrial production did not develop until after the Revolution. It was not until 1840 that the factory replaced the home as producer of goods. When machinery replaced handicraft production, businessmen became producers as well as wholesalers and suppliers.

During this period, the religious underpinnings of business were very important. Two basic ideologies developed. The first viewed wealth as a divine favor. Cotton Mather and Benjamin Franklin subscribed to this idea. The second viewpoint was expressed by John Woolman, a lawyer and a merchant, who incorporated William Penn's precept that merchants are stewards or trustees for the public good. During the eighteenth century and into the latter half of the nineteenth century, these two traditions created a tension that motivated businessmen toward good deeds. Gathering wealth and acting as stewards to the less fortunate became symbolic of the religious dimension of business, so much so that what has been called the "divine right of businessmen" appeared with the advent of the factory system. Businessmen perceived their role as business persons as directly related to God. However, in later years, a more restrictive view was that God gave control of property to Christian men who would protect the laborer. Still later, a more popular, broader perspective traced business stewardship indirectly to God, while subscribing to Social Darwinism and supporting the doctrines of Adam Smith and *laissez-faire* economists. Daniel Drew and John D. Rockefeller exemplified this latter view of the "Divine Right of Businessmen."

Underlying business ideologies evolved considerably over the forty years after the revolution. In his visit in 1831, Alexis de Tocqueville described in detail the American view of living, and especially of work. He perceived it as an "enlightened self-interest," a perspective that encourages daily self-denial for the sake of future prosperity. Furthermore, it is related to individualism. In his view, both tended to narrow a person's perspective. Another ideology that permeated business ethics, and is still felt today, is found in Adam Smith's *An Inquiry into the Wealth of Nations* (1776). Its overwhelming impact came with the development of the factory system and the advocates of big business and Social Darwinism – the idea that, in society, only the fittest should survive. Herbert Spencer, William Graham Sumner and other prophets of the new evolutionary social ideology, while concerned with the suffering of the poor, felt that progress could only come through long work, savings, and self-discipline. This approach thus became associated with what are known as "middle class virtues." It reflects differently the position of Lutheranism and Calvinism towards the need for hard work and a serious pursuit of one's "calling." A strong advocate of this position was Henry Demarest Lloyd, who used his position as a reporter on the *Chicago Tribune* to oppose the power of corporations, especially the railroads, and to propose his own moralistic approach to the social and economic problems in the USA.

Earlier American business ethics 1777–1890

Newer underlying ideologies of American business ethics can be found in the philosophical writings, especially in John Locke's position on private property and Jean Jacques Rousseau's proposals concerning the social contract. Practical applications of these views are exemplified in Andrew Carnegie's Gospel of Wealth and Henry Ford's Gospel of Production. John Locke, who made significant contributions in many areas of philosophy, had considerable influence first on the Founding Fathers and indirectly on the American constitution, and later on the development of the American business creed. He subscribed to the concept of natural human rights, and defended the right to private property. He argued that a person's right to self-preservation guarantees a right to those resources which are required to accomplish this goal, and that a person's labor is what contributes primarily to self-preservation. It is by "mixing" labor with land that a person acquires a right to land needed for sustaining himself and his family. For Locke, the primary function of society was to protect the natural rights of individuals, including the right to property.

The Enlightenment ideals of human reason and the rational reconstruction of society provided a perfect setting Jean Jacques Rousseau's philosophy. Freedom of humans from oppressive institutions was the essence of his beliefs. Through the Social Contract, which involved the voluntary subjection of every individual to what Rousseau called "the general will," people attempt to achieve the necessary ingredients of a civilized society without, however, sacrificing their basic rights or interests. The general will, as embodied in the social contract, was an expression of what is in everyone's interests, and as such is what all people truly desire. Thus, in Rousseau's cold-blooded phrase, if someone is coerced to act in accordance with the general will, he or she is "forced to be free."

In terms of business ethics, property and contract became important underlying philosophical ideologies . With reservations, Andrew Carnegie and Henry Ford applied Locke's and Rousseau's philosophical beliefs to the practical world of business. When the Industrial Revolution was in full swing, the belching of heavy smoke from the chimneys of factories was seen as a sign of successful manufacturing. Production – making things – was all important. Survival of the fittest became more important to business than the aforementioned stewardship tied to an earlier concept of business ethics. Carnegie believed that only the wealthy could endow society with what is necessary for cultural development. Only wealthy persons, e.g., Carnegie himself, could, through the vast fortunes they accumulated, contribute things such as libraries that were needed for social improvement. Moreover, the wealthy – not politicians or the common laborer – could best decide what was good for society in the long run. Distribution of wealth to the working class, even if used judicially for personal or family improvement, would not contribute to the good of society. Carnegie indeed espoused survival of the fittest in a practical way that reflected the business ethic of the time. It is no wonder that workers began seriously to form power groups by supporting labor unions, which led to large-scale confrontations between management and labor. These clashes signaled the death knell of the stewardship ideal. The 1886 Haymarket riots in Chicago exemplify the conflict between employer and employees during this period of industrial growth. By this time, the extensive and the expansive power of the so-called Robber Barons was perceived by the public as divisive and devastating to society in general, and to the small business person and the working class in particular.

The Robber Barons of the late nineteenth century followed business ideologies that were very different from previous ones. Unlike earlier business persons, for them God was no longer in business in any real sense. Self-interest became self-aggrandizement. Stewardship gave way to gaining power for personal use. The certainty of social purpose was lost, and means and ends were confused. Not surprisingly, the Robber Barons, in addition to building up their own empires, also set the stage for public resentment that led to legislation (such as the Sherman Antitrust Act in 1890 and the establishment of the Interstate Commerce Commission in 1886), muckraking newspaper reports on different industries (such as meat-packing), and paved the road to the New Deal. It seemed that business ethics was all business and no ethics. Names such as Mellon, Drew, Vanderbilt, Gould and Astor are still well known, but not as exemplars of business ethics, either then or now.

Another name that is still well known is Ford. Henry Ford was the leading advocate of what might be called the Gospel of Production. In a sense, this approach to business was refreshing. His goal was to organize production to do as much good as possible for everybody. Ford's ideas about production applied to some degree the principles of "scientific management" devised by Frederick Taylor as a means to greater productivity. By favoring higher wages, shorter hours, and planned activities for workers on the job,

Taylor's ideas undermined Spencer's "survival of the fittest," and led to a new phase in the history of American business ethics. Thus, in his own way, Henry Ford initiated a new era in American business ethics in addition to a new approach to production.

Although the contributions of persons and their ideologies to business and business ethics go back to English law and business practices, as events unfolded over the years, understandings of the role of the owner and the worker shifted dramatically. During the earliest times, owners had a sense of stewardship to employees and to society in general. They understood their role as having a public as well as a private dimension. However, the perspective of stewardship changed as America grew from family household operations to factory production. The use of machinery replaced the personal approach and individualism of the earliest business ethic. The use of steam to run machines in factories, and inventions such as railroads and automobiles, moved the Industrial Revolution into high gear. By 1894, the value of American business production surpassed the production of the UK, France and Germany combined. Except for the particular notions of individual business persons and their underlying philosophical views, no one set of ethical principles or practices emerged to guide the typical businessman or woman in the practice of business, nor was there any unified understanding of the ethical relation between employers and employees. In the late nineteenth century, the concepts underpinning business – power and rights – were exercised in such interacting arenas as courts of law, unions, trade associations and professional societies, but, with few exceptions, ethics was not a significant consideration in American business practice.

A mature American business ethics 1891–1963

The failure of controls in the late nineteenth century were reflected in the economic collapse of 1929 and in the years leading up to the New Deal. It was said that in the early twentieth century there was "poverty in the midst of plenty." According to some historians, the ideology of the time incorporated the philosophy of pragmatism, the psychology of behaviorism and the economics of institutionalism.

During this time, the academic approach to business ethics was still undeveloped. Most of the books specifically dealing with ethics in American business were highly general. Some provided an overview of issues or concerns, such as practical means to increase production while at the same time recognizing the rights of employees. Others limited themselves to the general direction of American business in a changing society. The authors did not deal with the overall problem of ethics in business.

One of the first comprehensive business ethics books – actually a textbook for college students – appeared in 1957. The author, Herbert Johnston, covered topics on a chapter-by-chapter basis. He included brief cases to illustrate in a practical manner the issues of a business situation. Each chapter generally commenced with a brief philosophical presentation (generally, the Natural Law theory) followed by acceptable ethical principles derived from the philosophical presentation. Ordinarily, there was a conclusion describing the correct ethical approach. The author dealt extensively with employee rights and obligations, like the "living wage." The Roman Catholic papal encyclicals were quoted in part to provide direction to Catholic university students. This format was more or less followed by a number of subsequent authors of business ethics textbooks. Another text, *Business and Society* (1963) by J. W. McGuire is thought by some to mark the beginning of the formal study of business and society.

Between 1957 and 1963, the years in which the books mentioned above were published, three important changes took place in the world of business that influenced and concerned business persons about their legal and ethical environment. First, the government proved that an alleged price fixing conspiracy among members of the electrical industry was true and punished the offenders with jail sentences and fines. Second, contrary to business's claims that only the electrical industry behaved illegally and unethically, an empirical study showed that most businesses, if not all, had unethical practitioners. Third, the 1964 Civil Rights Act and subsequent social legislation shifted the emphasis of business ethics from the individual business executive and manager to corporate activity.

The first change – price fixing – began with a newspaper reporter's investigation. The reporter wrote about the unusual coincidences in the pricing and bidding of large machines used in the making of electricity. Ultimately the US government investigated the allegations and the Kennedy administration, under Attorney General Robert Kennedy, produced evidence that, indeed, large manufacturers of electrical equipment were fixing prices. The government indicted the manufacturers for antitrust violations, and tried and won the case. Besides heavy fines, some of the conspirators were given prison sentences.

The business world was stunned. Big business up to this point had enjoyed a strong, positive reputation. Not only did business contribute substantially to providing goods and materials to win World War II, but, under the auspices of the government's Marshall plan, it helped to rebuild Europe and Japan. Business was also turning out products, such as automobiles and refrigerators, that were in short supply but in great demand. In short, the ethical position of business seemed invincible. The business world insisted that the price fixing was unique to the electrical industry, while the rest of business was law-abiding and ethical. However, this claim was not to go unchallenged.

The second change developed from a study on the ethics of business practioners. Raymond C. Baumhart, S. J., a doctoral candidate at the Harvard University School of Business Administration, sent out 1,700 questionnaires to all levels of business executives and managers. He followed up the questionnaire with face-to-face interviews with 100 of the respondents to verify the results. He subsequently wrote an article in the *Harvard Business Review* (1961) in which he claimed that most industries, if not all businesses in those industries, practice some form of unethical behavior. Indeed, he also stated that the employee's superiors had the most influence in producing these unethical, and sometimes illegal, actions.

The reaction to this ground breaking study was immediate. The government established an agency to deal with unethical business activity and, throughout the USA, business trade associations, colleges and universities, and churches – the American Management Association and Loyola University Chicago are only two of many examples – held workshops and seminars for improving business ethics in offices and plants. Even usually conservative business schools began showing an interest, and some actually initiated courses on business ethics.

Baumhart's article became a classic. Businesses gradually began to develop and incorporate workshops and in-house programs and training in business ethics. Some businesses, such as Johnson & Johnson, developed codes of ethics to assist employees in resolving problems in which ethics had considerable weight in the final outcome. (Johnson and Johnson expressed their values in a *Credo*, which became their guideline in dealing with the now-famous Tylenol disaster that required total recall of the product. One of the vice-presidents of this division stated that, when they were informed of the disaster, one of the first things they did was to apply the mandates of the company's *Credo*.)

After the Baumhart article, business ethics dealt primarily with the legal and ethical decisions of individual business persons. In general, it followed Locke's Natural Law approach to resolving problems. The practice of using business ethics case studies, a practice related to ancient traditions of ethical and legal casuistry, became a common method of investigating and resolving ethical problems in business. Typically these studies emphasize what the individual should do under specific circumstances, but they rarely dealt with the corporate structure within which these decisions had to be made.

A problem with the focus on cases is that sometimes the decision to take an ethical stand had to be made within the *ethos* of an industry that is already ethically corrupt in some way. The price-fixing scandal of the early 1960s showed how difficult it is to perform ethically when others, especially one's superiors, are acting unethically and even encouraging cooperation in unethical activities. The ability of the individual executive or manager to go against superiors is very limited, as the Baumhart study states. Lower level managers have little power to offset unethical practices in the corporation or industry. Baumhart suggests a different and, perhaps, difficult course of action: If you want to be ethical, find yourself an ethical boss. Of course, this places a considerable burden on the employee, perhaps an unreasonable and unrealistic burden.

Other concerns of business persons and ethicists during this period covered such topics as hiring and firing, safe working conditions, conflicts of interest, trade secrets, expense accounts and similar topics. Of great interest was the possibility of fraud and deception in relations with customers and competitors. Advertising was subjected to scrutiny not only for its effects on the individual customer, but also on the grounds of its own legitimacy. Although such general questions about legitimacy were the exception, not the rule; most of the concerns were personal: How should this executive or manager act in a responsible way, in this particular ethical problem?

During this time codes of ethics grew in popularity, and it is estimated that about 95 percent of larger corporations have them today. Codes vary considerably in their content. Some make very general statements about the overall goals of the business while others are quite specific, and go into great detail about many of the topics mentioned above. Most codes, however, make strong statements on topics such as avoiding conflict of interest, limitations on receiving and giving gifts, prohibitions of racial discrimination and sexual harassment, and protecting company property and proprietary information. Disciplinary action following an infraction of the company code is sometimes difficult to verify. Nevertheless, codes describe what is expected of company employees, and have became a source of information for employee behavior. Sometimes these codes were illustrated with examples of infractions and expected behavior in specific situations. Thus, they complemented the role of the business person and his or her individual ethic. This approach to business ethics was rapidly changing, and soon it would include society, its issues, its concerns and its problems. Business ethics would become "Business and Society" or "The Social Responsibilities of Business."

The rise of social issues in business ethics 1962–1970

The third change in business ethics came rather quickly after the price-fixing trouble and seemed to follow a shift in society's values in the post-Kennedy era. Beginning with the Supreme Court's *Brown* vs *the School Board of Topeka, Kansas* decision, the attitude towards racial discrimination began to change. The power of the federal government was felt in states where segregation was practiced in schools (including law and business schools), employment, police and fire departments, and even churches. Much of this segregation could be traced to the 1896 Supreme Court *Plessy* vs *Ferguson* decision regarding the "equal protection" clause of the 14th amendment to the constitution. This amendment was added after the Civil War to protect the freed slaves, who became American citizens. They were to be treated as equal to other citizens of the state in which they resided. However, in 1896, the Supreme Court interpreted the "equal protection" clause in terms of "separate but equal" facilities. Although the decision dealt specifically with accommodations in railroad cars, theoretically it implied that blacks and whites were to have the same facilities in all other areas – only separate. The *Brown* case, which was written by Chief Justice Earl Warren, stated that it was "unconscionable" for there to be this separation in education. From then on, the shift to genuine equality began its slow, painful course. States were forced by federal law to integrate their schools and the spirit of equality among races began to spread to other institutions, including business. A notable aid in achieving this goal was the historic 1964 Civil Rights Act, which Congress passed during the Johnson administration. President Lyndon Johnson then added Executive Order 11246 whereby any corporate entity (including businesses, schools, health care facilities, and so forth) which wanted a government contract had to engage in affirmative actions to accelerate the movement of minorities, including women, into the workforce. These two federal actions – the 1964 Civil Rights Act and Executive Order 11246 – set the stage for a dramatic shift in business ethics. The emphasis after the Baumhart survey was on the ethical decisions of individual executives and managers. The post-Johnson period gave business ethics a broader, social perspective.

After the 1964 Civil Rights Act and Executive Order 11246, discrimination in the work place was illegal. Eventually, it was perceived as unethical. Some classes of employees were "protected" against discrimination by law, and the 1964 Civil Rights Act (as amended) prohibited discrimination against all employees in hiring, promotion, termination, pay, fringe benefits and other aspects of employment on the basis of race, color, religion, sex, or national origin. Although much, but not all, discrimination in business had been directed against African Americans and women, other laws, such as the *American with Disabilities Act of 1990*, were passed to protect groups that were not covered in the original legislation.

The general nature of these and other laws made necessary clarification either through federal agency action or court decision. One of the most important Supreme Court decisions dealing with discriminatory practices in employment was the *1971 Griggs* vs *Duke Power Company* (401 US 424, 1971). The Court determined that it was not the employer's intention (in this case to upgrade the workers' education), but the consequences of the employer's actions that determine discrimination. This policy, called "disparate impact," is now used to analyze and resolve discrimination claims. An example is the airline (Republic, now a part of Northwest) that had a minimum height requirement of 5'2" for flight attendants. Statistical studies showed that half of Asian and Hispanic women could not be hired under this policy. Thus it was found discriminatory on the basis of its disparate impact on a protected class.

The change in the role of women in society in general has also had its impact on the role of women in the workplace. Highly educated, talented, and desiring a career, women entered business at unprecedented speed in the 1970s and 1980s. The "old boy" network was changing as well to let women in, albeit begrudgingly more often than not. The courts followed suit as more cases of discrimination against women were brought to their attention. Among the cases were victims of sexual harassment, exclusionary promotion policies, and women who received less pay for the same or similar work. American business ethics thus took a broader perspective as awareness of unjust discrimination against employees increased, and a willingness to deal with the problems caused by discrimination intensified.

However, problems concerning discrimination were not the only focus of business ethics. Leading the world (and needing its cooperation) in assessing the needs of the environment, Americans were faced with the pollution of land, air and water. As the government passed legislation to limit the amount of pollution, businesses had to rethink their role in society. Up to this time, business did not fret about sending toxic materials into the ground, the air or the water. It was believed, if it was considered at all, that nature would eventually recover. As the Earth became more populous, the disposal of waste became first a concern, then a problem, and finally a critical strategy for preserving the needs of society in the present and the future. The general approach was for government to set the standards and business to comply, but this strategy met with considerable resistance. Industries complained that it was difficult and expensive to meet the deadlines for the different forms of clean-up. They also were concerned about competition with businesses in foreign countries where environmental controls were weak or non-existent. In addition, business argued that pollution costs were opportunity costs; that is, American business might have to spend money for anti-pollution equipment instead of new machinery, plant modernizations, or new plants. They questioned the return on such a heavy investment in controlling pollution.

The debate about environmental problems took American business ethics to another turn in its history. This change in direction might be called "environmental business ethics." Ethicists began to see the environment as something more than land, air and water, and business ethicists began to see environmental protection as human protection. This new way of viewing the environment took an entirely different perspective on the relation between people and the environment, one that included more than could be physically measured in standard environmental impact statements. Environmental ethics thus attempted to shift the responsibility of business, its executives and its managers from simply controlling pollution, to issues of the overall quality of life. Consequently, in addition to fulfilling the mandates of civil rights legislation, business now had the responsibility to protect, and in some situations, to enhance the environment. This responsibility was given legal force in 1970, when the United States

Environmental Act created the Environmental Protection Agency (EPA) as an independent agent to administer federal laws dealing with environmental issues. Businesses could no longer escape the consequences of environmental degradation they caused.

Social and ethical problems in discrimination, and health, safety, and the environment were only the beginning of what by now had become almost a revolution in the way business is practiced. Still other social and ethical issues, especially those with implications for trading with foreign countries, soon became a part of the everyday concerns of business executives and managers. For example, in 1977 Congress passed the Foreign Corrupt Practices Act, which prohibited Americans from extending payments to high-ranking officials of foreign countries in exchange for special treatment over competitors. American business people complained that they would be in a non-competitive position since so many business persons from other countries were allowed to consider payoffs as legitimate business expenses. (This issue has created some strong negative attitudes in the formation of the European Union.) And there was more to come. Business also became concerned about political and social structures that permitted persons to be treated in an inhumane manner. These included apartheid, child labor, land division in less developed countries, and repressive political regimes.

All of these developments in business and business ethics became reflected in a newer concept called "social responsiveness," which is sensitive to social pressure but at the same time tends to become proactive. While social responsibility referred more to rights and obligations, social responsiveness reacted to power from others, primarily other interested parties. Socially conscious business executives and managers, as well as outside interest parties, led many ethicists (led by Ed Freeman) to refer to these people as "stakeholders," i.e., those who can affect, or be affected by, the business organization. This position recognizes that, in addition to shareholders, other members of the corporation and other groups in society have a stake in the organization. For example, the oil spill of the Valdez in Alaska, the toxic waste problem on the Love Canal in New York, and the precipitous plant closing in Kenosha, Wisconsin, illustrate the need for a broader definition of social responsibility and social responsiveness.

However, the stakeholder approach to business ethics is not the only one in play. Some ethicists, such as Robert Solomon, more recently have returned to the virtue ethics of Plato and Aristotle, in which the individual business person becomes immersed in the virtues of honesty, fairness, and benevolence. It is perhaps too early to determine the impact of this recent shift in emphasis among academics doing business ethics, but there can be no doubt that, at present, the field is more active, with a broader understanding of its methods and purpose, than at any time in the past.

Business ethics as a specific discipline

Not only did the content of business ethics shift during the 1960s and 1970s, but, as mentioned above, the philosophical approach to business ethics became much more varied. From their beginnings with the natural law theory of Locke, ethicists have been influenced by the utilitarianism of Bentham and his followers, the categorical imperative of Kant, and the distributive theory of justice of John Rawls. Text books and case books proliferated, written primarily by philosophers who specialized in applied ethics. Centers for research, conferences on business ethics and endowed chairs multiplied. Ultimately, the academic community recognized ethics and the social responsibility of business as a distinct discipline. Indeed, in 1971, the prestigious Academy of Management added a "social issues in management" division. In 1974, the accrediting agency for business schools, the American Assembly of Collegiate Schools of Business, granted business and society courses a prominent place in the core curriculum of business education. The University of Virginia now offers a doctoral degree in business ethics, and The Society of Business Ethics, founded by some of the original authors on this topic, has grown and proliferated. Indeed, European and Pacific Rim countries are using this operation as their working model. Incidentally, the term for national and international ethics in business has returned to a broader perception of the original; it is once again "business ethics" while it includes social issues.

American business ethics as global

Ethical problems in the international environment reflect many of those in the native country. Different cultural practices, different philosophies, different laws, even different religious roots make it difficult for foreign companies to attain legitimacy in host countries. The ethical question is easy to ask, but difficult to answer: Whose values are followed in a foreign environment?

The power of American business in the international arena is sometimes overwhelming. Foreign countries frequently react by limiting the ownership in a company in their country. Sometimes this leads to tragedy, as in the 1984 Union Carbide disaster. Sometimes it leads to sanctioned inhumane practices, like child labor in some less developed countries. Sometimes, the choice is between cultural relativism and ethical imperialism. In the first, the ethical standards of the country are followed, even though they are contrary to American law or practice. The second, ethical imperialism, occurs when the standards of the home country are followed or even imposed. Some ethicists say that the American firm should adhere to the higher, rather than the lower, standard. Other ethicists state that when American companies encounter "unbridgeable gaps," they should consider suspending business in the host country. As one might imagine, the debate on these issues is unresolved.

Conclusion

American business ethics has evolved significantly from the time of the Founding Fathers until the present. While religion seemed to imbue the early businessmen with a sense of social purpose, it now seems to be separate from ethics except in those individuals who feel that the secular theories of the ethicists are not sufficient. The arrogance of the divine right of businessmen has dramatically shifted to the rights of others, including employees, customers and competitors. The limited view of the classical owner exclusively to profits and return on investments shifted to the broader concept of "enlightened self-interest" to that of social responsibility and social responsiveness. Finally, the American business ethic has broadened its perspective to include other interest parties in society. Perhaps the newer notion of American business ethics, virtue ethics will be able to meld all these historical developments to produce an acceptable amalgamate called "The American Business Ethic." With the advent of

NAFTA, which currently includes Canada and Mexico, and might incorporate other countries in the near future, a term that would more accurately describe its future might be "The Business Ethics of the Americas."

Contemporary business ethicists might ponder two questions for future discussion. The questions relate to the ultimate responsibility in business decision making. The famous Nobel Laureate Milton Friedman asked this question, after declaring social responsibility of business to be "a subversive doctrine:" Who appointed or elected business executives and managers to determine what is good for the well-being of a nation? The second question is similar and refers to stakeholder management and virtue ethics: When the ultimate decision is made in a complex business situation, which of the stakeholders or virtue ethics proponents will assume responsibility for the decision? Obviously, the history of business ethics continues.

References

Baumhart, R. C. S. J. 1968: *Ethics in Business*. New York: Holt, Rinehart & Winston.

Further reading

Bellah, R., Madsen, R., Sullivan, W. M., Swidler, A., and Tipton, S. M. 1985: *Habits of the Heart*. Berkeley: University of California Press.
Cavanagh, G. F. 1990: *American Business Values*. Englewood Cliffs, New Jersey: Prentice-Hall.
Heilbroner, R. L. 1967: *The Worldly Philosophers*. New York: Simon and Schuster.
Galbraith, J. K. 1973: *Economics and the Public Purpose*. Boston: New American Library.
Jonsen, A. R. and Toulmin, S. 1988: *The Abuse of Casuistry: A History of Moral Reasoning*. Berkeley: University of California Press.
Rodgers, D. T. 1978: *The Work Ethic in Industrial America 1850–1920*. Chicago: University of Chicago Press.
Stone, C. D. 1975: *Where the Law Ends: The Social Control of Corporate Behavior*. New York: Harper.
Tawney, R. H. 1947: *Religion and the Rise of Capitalism*. New York: Mentor.
Walton, G. M. and Robertson, R. 1983: *History of the American Economy*. New York: Harcourt Brace Jovanovich.
Weber, M. 1958: *The Protestant Ethic and the Spirit of Capitalism*. Translated by T. Parsons. New York: Scribner.

28

Business ethics in Europe:
a tale of two efforts

HENK VAN LUIJK

Introduction

On business ethics, in the European tradition, two stories can be told: one from the outside and one from the inside. Both stories are about relatively recent events, because business ethics, as it presents itself today in Europe, has a short history. For the rest, the stories are strikingly different. The story told from the outside is the most common one and, at the same time, the flattest of the two. It reports some moderate successes and offers an outlook on some new initiatives, predominantly of an academic nature. The inside story is about a complicated growth process, serious obstacles, and an uncertain future. It is, by far, the most demanding to tell, but also the most intriguing to listen to. In what follows, the accent will be on the inside story, or, more modestly, on some major elements of it. To mark the difference, however, I start with a short version of the better known outside story, and I deliberately resist the temptation to open with a definition of *business ethics*, let alone with a definition of *Europe*. The stories themselves will have to do that job. There is no use in frenetically sharpening the knives without a ham on the table.

The outside story

Business ethics in Europe, in its present shape and form, made its first appearance in the early 1980s as a new course, gradually admitted to the curriculum of business schools and business administration faculties. It is a tone-setting start for, in this way, right from the beginning, the emphasis was on business ethics as an academic discipline. As such, the evolution of business ethics can be followed easily. Three criteria have proven to be sufficiently distinctive: material expansion, contacts laid, and themes studied. I restrict myself to the essentials; details are accessible in various sources.

With regard to *material expansion*, in 1983, the first European research position in business ethics was founded at what is now Sankt Gallen University in Switzerland. In 1984, the first full professorship of business ethics in Europe was established at Universiteit Nyenrode in The Netherlands. Fifteen years later, over twenty-five chairs can be counted all over Europe, and many persons with other academic positions are active in the field. Courses on "business ethics," "business and society," or "social responsibility in business" are taught at numerous places – universities and business

353

schools as well as polytechnics and professional educational institutions. Since 1992, the quarterly *Business Ethics: A European Review* has been published, as well as an Italian journal and a French one, the latter having been transformed recently into a regular publication in book form. Conferences, symposia and seminars are organized all over the continent and in the UK, not only by academic institutions, but also by professional organizations and, occasionally, by single corporations. The number of books published in the field is also far beyond the capacity of any person to follow, if only for the reason that they are written in twelve different languages. So far, a bright story indeed, except for the language inconvenience.

With regard to *mutual contacts*, the European Business Ethics Network (EBEN) deserves mention. Founded in 1987, by 1998 EBEN had 750 members, many of them from academia but also from the business world and the professions. EBEN brings together a substantial number of people interested in the moral quality of decision-making processes in business. In some European countries, national EBEN networks are established. They offer possibilities for meetings and joint initiatives on the basis of short-travel distances, shared issues, and the common language one finds within most national boundaries. EBEN may be the most visible association in European business ethics, but it certainly is not the only one. Again, a stimulating and, therefore, a promising picture.

For a major and for a minor reason, the outside story becomes more complicated when we look at the *themes studied*. The minor reason concerns the topics taken into consideration. European handbooks on business ethics, as far as available, cover the whole field of subjects one expects to find when people are talking about ethics in business, e.g., the rights and duties of employees, customers, suppliers and shareholders, environmental consequences of business, marketing and advertising practices, the role of the state, and international business relations. Over time, though, a certain alteration of subjects could be noticed as well, closely related to economic and social developments in Europe as a whole. Environmental issues, and questions regarding personnel policies in periods of restructuring and lay-offs, dominant in the mid-1980s, were followed by themes such as the ethics of mergers and hostile takeovers, the shaping of the European Union in a social, economic and monetary sense, international responsibilities of business, sense and nonsense of codes of conduct, the emergence of ethical auditing practices and ethical consultancy in business, and the topic of corporate governance. This link between themes studied and shifting focuses of attention in society at large may be a sign of a positive relationship between theory and practice, but it also involves the unpredictability of what is going to be the next item on the research agenda and a certain risk of superficiality in the way it is treated. Public interests often change before studies on previous subjects have been completed. A minor complication for those aware of it, one might say.

A major complication is of a local as well as a methodological nature. At stake here are differences in the style of reflection that hamper a mutual understanding across at least some of the national borders. For instance, differences occur where Spanish or Italian contributions to business ethics appear to originate in Roman Catholic doctrines and convictions that have largely lost their appeal in strongly secularized regions such as The Netherlands or Sweden. Differences, and subsequent difficulties, occur even more emphatically when British scholars and business people are confronted with

German treatises on the fundamental structure of economic rationality and the need for an elaborated "discourse ethics" as a basis for business ethics. Peter Ulrich's (1997) achievement – *Integrative Wirtschaftsethik. Grundlagen einer lebensdienlichen Ökonomie* (Integrative Business Ethics. Foundations of a Life-serving Economics) – even if it were to be translated in English, which seems unlikely, still would remain closed to those trained in an Anglo-Saxon style of reflection and analysis. The very few that, nevertheless, would be prepared to struggle with his book would probably end up wondering why five hundred pages were needed to make the point if, in their eyes, forty or fifty could have done the job as well. They would be wrong, but understandably so. It is not only the Channel that separates the British Isles from the European Continent. It is two centuries of divergent philosophical reflection and educational practices as well.

The outside story of business ethics in Europe is predominantly told from an academic perspective. It covers business ethics as an academic discipline, and presents a picture of steady growth: not spectacular maybe, but solid. By now, business ethicists in Europe have defined their field and competence, or so it seems. Fifteen years of academic efforts have not been in vain. The story, told this way, sounds fairly positive. Yet it leaves vital elements untold, and essential questions unasked. To tell a more adequate story, we have to make a shift from the outside perspective to the inside. Here, a closer look at some questions left open thus far can be helpful.

Open questions

Four such questions deserve our attention:

- Which target group or groups does business ethics in Europe envisage?
- What exactly is the reception of the ethicists' endeavors among their academic peers, and what is it in the business world?
- To what extent does the social and economic environment in Europe shape business ethics?
- Is it appropriate to present business ethics, first and foremost, as an academic discipline?

The questions, different in nature as they may seem, are nevertheless closely interrelated. The problem with them is that they are formulated against the background of a traditional academic idea of business ethics. In tackling them, we therefore may have to use the well-known philosophical tactic of answering a question by changing the subject. If so, we will do it overtly.

Target groups

From the outside view, business ethics is categorized as a branch of applied ethics. This says something about the target group or groups towards which the discipline is oriented. It says notably that, as in other varieties of applied ethics, business ethics will be mildly hybrid in its focus. The facts confirm this expectation, but in an unexpected way.

Ethicists active in any branch of applied ethics commonly aim at a double audience: their peers in other fields of ethics, and people practically involved in the specific field of their interest, be it medical ethics, environmental ethics, or media ethics. To this latter group, belong medical practitioners, environmental policymakers, or media experts, that the ethicists intend to support in their professional decisions, but also the general public, who make use of medical expertise or undergo the effects of environmental decisions and media influence – a multifarious focus, therefore. As a derivative of general ethics, which is considered to be the mother discipline in the field, the applied version has to prove, on the one hand, that it still belongs to the family. Therefore, it has to satisfy the authorities in the noble art of ethical thinking by living up to their standards of analysis and argumentation. On the other hand, as a help in the normative dilemmas that experts and ordinary people alike are facing in the real world, applied ethics has to show affinity with the issues at stake, at a minimum by speaking in terms that practitioners in business or other fields can understand.

In many places, the typical rule is that all varieties of applied ethics seek the proof of their right to exist, first and foremost, in the approval given by the mother science, as a seal of professionalism. Public acceptance by outside experts and users is most welcome, but of a secondary nature. However, this rule does not hold for business ethics in Europe. It is an exception, and shows signs of an atypical evolution in that, right from the beginning, it addressed itself explicitly and primarily to the business world in an attempt "to contribute to the moral quality of decision-making processes in business," as EBEN statements repeatedly proffered. At the outset, an "EBEN formula" was developed, saying that the aim of the network was to bring together representatives from business with people working at universities, in equal proportions. There were two reasons for this, one pragmatic and one principle-based. The pragmatic reason stated that it makes no sense to invest a great deal of energy in developing ethical insights for use in business if people actually working in the field do not hear you, or, in case they do hear you, do not understand what you are talking about. This reason sounds straightforward enough and is not really surprising. The principled reason, for its part, was based on the conviction that business ethicists are incapable of even knowing their subject unless they have developed a language in common with business representatives in a continuous process of exchange and debate. The latter reason is little less than revolutionary. For here, the basis of scientific competence is redefined. The authority to decide about the status and validity of business ethics is granted to its intended users as much as to its academic judges. An additional reason for this exceptional scientific position could be that, given the dispersed status of business administration as a science, to a large extent business ethics misses the intellectual counterpart that medical ethics finds in the medical sciences, or environmental ethics in the expertise of physicists, chemists and meteorologists.

In the background of this risky revolution, we find a cluster of motives, in which uncertainty, pretension, zeal, perspicacity, courage, a subcutaneous propensity to self-sacrifice, and a mild dose of misunderstandings all play their part.

The 1970s left many ethicists in Europe with the inextinguishable zeal to articulate, in a professional way, social criticisms diffusely existing in society at large. It also left them with the pretension that they were able to do so. Where business was at stake, they felt some uncertainty with regard to what to tackle first – the system or the symptoms – and how to proceed when bringing ethics to the Stock Exchange. Some were perspicacious enough to understand that a new agenda and a totally new language had to be developed, one not commonly to be found within academic circles. However, they made themselves victims of the naive assumption that the business world had at its disposal the vocabulary that the ethicists were looking for. To a large extent, the daring alliance sought with business was a leap in the dark. Thus, all too soon the risky revolution became a sobering experience. This will become clearer when we look at the reception of business ethics, or occasionally the non-reception, both by business and the academic ethical experts.

Reception

The welcome business ethics received from the business world was not especially warm. When business representatives started to notice scattered ethicists expressing themselves on subjects like the social responsibility of the corporation, their first question, although not voiced overtly, often was: "How dangerous are they, how much of a nuisance can they be?" They found out quickly that there was no serious danger, since most ethicists lacked the business expertise needed to make a real difference in business relations. In hindsight, this was a reasonable reaction. At its start, the new discipline mainly answered questions that were not asked by business. What ethicists positively did bring to the field were three things:

1   A sensitivity for the growing moral impact and importance of market relations
2   A set of long-standing scholarly tools to tackle moral dilemmas, not specifically designed, however, for use in business situations
3   Predominantly in German-speaking countries, a corpus of theoretical thinking about the limits of economic rationality

This was not bad for a start, but there was a long way to go yet.

The initial reception of business ethics in the circle of academic peers was hardly more embracing. Here, the discipline was facing two obstacles. The first one it shared with other branches of applied ethics: the already mentioned suspicion that applied ethical activities would not stand academic scrutiny for lack of scientific vigilance and theoretical depth, and would be largely superfluous in what they did have to offer. For to take a stance in a moral dilemma – for instance, as a surgeon in a hospital who must decide when to operate in a case of vital urgency, or as a personnel manager in a process of restructuring and lay-off – common sense and a bit of experience often are largely sufficient. You do not need to be a trained ethicist to find your way about in practical moral problems, and, in case you are one nonetheless, your contribution will add little to the common stock of ethical knowledge – so the objection went. In fact, what business ethicists faced, as did their colleagues in other fields of applied ethics, was a certain academic disdain for supposed professionals going out of the realm of ordinary practice and engaging themselves in the complexities of the bottom line.

The second obstacle was specific for the newly emerging field. Peers in academia proved to be skeptical also because they were convinced that, at the end of the day, ethics and business could not match. Ethicists active in business circles would inevitably end up providing services to "the system," the system of free market capitalism, that is, by offering moral justifications for tricky decisions that business people were going to take anyhow. Note that this objection was most vigorously raised in the mid-1980s, when the neo-Marxist wave that pervaded many a European university in the 1970s had not yet passed completely, and the triumph of market thinking was at its highest. There were serious prejudices implied in the objection, but those presenting it did have a point, or even two. For, at the start, the theoretical output of business ethics was rudimentary indeed; and because business ethicists were closer to economic power than any of their colleagues ever had been, the fear that they would stay close was at least understandable.

The first decade of business ethics in Europe was a cumulation of idiosyncrasies. For business ethicists, it was an uphill battle, a mixture of wonder, amusement and annoyance for business people, and a reason for distrust and cool distancing on the part of academic colleagues. Fortunately, time itself has caused the beginnings of a way out. Within a few years, the picture changed almost beyond recognition. Business people became receptive, peers interested, and business ethicists more modest. However, what changed most were the circumstances.

Changing circumstances

It is easier to sketch the state of affairs of business ethics in Europe in the late 1990s than to reconstruct the causes that led to its new posture. I first present the outlines, and then look for some explanatory reasons.

Most striking is the shift of attitudes in the business world. Fairly evident also is the modified judgment of representatives of academia. Real, but not really shocking, are developments among business ethicists themselves.

An example of a major development on the corporate level can be found in the Anglo-Dutch oil giant, Shell International. Executives within the company sometimes describe the evolution in a colloquial way by saying: "A long time we showed, towards the public, an attitude of 'See me,' not free of a certain arrogance: 'If you want to know who we are, just look at what we are doing – and be impressed.' Later we changed it into 'Trust me: We have considered things thoroughly, and there are good reasons why we are acting as we do.' Recently the perspective has changed again. Now it is the public saying: 'Show me.' Public trust has to be deserved by concrete actions of the corporation, not be based upon mere assertions." Also, in a more elaborate form, Shell is presenting itself with the help of a scheme of four phases that characterizes its corporate behavioral patterns since the middle of the century.

1 The first phase was "growth" and "return on investment." It lasted twenty-five years.
2 The second phase started in the early 1970s, when the "environment" became an independent factor in corporate policy. It lasts till today.
3 The third phase, from the nineties onward, and strongly accelerated by the Brent Spar affair and the troubles with the Ogoni people in Nigeria and the execution of one of their leaders, was marked by the insight that "We, as a company, must win a 'license to operate' from the general public." Thus, they acknowledged that a multinational corporation, powerful as it may be, has to accommodate itself to the expectations and requirements of society at large.

4   Recently, people on the executive level of Shell have understood that awareness of a "license to operate" is still too defensive a position. Their plea now is for a fourth phase, which the company explicitly accepts as a genuine corporate task, "to help people build a better world." The voice of these executives is being heard, and suggestions are gradually being incorporated in corporate policy.

The question can be raised whether this explicit corporate consciousness stands for a general trend in European business, or whether it remains an exception. We will have to come back to this point shortly. For the moment, it suffices to say that, in many European companies, increasing attention is paid to the social and ethical impact of corporate conduct and to issues of corporate governance. There is also an increase in the number of corporate codes, compliance strategies, and broadly designed in-control systems. Together, these phenomena indicate that, in a few years' time, European business leaders will have crossed a bridge that, a decade earlier, they failed even to notice.

The attitude of academic peers also has changed in the mid-1990s. Reluctantly in some cases, but irreversibly nevertheless, the acknowledgment arose that business ethics is here to stay, that it fulfills a demand of the market, and has proven its practical usefulness. The expectations concerning the *theoretical* contributions of business ethicists are still not very high, but this reservation is balanced by the recognition that ethicists active within the business world elaborate ways of tackling moral dilemmas and forms of practical moral reflection that hardly existed before. Also, by cultivating what, for a long time, was considered to be a moral wasteland, they uncover ethical issues that deserve serious scrutiny.

Less spectacular has been the route followed by the community of business ethicists. First and foremost, it is noteworthy that, by now, there *is* such a community on the European scene. Fifteen years of collective efforts have produced a critical mass of professionals devoted to the study of market morality and its implications. What is more, the critical mass is not amorphous any more, but articulate in age and competence. Early pioneers in the field have seen the rise of a second generation of colleagues, eager to play their role and to bring in their competencies. Less impressive, however, is the inside story when it comes to research programs. Much energy is invested in the development of tools for ethical support and intervention: dilemma training, methods of social and ethical auditing, guidelines for designing and reviewing corporate codes so that they offer more than just a list of dos and don'ts. Research programs properly speaking, though, remain rare. That is, one seldom finds well-grounded long-term projects that are jointly designed, cooperatively executed, and, in Lakatos' terms, theoretically and empirically progressive.

It is fair to say that, at the end of the 1990s, business ethics is infinitely more present, both in academia and in the real world, than when it made its first appearance in Europe in the mid-1980s. However, if this is true, can reasons be given for this almost spontaneous combustion?

Reasons

One reason is linked to semantics. Right from the beginning, the sheer *term* "business ethics," and its national equivalents "Wirtschaftsethik," "bedrijfsethiek," "éthique des affaires," "etica degli affari," sounded awkward and unappealing for European ears. It evoked the image of a self-appointed sovereign moral authority judging practices for which it never would be asked to take responsibility. The term built a blockade instead of a bridge. Almost inadvertently, however, in several European languages semantic equivalents arose that proved to be less offensive, and even had a certain attractiveness. They all circled around concepts like "responsible entrepreneurship," "Verantwortliches Unternehmen," "une gestion responsable des affaires." The punitive tone was gradually replaced by an appeal to responsible behavior, and judges became partners in concern.

Terms are productive only when social sentiments allow them to be so. This obviously was the case here. A social sentiment that has become ever stronger on the European scene is a sense of uncertainty with respect to the growing influence and power of business. The 1980s in Europe had shown the triumph of market ideology. After "the end of history," the victorious "Western" system proved very successful – economically speaking, that is, not socially, given the persistent unemployment rate in many European countries. "Never was the horizon so open," for market rules to take over. As a natural reaction, the general public felt the need to draw lines, to define clear social and environmental expectations, and to hold business accountable for the implications of its otherwise respected role.

Important to notice here is a striking difference between the European attitude towards business in the early 1970s and in the late 1990s. In the 1970s, a radical rejection of business in the name of grand new things to come was the message. Visionary as well as implacable, this project lacked roots in the established institutions and soon became a victim of vested interests. Since then, business in Europe has built for itself an unshakable position in the social fabric, while, at the same time, by its successes, it enabled more and more people to raise their voice without fear of being silenced by repressive intolerance. The 1990s present a new period of "coming of age in Europe." Groups involved in the shaping of society are strong enough to face each other as equals, recognizing that no one-sided victory will ever be won by whatever party. It is now on the basis of a real strength on both sides that "business" and "society" meet.

Not only relative positions of power were redefined in the last two decades of the century, but also basic social roles, or what may be called the pattern of responsibilities. The observation is frequently made that, since the 1980s, in many European countries "the government" is in a process of withdrawing itself from the public arena, leaving tasks that traditionally were considered to be "public," e.g., social insurances and pension systems, to private players such as corporations, branch organizations, or individual workers and citizens. Depending on one's political affinity, people see this process either as "the dismantlement of the welfare state" or as "the de-bureaucratization of the social system in view of empowerment of people and the promotion of efficiency and employability." Whatever the terms used, there are some serious flaws in the observation itself. For what is at stake is not a transfer of responsibility from one actor or agency to another, burdening the one and alleviating the other, but a reordering of responsibilities and, concomitantly, an overall increase and reordering of moral obligations. We witness a silent, but irreversible, process of social regrouping, in which previously separated tasks are now conceived as shared assignments, and in which the total sum of responsibilities not just remains equal, but grows according to the importance of the tasks. Corporate environmental policies can no longer be made dependent on governmental regulations. The defense of human rights, at home and abroad, cannot be seen anymore as the exclusive domain of public authorities. Employment measures exceed the power of governmental agencies. All these issues require concerted efforts that can neither be enforced by state representatives nor simply trusted to private good will alone. Creative alliances are needed, public/private partnerships, often of a temporary nature, that together are able to transform the social profile more than any law can accomplish. Different parties are involved in this process: administrative agencies, corporate bodies, non-governmental organizations, and single issue interest groups. They often feel uneasy in their new roles because they experience an evaporation of the solid division of labor they were accustomed to, but there is no way back – and the sheer necessity of cooperation can transform a social duty that initially feels like a threat into an opportunity of an unusual magnitude.

Sometimes this fundamental shift in the pattern of responsibilities is presented as a shift towards self-regulation. This observation is only partly correct. Often, the idea of self-regulation is that companies or branch organizations better anticipate upcoming regulations by making their own rules, thus preventing unwelcome public restrictions. However, though this may be true in single cases, it misses the point when it comes to the basic attitudes and commitments that are expected from present-day corporations. For what is required today, on the European business scene, is not just compliance with existing rules, or a clever anticipation of upcoming ones, or a voluntary conformation to something like the *Federal Sentencing Guidelines*. Public conviction requires business to acknowledge that it has an irreplaceable role to play in the protection of the natural environment and the fostering of common welfare. For companies in Europe today, to refrain from misdemeanors is not enough. An active commitment is expected as well, comparable to Shell's fourth phase – in concert with other players, public and private, no doubt, in a shifting pattern of responsibilities, certainly, but under the continuous condition of shared contributions. That, in the near future, European corporations can restrict themselves to compliance with some *European Sentencing Guidelines* is highly unlikely.

This brings us to a question that we have long postponed but that now can no longer be avoided: What are we talking about when we are talking about Europe?

Which Europe? What business ethics?

The first sentence in Norman Davies' (1996) monumental *Europe. A History* reads: "In the beginning, there was no Europe." And in the last sentence of the subsequent fifty-page introduction in which the author defines his subject, he says: "In the end, intellectual definitions raise more questions than they answer. It is the same with European history as with a camel. The practical approach is not to try and define it, but to describe it." What counts for European history counts for contemporary Europe as a cultural and political entity: we are, in fact, facing "a miracle of discord," in which distinct groups and cultures are fiercely unwilling to coagulate, and equally stubbornly refuse to fall apart. Europe is an experience, more than a definite content.

What does this mean for our theme: business ethics in the European tradition? It means that divergent ways of ethical thinking and commercial practice are kept together, not primarily by a common denominator like a shared history, or a common future, but by the recognition of an indelible belonging together, an experience that is stronger and more pervading to the extent that, almost paradoxically, less appeal is made to it. It makes sense to speak of "European business ethics," because people facing it, be they from inside or from outside Europe, recognize it whenever they see it.

Yet, this leaves us with an unsatisfactory outcome, because the phenomenon "Business Ethics in Europe" is made dependent on ephemeral experiences of recognition. Can the issue not be articulated in such a way that a more lasting impression results? There is indeed, such a way, and although it may at first glance look like a detour, let us try to sketch it briefly.

In the opening paragraph of this chapter, I indicated two questions that are fundamental in the context of our interest, but then I refrained from answering the questions of how to define "business ethics" and how to define "Europe." At the point where we are now in our inside story, it makes sense to take the two together, and state: to specify the stature of business ethics in Europe as a practice and as an academic discipline simultaneously, we need parameters that guide us towards an understanding of business ethics as a social institution in varying European contexts. By *"business ethics as a social institution,"* I mean a coherent set of concepts, practices, structures and interventions (co-)determining, in a reconstructable way, the moral stature and impact of business within a given social fabric. This set of factors may vary according to circumstances, but the basic ingredients will be present in most cases: ethical theories of a general and an intermediate nature concerning what morally speaking can be expected from business, auditing and training practices with regard to corporate responsibility, codes and other control systems developed to foster the moral quality of business processes, individual and collective initiatives and interventions of an individual and of an organizational nature, and a culture of transparency and openness stimulating mutual accountability among various business stakeholders. It is obvious that the reverse side, the absence of these ingredients or the explicit presence of moral unwillingness, will count heavily among the factors determining business ethics as a social institution – as a "practice," some would like to say – but then in a normatively negative sense. The leading question behind all these concepts, practices, structures and interventions remains: "What is the right thing to do for business in the given circumstances?" However, as a specific social institution in a given environment, business ethics, at the same time, is part and parcel of a larger institutional configuration, of which the actual legal system, the distribution of political power, and the degree of economic development are major components.

Now the idea is that, to grasp the place and role of business ethics in its European varieties – and probably in other contexts as well – we need parameters enabling us to analyze and make operational the set of theoretical and practical elements determining the actual shape of business ethics as a social institution in itself, *and* parameters to understand the wider institutional configuration within which it operates. Elsewhere, not yet distinguishing clearly between business ethics as a reconstructable entity in itself and the institutional surroundings of which it is an active part, I have suggested such an objective with the help of the following parameters: style of philosophical reflection, weight of ideological forces, state of economic development, distribution of social power, academic institutions and business education, and open or closed culture (van Luijk, 1997). In a rather impressionistic way, I have also tested the parameters, randomly pointing to morally relevant similarities and dissimilarities on the European business scene. Here I refer to another analytical framework, elaborated in view of "an exercise in applied institutional economics" by researchers of CPB, the Netherlands Bureau for Economic Policy Analysis, in a study entitled: *Challenging Neighbours. Rethinking German and Dutch Economic Institutions* (CPB, 1997). Their enterprise is not meant as a contribution to business ethics, but it is saturated with moral notions to such an extent that it may at least offer an indication of what a research project concerning business ethics as a social institution may look like.

The authors state: "Institutions are required to solve highly complex interdependent coordination problems under changing conditions" (CPB, 1997, p. 543). Since they are first and foremost interested in institutional economics, the authors connect the coordination problems they see to failures in the market system, i.e., to market failures. As issues that need coordination in this respect, they present these:

1 Unequally distributed *market power*
2 *Externalities*, defined as interdependencies between individual preferences or activities that are outside the price system and therefore not fully discounted in individual decisions (p. 48)
3 The *hold-up problem*, arising by changing bargaining power in the course of time, when the way back is blocked by high transaction costs and the final decision to proceed is not yet taken
4 *Uncertainty*, in connection with risk sharing, e.g., the risk of moral hazard and adverse selection, arising out of the lack of complete certainty about future events

Now market failures cannot be left to government interventions. Compensating measures will have to be developed within market relations as well. Four coordination mechanisms are listed by the authors: competition, control, common values and norms, and cooperative exchange. However, a clear-cut match between a coordination issue and a chosen mechanism is rare. A tradeoff in the form of a less than optimal solution will often be the inevitable outcome of coordination efforts. The authors present four dimensions on which tradeoffs are likely to occur. With regard to market power, the tradeoff is between diversity of products and services and economies of scale and scope. Externalities give rise to a tradeoff between experimentation and certainty, the internalization of externalities increasing public certainty but diminishing creative design. The hold-up problem, when approached with the help of the four coordination mechanisms, results in a tradeoff between external flexibility and commitment, flexibility with regard to the workforce, for example, being exchanged against commitment to employees once they are hired, whereas in the case of uncertainty and risk sharing the tradeoff is between incentives to face your own risks and solidarity with the unfortunate. Once they have developed this theoretical framework, the authors apply it to a series of German and Dutch institutions to find out what type of coordination mechanism best suits the kind of problems encountered in the field of, say, social protection, labor markets, corporate governance, and health care.

The framework contains some clear moral notions, such as solidarity, common values and norms, commitment, and cooperative exchanges. Its main orientation, no doubt, is towards problems of institutional economics. Yet, with regard to business ethics as a social institution, there are three striking similarities, and one dissimilarity. Business ethics, seen as a practical and reflective factor in the shaping of the social fabric, uses the same four coordination mechanism presented here: competition, control, common values and norms, and cooperative exchanges, be it in varying proportions. This is the first similarity. The second refers to the inevitable tradeoffs in the practice of business ethics. Almost always a price is paid to attain moral goals. However, moral tradeoffs will differ from the ones mentioned in the economic study, because there is a striking dissimilarity between the two coordinative approaches, given that ethics is directed to other coordination issues than is economics. Coordination problems in economics are linked to market failures. Coordination problems in business ethics relate to the interface between economic rules and moral requirements within the larger institutional context mentioned earlier. This, then, is the dissimilarity that can be noticed. However, there is a third similarity as well, of a different nature this time. The economic approach to social and institutional coordination is well-suited to varying national and cultural circumstances, as the authors of *Challenging Neighbours* (CPD, 1997) have proven with regard to Germany and The Netherlands. There is no reason why the same would not be true for an ethical approach along similar lines.

Conclusion

Is there a conclusion to be drawn from the meandering considerations developed up to here? We intended to tell the inside story of business ethics in Europe in the last two decades of the century. In that effort, we soon came across some open questions, and we deliberately left unanswered some others. The open questions were regarding the envisaged target groups of business ethics, the reception by academic peers and by the business world, the influence of social and economic factors on the shaping of business ethics, and the status of business ethics as an academic discipline. The questions initially left unanswered concerned the definition of "Europe" and of "business ethics." Where are we now?

The discussion of the first three out of the four open questions brought us to the tricky issues of '"Europe" as a shared experience and "business ethics" as a social institution. It brought us to some conclusions as well. Yes, there is something like European business ethics in the traditional sense – a set of courses and handbooks, and some consultancy activities, ordered along lines of schools of thought and preferences for topics studied – but there is more. Underneath the regular academic appearance, a much more complicated layer can be found where the need for social coordination, the experience of theoretico-practical partnerships, and the varieties of national cultures, economies and polities give rise to a much more opaque status of business ethics as a social institution, as a component, that is, in the concert of agencies and institutions that together contribute to a viable degree of social coordination. To elaborate business ethics at this specific level, we need conceptual instruments that, as yet, are only partly available. Coordination mechanisms are known, as we have seen. To determine which issues are in need of, and accessible to, moral coordination requires still a great deal of effort and cooperative exchange, as will the elaboration of the tradeoffs to be faced once business ethics has become acquainted with its new task, as demanding as it is promising. Additionally, to grasp the specificities of coordination issues and tradeoffs – in Europe as a whole and in its various constituencies – attention should be given to what distinguishes the bearers of the European experience, and what unites them. Then, in the years to come, business ethics will gradually acquire a *post-academic* status, never forgetting the school of its youth, returning there regularly and eagerly, but, at the same time, recognizing that wisdom is where the action is. The effort to develop business ethics as a social institution may become the specific European contribution to the field.

References

CPB Netherlands Bureau for Economic Policy Analysis 1997: *Challenging Neighbours. Rethinking German and Dutch Economic institutions.* Berlin, Heidelberg, New York: Springer.

Davies, N. 1996: *Europe. A History.* Oxford: Oxford University Press.

Luijk, H. van 1997: Business ethics in Western and Northern Europe: A search for effective alliances. *Journal of Business Ethics,* 16(14), 1579–87.

Ulrich, P. 1997: *Integrative Wirtschaftsethik. Grundlagen einer lebensdienlichen Ökonomie.* Haupt Bern.

Further reading

In van Luijk (1997), extensive references are given to bibliographies, country reports, institutions and organizations in the field of European business ethics. The Series: *Issues in Business Ethics* (H. van Luijk and P. Werhane (eds), Dordrecht and Boston: Kluwer) published papers delivered at subsequent Annual Conferences of the European Business Ethics Network (EBEN). Since 1998, the papers of the Annual Conferences of the EBEN have been published in a special issue of the *Journal of Business Ethics.* See also these publications:

Enderle, G. 1996: A comparison of business ethics in North America and Continental Europe. *Business Ethics. A European Review,* 5(1) 33–46.

Harvey, B. 1994: *Business Ethics. A European Approach.* New York and London: Prentice Hall.

Harvey, B., van Luijk, H. and Steinmann, H. (eds) 1994: *European Casebook on Business Ethics.* New York and London: Prentice Hall.

Mahoney, J. 1990: *Teaching Business Ethics in the UK, Europe and the USA. A Comparative Study.* London: The Athlone Press.

Mahoney, J. and Vallance, E. (eds) 1992: *Business Ethics in a New Europe.* Dordrecht and Boston: Kluwer.

29

Ethics and the regulatory environment

JEFFREY M. KAPLAN AND REBECCA S. WALKER

Introduction

Law and regulation play an important role in promoting ethical behavior. This is particularly so where the legal and regulatory system governs business conduct, as much of that conduct is sufficiently new (relatively speaking) or complex that its propriety cannot be determined by resort to traditional ethical precepts. The importance of law and regulation to business ethics is greater still where the focus is on the conduct of organizations (typically corporations) as opposed to individuals. Consensus does not exist on how conventional notions of actions and intentions – key to ethical theory generally – should be applied to organizations.

The concatenation of these two factors – the need for law and regulation to articulate standards of ethicality in business matters, and the inherent difficulty of determining by what thoughts or deeds a corporation should be judged – places a heightened burden on government to articulate the steps that corporations should take to require proper behavior by their employees. How the government is meeting that burden, and how businesses should respond to the government's lead, is the focus of this chapter.

Background

In the early 1600s, an English jurist, First Baron Edward Thurlow (1992) was attributed to have stated that a corporation could not be held liable for criminal wrongdoing because it has "no soul to be damned, and no body to be kicked." Since the 1909 Supreme Court decision of *New York Central Railroad* v. *United States*, 212 US 481, in which the Court held that a corporation can be liable for its employees' offenses – regardless of the existence of a soul or a body – corporate criminal liability has become a major part of the legal and regulatory landscape.

Because companies can be found criminally liable for the wrongdoing of their employees, and given that it is from the government that criminal law and civil regulations emanate, it is logical to expect the government to provide companies with guidance on how better to abide by the law. However, the government has traditionally been unwilling to provide either incentives or guidance to companies in the development of ethics programs, a fact that can perhaps be explained by a fear that such a definition could be used against it in litigation or otherwise, and perhaps by an unwillingness to cede policing to the business community (Sigler and Murphy, 1988). This reluctance may also reflect the government's lack of understanding of the potentially powerful impact such self-policing can have.

In the past few years, however, the law has undergone a dramatic transformation – increasingly providing shape and definition to the types of ethics programs that companies should develop and maintain. The existence of this legal guidance provides new opportunities for companies to obtain real comfort that they are doing the right thing. It also raises the bar for corporate ethics programs, placing increased pressure on companies not only to develop and maintain ethics programs, but continuously to improve them.

Thus, the question of how a company can create and maintain an effective ethics program – one that provides meaningful guidance to employees on regulatory and legal issues and that "catches" wrongdoing when it does occur – can now be answered, at least in part, by looking to guidelines articulated by the government in the criminal and regulatory context, as well as to judicial decisions in the realm of the civil law. The fact that such guidance is available – while perhaps expectable given the role that government should play in promoting ethical business conduct – is in fact a striking (and salutary) departure from the government's historical posture.

Incentives and guidance from the criminal law

In the late 1980s, partially in response to public opinion regarding the perceived disparity in the sentencing of criminal defendants, the federal government enacted the Sentencing Guidelines. The Guidelines create ranges within which a judge must sentence a defendant after considering certain enumerated factors, including the type and severity of offense and the defendant's criminal history. The initial Guidelines, which became effective in 1987, applied, for the most part, to individuals. However, in 1991, the organizational or "Corporate" Sentencing Guidelines came into effect.

The Corporate Sentencing Guidelines mandate more uniform (and much more severe) penalties for corporations convicted of criminal misconduct. They also provide a dramatic break from prior government policy regarding corporate compliance programs. Previously, ethics programs were only beneficial to corporations to the extent that they actually *prevented* misconduct and thus allowed a corporation to avoid criminal liability altogether or to avoid being a victim of an employee's misdeeds. The Guidelines, however, create incentives for companies to adopt corporate ethics programs by providing for significantly reduced penalties for those organizational defendants that have such programs in place prior to the offense for which they are convicted. Thus, in sentencing a corporation, if it is determined that "the offense occurred despite an effective program to prevent and detect violations of law," the court will reduce the fine by (depending on the size of the fine to begin with) anywhere from the thousands to the tens of millions of dollars (USSG §8C2.5(f)).

Far more valuable to potential defendants, however, is the fact that both federal and state prosecutors have taken the Guidelines' lead in exhibiting an unprecedented willingness to refuse to prosecute a company that had a compliance program in place prior to the offense. At a conference held by the US Sentencing Conference in September 1995, for example, several high-ranking federal prosecutors stated their willingness to consider ethics efforts in their determination of whether to charge a company with a crime (Kaplan, 1995). In addition, state governments are increasingly looking to ethics programs in determining whether to prosecute corporate wrongdoing (Correia and Breckenridge, 1997; Woo, 1993).

The above indicates the potential value of *having* an ethics program, but does not necessarily shed any light on the type of program a company should adopt and maintain. A closer look at the Corporate Sentencing Guidelines provides more specific guidance in that regard.

The Sentencing Guidelines articulate a definition of "an effective program to prevent and detect violations of law," which lists seven steps that organizations should take in establishing and maintaining an ethics program (USSG §8A1.2, Commentary, Application Note 3(k)). The steps are phrased in fairly general terms, but they provide useful guidance in fashioning an ethics program that will both meet with government approval (in the unfortunate event that the Corporate Sentencing Guidelines become applicable to a company) and be effective and useful.

The first step of an effective program according to the Sentencing Guidelines is that ethics standards and procedures must be tailored to a company's particular business and needs (USSG §8A1.2, Commentary, Application Note 3(k)(1)). Thus, the Sentencing Guidelines specify that, in determining the appropriate type of program for a given organization, consideration should be given to the likelihood that a particular offense will occur because of the nature of the business – for example, a company that handles toxic substances must establish standards for the handling and disposing of those substances – and the prior history of the organization (a company should be alert to prevent misconduct that has happened in the past) (USSG §8A1.2, Commentary, Application Note 3(k)(i–iii)).

Thus, before designing or fashioning modifications to an ethics program, a company should inventory its legal risks and design the program accordingly (Kaplan et al., 1993, ch. 6). Those in charge of designing or updating the program should obtain the knowledge of key personnel regarding prior detections of wrongdoing, "near misses" and areas of potential for wrongdoing. Ethics officers and others charged with developing self-policing programs can also better understand the risks they are seeking to prevent by reviewing documents from litigations, investigations, audits, and customer or employee complaints, seeking out information from other companies and public sources in the industry, and reviewing applicable government standards. It is obviously important, at this stage in developing or updating an ethics program, to prioritize the various aspects of the program based upon both the seriousness and likelihood of risks.

The second step in the Guidelines' definition of an effective ethics program requires that "[s]pecific individuals within high-level personnel" have "overall responsibility to oversee compliance" (USSG §8A1.2, Commentary, Application Note 3(k)(2)). This requirement dovetails with conventional wisdom about what it takes to make a compliance program work. The involvement of high-level personnel sends a message to lower-level employees and the government that the program is taken seriously and, on a practical level, actually leads to the program's achieving its stated goals because it is being implemented by those who have the ability to achieve results.

The third step in the Guidelines requires that a company use "due care not to delegate substantial discretionary authority" to individuals who have a propensity for illegal conduct (USSG §8A1.2, Commentary, Application Note 3(k)(3)). Again, this step reflects conventional wisdom regarding the need to have and promote conscientious and law-abiding employees, but it also points to the potential need to do background checks on employees who are assuming especially sensitive positions. It is important to remember this aspect of the Guidelines' seven steps with respect to transfers and promotions as well as new hires. Note, however, that managers must also be careful not to violate laws that protect employees' privacy, govern invasive investigative techniques, or prohibit various forms of discrimination, which could be violated by the careless implementation of procedures that have an unfair or disproportionate impact on protected groups; see, for example, 18 USCA §§2510–21 (1997) (prohibiting interception of wire and electronic communications); 29 USCA §§2001(3), 2002(2)(1997) (prohibiting use of polygraph results in most employment decisions); Civil Rights Act of 1964, 42 USCA §§2000e–2000e-4 (1997); Age Discrimination in Employment Act of 1967, 29 USCA §§621–634 (1985).

The fourth step in the Guidelines requires an organization to take steps "to communicate effectively its standards and procedures to all employees and other agents" (USSG §8A1.2, Commentary, Application Note 3(k)(4)). The first and most important manner of effective communication of ethics policies is a code of conduct, which, while not sufficient by itself, does have the very significant advantage of communicating the same message to every employee of the company. Codes of conduct should be as comprehensible and comprehensive as possible, and should provide sufficient detail about proper conduct to avoid employees' claiming that they were operating in a "gray area." Other means of communicating the company's policies include formal written policy statements (which are typically more detailed than codes), posters, and in larger companies or those in highly-regulated industries, formal training of employees (Kaplan et al., 1993, ch. 10). To avoid high penalties in case the ethics program fails to prevent wrongdoing and liability results, it is important that companies keep careful records of their communication of compliance policies to employees. This can be done by way of having employees sign acknowledgment forms indicating that they received and read the code of conduct or other ethics-related communications, as well as by having employees sign-in for training sessions.

The Guidelines' fifth step requires that a company take "reasonable steps to achieve compliance with its standards" by monitoring and auditing for violations, and by having a reporting system in place that allows employees to report misconduct by others (USSG §8A1.2, Commentary, Application Note 3(k)(5)). This step speaks more to the maintenance of a program rather than the establishment of one.

An effective audit program requires that audit procedures target both the types of offenses likely to occur (e.g., environmental rules for companies with environmental exposure; procurement requirements for government contractors, etc.) and also the operation of ethics procedures themselves. Thus, a company should audit its adherence to its own ethics policies. Examples include ensuring that the code of conduct has been distributed to, and code certifications signed by, all employees, that any scheduled training has occurred and that all relevant employees have attended, that auditing for violations of all significant risk areas has taken place, that any violations or other problems identified in the audit process have been addressed, and that the disciplinary process has been functioning as intended and adequately publicized.

The second part of the fifth step – a reporting system – requires at minimum a designated person (or people) to whom employees can report any possible misconduct. Larger companies often appoint an ombudsperson or install a "hotline" (staffed by its own employees or an outside provider) to meet this requirement. For smaller companies, less formal mechanisms – such as simply designating a high-ranking and well-respected employee – may be sufficient (Kaplan et al., 1993, ch. 12).

Regardless of the type of reporting mechanism adopted, certain policies and procedures can instill confidence among employees that the company genuinely wants to know when crimes or other illegal acts have been committed. These include allowing anonymous reporting; issuing written corporate policies that encourage whistleblowing; forbidding retaliation and following up with each complainant; keeping employees generally informed of what happens to complaints made through the system and what happens to complainants who utilize the system; and monitoring the treatment of whistleblowers over the long term. At the same time, so that the reporting mechanism is not abused, a company may wish to provide disciplinary measures for making a false or bad faith report.

The Sentencing Guidelines' sixth step requires that the ethics program be enforced consistently through "appropriate disciplinary mechanisms" (USSG §8A1.2, Commentary, Application Note 3(k)(6)). A disciplinary system serves to deter violations, to rehabilitate problem employees and to demonstrate to all concerned the company's commitment to effective compliance. Examples of discipline include informal and formal reprimands, demotion, financial penalties, suspension and discharge (Kaplan et al., 1993, ch. 14). The Guidelines specifically call for discipline not only of wrongdoers, but also of "individuals responsible for the failure to detect an offense" (USSG §8A1.2, Commentary, Application Note 3(k)(6)).

The seventh and final Sentencing Guidelines' factor requires that, when violations do occur, the company must take "all reasonable steps to respond appropriately to the offense and to prevent further similar offenses," including reporting the violation to the government (USSG §8A1.2, Commentary, Application Note 3(k)(7)). This obviously incorporates the sixth factor – discipline – but also specifically includes modifying aspects of the ethics program if necessary. For a company to be able to respond appropriately to violations of its ethics policies, the ethics officer (or committee) must receive any and all information regarding violations or other problems suggesting the need to reform the program. This requires effective communication, which can only be assured if there exists a system for communicating wrongdoing. In addition, a company must – to meet the government's definition of an effective ethics program – make a sincere effort to learn from violations or other problems. Lastly, this factor requires that, if the company is to receive credit for a violation in the context of being sentenced for unlawful conduct, the company must report the violation to the government. The Guidelines do allow for reasonable time for a company to conduct an internal investigation, and allowance is also given for a reasonable conclusion that no offense occurred (USSG §8A1.2, Commentary, Application Note 3(k)(7)).

370

Other regulatory incentives and guidance

The criminal law's recent but extensive articulation of the factors necessary for an effective ethics program are often echoed in the regulatory context. Interestingly, regulatory guidance regarding ethics programs is even more recent than guidance from the criminal law, despite the fact that the sole purpose of many government agencies is the regulation of corporate conduct in given industries. However, the regulatory context often does provide more specific details as to the manner in which effective ethics programs can be established and maintained.

For example, the Environmental Protection Agency (EPA) announced a policy in 1995 that provides for eliminating the "gravity component" of a civil fine – and agreeing not to recommend the case for criminal prosecution – when certain conditions are met (including voluntary disclosure and remediation of certain violations, cooperating with the EPA, taking steps to prevent a recurrence, and demonstrating a lack of repeat violations) and when the company discovered the violation through "either (a) an environmental audit that is systematic, objective, and periodic . . . or (b) a documented, systematic procedure or practice which reflects the regulated entity's due diligence in preventing, detecting, and correcting violations" (60 Fed. Reg. 66706, 66708 (1995)).

The EPA's standard for due diligence largely reflects that of the Sentencing Guidelines, but it also provides further guidance to companies as to the appropriate method for setting up and maintaining an effective ethics program, including requiring "periodic evaluation of the overall performance of the compliance management system" (60 Fed. Reg. 66706, 66711). Thus, the EPA's standard specifically requires that companies regularly evaluate and assess the effectiveness of their ethics programs (60 Fed. Reg. 66706, 66710–11). In addition, the EPA's standard calls for "appropriate incentives" to foster compliant behavior by employees – meaning that a company should not only discipline wrongdoers, but also reward those employees who demonstrate compliant behavior, like whistleblowing (60 Fed. Reg. 66706, 66711).

The Nuclear Regulatory Commission (NRC) is another governmental agency that provides both incentives and guidance to companies in the area of ethics programs. In 1996, the NRC issued a policy statement on freedom of employees in the nuclear industry to raise safety concerns without fear of retaliation (61 FR 24336 (1996)). The policy, while focused on the specific area of encouraging whistleblowers to report violations, also provides guidance to companies on the NRC's view of how to establish and maintain an effective compliance program.

Like the EPA, the NRC's policy statement echoes the Sentencing Guidelines, but, because of its focus on whistleblowing, it provides more specific guidance in that area than do the Guidelines. For example, the NRC's policy stresses the importance of training supervisors in the value of whistleblowers to the company and of incentive programs to encourage the reporting of wrongdoing (61 FR 24336 (1996)).

The Department of Health and Human Services also set forth its views on effective ethics and compliance when, in 1997, its Office of the Inspector General (OIG) issued a model compliance program for clinical laboratories that provide testing services for Medicare and Medicaid beneficiaries (61 FR 24336 (1996)). While much of the model program is specific to the industry, it also contains general points worth considering. The OIG policy, unlike the Guidelines, specifically calls for the involvement of the

Board of Directors in the compliance process. It also requires record retention for compliance-related documents and that compliance be an element in evaluating supervisors and managers.

Thus, while the policy statements of the EPA, the NRC and the Department of Health and Human Services are all, to a large extent, reflective of the Sentencing Guidelines' definition of "an effective program to prevent and detect violations of law," they are also more detailed articulations of how a company can maintain an effective ethics program – often providing specific guidance that the broad policy statement of the Sentencing Guidelines does not provide.

Civil incentives

The third realm of legal guidance to companies in the area of effective compliance programs is the civil law, where recent decisions of both federal and state courts provide both incentives and direction regarding maintaining effective ethics programs. The incentives are found in cases like the 1995 decision of the federal appeals court for the District of Columbia, *Gary* v. *Long* (59 F.3d 1391 (D.C. Cir. 1995), *cert. denied* 116 S. Ct. 569 (1995)) in which the court ruled that a company that had an effective sexual harassment policy could not be held liable for certain acts of sexual harassment by its employees. Thus, it is possible for companies to avoid civil liability altogether because of the existence of an effective ethics program.

Negative incentives also exist. In a landmark decision issued in 1996 by Delaware's Court of Chancery – one of the most important business courts in the country – the court held that the absence of a compliance program can lead to liability not only for a corporation, but also for its directors (Delaware Chancery Court 1996, p. 959). In that pathbreaking case, the court held that directors who fail to ensure the existence of adequate compliance measures may face liability for breach of their fiduciary duty of care to the corporation.

In the *Caremark* decision, Delaware's Chancery Court focused extensively on the Sentencing Guidelines, noting that, because of the significantly increased penalties that they mandate, they "offer powerful incentives for corporations today to have in place compliance programs to detect violations of law, promptly to report violations to appropriate public officials when discovered, and to take prompt, voluntary remedial efforts." (Delaware Chancery Court 1996, p. 969). *Caremark* offers more than mere incentives to establish and maintain an effective ethics program, however; it also offers guidance on *how* that can be done in its stressing the importance of Boards of Directors becoming involved in the shaping and maintenance of an ethics program.

Conclusion

A company may not have a soul or a body, but it presumably does have assets to be diminished, and the existence of the Corporate Sentencing Guidelines – embodying stiffer and more uniform penalties for companies found liable of criminal wrongdoing – should motivate companies to create and maintain effective ethics programs. Although first appearing in the context of criminal sanctions, it is laudable that the government has finally taken the initiative in assisting companies – who are, after all, judged by the actions of their employees – to behave lawfully and ethically. A smart company (assuming for the sake of argument that a company can have an intellect) will utilize the government's guidance, both to reap the internal rewards of a good ethics program and to minimize the harm that could befall the corporation if its soul is damned by a court of law.

References

Correia, E. and Breckenridge, L. P. 1997: State enforcement & settlement policies regarding internal compliance programs. *Corporate Conduct Quarterly*, 5(4), 61.

Delaware Chancery Court 1996: *In re Caremark International Inc. Derivative Litigation*, 698 A.2d, 959.

Kaplan, J. M. 1995: Government: With a good compliance program, firms may avert prosecution. *Ethikos*, November–December, 1.

Kaplan, J. M., Murphy, J., and Swenson, W. 1993: *Compliance Programs and the Corporate Sentencing Guidelines: Preventing Criminal and Civil Liability*. Deerfield, Ill.: Clark Boardman Callaghan.

Sigler, J. and Murphy, J. 1988: *Interactive Corporate Compliance: An Alternative to Regulatory Compulsion*. Westport, CT: Quorum Books.

Thurlow, E. 1992: In *The Oxford Dictionary of Quotations*, 4th edn, 697.

Woo, J. 1993: Self policing can pay off for companies, *The Wall Street Journal*, September 8, B5.

30

A passport for the corporate code: from Borg Warner to the Caux Principles*

LISA H. NEWTON

Introduction

The idea and development of the Corporate Code of Ethics have been well studied since Kenneth Goodpaster (1983) brought them into the philosophical arena in his account of the development of the Beliefs of Borg Warner. They remain a serious concern, but now we are in the throes of globalization. Can the codes that we are used to, based on good citizenship and justice for all stakeholders in a country of law, cross the oceans into lands where these are very much in question, and continue in business?

There is serious conflict on this point. We shall argue that conventional approaches miss some important problems, but that the concept of *kyosei*, introduced in connection with the Caux Principles, presents some unique possibilities of progress in this area.

Meanwhile, new global agreements on trade offer new challenges to any attempt at all to establish global ethical standards; we will conclude with an examination of some of the problems posed by such agreements.

Toeing the line at the millennium

Corporations continue to develop codes of ethics, and continue to believe that they do some good in the endless effort to persuade employees to comply with the law and to consider the ethical implications of their actions.

As evidence of continuing academic interest in the topic, we may cite Patrick E. Murphy's (1997) *80 Exemplary Ethics Statements*, a compilation with commentary of ethics statements from leading companies across the world. As evidence that code development, revision, and enforcement continue on the business scene, we may cite several recent moves in code development and revision: In December, 1996, Carole Gould reported in *The New York Times* that Fidelity Investments, the nation's largest mutual fund company, had just completed a revision of its code of ethics (effective January 1, 1997), and had further decided to make the code available to all of its shareholders. General Motors Corporation has also revised its code of ethics recently, on the side of stringency. From May 1, 1996 on, its 697,000 employees may accept as gifts only hats, caps, pens, and other small items, valued at less than $25. No one is

---

* Portions of this paper have been adapted from Newton (1997a, 1997b).

374

exempt (Smith, 1996). The best course, the policy advises, is to refuse any gift of any kind from any GM supplier. Meanwhile, in 1997, it was announced in *Ethically Speaking* that the Environmental Industry Association has initiated an ethics program named *Doing Our Best – A Matter of Integrity*, which contains not only a model code for members of the waste services and equipment manufacturing industries, but a resource kit from which companies can develop their own code of conduct, including a significant process for involving employees in developing and implementing the code. Interest and activity continue, even if they are not always undertaken willingly: Reporting in the *Boston Globe* on February 26, 1996, Richard Knox (1996) announced a "new code of ethics" for the HMOs (Health Maintenance Organizations) of the State of Massachusetts. A reading of the article quickly disabuses the reader of the outlandish notion that the profit cowboys of the HMOs have actually decided to moderate their conduct for the public good. No: this code is a set of "voluntary guidelines" issued by Massachusetts Attorney General Scott Harshbarger (soon thereafter to be candidate for governor of the state), presenting "community benefits" expectations for the HMOs to live up to. If you will not do a code of ethics yourself, the article implies, those with power to make life difficult will do it for you. In the same month, Dirk Johnson (1996) reported in *The New York Times* that the Laborers International Union of North America, mob-owned since its inception, had just adopted a "code of ethics" that made association with organized crime grounds for expulsion from the Union – pursuant, among other provisions, to an agreement extracted by the Justice Department in exchange for dropping RICO charges. One way or another, it seems, an effort to articulate the obligations of corporations to their various constituencies, once limited to a handful of excellent companies, is now accepted as an essential component of assuring the civic acceptability of the contemporary organization.

Howerer, we are now in a great era of globalization. It is not just that we have finally discovered the existence of other nations; that, it could be argued, we did in 1941 and the decades that followed. Nor is it just that we now have the technology to trade stock and currency anywhere in the world 24 hours of any arbitrary day. It is that with the collapse of the Warsaw Alliance and Communism, no voice or power opposes the domination of all economies by the Western Powers and Capitalism. In theory, as well as in political and economic viability, the market has triumphed. There is no further need, then, to justify the operations of the free market; there is no countervailing power. The US based corporation is welcome anywhere in the world. The question then becomes: Does the corporate code have its passport in order? Can it travel abroad without becoming entangled in unfamiliar procedures or laughed out of boardrooms in countries where gifts illegal here are required to do business at all?

Globalization is a phenomenon too vast for description in the confines of this space; the impacts go far beyond the work of the "multinational corporations," corporations without a country, virtually nations unto themselves, in which the new generation of business persons will seek their living. For purposes of this chapter, we will concentrate on the first wave of effects, specifically on the efforts made by US companies, accustomed to operating by codes of ethics at home, to carry on ethical dealings in operations abroad, whether in their own subsidiaries or in allied enterprises. In this section, we select three phenomena – three wrenching dislocations from the assumptions about the ethical conduct of business that have worked in the USA – that directly impact the possibility of continuing, developing, validating, or implementing a code of ethics in the multinational situation.

The first dislocation is the obvious one: the ethical rules and procedures that companies have adopted for use in the USA, based in part on the prevailing social norms and customs of the USA, cannot always be applied without modification in other cultures. Thomas Donaldson (1996, p. 49, p. 52) cites some examples of ham-handed culture-blind application of US rules abroad: the case of the required training video on sexual harassment, for instance, that left the religiously ultra-conservative Saudi Arabian managers "baffled and offended;" the case of the manager of a specialty-products company in China who turned in a pilfering employee to the local authorities, just as company policy required, not expecting that they would execute him, which they did. "If a company declared all gift giving unethical, it wouldn't be able to do business in Japan," Donaldson (p. 60) points out. Sticking by your ethical guns is a sign of integrity in the USA; it may be no more than ethical imperialism, or at least evidence of extreme cultural insensitivity, abroad. New occasions teach new duties; what was clearly right may now be surely wrong.

The alternative – an uncritical cultural relativism – is no improvement. It is tempting enough: "When in Rome, do as the Romans do," is not only likely to facilitate business deals with Romans; it also enables a serene, untroubled acceptance of any practices entailed in those deals, saving the intellectual energy needed to think about ethics and the emotional energy needed to insist on basic human rights when they are not respected in the culture with which we deal. Sometimes, Roman rules will do very well: after all, not all business ethics issues are of life-or-death importance. Insider trading laws and bribery regulation differ from nation to nation, and are nowhere as strict as in the USA. Sometimes, the cost of adopting the less rigorous ethics of other lands can be very expensive: Donaldson (1996, p. 52) points out that, for instance, it may well be in our long-term interest to teach the world higher standards of honesty when it comes to the theft of software.

Sometimes, it is indeed life and death with which we deal. Policy on treatment of women and education of children tends also to vary from nation to nation, and goods can often be produced much more cheaply by women who have no choice of employment and children who have no choice at all. We all benefit from the inexpensive shoes, toys and clothes made in Southeast Asia; but, at what point ought our corporations to object to the conditions under which they are made, to the point of breaking off relations with suppliers who subject their workers to intolerable conditions, as Levi Strauss did with the Tan family in China in 1992? (Donaldson, 1996, p. 54). We should do so at the point where practices violate the fundamental value of human life, the most basic of human rights, and the requirement of good citizenship, Donaldson suggests. His solution to the dilemma of carrying ethical practices across borders into unfamiliar territory is easy to prescribe, less so to follow: maintain a balance between resolute defense of principles and openness to new cultures by defining, very clearly, an ethical threshold below which your company's practices (and those of its suppliers and partners) will not fall, then working creatively with the rest of the culture to develop a hybrid ethic, a product of the home and host country's values in tension (Donaldson, 1996, p. 52, 54). Just get up on that high wire and walk across. If nothing else, Donaldson's work makes clear the difficulties of ethics, and shows how much effort we shall be put to to solve its problems. Would that every author on the subject of "international management" take the subject seriously. Right now, we seem to be teaching our students nothing at all. A quick and random look at business texts on the subject is not encouraging: most international management texts mention ethics, or codes of ethics, not at all, and few deal with the subject in any depth.

A code of ethics is invaluable, Donaldson (1996, p. 55) suggests, pointing out that Levi Strauss had relied on such a code when deciding how to deal with the Tans, but a "vision" code will not do the whole job. "Codes of conduct must provide clear direction about ethical behavior when the temptation to behave unethically is the strongest. The pronouncement in a code of conduct that bribery is unacceptable is useless unless accompanied by guidelines for gift-giving, payments to get goods through customs, and 'requests' from intermediaries who are hired to ask for bribes."

Donaldson's thesis, ultimately, is that we must have codes of ethics to guide management activities abroad, and that we can specify a "moral minimum," a set of "core human values," which define minimum ethical standards for all companies. The right to good health and the right to economic advancement and an improved standard of living are two core human values. The "Golden Rule" is a third. Ultimately, all codes must be based on an "overlapping consensus" where Western and non-Western values converge. Donaldson lays out a chart of those values, with the familiar liberty, equality, participation and human rights listed on the Western side, and an intriguing collection of alternate values on the Non-Western. These bear listing, since we will return to them later:

- *kyosei*: living and working together for the common good (from Japan)
- *dharma*: the fulfillment of inherited duty (from India)
- *santutthi*: the limitation of desire (Buddhist)
- *zakat*: almsgiving to the Muslim poor (Islam)

Donaldson argues that these values really reduce to the same core value as the American values: the worth of human life and dignity. He is probably wrong about the last three, which directly contradict essential items of US pluralism in a free market economy. *Zakat*, like the notion of "mitzvah," is simply an intratribal norm – it's your job to take care of your group – worthwhile in the group, but insufficiently universal to count as a value in a pluralist society. As for *santutthi*, it was E. F. Schumacher (1989) who first pointed out that Buddhism contained a series of principles which, if taken seriously, would destroy capitalism, by denying the legitimacy of unlimited consumer preference in a free market. There is no way to reconcile the purchase of our standard array of consumer appliances, not to mention $160 pairs of sneakers, with an ethic that requires that desires be limited to objects needed for life. *Dharma* flies in the face of freedom of contract; it is a sentimental notion with no validity in an immigrant society that specifically and emphatically liberates each generation from the limitations of the last. *Kyosei* also appears to be directly opposed to our most cherished convictions – we have always favored the autonomy of the individual in contrast to the collective good of the community – but *kyosei* is not, as the others are, simply irrelevant in a pluralist, capitalist, contractarian society. There may be potential here not only to help us to adjust to the demands of capitalism abroad, but perhaps, to some extent, to heal our own society. We will return to this in the next section.

Donaldson's approach (1996, p. 53) to these contrasting columns avoids the conflicts, heading instead for a "consensus" he has found among them all:

> First, individuals must not treat others simply as tools, in other words, they must recognize a person's value as a human being. Next, individuals and communities must treat people in ways that respect people's basic rights. Finally, members of a community must work together to support and improve the institutions on which the community depends.

The values consensus is summed up as respect for human dignity, respect for basic rights, and good citizenship. (Donaldson, 1996, p. 54) These must be the "starting point for all companies as they formulate and evaluate standards of ethical conduct at home and abroad" (p. 54). The ethical skeleton must be fleshed out by rules governing actual practices: the company must maintain a corporate culture in which "employees, customers, and suppliers are treated not as means to an end but as people whose intrinsic value must be acknowledged," the product and the workplace must be safe, relationships must not "violate human beings' rights to health, education, safety, and an adequate standard of living." For instance, "if employing children prevents them from receiving a basic education, the practice is intolerable" (p. 54).

Is Donaldson's the best approach to the ethical conduct of business on the international scene? At the very least, his insistence on the preservation of human rights abroad makes the starting point of the ethics trail visible, even to those who can see ethics and values only through US-tinted lenses.

When we follow that trail to the end, unfortunately, we have not reached solutions to the major ethical dilemmas of international business. As Manuel Velasquez (1995) points out, the actions by multinational corporations and their officers that strike us as clearly wrong are not well described in a framework of human rights and corporate codes. In a typical case, that of the aluminum companies in Jamaica between World War II and the oil crisis of 1973, Velasquez points out that the truly unethical practices that enriched the companies while impoverishing the island – "monopolization of markets, transfer price manipulation and tax avoidance, corporate limitations placed on the transfer of technology, and failure to disclose financial information to host governments" – figure in no corporate codes and have nothing to do with human rights (Velasquez, 1995, p. 871). (Nor have they much to do with "integrity," cornerstone of Richard De George's (1993) alternative approach which was criticized by Velasquez (1995, p. 871).) By way of contrast, Velasquez continues (p. 872), the international Organization for Economic Co-operation and Development's version of a corporate code of ethics (OECD, 1986) devotes considerable attention to just those problems:

> the obligation of multinationals to give due consideration to host countries' developmental and social needs; the obligation to provide adequate disclosure of information; the obligation to avoid transfer price manipulation; the obligation to avoid monopolistic practices and participation in cartels; the obligation to pay one's fair share of taxes; the obligation

to provide fair working conditions, and the obligation to transfer technology on reasonable terms and conditions.

Coming in 1986, the Guidelines could be of little help to Jamaica; clearly, they were built on the world's unhappy experience of decades of multinational corporate operations.

Donaldson's prescriptions may be out of reach as well as shy of the subject. His "bare minima" are impossible for some nations now, and could very well be beyond the capability of others even more needy. That "basic education," for example, to which "all children" are supposed to have a "right," is a Western innovation in many of the less developed countries. And are "sweatshops," for another example, the detested factories or other arrangements for the systematic economic exploitation of people with no other choices, the epitome of evil, or are they, for some nations, the only chance for development? A case for more of them can be made, on the grounds that, in the absence of exploitive employment, there will, in fact, be no employment at all, which cannot be good for the nation (Myerson, 1997; *The New York Times*, 1997). Where people have only bad options, it cannot help those people to take away the best of those options. Other possibilities may be more damaging in the long run: in many less developed nations, if the low-cost export production facilities (i.e. sweatshops) are taken away, the only remaining source of the employment and foreign currency needed to fuel economic development must come from the exploitation of a pristine natural environment; see, for example, De Palma (1995), Specter (1997) and Bonner (1997). Should the people sacrifice their forests for jobs? Which, in the long future, is more important? We are left, not with any clear or codeable answers, but with something far less specifiable. Into the foreseeable future, every decision will be problematic; we need a key just to let us in to the heart of the dilemmas.

Kyosei: Working together for the common good

That key may be in another approach – rather than subsuming those foreign candidates under human rights and human dignity, let us try a reverse procedure, and see if we can account for human rights and dignity with some of the values Donaldson mentions from abroad.

Kyosei is the most likely candidate, embodied as it is in the Caux Principles. The Caux Principles, published in 1992, have a history worth tracing; see http://www.cauxroundtable.org. Back in 1986, in the small town of Caux-sur-Montreux on a Swiss mountainside, a group of European business executives led by Frederik Philips (former president of Philips Electronics) and Olivier Giscard D'Estaing (vice chairman of France's leading business school) met to discuss the future shape of business ethics in a world gone suddenly capitalist. They were joined by some Japanese executives, and then, some years later, by a group of frustrated US businessmen, mostly from the Minneapolis area, who were trying to find some way of adapting their successful ethics initiatives to the new multinational endeavors in which they found themselves.

In 1992, the group decided to put out a first draft of some principles that would guide multinational corporations. The efforts to fit the US principles, essentially a

commitment to honesty and human rights, with Japanese communitarian presuppositions, in a European context, did not always go smoothly, but were ultimately successful.
Kenneth Goodpaster of St Thomas University, advisor to the group, records how they
settled on the basic principles that would stand as interpretive guides to the document
(Skelly, 1995):

> There were some tender moments when a few members felt the work they had done
> wasn't being recognized. . . . A breakthrough came when Jean-Loup Dherse of France
> argued forcefully for the Japanese communitarian concept of *kyosei* being supplemented
> by the Western European notion of the dignity of the human person. The healthy dynamic
> tension between *kyosei* and human dignity would underpin the whole document. And
> then we brought in The Minnesota Principles as the body of the CRT Principles document.

So the body of the document was essentially Minneapolis – essentially Dayton-
Hudson, Cargill, H. B. Fuller and Medtronic, to be exact. But the guiding principles –
kyosei and human dignity – were settled on in active debate on the scene.

Human dignity, fundamental value of all Western ethics, is familiar from Immanuel
Kant forward and, in any case, is spelled out in all the "stakeholder principles." *Kyosei*
is new. What does it mean?

In answer to that question, its major proponent has undertaken the definition.
Ryuzaburo Kaku (1997), CEO of Canon in Japan at the time of the Round Table conference, tracks the concept of *kyosei* as "harmony," "working together for the common
good," through a series of levels of work:

1   *Economic survival*: First, the company must prosper.
2   *Cooperating with labor*: There must be recognition throughout the company, labor
    and executives alike, that they are all in the same boat and must be loyal to each
    other, and cooperate with each other.
3   *Cooperating outside the company*: Respect and loyalty must be extended to, and
    expected from, suppliers and customers. Then the same cooperative spirit must
    be extended to competitors – not to form cartels and fix prices, but to engage in
    cooperative ventures – and to community groups.
4   *Global activism*: It is part of the responsibility of the multi-national corporation to
    help redress the "imbalances" of the world:
    (a)   Imbalances in *trade* (by, for instance, locating production facilities in the coun-
          try suffering an unfavorable trade balance)
    (b)   Imbalances in *technology* (by, for instance, putting R&D facilities in the host
          country, and training local people in advanced technology)
    (c)   Imbalances in *wealth* (by funding schools and health centers, for instance, in
          less developed countries)
    (d)   Imbalances in the *environment* (by using, and teaching the people to use,
          non-polluting technology, for instance; by working continuously for environ-
          mentally sustainable industry)
5   *The Government as* kyosei *partner*: Cooperation with government in redressing
    injustice and preserving the environment.

The common element in these steps is that harmony is the goal, preserved throughout; it does not change as you move from one group of stakeholders to the next. Harmony is the antithesis of that "imbalance" that Kaku sees as the major problem arising in the economic relations among nations, and in seeking it, we address, be it noted, the problems enumerated by Velasquez. We also address most problems lumped under "human rights" or "human dignity": cooperation with the workers is incompatible with "sweatshops," *unless* (taking note of the questions raised above) workers and management genuinely agree that for the moment, production at subsistence wages is essential to build the company, and that management will share in the sufferings imposed on the workers. Real cooperation with the communities is incompatible with the callous layoffs of workers by faraway Boards of Directors anxious to please Wall Street.

"Working together for the common good" is one definition of *kyosei* given by Kaku and others of its exponents. Others are possible; the key to them all is the basic combination of the Japanese characters, "the working-together life." For the point is that the common good (in the sense of widely shared prosperity) may well come from working together, and probably will, but the working together is a value in itself, because it is enjoyable, and because it makes all the participants better and more generous people, by bringing them out of themselves. This is, in culturally novel form, the value of "community," mutual loyalty or fidelity, an undercurrent value in the fiercely individualistic Anglo-American tradition. Key proponents of this value in modern form include Bradley (1876) and Royce (1969). The core of this value is that the shared life is better *for its own sake*, not (merely) as a means to other ends. It is interesting to note, from the exposition above, that Kaku derives the necessity of each step from the inadequacy of the previous one – *not* inadequacy in achieving some business goal, or even some broader altruistic social objective, but inadequacy in enabling the members of the company themselves to take a truly broad, inclusive view of the others in their world. The sharing is for the sake of the sharers.

For this reason, Ken Goodpaster has noted the similarity between *kyosei* and what we call "the moral point of view" – the requirement that we take all participants in a situation seriously as ends in themselves, and genuinely endeavor to frame each problem from their perspectives as well as our own. This requirement underlies the values of "human rights" and "human dignity," to complete the derivation begun above. We adopt the moral point of view not just to recognize their legitimate rights and interests, as the Common Law would have us do, but also to become, ourselves, the kind of people who readily share with others because they want to, and to help the others become so also, just because that is a better sort of person to be. We include others in our moral framework not for their sake, reluctantly sacrificing part of our individual interest to make room for theirs, but for our own sake, gladly entering the role of sharer because it seems better to live that way.

How does the introduction of this concept improve the way we develop and implement trans-national codes of ethics for our MNCs? *Kyosei* has three capabilities inaccessible for human rights based codes, as long as such codes are interpreted strictly in accordance with the Western traditions of law and ethics.

First, while not for one moment attacking human rights, it can consistently empower managers and ask employees that, in certain situations, those rights not be asserted or exercised for the sake of the common good, and for the sake of the community itself that grounds those rights. Note how quickly Kaku sat down with his unions, foregoing his management prerogatives to extract productivity, and cheerfully requesting them to suspend their right of adversarial demands. By the time he was done talking with his stakeholders, Kaku had permission to invest very heavily in R & D, enterprises that require large expenditures now in return for an uncertain profit far down the line. The workers accepted the pay, lower than it might have been. In a US company, we would have to have similar conversations with the shareholders, asking them to forego a small amount of dividend income and expected stock price rise for such research; with the Board of Directors, asking them to authorize a research-friendly company policy even over Wall Street's objections; and with the CEO, asking him to forego a million or two of this year's bonus which, by his contract, he had earned.

The second capability is to embrace the local community as a full partner, requiring that the company care for the local community. When profits are sagging in a local facility, companies tend to downsize the workforce or close the plant to cut costs. To make sure that these moves cause no trouble for the managers, the company lawyers are asked to review legal liability prior to making the moves. When the lawyers have finished their work, the whole effort of downsizing and closing is turned over to the Human Resources Department, which has no authority to change any decisions, and to the Public Relations Department, also not in the decision loop. The decision passes from finance to law to powerless executors, with no inclusion of the employees, and no inclusion of representatives of the communities affected. When the people who have been hurt by the decision try to discuss it with the company, to see if alternatives can be found, and to present proposals for keeping the operation going at lower cost, there is no one in sight who had any part of the original decision or could have any part in any revision. The flunkies who are charged with explaining it to the community generally know nothing about why it was made, or know better than to present the real reasons. They certainly are not, for instance, about to explain that this CEO was hired to push the price of the stock up, and that layoffs generally do just that. So they talk regretfully about how sad the company is that business necessitated this decision, how sorry for the unemployed, and proceed with their work of extracting corporate investment from the community without delay and, preferably, without violence. *Kyosei* would require that the community be included from the beginning of the decision process to the end, and that the final decision be worked out in consensus. Of course, that would rule out certain sorts of reasons for layoffs and closings; but perhaps, that is how it should be.

The third capability is the protection of the natural environment. For *kyosei* encompasses the community collectively – not just as the sum of those living there now, but, as Edmund Burke (1973, p. 110) would put it, as "a partnership . . . between those who are living, those who are dead, and those who are to be born." Seen as a being, whose life and energy transcend those now alive, the community can rationally, and without violation of rights, restrict the freedom of all those now living to protect the interests of the unborn to the last generation, and that is precisely what environmental protection does.

Kyosei, then, does a good conceptual job of covering the normal moral commitments of corporate codes in the USA: respect for human rights, preservation of openness and honesty, concern for safety and welfare of worker, customer, and member of the community. But, it goes further than that – allowing us to prevent the most egregious abuses of capitalism against which there can be no law, and allowing us to work systematically to preserve the natural environment.

Crisis: danger and opportunity

If we flesh out the general moral imperative to respect humanity, whether in oneself or in others, with the notion of *kyosei* or community, we have the basis for a corporate code that can answer the objections that Manuel Velasquez raises against the human rights models of Thomas Donaldson and Richard De George, and can go on to serve the broader community, the natural environment, and the generations of the unborn. We are presented with our greatest opportunity to develop guidelines for multinational corporations that will help them to address the real problems of the global future.

Just at this moment, though, we are also confronted with our gravest danger to any values-based agreements on the global conduct of business. Consider the case of the tunafish, or, more accurately, the spinning dolphin. As most of us are aware, the dolphins – air-breathers, like us – tend to gather in the same waters as the increasingly valuable tunafish. When the fishers net the tuna, they tend to net the dolphins too; unless precautions are taken, the sounding tuna will drag the net under and drown the dolphins. Precautions to save the dolphin are not without cost: special nets have to be purchased, and the operation takes more time and risks losing tuna in the process, as the edges of the nets must be lowered after the initial closure to let the dolphins escape. Nevertheless, US consumers had indicated their willingness to pay that cost to save the dolphin, and at the end of the 1980s, the Pelly Amendment of the Fisherman's Protective Act required that all tuna packaged in the USA had to be "dolphin-safe" – caught in a manner that allowed the dolphins to be released. After the North American Free Trade Agreement (NAFTA) went into effect, forbidding North American countries to erect tariffs, or other trade barriers that acted as tariffs, against each other's goods, Mexico started exporting tuna to the USA. The Mexicans did not use dolphin-safe fishing methods, so the tuna was turned back at the border as illegally gotten. Mexico appealed to an arbitration panel enforcing the General Agreement on Tariffs and Trade (GATT), which ruled in 1992 that the US law in fact violated GATT rules. We could no longer refuse to take the Mexican tuna, less expensive because it costs less to catch tuna without dolphin precautions, and offer it for sale – presumably at prices that would undercut the US producers until they, too, abandoned all efforts to save dolphins.

The ruling caused an uproar, among environmentalists first, but also among those who had feared all along that international agreements meant the loss of national sovereignty. The instant implication was that every law the USA had passed to preserve social good from rampant capitalist exploitation – starting with the abolition of slavery! – was straw before the autonomous scythe of unfettered global capitalism. We could not exclude goods made by prison labor, child labor, slave labor, no matter what laws we had passed or agreements we had reached among our own multinational companies, so long as the producing country was a signatory to one of our trade agreements. The uproar continues: GATT promised to reconsider, proposed exceptions have been brought forward, and in the latest (as of this writing) move, President William Clinton and his industry backers were roundly defeated in their effort to get "fast-track" power for the President to negotiate even more trade agreements. The coalition that defeated "fast-track" was an almost comical amalgam of groups that have never spoken to each other before: labor unions, environmentalists, and right-wing defenders of national sovereignty. Yet only the existence of such odd groups, at this point, guarantees that any code of ethics, domestic or international, will be able to enforce its strictures on the market.

We have often asked, in this country: Do we have the political will to save our industries, our communities, to save our natural beauty for our grandchildren? The answer has not always been encouraging. Now, we have to ask that question as a world. That does not make it any easier, but it is an appropriate challenge, for from now on, we will have to do everything that we do as the whole world, not as ourselves in our own country alone.

References

Bonner, R. 1997: Westerners angle for mining stakes in Congo. *The New York Times*, Tuesday, June 17, D4.

Bradley, F. H. 1876: My station and its duties. *Ethical Studies*. Essay V, London. Reprinted in 1967: A. I. Melden (ed.) *Ethical Theories: A Book of Readings*, 2nd edn. Englewood Cliffs, NJ: Prentice Hall, 450–81.

Burke, E. 1973: *Reflections on the Revolution in France*. Garden City, NY: Anchor Books, 15–266. Bound with Paine, *The Rights of Man*.

De George, R. 1993: *Competing with Integrity in International Business*. New York: Oxford University Press.

De Palma, A. 1995: In Suriname's rain forests, a fight over trees vs. jobs. *The New York Times*, Monday, September 4, 1 & 5.

Donaldson, T. 1996: Values in tension: Ethics away from home. *Harvard Business Review*, September–October 48–62.

Ethics Center in Santa Clara 1997: Ethically Speaking. Newsletter of the Association for Practical and Professional Ethics, 6(1), 7.

Goodpaster, K. 1983: Harvard Business School Case 9-383-091.

Johnson, D. 1996: At prosecutors' prodding, laborers' union opens up elections. *New York Times*, February 2, 14.

Kaku, R. 1997: The Path of Kyosei. *Harvard Business Review*, p. 55.

Knox, R. A. 1996: New code of ethics to govern HMOs. *Boston Globe*, February 26, 13.

Murphy, P. E. 1997: 80 Exemplary Ethics Statements.

Myerson, A. R. 1997: In principle, a case for more "Sweatshops." *The New York Times*, Sunday June 22, E5.

Newton, L. H. 1997a: Who speaks for the trees? Considerations for any trans-national code. In O. Williams, C.S.C. (ed.), *Global Codes of Conduct: An Idea Whose Time Has Come?* Notre Dame, Indiana: Notre Dame University, September.

Newton, L. H. 1997b: A scaffold for Muir: A logic for environmental protection. In P. Werhane (ed.), *Environmental Challenges to Business*. Derived from the 1997 Ruffin Lectures in Business Ethics at the Olsson Center for Applied Ethics, Darden School, University of Virginia, Charlottesville, Virginia.

OECD 1986: *OECD Guidelines*. Paris: OECD (Organization for Economic Co-operation and Development).

Royce, J. 1969: The philosophy of loyalty. In J. J. McDermott (ed.), *Basic Writings*, vol. 2. Chicago: University of Chicago Press, 855–1013.

Schumacher, E. F. 1989: *Small is Beautiful: Economics As If People Mattered*, 2nd edn. New York: Harper and Row. First published in 1973.

Skelly, J. 1995: The rise of international ethics: The Caux Round Table Principles for business ethics. *Business Ethics*, March–April supplement, 2–5.

Smith, D. 1996: A new look at ethics. *Ward's Auto World*, 32(8), 21–6.

South Bend, IN: University of Notre Dame Press.

Specter, M. 1997: Pristine Russian Far East sees its fate in gold. *The New York Times*, Monday, June 9, A1 & A8.

The New York Times 1997: Letters: In Mexico, sweatshops are where the jobs are. Wednesday, June 25.

Velasquez, M. 1995: International business ethics. *Business Ethics Quarterly*, 5(4), October, 865–82.

31

Investigations and due process

JOAN ELISE DUBINSKY

Rules of conduct

Every group of human beings sets rules for how its members ought to behave. These behavioral rules set the norm for individual conduct. Behavioral rules generally describe the minimally expected conduct of members and those who aspire to become members. Each member, to be a member, learns those expectations and, in some fashion, sets out to follow those rules. Individuals are expected to learn what is required of them to participate in the group, and to bring their own conduct into line with these minimum expectations. The setting of conduct rules by groups occurs in families, communities, civic organizations, social clubs, schools, and, of course, business organizations.

Rule setting by businesses is generally more obvious and forthright than rule setting within families or social clubs. Within a business context, it makes perfect sense to establish conduct rules, write them down, and to distribute them. In a commercial organization, the rules of social compact may be known as laws, regulations, directives, policies, procedures, standard operating procedures, or protocols. Determining which rules are superior to the others describes their internal hierarchy. In other words, some rule will always "trump" the others. Understanding this hierarchy is best left to jurisprudence. (For our purposes, however, we will call all of these written business conduct expectations the *organic laws* of a business entity.) Within a family, however, one rarely sees written rules regarding meal times, expenditures, or visits to relatives.

Just as groups feel a need to set rules to control and guide behavior, so do some individuals feel a need to rebel against those rules. Not everyone, when acting alone, desires to follow the group's rules. Someone will always break the rules. There will always be rule followers, rule breakers, and those who delight in testing the limits.

Investigations defined

When we believe that someone – whether a current member of our group or an aspiring member – breaks the rules of our group's minimally expected standards of conduct, we want to know about it. *Knowing about it*, at its most fundamental level, is the definition of an investigation.

There is something very compelling about an investigation. Inquiring into what happened, and why, feeds a fundamental human need. People are consistently intrigued about fact finding and inquiries. This delight in "knowing about it" is seen in social, business and family gatherings. The quest to know what happened and why fills our courtrooms, television sets and movie screens, newspapers, gossip columns and telephone wires. Adults and teenagers are fascinated about this backward-looking inquiry into someone else's conduct. (How else can we explain the public's fascination with the criminal and civil trials of O. J. Simpson, or the criminal trial of Timothy McVeigh?)

Knowing what happened and why fills a substantial portion of our business and professional lives. In a business context, investigations consume the greater portion of the work time of numerous professionals. Auditors, lawyers, human resources managers, security personnel, law enforcement agents, compliance practitioners and ethics officers devote much of their professional efforts to investigating or "knowing about it." Typically, these professionals rely upon their experiences, skill and knowledge to find out what occurred. Using some type of structured inquiry, they respond to the allegation that someone's behavior has slipped beneath the norm. If a rule of conduct has been broken, businesses have professionals who make it their business to know about it.

By their very nature, investigations focus upon individuals within a social context. Outside of a group context, the concept of investigations just does not make sense. Just as "knowing about it" seems to be a fundamental part of the human experience, so does the sense that *how* others *"know about it"* must be accomplished with fairness in mind. By living and working in groups, we humans tend to subject ourselves to rules. We expect that these rules will apply to all members of our groups. From this recognition, we have the fundamental alliance of fairness, or justice, with the concept of communal expectations and standards. If a member of our group receives different treatment – i.e., non equality of treatment – then we seek out good reasons for this difference in treatment. Fair treatment of individuals, groups and organizations is a baseline premise for any effort to investigate allegations into the breaking of the rules of social compact or the organic laws of a corporate group.

The theory behind due process

Under US law, this concept of fairness as applied to investigations is frequently intermingled with the constitutional right to due process. In its most legalistic sense, due process describes the substantive and procedural efforts we undertake prior to the deprivation or removal of fundamental rights of liberty and property by the government. Due process, deriving from the 14th amendment to the US Constitution, acts as a limit or brake upon governmental action against individuals. (US Constitution, amendment XIV, section 1, states in pertinent part: "nor shall any State deprive any person of life, liberty or property, without due process of law . . .".) We find it abhorrent, as a matter of jurisprudence, to permit an elected government or its official representative to take away one's liberty or property without fair treatment. Procedurally, we interpret fair treatment to require some type of notice and some type of hearing. Under law, a person is entitled to advance notice and a hearing before the government deprives this individual of life, liberty or property.

Lawyers have spent considerable legal effort determining which rights involve liberty and property so that the admonitions of the 14th Amendment can be followed. Is government employment a property right or a mere benefit? (*Harvard Law Review*, 1984) Does it matter whether the employment is offered by a state or by the federal government? Is employment different from welfare benefits, or health insurance for military families? Under what circumstances – and how – can these types of relationships be altered or terminated? Answers to these questions range far beyond the scope of this chapter. Yet, we should at least wonder about the nature of life, liberty, property, employment, privileges, and benefits before we consider what is a fair process whereby such elemental rights can be abridged.

The primary concerns of procedural due process are the type of notice given and the type of hearing provided before the government can abridge liberty or property interests. Of equal interest but far beyond the scope of this chapter are the differences between procedural due process and substantive due process. Procedural due process ensures that governmental action is constrained before liberty or property are withdrawn, via the requirements of notice and hearing. Substantive due process, on the other hand, protects individuals from arbitrary and irrational government actions, "regardless of the fairness of the procedures used to implement them." *Daniels* v. *Williams*, 474 US 327, 331 (1986).

Post-deprivation notice or hearing fail to satisfy the requirements of the 14th Amendment. It is what happens *before* a right is abridged that matters.

The parameters of notice and hearing regularly appear upon the docket of the US Supreme Court. A number of frequently asked questions come before our highest judicial body. What kind of hearing should be provided? How trial-like must the proceedings be? Must the inquiry be merely reasonable, based upon the types of information and evidence which reasonable people rely upon in their everyday dealings? Should the evidence be more rigorously presented before action is taken? How much proof is needed before a decision can be reached? How much of an opportunity to be heard is sufficient? (For example, see: *Bishop* v. *Wood*, 426 US 341 (1976), stating that employment at will under state law does not confer a property right upon the employee; *Cleveland Bd. of Educ.* v. *Loudermill*, 470 US 532 (1985), holding that state law providing only "for cause" termination does confer a property right; *Board of Regents* v. *Roth*, 408 US 564 (1972), holding that an untenured assistant professor did not have a legitimate claim of entitlement to continued employment to entitle him to a procedural due process hearing; *Mathews* v. *Eldridge*, 424 US 319 (1976), setting a three-part inquiry when addressing whether a pre-termination hearing did in fact afford proper due process.)

The best guidance concerning the type of due process hearing to be provided stems from the Supreme Court's decision in *Mathews* v. *Eldridge*. Here, the Court established a three-part test that weighs the interests of the government against the interests of the individuals affected by the government's conduct: first, the court must consider the private interest of the individual affected by the governmental action; second, the court must gauge the risk of erroneous deprivation under the notice and hearing procedures currently afforded by the government; and finally, the court must consider the government's interest in the added expense of providing a more comprehensive hearing.

A due process model for business ethicists

This, then, offers a simple introduction to the theory of due process within the US legal system. When we turn to business ethics, however, the concept becomes much broader, and somewhat less well-defined. Due process is more than just a legal theory or a constitutional right. It helps us to protect our rules of social compact and capacity to "know about it" when our groups' organic laws may be broken.

Though the concept of due process, in its most pure sense, applies only to governmental action, we have seen the concept expanded to include other non-governmental situations where notice and hearing are expected. Investigations conducted in a business setting generally involve some type of notice and some type of hearing. In this context, non-governmental entities, such as privately held and publicly traded corporations, begin to wonder about the due process requirements for their own internal activities. As a result, investigations, notice and hearing are inherently linked.

There is a role for due process outside of the context of the 14th Amendment and the government. Private organizations can and should consider the basic elements of due process. We cannot find facts and determine what has occurred without first providing notice that an investigation has begun, and an opportunity for those involved in the situation to be heard. Fairness requires that we treat with respect both the individual bringing a complaint of rule breaking and the individual who has been accused of rule breaking. The manner by which the investigation is conducted sheds light on the fairness of the process we provide. We tangibly demonstrate respect through the notice we give and the hearing process we follow. So, in this broader context, due process concepts *do* apply to *all* business groups – whether public, private, government, or non-profit in status and structure.

Investigation (the "knowing about it") focuses on how we come to closure about what has occurred. Due process, for our purposes, focuses on how we treat the individuals whose actions either have initiated our investigation or whose actions are the subject of our investigations. In other words, *investigation* addresses fact finding while *due process* addresses fair treatment of the individuals involved in the fact finding. If we were to draw a visual model, we would see the yin/yang diagram of Taoism. On one side, we write "Investigations," with "Notice," "Fact finding" and "Hearing" intertwined. On the other side of the diagram, we write the words "Due process," with "Fair treatment" and "Respect" intertwined.

As business ethicists, we are properly concerned with both parts of this diagram. We consciously allow ourselves to move beyond the legal requirements and constitutional constraints of notice and hearing, procedural and substantive due process. We know from experience that ethics officers and compliance practitioners spend much of their business lives conducting investigations. Investigations follow naturally from the letters, complaints, calls and anonymous notes that find their way to the desk of an ethics officer. Ethics officers may be chartered to receive, investigate, and resolve a myriad of corporate complaints. Ethics officers publicize their availability so that employees feel comfortable coming forward with reports and concerns about wrongdoing. These concerns range from allegations of fraud and abuse, code violations, unfair employment practices, and the inequitable distribution of wages and benefits to more mundane requests for an interpretation of a corporate gift-giving policy.

How we go about conducting these inquiries reveals much about our corporations' commitments to business ethics.

Who should conduct an investigation?

A corporate commitment to respect individuals and provide fair treatment is insufficient. We must also ask about the nature and characteristics of the people chosen to provide notice and hearing. There are some important distinctions among the categories of professionals who are asked to conduct investigations. As we look at the "who" question, we will also encounter questions about privilege and disclosure.

Just as with many other human pursuits, investigations can be outcome-determinative. How the inquiry proceeds and the findings reached can, unfortunately, be influenced by the investigators, themselves. When lawyers are asked to conduct an internal investigation, legal risk-prevention and the avoidance of liability may be paramount considerations. When internal auditors are asked to conduct an internal investigation, the effectiveness of internal control systems may be paramount. When human resources managers conduct an investigation, issues of organizational behavior are paramount. The individualized concerns upon which various professionals focus will surface during the course of an investigation. This is not to say that professionals are "professionally blind" to concerns outside of their training. Rather, these inherent biases may influence the ultimate conclusions about what, in fact, did happen. Certainly, these biases influence the kinds of questions that will be asked during an investigation.

Investigations into allegations of wrongdoing do not occur in a vacuum – divorced from their environmental context. For instance, many ethics officers observe an increase in complaints about employment discrimination following any single training program or presentation about sexual harassment. Generally, the ethics office receives additional inquiries after any internal communication reminding employees about their ethical obligations, or advising them of the availability of a "hotline" or "helpline." Press attention to allegations of corporate wrongdoing may stimulate employees of other organizations to come forward with concerns about their own employer's activities.

Where corporations have experienced serious instances of criminal wrongdoing, internal investigations conducted by either inside or outside counsel are the preferred manner for response. When coupled with government pressure for voluntary disclosure of suspected wrongdoing, corporations may prefer the protections which counsel provide in the conduct of these investigations. Conducting a sensitive internal investigation under protection of the attorney–client privilege is a powerful incentive to involve counsel at the earliest indication of significant wrongdoing. (The attorney–client privilege protects the confidentiality of communications between client – whether an individual or a corporation – and his or her attorney.) Where the privilege obtains, the advice provided by counsel is protected from public disclosure or discovery – unless the corporate client decides to waive that privilege. In *Upjohn* v. *United States*, 449 US 383 (1981), the Supreme Court upheld a corporation's claim of attorney–client privilege over communications between the corporation's counsel and its lower-level managers as part of an internal investigation into payments by its foreign subsidiary to foreign government officials to secure government business. The Court emphasized the dual purpose of the privilege: "to protect not only the giving of professional advice to those who can act on it but also the giving of information to the lawyer to enable him to give sound advice" (p. 390). This privilege can be used to protect the investigation itself, the legal advice provided, and the ultimate determinations from public discovery in subsequent litigation. By involving counsel as the investigators, a corporation gains the option to hoist a shield against certain types of adverse publicity.

The government, in the exercise of its prosecutorial discretion, can extend a tempting lure to corporations. In exchange for the voluntary disclosure of wrongdoing, coupled with the results of or access to internal investigations, a corporation may be able to avoid a criminal indictment or, if that fails, receive less onerous treatment in light of its cooperative stance with the Department of Justice. The Department of Defense has a formal process for voluntary disclosure for certain government contractors. The Department will enter into formal agreements, called "XYZ Agreements," with defense contractors who disclose wrongdoing. Such an agreement can lessen the potential for a suspension order or debarment provided that restitution, corrective action, and other types of self-policing initiatives are instituted. Where a company exercises its option to cooperate, it may voluntarily disclose information that could have been protected via the attorney–client privilege. In exchange, it may gain something even more valuable. Waiving the privilege may be a small price to pay if the result is either

- no prosecution whatsoever; or
- leniency in sentencing.

In such situations, the active involvement and leadership of counsel is imperative to protect the corporation from significant harm. However, in such instances, due attention to fair treatment, respect and individual rights may suffer. Corporate counsel serves a single client who is the corporate entity. The individual officers, executives, managers and employees who may be subjects, targets or witnesses to an inquiry may find their rights less well protected than those of the corporation. For a legalistic view of privilege, confidentiality and internal investigations, see Mulroy and Thesing (1989).

Many attorneys, when asked to conduct internal investigations, take great care in warning those whom they interview that the attorney's role is to protect the company, not the accuser or the accused. These "Miranda" style warnings, though well placed from the perspective of protecting the corporate client, can result in reluctance or non-cooperation on the part of those from whom the attorney seeks information. These warnings (sometimes even reduced to formal memoranda) inhibit the due process side of the investigatory model. Fairness and respect for the interviewee are not well served when the investigator takes great care to remind all present that it is the corporation's rights that are deserving of protection, not the individuals involved in the matter. As a result, the rights of the company and the rights of the individuals frequently conflict.

We know that counsel do not conduct all internal investigations. Modern business cannot afford this amount of lawyering (Dubinsky, 1997). Detailing in-house counsel to conduct all internal fact finding requires dedicated legal staff who may do nothing other than investigations. Asking outside counsel to conduct all fact-finding activities is prohibitively costly. An alternative may be to ask other professionals, such as ethics officers, human resources managers, employee relations officers, internal auditors, and security personnel, to conduct internal investigations. Determining who should be the proper internal authority to do the work can be challenging. Professional expertise, rivalry and credentials may enter into that decision.

Where we pay attention to the due process considerations of internal investigations, we focus less on the professional training of the investigator and more on individual capabilities. There exist specific characteristics of good internal investigators that deserve recognition. Regardless of how the work load is allocated, an effective and thorough internal investigation is predicated upon the work of a knowledgeable and thorough professional. A good outcome can rest upon the selection of the investigator.

When selecting an investigator, four characteristics come to mind:

1   *Recognized status and stature*
    The investigator must have sufficient corporate "clout" so that his or her calls are returned. The accused and the accuser alike must take the investigation and the investigator seriously.
2   *Objectivity and impartiality*
    The investigator may not have, nor even appear to have, bias or predisposition towards any of the individuals involved in the situation.
3   *Ability to suspend or withhold judgment*
    The investigator must not reach conclusions prematurely, or issue snap judgments until all of the fact finding has been completed and the analysis concluded. Only then should the investigator reveal his or her impressions and determinations.
4   *Ability to communicate clearly, orally and in writing*
    Before, during and after the investigation, the investigator will need to communicate clearly and concisely. While remedies may be communicated orally in a final management briefing, often the results of the fact finding itself are reduced to writing in the form of a final file report.

Notice and hearing: conducting the investigation

Recognizing that most internal investigations are not conducted by counsel under privilege, there are specific steps and techniques that can improve the quality of an internal investigation. Such investigative techniques are rarely taught outside of forensic classes for auditors or law enforcement personnel. Experience has identified a set of ten critical steps for an effective investigation.

1   Take employee complaints seriously.
2   Determine the nature of the complaint or concern.
3   Distinguish between confidentiality and privacy.
4   Act with timeliness.
5   Meet with the manager or the accused.
6   Prepare a plan and complete the investigation.
7   Document the investigation.
8   Reach a conclusion and suggest a set of remedies.
9   Deliver the message.
10 Conduct appropriate follow-up.

These steps can be broken into two groups of five steps each – corresponding to the "notice and hearing" aspects of the due process model. The concept of notice – advising an individual that he or she has been accused of violating some organic corporate law – constitutes steps 1 though 5, above. During this phase of the internal investigation, the investigator clarifies the issues and ensures that the individuals most involved in the situation are informed that

- a concern has been raised;
- the matter is potentially significant;
- an inquiry will be made; and
- their cooperation is sought.

The hearing part of the due process model constitutes steps 6 through 10. This phase focuses upon gathering data (whether qualitative or quantitative) about what occurred and reaching some logical conclusions. Though we use the word "hearing" when discussing the fairness and respect aspects of due process, a courtroom style hearing is rarely conducted. Over the course of the investigation, the investigator gathers, sifts, weighs, and analyzes information. He or she reaches some conclusions about the weight of evidence gathered and the credibility of witnesses interviewed. Collectively, this process constitutes the hearing side of the equation – the "knowing about it." (*Kestenbaum* v. *Pennzoil Company*, 766 P. 2d 280 (NM 1988), cert. denied 109 S.Ct. 3163 (1989) is an insightful and somewhat frightening case about the nature of internal investigations and the standards of good investigative practices in a matter involving sexual harassment allegations.)

Consequences of an investigation: the perspective of the accused

No matter how good the investigative techniques, and no matter how fair and just the procedures followed, every internal corporate investigation has consequences. For the accused and the accuser, these consequences are significant and potentially adverse. However, from the perspective of the corporation itself, the ramifications of *not* investigating an allegation of wrongdoing are of even greater moment. We will now examine these risks.

The likely end result of many investigations is the imposition of disciplinary action or discharge. Adverse action, in the context of one's employment relationship, often follows an internal investigation into some kind of wrongdoing. Once all is said and done, and we "know about it," we expect that something concrete will be done to bring the matter to a close. More often than not, the individual accused of breaking the group's organic law receives some kind of corporate punishment.

For the individual or individuals accused of wrongdoing, investigations never result in positive benefits or employment gain. Those accused of wrongdoing quickly appreciate this unsavory truth. Even where the individual is exonerated of all allegations of misconduct, he or she still has suffered through what may be a lengthy and emotionally draining exercise. From the perspective of the accused, the best outcome will be the clearing of one's name and the maintenance of the proceedings in strict confidence. No rational business person lists as a career goal the opportunity to be the target of an internal corporate investigation.

The accused faces many significant business risks:

- Time spent in defending oneself against an accusation is time lost from other business pursuits.
- Money spent on legal fees cannot be recouped.
- One's reputation can be tarnished merely through the adverse associations others may draw.
- Fearing for their own job security, colleagues may ostracize the accused.
- Disciplinary action (even as mild as a written file memorandum) can impede career advancement and promotion.
- Forced resignations or involuntary terminations will haunt an employee for the remainder of his or her working days.

These risks exist *regardless* of the merits of the initial accusation, the quality of the investigation, the skills of the investigator, or the final determination about what happened. Whatever the results, the individual accused of wrongdoing will suffer harm. The innocent individual who has been wrongfully accused can suffer business risks just as easily as the individual who has broken the organic laws of his or her corporation. Exoneration comes only *after* notice and hearing. In this respect, the procedural due process aspects of an investigation may protect constitutionally guaranteed rights – but only at considerable cost to those who stand to lose employment or other property rights.

No amount of precise notice and careful hearing practices will eliminate these risks. At best, due process considerations *may* reduce some of the risks which the accused *will* face.

Consequences of an investigation: the perspective of the accuser

Others in the investigatory cast of characters also face significant consequences. The individual bringing the allegations of misconduct may not face discipline or discharge merely because he or she has brought a concern to the attention of management. Many organizations take special effort to reassure employees that they will not suffer retaliation or retribution because they have identified concerns about possible misconduct. Many corporate codes of conduct include explicit protections for those who, in good faith, bring forth concerns or complaints. Other corporations, sensing the need to ferret out all possible situations where misconduct may have occurred, impose upon employees a "talk or walk" policy; i.e., employees who suspect misconduct but fail to report it promptly may themselves face dismissal. Some major corporations have developed training programs specifically addressing the fear of retaliation. However, the individual making a complaint (regardless of the merit, completeness, or accuracy of the allegations) faces a separate set of risks or potential harms.

For this analysis, we presume that the accuser acts in good faith to bring forward suppositions about misconduct. (There are, no doubt, situations where the accuser acts in bad faith and with malice. One can only hope that such situations are rare.) Accusers may base their concerns on gossip or innuendo; more frequently, however, they have heard, seen or learned something out of the ordinary that raises doubts about proper business conduct. They may have reached tentative conclusions in their own minds about what has occurred. They want to "know about it." More importantly, they want to know whether these actions – if they occurred – represent acceptable conduct within the context of their own organization.

The good faith accuser may ultimately be proven wrong in his or her suppositions. The conduct he or she observed may not have occurred, or if it did, this conduct may not have violated the corporation's organic law. The ultimate outcome of the internal investigation, however, does not reduce the personal risks which the accuser faces. These risks are faced as the accuser decides to come forward with his or her concerns. They must be weighed long before the "end" of the story is reached. The accuser ought to consider these risks *before* filing a report, calling a "hotline" or "helpline," or blowing the whistle to an outside regulatory agency.

The accuser's perspective must take account of, recognize and evaluate several distinct risks:

- Time spent in bringing an accusation is time lost from other business pursuits.
- Emotional energy once spent cannot be regained or transferred to other more positive activities.
- Once brought, an accusation of misconduct against a colleague fatally damages the informal ties of business friendship and collegiality.
- The teller of tales, as we have learned from our days in elementary school, is disliked and possibly shunned.
- Fear for one's own job security may lead other colleagues to ostracize a business associate who is viewed as a tattler or whistleblower.
- Knowledge that one has been the precipitating cause of a colleague's disciplinary action or dismissal is an extremely heavy psychological burden.
- Memories of participation in a serious internal investigation can haunt an employee for the remainder of his or her working days.

The corporate obligations that "trump" these investigatory risks

Viewed dispassionately, the harms and adverse consequences of internal investigations may dissuade a rational person from bringing forward allegations or from participating in any type of inquiry. When facing this set of risks, why would any rational person want to become involved? Certainly, the risks which an accuser should weigh before speaking up are significant and replete with harm. The risks which the accused will face are substantial and long-lasting. In the idiom of late twentieth-century American business, both accused and accuser – once involved in an internal investigation – face "career limiting gestures." If dispassionate self-interest were the primary motivating force, no employee in his or her right mind would willingly participate. No amount of notice and hearing mitigates these risks, or reduces these harms.

Classical utilitarian analysis focuses on harms and benefits distributed among members of social groups, and as experienced by the social group itself. Here, however, we have a more narrow analysis. When considering the risks facing accused and accuser, we are weighing and measuring only harms and harms. For the individuals involved, there are few real benefits gained by voluntary participation in an internal investigation. The question becomes whose harms and risks are greater, not how the harms can be balanced by benefits.

The current legal environment obligates corporations to engage in self policing, self-regulating, and self-investigatory conduct. The risks and harms which accuser and accused, as individuals, will face are just not relevant. If the corporation fails to investigate a matter involving alleged wrongdoing, its very corporate existence can be threatened. The downside risks which a business will face should it fail to investigate a matter of consequence are tremendous. For a rational corporation, there is no choice but to conduct internal investigations into allegations of wrongdoing, abuse, waste, fraud and misconduct. When the corporation's own organic laws or the laws of the governments under whose jurisdiction the business operates are violated, the corporation *must* know about it. Internal investigations are not optional.

The Federal Sentencing Guidelines for Organizations strongly encourage corporations to implement mechanisms for the reporting and investigating of possible offenses and wrongdoing (Jordan and Murphy, 1996). The Guidelines establish seven elements – or mitigating factors – that are designed to reduce the likelihood of criminal misconduct by organizations and their employees. One of those factors speaks directly to the corporate duty to investigate:

> The organization must take reasonable steps to achieve compliance with its standards, e.g., by utilizing monitoring and auditing systems reasonably designed to detect criminal conduct by its employees and other agents and by having in place and publicizing a reporting system whereby employees and other agents can report criminal conduct by others within the organization without fear of retribution.

For organizations accused of wrongdoing, these same seven factors may serve as mitigating factors to reduce mandatory criminal sanctions. The very real specter of substantial criminal and civil penalties or incarceration is a powerful motivating factor for organizations to conduct internal investigations into wrongdoing – without regard to the personal risks which the participants will face.

Avoidance of corporate civil or criminal liability is a powerful motivating force arguing in favor of conducting internal investigations. However, other business considerations likewise compel an organization to conduct an investigation.

Organizations generally crave knowledge about their own activities:

- Managers need facts to make predictions about future business pursuits.
- Facts cannot be known without benefit of some type of investigation or inquiry.

Consider the simple example of a workplace injury. Almost all modern corporations maintain safety committees to investigate why an injury or accident occurred. Knowing an accident's cause generally will help prevent its repetition.

There are other reasons why corporations opt to conduct internal investigations, regardless of the risks and harms which individuals will face as a result of the formal inquiry. No business executive welcomes additional government oversight, resident government auditors, or court appointed monitors. Corporations, whether privately held or publicly traded, place great value on the fact that they are not part of the government. In short, private enterprise cherishes its privacy. Conducting a private and internal investigation into alleged misconduct tends to reinforce that sense of privacy. Executives have articulated the fear that if they fail to conduct internal investigations when circumstances warrant the inquiry, then the government will do so, filling any void. Investigations conducted by court appointed monitors, external auditors, or the Inspectors General of a governmental agency are intrusive and frightening. For a private business, there is no real choice between conducting an internal investigation or responding to an investigation sponsored by the federal government. Though we generally want "to know about it," we want to keep that knowledge to ourselves.

Finally, corporations understand and accept their overlapping and complex obligations to their stakeholders. These internal and external constituencies want their organizations to be well run, well led, and well governed. Knowing what happened and why, enforcing internal compliance rules, and remaining law abiding are of genuine interest. For a stockholder, this may be called protecting one's investment. For an employee, it may be called protecting one's future. For an executive, it may be called protecting one's reputation.

A request for fundamental fairness

For all the preceding reasons, corporations have no choice but to conduct internal investigations into allegations of criminal misconduct as well as allegations that their own organic laws have been broken. A study of how this is accomplished provides keen insight into the very nature, commitments and virtues of the organization itself. Notice and hearing, fact finding, investigations, due process, respect and fairness all play a part.

From a corporate perspective, not acting is by far more risky than acting. Though the accuser and the accused face substantial individual risks stemming from the very nature of an investigation, the risks facing the corporation are much greater if it chooses not to conduct an investigation. The balance point among these competing risks and harms is, fundamentally, due process and the concepts of notice and hearing. How the corporation conducts its investigation can minimize the risks facing the accused and the accuser. How the organization goes about "knowing about it" is critical.

Though the act of investigation is not optional for the organization, there are many options when the organization considers how it should conduct an investigation. By taking care to protect the reputations of the individuals involved, by acting in an even-handed manner, by conducting a careful inquiry, and by refraining from leaping into a judgment prematurely, organizations can still "know about it" in a fair fashion. The attributes of a good investigator are, in fact, the same attributes which a corporation should adopt when it undertakes to conduct any internal investigation.

Corporations, just as governments, ought to be fundamentally fair. Fairness is demonstrated when investigations are conducted systematically, objectively and without prejudgment. When corporate rules are broken, we do want to know about it. And, we have an obligation to know about it in a fashion that accords due process to the accuser and the accused. The concepts of notice and hearing enable private business to do just that.

References

Dubinsky, J. 1997: What lawyers should know about business ethics. *Law Governance Review*, Summer, 13–23.

Harvard Law Review 1984: Developments in the law – public employment. 97, 1611, 1780–1800.

Jordan, K. S. and Murphy, J. E. 1996: *Compliance Programs: What the Government Really Wants*, ACCA Docket (July/August).

Mulroy, T. R., Jr and Thesing, W. J. Jr 1989: Confidentiality concerns in internal corporate investigations. *Tort & Insurance Law Journal*, 25, 48 (Fall).

32

Ethics and corporate leadership

KEITH DARCY

The world in which we live

We live in a world changing at hyper-speed. The landscape that we were once familiar with has been turned upside down. The Berlin Wall is gone. The Germanys are united. The "Evil Empire" – the Soviet Union – does not exist anymore. Communism is dying. Apartheid is dead, and Nelson Mandela is not only free, but he is President of the free Republic of South Africa which has completed a public forum – the Truth Commission – to openly discuss its worst sins.

It is an age of globalization. Economic cooperation is replacing ideological differences. EU, NAFTA and APEC evidence regional cooperation. The introduction of the "euro" signals the first step toward a united economic state of Europe. The World Trade Organization represents the emergence of economic cooperation and free trade around the world. The implications to business are staggering: Chrysler Corporation is owned by Daimler Benz; Amoco was purchased by British Petroleum; Bankers Trust Company is soon-to-be part of Deutsche Bank; Random House is owned by Bertelsmann; and Citigroup is everywhere.

It is an age of technology. Fiberoptics and satellites are moving us to a single world-wide information network. We can now communicate anything, to anyone, anywhere, and by any form – voice, data, text, image – at the speed of light. Our desktop PCs today have more computing capacity than the mainframes that NASA used to put a man on the Moon.

It is an age of re-engineering, restructuring, rightsizing, reorganizing, and flattening our organizations. As employees reluctantly trade the comforts of the old social contract for some yet-to-be-defined understanding, the toll on human worth and dignity has been harsh. Dependence upon, and loyalty to, the company has been replaced by estrangement and cynicism. We are challenged to find new ways to recreate inter-dependencies and search for new ways to experience "community" in our organizations.

It is an age of information. Knowledge, it is said, doubles every five years, and we sometimes wonder why we make short-term decisions. Information is now instantaneously available and globally abundant. The secret of leadership, we discover, is that there are no secrets. Quite simply, in this age of information, there is no place to hide anymore, whether it is:

- an oil spill in Alaska;
- a nuclear meltdown in Chernobyl;

- an intern's relationship with the President in the White House;
- child labor practices in Vietnam;
- corruption in the emerging markets;
- the cancer-causing effects of tobacco;
- unacceptable sales practices in the securities and insurance industries;
- the absence of women and minorities on boards and in top management;
- the growing compensation gap between the executive suite and the plant floor.

Information is like a virus that requires truth, and truth demands freedom. When people become aware of alternatives, revolutions occur. This, indeed, is an age of revolutions.

Perhaps, as Alvin Toffler (1970) defined the title of his best selling book, we are experiencing "future shock," i.e. "disorientation due to premature accelerated change." Given the velocity of change in today's world, we have become confused and disoriented. As the once familiar maps and guideposts blur, we grope into the future, seeking some new understanding of world order and our place in it.

We stand at the end of an age, and at the beginning of a time not yet defined. Uniquely, we have the opportunity to participate in defining it. Thus is the call of leadership.

Leadership today

All of this change begs the question: "What kind of leadership is required to lead us in this new age?" Indeed, who are today's leaders? Is it Bill Clinton or Tony Blair? Is it Lou Gerstner, Bill Gates, or Al Dunlap? Or perhaps it is Libby Dole, Sandra Day O'Connor, or Martha Stewart. What makes these people – or anyone else – a leader? Is it fame, status, money, or power?

Leadership today has become a celebrity watch. *Newsweek, Time, Business Week, Fortune,* and *Forbes* all regularly feature personalities who are "hot." As we peer into their private lives, we observe their reading lists, their work habits, their food tastes, and their hobbies as if these small details carry messages of profound significance about leadership (Burns, 1978, p.1). One thing we know for sure: in this age of media and information, the closer we know our leaders, the more apparent it becomes how little we truly know about the subject matter of leadership.

Ethics today

Ethics comes from the Greek word ethos, which means "customs" or "traditions." Ethics represents the customary beliefs, social norms, and common values of society. In a world changing at hyper-speed today, however, our common beliefs are no longer common.

For example, witness the seismic events in Washington through the "Monicagate" impeachment hearings. Our reaction to them clearly suggests that we – as a nation, and as individuals – were divided and left straddling either side of the moral fault line, more concerned with our economic well-being and self-interest than the obvious failures of leadership.

Indeed, at the heart of this political circus in Washington are much deeper questions. They are not political questions. They are personal questions: questions about us; questions of values; questions of beliefs. They are the most fundamental questions in our life's journey:

- Who am I?
- What are the values and beliefs that define who I am?
- How do I act on these values and beliefs?

Following these are the even larger questions:

- Who are we as a community of people?
- What do we value, hold to be important?

Ultimately, however, it is not important what we say we believe in. It is what we do with our beliefs that count. Clearly, words without the actions are an empty chalice.

Values and beliefs are the subatomic particles that make up our ethical DNA. How we behave, according to the ancient Greeks, expresses our character. Ethics, therefore, represents the choices we make – and the way we express our choices is both through our actions as well as our inactions, i.e., when confronted by a situation and we do not act, we choose *not* to act – no one is uncommitted.

Eric Fromm, the twentieth-century German philosopher, once wrote (1976), "We are what we are devoted to, and what we are devoted to motivates our conduct." Indeed, what are we devoted to? Is it our economic status? Are we devoted to our jobs? Is it our title, our committees, prestige, fame, or perhaps power?

Fromm follows with an even deeper question: "If I am what I have, and what I have is lost, who then am I?" If someone takes away my job, money, title and concomitant power, who am I?

Indeed, it is these deeper questions that evoke our character, and our character is the foundation of leadership.

What is leadership?

The dictionary tells us that to lead is "to go before, or with, to show the way; to guide in direction, course, or action" (Barnhart, 1963). In business, who are these people? Where are these people? How do leaders distinguish themselves from managers and followers?

Managers plan, organize, schedule, budget, and facilitate the completion of tasks necessary to achieve corporate objectives. Managers, it has been said, are responsible for the physical resources of the firm.

Leaders, on the other hand, are said to create visions, inspire, are committed and evoke commitment, see opportunities that evade others, look at what is possible, translate vision into action, and have aspirations and empathy. Leaders are responsible for mobilizing the emotional and spiritual resources of the firm (Kouzes and Posner, 1995).

Posner and Kouzes, in their research about leadership, have regularly asked the question "What values do you most admire in leaders?" The answers over many years and many different groups includes such values as honesty, competence, vision, inspiration, intelligence, fairness, etc. Interestingly, and perhaps not surprisingly, "honesty" is always the most important value among individuals and groups. Some of the quotes from their research are noteworthy (Kouzes and Posner, 1995):

- "We appreciate people who express values, even on tough positions. At least they stand for something."
- "We simply don't trust someone who does not tell us their value or standards."
- "People must walk the talk, do what they say. Where agreements are not kept – where there are false promises – there are deceptions."

For sure, there are many different "schools" of leadership. Trait theory suggests that leadership is rooted in biology, and is naturally endowed. Leaders, it is believed, are born, not made. Situational leadership suggests that leadership is not biologically determined, but rather a function of matching the appropriate skills to situational conditions. Organizational leadership is a function of role in a hierarchical organization where the skills and responsibilities at each level are clearly defined. Visionary leadership believes the critical ingredient is vision and the ability to mobilize people toward a meaningful future (Bennis and Nanus, 1985).

Warren Bennis, alternatively, suggests there are several "myths" of leadership of which we must be wary:

- Leadership is a rare skill.
- Leaders are born not made.
- Leaders are charismatic.
- Leadership exists only at the top (Bennis and Nanus, 1985).

We must pay careful attention to this message. Bennis is telling us as clearly as we can listen that leadership is not limited, but pervasive. It exists everywhere in our organizations from the CEO right down to the custodian. Also, leadership derives from our experiences, not biology. The word "character" comes from the Greek charakter, which literally means "engraving tool." We are, indeed, the sum of our experiences – experiences which are indelibly engraved upon us – and our character is shaped by, and speaks from, these experiences. Victor Frankl (1959) even suggests that man's search for meaning may be found in the midst of our most painful experiences. It is the fuel that propels us to lead. Leadership, thus, is born in the midst of our deepest experiences. To be actualized, these experiences must be evoked and nurtured.

For sure, there has been an evolving understanding of leadership. One such definition suggests that leadership is making followers do what followers would otherwise not do (Burns, 1978, p. 18). This is sometimes referred to as Theory X leadership. It assumes people are lazy, do not want to work, and will not unless some strong action is taken. This understanding of leadership underlies some of Frederick Taylor's early work in management science.

Yet another understanding of leadership suggest it involves making followers act for certain goals that represent the values and motivation, wants and needs, goals and aspirations of both followers and leaders (Burns, 1978, p. 19). Leadership here introduces the importance of relationship between followers and leaders. It is, in fact, seen as an inseparable relationship, which is based on shared values and purpose – and the absence of that relationship is nothing more than raw power.

Power, of course, is well understood in organizational life. Power is a zero sum game. The way the game is played, simply, is: "If I have more, you have less." It is built upon self-interest and the desire to destroy the competition or any perceived threat (Burns, 1978, p. 18). It is a very dangerous game.

It is only in contrast to this zero sum game of power that we can begin to understand the real significance of "empowerment." Empowerment understands that each of us is born with unlimited human potential, which we barely, under the best of circumstances, utilize in our lifetime. In contrast to the dark game of power, empowerment suggests we can unleash the unlimited human potential that resides within the fullness of all of our people. In doing so, we open up our organizations to the extraordinary diversity of skills, backgrounds, and experiences people bring to work each day.

There is an emerging bias towards understanding leadership as a relationship based upon shared values and purpose. In addition, we are evolving towards a sense of leadership that can also be transformational, i.e. where leaders and followers raise one another to higher levels of motivation and human understanding (Burns, 1978, p. 4). By satisfying the higher needs, it engages the full person.

This is the essence of integrity. Integrity has its origins in the Latin integer, which means "whole" or "complete." What does it mean to be a whole or complete person? What does it mean to know who you are, what you value and believe, and how to live out those values and beliefs wholly and completely in this world? Integrity, therefore, is that sense of alignment we seek between our deepest held beliefs and our everyday actions and decisions. Our challenge is to shrink the gap in this world of everyday contradictions between our stated beliefs and our actions. For, what are the words without the actions but an empty chalice?

Leadership ultimately involves authenticity, and authenticity demands integrity. Therein lie the seeds of the leadership paradox.

The human materials of leadership

No matter how we ultimately define this evolving understanding of leadership, more important may be the task of discovering where we find the human materials to produce such leaders for our organizations.

Maslow, in his *Hierarchy of Human Needs*, offers us some challenges and clues. Maslow, in his landmark work, suggested there is a hierarchy of human need, and each must be satisfied before we can achieve the next level. The first stage of human need is for food, shelter, clothing and the very fundamentals of life, without which we die. Having satisfied this, we evolve to the need for safety, i.e. to be free from fear and insecurity. Having satisfied this, we will seek out affection and belongingness, that sense of being in community with others. Having satisfied this, we will seek to achieve self-esteem, that deeper sense of who we are. Finally, Maslow holds out the unattainable goal of self-actualization, the fulfillment of our human potential (Mahesh, 1993).

Observing Maslow in the context of organizational life, we must ask the question: How are companies doing in developing people through the stages of Maslow's hierarchy? We need not go too far in groping for an answer: "Not very well." In this day and age of downsizing, rightsizing, RIFs, re-engineering, and restructurings, we are threatening a community of people at the very core of their existence. For those of us who are the lucky "survivors," how can we possibly feel free from fear and insecurity? In fact, we have replaced security – the old social contract – with fear, competition, and cynicism. How do we, in the wake of this mass destruction of human spirit, develop a sense of affection and belongingness? How do we, in fact, help people experience the beginning of self-esteem? Where will our highly evolved, principle-centered leaders come from? The challenge in terms of organizational development is clear.

Lawrence Kohlberg, the late Harvard professor, also offers us some clues in the genetic development of leaders through his work on the theory of moral development. Kohlberg indicates there are essentially three stages of moral development: pre-conventional, conventional, and the post-conventional stages. He is signaling to us in his language that there is a norm – a conventional phase – and that something precedes it and something may follow from it. Not unlike Maslow, Kohlberg (1981) suggest we must satisfy one phase before moving on.

The pre-conventional phase of moral development is sometimes referred to as the pre-adolescent phase. It is the phase in which we learn to defer to power and punishment. It is where we learn there are rewards and punishments for good and bad behavior. It is where we develop a sense of personal responsibility.

The conventional phase emphasizes conformity. We seek to gain acceptance through conformance with the standards and norms. We understand the formal and informal rules that guide and govern our behavior, e.g. the laws of society; the policies of organizations. It is, similar to Maslow, where we seek affection and belongingness. Right and wrong are often determined by the group rather than the merits of the action.

The post-conventional phase is where we develop an orientation toward a more principled life. We begin seeking higher moral ground. It is the phase where we seek logic and consistency in our actions and behaviors. One does good for no other reason that it is intrinsically right, regardless of the consequences. It is the phase in which we seek alignment of our deepest values and beliefs in our day-to-day actions, decisions, and the way in which we engage the world.

Kohlberg's first two phases of moral development are externally derived. It is where our understanding of what's right and wrong is developed external to ourselves, e.g. parents, laws, policies. We comply with the rules of order, and conform to group norms. It is not until we reach the post-conventional phase that we begin to internalize our values, our sense of right and wrong.

In observing organizational life, almost all of our corporations are mired in Kohlberg's first and second stages. Compliance with the externals laws and regulations, or with internal company policies, is the norm. By itself, this is useful and necessary, but how can we help people to develop their sense of values, their deepest held beliefs? How can we institutionalize the values, and help people to internalize them? How can we develop policies, practices, procedures, financial goals, compensation and reward systems, and corporate goals that reinforce these values? How can we contribute to the development of whole or complete people? What do we need to do differently to treat people as ends unto themselves, rather than automatons who are merely a means to some corporate end, some short-term financial gain?

Ethics and corporate leadership

For corporate leaders, it is becoming increasingly difficult to navigate the waters of today's uncertain, ever-changing environment which point toward the exciting yet frightening possibilities of the twenty-first century. Change is an unwelcome stranger, and despite the steady economic growth of recent years, fear and uncertainty continually permeates our organizations. In the midst of extraordinary change, leaders must paint a meaningful and compelling vision. Leadership derives from trust, and trust is built upon a common understanding between people. As our common understanding becomes increasingly blurred, ethics is the language that realigns leaders with their employees, customers, shareholders, suppliers, regulators, and the communities in which they operate (Bennis, 1998). Ethics, therefore, is not just a personal matter, but interpersonal.

Developing a sense of shared values – a set of beliefs against which all decisions can be measured and tested – is increasingly the basis on which long-term strategies and their successful implementation are built. In this environment, the failure of leadership to align ethics and values to their business strategies and operating plans bears potentially heavy costs and certainly many lost opportunities.

Anyone who has spent five minutes in the executive suite knows that a strategy that is incompatible with an organization's culture will be difficult, if not impossible, to achieve. The street is littered with many unsuccessful mergers and acquisitions between companies whose cultures are different. Successful implementation of a strategy requires not only the physical and intellectual commitment of its people, but also a sense of shared values and purpose, along with their emotional and spiritual commitment.

Times of great change in organizations add stress and anxiety which can contribute to an environment for wrongful behavior, often beginning in innocence and without awareness. Absent a strong values system in organizations where there is a culture that openly acknowledges what is right and wrong, loyalty blunders can become commonplace. There are many examples where a conspiracy of silence has been costly to organizations.

Recent new legal challenges have raised the stakes even higher and make the failure to integrate ethics and values into a corporation's business plans increasingly dangerous, and potentially fatal. For example, the US Sentencing Commission issued guidelines in November, 1991 that have fundamentally and irrevocably altered the scope, definition, and relationship of management and corporate responsibility (Kaplan et al., 1994). In the most significant government campaign ever waged against white collar and other economic crimes, top executives and others responsible for the management and policy making of the company may now be subject to substantial personal risks – including fines and jail sentences – where there have been legal violations by employees conducting business. Willful ignorance is no longer a defense.

Companies, along with their officers and directors, may now be held criminally liable for the behavior of their employees, even though an employee may have acted contrary to explicit instructions. Mandatory fines – up to $290 million or more as some companies have experienced – may be levied against the company. These guidelines now clearly place the responsibility for corporate values and employee behavior squarely on corporate leadership. Those leaders who ignore these guidelines do so at their own peril. Just ask some former executives at Salomon Brothers, Daiwa Bank and elsewhere.

These risks are even greater today given the universal availability of information. Corporations are increasingly subject to criticism by the media, competitors, social critics, the general public, regulators and even employees themselves. Telecommunication advances have virtually eliminated the communications "float" which formerly acted to cushion the company and its stakeholders from the shock of awareness. Society today is more informed. Gaps are emerging in our common understanding and misalignment of our stated values is becoming increasingly visible. These contradictions, at a minimum, breed credibility gaps that call into question our relationships with other stakeholders. At stake is our trust with one another.

Clearly, leaders and their organizations will not be able to buy the loyalty of this generation of workers. Today's employees are loyal to their profession and to the people they trust and respect, not necessarily the organization. They want to work with leaders whose action they can trust and who, in turn, trust them. Today's workers want to be respected and valued not just for their expertise, but also for the diversity of their backgrounds, perspectives and experiences.

In the midst of this changing environment, employees are increasingly saying they want to be identified with a company that stands for something more than just short-term financial gain. They want to work for a company that has a meaningful vision, a true mission, in which the organization's goals and values align with their own. They want to take pride in what they produce. They want to admire the people they work with.

Leaders must develop a culture where employees are encouraged to discuss their day-to-day dilemmas. Lines of communication must be open to stakeholders inside and outside the firm. Today's leader must create an organizational culture unhampered by fear. Such leaders are committed to problem finding, not just problem solving. They must embrace error, even failure, because it teaches more than problem solving. They encourage healthy dissent and reward those brave enough to say no.

The payoff is even more significant. This trust, once developed, will extend to customers, regulators, and the public. It will develop a renewed sense of pride, dedication, and loyalty to the company.

The starting point for all this begins with the words and the actions of top management. A CEO that acts on and openly discusses values and concerns for the various stakeholders is a crucial first step in aligning a company's culture with its business objectives. However, where there are actions that cannot be spoken about, or words that cannot be put into action, corporation moral development will be undermined by cynicism. Top management must be prepared to "walk the talk" and to set the standards for the company, no matter what the price. As Dante once wrote, "The hottest places in hell are reserved for those who in times of great moral crisis maintain their neutrality" (Mandelbaum, 1980).

Leaders must find ways to integrate ethics and values into their day-to-day decisions. The risks for failing to do so are extreme, as are the lost opportunities. Policies, practices, procedures, financial goals and compensation and reward systems must be examined for the values they signal and must reinforce the desired culture and core values an organization seeks. Leaders must find ways to shrink the gap between the formal organization – the published policies – and the informal organization, i.e. the silent, invisible "way things really get done around here."

Leadership in the twenty-first century

Where are the people that provide us with this sense of leadership that our organizations so desperately needs? Where will we find them?

A company is simply a community of people with common interests and shared values banded together to achieve a common goal. The leaders of tomorrow are sitting there in our organizations today. They are on the floor below us, down the hall, or even in the next cubicle right now. In looking closely at them, what we discover is that there is no distinction based upon social class, organizational rank, gender, race, national origin, color of skin, ethnic background, religion, sexual preference, age, or physical or mental condition. The common mark of these leaders are the deep inner values they have formed through the years of experiences, and their commitment to stay true to those values which have been forged and hardened by change (Bennis, 1988). They are people who devote their professional lives to service and meeting the needs of others. They are people who are committed to something beyond themselves.

The ultimate challenge for today's leaders is to prepare the leaders of tomorrow. The laurel will go to the leader who is not focused on personal achievement, but who is committed to unleashing other people's talents, creativity, and unlimited human potential. These leaders know that life is not a problem to be solved, but a mystery to be lived. These leaders know that we must be faithful to something greater than the sound of our own voice (Campbell and Moyers, 1988). These leaders know that if we want our companies to be successful and vitalized, they must be inhabited by growing and vitalized individuals.

References

Barnhart, C. 1963: *The American College Dictionary*. New York: Random House, p. 693
Bennis, W. 1988: Leaders on leadership. *Harvard Business Review*, Boston, MA, p. 36.
Bennis, W., and Nanus, B. 1985: *Leaders*. New York: Harper & Row.
Burns, J. MacG. 1978: *Leadership*. New York: Harper & Row.
Campbell, J. with Moyers, B. 1988: *The Power of Myth: The Hero's Adventure*. PBS. A production of Apostrophe S. Productions in association with Public Affairs Television and Alvin Perlmatter Inc. Series producer: C. Tatge. Executive producers: J. Konner and A. H. Perlmutter. Executive editor: B. Moyers.
Frankl, V. 1959: *Man's Search for Meaning*. New York: Washington Square Press.
Fromm, E. 1976: *To Have or To Be*. New York: Bantam Books.
Kaplan, J., Murphy, J., and Swenson, W. 1994: *Compliance Programs and the Corporate Sentencing Guidelines*. New York: Clark, Boardman & Callaghan.
Kohlberg, L. 1981: *The Philosophy of Moral Development*. San Francisco, CA: Harper & Row.
Kouzes, J. M. and Posner, B. 1995: *The Leadership Challenge*. San Francisco, CA: Jossey-Bass Inc.
Mahesh, V. S. 1993: *Thresholds of Motivation*. New Dehli, India: Tata McGraw-Hill.

Mandelbaum, A. 1980: The Divine Comedy of Dante Alighieri, Vol. 1, Interno. New York: Bantram.

Toffler, A. 1970: *Future Shock*. New York: Random House, p. 2.

Further reading

Colby, A. and Kohlberg, L. 1987: *The Measurement of Moral Judgment*, Vol 1–2. New York: Cambridge University Press.

Collins, J. and Porras, J. 1994: *Built to Last*. New York: Harper-Collins.

Conger, J. A. & Associates 1994: *Spirit At Work*. San Francisco, CA: Jossey Bass.

Covey, S. 1990: *Principle Centered Leadership*. New York: Fireside.

DeFoore, B. and Renesch, J. (eds) 1995: *Rediscovering the Soul of Business*. San Francisco, CA: Sterling & Stone.

Fox, M. 1994: *The Reinvention of Work*. San Francisco, CA: Harper.

Fukuyama, F. 1995: *Trust*. New York: The Free Press.

Gardner, J. 1990: *On Leadership*. New York: The Free Press.

Gilligan, C. 1982: *In A Different Voice*. Cambridge, MA: Harvard University Press.

Greenleaf, R. K. 1970: *The Servant Leader*. Newton Centre, MA: The Robert K. Greenleaf Centre.

Handy, C. 1994: *The Age of Paradox*. Boston, MA: Harvard Business School Press.

Hesselbein, F., Goldsmith, M., and Beckhard, R. (eds) 1996: *The Leader of the Future*. San Francisco, CA: Jossey-Bass.

Kotter, J. 1988: *The Leadership Factor*. New York: The Free Press.

Liebig, J. 1994: *Merchants of Vision*. San Francisco, CA: Berret-Koehler.

Noer, D. 1995: *Healing The Wounds*. San Francisco, CA: Jossey-Bass Publishers.

O'Toole, J. 1995: *Leading Change*. San Francisco, CA: Jossey-Bass Publishers.

Scherer, J. 1993: *Work And The Human Spirit*. Spokane, WA: John Scherer & Associates.

Solomon, R. 1992: *Ethics and Excellence*. New York: Oxford University Press.

Teilhard De Chardin, P. 1980: *The Heart of The Matter*. New York: Harcourt Brace & Company.

Walton, C. 1988: *The Moral Manager*. Cambridge, MA: Ballinger.

Wheatley, M. 1992: *Leadership and the New Science*. San Francisco, CA: Berret-Koehler.

Bibliography

At the end of each chapter, texts are listed which relate specifically to the contributors' own topic of interest. This bibliography lists recent books that deal primarily with business ethics. It is not intended to be a comprehensive listing of all books about applied ethics or ethical theory, but may provide a useful source for interested readers.

Adams, D. M. and Maine, E. W. 1997: *Business Ethics for the 21st Century*. Mountain Views, CA: Mayfield.

Aguilar, F. J. 1994: *Supercharging Corporate Performance: Business Ethics in Action*. Oxford: Oxford University Press.

Albrecht, S. 1998: *Ethical Workplace*. Menlo Park, CA: Crisp Publications.

American College Staff 1995: *Readings and Applications in Ethics for Field Managers*. Bryn Mawr, Penn.: American College.

Andrews, K. R. (ed.) 1989: *Ethics in Practice: Managing the Moral Corporation*. Boston, MA: Harvard Business School Press.

Anon, 1990: *Ethical Considerations in Corporate Takeovers*. Georgetown University Press.

Arganda, A. (ed.) 1995: *The Ethical Dimension of Financial Institutions and Markets*. New York: Springer-Verlag.

Atkinson, G. and Kennedy, R. G. 1989: *The Ethical Profession of Business*. St Paul, MN: Saint Thomas Technology Press.

Badaracco, J. L. Jr 1994: *Business Ethics: Roles and Responsibilities*. Burr Ridge, IL: Irwin-McGraw-Hill.

Badaracco, J. L. Jr 1997: *Defining Moments: When Managers Must Choose Between Right and Right*. Boston, MA: Harvard Business School Press.

Bain, B. (ed.) 1994: *Managing Business Ethics*. Newton, MA: Butterworth-Heinemann.

Baker, H. K. (ed.) 1994: *Good Ethics: The Essential Element of a Firm's Success*. New York: Association for Investment Management and Research.

Baker, H. K., Veit, E. T., and Murphy, M. R. 1995: *Ethics in the Investment Profession: An International Survey*. Charlottesville, VA: Institute of Chartered Financial Analysts, Research Foundation.

Baron, D. P. 1995: *Business and Its Environment*. Upper Saddle River, NJ: Prentice-Hall.

Barry, N. P. 1991: *The Morality of Business Enterprise*. New York: Macmillan.

Bartee, E. M. 1993: *America's Mount Olympus: What's Really Gone Wrong in Corporate America and How Its Shareholders Can Fix It*. Lebanon, TN: Henderson Group.

Barton, L. 1994: *Ethics: The Enemy in the Workplace*. Belmont, CA: South-Western, ITP.

Beauchamp, T. L. and Bowie, N. E. (eds) 1997: *Ethical Theory and Business*. Upper Saddle River, NJ: Prentice-Hall.

Becker, G. K. (ed.) 1996: *Ethics in Business and Society: Chinese and Western Perspectives*. New York: Springer-Verlag.

Beekun, R. I. 1996: *Islamic Business Ethics*. Herndon, VA: International Institute of Islamic Thought.

Behrman, J. N. 1988: *Essays on Ethics in Business and the Professions*. Upper Saddle River, NJ: Prentice-Hall.

Bennis, W. G. 1993: *An Invented Life: Meditations on Leadership and Change*. Reading, MA: Addison Wesley Longman.

Berenbeim, R. E. 1987: *Corporate Ethics*. New York: The Conference Board.

Berry, L. D. 1996: *The Power of Internal Marketing: Building a Values-Based Corporate Culture*. New Orleans, LA: Good Reading Books.

Bird, F. B. 1996: *The Muted Conscience: Moral Silence and the Practice of Ethics in Business*. Westport, CT: Greenwood.

Birsch, D. and Fielder, J. (eds) 1994: *The Ford Pinto Case: A Study in Applied Ethics, Business, and Technology*. State University of New York Press.

Blanchard, K. H. and O'Connor, M. 1996: *Managing by Values*. San Francisco, CA: Berrett-Koehler Publishers.

Blanchard, K. H. and Peale, N. V. 1988: *The Power of Ethical Management: Why the Ethical Way Is the Profitable Way – in Your Life and in Your Business*. New York: William Morrow & Co.

Block, W. 1991: *Defending the Undefendable*. San Francisco, CA: Fox & Wilkes.

Boatright, J. R. 1994: *Cases in Ethics and the Conduct of Business*. Upper Saddle River, NJ: Prentice-Hall.

Boatright, J. R. 1996: *Ethics and the Conduct of Business*. Upper Saddle River, NJ: Prentice-Hall.

Bohlman, H. M. and Dundas, M. J. 1996: *The Legal, Ethical and International Environment of Business*. St Paul, MN: West Publishing Corp.

Boothe, P. H. (ed.) 1991: *To Be or Not to Be an SOB: A Reaffirmation of Business Ethics*. Forth Worth, TX: Unicorn Press.

Bowie, N. E. 1999: *Business Ethics: A Kantian Perspective*. Oxford: Blackwell.

Bowie, N. E. and Duska, R. 1989: *Business Ethics*. Upper Saddle River, NJ: Prentice-Hall.

Bowie, N. E. and Freeman, R. E. (eds) 1992: *Ethics and Agency Theory: An Introduction*. Oxford: Oxford University Press.

Boylan, M. 1995: *Ethical Issues in Business*. Troy, MO: Harcourt Brace College Publishers.

Brady, F. N. 1989: *Ethical Managing: Rules and Results*. Upper Saddle River, NJ: Prentice-Hall.

Brady, F. N. 1997: *Ethical Universals in International Business*. New York: Springer-Verlag.

Braybrooke, D. 1983: *Ethics in the World of Business*. Lanham, MD: Rowman & Littlefield.

Briner, B. 1996: *The Management Methods of Jesus: Ancient Wisdom for Modern Business*. Nashville, TN: Thomas Nelson Inc.

Brooks, T. 1995: *Accountability: It All Depends on What You Mean*. Englewood, CO: Akkad Press.

Buchanan, A. 1985: *Ethics, Efficiency and the Market*. Lanham MD: Rowman & Littlefield.

Buchholz, R. A. 1989: *Fundamental Concepts and Problems in Business Ethics*. Upper Saddle River, NJ: Prentice-Hall.

Buchholz, R. A. and Rosenthal, S. B. 1997: *Business Ethics: The Pragmatic Path Beyond Principles to Process*. Upper Saddle River, NJ: Prentice-Hall.

Burkett, L. 1992: *Business by the Book: The Complete Guide of Biblical Principles for Business Men and Women*. Nashville, TN: Thomas Nelson Inc.

Callahan, J. C. (ed.) 1988: *Ethical Issues in Professional Life*. Oxford: Oxford University Press.

Campbell, L. A. (ed.) 1993: How to Develop a Code of Conduct. Altamonte Springs, FL: Institute of Internal Auditors, Inc.

Campbell, L. A. (ed.) 1996: *Assessing Organizational and Individual Ethics*. Altamonte Springs, FL: Institute of Internal Auditors, Inc.

Cannon, T. 1994: *Corporate Responsibility: Issues in Business Ethics, Governance and Responsibilities*. Philadelphia, PA: Trans-Atlantic.

410

Carroll, A. B. 1993: *Business and Society: Ethics and Stakeholder Management.* Belmont, CA: South-Western, ITP.

Casey, A. V. 1997: *Casey's Law: If Something Can Go Right, It Should.* New York: Arcade Publishing.

Castro, B. (ed.) 1996: *Business and Society: A Reader in the History, Sociology, and Ethics of Business.* Oxford University Press.

Causey, D. Y. Jr and Causey, S. A. 1995: *Duties and Liabilities of Public Accountants.* Mississippi State, MS: Accountants Press.

Cavanagh, G. F. 1997: *American Business Values.* Upper Saddle River, NJ: Prentice-Hall.

Cavanagh, G. F. and McGovern, A. F. 1988: *Ethical Dilemmas in the Modern Corporation.* Englewoods Cliff, NJ: Prentice-Hall.

Chakraborty, S. K. 1998: *Values and Ethics for Organizations: Theory and Practice.* New York: Oxford University Press.

Chatfield, C. A. 1997: *The Trust Factor: The Art of Doing Business in the 21st century.* Santa Fe, NM: Sunstone Press.

Childs, J. M. Jr 1995: *Ethics in Business: Faith at Work.* Minneapolis, MN: Fortress Press.

Chonko, L. B. 1995: *Ethical Decision-Making in Marketing.* Thousand Oaks, CA: Sage Publications.

Chryssides, G. D. and Kaler, J. H. 1993: *An Introduction to Business Ethics.* New York: Chapman & Hall.

Chryssides, G. D. and Kaler, J. H. 1996: *Essentials of Business Ethics.* Hightstown, NJ: McGraw-Hill.

Ciulla, J. B. 1998: *Ethics, the Heart of Leadership.* Westport, CT: Greenwood Publishing Group.

Clark R. W. and Lattal, A. D. 1993: *Workplace Ethics: Winning the Integrity Revolution.* Lanham, MD: Rowman and Littlefield.

Clarke, F. L. and Oliver, K. G. 1997: *Corporate Collapse: Regulatory, Accounting and Ethical Failure.* Portchester, NY: Cambridge University Press.

Cohen, B. and Greenfield, J. 1997: *Ben and Jerry's Double-Dip Capitalism: Lead with Your Values and Make Money Too.* Old Tappan, NJ: Simon & Schuster Inc.

Collins D. 1994: *Ethical Dilemmas in Accounting.* Belmont, CA: South-Western, ITP.

Collins, D. and O'Rourke, T. 1993: *Ethical Dilemmas in Business.* Belmont, CA: South-Western, ITP.

Collins, D. and O'Rourke, T. 1994: *Ethical Dilemmas in Every Department of Big Mess,* Belmont, CA: South-Western, ITP.

Conrad, C. and Dervin, B. (eds) 1993: *The Ethical Nexus: Communication, Values, and Organizational Decisions.* Stanford, CT: Ablex Publishing Corp.

Conry, E. J. 1995: *Moral Partners: Building Moral Character for Business.* Thousand Oaks, CA: Sage Publications.

Conry, E. J. 1997: *Ethics and Evidence: Developing Ethical Character in Professionals.* Thousand Oaks, CA: Sage Publications.

Cooke, R. 1998: *Tools for Individual and Group Learning: Ethical Decision Challenge.* New York: AMACOM Books / American Management Association.

Cowan, J. 1992: *Small Decencies: Reflections and Meditations on Being Human at Work.* New York: Harper Collins Publishers.

Cowan, R. and Rizzo, M. J. (eds) 1995: *Profits and Morality.* University of Chicago Press.

Danley, J. R. 1994: *The Role of the Modern Corporation in a Free Society.* University of Notre Dame Press.

Davies, P. W. 1997: *Current Issues in Business Ethics.* New York: Routledge Inc.

De Geer, H. (ed.) 1994: *Business Ethics in Progress.* New York: Springer-Verlag.

De George, R. T. 1993: *Competing with Integrity in International Business.* New York: Oxford University Press.

De George, R. T. 1994: *Business Ethics.* Upper Saddle River, NJ: Prentice-Hall.

De Mente, B. L. 1994: *Chinese Etiquette and Ethics in Business*. Lincolnwood, IL: NTC Publishing Corp.

De Mente, B. L. 1994: *Japanese Etiquette and Ethics in Business*. Lincolnwood, IL: NTC Publishing Corp.

De Mente, B. L. 1994: *Korean Etiquette and Ethics in Business*. Lincolnwood, IL: NTC Publishing Corp.

Defoore, B. and Renesch, J. R. (eds) 1995: *Rediscovering the Soul of Business: A Renaissance of Values*. San Francisco, CA: New Leaders Press.

DesJardins, J. R. and McCall, J. J. (eds) 1995: *Contemporary Issues in Business Ethics*. Belmont, CA: Wadsworth, ITP.

Devine, G. 1996: *Responses to 101 Questions on Business Ethics*. Mahwah, NJ: Paulist Press.

Dewey, O. 1969: *Moral Views of Commerce, Society and Politics in Twelve Discourses*. New York: Augustus M. Kelley Publishers.

Di Norcia, V. 1998: *Hard Like Water: Ethics in Business*. Oxford: Oxford University Press.

Diamond, S. 1990: *The Reputation of the American Businessman*. Magnolia, MA: Peter Smith Publishing Inc.

Dienhart, J. W. 1997: *Business Ethics*. Santa Barbara, CA: ABC-CLIO, Inc.

Dobson, J. (ed.) 1997: *Finance Ethics: The Rationality of Virtue*. Lanham, MD: Rowman & Littlefield.

Donaldson, J. 1989: *Business Ethics: A European Casebook*. San Diego, CA: Academic Press.

Donaldson, L. and Wilson, D. 1995: *Russian Etiquette and Ethics in Business*. Lincolnwood, IL: NTC.

Donaldson, T. 1989: *The Ethics of International Business*. New York: Oxford University Press.

Donaldson, T. and Dunfee, T. W. (eds) 1997: *Ethics in Business and Economics* (2 vols). Brookfield, UT: Ashgate Publishing Co.

Donaldson, T. and Freeman, R. E. (eds) 1994: *Business as a Humanity*. Oxford: Oxford University Press.

Donaldson, T. and Gini, A. R. (eds) 1995: *Case Studies in Business Ethics*. Upper Saddle River, NJ: Prentice-Hall.

Donaldson, T. and Werhane, P. H. 1983: *Ethical Issues in Business*. Upper Saddle River, NJ: Prentice-Hall.

Donaldson, T. and Werhane, P. H. (eds) 1995: *Ethical Issues in Business: A Philosophical Approach*. Upper Saddle River, NJ: Prentice-Hall.

Edwards, J. D. and Hermanson, R. H. 1993: *Essentials of Financial Accounting with Ethics Cases*. Burr Ridge, IL: Irwin Professional Publications.

Edwards, J. D. and Hermanson, R. H. 1993: *Essentials of Managerial Accounting with Ethics Cases*. Burr Ridge, IL: Irwin Professional Publications.

Eells, R. and Nehemkis, P. 1984: *Corporate Intelligence and Espionage: A Blueprint for Executive Decision Making*. New York: Free Press.

Elfstrom, G. 1991: *Moral Issues and Multinational Corporations*. New York: Saint Martin's Press.

Enderle, G., Almond, B., and Argandona, A. (eds) 1990: *People in Corporations: Ethical Responsibilities and Corporate Effectiveness*. Norwell, MA: Kluwer Academic Publishers.

Engelbourg, S. 1980: *Power and Morality: American Business Ethics, 1840–1914*. Westport, CT: Greenwood Publishing Group.

Falsey, T. A. 1989: *Corporate Philosophies and Mission Statements: A Survey and Guide for Corporate Communicators and Management*. Westport, CT: Greenwood Publishing Group.

Ferrell, O. C. 1993: *Business Ethics*. Boston: Houghton Mifflin.

Ferrell, O. C. and Gardiner, G. (eds) 1991: *In Pursuit of Ethics: Tough Choices in the World of Work*. St Louis, MO: Smith Collins.

Fisher, B. D. and Phillips, M. J. 1997: *The Legal, Ethical and Regulatory Environment of Business*. Belmont, CA: South-Western, ITP.

Fitzpatrick, R. L. 1996: *False Profits: Seeking Spiritual Deliverance in Pyramid Schemes and Multi-Level Marketing*. Charlotte, NC: Herald Press.

Francis, R. D. 1994: *Business Ethics in Australia: A Practical Guide*. Holmes Beach, FL: Gaunt.

Fredrick, C. and Atkinson, C. 1997: *Women, Ethics and the Workplace*. Westport, CT: Greenwood Publishing Group.

Frederick, W. C. 1995: *Values, Nature, and Culture in the American Corporation*. Oxford: Oxford University Press.

Frederick, W. C. and Preston, L. E. (eds) 1990: *Business Ethics: Research Issues and Empirical Studies*. Stanford, CT: Jai Press.

French, P. 1994: *Corporate Ethics*. Troy, MD: Harcourt Brace College Publishers.

French, P., Nesteruk, J., and Risser, D. T., with Abbarno, J. 1992: *Corporations in the Moral Community*. New York: Harcourt Brace Janovich.

French, W. A. 1994: *Practical Business Ethics*. Upper Saddle River, NJ: Prentice-Hall.

Gambling, T. and Karim, R. A. 1991: *Business and Accounting Ethics in Islam*. Herndon, VA: Cassell.

Garrett, T. M. and Klonoski, R. J. 1985: *Business Ethics*. Upper Saddle River, NJ: Prentice-Hall.

Gilbert, D. R. 1996: *Ethics Through Corporate Strategy*. Oxford: Oxford University Press.

Glenn, J. R. 1986: *Ethics in Decision Making*. New York: John Wiley & Sons.

Goodpaster, K. E., Nash, L. L., and Matthews, J. B. 1997: *Policies and Persons: A Casebook in Business Ethics*. Hightstown, New York: McGraw-Hill.

Gordon, D. and Sheamur, J. (eds) 1993: *The Morals of Markets and Related Essays*. Indianapolis, IN: H. B. Acton.

Gortner, H. F. 1991: *Ethics for Public Managers*. Westport, CT: Greenwood Publishing Group.

Grace, D. and Cohen, S. 1996: *Business Ethics: Australian Problems and Cases*. Oxford: Oxford University Press.

Grayson, L., Woolston, H., and Tanega, J. 1993: *Business and Environmental Accountability*. Mahwah, NJ: Lawrence Erlbaum Assoc., Inc.

Green, R. M. 1993: *The Ethical Manager: A New Method for Business Ethics*. Upper Saddle River, NJ: Prentice-Hall.

Griseri, P. and Groucutt, J. 1996: *In Search of Business Ethics*. New York: State Mutual Book & Periodical Service.

Grote, J. and McGeeney, J. 1997: *Clever As Serpents: Business Ethics and Office Politics*. Collegeville, MA: The Liturgical Press.

Guerand K. and Burrow, J. 1995: *Business Principles and Management*. Belmont, CA: South-Western, ITP.

Guy, M. E. 1990: *Ethical Decision-Making in Everyday Work Situations*. Westport, CT: Greenwood Publishing Group.

Hadley, A. T. 1973: *Standards of Public Morality*. New York: Arno Press.

Halbert, T. and Ingulli, E. (eds) 1996: *Law and Ethics in the Business Environment*. Anaheim, CA: West Publishers.

Hall, S. S. (ed.) 1992: *Ethics in Hospitality Management: A Book of Readings*. East Lansing, MI: Educational Institute of the American Hotel & Motel Association.

Hall, W. D. 1993: *Making the Right Decision: Ethics for Managers*. Arthur Anderson paperbook. New York: John Wiley & Sons.

Hamada, T. and Sibley, W. E. (eds) 1994: *Anthropological Perspectives on Organizational Culture*. Lanham, MD: University Press of America.

Hammon, A. D. 1985: *The Business of Integrity*. Loveland, CO: Foundation House.

Hancock, W. A. 1991: *Corporate Counsel's Guide to Business Ethics Policies*. Business Laws, Inc.

Hansen, J. L. and Christensen, P. A. 1995: *Invisible Patterns: Ecology and Wisdom in Business and Profit*. Westport, CT: Greenwood Publishing Group.

413

Hartley, R. F. 1993: *Business Ethics: Violations of the Public Trust*. New York: John Wiley & Sons.

Hartmann, E. M. 1996: *Organizational Ethics and the Good Life*. Oxford: Oxford University Press.

Harvard Business Review Staff 1991: *Ethics at Work*. Boston, MA: Harvard Business School Publishing.

Harvey, B. (ed.) 1991: *Market Morality and Company Size*. Norwell, MA: Kluwer Academic Publishers.

Harvey, B. (ed.) 1994: *Business Ethics: A European Approach*. Upper Saddle River, NJ: Prentice-Hall.

Harvey, B., van Luijk, H., and Steinmann, H. (eds) 1994: *European Casebook on Business Ethics*. Upper Saddle River, NJ: Prentice-Hall.

Harwood, S. 1996: *Business as Ethical and Business as Usual*. Sudbury, MA: Jones and Bartlett Publishers Inc.

Henderson, V. E. 1992: *What's Ethical in Business?* Hightstown, NJ: McGraw-Hill.

Hendry, J. and Sorell, T. 1994: *Business Ethics*. Woburn, MA: Butterworth-Heinemann.

Herman, S. W. 1998: *Durable Goods: A Conventional Ethic for Management and Employees*. University of Notre Dame.

Hess, J. D. 1977: *Ethics in Business and Labor*. Ann Arbor, MI: Books on Demand.

Higginson, R. and Moore, G. 1997: *Apocalypse! The Business Ethics Game*. New York: John Wiley & Sons.

Hill, A. 1997: *Just Business: Christian Ethics for the Marketplace*. Downers Grove, IL: InterVarsity Press.

Hodapp, P. F. 1994: *Ethics in the Business World*. Melbourne, FL: Krieger Publishing Co.

Hoffman, W. M. 1986: *Ethics and the Multinational Enterprise*. Proceedings of the Sixth National Conference on Business. Lanham, MD: University Press of America.

Hoffman, W. M. and Frederick, R. E. (eds) 1994: *Business Ethics: Readings and Cases in Corporate Morality*. Hightstown, NJ: McGraw-Hill.

Hoffman, W. M., Frederick, R. E., and Petry, E. S. (eds) 1990: *Business, Ethics and the Environment: The Public Policy Debate*. Westport, CT: Greenwood Publishing Group.

Hoffman, W. M., Frederick, R. E., and Petry, E. S. (eds) 1990: *The Corporation, Ethics and the Environment*. Westport, CT: Greenwood Publishing Group.

Hoffman, W. M., Kamm, J. B., and Frederick, R. E. (eds) 1996: *The Ethics of Accounting and Finance: Trust, Responsibility and Control*. Westport, CT: Quorum Books.

Hoffman, W. M., Lange, A. E., and Fedo, D. A. (eds) 1986: *Ethics, October 10 and 11, 1985*. Lanham, MD: University Press of America.

Hoffman, W. M., Kamm, J. B., Frederick, R. E., and Petry, E. S. (eds) 1993: *Emerging Global Business Ethics*. Westport, CT: Greenwood Publishing Group.

Hoivik, H. V. and Follesdal, A. (eds) 1995: *Ethics and Consultancy: European Perspectives*. Norwell, MA: Kluwer Academic Publishers.

Hopkins, W. E. 1997: *Ethical Dimensions of Diversity*. Thousand Oaks, CA: Sage Publications.

Horn, N. (ed.) 1980: *Legal Problems of Codes of Conduct for Multinational Enterprises*. Norwell, MA: Kluwer Academic Publishers.

Hosmer, LaRue T. 1993: *Moral Leadership in Business*. Burr Ridge, IL: Richard D. Irwin.

Hosmer, LaRue T. 1995: *The Ethics of Management*. Burr Ridge, IL: Irwin Professional Publications.

Iannone, A. P. (ed.) 1989: *Contemporary Moral Controversies in Business*. Oxford: Oxford University Press.

Inoue, S. 1997: *Putting Buddhism to Work: A New Approach to Management and Business*. Oxford University Press.

Jackall, R. 1989: *Moral Mazes: The World of Corporate Managers*. Oxford: Oxford University Press.

Jackson, J. 1996: *An Introduction to Business Ethics*. Oxford: Blackwell.

Jackson, J. H., Miller, R. L., and Miller, S. G. 1997: *Business and Society Today: Managing Social Issues*. Anaheim, CA: West Publishers.

Jacobs, J. 1994: *Systems of Survival: A Dialogue on the Moral Foundations of Commerce and Politics.* New York: Random House.

Jennings, M. M. 1995: *Case Studies in Business Ethics.* Anaheim, CA: West Publishers.

Jennings, M. M. 1999: *Business: Its Legal, Ethical, and Global Environment.* Austin, TX: South-Western Publishers.

Jeremy, D. J. 1988: *Business and Religion in Britain.* Brookfield, UT: Ashgate Publishing Co.

Johnson, P. and Smith, K. (eds) 1996: *Business Ethics.* New York: Routledge Inc.

Jones, B. M. 1998: *Simply the Best: Great Business Hits: A Look at "Top Twenty" Principles and Ethical Standards Behind Sales and Business Success.* Murray, UT: Business Resource Publishers.

Jones, D. G. and Bennett, P. (eds) 1986: *Bibliography of Business Ethics, 1981–1985*: University of Virginia: Edwin Mellen Press.

Jones, D. G. and Troy, H. (eds) 1982: *A Bibliography of Business Ethics, 1976–1980.* University Press of Virginia.

Jones, I. and Pollitt, M. G. 1998: *The Role of Business Ethics in Economic Performance.* New York: Saint Martin's Press.

Jung, L. and Levine, A. 1987: *Business Ethics in Jewish Law.* New York: Hebrew Publishing Co.

Kanungo, R. N. and Mendonca, M. 1995: *The Ethical Dimensions of Leadership.* Thousand Oaks, CA: Sage Publications.

Kapstein, M. 1998: *Ethics Management: Auditing and Developing the Ethical Content of Organizations.* Boston: Kluwer Academic Publishers

Katchmer, G. A. Jr and Murray, A. D. (eds) 1995: *Professional Budo: Ethics, Chivalry and the Samurai Code.* Roslindale, MA: YMAA Publication Center.

Kaufman, A., Zacharias, L., and Karson, M. 1995: *Managers vs. Owners: The Struggle for Corporate Control in American Democracy.* Oxford: Oxford University Press.

Kelly, C. M. 1988: *The Destructive Achievers: Power and Ethics in the American Corporation.* Reading, MA: Addison Wesley Longman.

Kidder, R. M. 1996: *How Good People Make Tough Choices.* Old Tappan, NJ: Simon & Schuster Inc.

Kile, D. A. 1995: *Business Conduct and Ethics: How to Set up a Self-Governance Program.* Chesterland, OH: Business Laws, Inc.

Klein, S. 1994: *Business Ethics: Reflections from a Platonic Point of View.* New York: Peter Lang.

Koslowski, P. (ed.) 1992: *Ethics in Economics, Business, and Economic Policy.* New York: Springer-Verlag.

Koslowski, P. 1997: *Business Ethics in East Central Europe.* New York: Springer-Verlag.

Koslowski, P. and Shionoya, Y. (eds) 1994: *The Good and the Economical: Ethical Choices in Economics and Management.* New York: Springer-Verlag.

Kransdorff, A. 1998: *Corporate Amnesia: Keeping Know-How Within the Company.* Woburn, MA: Butterworth-Heinemann.

Kreuger, D. A., Shriver, D. W. Jr, and Nash, L. L. 1996: *The Business Corporation and Productive Justice.* Nashville, TN: Abingdon.

Kuhn, J. W. and Shriver, D. W. Jr 1991: *Beyond Success: Corporations and Their Critics in the 1990s.* New York: Oxford University Press.

Kultgen, J. 1988: *Ethics and Professionalism.* University of Pennsylvania Press.

Ladenson, R. F. 1995: *Ethics in the American Workplace: Policies and Decisions.* Horsham, PA: LRP.

Landekich, S. (ed.) 1989: *Corporate Codes of Conduct.* Montvale, NJ: National Association of Accountants.

Lane, C. and Bachmann, R. (eds) 1998: *Trust Within and Between Organizations: Conceptual Issues and Empirical Applications.* Oxford: Oxford University Press.

Lange, H., Lohr, A., and Steinmann, H. 1997: *Working Across Cultures: Ethical Perspectives for Intercultural Management.* Norwell, MA: Kluwer Academic Publishers.

Langford, D. 1998: *Business Computer Ethics.* Reading, MA: Addison Wesley Longman.

415

Larmer, R. A. (ed.) 1995: *Ethics in the Workplace: Selected Readings in Business Ethics.* Anaheim, CA: West Publishers.

Larson, A. and Freeman, R. E. 1997: *Women's Studies and Business Ethics: Toward a New Conversation.* New York: Oxford University Press.

LeClair, D. T., Ferrell, O. C., and Fraedrich, J. P. 1998: *Integrity Management: A Guide to Managing Legal and Ethical Issues in the Workplace.* University of Tampa.

Ledenva, A. 1998: *Russia's Economy of Favours: Blat, Networking and Informal Exchanges.* Cambridge University Press.

Lewis, A. and Warneryd, E. (eds) 1994: *Ethics and Economic Affairs.* New York: Routledge Inc.

Liebig, J. E. 1991: *Business Ethics: Profiles in Civic Virtue.* Golden, Colerado: Fulcrum.

Lingenfelter, S. 1992 (ed.): *Ethics in the Russian Marketplace: An Anthology.* Wheaton, IL: Billy Graham Center.

Lippke, R. L. 1995: *Radical Business Ethics.* Lanham, MD: Rowman & Littlefield.

Ludwig, D. C. (ed.) 1993: *Business and Society in a Changing World Order.* Lewiston, NY: Edwin Mellen Press.

Lufrano, R. J. 1996: *Honorable Merchants: Commerce and Self-cultivation in Late Imperial China.* University of Hawaii Press.

Lynch, J. J. 1994: *Banking and Finance: Managing the Moral Dimension.* New York: American Educational Systems.

Lynch, S. 1997: *Arrogance and Accords: The Inside Story of the Honda Scandal.* Irving, TX: Pecos Press.

MacAdam, M. N. 1996: *Intentional Integrity.* Nashville, TN: Broadman & Holman.

MacAdams, T. and Freeman, J. 1993: *Law, Business and Society.* Burr Ridge, IL: Richard D. Irwin.

Machan, T. R. (ed.) 1988: *Commerce and Morality: Alternative Essays in Business Ethics.* Lanham, MD: Rowman & Littlefield.

Mahoney, J. 1990: *Teaching Business Ethics in the U. K., Europe and the USA: A Comparative Study.* London: The Athlone Press.

Mahoney, J. and Vallance, E. (eds) 1992: *Business Ethics in a New Europe.* Dordrecht, Boston: Kluwer.

Mangel, G. D. 1995: *Corporate's Struggle with Ethics (The Lures and the Lies): A Guide to Climbing the Corporate Ladder.* Waterloo, Iowa: A. M. Publishing.

Manley, W. Jr 1991: *Executive's Handbook of Model Business Conduct Codes.* Upper Saddle River, NJ: Prentice-Hall.

Manley, W. Jr and Shrode, W. A. 1990: *Critical Issues in Business Conduct: Legal, Ethical, and Social Challenges for the 1990s.* Westport, CT: Greenwood Publishing Group.

Marcus, A. A. 1995: *Business and Society: Strategy, Ethics, and the Global Economy.* Burr Ridge, IL: Richard D. Irwin.

Mason, R. O., Mason, F. M., and Culnan, M. J. 1995: *Information and Responsibility: The Ethical Challenge.* Thousand Oaks, CA: Sage Publications.

May, W. W. 1992: *Business Ethics and the Law: Beyond Compliance.* New York: Peter Lang.

McAdams, T. and Pincus, L. B. 1996: *The Legal Environment of Business: Ethical and Public Policy Contexts.* Burr Ridge, IL: Richard D. Irwin.

McCann, D. P., Roels, S. J., and Stackhouse, M. L. (eds) 1995: *On Moral Business: Classical Contemporary Resources for Ethics in Economic Life.* Grand Rapids, MI: William B. Eerdmans Publishing Co.

McCoy, C. S. 1985: *Management of Values: The Ethical Difference in Corporate Policy and Performance.* Boston, MA: Pittman.

McGee, R. W. (ed.) 1992: *Business Ethics and Common Sense.* Westport, CT: Greenwood Publishing Group.

Mellema, G. 1994: *The Bottom Line: Making Christian Choices in the Marketplace.* Grand Rapids, MI: CRC Publications.

Menken, D. L. 1988: *Faith, Hope and the Corporation: Sharpening Your Business Philosophy and Business Ethics.* Saint Paul, MN: Phrontisterion.

Messick, D. M. and Tenbrunsel, A. E. (eds) 1996: *Codes of Conduct: Behavioral Research into Business Ethics.* New York: Russell Sage Foundation.

Michalos, A. C. 1995: *A Pragmatic Approach to Business Ethics.* Thousand Oaks, CA: Sage Publications.

Minus, P. M. 1993: *The Ethics of Business in a Global Economy.* Norwell, MA: Kluwer Academic Publishers.

Moore, B. Jr 1998: *Moral Aspects of Economic Growth, and Other Essays.* Cornell University Press.

Moorthy, R. S., De George, R. T., Donaldson, T., Ellos, W. J., Solomon R. C., and Textor, R. B. 1998: *Uncompromising Integrity: Motorola's Global Challenge.* Motorola University Press.

Murphy, K. 1992: *Honesty in the Workplace.* Pacific Grove, CA: Brooks Cole.

Murphy, P. E. 1997: *Eighty Exemplary Ethics Statements.* University of Notre Dame Press.

Nash, L. L. 1990: *Good Intentions Aside: A Manager's Guide to Resolving Ethical Problems.* Boston, MA: Harvard Business School Publishing.

Nash, L. L. 1994: *Believers in Business.* Nashville, TN: Thomas Nelson Inc.

Natale, S. M. 1987: *Ethics and Morals in Business.* Birmingham, AL: Religious Education Press.

Natale, S. M. and Wilson, J. B. (eds) 1990: *The Ethical Contexts for Business Conflicts.* Lanham, MD: University Press of America.

Nave, J. R. 1987: *The Quest for Success Rediscovering American Business Values.* Blackbutte Ranch, OR: Windemere Press Inc.

Nelson, C. A. and Cavey, R. D. 1991: *Ethics, Leadership and the Bottom Line: An Executive Reader.* Great Barrington, MA: North River.

Newton, L. H. and Ford, M. M. 1996: *Taking Sides: Clashing Views on Controversial Issues in Business Ethics.* Dubugne, IA: WCB/McGraw-Hill.

Newton, L. H. and Schmidt, D. 1995: *Wake up Calls: Classic Cases in Business Ethics.* Belmont, CA: Wadsworth, ITP.

Nielsen, R. P. 1996: *The Politics of Ethics: Methods for Acting, Learning and Sometimes Fighting with Others in Addressing Ethics Problems in Organizational Life.* New York: Oxford University Press.

Nix, W. H. 1997: *Transforming Your Workplace for Christ.* Nashville, TN: Broadman & Holman.

Novak, R. 1991: *Toward a Theology of the Corporation.* Washington, DC: American Enterprise Institute for Public Policy Research.

Oakes, G. 1990: *The Soul of the Salesman: The Moral Ethos of Personal Sales.* Atlantic Heights, NJ: Humanities Press.

Ottensmeyer, E. J. and McCarthy, G. D. 1996: *Ethics in the Workplace.* Hightstown, NJ: McGraw-Hill.

Oz, E. 1993: *Ethics for an Information Age.* Business & Educational Technologies. ISBN: 0-697204626.

O'Neill, A. M. 1986: *Etica Comercial: Una Filosofia para la Libre Empresa.* University of Puerto Rico Press.

O'Neil J. 1998: *The Market: Ethics, Knowledge and Politics.* New York: Routledge Inc.

Paine, L. S. 1996: *Cases in Leadership, Ethics and Organizational Integrity: A Strategic Perspective.* Burr Ridge, IL: Richard D. Irwin.

Pamental, G. L. 1988: *Ethics in the Business Curriculum: A Preliminary Survey of Undergraduate Business Programs.* Lanham, MD: University Press of America.

Parker, D. and Hall, B. (eds) 1991: *Management by Slime and Grime.* Redwood City, CA: Gerhard Flemming.

417

Parker, D. B., Swope, S., and Baker, B. 1990: *Ethical Conflicts in Information and Computer Science, Technology, and Business*. Wellesley, MA: QED Information Systems.

Parker, M. (ed.) 1998: *Ethics and Organizations*. Thousand Oaks, CA: Sage

Parks, R. H. 1996: *The Witch Doctor of Wall Street: A Noted Financial Expert Guides You Through Today's Voodoo Economics*. Amherst, NY: Prometheus Books.

Paul, K. (ed.) 1987: *Business Environment and Business Ethics*. Cambridge, MA: Ballinger Publishing Co.

Paul, K. (ed.) 1991: *Contemporary Issues in Business Ethics and Politics*. Lewiston, NY: Edwin Mellen Press.

Pearson, G. 1995: *Integrity in Organizations: An Alternative Business Ethic*. Hightstown, NJ: McGraw-Hill.

Peterson, C.D. 1997: *On Your Own: Discovering Your New Life and Career Beyond the Corporation*. New York: John Wiley & Sons.

Petrick, J. A. and Quinn, J. F. 1997: *Management Ethics: Integrity at Work*. Thousand Oaks, CA: Sage Publications.

Pfeiffer, R. S. and Forsberg, R. P. 1992: *Ethics on the Job: Cases and Strategies*. Belmont, CA: Wadsworth, ITP.

Pincus, L. B. 1997: *Perspectives in Business Ethics*. Burr Ridge, IL: Irwin Professional Publications.

Piper, T. R., Gentile, M. C., and Parks, S. D. 1993: *Can Ethics Be Taught? Perspectives, Challenges, and Approaches at the Harvard Business School*. Boston, MA: Harvard Business School Press.

Pivar, W. H. and Harian, D. L. 1995: *Real Estate Ethics Good Ethics = Good Business*. New York: State Mutual Book & Periodical Service.

Pratley, P. 1995: *The Essence of Business Ethics*. Upper Saddle River, NJ: Prentice-Hall.

Primeaux, P. D. 1999: *Reinventing the American Dream: The Ethics of Business and the Business of Ethics*. Bethesda, MD: International Scholars.

Prindl, A. R. and Prodhan, B. (eds) 1994: *Ethical Conflicts in Finance: The ACT Guide*. Oxford: Blackwell.

Pritchett, P. 1991: *The Ethics of Excellence*. Dallas, TX: Pritchett & Associates.

Protho, J. W. 1970: *Dollar Decade: Business Ideas in the 1920s*. Westport, CT: Greenwood Publishing Group.

Rackley, R. R. 1997: *Ethics, Insurance Perspectives and Insurance Contract Analysis (For CPCU 1)*. Baton Rouge, LA: Insurance Achievement, Inc.

Radin, M. 1976: *The Lawful Pursuit of Gain*. New York: Arno Press.

Rae, S. B. and Wong, K. L. 1996: *Beyond Integrity: A Judeo-Christian Approach to Business Ethics*. Grand Rapids, MI: Zondervan.

Reder, A. 1995: *In Pursuit of Principle and Profit: Business Success Through Social Responsibility*. New York: Putnam.

Reeves, F. 1993: *Business Ethics*. Denton, TX: RonJon.

Reeves-Ellington, R. H. and Anderson, A. 1997: *Business, Commerce, and Social Responsibility: Beyond Agenda*. Lewiston, NY: The Edwin Mellen Press.

Rich, A. 1997: *Business and Ethics: The Ethics of Economic Systems*. Winonadale, IN: Eisenbrauns.

Richardson, J. E. (ed.) 1995: *Annual Editions: Business Ethics, 95–96*. Guilford, CT: Dushkin.

Richardson, J. E. (ed.) 1997: *Annual Editions: Business Ethics, 97–98*. Madison, WI: Brown & Benchmark.

Ringleb, A. H., Meiners, R. E., and Edwards, F. L. 1995: *Managing in the Legal Environment*. Anaheim, CA: West Publishers.

Roleff, T. L. 1996: *Business Ethics*. San Diego, CA: Greenhaven Press Inc.

Salkin, J. K.: 1994: *Being God's Partner: How to Find the Hidden Link Between Spirituality and Your Work*. Woodstock, UT: Jewish Lights Publishing.

Sanders, M. (ed.) 1989: *Ethics in Business: A Guide for Managers*. Menlo Park, CA: Crisp Publications.

Sarasin, C. (ed.) 1995: *Facing Public Interest: Ethical Challenges to Business Policy and Corporate Communications*. Norwell, MA: Kluwer Academic Publishers.

Schlegelmilch, B. 1998: *Marketing Ethics: An International Perspective*. Boston: International Thomson.

Shafritz, J. M. and Madsen, P. (eds) 1990: *The Essentials of Business Ethics*. New York: NAL Dutton.

Shaw, W. M. 1991: *The Structure of the Legal Environment: Law, Ethics and Business*. Boston, MA: PWS.

Shaw, W. H. 1999: *Business Ethics*. Belmont, CA: Wadsworth, ITP.

Shaw, W. H. and Barry, V. 1997: *Moral Issues in Business*. Belmont, CA: Wadsworth, ITP.

Shelton, K. (ed.) 1998: *Integrity at Work: Dealing with Differing Standards of Ethics, Values, and Principles*. Prove, UT: Executive Excellence Publishing.

Sikula, A. F. Sr 1995: *Moral Management: Integrating Ethics*. Burr Ridge, IL: Irwin Professional Publications.

Smith, N. C. and Quelch, J. A. 1994: *Ethics in Marketing: Selected Material*. Burr Ridge, IL: Richard D. Irwin.

Smith, S. M. 1993: *Practical Ethics for the Federal Employee*. Huntsville, AL: FPMI Communications.

Smye, M. D. and Wright, L. 1996: *Corporate Abuse: How Lean and Mean Robs People and Profits*. New York: Macmillan.

Snell, R. 1993: *Developing Skills for Ethical Management: Providing Ethical Developments for Managers*. New York: Chapman & Hall.

Snoeyenbos, M., Almeder R., and Humber J. (eds) 1992: *Business Ethics*. Buffalo, NY: Prometheus Books.

Solomon, R. C. 1993: *Ethics and Excellence: Cooperation and Integrity in Business*. Oxford: Oxford University Press.

Solomon, R. C. 1994: *A New World of Business: Ethics and Free Enterprise in the Global 1990s*. Lanham, MD: Rowman & Littlefield.

Solomon, R. C. 1994: *Above the Bottom Line: An Introduction to Business Ethics*. Troy, MO: Harcourt Brace College Publishers.

Solomon, R. C. 1997: *It's Good Business: Ethics and Free Enterprise for the New Millennium*. Lanham, MD: Rowman & Littlefield.

Sonnenberg, F. K. 1993: *Managing with a Conscience: How to Improve Performance Through Integrity, Trust, and Commitment*. Hightstown, NJ: McGraw-Hill.

Stewart, D. 1995: *Business Ethics*. Hightstown, NJ: McGraw-Hill.

Stewart, S. and Donleavy, G. (eds) 1995: *Whose Business Values? Some Asian and Cross Cultural Perspectives*. Wilmore, KY: Coronet Books.

Stock, G. 1991: *The Book of Questions: Business, Politics and Ethics*. New York: Workman Publishing Co.

Stone, C. D. 1991: *Where the Law Ends: The Social Control of Corporate Behavior*. Prospect Heights, IL: Waveland Pr. Inc.

Stuart, B. and Stuart, I. 1996: *Writing, Ethics, and Group Projects for Accounting*. Belmont, CA: South-Western, ITP.

Stuhr, J. J. 1990: *Morals and the Media: Information, Entertainment, and Manipulation*. University of Oregon Books.

Sutton, B. (ed.) 1993: *The Legitimate Corporation: Essential Readings in Business Ethics and Corporate Governance*. Oxford: Blackwell.

Taeusch, C. F. 1973: *Policy and Ethics in Business*. New York: Arno Press.

Tamasy, R. J. (ed.) 1995: *Jesus Works Here: Leading Christians in Business Talk about How You Can Walk with Christ Through Stress, Change and Other Challenges of the Workplace*. Nashville, TN: Broadman & Holman.

Toenjes, R. 1996: *Cases of Virtue and Business Ethics*. Dubuque, IA: Kendall Hunt.

Toffler, B. L. 1986: *Managers Talk Ethics: Making Tough Choices in a Competitive Business World*. New York: John Wiley & Sons.

Tome, W. 1986: *Business Ethics: An Introduction Business Values for a Pluralist Society*. University of Scranton Press.

Treviño, L. K. and Nelson, K. A. 1995: *Managing Business Ethics: Straight Talk about How to Do It Right*. New York: John Wiley & Sons.

Trice, E. (ed.) 1995: *Corporate Diplomacy: Principled Leadership for the Global Community*. Washington, DC: Center for Strategic & International Studies.

Tucker, E. W. and Henkel, J. W. 1998: *The Legal and Ethical Environment of Business*. Upland: PA: Diane Publishing Co.

Tuleja, T. 1987: *Beyond the Bottom Line: How Business Leaders Are Turning Principles into Profits*. New York: Penguin Books.

Vallance, E. 1995: *Business Ethics at Work*. Cambridge University Press.

Van Dam, C. and Stallaert, L. M. 1978: *Trends in Business Ethics: Implications for Decision Making*. Norwell, MA: Kluwer Academic Publishers.

Vanberg, V. 1987: *Morality and Economics: De Moribus Est Disputandum*. Bowling Green State University.

Veit, E. T. and Murphy, M. R. 1992: *Ethics in the Investment Profession: A Survey*. Charlottesville, VA: Institute of Chartered Financial Analysts, Research Foundation.

Velazquez, M. 1997: *Business Ethics*. Upper Saddle River, NJ: Prentice-Hall.

Vernon, H. 1997: *Business and Society: A Managerial Approach*. Burr Ridge, IL: Irwin Professional Publications.

Walton, C. C. 1988: *The Moral Manager*. Cambridge, MA: Ballinger.

Walton, C. C. 1990: *Enriching Business Ethics*. New York: Plenum.

Walton, C. C. 1992: *Corporate Encounters: Law and Ethics in the Business Environment*. Fort Worth, TX: Dryden.

Wartick, S. L. and Wood, D. J. (eds) 1997: *International Business and Society*. Oxford: Blackwell.

Watson, C. E. 1991: *Managing with Integrity: Insights from America's CEOs*. Westport, CT: Greenwood Publishing Group.

Weber, C. E. 1995: *Stories of Virtue in Business*. Lanham, MD: University Press of America.

Weckert, J. and Adeney, D. 1997: *Computer and Information Ethics*. Westport, CT: Greenwood Publishing Group.

Weiss, J. W. 1993: *Business Ethics: A Managerial, Stakeholder Approach*. Belmont, CA: South-Western, ITP.

Weiss, J. W. 1995: *Organizational Behavior and Change: Managing Diversity, Cross Cultural Dynamics and Ethics*. Anaheim, CA: West Publishers.

Weiss, J. W. 1998: *Business Ethics*. Troy, MO: Harcourt Brace College Publishers.

Werhane, P. and D'Andrade, K. (eds) 1985: *Profit and Responsibility: Issues in Business and Professional Ethics*. Lewiston, NY: Edwin Mellen Press.

Werhane, P. and Freeman, R. E. (eds) 1996: *The Blackwell Encyclopedic Dictionary of Business Ethics*. Oxford: Blackwell.

White, T. I. 1993: *Business Ethics: A Philosophical Reader*. Upper Saddle River, NJ: Prentice-Hall.

Wienen I. 1997: *Impact of Religion on Business Ethics in Europe and the Muslim World: Islamic vs. Christian Tradition*. New York: Peter Lang.

Wilbur, J. B. III 1992: *The Moral Foundations of Business Practice*. Lanham, MD: University Press of America.

Williams, G. J. 1992: *Ethics in Modern Management*. Westport, CT: Greenwood Publishing Group.

Williams, O. F. 1998: *The Moral Imagination: How Literature and Films Can Stimulate Ethical Reflection in the Business World*. University of Notre Dame Press.

Williams, O. F., Reilly, F. K., and Houck, J. W. (eds) 1989: *Ethics and the Investment Industry.* Lanham, MD: Rowman & Littlefield.

Wines, W. A. and Anderson, S. C. 1994: *Readings in Business Ethics and Social Responsibility.* Dubuque, IA: Kendall Hunt.

Wood, D. J. 1994: *Business and Society.* New York: Harper Collins College Publishers.

Wuthnow, R. 1996: *Poor Richard's Principle: Restoring the American Dream by Recovering the Moral Dimension of Work, Business, and Money.* Princeton University Press.

Yu, X., Lu, X., Liu, F., Shang, R., and Enderle, G. (eds) 1997: *Economic Ethics and Chinese Culture.* Washington, DC: Council for Research in Values & Philosophy.

Zadek, S., Pruzan, P., and Evans, R. (eds) 1997: *Building Corporate Accountability: Emerging Practice in Social and Ethical Accounting and Auditing.* New York: Island Press.

Zinn, L. M. 1996: *E Is for Ethics: Essentials for Entrepreneurs.* Boulder, CO: Lifelong Learning Options.

Appendix A: Business ethics: electronic resources

Over the past few years the number of web pages devoted to business ethics and related issues has increased dramatically. What follows is at best a partial list. However, from the sites listed it should be possible to find links to most business ethics web pages.

Institute for Business and Professional Ethics
     www.depaul.edu/ethics/
The Carol and Lawrence Zicklin Center for Business Ethics Research
     rider.wharton.upenn.edu/~ethics/zicklin/
Ethics Resource Center
     www.ethics.org
The Society for Business Ethics
     www.luc.edu/depts/business/sbe/index.htm
Centre for Applied Ethics
     www.ethics.ubc.ca/resources/
Academy of Management: Social Issues in Management Division
     cac.psu.edu/~plc/sim/sim.html
Olsson Center for Applied Ethics
     www.darden.virginia.edu/research/olsson/olsson.htm
International Society of Business, Economics and Ethics
     www.nd.edu/~isbee/
Ethics Officer Association
     www.eoa.org/
American Philosophical Association
     www.udel.edu/apa/
Ethics on the World Wide Web
     www5.fullerton.edu/les/ethics_list.html
The Business Ethics listserv
     buseth-1@listserv.acsu.buffalo.edu

Appendix B: Domestic and international business ethics organizations

The information in this appendix is supplied by the Center for Business Ethics.

Centers and organizations working in business ethics

This information is correct as at December 1998.

A. Alfred Taubman Center for Public Policy,
Policy and American Institutions,
Thomas Anton,
Brown University,
Box 1977,
Providence, RI 02912
Tel: 401-863-2201
Fax: 401-863-2452

Academy of Management,
Pace University,
Nancy Urbanowicz – Executive Director,
PO Box 3020,
Bricliss Manor, NY 10510
Tel: 914-923-2607
Fax: 914-923-2615

Alliance of Work/Life Professionals,
Stephanie Trapp – Executive Director,
514 King Street Suite 420,
Alexandria, VA 22314
Tel: 800-874-9383
Fax: 703-684-6048

American Council on Consumer Interest (ACCI),
Anita Metzin – Executive Director,
240 Stanley Hall,
University of Missouri,
Columbia, MO 65211
Tel: 573-882-3817
Fax: 573-884-6571

American Enterprise Institute for Public Policy Research,
Christopher DeMuth – Executive Director,
1150 17th Street, N.W.,
Washington, DC 20036
Tel: 202-862-5800
Fax: 202-862-7177

American Institutes for Research (AIR),
Center for Community Research,
PO Box 1113,
Palo Alto, CA 94302
Tel: 415-493-3550
Fax: 415-858-0958
email: brossi@air-ca.org/air-dc.org/
comm/comm.html

Arthur Anderson Center for Professional Education,
Herb Desch, Executive Director,
1405 North Fifth Avenue,
St Charles, IL 60174
Tel: 630-377-3100
Fax: 630-584-7212

Association for Practical & Professional Ethics,
Brian Schrag, Executive Secretary,
Indiana University,
618 East 3rd Street,
Bloomington, IN 47405
Tel: 812-855-6450
Fax: 812-855-3315
email: appe@ucs.indiana.edu

Association of Professional Responsibility Lawyers,
c/o American Bar Association c/o Kristen Dell,
Center for Professional Responsibility,
150 East Wilson Bridge Road, Suite 200,
Worthington, OH 43085
Tel: 213-626-7300
Fax: 614-436-2865

Business Enterprise Trust, The Kathleen Meyer,
Executive Director,
706 Cowper Street,
Palo Alto, CA 94301
Tel: 650-321-5100
Fax: 650-321-5774
email: bet@betrust.org
www.betrust.org

Business Ethics Section of the Academy of Legal Studies in Business,
Dan Herron, Executive Secretary,
Department of Finance,
Miami University,
120 Upham Hall,
Oxford, OH 45056
Tel: 800-831-2903

Business Ethics Strategies, Inc./BEST,
PO Box 275,
New York, NY 10044-0205
Tel: 212-691-1224
Fax: 212-741-8756

Business for Social Responsibility (BSR),
609 Mission Street 2nd floor,
San Francisco, CA 94103-3722
Tel: 415-537-0888
Fax: 415-537-0889

Business, Government, and Society Research Institute,
University of Pittsburgh,
Katz Graduate School of Business,
c/o Barry Mitnick,
261 Mervis Hall,
Pittsburgh, PA 15260
Tel: 412-648-1555
Fax: 412-648-1693

Campaign Finance Board,
Jeanne Olson,
First Floor, S. Centennial Building,
658 Cedar Street,
St Paul, MN 55155
Tel: 651-296-1720
Fax: 651-296-1722

Carnegie Council on Ethics and International Affairs,
Dr Joel Rosenthal, President,
Merrill House,
170 East 64th Street,
New York, NY 10021-7478
Tel: 212-838-4120
Fax: 212-752-2432

Carol and Lawrence Zicklin Center for Business Ethics Research,
Lauretta Tomasco, Associate Director,
The Wharton School,
The University of Pennsylvannia,
Philadelphia, PA 19104-6369
Tel: 215-898-7691
email: tomascol@wharton.upenn.edu

Cary M. Maguire Center for Ethics and Public Responsibility,
Richard O. Mason – Executive Director,
Southern Methodist University,
PO Box 750316,
Dallas, TX 75275
Tel: 214-768-4255
Fax: 214-768-3391

Center for Advance Study in the Behavioral Sciences,
Neil Smellser,
75 Alta Road,
Stanford, CA 94305
Tel: 650-321-2052
Fax: 650-321-1192

Center for the Advancement of Applied Ethics,
Peter Madsen, Director,
Carnegie Mellon University,
Baker Hall,
Pittsburgh, PA 15213
Tel: 412-268-5703
Fax: 412-268-6074

Center for the Advancement of Ethics and Character,
Kevin Ryan, Director,
605 Commonwealth Avenue,
Boston, MA 02215
Tel: 617-353-3262
Fax: 617-353-3924

Center for Applied Christian Ethics,
Dr Allen Johnson, Director,
Bible Department,
Wheaton College,
Wheaton, IL 60187
Tel: 630-752-5886
Fax: 630-752-5731

Center for Applied Ethics,
Duke University,
PO Box 90287,
Durham, NC 27708-0287
Tel: 919-660-5204
Fax: 919-660-5219

Center for Applied Philosophy and Ethics,
Robert J. Baum, Director,
330 Griffin-Floyd Hall,
PO Box 118545,
University of Florida,
Gainesville, FL 32611-8545
Tel: 352-392-2084
Fax: 352-392-5577

Center for Applied & Professional Ethics,
Hilde Nelson, Director,
Department of Philosophy,
801 McClung Tower,
University of Tennessee,
Knoxville, TN 37996-0480
Tel: 423-974-3255
Fax: 423-974-3509

Center for Business and Democracy,
Barbara Mossberg, Director,
Goddard College, 123 Pitkin Rd,
Plainfield, VT 05667
Tel: 802-454-8311
Fax: 802-454-8017

Center for Business Ethics,
W. Michael Hoffman,
Executive Director,
Bentley College,
Waltham, MA 02154-4705
Tel: 781-891-2981
Fax: 781-891-2988
email: cbeinfo@Bentley.edu
www.Bentley.edu/resource/cbe

Center for Business/Religion/ Professions,
Jim Craig, Director,
Pittsburgh Theological Seminary,
616 N. Highland Avenue,
Pittsburgh, PA 15206
Tel: 412-362-5610
Fax: 412-363-3260

Center for Clinical Bioethics,
Edmund Pellergiano – Director,
Georgetown University,
400 Reservoir Road N.W.,
Washington, DC 20007
Tel: 202-687-8999
Fax: 202-687-8955

Center for Corporate Community Relations, The,
Bradley Googins – Executive Director,
Boston College,
36 College Rd.,
Chestnut Hill, MA 02167-3835
Tel: 617-552-4545
Fax: 617-552-8499
email: cccr@bc.edu
www.bc.edu/cccr

Center for Corporate Public Involvement,
Ms Shawn Haufman,
1001 Pennsylvania Avenue, N.W.,
5th. Flr,
Washington, DC 20004-2599
Tel: 202-624-2425
Fax: 202-624-2319

Center for Creative Leadership,
John Alexander, Acting President,
One Leadership Place,
Greensboro, NC 27410
or
PO Box 26300,
Greensboro, NC 27438
Tel: 336-288-7210
Fax: 336-288-3999

Center for Ethics,
Elaine Englehardt,
Ethics Center,
Utah Valley State College,
800 West 1200 South,
Orem, Ut 84058
Tel: 801-222-8405
Fax: 801-226-8938

Center for Ethics,
The University of Tampa,
Debbie Thorne LeClair, Ph.D,
401 W. Kennedy Blvd., Box 61-F,
Tampa, FL 33606-1490
Tel: 813-258-7415
Fax: 813-258-7408

Center for Ethics,
David Ozar, Director,
Loyola University of Chicago,
6525 N. Sheridan Road,
Chicago, IL 60626
Tel: 773-508-8349 ext 8352
Fax: 773-508-8879
www.luc.edu/depts/ethics/

Center for Ethics and Business,
Dr Thomas White,
Loyola Marymount University,
7900 Loyola Blvd.
Los Angeles, CA 90045-8385
Tel: 310-338-4523
Fax: 310-338-3000
email: twhite@lmumail.lmu.edu

Center for Ethics in Public Policy and the Professions,
Dr James W. Fowler, Director,
Emory University,
1462 Clifton Road,
Dental Bldg. Ste. 302,
Atlanta, GA 30322
Tel: 404-727-4954
Fax: 404-727-7399

Center for Ethics and Religious Values in Business,
Oliver Williams, Co-Director,
College of Business Administration,
University of Notre Dame,
Notre Dame, IN 46556
Tel: 219-631-6072
Fax: 219-631-5255

Center for Ethics & Social Policy,
Dr Claire Fischer,
Graduate Theological Union,
2400 Ridge Road,
Berkeley, CA 94709
Tel: 510-649-2560
Fax: 510-649-2565

Center for Ethics Studies,
Robert Ashmore, Acting Director,
Academic Support Facility, Rm. 336,
Marquette University, PO Box 1881,
Milwaukee, WI 53201-1881
Tel: 414-288-7221
Fax: 414-288-5826

Center for Law and Social Policy,
Alan Houseman,
1616 P Street, N.W., Suite 150,
Washington, DC 20036
Tel: 202-328-5140
Fax: 202-328-5195 or 202-328-5197
www.clasp.org

Center for Media and Literacy,
Elizabeth Thoman,
4727 Wilshire Boulevard, Suite 403,
Los Angeles, CA 90010
Tel: 323-931-4177
Fax: 323-931-4474

Center on Philanthropy,
Dr Eugene Tempel, Executive Director,
Indiana University,
550 W. North St.,
Suite 301,
Indianapolis, IN 46202-3162
Tel: 317-274-4200
Fax: 317-684-8900

Center for Professional Ethics,
John R. Wilcox, Director,
Manhattan College,
Bronx, NY 10471
Tel: 718-862-7442
Fax: 718-862-8044
JWilcox@Manhattan.edu

Center for Professional Ethics,
Robert Lawry, Director,
233 Yost Hall,
Case Western Reserve University,
10900 Euclid Ave.,
Cleveland, OH 44106-7057
Tel: 216-368-5349
Fax: 216-368-5163

Center for Public Policy and Contemporary Issues,
Richard Lamm,
University of Denver,
2199 S. University Blvd,
Denver, CO 80208
Tel: 303-871-3400
Fax: 303-871-3066

Center for Religion, Ethics and Social Policy (CRESP),
Wessells Anke, Coordinator,
Cornell University,
Anabel Taylor Hall,
Ithaca, NY 14853
Tel: 607-255-5027
Fax: 607-255-9985

Center for Study of Business and Government,
Dr Gloria Thomas,
Bernard M. Baruch College,
City University of New York,
17 Lexington Avenue 23rd Street,
Box E0929,
New York, NY 10010
Tel: 212-802-6580
Fax: 212-802-6555

Center for the Study of Ethical Development,
James Rest,
206 Burton Hall,
University of Minnesota,
178 Pillsbury Drive,
Minneapolis, MN 55455
Tel: 612-624-0876
Fax: 612-624-8241

Center for the Study of Ethical Issues in Business,
David Messick, Director,
Kellogg Graduate School of
  Management,
Northwestern University OB-KGSM,
Evanston, IL 60208
Tel: 847-491-8074
Fax: 847-467-2153

Center for the Study of Ethics,
Elaine Englehardt, Ph.D,
Utah Valley State College,
800 West 1200 South,
Orem, UT 84058-5999
Tel: 801-222-8000 Ext. 8129
Fax: 801-222-8938

Center for the Study of Ethics and the Professions,
Dr Vivian Weil, Director,
Stewart Building Room 102,
Illinois Institute of Technology,
10 West 31st,
Chicago, IL 60616-3793
Tel: 312-567-3017
Fax: 312-567-3016

Center for Study of Ethics in Society,
Michael S. Pritchard, Director,
Moore Hall Room 311,
Western Michigan University,
Kalamazoo, MI 49008
Tel: 616-387-4380
Fax: 616-387-4390

Center for the Teaching and Study of Applied Ethics,
Steve Kalish,
College of Law,
University of Nebraska-Lincoln,
PO Box 830902,
Lincoln, NE 68583-0902
Tel: 402-472-1248
Fax: 402-472-5185

Center for Values and Social Policy,
Graham Oddie, Director,
Dept. of Philosophy, Campus Box 232,
University of Colorado at Boulder,
Boulder, CO 80309-0232
Tel: 303-492-6364
Fax: 303-492-8386

Center on Work & Family,
Boston University,
232 Bay State Road,
Boston, MA 02215
Tel: 617-353-7225
Fax: 617-353-7220

Clearinghouse for Information About Values & Ethics,
Dr Albert Teich, Director,
Organization & Human Systems
  Development,
Directorate for Science and Policy
  Programs,
American Association for the
  Advancement of Science,
1200 New York Avenue, N.W.,
Washington, DC 20005
Tel: 202-326-6600
Fax: 202-289-4950

Coalition for Environmentally Responsible Economies (CERES),
11 Arlington St 6th Floor,
Boston, MA 02111
Tel: 617-451-0927
Fax: 617-247-0700
www.ceres.org

Committee for Economic Development (CED),
477 Madison Avenue,
New York, NY 10022
Tel: 212-688-2063
Fax: 212-758-9068
www.ced.org

Committee on Ethics in the Public Service,
National Academy of Public
   Administration,
1120 G Street, N.W., Suite 850,
Washington, DC 20005-3821
Tel: 202-347-3190
Fax: 202-393-0993

Committee on Professional Ethics, Rights and Freedom,
Jim Biggs, Executive Director,
American Political Science Association,
1527 New Hampshire Avenue, N.W.,
Washington, DC 20036
Tel: 202-483-2512 x 105
Fax: 202-483-2657

Common Cause,
Ann McBride, President,
1250 Connecticut Ave. N.W., Ste. 600,
Washington, DC 20036
Tel: 202-833-1200
Fax: 202-659-3716

Computer Professionals for Social Responsibility,
Duff Axsom,
PO Box 717,
Palo Alto, CA 94302
Tel: 650-322-3778
Fax: 650-322-4748

Conference Board, The,
Richard Cavanagh, President,
845 Third Avenue,
New York, NY 10022-6679
Tel: 212-759-0900
Fax: 212-980-7014
Info@conference-board.org

Council on Economic Priorities (CEP),
Alice Tetter-Marlin, Director,
30 Irving Place, 9th. Flr.,
New York, NY 10003-2386
Tel: 212-420-1133
Fax: 212-420-0988 or 800-729-4237
www.accesspt.com/cep

Council of Ethical Organizations,
Mark Pastin,
Chair and President,
214 S. Payne Street,
Alexandria, VA 22314
Tel: 703-683-7916
Fax: 793-299-8386

Council for Ethics in Economics,
David C. Smith, President,
3rd Floor,
125 East Broad Street,
Columbus, OH 43215
Tel: 614-221-8661
Fax: 614-221-8707
www.businessethics.org
email: mazurt@businessethics.org

Defense Industry Initiative on Business Ethics and Conduct,
c/o Alan R. Yuspeh, Coordinator,
Howrey & Simon,
1299 Pennsylvania Avenue, N.W.,
Washington, DC 20004-2402
Tel: 202-783-0800
Fax: 202-383-6610

Emerson Electric Center for Business Ethics,
Dr James E. Fisher, Director,
School of Business Administration,
Saint Louis University,
3674 Lindell Blvd.,
St Louis, MO 63108
Tel: 314-977-3836
Fax: 314-977-1647

Environmental Media Association (EMA),
10780 Santa Monica Blvd., Suite 210,
Los Angeles, CA 90034
Tel: 310-446-6244
Fax: 301-446-6255
email: ema@epg.org
www.ema-online.org

Ethics Center,
Peggy Desautels,
University of South Florida,
100 Fifth Avenue South,
St Petersburg, FL 33701-5016
Tel: 727-553-3172
Fax: 727-553-3169

Ethics in Public Service Network,
Department of Public
    Administration,
HPB, Room 202,
University of Central Florida,
Orlando, FL 32816-1395
Tel: 407-823-2604
Fax: 407-823-5651

Ethics Institute, The,
Dean Steven Bahls,
Capital University Law and Graduate
    Center,
303 Broad Street,
Columbus, OH 43215-5683
Fax: 614-445-7125

Ethics Institute,
Ronald M. Greene,
    Director,
Dartmouth College,
6031 Parker House,
Hanover, NH 03755
Tel: 603-646-1263
Fax: 603-646-2652

Ethics Officer Association,
c/o Center for Business
    Ethics,
30 Church Street,
Suite 331,
Belmont, MA 02178
Tel: 617-484-9400
Fax: 617-484-8330
email: epetry@EOA.org

Ethics Resource Center Inc.,
Michael Daigneault, President,
1747 Pennsylvania Ave, N.W., Suite 400,
Washington, DC 20005
Tel: 202-737-2258
Fax: 202-737-2227
email: ethics@ethics.org
www.ethics.org

Families & Work Institute,
330 Seventh Avenue,
New York, NY 10001
Tel: 212-465-2044
Fax: 212-465-8637
www.familiesandworkinst.org

Forum for Policy Research,
Graduate Department of Public Policy
    and Administration,
Rutgers, the State University of New
    Jersey,
401 Cooper Street,
Camden, NJ 08102
Tel: 609-225-6311
Fax: 609-225-6559

**George W. Romney Institute of
    Public Management,**
Marriott School of Management,
760 Tanner Building,
Provo, UT 84602-3158
Tel: 801-378-4221
Fax: 801-378-9975
email: mpa@byu.edu
msm.byu.edu/programs/mpa/

Hall Center for Humanities,
University of Kansas,
211 Wadkins Home,
Lawrence, KS 66045
Tel: 785-864-4798
Fax: 785-864-3884

Healthy Companies Institute,
1420 16th Street NW,
Washington, DC 20036
Tel: 202-234-9288
Fax: 202-234-9289

Henry Salvatori Center,
Charles R. Kesler, Director,
Pitzer Hall,
Claremont McKenna College,
850 Columbia,
Claremont, CA 91711
Tel: 909-621-8201
Fax: 909-621-8416

Hoffberger Center for Professional Ethics,
Dr Alfred Guy, Director,
University of Baltimore,
1420 N. Charles Street,
Baltimore, MD 21201-5779
Tel: 410-837-5324
Fax: 410-837-4783

Human Economy Center,
John Applegath,
Department of Economics, MSU 14,
Mankato State University,
PO Box 8400,
Mankato, MN 56002-8400
Tel: 507-389-5325

Humanities and Philosophy Dept.,
Utah Valley State College,
800 West 1200 South,
Orem, UT 84058
Tel: 801-222-8352
Fax: 801-222-8938

Indiana University Center on Philanthropy,
Eugene Temple – Executive Director,
550 West North St, Suite 301,
Indianapolis, IN 46202-3162
Tel: 317-274-4200
Fax: 317-684-8968

Initiative for a Competitive Inner City,
One Metro Tech Center North, 11ᵗʰ Fl.,
Brooklyn, NY 11201
Tel: 718-722-7390
Fax: 718-858-6108
email: initiative@aol.com

Institute for Absolute Ethics,
Mr McNair, Director,
4090 North Lake Creek Cove,
Suite 1,
A Division of Executive Leadership Foundation,
Tucker, GA 30084
Tel: 770-270-1818
Fax: 770-491-9039

Institute for Applied and Professional Ethics,
Arthur Zucker,
207 R. Tech,
Dept. of Philosophy,
Ohio University,
Athens, OH 45701-2979
Tel: 740-593-4596
Fax: 740-593-4597

Institute for Business and Management Administration,
Dr Widdick Berman,
Chair,
Iona College,
715 North Avenue,
New Rochelle, NY 10801
Tel: 914-633-2262

Institute for Business & Professional Ethics,
Laura B. Pincas Hartman,
Director,
DePaul University,
One East Jackson Blvd.,
Suite 7000,
Chicago, IL 60604-2287
and
University of Wisconsin,
52 Granger Hall,
975 University Ave.,
Madison, WI 53706
Tel: 608-262-7920
Fax: 608-262-8773
www.depaul.edu.ethics

433

Institute for Christian Ethics,
Dr Dickson Sutherland,
Stetson University,
PO Box 8367,
DeLand, FL 32720-3757
Tel: 904-822-7364
Fax: 904-822-8936

Institute for Consumer Responsibility,
Todd Putnam,
3618 Wallingford Ave N,
Seattle, WA 98103
Tel: 206-632-5230

Institute for Ethics and Policy Studies,
Craig Walton, Director,
University of Nevada,
Las Vegas,
4505 Maryland Parkway,
Las Vegas, NV 89154-5049
Tel: 702-895-4029
Fax: 702-895-4673

Institute for Global Ethics, The,
Rushworth M. Kidder,
President,
11-13 Main St,
PO Box 563,
Camden, ME 04843
Tel: 207-236-6658
Fax: 207-236-4014

Institute of International Business Ethics,
Dr Bodo B. Schlegelmilch,
Director,
Thunderbird,
15249 N. 59th Avenue,
Glendale, AZ 85306-6000
Tel: 602-978-7011
Fax: 602-843-6143

Institute for Leadership and Continuing Education,
Katherine Oakley, Director,
College of St Catherine,
2004 Randolph Avenue,
PO F8,
St Paul, MN 55105
Tel: 612-690-6819
Fax: 612-690-6024

Institute for Philosophy and Public Policy,
William Galston,
University of Maryland,
3111 Van Munching Hall,
College Park, MD 20742
Tel: 301-405-6347
Fax: 301-314-9346

Interfaith Center on Corporate Responsibility (ICCR),
Mr Tim Smith, Director,
475 Riverside Drive,
Room 550,
New York, NY 10115-0500
Tel: 212-870-2295
Fax: 212-870-2023

International Association for Business and Society,
c/o Sage Publications, Inc.,
David McCune, President,
2455 Teller Road,
Newbury Park, CA 91320
Tel: 805-499-0721
Fax: 805-499-0871

International Business Ethics Institute,
Lori Tansey, President,
1000 Connecticut Ave., NW,
Suite 503,
Washington, DC 20038
Tel: 202-296-6938
Fax: 202-296-5897

International Center for Ethics in Business,
Richard De George,
   Director,
School of Business,
University of Kansas,
Lawrence, KS 66045
Tel: 785-864-3976
Fax: 785-864-4298

International Center for Ethics, Justice and Public Life,
Daniel Ferris – Executive
   Director,
Mail stop 086 PO Box 9110,
Brandeis University,
Waltham, MA 02254-9110
Tel: 781-736-8577
Fax: 781-736-8561

International Reform Federation,
Suite 200, Braddock Building,
205 Tuckerton Road,
Medford, NJ 08055
Tel: 609-985-7724

Investor Responsibility Research Center,
Scott Senn, Executive Director,
1350 Connecticut Avenue, N.W.
Suite 700,
Washington, DC 20036-1701
Tel: 202-833-0700
Fax: 202-833-3555

James MacGregor Burns Academy of Leadership,
University of Maryland,
1107 Taliaferro Hall,
College Park, MD 20742
Tel: 301-405-5751
Fax: 301-405-6402

John F. Connelly Program in Business Ethics,
George G. Brenkert, Director,
The McDonough School of Business,
Georgetown University,
37th and O Streets NW,
209 Maguire,
Washington, DC 20057
Tel: 202-687-7626
Fax: 202-687-7351

Josephson Institute for Advancement of Ethics,
Rosa Maulini, CEO/CFO,
4640 Admiralty Way, Suite 1001,
Marina Del Rey, CA 90292-6610
Tel: 310-306-1868
Fax: 310-827-1864 or 800-711-2670
email: cc@jiethics.org

Kegley Institute of Ethics,
Christopher Meyers, Director,
California State University at Bakersfield,
9001 Stockdale Highway,
Bakersfield, CA 93311-1099
Tel: 805-664-3149
Fax: 805-665-6904

Kennedy Institute of Ethics,
Leroy Walters, Director,
Georgetown University,
37th N.O. Street N.W. 4th Fl.
   Healy Hall,
Washington, DC 20057-1212
Tel: 202-687-6774
Fax: 202-687-8089

Law, Medicine, and Ethics Program,
George Annas, Director,
Boston University School of Public
   Health,
715 Albany Street,
Boston, MA 02118
Tel: 617-638-4626
Fax: 617-414-1464

Lincoln Center for Applied Ethics,
Marianne M. Jennings Director,
PO Box 874806,
Arizona State University,
Tempe, AZ 85287-4806
Tel: 602-965-2710
Fax: 602-965-3995

Management Institute for Environment & Business (MEB),
A Program of the World Resources Institute (WRI),
1709 New York Avenue NW,
Suite 700,
Washington, DC 20006
Tel: 202-638-6300
Fax: 202-638-0036
www.wri.org/wri/meb/

Markkula Center for Applied Ethics,
Father Thomas Shanks, Director,
Santa Clara University,
500 El Camino Rio,
Santa Clara, CA 95053
Tel: 408-554-5319
Fax: 408-554-2373
email: ethics@scu.edu

Media Ethics,
c/o Mass Communication,
Prof. Emmanuel Paraschos,
Emerson College,
100 Beacon Street,
Boston, MA 02116-1596
Tel: 617-824-8500
Fax: 617-824-8804

Minnesota Center for Corporate Responsibility,
1000 La Salle Avenue, #153,
Minneapolis, MN 55403-2005
Tel: 612-962-4120
Fax: 612-962-4125
email: MCCR_UST@stthomas.edu

Minnesota Network for Institutional Ethics Committees,
2550 University Ave, West Suite 350 South,
St Paul, MN 55114
Tel: 612-645-4545
Fax: 651-645-0002

National Center for Employee Ownership,
1201 Martin Luther King, Jr Way,
Oakland, CA 94612
Tel: 510-272-9461
Fax: 510-272-9510
email: nceo@nceo.org
www.nceo.org/

National Humanities Center,
Robert Connor,
7 Alexander Drive,
Research Triangle Park, NC 27709
Tel: 919-549-0661
Fax: 919-990-8535

National Institute for Engineering Ethics,
National Society of Professional Engineers,
Philip E. Ulmer – President,
1420 King Street,
Alexandria, VA 22314-2715
Tel: 703-684-2840
Fax: 703-519-3763

New England Work & Family Association,
Boston University,
232 Bay State Road,
Boston, MA 02215
Tel: 617-353-7225
Fax: 353-7220

Nine to Five, National Association of Working Women,
238 W. Wisconsin Ave., Suite 700,
Milwaukee, WI 53203-2308
Tel: 414-274-0925
Fax: 414-272-2870

Northwest Ethics Institute,
Raymond T. Cole, Executive Director,
2729 Northeast 87th Street,
PO Box 15901,
Seattle, WA 98115-3455
Tel: 206-623-1572
Fax: 206-441-7362

Olsson Center for Applied Ethics,
R. Edward Freeman,
Darden Graduate School of Business
    Administration,
University of Virginia,
PO Box 6550,
Charlottesville, VA 22906-6550
Tel: 804-924-7247
Fax: 804-924-6378

One Small Step,
The United Way,
50 California Sret, Suite 200,
San Francisco, CA 94111-4696
Tel: 415-772-4315
Fax: 415-391-8302

Organizational Ethics Associates,
3505 Arborcrest Court,
Cincinnati, OH 45236
Tel: 513-984-2820
Fax: 513-984-2820

Points of Light Foundation,
1400 I Street NW, Suite 800,
Washington, DC 20006
Tel: 202-729-8000
Fax: 202-729-8100

**Poynter Center for the Study
    of Ethics in American
    Institutions,**
David H. Smith, Director,
Indiana University,
618 East 3rd Street,
Bloomington, IN 47405
Tel: 812-855-0261
Fax: 812-855-3315

Practical Ethics Center,
Deni Elliot,
1000 East Beckwest,
University of Montana,
Missoula, Montana 59812
Tel: 406-243-5744

Program in Applied Ethics,
John Carroll University,
University Heights,
Cleveland, OH 44118
Tel: 216-397-4466

Program in Applied Ethics,
Lisa Newton, Director,
Fairfield University,
Fairfield, CT 06430
Tel: 203-254-4000 Ext. 2282

Programs in Business Ethics,
William W. May, Director,
School of Religion,
University of Southern California,
Los Angeles, CA 90089-0355
Tel: 213-740-0276

**Program in Ethics and the
    Professions,**
Professor Dennis Thompson,
    Director,
Harvard University,
79 Kennedy Street,
Cambridge, MA 02138
Tel: 617-495-1336
Fax: 617-496-6104

**Program on Ethics and
    Public Life,**
Henry Shue, Director,
Cornell University,
117 Stimson Hall,
Ithaca, NY 14853-7101
Tel: 607-255-8515
Fax: 607-255-8649

Program for Ethics, Science and the Environment,
Kathleen Moore, Chair,
Dept. of Philosophy,
Hovland Hall,
Oregon State University,
Corvallis, OR 97331-3902
Tel: 541-737-5648
Fax: 541-737-2571

Program in Ethics in Society,
Fred Dretske, Chair,
c/o Dept. of Philosophy,
Stanford University,
Stanford, CA 94305-2155
Tel: 415-723-0997
Fax: 415-723-0985

Public Citizen,
Joan Claybrook,
1600 20th Street. NW,
Washington, DC 20009
Tel: 202-588-1000

Public Policy Research Center,
University of Missouri at St Louis,
Room 362SSB,
8001 Natural Bridge Road,
St Louis, MO 63121
Tel: 314-553-5273

Research Center on Computing and Society,
Southern Connecticut State University,
Mr Michael J. Adanti – President,
501 Crescent Street,
New Haven, CT 06515
Tel: 203-392-5200
Fax: 203-392-6597

Resources for Ethics & Management,
14 Cornell Road,
West Hartford, CT 06107
Tel: 860-521-9233
Fax: 860-521-4697
email: 75132.171@compuserve.com

Robert K. Greenleaf Center for Servent Leadership,
Larry Spears, Executive Director,
921 E. 86th Street Suite 200,
Indianapolis, IN 46240
Tel: 317-259-1241
Fax: 317-259-0560

School of Business Administration,
Steven N. Brenner,
Portland State University,
Portland, OR 97207-0751
Tel: 503-725-4768
Fax: 503-725-5850

Silha Center for the Study of Media Ethics and Law,
William Babcock,
111 Murphy Hall,
University of Minnesota,
School of Journalism,
206 Church Street, S.E.,
Minneapolis, MN 55455-0418
Tel: 612-625-3421
Fax: 612-626-8012

Social Investment Forum,
PO Box 57216,
1612 K Street N.W.,
Washington, DC 20006
Tel: 202-872-5319
Fax: 202-331-8166
email: Info@socialinvest.org
www.socialinvest.org

Social Philosophy and Policy Center,
Fred Miller,
Bowling Green State University,
Bowling Green, OH 43403
Tel: 419-372-2536
Fax: 419-372-8738

Social Venture Network (SVN),
PO Box 29221,
San Francisco, CA 94129-0221
Tel: 415-561-6501
Fax: 415-561-6435
email: svn@well.com
www.svn.org

**Society for the Advancement of
  Socio-Economics,**
Richard Coughlin, Executive Director,
2808 Central S.E.,
Albuquerque NM 87106

Society for Business Ethics,
Ronald Duska, Executive Director,
The American College,
270 S. Bryn Mawr Ave.,
Bryn Mawr, PA 19010
Tel: 610-526-1387
Fax: 610-526-1359
email: rduska@aol.com

Stein Institute of Law and Ethics,
Professor Mary C. Daly,
Fordham University School of Law,
140 West 62nd Street,
New York, NY 10023-7485
Tel: 212-636-6838
Fax: 212-636-6899

University Center for Human Values,
Louis Marx Hall,
Princeton University,
Princeton, NJ 08544-1006
Tel: 609-258-4798
Fax: 609-258-2729

Vesper Society, The,
Claude Whitmyer,
151 Portero Avenue,
San Francisco, CA 94103
Tel: 415-648-2667

**Warren W. Hobbie Center for Values
  and Ethics,**
Dr Lawrence Brasher,
Catawba College,
2300 West Innes Street,
Salisbury, NC 28144-2488
Tel: 704-637-4429
Fax: 704-637-4736

**William B. and Evelyn Burkenroad
  Institute For the Study of Ethics &
  Leadership in Management,**
Arthur P. Brief, Director,
A. B. Freeman School of Business,
Tulane University,
New Orleans, LA 70118
Tel: 504-865-5662
Fax: 504-862-8742

Centers and institutions working in business ethics (international)

This information is correct as at September 1998.

Australia

**Australian Association for
  Professional and Applied Ethics,**
PO Box A2526,
Sydney South NSW 1235,
AUSTRALIA
Tel: 61-2-9385-2320
Fax: 61-2-9385-1029
email: s.cohen@unsw.edu.au
http://www.arts.unsw.edu.au/aapae/

**Australian Institute of Ethics and
  the Professions,**
University of Queensland,
St Lucia Queensland 4067,
AUSTRALIA
Tel: 011-61-7-3842-6612
Fax: 015-61-7-3870-5124
email: h.munro@mailbox.uq.edu.au

The Centre for the Study of Ethics,
Queensland University of Technology,
School of Humanities,
Beams Road,
Carseldine QLD 4034,
AUSTRALIA
Tel: 07-3864-4563
Fax: 07-3864-4719
email: n.preston@qut.edu.au
http://www.qut.edu.au/arts/human/ethics

The St James Ethics Centre,
GPO Box 3599,
Sydney 2001 New South Wales,
AUSTRALIA
Tel: 02-9241-2799
Fax: 02-9251-3985

Belgium

Centrum voor Ethiek,
K. Boey,
Director,
UFSIA,
Prirsstraat 13,
B-2000 Antwerp,
BELGIUM

Chaire Hoover d'Ethique
Economique et Sociale,
Universite Catholique de Louvain,
3 Place Montesquieu,
1348 Louvain-La-Neuve,
BELGIUM
Tel: 32-10-473951
Fax: 32-10-473952
email: vanparijs@etes.ucl.ac.be
www.econ.ucl.ac.be/etes/home.html

Service de recherche et
d'information et ethique de
placement,
Vincent Commenne,
Chairman,
Moensberg 101,
B-1180 Brussels,
BELGIUM

Brazil

FIDES (Fundacao Instituto de
Desenvolvimento Empresarial e
Social),
Rua Santanesia, 528,
Sao Paulo, SP,
BRAZIL
Tel: 5511-212-8292
Fax: 5511-212-8299

Canada

Canadian Centre for Ethics &
Corporate Policy,
George Brown House,
2nd floor,
50 Baldwin Street,
Toronto, Ontario M5T1L4,
CANADA
Tel: (416)348-8691
Fax: (416)348-8689
email: ethicctr@interlog.com
http://www.ethiccentre.com

Centre for Accounting
Ethics,
University of Waterloo,
School of Accountancy,
http://arts.uwaterloo.ca/acct/ethics,
Waterloo, ON N2L 3G1,
CANADA
Tel: 519-885-1211 x2770
email: mlemon@uwaterloo.ca

Center for Applied Ethics,
Michael McDonald, Director,
University of British
Columbia,
Vancouver, BC V6T 1Z2,
CANADA
Tel: 604-822-5139
Fax: 604-822-8627
email: ethics@interchg.ubc.ca
www.ethics.ubc.ca

Center for Professional and Applied Ethics,
Arthur Schafer, Director,
University of Manitoba,
Winnipeg Manitoba,
CANADA R3T 2N2

Clarkson Centre for Business Ethics,
Richard LeBlanc, Associate Director,
Rotman School of Management,
University of Toronto,
105 St George Street,
Toronto, Ontario M5S 3E6,
CANADA

Groupe de recherche Ethos,
Universite du Quebec a Rimouski,
200 dea Ursulines,
Rimouski, Quebec B5L 3A1,
CANADA
Tel: (204)474-9107

Westminster Institute for Ethics and Human Values,
Dr Abbyann Lynch, Director,
Westminister College,
361 Windermere Rd,
London, Ontario,
CANADA N6G 2K3

The North-South Institute,
Gail Whiteman,
55 Murray Suite 200,
Ottawa, K1N 5M3,
CANADA
Tel: 613-241-3535
Fax: 613-241-7435
email: whiteman_nsi-ins.ca
http://www.nsi.ins.ca

Occupational Ethics Group,
Jack Stevenson, Co-Chair,
University of Toronto,
Department of Philosophy,
Toronto, Ontario M5S 1A1,
CANADA

Taskforce on the Churches and Corporate Responsibility,
129 St Clair Avenue West,
Toronto, Ontario M4V 1N5,
CANADA
Tel: 416-923-1758
Fax: 416-927-7554
email: tccr@web.net

China

Centre for Applied Ethics,
Prof. Gerhold K. Becker,
Hong Kong Baptist College,
224, Waterloo Road,
Kowloon, Hong Kong,
CHINA
Tel: (852)-339 7291
Fax: (852)-339 7379

Hong Kong Ethics Development Centre,
1 F, Tung Wah Mansion,
199-203 Hennessy Road,
Wanchai Hong Kong,
CHINA
Tel: 2587-9812
Fax: 2824 9766
email: hkedc@chevalier.net

Denmark

Centre for Ethics and Law in Nature and Society,
Peter Kemp,
Valkendorfsgade 30, III,
1151 Copenhagen K,
DENMARK
Tel: 45-3369-1616
Fax: 45-3369-1617
e-mail: ethiclaw@inet.uni-c.dk
http://www.inet.unic.dk/home/
centre_for_ethics_and_law/

441

England

Action for Corporate Responsibility,
Sheena Carmichael,
4 Beau Gate,
Glasgow G12 9EE,
SCOTLAND

Board for Social Responsibility,
Ruth Badger,
Church House,
Great Smith Street,
London SW1P 3NZ,
ENGLAND
Tel: 0171-340-0306
Fax: 0171-233-2576
email: rbadger.clara.net

**Centre for Business and
Professional Ethics,**
Jennifer Jackson, Director,
The University of Leeds,
Leeds, LS2 9JT,
ENGLAND
Tel: 0113-233-3280
Fax: 0113-233-3265
email: j.c.jackson@leeds.ac.uk

**Center for Business and Public
Sector Ethics,**
Rosemund Thomas,
6 Croftgate,
Fulbrooke Road,
Cambridge CB3 9EG,
ENGLAND

Institute of Business Ethics,
Stanley Kiaer, Director,
12 Palace Street,
London SW1E 5JA,
ENGLAND
Tel: 0171-931-0495
Fax: 0171-821-5819
email: info@ibe.org.uk
www.ibe.org.uk

**Social Values Research
Centre,**
Society for Applied Philosophy,
Brenda Almond, Honorary
Secretary,
University of Hull,
Hull HU6 7RX,
ENGLAND

France

Centre d'Ethique de L'Enterprise,
J. L. Flinois,
45 rue de L'Universite,
75005 Paris,
FRANCE

Ethique des Affaires,
J. Mousse,
E.D.H.E.C.,
rue Monsieur 15,
F-75007 Paris,
FRANCE

Germany

**Association for Ethics Education
and Management,**
Joachim Kreutzham, Executive
Director,
Hindenburgplatz 3,
D-3200 Hildesheim,
GERMANY

**Betriebwirtschaftliches
Institut,**
H. Steinmann,
Friedrich Alex Universität,
Postfach 3931,
Lange Gasse 20,
D 8500 Nürnberg,
GERMANY
Tel: 49-911-5302-314
Fax: 49-911-5302-474
email: wsuf00@wsrz2.wiso.
uni-erlangen.de

Global Ethic Foundation,
Waldhäuser Straße 23,
D-72076 Tübingen,
GERMANY
Tel: 49-7071-626 46
Fax: 49-7071-6101 40
email: office@stiftung-weltethos.
   uni-tuebingen.de
http://www.uni-tuebingen.de/
   stiftung-weltethos

Transparency International,
Peter Eigen, Chairman,
Hardenbergplatz 2,
D-10623 Berlin,
GERMANY

Hungary

Business Ethics Center,
Dr Laszlo Zsolnai, Director,
Budapest University of Economic Sciences,
1053 Budapest,
Veres Palne u. 36.,
HUNGARY
Tel: 36-1-318-3037
Fax: 36-1-318-3037
email: zsolnai@mercur.bke.hu

Business Ethics Center,
Laszlo Radacsi, Assistant Professor,
Budapest University of Economic Sciences,
1053 Budapest,
Veres Palne u. 36.,
HUNGARY

Italy

Center for Ethics, Law & Economics,
Prof. Lorenzo Sacconi,
Director CELE,
Corso Matteotti, 22,
21053 Castellanza – Varese,
ITALY
Tel: ++39.331572307
Fax: ++39.331572229
email: lsacconi@liuc.it

Etica degli Affari,
Stefano Frega,
Prospecta Publisher,
Via Tizino, n. 11,
Milan, 20145,
ITALY

Japan

The Institute of Moralogy,
Mototoka Hircike, President,
2-1-1, Hikarigaoka, Hashiwa-shi,
Chiba-Ken, 277,
JAPAN

The Institute of Moralogy,
Dr Yukimas Nagayasu,
Research Department, Economic
   Section,
2-1-1 Hikarigaoka,
Kashiwa City, Chiba,
JAPAN 277

**Institute of the Study of Social
   Justice,**
Anselmo Mataix, Director,
Sophia University,
7-1, Kioicho, Chiyoda-ku,
JAPAN 102

Takaji Hishiyama,
Senior Managing Director,
Mitsubishi Petroleum Development
   Co., Ltd,
New Pier Takeshiba South Tower, 6F,
1-16-1, Kaigan, Minato-ku,
Tokyo 105, JAPAN
Tel: 3-5403-2611
Fax: 3-5403-2626

**Japan Society for Business
   Ethics,**
M. Mizutani Jabes, Chairman,
2-17-18 Tsuru Maki,
Setagaya, Tokyo,
JAPAN

Luxembourg

International Affairs, Law and Ethics Division,
LUX Conference,
SC, 74 Rue Ermesinde,
L-1469,
LUXEMBOURG
Tel: (352) 47-471928

Mexico

Ethical and Values Center,
Lic. Magdalena Medlich Ducoulombier,
I.T.E.S.M. Campus Monterrey,
CEDES 8vo. Piso,
Eugenio Garzo Sada 2501 Sur.
   Tecnologio,
C.P. 64849 Monterrey, N.L. MEXICO
Tel: (8) 3284254
Fax: (8) 3582000 x4346
email: mmedlich@campus.mty.itesm.mx

Instituto Tecnologico y de Estudios,
Juan Gerado Garza,
Superiores De Monterrey,
Sucursal de Correos "J",
C.P. 64849 Monterrey, N.L.,
MEXICO

Netherlands

Centre for Bioethics and Health Law,
University of Utrecht,
PO Box 80.105,
3508 TC Utrecht,
THE NETHERLANDS

Ethiek van Economie en Bedrijf,
E.J.J.M. Kimman,
Iniversiteit Maastricht,
Department of Economics,
P.O.B. 616,
6200 MD Maastricht,
THE NETHERLANDS
Tel: 31-43-388-3821
Fax: 31-43-326-1555
email: kimman@algec.unimaas.nl

European Institute for Business Ethics,
Henk J. L. van Luijk, Academic
   Director,
Nijenrode University,
Straatweg 25,
3621 BG Breukelen,
THE NETHERLANDS
Tel: 31-3462-91290
Fax: 31-3462-65453
email: vanluijk@nijenrode.nl

New Zealand

Unitec Institute of Technology,
Gael M. McDonald, Dean,
Faculty of Business,
Carrington Road,
Private Bag,
Auckland 92025,
NEW ZEALAND
Tel: 649-849-4180
Fax: 649-815-2927

Norway

Center for Ethics & Leadership,
Heidi von Weltzien Hoivik,
   PhD,
Director,
Norwegian School of Management,
NORWAY
Tel: 47-67-570500 x736
Fax: 47-67-570520
email: heidi.hoivik@bi.no

Norwegian National Committee for Research Ethics in the Social Sciences and the Humanities,
Gaustadalleen 21,
N-0371 Oslo,
NORWAY
Tel: 47-22-95-87-82
Fax: 47-22-95-84-92
email: dagel@sn.no

Spain

Ética, Economía y Dirección (Spanish branch of the European Business Ethics Network),
José Luis Fernández, President,
Universidad Pontificia Comillas de Madrid,
ICADE,
Alberto Aguilera, 23,
28015 Madrid, SPAIN
Tel: 34-91-542-2800
Fax: 34-91-559-6569
email:jlfernandez@psc.upco.es
http://www.upco.es

Instituto de Ciencias,
Para la Familia,
Marta Dalfo,
Servicio de Documentación,
Universidad de Navarra,
Edificio Los Nogales,
31080 Pamplona,
SPAIN
Tel: 25 27 00

Sweden

The Swedish Council for Management and Work Life Issues,
Hans De Geer,
PO Box 5042, Stockholm, SWEDEN

Switzerland

Ethics & Business,
Dr Peter F. Mueller, President,
Zurichbergstr. 46a,
8044 Zurich,
SWITZERLAND

Institute for Business Ethics,
University of St Gallen,
Guisanstrasse 11,
CH-9010 St Gallen,
SWITZERLAND
Tel: 41-71-2242644
Fax: 41-71-2242881
email: ethik@unisg.ch
http://www.iwe.unisg.ch

Institute for Social Ethics,
Hans-Balz Peter, Director,
Sulgenauweg 26,
Ch-3007 Berne,
SWITZERLAND

Venezuela

Instituto de Estudios,
Superiores de Administración (IESA),
Dr Rogelio Perez-Perdomo,
Professor of Business Ethics,
Apartado Postal 1640,
Caracas 1010-A,
VENEZUELA
email: rperez@newton.iesa.edu.ve

Index

A Companion to Business Ethics
Edited by Robert E. Frederick

In a series of articles specifically commissioned
for this volume, some of today's most
distinguished business ethicists survey the main
areas of interest and concern in the field of
business ethics.

Sections of the book cover topics such as the
often uneasy relationship between business
ethics and capitalism, the link between business
ethics and ethical theory, how ethics applies to
specific problems in the business world, the
connection between business ethics and related
academic disciplines, and the practice of
business ethics in modern corporations.

The book can be used as a comprehensive text
for introductory or advanced courses in business
ethics, as a reference for teachers and writers in
the field, or as a guide for other academic or
business persons who wish to become familiar
with the central issues in the field. To enhance
its usefulness as a reference work, the volume
includes bibliographies of the relevant literature,
a list of internet sources for material on business
ethics, and an extensive index.